English
Novel
Explication

Supplement V

Compiled by
Christian J. W. Kloesel

ARCHON BOOKS / Hamden, Connecticut
1994

© 1994 The Shoe String Press, Inc.
All rights reserved.
First published 1994 as an Archon Book,
an imprint of The Shoe String Press, Inc.,
Hamden, Connecticut 06514.

Library of Congress Cataloging-in-Publication Data
(Revised for volume 5)

English novel explication. Supplement.
Supplements: English novel explication /
compiled by Helen H. Palmer & Anne Jane Dyson.
Supplement I / compiled by Peter L. Abernethy,
Christian J. W. Kloesel, Jeffrey R. Smitten;
supplement II / compiled by Christian J. W. Kloesel,
Jeffrey R. Smitten; supplements III–V / compiled
by Christian J. W. Kloesel.
Includes bibliographical references and indexes.
1. English fiction—Explication—Bibliography.
I. Abernethy, Peter L.   II. Kloesel, Christian J. W.
III. Smitten, Jeffrey R.   IV. Title: English novel explication

Z2014.F5P26 Suppl. [PR821]   016.823′009   84-137107
ISBN 0-208-01464-0 (v. 1)
ISBN 0-208-02308-9 (v. 5: alk. paper)

The paper used in this publication meets the minimum
requirements of American National Standard
for Information Sciences—Permanence of Paper
for Printed Library Materials,
ANSI Z39.48–1984. ∞

Printed in the United States of America

For Alicia

CONTENTS

PREFACE

This fifth supplement extends the *English Novel Explication* series from the second half of 1989 through the first half of 1993. Accordingly, it has been my primary responsibility to gather materials published in those four years, although I have added a few earlier items not included in the fourth supplement, as well as everything published in 1993 that had arrived in nearby libraries. But readers should be reminded that it has not been possible to include all items published in those four years, especially those appearing toward the very end of the period. Because *English Novel Explication* is a continuing series, it must have a fixed date of publication, and that date cannot be affected by printing and library binding schedules or by the inevitable delays in acquisitions, cataloguing, interlibrary loans, and the return of charged or overdue books. Consequently, readers not finding an item they expect to be here must consult the next supplement.

The scope of the present supplement is the same as that of the four previous ones. The very broad definition of the term "novel" is again based on Ernest A. Baker's *History of the English Novel,* and that is why such works as Malory's *Le Morte Darthur,* Bunyan's *The Pilgrim's Progress,* Swift's *Gulliver's Travels,* Johnson's *Rasselas,* and Orwell's *Down and Out in Paris and London* are included. An "English" novelist is a writer born in England, Scotland, Wales, Ireland, or the British Commonwealth who has lived in Great Britain during some significant portion of her/his creative years. This definition excludes writers like Brian Moore and Henry James, and it includes others like Doris Lessing, Malcolm Lowry, V. S. Naipaul, and Olive Schreiner. By "explication" is meant the interpretation of the significance and meaning of a novel. Consequently, discussions of theme, imagery, symbolism, diction and structure are included here (even those of the poststructuralist, deconstructionist, and semiotic kind), whereas those wholly or exclusively devoted to sources and influence, critical reception, biography, or bibliography are excluded.

The format of the present supplement is similar to that of the four earlier ones. I have abbreviated book titles to conserve space; full titles, together with complete bibliographical information, may be found in the *List of Books Indexed* at the end of the volume. In addition, I have used the generally accepted abbreviations of the journals of the American and Australian Modern Language Associations (*PMLA* and *AUMLA*), and have abbreviated several frequently repeated words in journal and serial titles. These words include, without periods, Academy (Acad), American (Am), Association (Assoc), British (Brit), Bulletin (Bull), Century (Cent), Chronicle (Chron), College (Coll), Comparative (Compar), Conference (Conf), Contemporary (Contemp), Critical (Crit), Department (Dept), English (Engl), History (Hist), Humanities (Hum), Institute (Inst), International (Intl), Journal (J), Language (Lang), Library (Lib), Linguistics (Ling), Literary (Liter), Literature (Lit), Magazine (Mag), Modern (Mod), Newsletter (Newsl), Philological (Philol), Philosophy (Philos), Proceedings (Proc), Psychology (Psych), Publications (Publs), Quarterly (Q), Religion (Rel), Research (Res), Review (R), Society (Soc), Studies (Stud), Supplement (Suppl), Transactions (Trans), University (Univ), and Yearbook

(Yrbk). A few abbreviations, like *ANQ, ELH, LIT, PTL,* or *S,* are themselves journal titles. In another matter—the same article treating two or more of a single author's novels—I have returned to the practice of the first supplement, with full citations in all instances; for though the practice of abbreviating subsequent citations may be useful for such rarely cited or moderately productive novelists as Susan Ferrier, Ronald Firbank, Naomi Mitchison, and Liam O'Flaherty, it unnecessarily complicates the reader's task in such productive and much-discussed authors as Charles Dickens, George Eliot, D. H. Lawrence, Doris Lessing, and Virginia Woolf.

Readers should remember that, as in the four previous supplements, page numbers in a citation correspond, in most instances, to the passage of explication for a given novel and not necessarily to the entire article or book. When an entire book is devoted to explication of the novel under which it appears, it is sometimes listed without page numbers.

As always, I am grateful to the library staffs at Indiana University–Purdue University at Indianapolis and Indiana University at Bloomington—as well as to English novelists and the critics who explicate them.

Indianapolis, Indiana   C.J.W.K.
October 1993

PETER ACKROYD

Chatterton, 1987

Finney, Brian. "Peter Ackroyd, Postmodernist Play and *Chatterton.*" *Twentieth Cent Lit* 38 (1992), 249–60.

Hawksmoor, 1985

Herman, Luc. "The Relevance of History: *Der Zauberbaum* (1985) by Peter Sloterdijk and *Hawksmoor* (1985) by Peter Ackroyd," in Theo D'Haen and Hans Bertens, eds., *History and Post-War Writing,* 107–24.

Lee, Alison. *Realism and Power,* 68–73, 83–87.

RICHARD ADAMS

Watership Down, 1972

Schmoll, Edward A. "Homeric Reminiscence in *Watership Down.*" *Classical and Mod Lit* 10 (1989), 21–26.

WILLIAM HARRISON AINSWORTH

Jack Sheppard, 1839

Chittick, Kathryn. *Dickens and the 1830s,* 153–62.
Drexler, Peter. *Literatur, Recht, Kriminalität,* 147–49.
Reed, John R. *Victorian Will,* 206–8.

RICHARD ALDINGTON

All Men are Enemies, 1933

Doyle, Charles. *Richard Aldington,* 158–63.
Gindin, James. *British Fiction,* 33–36.

The Colonel's Daughter, 1931

Doyle, Charles. "Aldington's Novels: An Orthodox Introduction," in Charles Doyle, ed., *Richard Aldington,* 88–89.
Doyle, Charles. *Richard Aldington,* 151–53.

Death of a Hero, 1929

Doyle, Charles. "Aldington's Novels: An Orthodox Introduction," in Charles Doyle, ed., *Richard Aldington,* 86–88.
Doyle, Charles. *Richard Aldington,* 1–5, 126–38, 141–43, 302–5.
Gindin, James. *British Fiction,* 27–32.
Onions, John. *English Fiction and Drama,* 68–76.
Tylee, Claire M. *The Great War,* 4–6, 235–37, 240–43.

Rejected Guest, 1939

Doyle, Charles. "Aldington's Novels: An Orthodox Introduction," in Charles Doyle, ed., *Richard Aldington,* 90–91.
Doyle, Charles. *Richard Aldington,* 199–230.
Gindin, James. *British Fiction,* 39–42.

Women Must Work, 1934

> Doyle, Charles. "Aldington's Novels: An Orthodox Introduction," in Charles Doyle, ed., *Richard Aldington*, 89–90.
> Doyle, Charles. *Richard Aldington*, 164–68.
> Gindin, James. *British Fiction*, 36–39.

BRIAN ALDISS

Frankenstein Unbound, 1973

> Borgmeier, Raimund. "Frankenstein Unbound: Mary Shelley's Novel From the Perspective of Science Fiction," in Günter Ahrends and Hans-Jürgen Diller, eds., *English Romantic Prose*, 149–60.

Helliconia, 1982–1985

> Terrel, Denise. "Au coeur du Labyrinthe: le phagor dans la trilogie de *Helliconia* de Brian Aldiss." *Etudes Anglaises* 41 (1988), 307–17.

WILLIAM ALEXANDER

Johnny Gibb of Gushetneuk, 1871

> Letley, Emma. *From Galt to Douglas Brown*, 131–49.

ROSE LAURE ALLATINI

Despised and Rejected, 1918

> Tylee, Claire M. *The Great War*, 121–29.

GRANT ALLEN

The Woman Who Did, 1895

> Ardis, Ann L. *New Women, New Novels*, 51–53.

MARGERY ALLINGHAM

Hide My Eyes, 1958

> Asbee, Sue. "Margery Allingham and Reader Response," in Clive Bloom, ed., *Twentieth-Century Suspense*, 169–73.

The Tiger in the Smoke, 1957

> Knowles, Sebastian D. G. *A Purgatorial Flame*, 216–20.

Traitor's Purse, 1941

> Asbee, Sue. "Margery Allingham and Reader Response," in Clive Bloom, ed., *Twentieth-Century Suspense*, 161–69.

KINGSLEY AMIS

The Alteration, 1976

Bradford, Richard. *Kingsley Amis*, 63–66.
Everett, Barbara. "Kingsley Amis: Devils and Others," in Dale Salwak, ed., *Kingsley Amis*, 92–97.
Helbig, Jörg. "Thema und Variation: Kingsley Amis' *The Alteration* als postmoderne Spielart des historischen Romans." *Germanisch-Romanische Monatsschrift* 42 (1992), 444–49.
Moseley, Merritt. *Understanding Kingsley Amis*, 108–13.

The Anti-Death League, 1966

Bradford, Richard. *Kingsley Amis*, 49–54.
Moseley, Merritt. *Understanding Kingsley Amis*, 72–79.

Difficulties With Girls, 1988

Bradford, Richard. *Kingsley Amis*, 99–102.
Moseley, Merritt. *Understanding Kingsley Amis*, 160–66.
Taylor, D. J. *A Vain Conceit*, 48–50.

Ending Up, 1974

Bradford, Richard. *Kingsley Amis*, 94–96.
Moseley, Merritt. *Understanding Kingsley Amis*, 130–37.

The Folks That Live on the Hill, 1990

Moseley, Merritt. *Understanding Kingsley Amis*, 166–71.

Girl, 20, 1971

Bradford, Richard. *Kingsley Amis*, 81–84.
Moseley, Merritt. *Understanding Kingsley Amis*, 122–31.

The Green Man, 1969

Bradford, Richard. *Kingsley Amis*, 54–60.
Moseley, Merritt. *Understanding Kingsley Amis*, 85–90.

I Like It Here, 1958

Bradford, Richard. *Kingsley Amis*, 38–42.
Gindin, James. "Changing Social and Moral Attitudes," in Dale Salwak, ed., *Kingsley Amis*, 137–39.
Moseley, Merritt. *Understanding Kingsley Amis*, 33–38.

I Want It Now, 1969

Bradford, Richard. *Kingsley Amis*, 77–81.
Moseley, Merritt. *Understanding Kingsley Amis*, 79–85.

Jake's Thing, 1978

Bradford, Richard. *Kingsley Amis*, 84–89.
Macleod, Norman. "The Language of Kingsley Amis," in Dale Salwak, ed., *Kingsley Amis*, 118–29.
Moseley, Merritt. *Understanding Kingsley Amis*, 137–44.

Wilson, Keith. "Jim, Jake and the Years Between," in Dale Salwak, ed., *Kingsley Amis*, 76–88.

Lucky Jim, 1954

Bergonzi, Bernard. *Wartime and Aftermath,* 135–36, 143–47.

Bradford, Richard. *Kingsley Amis,* 23–33.

Eastman, John K. "Dissimilar Discourses: The Realism of Amis's Conversations in *Lucky Jim.*" *Revista Alicantina de Estudios Ingleses* 2 (1989), 43–51.

Moseley, Merritt. *Understanding Kingsley Amis,* 18–27.

Rossen, Janice. *The University in Modern Fiction,* 75–83.

Taylor, D. J. *A Vain Conceit,* 46–48.

Wilkinson, John. "Conventions of Comedies of Manners and British Novels about Academic Life," in Bege K. Bowers and Barbara Brothers, eds., *Reading and Writing,* 209–12.

Wilson, Keith. "Jim, Jake and the Years Between," in Dale Salwak, ed., *Kingsley Amis,* 76–88.

The Old Devils, 1986

Bradford, Richard. *Kingsley Amis,* 96–99.

Everett, Barbara. "Kingsley Amis: Devils and Others," in Dale Salwak, ed., *Kingsley Amis,* 89–93, 97–99.

Gindin, James. "Changing Social and Moral Attitudes," in Dale Salwak, ed., *Kingsley Amis,* 145–48.

Moseley, Merritt. *Understanding Kingsley Amis,* 154–60.

One Fat Englishman, 1963

Moseley, Merritt. *Understanding Kingsley Amis,* 64–72.

The Riverside Villas Murder, 1973

Bradford, Richard. *Kingsley Amis,* 60–62.

Moseley, Merritt. *Understanding Kingsley Amis,* 101–5.

Russian Hide-and-Seek, 1980

Aldiss, Brian. "'im," in Dale Salwak, ed., *Kingsley Amis,* 44–46.

Bradford, Richard. *Kingsley Amis,* 66–69.

Moseley, Merritt. *Understanding Kingsley Amis,* 113–18.

Stanley and the Women, 1984

Bradford, Richard. *Kingsley Amis,* 88–93.

Moseley, Merritt. *Understanding Kingsley Amis,* 146–54.

Take A Girl Like You, 1960

Bradford, Richard. *Kingsley Amis,* 42–45.

Moseley, Merritt. *Understanding Kingsley Amis,* 38–46.

That Uncertain Feeling, 1955

Bradford, Richard. *Kingsley Amis,* 33–38.

Moseley, Merritt. *Understanding Kingsley Amis,* 27–33.

MARTIN AMIS

Money, 1984

Doan, Laura L. " 'Sexy Greedy *Is* the Late Eighties': Power Systems in Amis's *Money* and Churchill's *Serious Money.*" *Minnesota R* 34–35 (1990), 69–80.

Massie, Allan. *The Novel Today,* 47–48.

Time's Arrow, 1991

Slater, Maya. "Problems When Time Moves Backwards: Martin Amis's *Time's Arrow.*" *English* 42 (1993), 141–52.

MICHAEL ARLEN

The Green Hat, 1924

Bracco, Rosa Maria. *'Betwixt and Between,'* 25–27.

PENELOPE AUBIN

The Life of Charlotta DuPont, 1736

Williamson, Marilyn L. *Raising Their Voices,* 251–53.

JANE AUSTEN

Emma, 1816

Benson, Mary Margaret. "Mothers, Substitute Mothers, and Daughters in the Novels of Jane Austen." *Persuasions* 11 (1989), 117–18.

Berendsen, Marjet. *Reading Character,* 38–173.

Boardman, Michael M. *Narrative Innovation,* 78–83.

Booth, Alison. *Greatness Engendered,* 127–29.

Bull, J. A. *The Framework of Fiction,* 103–9.

Campbell, Susie. "The Significance of Games in *Emma,*" in Linda Cookson and Bryan Loughrey, eds., *Critical Essays,* 34–44.

Crosby, Christina. "Facing the Charms of *Emma.*" *New Orleans R* 16:1 (1989), 88–97.

Davis, Patricia D. "Jane Austen's Use of Frank Churchill's Letters in *Emma.*" *Persuasions* 10 (1988), 34–38.

Dussinger, John A. *In the Pride of the Moment,* 30–40, 53–64, 131–36, 159–68.

Dwyer, June. *Jane Austen,* 89–99.

Favret, Mary A. *Romantic Correspondence,* 154–66.

Fergus, Jan. *Jane Austen,* 151–56.

Finch, Casey, and Peter Bowen. " 'The Tittle-Tattle of Highbury': Gossip and the Free Indirect Style in *Emma.*" *Representations* 31 (1990), 1–15.

Fishelov, David. "Types of Character, Characteristics of Type," in John V. Knapp, ed., *Literary Character,* 83–84.

Flavin, Louise. "Free Indirect Discourse and the Clever Heroine of *Emma.*" *Persuasions* 13 (1991), 50–57.

Gard, Roger. *Jane Austen's Novels,* 155–81.

Gibson, Andrew. "'Imaginism' and Objectivity in *Emma,*" in Linda Cookson and Bryan Loughrey, eds., *Critical Essays,* 69–79.

Gross, Gloria Sybil. "Jane Austen and Psychological Realism: 'What Does a Woman Want?,'" in Bege K. Bowers and Barbara Brothers, eds., *Reading and Writing,* 21–31.

Hardy, Barbara. "The Talkative Woman in Shakespeare, Dickens and George Eliot," in Sally Minogue, ed., *Problems for Feminist Criticism,* 29–30.

Harrison, Bernard. *Inconvenient Fictions,* 148–52.

Hirsch, Marianne. *The Mother/Daughter Plot,* 58–61.

Hodge, Robert. *Literature as Discourse,* 151–54.

Holderness, Graham. "Disliking the Heroine in *Emma,*" in Linda Cookson and Bryan Loughrey, eds., *Critical Essays,* 81–91.

Hollindale, Peter. "Age and Patronage in *Emma,*" in Linda Cookson and Bryan Loughrey, eds., *Critical Essays,* 105–14.

Holly, Grant I. "*Emma* grammatology." *Stud in Eighteenth-Cent Culture* 19 (1989), 39–50.

Hudson, Glenda A. *Sibling Love and Incest,* 50–55.

Jay, Penny. "A Changing View: Jane Austen's Landscapes." *Sydney Stud in Engl* 15 (1989–90), 58–60.

Kenney, Catherine. "The Mystery of *Emma* . . . or The Consummate Case of the Least Likely Heroine." *Persuasions* 13 (1991), 138–45.

Lauber, John. *Jane Austen,* 79–94.

Levin, Amy K. *The Suppressed Sister,* 50–52.

McAleer, John. "What a Biographer Can Learn about Jane Austen from *Emma.*" *Persuasions* 13 (1991), 69–79.

MacDonagh, Oliver. *Jane Austen,* 129–37, 143–45.

McMaster, Juliet. "The Secret Languages of *Emma.*" *Persuasions* 13 (1991), 119–31.

Mallett, Phillip. "On Liking Emma." *Durham Univ J* 84 (1992), 249–54.

Mandel, Miriam B. "Fiction and Fiction-Making: *Emma.*" *Persuasions* 13 (1991), 100–103.

Marshall, Mary Gaither. "Jane Austen and the MTV Generation: Teaching *Emma* at a Community College." *Persuasions* 13 (1991), 104–7.

Mei, Huang. *Transforming the Cinderella Dream,* 95–98.

Meihuizen, Dorothea. "The Relevance and Importance of *Emma* to Matric Pupils." *CRUX* 21:4 (1991), 24–32.

Meyersohn, Marylea. "Jane Austen's Garrulous Speakers: Social Criticism in *Sense and Sensibility, Emma,* and *Persuasion,*" in Bege K. Bowers and Barbara Brothers, eds., *Reading and Writing,* 40–45.

Milligan, Ian. *Studying Jane Austen,* 89–122.

Moler, Kenneth L. "'Group Voices' in Jane Austen's Narration." *Persuasions* 13 (1991), 9–11.

Monk, Leland. "Murder She Wrote: The Mystery of Jane Austen's *Emma.*" *J of Narrative Technique* 20 (1990), 342–51.

Nardin, Jane. "Propriety versus Morality in Jane Austen's Novels." *Persuasions* 10 (1988), 74–75.

Neale, Catherine. "*Emma:* The Role of Heroine and the Role of Woman," in Linda Cookson and Bryan Loughrey, eds., *Critical Essays,* 56–67.

Oakleaf, David. "Marks, Stamps, and Representations: Character in Eighteenth-Century Fiction." *Stud in the Novel* 23 (1991), 301–2.

Odom, Keith C. *Jane Austen,* 111–30.

Parker, Mark. "The End of Emma: Drawing the Boundaries of Class in Austen." *JEGP* 91 (1992), 344–59.

Parkinson, Kathleen. "Courtship and Marriage in *Emma,*" in Linda Cookson and Bryan Loughrey, eds., *Critical Essays,* 21–32.

Pinsent, Pat. " 'There is a whole larger world outside, of which she says nothing': Discuss this View of Jane Austen in Relation to *Emma,*" in Linda Cookson and Bryan Loughrey, eds., *Critical Essays,* 9–19.

Preus, Nicholas E. "Sexuality in *Emma:* A Case History." *Stud in the Novel* 23 (1991), 196–213.

Punter, David. *The Romantic Unconscious,* 137–38.

Reid-Walsh, Jacqueline. "Governess or Governor?: The Mentor/Pupil Relation in *Emma.*" *Persuasions* 13 (1991), 108–15.

Ross, Deborah. *The Excellence of Falsehood,* 185–98, 204–205.

Schwarz, Daniel R. *The Transformation,* 131–33.

Spacks, Patricia Meyer. "Women and Boredom: The Two Emmas." *Yale J of Criticism* 2:2 (1989), 191–204.

Spencer-Ellis, Mark. "Definition and Self-Definition," in Linda Cookson and Bryan Loughrey, eds., *Critical Essays,* 46–54.

Steig, Michael. *Stories of Reading,* 167–69.

Stevenson, John Allen. *The British Novel,* 110–28.

Stovel, Bruce. "Emma's Search for a True Friend." *Persuasions* 13 (1991), 58–67.

Swingle, L. J. "The Reader and the Virgin: What Next?," in Lloyd Davis, ed., *Virginal Sexuality,* 36–39.

Thaden, Barbara Z. "Figure and Ground: The Receding Heroine in Jane Austen's *Emma.*" *South Atlantic R* 55:1 (1990), 47–60.

Tobin, Beth Fowkes. "The Moral and Political Economy of Property in Austen's *Emma.*" *Eighteenth-Cent Fiction* 2 (1990), 229–54.

Toker, Leona. *Eloquent Reticence,* 84–104.

Turner, Christopher. "Aspects of Comedy in *Emma,*" in Linda Cookson and Bryan Loughrey, eds., *Critical Essays,* 93–103.

Uphaus, Robert W. *The Idea of the Novel,* 108–10.

Warren, Leland E. "The Conscious Speakers: Sensibility and the Art of Conversation Considered," in Syndy McMillen Conger, ed., *Sensibility in Transformation,* 36–38.

Watts, Cedric. "The Limitations of *Emma,*" in Linda Cookson and Bryan Loughrey, eds., *Critical Essays,* 116–23.

Watts, Cedric. *Literature and Money,* 130–37.

Wilkie, Brian. "Jane Austen: *Amor* and Amoralism." *JEGP* 91 (1992), 536–43.

Wiltshire, John. *Jane Austen and the Body*, 110–54.

Zaal, J. "Is *Emma* Still Teachable?" *CRUX* 22:3 (1988), 61–68.

Lady Susan, 1871

Dwyer, June. *Jane Austen*, 113–17.

Favret, Mary A. *Romantic Correspondence*, 139–46.

Fergus, Jan. *Jane Austen*, 72–74, 119.

Gard, Roger. *Jane Austen's Novels*, 27–44.

Gard, Roger. "*Lady Susan* and the Single Effect." *Essays in Criticism* 39 (1989), 305–25.

Kaplan, Deborah. *Jane Austen among Women*, 158–70.

MacDonagh, Oliver. *Jane Austen*, 20–28.

Odom, Keith C. *Jane Austen*, 42–49.

Winnifrith, Tom. "Jane Austen's Adulteress." *Notes and Queries* 235 (1990), 18–20.

Love and Friendship, 1922

Fraiman, Susan. *Unbecoming Women*, 64–69.

Kaplan, Deborah. *Jane Austen among Women*, 144–46.

Mansfield Park, 1814

Armstrong, Isobel. *Jane Austen*, 43–104.

Benson, Mary Margaret. "Mothers, Substitute Mothers, and Daughters in the Novels of Jane Austen." *Persuasions* 11 (1989), 121–22.

Boardman, Michael M. *Narrative Innovation*, 78–88.

Bowden, Martha F. "What Does Lady Bertram Do?" *Engl Lang Notes* 30:2 (1992), 30–32.

Chazal, Roger. "*Mansfield Park* et l'emblème de l'oiseleur." *Etudes Anglaises* 44 (1991), 185–99.

Cohen, Paula Marantz. "The Anorexic Syndrome and the Nineteenth-Century Domestic Novel," in Lilian R. Furst and Peter W. Graham, eds., *Disorderly Eaters*, 133–37.

Cohen, Paula Marantz. *The Daughter's Dilemma*, 59–87.

Dussinger, John A. *In the Pride of the Moment*, 27–30, 181–83.

Dussinger, John A. "Madness and Lust in the Age of Sensibility," in Syndy McMillen Conger, ed., *Sensibility in Transformation*, 96–99.

Dwyer, June. *Jane Austen*, 77–88.

Emprin, Ginette. "Fanny Price: une certaine idée de la jeunesse." *Etudes Anglaises* 44 (1991), 143–50.

Fergus, Jan. *Jane Austen*, 145–50.

Ferguson, Moira. "*Mansfield Park:* Slavery, Colonialism, and Gender." *Oxford Liter R* 13:1–2 (1991), 118–39.

Fowler, Kathleen L. "Apricots, Raspberries, and Susan Price! Susan Price!: *Mansfield Park* and Maria Edgeworth." *Persuasions* 13 (1991), 28–32.

Galperin, William. "The Theatre at Mansfield Park: From Classic to Romantic Once More." *Eighteenth-Cent Life* 16:3 (1992), 247–68.

Gard, Roger. *Jane Austen's Novels*, 121–54.

Goubert, Pierre. "La position morale de Jane Austen dans *Mansfield Park.*" *Etudes Anglaises* 43 (1990), 1–12.

Halperin, John. J*ane Austen's Lovers*, 27–46.

Holway, Tatiana M. "The Game of Speculation: Economics and Representation." *Dickens Q* 9 (1992), 105–7.

Horwitz, Barbara J. *Jane Austen and the Question of Women's Education*, 136–39, 152–55.

Hudson, Glenda A. "Mansfield Revisited: Incestuous Relationships in Jane Austen's *Mansfield Park.*" *Eighteenth-Cent Fiction* 4 (1991), 53–68.

Hudson, Glenda A. *Sibling Love and Incest*, 35–50, 87–90, 112–16.

Jarvis, W. A. W. "The Ships in *Mansfield Park.*" *Persuasions* 10 (1988), 31–33.

Jay, Penny. "A Changing View: Jane Austen's Landscapes." *Sydney Stud in Engl* 15 (1989–90), 56–58.

Lauber, John. *Jane Austen*, 61–78.

Laurence, Patricia Ondek. *The Reading of Silence*, 67–72.

Litvak, Joseph. *Caught in the Act*, 1–26, 32–34.

McCawley, Dwight. "Hostility and Aggression: Jane Austen's Inner Plot." *Mid-Hudson Lang Stud* 12:2 (1989), 16–26.

MacDonagh, Oliver. *Jane Austen*, 7–19.

Marshall, David. "True Acting and the Language of Real Feeling: *Mansfield Park.*" *Yale J of Criticism* 3 (1989), 87–106.

Mei, Huang. *Transforming the Cinderella Dream*, 75–104.

Mellor, Anne K. "Why Women Didn't Like Romanticism: The Views of Jane Austen and Mary Shelley," in Gene W. Ruoff, ed., *The Romantics and Us*, 280–81.

Milligan, Ian. *Studying Jane Austen*, 64–88.

Minma, Shinobu. "*Mansfield Park* and English Society in the Early Nineteenth Century." *Stud in Engl Lit* (Tokyo) English Nr. 1990, 39–56.

Moler, Kenneth L. "'Group Voices' in Jane Austen's Narration." *Persuasions* 13 (1991), 9.

Morgan, Susan, and Susan Kneedler. "Austen's Sexual Politics." *Persuasions* 12 (1990), 19–23.

Nordell, Robert. "Confrontation and Evasion: Argument Scenes in *Mansfield Park* and *Pride and Prejudice.*" *Engl Stud in Africa* 36:1 (1993), 22–26.

Odom, Keith C. *Jane Austen*, 91–113.

Perkins, Pam. "A Subdued Gaiety: The Comedy of *Mansfield Park.*" *Nineteenth-Cent Lit* 48 (1993), 1–25.

Ralph, Phyllis C. *Victorian Transformations*, 66–70.

Ray, Joan Klingel. "Jane Austen's Case Study of Child Abuse: Fanny Price." *Persuasions* 13 (1991), 16–24.

Raymer, Robyn. "Jane Austen, Fanny Price, and Anne Elliot." *Spectrum* 31 (1989), 141–55.

Ross, Deborah. *The Excellence of Falsehood,* 187–95.

Skinner, John. "Exploring Space: The Constellations of *Mansfield Park.*" *Eighteenth-Cent Fiction* 4 (1992), 125–48.

Snyder, William C. "Mother Nature's Other Natures: Landscape in Women's Writing, 1770–1830." *Women's Stud* 21 (1992), 150–55.

Steig, Michael. *Stories of Reading,* 159–79.

Sutherland, Kathryn. "*Jane Eyre*'s Literary History: The Case for *Mansfield Park.*" *ELH* 59 (1992), 409–37.

Wilkie, Brian. "Jane Austen: *Amor* and Amoralism." *JEGP* 91 (1992), 553–55.

Wilkie, Brian. "Structural Layering in Jane Austen's Problem Novels." *Nineteenth-Cent Lit* 46 (1992), 517–20, 528–44.

Wiltshire, John. *Jane Austen and the Body,* 62–109.

Winnifrith, Tom. "Jane Austen's Adulteress." *Notes and Queries* 235 (1990), 18–20.

Yarrow, Dorothy F. "*Mansfield Park* and *Wives and Daughters.*" *Gaskell Soc Newsl* 12 (1991), 4–5.

Yeazell, Ruth Bernard. *Fictions of Modesty,* 143–68.

Northanger Abbey, 1818

Banerjee, A. "Dr. Johnson's Daughter: Jane Austen and *Northanger Abbey.*" *Engl Stud* 71 (1990), 113–24.

Benson, Mary Margaret. "Mothers, Substitute Mothers, and Daughters in the Novels of Jane Austen." *Persuasions* 11 (1989), 120–21.

Dussinger, John A. " 'The Glory of Motion': Carriages and Consciousness in the Early Novel," in H. George Hahn, ed., *The Country Myth,* 214–18.

Dussinger, John A. *In the Pride of the Moment,* 114–16, 151–53.

Dwyer, June. *Jane Austen,* 43–52.

Fergus, Jan. *Jane Austen,* 95–101.

Gard, Roger. *Jane Austen's Novels,* 45–59.

Hudson, Glenda A. *Sibling Love and Incest,* 81–84.

Jay, Penny. "A Changing View: Jane Austen's Landscapes." *Sydney Stud in Engl* 15 (1989–90), 49–51.

Lanser, Susan Sniader. *Fictions of Authority,* 61–63, 67–72, 77–80.

Loveridge, Mark. "*Northanger Abbey;* or, Nature and Probability." *Nineteenth-Cent Lit* 46 (1991), 1–29.

MacDonagh, Oliver. *Jane Austen,* 81–88.

Miles, Robert. *Gothic Writing,* 143–59.

Milligan, Ian. *Studying Jane Austen,* 12–30.

Morrison, Paul. "Enclosed in Openness: Northanger Abbey and the Domestic Carceral." *Texas Stud in Lit and Lang* 33 (1991), 1–21.

Odom, Keith C. *Jane Austen,* 59–67.

Roberts, Bette B. "The Horrid Novels: *The Mysteries of Udolpho* and

Northanger Abbey," in Kenneth W. Graham, ed., *Gothic Fictions,* 89–111.

Shaw, Narelle. "Free Indirect Speech and Jane Austen's 1816 Revision of *Northanger Abbey.*" *Stud in Engl Lit, 1500–1900* 30 (1990), 591–99.

Smith, Amy Elizabeth. "'Julias and Louisas': Austen's *Northanger Abbey* and the Sentimental Novel." *Engl Lang Notes* 30:1 (1992), 33–40.

Tropp, Martin. *Images of Fear,* 12–27.

Wiesenfarth, Joseph. *Gothic Manners,* 3–6.

Williams, Michael. "*Northanger Abbey:* Some Problems of Engagement." *Unisa Engl Stud* 25:2 (1987), 8–17.

Persuasion, 1818

Benson, Mary Margaret. "Mothers, Substitute Mothers, and Daughters in the Novels of Jane Austen." *Persuasions* 11 (1989), 118–19.

Boardman, Michael M. *Narrative Innovation,* 75–83, 88–103.

Dussinger, John A. *In the Pride of the Moment,* 48–49, 158–59, 170–74.

Dwyer, June. *Jane Austen,* 101–11.

Favret, Mary A. *Romantic Correspondence,* 165–75.

Fergus, Jan. *Jane Austen,* 164–69.

Fitzgerald, Jennifer. "Jane Austen's *Persuasion* and the French Revolution." *Persuasions* 10 (1988), 39–42.

Gard, Roger. *Jane Austen's Novels,* 182–207.

Hudson, Glenda A. *Sibling Love and Incest,* 91–96, 116–18.

Jay, Penny. "A Changing View: Jane Austen's Landscapes." *Sydney Stud in Engl* 15 (1989–90), 61–62.

Kastely, James L. "*Persuasion:* Jane Austen's Philosophical Rhetoric." *Philos and Lit* 15 (1991), 74–87.

Knox-Shaw, Peter. "*Persuasion,* Byron, and the Turkish Tale." *R of Engl Stud* 44 (1993), 47–69.

Lauber, John. *Jane Austen,* 95–106.

Levin, Amy K. *The Suppressed Sister,* 45–49.

MacDonagh, Oliver. *Jane Austen,* 98–108.

Meyersohn, Marylea. "Jane Austen's Garrulous Speakers: Social Criticism in *Sense and Sensibility, Emma,* and *Persuasion,*" in Bege K. Bowers and Barbara Brothers, eds., *Reading and Writing,* 45–47.

Milligan, Ian. *Studying Jane Austen,* 123–39.

Odom, Keith C. *Jane Austen,* 131–51.

Orange, Michael. "Aspects of Narration in *Persuasion.*" *Sydney Stud in Engl* 15 (1989–90), 63–71.

Ralph, Phyllis C. *Victorian Transformations,* 70–76.

Raymer, Robyn. "Jane Austen, Fanny Price, and Anne Elliot." *Spectrum* 31 (1989), 144–55.

Taylor, Roselle. "Point of View and Estrangement in *Persuasion.*" *Publs of the Arkansas Philol Assoc* 15 (Special Issue—April 1989), 97–107.

Warhol, Robyn. "The Look, the Body, and the Heroine: A Feminist Narratological Reading of *Persuasion.*" *Novel* 26 (1992), 5–18.

Wilkes, G. A. "Autumn at Uppercross: A Note on the Use of Landscape in *Persuasion.*" *Sydney Stud in Engl* 16 (1990–91), 137–42.

Wilkie, Brian. "Jane Austen: *Amor* and Amoralism." *JEGP* 91 (1992), 551–52.

Wiltshire, John. *Jane Austen and the Body,* 155–96.

Pride and Prejudice, 1813

Alexander, Edward. "A Biblical Source for *Pride and Prejudice?* The Bennet Girls and Zeophehad's Daughters." *Engl Lang Notes* 29:4 (1992), 57–58.

Armstrong, Nancy. "The Rise of Feminine Authority in the Novel," in Mark Spilka and Caroline McCracken-Flesher, eds., *Why the Novel Matters,* 106–9.

Bennett, Paula. "Family Plots: *Pride and Prejudice* as a Novel about Parenting," in Marcia McClintock Folsom, ed., *Approaches,* 134–39.

Benson, Mary Margaret. "Mothers, Substitute Mothers, and Daughters in the Novels of Jane Austen." *Persuasions* 11 (1989), 122–24.

Boardman, Michael M. *Narrative Innovation,* 59–61.

Brattin, Joel J. "The Misdated Express in *Pride and Prejudice.*" *Publs of the Missouri Philol Assoc* 13 (1988), 54–56.

Bromberg, Pamela S. "Teaching about the Marriage Plot," in Marcia McClintock Folsom, ed., *Approaches,* 126–33.

Brown, Julia Prewitt. "The 'Social History' of *Pride and Prejudice,*" in Marcia McClintock Folsom, ed., *Approaches,* 57–66.

Carr, Jean Ferguson. "The Polemics of Incomprehension: Mother and Daughter in *Pride and Prejudice,*" in Florence Howe, ed., *Tradition and the Talents of Women,* 68–82.

Copeland, Edward. "The Economic Realities of Jane Austen's Day," in Marcia McClintock Folsom, ed., *Approaches,* 33–45.

Derry, Stephen. "Jane Austen's Use of *The Vicar of Wakefield* in *Pride and Prejudice.*" *Engl Lang Notes* 28:3 (1991), 25–27.

Dowling, William C. "*Evelina* and the Genealogy of Literary Shame." *Eighteenth-Cent Life* 16:3 (1992), 215–19.

Duckworth, Alistair M. "Fiction and Some Uses of the Country House Setting from Richardson to Scott," in H. George Hahn, ed., *The Country Myth,* 236–39.

Dussinger, John A. *In the Pride of the Moment,* 23–27, 41–44, 102–4, 121–28, 156–59.

Dwyer, June. *Jane Austen,* 65–75.

Enomoto, Yoshiko. "*Machiko* and *Pride and Prejudice.*" *Compar Lit Stud* 28 (1991), 245–58.

Erlebach, Peter. *Theorie und Praxis des Romaneingangs,* 185–92.

Fergus, Jan. *Jane Austen,* 81–86.

Folsom, Marcia McClintock. "'Taking Different Positions': Knowing and Feeling in *Pride and Prejudice,*" in Marcia McClintock Folsom, ed., *Approaches,* 100–114.

Fraiman, Susan. "Peevish Accents in the Juvenilia: A Feminist Key to

Pride and Prejudice," in Marcia McClintock Folsom, ed., *Approaches,* 74–80.

Fraiman, Susan. *Unbecoming Women,* 59–87.

Frost, Cy. "Autocracy and the Matrix of Power: Issues of Propriety and Economics in the Work of Mary Wollstonecraft, Jane Austen, and Harriet Martineau." *Tulsa Stud in Women's Lit* 10 (1991), 261–64.

Gard, Roger. *Jane Austen's Novels,* 96–120.

Giles, Paul. "The Gothic Dialogue in *Pride and Prejudice.*" *Text & Context* 2:1 (1988), 68–75.

Goubert, Pierre. "L'implicite dans *Pride and Prejudice.*" *Etudes Anglaises* 44 (1991), 179–83.

Halperin, John. "Inside *Pride and Prejudice.*" *Persuasions* 11 (1989), 37–45.

Harris, Jocelyn. "The Influence of Richardson on *Pride and Prejudice,*" in Marcia McClintock Folsom, ed., *Approaches,* 94–99.

Harris, R. Allen. "Social Definition in *Pride and Prejudice:* An Exercise in Extensional Semantics." *Engl Stud in Canada* 17 (1991), 163–75.

Heilman, Robert Bechtold. *The Workings of Fiction,* 79–98.

Heldman, James. "How Wealthy Is Mr. Darcy—*Really?* Pounds and Dollars in the World of *Pride and Prejudice.*" *Persuasions* 12 (1990), 38–49.

Hudson, Glenda A. "'Precious Remains of the Earliest Attachment': Sibling Love in Jane Austen's *Pride and Prejudice.*" *Persuasions* 11 (1989), 125–30.

Hudson, Glenda A. *Sibling Love and Incest,* 69–71, 73–76, 104–8, 126–28.

Jay, Penny. "A Changing View: Jane Austen's Landscapes." *Sydney Stud in Engl* 15 (1989–90), 54–55.

Kaplan, Deborah. *Jane Austen among Women,* 182–204.

Kaplan, Deborah. "*Pride and Prejudice* and Jane Austen's Female Friendships," in Marcia McClintock Folsom, ed., *Approaches,* 81–88.

Kneedler, Susan. "The New Romance in *Pride and Prejudice,*" in Marcia McClintock Folsom, ed., *Approaches,* 152–63.

Knuth, Deborah J. "Sisterhood and Friendship in *Pride and Prejudice:* Need Happiness be 'Entirely a Matter of Chance?'" *Persuasions* 11 (1989), 99–107.

Koppel, Gene. "*Pride and Prejudice:* Conservative or Liberal Novel—Or Both? (A Gadamerian Approach)." *Persuasions* 11 (1989), 132–39.

Lacour, Claudia Brodsky. "Austen's *Pride and Prejudice* and Hegel's 'Truth in Art': Concept, Reference, and History." *ELH* 59 (1992), 597–619.

Langland, Elizabeth. "A Feminist and Formalist Approach to Close Reading," in Marcia McClintock Folsom, ed., *Approaches,* 140–47.

Lauber, John. *Jane Austen,* 41–59.

Levin, Amy K. *The Suppressed Sister,* 39–45.

McAleer, John. "The Comedy of Social Distinctions in *Pride and Prejudice.*" *Persuasions* 11 (1989), 70–76.

McCawley, Dwight. "Assertion and Aggression in the Novels of Jane Austen." *Persuasions* 11 (1989), 77–84.

McCawley, Dwight. "Hostility and Aggression: Jane Austen's Inner Plot." *Mid-Hudson Lang Stud* 12:2 (1989), 16–26.

MacDonagh, Oliver. *Jane Austen,* 32–35, 89–96.

McMaster, Juliet. "Talking about Talking," in Marcia McClintock Folsom, ed., *Approaches,* 167–73.

Meyersohn, Marylea. "The Duets of *Pride and Prejudice,*" in Marcia McClintock Folsom, ed., *Approaches,* 148–51.

Michaelson, Patricia Howell. "Reading *Pride and Prejudice.*" *Eighteenth-Cent Fiction* 3 (1990), 65–76.

Milligan, Ian. *Studying Jane Austen,* 44–63.

Moler, Kenneth L. " 'Group Voices' in Jane Austen's Narration." *Persuasions* 13 (1991), 8–9.

Moler, Kenneth L. "Literary Allusion in *Pride and Prejudice,*" in Marcia McClintock Folsom, ed., *Approaches,* 89–93.

Moler, Kenneth L. *"Pride and Prejudice,"* 17–100.

Nardin, Jane. "Propriety versus Morality in Jane Austen's Novels." *Persuasions* 10 (1988), 73–74.

Nicoletta, Daniela. *Vibrazione e risonanza,* 28–37.

Nordell, Robert. "Confrontation and Evasion: Argument Scenes in *Mansfield Park* and *Pride and Prejudice.*" *Engl Stud in Africa* 36:1 (1993), 17–22, 25–26.

Odom, Keith C. *Jane Austen,* 41–44, 71–90.

Parker, Jo Alyson. *"Pride and Prejudice:* Jane Austen's Double Inheritance Plot." *REAL: Yrbk of Res in Engl and Am Lit* 7 (1990), 159–88.

Perry, Ruth. "Home at Last: Biographical Background to *Pride and Prejudice,*" in Marcia McClintock Folsom, ed., *Approaches,* 46–55.

Phelan, James. *Reading People,* 43–60.

Polhemus, Robert M. *Erotic Faith,* 28–54.

Ralph, Phyllis C. *Victorian Transformations,* 76–86.

Schaffer, Julie. "Not Subordinate: Empowering Women in the Marriage Plot—The Novels of Frances Burney, Maria Edgeworth, and Jane Austen." *Criticism* 34 (1992), 64–68.

Scheuermann, Mona. *Her Bread to Earn,* 201–21.

Sherrod, Barbara. *"Pride and Prejudice:* A Classic Love Story." *Persuasions* 11 (1989), 66–69.

Smith, Johanna M. " 'I Am a Gentleman's Daughter': A Marxist-Feminist Reading of *Pride and Prejudice,*" in Marcia McClintock Folsom, ed., *Approaches,* 67–73.

Snyder, William C. "Mother Nature's Other Natures: Landscape in Women's Writing, 1770–1830." *Women's Stud* 21 (1992), 148–50.

Stovel, Bruce. "Secrets, Silence, and Surprise in *Pride and Prejudice.*" *Persuasions* 11 (1989), 85–91.

Stovel, Bruce. "Surprise in *Pride and Prejudice,*" in Marcia McClintock Folsom, ed., *Approaches,* 115–25.

Tave, Stuart M. *Lovers, Clowns, and Fairies,* 58–88.

Urquhart, Alan. "'Wit' and 'Impertinence': The Elision of Class Difference in *Pride and Prejudice.*" *Sydney Stud in Engl* 16 (1990–91), 78–101.

Ward, David Allen. "Austen's *Pride and Prejudice.*" *Explicator* 51 (1992), 18–19.

Wiesenfarth, Joseph. *Gothic Manners,* 25–40.

Wilkie, Brian. "Jane Austen: *Amor* and Amoralism." *JEGP* 91 (1992), 543–51.

Wilkie, Brian. "Structural Layering in Jane Austen's Problem Novels." *Nineteenth-Cent Lit* 46 (1992), 520–22.

Wingard, Sara. "Reversal and Revelation: The Five Seasons of *Pride and Prejudice.*" *Persuasions* 11 (1989), 92–97.

Sanditon, 1925

Dwyer, June. *Jane Austen,* 118–24.

Fergus, Jan. *Jane Austen,* 168–70.

Gard, Roger. *Jane Austen's Novels,* 208–21.

Lauber, John. *Jane Austen,* 111–17.

MacDonagh, Oliver. *Jane Austen,* 149–66.

Miller, D. A. "The Late Jane Austen." *Raritan* 10:1 (1990), 69–79.

Noll-Wiemann, Renate. "Jane Austens Fragmente." *Anglia* 110 (1992), 368–94.

Odom, Keith C. *Jane Austen,* 153–63.

Wiltshire, John. *Jane Austen and the Body,* 197–221.

Sense and Sensibility, 1811

Benedict, Barbara M. "Jane Austen's *Sense and Sensibility:* The Politics of Point of View." *Philol Q* 69 (1990), 453–68.

Benson, Mary Margaret. "Mothers, Substitute Mothers, and Daughters in the Novels of Jane Austen." *Persuasions* 11 (1989), 119–20.

Braun, Eva. "Whose Sense? Whose Sensibility? Jane Austen's Subtlest Novel." *Persuasions* 12 (1990), 131–33.

David, Gail. *Female Heroism,* 113–43.

Dorsey, Shelly. "Austen, Forster, and Economics." *Persuasions* 12 (1990), 54–59.

Dussinger, John A. *In the Pride of the Moment,* 116–20.

Dwyer, June. *Jane Austen,* 53–63.

Easton, Celia A. "*Sense and Sensibility* and the Joke of Substitution." *J of Narrative Technique* 23 (1993), 114–24.

Favret, Mary A. *Romantic Correspondence,* 145–55.

Fergus, Jan. *Jane Austen,* 88–94.

Gard, Roger. *Jane Austen's Novels,* 70–95.

Hatch, Ronald B. "'Lordship and Bondage': Women Novelists of the Eighteenth Century." *REAL: Yrbk of Res in Engl and Am Lit* 8 (1991/ 92), 240–42.

Heilman, Robert Bechtold. *The Workings of Fiction,* 79–81.

Horwitz, Barbara J. *Jane Austen and the Question of Women's Education,* 101–4.

Hudson, Glenda A. *Sibling Love and Incest,* 56–60, 76–81.

Humphrey, Mary Jane. "Mrs. Palmer and Her Laughter." *Persuasions* 13 (1991), 13–15.

Jay, Penny. "A Changing View: Jane Austen's Landscapes." *Sydney Stud in Engl* 15 (1989–90), 51–54.

Kaplan, Laurie, and Richard S. Kaplan. "What is Wrong with Marianne? Medicine and Disease in Jane Austen's England." *Persuasions* 12 (1990), 117–30.

Kaufmann, David. "Law and Propriety, *Sense and Sensibility:* Austen on the Cusp of Modernity." *ELH* 59 (1992), 385–404.

Kroeber, Karl. "Jane Austen as an Historical Novelist: *Sense and Sensibility.*" *Persuasions* 12 (1990), 10–18.

Lauber, John. *Jane Austen,* 27–40.

Levin, Amy K. *The Suppressed Sister,* 35–39.

MacDonagh, Oliver. *Jane Austen,* 53–65.

Meyersohn, Marylea. "Jane Austen's Garrulous Speakers: Social Criticism in *Sense and Sensibility, Emma,* and *Persuasion,*" in Bege K. Bowers and Barbara Brothers, eds., *Reading and Writing,* 36–40.

Milligan, Ian. *Studying Jane Austen,* 31–43.

Nardin, Jane. "Propriety versus Morality in Jane Austen's Novels." *Persuasions* 10 (1988), 70–73.

Odom, Keith C. *Jane Austen,* 49–58.

Roeder, Sharlene. "The Fall on High-church Down in Jane Austen's *Sense and Sensibility.*" *Persuasions* 12 (1990), 117–18.

Ross, Deborah. *The Excellence of Falsehood,* 176–79.

Ruoff, Gene W. *Jane Austen's "Sense and Sensibility,"* 33–113.

Spacks, Patricia Meyer. "The Problem of the Interesting." *Persuasions* 12 (1990), 71–78.

Thompson, James. "Sense and Sensibility: Finance and Romance," in Syndy McMillen Conger, ed., *Sensibility in Transformation,* 151–67.

Thomsen, Inger Sigrun. "Dangerous Words and Silent Lovers in *Sense and Sensibility.*" *Persuasions* 12 (1990), 134–38.

Tsomondo, Thorell. "Imperfect Articulation: A Saving Instability in *Sense and Sensibility.*" *Persuasions* 12 (1990), 99–109.

Wallace, Tara Ghoshal. "*Sense and Sensibility* and the Problem of Feminine Authority." *Eighteenth-Cent Fiction* 4 (1992), 149–63.

Wilkie, Brian. "Jane Austen: *Amor* and Amoralism." *JEGP* 91 (1992), 552–53.

Wilkie, Brian. "Structural Layering in Jane Austen's Problem Novels." *Nineteenth-Cent Lit* 46 (1992), 522–28.

Wiltshire, John. *Jane Austen and the Body,* 24–61.

The Watsons, 1871

Dwyer, June. *Jane Austen,* 117–18.

Fergus, Jan. *Jane Austen,* 114–19.

Kaplan, Deborah. *Jane Austen among Women,* 170–81.

Lauber, John. *Jane Austen,* 107–10.

MacDonagh, Oliver. *Jane Austen,* 28–32.

Noll-Wiemann, Renate. "Jane Austens Fragmente." *Anglia* 110 (1992), 368–94.
Odom, Keith C. *Jane Austen,* 67–69.

ROBERT BAGE

Hermsprong, or Man as He Is Not, 1796

Hall, K. G. *The Exalted Heroine,* 123–38.
Scheuermann, Mona. *Her Bread to Earn,* 152–68.

ENID BAGNOLD

The Squire, 1938

Cosslett, Tess. "Childbirth from the Woman's Point of View in British Women's Fiction: Enid Bagnold's *The Squire* and A. S. Byatt's *Still Life.*" *Tulsa Stud in Women's Lit* 8 (1989), 263–83.

BERYL BAINBRIDGE

Young Adolf, 1978

Schaffeld, Norbert. *Die Darstellung des nationalsozialistischen Deutschland,* 26–43.

ROBERT MICHAEL BALLANTYNE

The Coral Island, 1858

Loxley, Diana. *Problematic Shores,* 115–26.
Michel-Michot, Paulette. "The Myth of Innocence: *Robinson Crusoe, The Coral Island* and *Lord of the Flies,*" in Jeanne Delbaere, ed., *William Golding,* 35–36, 40–41, 43–44.
Wall, Barbara. *The Narrator's Voice,* 68–70.

The Gorilla Hunters, 1861

Bristow, Joseph. *Empire Boys,* 107–9.

J. G. BALLARD

The Atrocity Exhibition, 1969

Stephenson, Gregory. *Out of the Night,* 63–68.

Concrete Island, 1974

Ruddick, Nicholas. *Ultimate Island,* 90–93.
Stephenson, Gregory. *Out of the Night,* 74–80.

Crash, 1972

Baudrillard, Jean. "Ballard's *Crash.*" *Science-Fiction Stud* 18 (1991), 313–30.
Caserio, Robert L. "Mobility and Masochism: Christine Brooke-Rose and

J. G. Ballard," in Mark Spilka and Caroline McCracken-Flesher, eds., *Why the Novel Matters*, 320–22.

Foster, Dennis A. "J. G. Ballard's Empire of the Senses: Perversion and the Failure of Authority." *PMLA* 108 (1993), 523–27.

Hollinger, Veronica. "Specular SF: Postmodern Allegory," in Nicholas Ruddick, ed., *State of the Fantastic*, 30–33.

McKee, Alan. "Intentional Phalluses: The Male 'Sex' in J. G. Ballard." *Foundation* 57 (1993), 62–66.

Ruddick, Nicholas. "Ballard/*Crash*/Baudrillard." *Science-Fiction Stud* 19 (1992), 354–59.

Ruddick, Nicholas. *Ultimate Island*, 158–63.

Stephenson, Gregory. *Out of the Night*, 68–74.

The Crystal World, 1966

Stephenson, Gregory. *Out of the Night*, 57–61.

The Day of Creation, 1987

Stephenson, Gregory. *Out of the Night*, 134–42.

The Drought, 1964

Stephenson, Gregory. *Out of the Night*, 50–56.

The Drowned World, 1962

Malmgren, Carl D. *Worlds Apart*, 131–38.
Ruddick, Nicholas. *Ultimate Island*, 155–58.
Stephenson, Gregory. *Out of the Night*, 46–50.

Empire of the Sun, 1984

Caserio, Robert L. "Mobility and Masochism: Christine Brooke-Rose and J. G. Ballard," in Mark Spilka and Caroline McCracken-Flesher, eds., *Why the Novel Matters*, 322–26.

Foster, Dennis A. "J. G. Ballard's Empire of the Senses: Perversion and the Failure of Authority." *PMLA* 108 (1993), 527–31.

Stephenson, Gregory. *Out of the Night*, 128–34.

Hello America, 1981

Stephenson, Gregory. *Out of the Night*, 123–28.

High-Rise, 1975

McKee, Alan. "Intentional Phalluses: The Male 'Sex' in J. G. Ballard." *Foundation* 57 (1993), 62–66.
Ruddick, Nicholas. *Ultimate Island*, 163–67.
Stephenson, Gregory. *Out of the Night*, 80–84.

Running Wild, 1988

Foster, Dennis A. "J. G. Ballard's Empire of the Senses: Perversion and the Failure of Authority." *PMLA* 108 (1993), 519–23.
Stephenson, Gregory. *Out of the Night*, 142–46.

The Unlimited Dream Company, 1979

McKee, Alan. "Intentional Phalluses: The Male 'Sex' in J. G. Ballard." *Foundation* 57 (1993), 62–66.
Stephenson, Gregory. *Out of the Night,* 117–23.

The Wind from Nowhere, 1962

Ruddick, Nicholas. *Ultimate Island,* 153–55.
Stephenson, Gregory. *Out of the Night,* 42–46.

JOHN BANIM

The Boyne Water, 1826

Escarbelt, Bernard. "Historical Glimpses: John Banim," in Jacqueline Genet, ed., *The Big House in Ireland,* 85–87.

The Nowlans, 1826

Escarbelt, Bernard. "Historical Glimpses: John Banim," in Jacqueline Genet, ed., *The Big House in Ireland,* 87–89.

JOHN BANVILLE

Birchwood, 1973

Brown, Terence. "Redeeming the Time: The Novels of John McGahern and John Banville," in James Acheson, ed., *The British and Irish Novel,* 165–67.
Burgstaller, Susanne. "'This Lawless House': John Banville's Post-Modernist Treatment of the Big-House Motif in *Birchwood* and *The Newton Letter,*" in Otto Rauchbauer, ed., *Ancestral Voices,* 239–46.
Cornwell, Neil. *The Literary Fantastic,* 173–77.
Cronin, Gearóid. "John Banville and the Subversion of the Big House Novel," in Jacqueline Genet, ed., *The Big House in Ireland,* 218–21, 226–29.
Imhof, Rüdiger. *John Banville,* 53–73.
Lernout, Geert. "Banville and Being: *The Newton Letter* and History," in Joris Duytschaever and Geert Lernout, eds., *History and Violence,* 69–74.
McMinn, Joseph. *John Banville,* 30–45.
O'Neill, Patrick. "John Banville," in Rüdiger Imhof, ed., *Contemporary Irish Novelists,* 209–11.

The Book of Evidence, 1989

McMinn, Joseph. *John Banville,* 109–23.

Doctor Copernicus, 1976

Brown, Terence. "Redeeming the Time: The Novels of John McGahern and John Banville," in James Acheson, ed., *The British and Irish Novel,* 167–69.

Imhof, Rüdiger. *John Banville*, 74–103.

McMinn, Joseph. *John Banville*, 46–67.

O'Neill, Patrick. "John Banville," in Rüdiger Imhof, ed., *Contemporary Irish Novelists*, 211–13.

Kepler, 1981

Brown, Terence. "Redeeming the Time: The Novels of John McGahern and John Banville," in James Acheson, ed., *The British and Irish Novel*, 167–69.

Imhof, Rüdiger. *John Banville*, 104–39.

McMinn, Joseph. *John Banville*, 68–87.

O'Neill, Patrick. "John Banville," in Rüdiger Imhof, ed., *Contemporary Irish Novelists*, 213–15.

Mefisto, 1986

Brown, Terence. "Redeeming the Time: The Novels of John McGahern and John Banville," in James Acheson, ed., *The British and Irish Novel*, 170–71.

Cornwell, Neil. *The Literary Fantastic*, 176–84.

Fiérobe, Claude. "Cygnes et Signes: Swan dans *Mefisto* de John Banville." *Etudes Irlandaises* 16:1 (1991), 97–106.

Imhof, Rüdiger. *John Banville*, 153–70.

McMinn, Joseph. *John Banville*, 98–108.

O'Neill, Patrick. "John Banville," in Rüdiger Imhof, ed., *Contemporary Irish Novelists*, 218–22.

The Newton Letter, 1982

Burgstaller, Susanne. " 'This Lawless House': John Banville's Post-Modernist Treatment of the Big-House Motif in *Birchwood* and *The Newton Letter,*" in Otto Rauchbauer, ed., *Ancestral Voices*, 246–54.

Cronin, Gearóid. "John Banville and the Subversion of the Big House Novel," in Jacqueline Genet, ed., *The Big House in Ireland*, 221–29.

Imhof, Rüdiger. *John Banville*, 140–52.

Lernout, Geert. "Banville and Being: *The Newton Letter* and History," in Joris Duytschaever and Geert Lernout, eds., *History and Violence*, 74–77.

McMinn, Joseph. *John Banville*, 88–97.

O'Neill, Patrick. "John Banville," in Rüdiger Imhof, ed., *Contemporary Irish Novelists*, 216–18.

Nightspawn, 1971

Imhof, Rüdiger. *John Banville*, 36–52.

McMinn, Joseph. *John Banville*, 21–29.

O'Neill, Patrick. "John Banville," in Rüdiger Imhof, ed., *Contemporary Irish Novelists*, 208–9.

JAMES BARKE

Major Operation, 1936

Croft, Andy. *Red Letter Days,* 276–79.

Malzahn, Manfred. "Coming to Terms with Industrial Scotland: Two 'Proletarian' Novels of the 1930s," in Joachim Schwend and Horst W. Drescher, eds., *Studies in Scottish Fiction,* 194–203.

Whyte, Christopher. "Imagining the City: The Glasgow Novel," in Joachim Schwend and Horst W. Drescher, eds., *Studies in Scottish Fiction,* 325–27.

JANE BARKER

Exilius, or, The Banished Roman, 1715

Wikborg, Eleanor. "The Expression of the Forbidden in Romance Form: Genre as Possibility in Jane Barker's *Exilius.*" *Genre* 22 (1989), 3–18.

Williamson, Marilyn L. *Raising Their Voices,* 247–49.

Love Intrigues, 1713

Williamson, Marilyn L. *Raising Their Voices,* 245–47.

A Patch-Work Screen for the Ladies, 1723

Donovan, Josephine. "Women and the Rise of the Novel: A Feminist-Marxist Theory." *Signs* 16 (1991), 460–62.

Williamson, Marilyn L. *Raising Their Voices,* 249–51.

JULIAN BARNES

Before She Met Me, 1982

Higdon, David Leon. "'Unconfessed Confessions': The Narrators of Graham Swift and Julian Barnes," in James Acheson, ed., *The British and Irish Novel,* 177–79.

Millington, Mark I., and Alison S. Sinclair. "The Honourable Cuckold: Models of Masculine Defence." *Compar Lit Stud* 29 (1992), 13–17.

Flaubert's Parrot, 1984

Higdon, David Leon. "'Unconfessed Confessions': The Narrators of Graham Swift and Julian Barnes," in James Acheson, ed., *The British and Irish Novel,* 175, 179–81.

Lee, Alison. *Realism and Power,* 1–4, 36–40.

Scott, James B. "Parrot as Paradigms: Infinite Deferral of Meaning in *Flaubert's Parrot.*" *Ariel* 21:3 (1990), 57–68.

Shiner, Larry. "Flaubert's Parrot, Agee's Swan: From 'Reality Effect' to 'Fiction Effect.'" *J of Narrative Technique* 20 (1990), 167–78.

A History of the World in 10 1/2 Chapters, 1989

Raucq-Hoorickx, Isabelle. "Julian Barnes' *History of the World in 10 1/2 Chapters:* A Levinasian Deconstructionist Point of View." *Le Langage et l'Homme* 26:1 (1991), 47–54.

Metroland, 1980

> Higdon, David Leon. "'Unconfessed Confessions': The Narrators of Graham Swift and Julian Barnes," in James Acheson, ed., *The British and Irish Novel,* 175–77.

EATON STANNARD BARRETT

The Heroine; or Adventures of a Fair Romance Reader, 1813

> Kelly, Gary. "Unbecoming a Heroine: Novel Reading, Romanticism, and Barrett's *The Heroine.*" *Nineteenth-Cent Lit* 45 (1990), 226–41.

JAMES MATTHEW BARRIE

Peter and Wendy, 1911

> Honig, Edith Lazaros. *Breaking the Angelic Image,* 101–8.
> Wall, Barbara. *The Narrator's Voice,* 23–29.

Peter Pan in Kensington Gardens, 1906

> Gilead, Sarah. "Magic Abjured: Closure in Children's Fantasy Fiction." *PMLA* 106 (1991), 285–87.
> Wall, Barbara. *The Narrator's Voice,* 23–29.

Sentimental Tommy, 1895

> Jack, R. D. S. "Art, Nature and Thrums," in Joachim Schwend et al., eds., *Literatur im Kontext,* 155–63.
> Letley, Emma. *From Galt to Douglas Brown,* 233–44.

RALPH BATES

The Olive Field, 1936

> Croft, Andy. *Red Letter Days,* 319–22.

THOMAS BATY

Beatrice the Sixteenth, 1909

> Patai, Daphne, and Angela Ingram. "Fantasy and Identity: The Double Life of a Victorian Sexual Radical," in Angela Ingram and Daphne Patai, eds., *Rediscovering Forgotten Radicals,* 265–69.

SAMUEL BECKETT

Company, 1980

> Amiran, Eyal. *Wandering and Home,* 40–41, 58–59, 69–70.
> Astro, Alan. *Understanding Samuel Beckett,* 198–203.
> Beer, Ann. "Beckett's 'Autography' and the Company of Languages." *Southern R* (Baton Rouge) 27 (1991), 771–91.

Bersani, Leo, and Ulysse Dutoit. "Beckett's Sociability." *Raritan* 12:1 (1992), 10–19.

Brienza, Susan. "Clods, Whores, and Bitches: Misogyny in Beckett's Early Fiction," in Linda Ben-Zvi, ed., *Women in Beckett*, 102–3.

Carey, Phyllis. "Samuel Beckett's *coup de grâce*." *Notes on Mod Irish Lit* 1 (1989), 23–26.

Cismaru, Alfred. "*Isms* and Godots versus Egos and Individuals: The Beckettian Stand." *Midwest Q* 31 (1990), 514–22.

Handwerk, Gary. "Alone with Beckett's *Company*." *J of Beckett Stud* 2:1 (1992), 65–78.

Hicks, Jim. "Partial Interpretations and *Company:* Beckett, Foucault, et al. and the Author Question." *Stud in Twentieth-Cent Lit* 17 (1993), 309–22.

Jewinski, Ed. "Beckett's *Company,* Post-structuralism, and *Mimetalogique,*" in Lance St. John Butler and Robin J. Davis, eds., *Rethinking Beckett*, 141–58.

Krance, Charles. "Beckett's *Encores:* Textual Genesis as *Still*-Life Performance." *Essays in Theatre* 8 (1990), 121–26.

Krance, Charles. "*Worstward Ho* and *On*-words: Writing to(wards) the Point," in Lance St. John Butler and Robin J. Davis, eds., *Rethinking Beckett*, 124–26.

Lyons, Charles R. "Male or Female Voice: The Significance of the Gender of the Speaker in Beckett's Late Fiction and Drama," in Linda Ben-Zvi, ed., *Women in Beckett*, 151–54, 157–60.

Watson, David. *Paradox and Desire*, 147–54.

How It Is, 1964

Alvarez, A. *Beckett*, 76–84.

Amiran, Eyal. *Wandering and Home*, 162–68.

Astro, Alan. *Understanding Samuel Beckett*, 93–112.

Bersani, Leo, and Ulysse Dutoit. "Beckett's Sociability." *Raritan* 12:1 (1992), 3–10.

Breuer, Rolf. "Paradox in Beckett." *Mod Lang R* 88 (1993), 572.

Foster, Paul. *Beckett and Zen*, 231–57.

Heise, Ursula K. "*Erzählzeit* and Postmodern Narrative: Text as Duration in Beckett's *How It Is*." *Style* 26 (1992), 245–64.

Hill, Leslie. *Beckett's Fiction*, 133–40.

Rabinovitz, Rubin. *Innovation*, 140–42.

Ricks, Christopher. *Beckett's Dying Words*, 109–10, 115–16, 137–39.

Topsfield, Valerie. *The Humour of Samuel Beckett*, 120–26.

Watson, David. *Paradox and Desire*, 86–88, 90–94, 96–103.

Ill Seen Ill Said, 1982

Beer, Ann. "Beckett's 'Autography' and the Company of Languages." *Southern R* (Baton Rouge) 27 (1991), 771–91.

Cismaru, Alfred. "*Isms* and Godots versus Egos and Individuals: The Beckettian Stand." *Midwest Q* 31 (1990), 514–22.

Graver, Lawrence. "Homage to the Dark Lady: *Ill Seen Ill Said,*" in Linda Ben-Zvi, ed., *Women in Beckett,* 142–48.

Krance, Charles. "*Worstward Ho* and *On*-words: Writing to(wards) the Point," in Lance St. John Butler and Robin J. Davis, eds., *Rethinking Beckett,* 132–38.

Lyons, Charles R. "Male or Female Voice: The Significance of the Gender of the Speaker in Beckett's Late Fiction and Drama," in Linda Ben-Zvi, ed., *Women in Beckett,* 151–54, 157–60.

Moorjani, Angela B. "The Magna Mater Myth in Beckett's Fiction: Subtext and Subversion," in Linda Ben-Zvi, ed., *Women in Beckett,* 138–39.

Watson, David. *Paradox and Desire,* 154–61.

The Lost Ones, 1971

Amiran, Eyal. *Wandering and Home,* 165–69.

Brienza, Susan. "Clods, Whores, and Bitches: Misogyny in Beckett's Early Fiction," in Linda Ben-Zvi, ed., *Women in Beckett,* 103.

Hansford, James. "*The Lost Ones:* The One and the Many." *Stud in Short Fiction* 26 (1989), 125–33.

Rabinovitz, Rubin. *Innovation,* 160–62.

Malone Dies, 1956

Alexander, Marguerite. *Flights from Realism,* 58–60.

Alvarez, A. *Beckett,* 63–68.

Astro, Alan. *Understanding Samuel Beckett,* 68–81.

Amiran, Eyal. *Wandering and Home,* 59–60, 111–15, 204–6.

Breuer, Rolf. "Paradox in Beckett." *Mod Lang R* 88 (1993), 568–69.

Foster, Paul. *Beckett and Zen,* 186–202.

Häufle, Heinrich. "Erzählerlaunen: Zu einem narrativen Verfahren in S. Becketts *Malone meurt.*" *Zeitschrift für Französische Sprache und Literatur* 101 (1991), 19–34.

Harrington, John P. *The Irish Beckett,* 159–65.

Harrington, John P. "A Note on *Malone Dies* and Local Phenomena." *J of Beckett Stud* 1:1–2 (1992), 141–43.

Hill, Leslie. *Beckett's Fiction,* 45–49, 62–66, 70–72, 100–108.

Mays, J. C. C. "Irish Beckett: A Borderline Instance," in S. E. Wilmer, ed., *Beckett in Dublin,* 134–37.

Phillips, K. J. *Dying Gods in Twentieth-Century Fiction,* 54–64.

Rabinovitz, Rubin. *Innovation,* 5–6, 31–33, 69–71, 96–100, 109–10, 199–200.

Rabinovitz, Rubin. "Repetition and Underlying Meanings in Samuel Beckett's Trilogy," in Lance St. John Butler and Robin J. Davis, eds., *Rethinking Beckett,* 31–65.

Rabinovitz, Rubin. "Stereoscopic or Stereotypic: Characterization in Beckett's Fiction," in Linda Ben-Zvi, ed., *Women in Beckett,* 110–12.

Ricks, Christopher. *Beckett's Dying Words,* 1–3, 111–16, 118–20, 142–44.

Roig, Michel. "*Malone meurt:* perspectives baroques." *Roman 20–50* 4 (1987), 101–7.

Roig, Michel. *"Malone meurt:* roman à voir." *Littératures* 20 (1989), 133–40.

Thomas, Ronald R. *Dreams of Authority,* 280–90.

Toyama, Jean Yamasaki. *Beckett's Game,* 45–58.

Mercier and Camier, 1970

Alvarez, A. *Beckett,* 54–57.

Amiran, Eyal. *Wandering and Home,* 102–8.

Campbell, Julie. "Pilgrim's Progress/Regress/Stasis: Some Thoughts on the Treatment of the Quest in Bunyan's *Pilgrim's Progress* and Beckett's *Mercier and Camier."* *Compar Lit Stud* 30 (1993), 137–52.

Harrington, John P. *The Irish Beckett,* 149–55.

Ricks, Christopher. *Beckett's Dying Words,* 69–73, 76–78.

Topsfield, Valerie. *The Humour of Samuel Beckett,* 63–70.

Molloy, 1955

Alexander, Marguerite. *Flights from Realism,* 54–58.

Alvarez, A. *Beckett,* 57–63.

Amiran, Eyal. *Wandering and Home,* 39–42, 107–11.

Astro, Alan. *Understanding Samuel Beckett,* 51–67.

Breuer, Rolf. "Paradox in Beckett." *Mod Lang R* 88 (1993), 566–68.

Cantrell, Carol Helmstetter. "Cartesian Man and the Woman Reader: A Feminist Approach to Beckett's *Molloy,"* in Linda Ben-Zvi, ed., *Women in Beckett,* 117–29.

Dettmar, Kevin J. H. "The Figure in Beckett's Carpet: *Molloy* and the Assault on Metaphor," in Lance St. John Butler and Robin J. Davis, eds., *Rethinking Beckett,* 72–86.

Foster, Paul. *Beckett and Zen,* 155–85.

Gauer, Denis. *"Molloy* et l'objet sans nom: l'appel du sens et le fil du rasoir." *Etudes Irlandaises* 16:2 (1991), 55–66.

Harrington, John P. *The Irish Beckett,* 157–59.

Hill, Leslie. *Beckett's Fiction,* 66–69, 72–74, 76–78, 83–99.

Mays, J. C. C. "Irish Beckett: A Borderline Instance," in S. E. Wilmer, ed., *Beckett in Dublin,* 134–37.

Moorjani, Angela. "A Cryptanalysis of Beckett's *Molloy,"* in Joseph H. Smith, ed., *The World of Samuel Beckett,* 53–70.

Moorjani, Angela B. "The Magna Mater Myth in Beckett's Fiction: Subtext and Subversion," in Linda Ben-Zvi, ed., *Women in Beckett,* 134–38.

Rabinovitz, Rubin. *Innovation,* 37–55, 65–71, 77–79, 90–92, 96–99.

Rabinovitz, Rubin. "Repetition and Underlying Meanings in Samuel Beckett's Trilogy," in Lance St. John Butler and Robin J. Davis, eds., *Rethinking Beckett,* 31–65.

Rabinovitz, Rubin. "Stereoscopic or Stereotypic: Characterization in Beckett's Fiction," in Linda Ben-Zvi, ed., *Women in Beckett,* 110–12.

Richardson, Brian. "Causality in *Molloy:* Philosophic Theme, Narrative Transgression, and Metafictional Paradox." *Style* 26 (1992), 66–75.

Rolin-Ianziti, Jeanne. "L'Evaluation comme procédé de construction du récit: le cas de *Molloy*." *Australian J of French Stud* 25 (1988), 267–79.

Thomas, Ronald R. *Dreams of Authority*, 280–90.

Topsfield, Valerie. *The Humour of Samuel Beckett*, 75–81.

Toyama, Jean Yamasaki. *Beckett's Game*, 19–40.

Watson, David. *Paradox and Desire*, 63–68.

Murphy, 1938

Acheson, James. "Beckett and the Heresy of Love," in Linda Ben-Zvi, ed., *Women in Beckett*, 70–72, 76–77.

Alexander, Marguerite. *Flights from Realism*, 32–36.

Alvarez, A. *Beckett*, 33–40.

Amiran, Eyal. *Wandering and Home*, 33–35, 58–60, 90–97, 131–33.

Astro, Alan. *Understanding Samuel Beckett*, 36–42.

Brienza, Susan. "Clods, Whores, and Bitches: Misogyny in Beckett's Early Fiction," in Linda Ben-Zvi, ed., *Women in Beckett*, 96–98.

Culik, Hugh. "Mathematics as Metaphor: Samuel Beckett and the Esthetics of Incompleteness." *Papers on Lang & Lit* 29 (1993), 140–45.

DiBattista, Maria. *First Love*, 216–21.

Foster, Paul. *Beckett and Zen*, 123–27.

Gagliardo, Francesca. "La partita a scacchi in *Murphy* di S. Beckett: Follia matematica o indagine psicologia?" *Confronto Letterario* 8:15 (1991), 183–87.

Harrington, John P. *The Irish Beckett*, 82–108.

Kiberd, Declan. "Beckett and the Life to Come," in S. E. Wilmer, ed., *Beckett in Dublin*, 78–80.

Rabinovitz, Rubin. *Innovation*, 14–15, 194–95, 203–4.

Ricks, Christopher. *Beckett's Dying Words*, 6–8, 57–60, 98–101.

Topsfield, Valerie. *The Humour of Samuel Beckett*, 43–48.

Watson, David. *Paradox and Desire*, 48–50.

Wood, Rupert. "Murphy, Beckett; Geulincx, God." *J of Beckett Stud* 2:2 (1993), 27–48.

The Unnamable, 1958

Alexander, Marguerite. *Flights from Realism*, 60–62.

Alvarez, A. *Beckett*, 68–76.

Amiran, Eyal. *Wandering and Home*, 19–21, 38–40, 52–54, 59–61, 116–22, 149–51, 159–64, 189–91.

Astro, Alan. *Understanding Samuel Beckett*, 81–94.

Breuer, Rolf. "Paradox in Beckett." *Mod Lang R* 88 (1993), 577–80.

Fitch, B. T. "Evolution d'une œuvre, révolution d'une forme: du roman au texte chez Beckett," in G. T. Harris and P. M. Wetherill, eds., *Littérature et révolutions*, 289–303.

Foster, Paul. *Beckett and Zen*, 203–30.

Hanson, Susan. "On Translation and M/Others: Samuel Beckett's *The Unnamable*." *Translation Perspectives* 5 (1990), 131–46.

Harrington, John P. *The Irish Beckett*, 166–71.

Hill, Leslie. *Beckett's Fiction*, 79–83, 116–22.

Mays, J. C. C. "Irish Beckett: A Borderline Instance," in S. E. Wilmer, ed., *Beckett in Dublin*, 134–37.

Rabinovitz, Rubin. *Innovation*, 23–26, 31–32, 65–71, 96–100, 199–201.

Rabinovitz, Rubin. "Repetition and Underlying Meanings in Samuel Beckett's Trilogy," in Lance St. John Butler and Robin J. Davis, eds., *Rethinking Beckett*, 31–65.

Rabinovitz, Rubin. "Stereoscopic or Stereotypic: Characterization in Beckett's Fiction," in Linda Ben-Zvi, ed., *Women in Beckett*, 110–12.

Sherzer, Dina. "Samuel Beckett, Linguist and Poetician: A View from *The Unnamable.*" *SubStance* 56 (1988), 87–98.

Thomas, Ronald R. *Dreams of Authority*, 261–63, 280–90.

Topsfield, Valerie. *The Humour of Samuel Beckett*, 87–93.

Toyama, Jean Yamasaki. *Beckett's Game*, 61–78.

Watson, David. *Paradox and Desire*, 32–35, 40–44, 46–48, 50–52.

Watt, 1953

Acheson, James. "A Note on the Ladder Joke in *Watt.*" *J of Beckett Stud* 2:1 (1992), 115–16.

Alvarez, A. *Beckett*, 40–46.

Amiran, Eyal. *Wandering and Home*, 29–32, 58–60, 97–103.

Astro, Alan. *Understanding Samuel Beckett*, 42–49.

Axelrod, M. R. *The Politics of Style*, 61–86.

Breuer, Rolf. "Three Notes on Beckett." *J of Beckett Stud* 1:1–2 (1992), 145–46.

Brienza, Susan. "Clods, Whores, and Bitches: Misogyny in Beckett's Early Fiction," in Linda Ben-Zvi, ed., *Women in Beckett*, 98–101.

Büttner, Gottfried. "A New Approach to *Watt,*" in Lance St. John Butler and Robin J. Davis, eds., *Rethinking Beckett*, 169–78.

Culik, Hugh. "Mathematics as Metaphor: Samuel Beckett and the Esthetics of Incompleteness." *Papers on Lang & Lit* 29 (1993), 147–50.

Foster, Paul. *Beckett and Zen*, 128–54.

Harrington, John P. "The Galls in Samuel Beckett's *Watt.*" *Notes on Mod Irish Lit* 2 (1990), 6–9.

Harrington, John P. *The Irish Beckett*, 109–42.

Hill, Leslie. *Beckett's Fiction*, 20–35.

Montgomery, Angela. "Beckett and Science: *Watt* and the Quantum Universe." *Compar Criticism* 13 (1991), 171–81.

Mooney, Michael E. "*Watt:* Samuel Beckett's Sceptical Fiction," in Lance St. John Butler and Robin J. Davis, eds., *Rethinking Beckett*, 160–67.

O'Neill, Patrick. *The Comedy of Entropy*, 234–47.

Rabinovitz, Rubin. *Innovation*, 20–34, 177–78.

Ricks, Christopher. *Beckett's Dying Words*, 74–76.

Topsfield, Valerie. *The Humour of Samuel Beckett*, 48–57.

Watson, David. *Paradox and Desire*, 17–19.

WILLIAM BECKFORD

Vathek, 1786

Baridon, Michel. "Vathek—Megalomaniac Caliph or Pundit of the Avant-Garde?," in Kenneth W. Graham, ed., *"Vathek" and the Escape from Time,* 73–94.

Cope, Kevin L. "Moral Travel and the Pursuit of Nothing: *Vathek* and *Siris* as Philosophical Monologue." *Stud in Eighteenth-Cent Culture* 18 (1988), 167–82.

Cope, Kevin L. "William Beckford's *Vathek* as Philosophical Monologue." *Stud on Voltaire and the Eighteenth Cent* 265 (1989), 1673–76.

Craig, Randall. "*Vathek:* The Inversion of Romance," in Kenneth W. Graham, ed., *"Vathek" and the Escape from Time,* 113–27.

Fothergill, Brian. "The Influence of Landscape and Architecture on the Composition of *Vathek,"* in Kenneth W. Graham, ed., *"Vathek" and the Escape from Time,* 33–46.

Frank, Frederick S. "The Gothic *Vathek:* The Problem of Genre Resolved," in Kenneth W. Graham, ed., *"Vathek" and the Escape from Time,* 157–70.

Garrett, John. "Ending in Infinity: William Beckford's Arabian Tale." *Eighteenth-Cent Fiction* 5 (1992), 15–34.

Gill, R. B. "The Enlightened Occultist: Beckford's Presence in *Vathek,"* in Kenneth W. Graham, ed., *"Vathek" and the Escape from Time,* 131–43.

Hagstrum, Jean H. *Eros and Vision,* 59–61.

Hyland, Peter. "*Vathek,* Heaven and Hell," in Kenneth W. Graham, ed., *"Vathek" and the Escape from Time,* 145–54.

Klein, Jürgen. "*Vathek* and Decadence," in Kenneth W. Graham, ed., *"Vathek" and the Escape from Time,* 173–95.

Maynard, Temple J. "Eschewing Present Pleasure for an Eternity of Bliss: The Irreligious Motivation of Beckford's Protagonists in *Vathek.*" *Stud on Voltaire and the Eighteenth Cent* 265 (1989), 1676–79.

Maynard, Temple J. "The Movement Underground and the Escape from Time in Beckford's Fiction," in Kenneth W. Graham, ed., *"Vathek" and the Escape from Time,* 9–28.

Meyer, Eric. "'I Know Thee Not, I Loathe Thy Race': Romantic Orientalism in the Eye of the Other." *ELH* 58 (1991), 665–68.

Napier, Elizabeth R. *The Failure of Gothic,* 64–68.

Potkay, Adam. "Beckford's Heaven of Boys." *Raritan* 13:1 (1993), 73–86.

Probyn, Clive T. *English Fiction,* 172–75.

Svilpis, J. E. "Orientalism, Fantasy, and *Vathek,"* in Kenneth W. Graham, ed., *"Vathek" and the Escape from Time,* 49–70.

Varma, Devendra P. "Beckford Treasures Rediscovered: Mystic Glow of Persian Sufism in *Vathek,"* in Kenneth W. Graham, ed., *"Vathek" and the Escape from Time,* 97–109.

SYBILLE BEDFORD

Jigsaw, 1989

Evans, Robert Owen. "Sybille Bedford: A Paradise of Dainty Devices," in Robert E. Hosmer, Jr., ed., *Contemporary British Women Writers,* 17–19.

A Legacy, 1956

Evans, Robert Owen. "Sybille Bedford: A Paradise of Dainty Devices," in Robert E. Hosmer, Jr., ed., *Contemporary British Women Writers,* 1–13.

MAX BEERBOHM

Zuleika Dobson, 1911

Gagnier, Regenia. "Evolution and Information, or Eroticism and Everyday Life, in *Dracula* and Late Victorian Aestheticism," in Regina Barreca, ed., *Sex and Death,* 154–55.

Kiernan, Robert F. *Frivolity Unbound,* 38–48.

Riewald, J. G. *Remembering Max Beerbohm,* 112–14, 124–27, 165–66.

Rossen, Janice. *The University in Modern Fiction,* 108–9, 112–14.

Wiesenfarth, Joseph. *Gothic Manners,* 187–91.

APHRA BEHN

The Fair Jilt, 1688

Pearson, Jacqueline. "Gender and Narrative in the Fiction of Aphra Behn." *R of Engl Stud* 42 (1991), 51–53.

Woodcock, George. *Aphra Behn,* 199–201.

The History of the Nun; or, The Fair Vow-Breaker, 1689

Craft, Catherine A. "Reworking Male Models: Aphra Behn's *Fair Vow-Breaker,* Eliza Haywood's *Fantomina,* and Charlotte Lennox's *Female Quixote." Mod Lang R* 86 (1991), 832–38.

Pearson, Jacqueline. "Gender and Narrative in the Fiction of Aphra Behn." *R of Engl Stud* 42 (1991), 50–51.

Woodcock, George. *Aphra Behn,* 206–8.

Love Letters Between a Nobleman and His Sister, 1683–1687

Gardiner, Judith Kegan. "The First English Novel: Aphra Behn's *Love Letters,* The Canon, and Women's Tastes." *Tulsa Stud in Women's Lit* 8 (1989), 201–19.

Jacobs, Naomi. *The Character of Truth,* 11–13.

Jacobs, Naomi. "The Seduction of Aphra Behn." *Women's Stud* 18 (1991), 395–401.

Pearson, Jacqueline. "Gender and Narrative in the Fiction of Aphra Behn." *R of Engl Stud* 42 (1991), 53–56, 179–84.

Starr, G. A. "Aphra Behn and the Genealogy of the Man of Feeling." *Mod Philology* 87 (1990), 368–72.

Wehrs, Donald R. "*Eros*, Ethics, Identity: Royalist Feminism and the Politics of Desire in Aphra Behn's *Love Letters*." *Stud in Engl Lit, 1500–1900* 32 (1992), 461–74.

Williamson, Marilyn L. *Raising Their Voices*, 214–16.

Oroonoko, 1688

Erickson, Robert A. "Mrs A. Behn and the Myth of Oroonoko-Imoinda." *Eighteenth-Cent Fiction* 5 (1993), 201–16.

Erlebach, Peter. *Theorie und Praxis des Romaneingangs*, 136–40.

Ferguson, Margaret W. "Juggling the Categories of Race, Class and Gender: Aphra Behn's *Oroonoko*." *Women's Stud* 19 (1991), 159–75.

Ferguson, Moira. "*Oroonoko:* Birth of a Paradigm." *New Liter Hist* 23 (1992), 339–56.

Hutner, Heidi. "Aphra Behn's *Oroonoko:* The Politics of Gender, Race, and Class," in Dale Spender, ed., *Living by the Pen*, 39–50.

Pearson, Jacqueline. "Gender and Narrative in the Fiction of Aphra Behn." *R of Engl Stud* 42 (1991), 184–90.

Ross, Deborah. *The Excellence of Falsehood*, 18–20, 29–38.

Starr, G. A. "Aphra Behn and the Genealogy of the Man of Feeling." *Mod Philology* 87 (1990), 362–68.

Woodcock, George. *Aphra Behn*, 16–26, 202–6, 230–35.

ANNA MARIA BENNETT

Agnes De-Courci, 1789

Grundy, Isobel. "'A novel in a series of letters by a lady': Richardson and Some Richardsonian Novels," in Margaret Anne Doody and Peter Sabor, eds., *Samuel Richardson*, 229–31.

ARNOLD BENNETT

Anna of the Five Towns, 1902

Scheick, William J. *Fictional Structure & Ethics*, 66–74.

Stovel, Nora Forster. "'A Great Kick at Misery': Lawrence's and Drabble's Rebellion Against the Fatalism of Bennett," in Keith Cushman and Dennis Jackson, eds., *D. H. Lawrence's Literary Inheritors*, 131–54.

The Card, 1911

Killam, G. D. *Arnold Bennett: "The Card,"* 14–43.

Clayhanger, 1910

Carey, John. *The Intellectuals and the Masses*, 163–64, 168–70.

Trodd, Anthea. *A Reader's Guide*, 48–52.

Hilda Lessways, 1911

> Harris, Janice H. "Lawrence and the Edwardian Feminists," in Michael Squires and Keith Cushman, eds., *The Challenge of D. H. Lawrence,* 64–66.
> Trodd, Anthea. *A Reader's Guide,* 67–69.

Lord Raingo, 1926

> Harvie, Christopher. *The Centre of Things,* 156–59.

A Man from the North, 1898

> Carey, John. *The Intellectuals and the Masses,* 160–62.

The Old Wives' Tale, 1908

> Carey, John. *The Intellectuals and the Masses,* 166–68, 176–78.
> Tindall, Gillian. *Countries of the Mind,* 117–18, 166–69.

The Pretty Lady, 1918

> Orel, Harold. *Popular Fiction in England,* 203–13.

E. C. BENTLEY

Trent's Last Case, 1913

> Paul, Robert S. *Whatever Happened to Sherlock Homes?,* 97–99.

JOHN BERGER

Corker's Freedom, 1964

> Papastergiadis, Nikos. *Modernity as Exile,* 171–74.

The Foot of Clive, 1962

> Papastergiadis, Nikos. *Modernity as Exile,* 156–66.

G., 1972

> Papastergiadis, Nikos. *Modernity as Exile,* 175–80.
> Weibel, Paul. *Reconstructing the Past,* 11–48, 97–122.

A Painter of Our Time, 1959

> Hassam, Andrew. *Writing and Reality,* 74–78.
> Papastergiadis, Nikos. *Modernity as Exile,* 146–56.

BERNARD BERGONZI

The Roman Persuasion, 1981

> Woodman, Thomas. *Faithful Fictions,* 53–55, 140–41.

C. A. G. BERTRAM

Men Adrift, 1935

> Croft, Andy. *Red Letter Days,* 271–75.

WALTER BESANT

All Sorts and Conditions of Man, 1882

> Neetens, Wim. "Problems of a 'Democratic Text': Walter Besant's Impossible Story." *Novel* 23 (1990), 247–64.
> Neetens, Wim. *Writing and Democracy,* 41–61.

The Inner House, 1888

> Suvin, Darko. "Counter-Projects: William Morris and the Science Fiction of the 1880s," in Florence S. Boos and Carole G. Silver, eds., *Socialism and . . . William Morris,* 94–95.

DAN BILLANY AND DAVID DOWIE

The Cage, 1949

> Munton, Alan. *English Fiction,* 54–60.

RICHARD D. BLACKMORE

Lorna Doone, 1869

> Gardner, Barry. *Who Was Lorna Doone?,* 5–35.

ALGERNON BLACKWOOD

The Centaur, 1911

> Joshi, S. T. *The Weird Tale,* 94–97.

The Education of Uncle Paul, 1909

> Joshi, S. T. *The Weird Tale,* 121–23.

The Human Chord, 1910

> Joshi, S. T. *The Weird Tale,* 109–11.
> Punter, David. *The Romantic Unconscious,* 108–9.

Julius Le Vallon, 1916

> Joshi, S. T. *The Weird Tale,* 97–101.

GEORGE BLAKE

The Shipbuilders, 1935

> Malzahn, Manfred. "Coming to Terms with Industrial Scotland: Two 'Proletarian' Novels of the 1930s," in Joachim Schwend and Horst W. Drescher, eds., *Studies in Scottish Fiction,* 194–203.
> Whyte, Christopher. "Imagining the City: The Glasgow Novel," in Joachim Schwend and Horst W. Drescher, eds., *Studies in Scottish Fiction,* 327–30.

PHYLLIS BOTTOME

The Mortal Storm, 1937

Brothers, Barbara. "British Women Write the Story of the Nazis: A Conspiracy of Silence," in Angela Ingram and Daphne Patai, eds., *Rediscovering Forgotten Radicals,* 248–51.

Croft, Andy. *Red Letter Days,* 324–26.

ELIZABETH BOWEN

The Death of the Heart, 1938

Dukes, Thomas. "The Unorthodox Plots of Elizabeth Bowen." *Stud in the Hum* 16 (1989), 16–20.

Gindin, James. *British Fiction,* 113–18.

Lassner, Phyllis. *Elizabeth Bowen,* 97–119.

Rossen, Janice. *The University in Modern Fiction,* 21–23.

Tindall, Gillian. *Countries of the Mind,* 234–36.

Eva Trout, 1969

Wyatt-Brown, Anne M. "The Liberation of Mourning in Elizabeth Bowen's *The Little Girls* and *Eva Trout,*" in Anne M. Wyatt-Brown and Janice Rossen, eds., *Aging and Gender,* 164–72, 177–83.

Friends and Relations, 1931

Coates, John. "The Tree of Jesse and the Voyage Out: Stability and Disorder in Elizabeth Bowen's *Friends and Relations.*" *Durham Univ J* 84 (1992), 291–302.

Halperin, John. *Jane Austen's Lovers,* 196–98.

Lassner, Phyllis. *Elizabeth Bowen,* 48–55.

The Heat of the Day, 1949

Bergonzi, Bernard. *Wartime and Aftermath,* 86–88.

Caserio, Robert L. "The Heat of the Day: Modernism and Narrative in Paul de Man and Elizabeth Bowen." *Mod Lang Q* 54 (1993), 268–84.

Dukes, Thomas. "Desire Satisfied: War and Love in *The Heat of the Day* and *Moon Tiger.*" *War, Lit, and the Arts* 3:1 (1991), 75–97.

Dukes, Thomas. "The Unorthodox Plots of Elizabeth Bowen." *Stud in the Hum* 16 (1989), 20–22.

Gindin, James. *British Fiction,* 124–29.

Lassner, Phyllis. *Elizabeth Bowen,* 120–40.

Lassner, Phyllis. "Reimagining the Arts of War: Language and History in Elizabeth Bowen's *The Heat of the Day* and Rose Macaulay's *The World My Wilderness.*" *Perspectives on Contemp Lit* 14 (1988), 30–37.

McCormack, W. J. *Dissolute Characters,* 214–30, 236–40.

The House in Paris, 1935

> Dukes, Thomas. "The Unorthodox Plots of Elizabeth Bowen." *Stud in the Hum* 16 (1989), 10–15.
>
> Gindin, James. *British Fiction,* 118–20.
>
> Lassner, Phyllis. *Elizabeth Bowen,* 73–96.

The Last September, 1929

> Coates, John. "Elizabeth Bowen's *The Last September:* The Loss of the Past and the Modern Consciousness." *Durham Univ J* 82 (1990), 205–16.
>
> Cronin, Gearóid. "The Big House and the Irish Landscape in the Work of Elizabeth Bowen," in Jacqueline Genet, ed., *The Big House in Ireland,* 143–60.
>
> Gindin, James. *British Fiction,* 109–11, 117–19.
>
> Halperin, John. *Jane Austen's Lovers,* 194–96.
>
> Lassner, Phyllis. *Elizabeth Bowen,* 26–47.
>
> Reynolds, Lorna. *"The Last September:* Elizabeth Bowen's Paradise Lost," in Otto Rauchbauer, ed., *Ancestral Voices,* 149–56.
>
> Scanlan, Margaret. *Traces of Another Time,* 40–50.
>
> Weekes, Ann Owens. *Irish Women Writers,* 86–107.

The Little Girls, 1964

> Coates, John. "False History and True in *The Little Girls." Renascence* 44 (1992), 83–103.
>
> Kemp, Sandra. "But One Isn't Murdered: Elizabeth Bowen's *The Little Girls,"* in Clive Bloom, ed., *Twentieth-Century Suspense,* 130–41.
>
> Wyatt-Brown, Anne M. "The Liberation of Mourning in Elizabeth Bowen's *The Little Girls* and *Eva Trout,"* in Anne M. Wyatt-Brown and Janice Rossen, eds., *Aging and Gender,* 164–77.

To the North, 1932

> Coates, John. "Moral Choice in Elizabeth Bowen's *To the North." Renascence* 43 (1991), 241–67.
>
> Gindin, James. *British Fiction,* 118–21.
>
> Lassner, Phyllis. *Elizabeth Bowen,* 55–72.
>
> Tindall, Gillian. *Countries of the Mind,* 207–8.

A World of Love, 1955

> Leray, Josette. "Elizabeth Bowen's *A World of Love,"* in Jacqueline Genet, ed., *The Big House in Ireland,* 163–75.

MALCOLM BRADBURY

The History Man, 1975

> Acheson, James. "The Small Worlds of Malcolm Bradbury and David Lodge," in James Acheson, ed. *The British and Irish Novel,* 80–82.
>
> Eykman, Christoph. *Der Intellektuelle,* 83–86.

Rates of Exchange, 1983

Acheson, James. "The Small Worlds of Malcolm Bradbury and David Lodge," in James Acheson, ed. *The British and Irish Novel,* 82–84.

Stepping Westward, 1965

Böhm, Rudolf. "Malcolm Bradbury, *Stepping Westward:* Das Dilemma des Liberalismus," in Joachim Schwend et al., eds., *Literatur im Kontext,* 265–75.

MARY ELIZABETH BRADDON

Aurora Floyd, 1863

Drexler, Peter. *Literatur, Recht, Kriminalität,* 182–84.

Lady Audley's Secret, 1862

Briganti, Chiara. "Gothic Maidens and Sensation Women: Lady Audley's Journey from the Ruined Mansion to the Madhouse." *Victorian Lit and Culture* 19 (1991), 189–209.

Cvetkovich, Ann. *Mixed Feelings,* 45–70.

Drexler, Peter. *Literatur, Recht, Kriminalität,* 184–87.

Kayman, Martin A. *From Bow Street to Baker Street,* 183–88.

Litvak, Joseph. *Caught in the Act,* 141–45.

Matus, Jill L. "Disclosure as 'Cover-up': The Discourse of Madness in *Lady Audley's Secret.*" *Univ of Toronto Q* 62 (1993), 334–52.

Morris, Virginia B. *Double Jeopardy,* 91–98.

Tuss, Alex J., SM. *The Inward Revolution,* 89–97.

JOHN BRAINE

Room at the Top, 1957

Bergonzi, Bernard. *Wartime and Aftermath,* 147–49.

Jourdain, Claude. "La femme reconnue: les femmes dans le roman de Braine." *Caliban* 27 (1990), 61–72.

Marwick, Arthur. "*Room at the Top:* The Novel and the Film," in Arthur Marwick, ed., *The Arts, Literature, and Society,* 249–79.

JOHN BRODERICK

The Pilgrimage, 1961

Lubbers, Klaus. "John Broderick," in Rüdiger Imhof, ed., *Contemporary Irish Novelists,* 80–82.

ANNE BRONTË

Agnes Grey, 1847

Baldridge, Cates. "*Agnes Grey*—Brontë's *Bildungsroman* That Isn't." *J of Narrative Technique* 23 (1993), 31–44.

Chitham, Edward. *A Life of Anne Brontë,* 8–12, 72–75, 105–7, 124–29, 134–36, 194–96.

Freeman, Janet H. "Telling Over *Agnes Grey.*" *Cahiers Victoriens et Edouardiens* 34 (1991), 109–25.

Knapp, Bettina L. *The Brontës,* 79–91.

Langland, Elizabeth. *Anne Brontë,* 97–118.

Lanser, Susan Sniader. *Fictions of Authority,* 177–81.

Winnifrith, Tom. *The Brontës and Their Background,* 56–58, 182–88.

The Tenant of Wildfell Hall, 1848

Chitham, Edward. *A Life of Anne Brontë,* 134–37, 139–55.

Gordon, Felicia. *A Preface to the Brontës,* 175–81.

Knapp, Bettina L. *The Brontës,* 91–100.

Langland, Elizabeth. *Anne Brontë,* 46–54, 119–48.

Langland, Elizabeth. "The Voicing of Feminine Desire in Anne Brontë's *The Tenant of Wildfell Hall,*" in Antony H. Harrison and Beverly Taylor, eds., *Gender and Discourse,* 111–22.

Martin, Françoise. "*The Tenant of Wildfell Hall:* portrait de l'artiste en jeune femme." *Cahiers Victoriens et Edouardiens* 34 (1991), 95–105.

Shires, Linda M. "Of Maenads, Mothers, and Feminized Males: Victorian Readings of the French Revolution," in Linda M. Shires, ed., *Rewriting the Victorians,* 160–62.

Winnifrith, Tom. *The Brontës and Their Background,* 59–61, 140–42, 186–89.

CHARLOTTE BRONTË

Jane Eyre, 1847

Albertazzi, Silvia. *Il sogno gotico,* 89–118.

Armstrong, Nancy. "The Rise of Feminine Authority in the Novel," in Mark Spilka and Caroline McCracken-Flesher, eds., *Why the Novel Matters,* 103–5.

Atkins, Elizabeth. "*Jane Eyre* Transformed." *Lit/Film Q* 21 (1993), 54–60.

Auerbach, Emily. *Maestros, Dilettantes, and Philistines,* 54–56.

Birkner, Gerd. "Charlotte Brontës *Jane Eyre*—das Selbst als Pneuma," in Gregory Claeys and Liselotte Glage, eds., *Radikalismus in Literatur und Gesellschaft,* 183–200.

Bock, Carol. *Charlotte Brontë,* 69–108.

Boumelha, Penny. *Charlotte Brontë,* 24–28, 58–77.

Brinton, Laurel J. "The Historical Present in Charlotte Brontë's Novels: Some Discourse Functions." *Style* 26 (1992), 221–41.

Butler, Gerald J. *Love and Reading*, 97–101, 162–65.

Chitham, Edward. *A Life of Anne Brontë*, 139–43.

Craig, Randall. "Logophobia in *Jane Eyre*." *J of Narrative Technique* 23 (1993), 92–110.

De Jong, Mary G. "Different Voices: Moral Conflict in *Jane Eyre, The Mill on the Floss*, and *Romola*." *CEA Critic* 51:2–3 (1989), 55–58.

DeLamotte, Eugenia C. *Perils of the Night*, 193–228.

Delourme, Chantal. "La mémoire fécondée. Réflexions sur l'intertextualité: *Jane Eyre, Wide Saragasso Sea*." *Etudes Anglaises* 42 (1989), 257–68.

Derwin, Susan. *The Ambivalence of Form*, 94–112.

Dole, Carol M. "The Nature World in *Jane Eyre* and *Wide Saragasso Sea*." *West Virginia Univ Philol Papers* 37 (1991), 60–66.

Easson, Angus. "Jane Eyre's 'Three-Tailed Bashaw,' Again." *Notes and Queries* 235 (1990), 425.

Eberhart, Connie L. "Jane Eyre: A Daughter of the Lady in Milton's *Comus*." *Univ of Mississippi Stud in Engl* 8 (1990), 80–90.

Farr, Judith. "Charlotte Brontë, Emily Brontë and the 'Undying Life' Within." *Victorians Inst J* 17 (1989), 92–96.

Federico, Annette. "'A cool observer of her own sex like me': Girl-Watching in *Jane Eyre*." *Victorian Newsl* 80 (1991), 29–33.

Fraiman, Susan. *Unbecoming Women*, 88–120.

Freeman, Jane. "Character Foils and Games in *Jane Eyre*." *Brontë Newsl* 7 (1988), 2–3.

Gates, Barbara. "Down Garden Paths: Charlotte Brontë's Haunts of Self and Other." *Victorian Newsl* 83 (1993), 37–38.

Gezari, Janet. *Charlotte Brontë and Defensive Conduct*, 59–89.

Goodrich, Norma Lorre. *Heroines*, 236–40.

Gordon, Felicia. *A Preface to the Brontës*, 109–11, 129–32, 136–55.

Heilman, Robert Bechtold. *The Workings of Fiction*, 43–46, 107–9, 111–13.

Hogge, Quentin, and Penelope Hogge. "Conflict in *Jane Eyre*." *CRUX* 24:1 (1990), 13–15.

Imlay, Elizabeth. *Charlotte Brontë and the Mysteries of Love*, 1–204.

Knapp, Bettina L. *The Brontës*, 144–64.

Langland, Elizabeth. *Anne Brontë*, 42–46, 50–54.

Lanser, Susan Sniader. *Fictions of Authority*, 176–78, 181–93.

Lawson, Kate. "Madness and Grace: Grace Poole's Name and Her Role in *Jane Eyre*." *Engl Lang Notes* 30:1 (1992), 46–49.

Lerner, Laurence. "Bertha and the Critics." *Nineteenth-Cent Lit* 44 (1989), 273–300.

Litvak, Joseph. *Caught in the Act*, 27–73.

London, Bette. "The Pleasures of Submission: *Jane Eyre* and the Production of the Text." *ELH* 58 (1991), 195–210.

Lundberg, Patricia Lorimer. "The Dialogic Search for Community in Charlotte Brontë's Novels." *J of Narrative Technique* 20 (1990), 301–4.

Macpherson, Pat. *Reflecting on Jane Eyre*, 1–118.

Mei, Huang. *Transforming the Cinderella Dream,* 105–17.

Meyer, Susan. "Colonialism and the Figurative Strategy of *Jane Eyre.*" *Victorian Stud* 33 (1990), 247–68.

Michie, Elsie. "From Simianized Irish to Oriental Despots: Heathcliff, Rochester and Racial Difference." *Novel* 25 (1992), 125–40.

Miecznikowski, Cynthia. " 'Do you never laugh, Miss Eyre?': Humor, Wit and the Comic in *Jane Eyre.*" *Stud in the Novel* 21 (1989), 367–77.

Milbank, Alison. *Daughters of the House,* 140–48.

Miles, Robert. *"Jane Eyre,"* 7–84.

Moore, Richard. *"Jane Eyre:* Love and the Symbolism of Art." *Crit Survey* 3:1 (1991), 44–52.

Nestor, Pauline. *Charlotte Brontë's "Jane Eyre,"* 33–95.

Odom, Keith C. "Charlotte Brontë's Uses of Byron and Goethe for the Contrasted Heroes in *Jane Eyre.*" *Brontë Newsl* 9 (1990), 5–6.

Parkin-Gounelas, Ruth. *Fictions of the Female Self,* 55–57.

Peters, Joan D. "Finding a Voice: Towards a Woman's Discourse of Dialogue in the Narration of *Jane Eyre.*" *Stud in the Novel* 23 (1991), 217–33.

Ralph, Phyllis C. *Victorian Transformations,* 87–112.

Randriambeloma-Rakotoanosy, Ginette. *Rencontres,* 75–166.

Rea, Joanne E. "Brontë's *Jane Eyre.*" *Explicator* 50 (1992), 75–77.

Reger, Mark. "Brontë's *Jane Eyre.*" *Explicator* 50 (1992), 213–15.

Ren, Shyh-jong. "A Comparative Study of Religious Growth in Charlotte Brontë's *Jane Eyre* and Endo Shusaku's *Silence.*" *Lang and Lit* 14 (1990), 1–24.

Roy, Parama. "Unaccommodated Woman and the Poetics of Property in *Jane Eyre.*" *Stud in Engl Lit, 1500–1900* 29 (1989), 713–26.

Schacht, Paul. "Jane Eyre and the History of Self-Respect." *Mod Lang Q* 52 (1991), 423–53.

Sharpe, Jenny. *Allegories of Empire,* 27–55.

Shires, Linda M. "Of Maenads, Mothers, and Feminized Males: Victorian Readings of the French Revolution," in Linda M. Shires, ed., *Rewriting the Victorians,* 155–58.

Shuttleworth, Sally. "Psychological Definition and Social Power: Phrenology in the Novels of Charlotte Brontë," in John Christie and Sally Shuttleworth, eds., *Nature Transfigured,* 132–47.

Spignesi, Angelyn. *Lyrical-Analysis,* 9–312.

Sutherland, Kathryn. *"Jane Eyre's* Literary History: The Case for *Mansfield Park.*" *ELH* 59 (1992), 409–37.

Tayler, Irene. *Holy Ghosts,* 168–80.

Thomas, Ronald R. *Dreams of Authority,* 146–74.

Thorpe, Michael. " 'The Other Side': *Wide Saragasso Sea* and *Jane Eyre,*" in Pierrette M. Frickey, ed., *Critical Perspectives,* 178–84.

Tindall, Gillian. *Countries of the Mind,* 15–17.

Tyson, Nancy Jane. "Altars to Attics: The State of Matrimony in Brontë's *Jane Eyre,*" in Sara Munson Deats and Lagretta Tallent Lenker, eds., *The Aching Hearth,* 95–104.

Vesterman, William. "Mastering the Free Spirit: Status and Contract in Some Fictional Polities." *Eighteenth-Cent Life* 16:3 (1992), 184–86.

Watts, Cedric. *Literature and Money*, 144–46.

Weber, Ingeborg. "Weibliche Wut und literarischer Wahnsinn: Zu einer feministischen Lesart von *Jane Eyre*," in Therese Fischer-Seidel, ed., *Frauen und Frauendarstellung*, 65–84.

Williams, Carolyn. "Closing the Book: The Intertextual End of *Jane Eyre*," in Jerome J. McGann, ed., *Victorian Connections*, 60–87.

Williams, Judith. *Perception and Expression*, 19–52.

Winnifrith, Tom. *The Brontës and Their Background*, 20–23, 49–55, 166–71.

Winnifrith, Tom, and Edward Chitham. *Charlotte and Emily Brontë*, 1–4, 34–38, 54–57, 110–14, 120–23.

Wolstenholme, Susan. *Gothic (Re)Visions*, 58–60.

Young, Arlene. "The Monster Within: The Alien Self in *Jane Eyre* and *Frankenstein*." *Stud in the Novel* 23 (1991), 325–37.

The Professor, 1857

Bock, Carol. *Charlotte Brontë*, 54–68.

Boumelha, Penny. *Charlotte Brontë*, 20–23, 38–57.

Brinton, Laurel J. "The Historical Present in Charlotte Brontë's Novels: Some Discourse Functions." *Style* 26 (1992), 221–41.

Bruce, Donald Williams. "Charlotte Brontë in Brussels: *The Professor* and *Villette*." *Contemp R* 254 (1989), 321–28.

Chitham, Edward. *A Life of Anne Brontë*, 134–36.

Gates, Barbara. "Down Garden Paths: Charlotte Brontë's Haunts of Self and Other." *Victorian Newsl* 83 (1993), 36–37.

Gezari, Janet. *Charlotte Brontë and Defensive Conduct*, 30–58.

Johnston, Ruth D. "*The Professor:* Charlotte Brontë's Hysterical Text, or Realistic Narrative and the Ideology of the Subject from a Feminist Perspective." *Dickens Stud Annual* 18 (1989), 353–77.

Knapp, Bettina L. *The Brontës*, 136–44.

Lundberg, Patricia Lorimer. "The Dialogic Search for Community in Charlotte Brontë's Novels." *J of Narrative Technique* 20 (1990), 297–301.

Parkin-Gounelas, Ruth. *Fictions of the Female Self*, 54–71.

Tayler, Irene. *Holy Ghosts*, 159–68.

Williams, Judith. *Perception and Expression*, 7–18.

Winnifrith, Tom. *The Brontës and Their Background*, 160–67.

Winnifrith, Tom, and Edward Chitham. *Charlotte and Emily Brontë*, 49–50, 83–84, 91–93.

Shirley, 1849

Arnold, Margaret J. "*Coriolanus* Transformed: Charlotte Brontë's Use of Shakespeare in *Shirley*," in Marianne Novy, ed., *Women's Re-visions of Shakespeare*, 76–88.

Basham, Diana. *The Trial of Woman*, 61–67.

Bock, Carol. *Charlotte Brontë*, 109–26.

Boumelha, Penny. *Charlotte Brontë*, 28–32, 78–99.

Brinton, Laurel J. "The Historical Present in Charlotte Brontë's Novels: Some Discourse Functions." *Style* 26 (1992), 228–41.

Datta, Sangeeta. "Charlotte Brontë and the Woman Question," in Jasodhara Bagchi, ed., *Literature, Society and Ideology*, 205–6.

Gates, Barbara. "Down Garden Paths: Charlotte Brontë's Haunts of Self and Other." *Victorian Newsl* 83 (1993), 38–40.

Gezari, Janet. *Charlotte Brontë and Defensive Conduct*, 90–124.

Gorak, I. E. "Border Countries: *Wuthering Heights* and *Shirley* as Regional Novels." *Criticism* 32 (1990), 449–67.

Gordon, Felicia. *A Preface to the Brontës*, 79–80, 132–34.

Heilman, Robert Bechtold. *The Workings of Fiction*, 50–53, 109–11, 113–15, 205–29.

Keen, Suzanne. "Narrative Annexes in Charlotte Brontë's *Shirley*." *J of Narrative Technique* 20 (1990), 107–18.

Knapp, Bettina L. *The Brontës*, 164–71.

Langland, Elizabeth. *Anne Brontë*, 51–54.

Lashgari, Deirdre. "What Some Women Can't Swallow: Hunger as Protest in Charlotte Brontë's *Shirley*," in Lilian R. Furst and Peter W. Graham, eds., *Disorderly Eaters*, 141–52.

Lawson, Kate. "The Dissenting Voice: *Shirley*'s Vision of Women and Christianity." *Stud in Engl Lit, 1500–1900* 29 (1989), 729–42.

Lundberg, Patricia Lorimer. "The Dialogic Search for Community in Charlotte Brontë's Novels." *J of Narrative Technique* 20 (1990), 304–7.

Mineo, Ady. "Identità femminile tra quotidianità e mito in *Shirley* di Charlotte Brontë," in A. Arru and M. T. Chialant, eds., *Il racconto delle donne*, 213–32.

Parkin-Gounelas, Ruth. *Fictions of the Female Self*, 42–46.

Reifel, Karen F. " 'And what is your reading . . . ?': Self-Definition in Charlotte Brontë's *Shirley*." *Cahiers Victoriens et Edouardiens* 34 (1991), 31–41.

Tayler, Irene. *Holy Ghosts*, 180–99.

Williams, Judith. *Perception and Expression*, 53–78.

Winnifrith, Tom. *The Brontës and Their Background*, 30–32, 171–76.

Winnifrith, Tom, and Edward Chitham. *Charlotte and Emily Brontë*, 36–37.

Zlotnick, Susan. "Luddism, Medievalism and Women's History in *Shirley*: Charlotte Brontë's Revisionist Tactics." *Novel* 24 (1991), 282–95.

Villette, 1853

Bock, Carol. *Charlotte Brontë*, 127–48.

Bock, Carol A. "Charlotte Brontë's Storytellers: The Influence of Scott." *Cahiers Victoriens et Edouardiens* 34 (1991), 26–28.

Boone, Joseph A. "Depolicing *Villette*: Surveillance, Invisibility, and the Female Erotics of 'Heretic Narrative.' " *Novel* 26 (1992), 20–42.

Boumelha, Penny. *Charlotte Brontë*, 32–36, 100–122.

Briganti, Chiara. "Charlotte Brontë's *Villette*: The History of Desire." *West Virginia Univ Philol Papers* 35 (1989), 8–20.

Brinton, Laurel J. "The Historical Present in Charlotte Brontë's Novels: Some Discourse Functions." *Style* 26 (1992), 221–41.

Bruce, Donald Williams. "Charlotte Brontë in Brussels: *The Professor* and *Villette.*" *Contemp R* 254 (1989), 321–28.

Cheng, Anne A. "Reading Lucy Snowe's Cryptology: Charlotte Brontë's *Villette* and Suspended Mourning." *Qui Parle* 4:2 (1991), 75–90.

Crosby, Christina. *The Ends of History,* 110–43.

Datta, Sangeeta. "Charlotte Brontë and the Woman Question," in Jasodhara Bagchi, ed., *Literature, Society and Ideology,* 206–8.

DeLamotte, Eugenia C. *Perils of the Night,* 229–89.

Edgecombe, Rodney Stenning. "Odic Elements in Charlotte Brontë's *Villette.*" *Mod Lang R* 87 (1992), 817–26.

Feinberg, Monica L. "Homesick: The Domestic Interiors of *Villette.*" *Novel* 26 (1993), 170–91.

Fletcher, Luann McCracken. "Manufactured Marvels, Heretic Narratives, and the Process of Interpretation in *Villette.*" *Stud in Engl Lit, 1500–1900* 32 (1992), 723–42.

Fraiman, Susan. *Unbecoming Women,* 97–99.

Gates, Barbara. "Down Garden Paths: Charlotte Brontë's Haunts of Self and Other." *Victorian Newsl* 83 (1993), 40–42.

Gezari, Janet. *Charlotte Brontë and Defensive Conduct,* 125–70.

Gordon, Felicia. *A Preface to the Brontës,* 156–74.

Heilman, Robert Bechtold. *The Workings of Fiction,* 46–50, 104–7.

Johnson, Patricia E. " 'This Heretic Narrative': The Strategy of the Split Narrative in Charlotte Brontë's *Villette.*" *Stud in Engl Lit, 1500–1900* 30 (1990), 617–29.

Kelly, Mary Ann. "Paralysis and the Circular Nature of Memory in *Villette.*" *JEGP* 90 (1991), 342–60.

Knapp, Bettina L. *The Brontës,* 172–81.

Lawrence, Karen. "The Cypher: Disclosure and Reticence in *Villette,*" in Florence Howe, ed., *Tradition and the Talents of Women,* 87–99.

Lawson, Kate. "Reading Desire: *Villette* as 'Heretic Narrative.' " *Engl Stud in Canada* 17 (1991), 53–70.

Litvak, Joseph. *Caught in the Act,* 75–107.

Lundberg, Patricia Lorimer. "The Dialogic Search for Community in Charlotte Brontë's Novels." *J of Narrative Technique* 20 (1990), 307–10.

Mei, Huang. *Transforming the Cinderella Dream,* 117–39.

Milbank, Alison. *Daughters of the House,* 148–57.

Minogue, Sally. "Gender and Class in *Villette* and *North and South,*" in Sally Minogue, ed., *Problems for Feminist Criticism,* 79–106.

Newsom, Robert. "*Villette* and *Bleak House:* Authorizing Women." *Nineteenth-Cent Lit* 46 (1991), 54–81.

Parkin-Gounelas, Ruth. *Fictions of the Female Self,* 71–76.

Polhemus, Robert M. *Erotic Faith,* 79–107.

Pollack, Mary S. "Mending the World: Intersubjectivity in Charlotte Brontë's *Villette.*" *Cahiers Victoriens et Edouardiens* 34 (1991), 47–60.

Tayler, Irene. *Holy Ghosts,* 200–286.

Vrettos, Athena. "From Neurosis to Narrative: The Private Life of the Nerves in *Villette* and *Daniel Deronda.*" *Victorian Stud* 33 (1990), 559–79.

Watkins, Susan. "Epiphany and Subjectivity in Charlotte Brontë's *Villette,*" in Philip Shaw and Peter Stockwell, eds., *Subjectivity and Literature,* 49–56.

Williams, Judith. *Perception and Expression,* 79–141.

Winnifrith, Tom. *The Brontës and Their Background,* 46–49, 176–82.

Winnifrith, Tom, and Edward Chitham. *Charlotte and Emily Brontë,* 82–85, 87–89, 91–93.

Wolstenholme, Susan. *Gothic (Re)Visions,* 57–78.

Yeazell, Ruth Bernard. *Fictions of Modesty,* 169–93.

EMILY BRONTË

Wuthering Heights, 1847

Armstrong, Nancy. "Emily's Ghost: The Cultural Politics of Victorian Fiction, Folklore, and Photography." *Novel* 25 (1992), 245–62.

Barreca, Regina. "The Power of Excommunication: Sex and the Feminine Test in *Wuthering Heights,*" in Regina Barreca, ed., *Sex and Death,* 227–39.

Bazin, Claire. "Heathcliff ou L'Amour de L'Argent." *Cahiers Victoriens et Edouardiens* 35 (1992), 71–80.

Bazin, Claire. "Is Mr. Heathcliff a Man?" *Cahiers Victoriens et Edouardiens* 34 (1991), 71–78.

Berman, Jeffrey. *Narcissism and the Novel,* 78–80, 85–112.

Chitham, Edward. *A Life of Anne Brontë,* 133–35, 143–46, 149–52.

Cohen, Paula Marantz. *The Daughter's Dilemma,* 89–113.

David, Gail. *Female Heroism,* 143–63.

DeLamotte, Eugenia C. *Perils of the Night,* 127–39.

Erlebach, Peter. *Theorie und Praxis des Romaneingangs,* 212–20.

Farr, Judith. "Charlotte Brontë, Emily Brontë and the 'Undying Life' Within." *Victorians Inst J* 17 (1989), 96–101.

Frantz, Andrea Breemer. *Redemption and Madness,* 45–51.

Galef, David. "Keeping One's Distance: Irony and Doubling in *Wuthering Heights.*" *Stud in the Novel* 24 (1992), 242–49.

Gezari, Janet. *Charlotte Brontë and Defensive Conduct,* 125–42.

Goldfarb, Russell M. "The Survival of Nelly Dean in *Wuthering Heights.*" *CEA Critic* 51:4 (1989), 53–63.

Goodheart, Eugene. *Desire and Its Discontents,* 97–111.

Goodheart, Eugene. "Family, Incest and Transcendence in *Wuthering Heights,*" in Ann B. Dobie, ed., *Explorations,* 34–50.

Gorak, I. E. "Border Countries: *Wuthering Heights* and *Shirley* as Regional Novels." *Criticism* 32 (1990), 449–67.

Gordon, Felicia. *A Preface to the Brontës,* 189–207.

Haggerty, George E. *Gothic Fiction,* 65–80.

Hodge, Robert. *Literature as Discourse,* 52–57.

Hoenselaars, A. J. "Emily Brontë, *Hamlet,* and *Wilhelm Meister."* *Notes and Queries* 237 (1992), 177–78.

Horatschek, Annegreth. " 'In true gossip's fashion'? Das domestizierte Bewußtsein der Nelly Dean." *Poetica* 21 (1989), 353–88.

Kegler, Adelheid. "Silent House: MacDonald, Brontë and Silence Within the Soul," in Kath Filmer, ed., *The Victorian Fantasists,* 120–23.

Knapp, Bettina L. *The Brontës,* 107–32.

Knoepflmacher, U. C. *Emily Brontë: "Wuthering Heights,"* 1–127.

Lavabre, Simone. "Féminisme et liberté dans *Wuthering Heights."* *Cahiers Victoriens et Edouardiens* 34 (1991), 63–70.

Michie, Elsie. "From Simianized Irish to Oriental Despots: Heathcliff, Rochester and Racial Difference." *Novel* 25 (1992), 125–40.

Miles, Peter. *"Wuthering Heights,"* 51–93.

Miller, J. Hillis. *Victorian Subjects,* 205–6.

Mills, Sara, Lynne Pearce, Sue Spaull, and Elaine Millard. *Feminist Readings,* 30–33, 34–36, 38–40, 43–46, 73–77, 162–70.

Newman, Beth. " 'The Situation of the Looker-On': Gender, Narration, and Gaze in *Wuthering Heights."* *PMLA* 105 (1990), 1029–39.

Polhemus, Robert M. *Erotic Faith,* 108–36.

Pratt, Linda Ray. " 'I Shall Be Your Father': Heathcliff's Narrative of Paternity." *Victorians Inst J* 20 (1992), 13–34.

Punter, David. *The Romantic Unconscious,* 137–38.

Ralph, Phyllis C. *Victorian Transformations,* 113–33.

Randriambeloma-Rakotoanosy, Ginette. *Rencontres,* 75–166.

Ru, Yi-ling. *The Family Novel,* 34–36.

Scheick, William J. *Fictional Structure & Ethics,* 25–28.

Smith, Sheila. " 'At once strong and eerie': The Supernatural in *Wuthering Heights* and its Debt to the Traditional Ballad." *R of Engl Stud* 43 (1992), 498–517.

Sorensen, Katherine M. "From Religious Ecstasy to Romantic Fulfillment: John Wesley's *Journal* and the Death of Heathcliff in *Wuthering Heights."* *Victorian Newsl* 82 (1992), 1–4.

Steig, Michael. *Stories of Reading,* 41–62.

Stevens, W. Kera. "The Devil on the Moors and in the 'Sertão': Modes of Fantasy in *Wuthering Heights* and *Grande Sertão: Veredas."* *Estudos Anglo-Americanos* 12–13 (1988–89), 134–39.

Tayler, Irene. *Holy Ghosts,* 72–109.

Thomas, Ronald R. *Dreams of Authority,* 112–34.

Tindall, Gillian. *Countries of the Mind,* 12–14.

Weber, Jean Jacques. *Critical Analysis of Fiction,* 93–106.

Wiesenfarth, Joseph. *Gothic Manners,* 63–82.

Williams, Anne. " 'The Child is Mother of the Man': The 'Female Aesthetic' of *Wuthering Heights."* *Cahiers Victoriens et Edouardiens* 34 (1991), 81–93.

Williams, Meg Harris, and Margot Waddell. *The Chamber of Maiden Thought,* 126–42.

Winnifrith, Tom. *The Brontës and Their Background,* 67–73, 189–94.

Winnifrith, Tom, and Edward Chitham. *Charlotte and Emily Brontë,* 53–58, 71–73, 78–81, 108–13.

Woodring, Carl. *Nature into Art,* 107–11.

Yocum, Kathleen A. "Brontë's *Wuthering Heights.*" *Explicator* 48 (1989), 21–22.

EMMA BROOKE

A Superfluous Woman, 1894

Ardis, Ann L. *New Women, New Novels,* 112–13.

FRANCES BROOKE

The History of Emily Montague, 1769

Benedict, Barbara M. "The Margins of Sentiment: Nature, Letter, and Law in Frances Brooke's Epistolary Novels." *Ariel* 23:3 (1992), 13–23.

Merrett, Robert. "The Politics of Romance in *The History of Emily Montague.*" *Canadian Lit* 133 (1992), 92–107.

Sellwood, Jane. "'A little acid is absolutely necessary': Narrative as Coquette in Frances Brooke's *The History of Emily Montague.*" *Canadian Lit* 136 (1993), 60–75.

Lady Julia Mandeville, 1763

Benedict, Barbara M. "The Margins of Sentiment: Nature, Letter, and Law in Frances Brooke's Epistolary Novels." *Ariel* 23:3 (1992), 10–13.

Mullan, John. *Sentiment and Sociability,* 132–34.

HENRY BROOKE

The Fool of Quality, 1764–1770

Mullan, John. *Sentiment and Sociability,* 133–35.

Probyn, Clive T. *English Fiction,* 152–55.

CHRISTINE BROOKE-ROSE

Amalgamemnon, 1984

Hawkins, Susan E. "Innovation/History/Politics: Reading Christine Brooke-Rose's *Amalgamemnon.*" *Contemp Lit* 32 (1991), 58–73.

Little, Judy. "*Amalgamemnon* and the Politics of Narrative." *R of Contemp Fiction* 9:3 (1989), 134–37.

Thru, 1975

Berressem, Hanjo. "*Thru* the Looking Glass: A Journey into the Universe of Discourse." *R of Contemp Fiction* 9:3 (1989), 128–33.

Xorandor, 1986

Caserio, Robert L. "Mobility and Masochism: Christine Brooke-Rose and J. G. Ballard," in Mark Spilka and Caroline McCracken-Flesher, eds., *Why the Novel Matters,* 310–11, 326–27.

Hawkins, Susan E. "Memory and Discourse: Fictionalizing the Present in *Xorandor.*" *R of Contemp Fiction* 9:3 (1989), 138–44.

ANITA BROOKNER

Family and Friends, 1985

Sadler, Lynn Veach. *Anita Brookner,* 68–94.

A Friend from England, 1987

Sadler, Lynn Veach. *Anita Brookner,* 117–39.

Hotel du Lac, 1984

Baxter, Gisèle Marie. "Clothes, Men and Books: Cultural Experiences and Identity in the Early Novels of Anita Brookner." *English* 42 (1993), 126–37.

Hosmer, Robert E., Jr. "Paradigm and Passage: The Fiction of Anita Brookner," in Robert E. Hosmer, Jr., ed., *Contemporary British Women Writers,* 34–40.

Medrano, Isabel. "La dimensión espacio-temporal de *Hotel du Lac.*" *Epos* 6 (1990), 411–22.

Sadler, Lynn Veach. *Anita Brookner,* 54–67.

Latecomers, 1988

Hosmer, Robert E., Jr. "Paradigm and Passage: The Fiction of Anita Brookner," in Robert E. Hosmer, Jr., ed., *Contemporary British Women Writers,* 40–45.

Look at Me, 1983

Monnickendam, Andrew. "Anita Brookner: A Scottish Novelist?—Ethnocentricity and Cultural Identity in her Early Fiction," in Joachim Schwend et al., eds., *Literatur im Kontext,* 297–305.

Sadler, Lynn Veach. *Anita Brookner,* 35–53.

A Misalliance, 1986

Sadler, Lynn Veach. *Anita Brookner,* 95–116.

Providence, 1982

Baxter, Gisèle Marie. "Clothes, Men and Books: Cultural Experiences and Identity in the Early Novels of Anita Brookner." *English* 42 (1993), 126–37.

Hosmer, Robert E., Jr. "Paradigm and Passage: The Fiction of Anita Brookner," in Robert E. Hosmer, Jr., ed., *Contemporary British Women Writers,* 30–34.

Monnickendam, Andrew. "Anita Brookner: A Scottish Novelist?—Ethnocentricity and Cultural Identity in her Early Fiction," in Joachim Schwend et al., eds., *Literatur im Kontext,* 297–305.

Sadler, Lynn Veach. *Anita Brookner,* 20–34.

A Start in Life, 1981

Baxter, Gisèle Marie. "Clothes, Men and Books: Cultural Experiences and Identity in the Early Novels of Anita Brookner." *English* 42 (1993), 126–37.

Monnickendam, Andrew. "Anita Brookner: A Scottish Novelist?—Ethnocentricity and Cultural Identity in her Early Fiction," in Joachim Schwend et al., eds., *Literatur im Kontext,* 297–305.

Sadler, Lynn Veach. *Anita Brookner,* 8–19.

ALEC BROWN

Daughters of Albion, 1935

Croft, Andy. *Red Letter Days,* 140–43.

GEORGE DOUGLAS BROWN

The House with the Green Shutters, 1901

Sellin, Bernard. "George Douglas Brown's *The House with the Green Shutters:* A Sense of Place," in Joachim Schwend et al., eds., *Literatur im Kontext,* 173–82.

GEORGE MACKAY BROWN

Greenvoe, 1972

Mergenthal, Silvia. " 'The Double Man': Sprache und Region bei George Mackay Brown und Edwin Morgan." *Anglia* 110 (1992), 412–16.

Robb, David S. "*Greenvoe:* A Poet's Novel." *Scottish Liter J* 19:1 (1992), 47–59.

JOHN BRUNNER

Stand on Zanzibar, 1968

Auffret-Boucé, Hélène. "*Stand on Zanzibar* ou l'art du gerbage." *Etudes Anglaises* 41 (1988), 345–54.

Greven-Borde, Hélène. "Utopie et science-fiction: le discours des bâtisseurs de cités." *Etudes Anglaises* 41 (1988), 286–90.

Schaffer, Carl. "Exegeses on *Stand on Zanzibar*'s Digressions into Genesis," in Olena H. Saciuk, ed., *The Shape of the Fantastic,* 193–99.

MARY BRUNTON

Discipline, 1814

Lanser, Susan Sniader. *Fictions of Authority,* 177–81.

Self-Control, 1811

    Ackley, Katherine Anne. "Violence Against Women in the Novels of Early British Women Writers," in Dale Spender, ed., *Living by the Pen,* 212–15.

    McKerrow, Mary. "Joanna Baillie and Mary Brunton: Women of the Manse," in Dale Spender, ed., *Living by the Pen,* 167–70.

WINIFRED BRYHER

Gate to the Sea, 1958

    Hoberman, Ruth. "Multiplying the Past: Gender and Narrative in Bryher's *Gate to the Sea.*" *Contemp Lit* 31 (1990), 354–70.

JOHN BUCHAN

The Dancing Floor, 1926

    Donald, Miles. "John Buchan: The Reader's Trap," in Clive Bloom, ed., *Spy Thrillers,* 59–72.

Greenmantle, 1916

    Butts, Dennis. "The Hunter and the Hunted: The Suspense Novels of John Buchan," in Clive Bloom, ed., *Spy Thrillers,* 47–57.

    Donald, Miles. "John Buchan: The Reader's Trap," in Clive Bloom, ed., *Spy Thrillers,* 59–72.

    Orel, Harold. *Popular Fiction in England,* 184–90.

    Stafford, David. *The Silent Game,* 61–62, 65–66.

The Island of Sheep, 1936

    Butts, Dennis. "The Hunter and the Hunted: The Suspense Novels of John Buchan," in Clive Bloom, ed., *Spy Thrillers,* 47–57.

John Macnab, 1925

    MacLachlan, Christopher. "John Buchan's Novels about Scotland," in Joachim Schwend and Horst W. Drescher, eds., *Studies in Scottish Fiction,* 55–64.

    Young, Michael. "The Rules of the Game: Buchan's *John Macnab.*" *Stud in Scottish Lit* 24 (1989), 194–211.

Mr. Standfast, 1918

    Butts, Dennis. "The Hunter and the Hunted: The Suspense Novels of John Buchan," in Clive Bloom, ed., *Spy Thrillers,* 47–57.

    Donald, Miles. "John Buchan: The Reader's Trap," in Clive Bloom, ed., *Spy Thrillers,* 59–72.

Prester John, 1910

    Donald, Miles. "John Buchan: The Reader's Trap," in Clive Bloom, ed., *Spy Thrillers,* 59–72.

The Thirty-Nine Steps, 1915

Butts, Dennis. "The Hunter and the Hunted: The Suspense Novels of John Buchan," in Clive Bloom, ed., *Spy Thrillers,* 47–57.
Orel, Harold. *Popular Fiction in England,* 177–81.
Stafford, David. *The Silent Game,* 56–57, 58–59.
Trotter, David. "The Politics of Adventure in the Early British Spy Novel," in Wesley K. Wark, ed., *Spy Fiction,* 50–53.

The Three Hostages, 1924

Butts, Dennis. "The Hunter and the Hunted: The Suspense Novels of John Buchan," in Clive Bloom, ed., *Spy Thrillers,* 47–57.
Donald, Miles. "John Buchan: The Reader's Trap," in Clive Bloom, ed., *Spy Thrillers,* 59–72.

Witch Wood, 1927

MacLachlan, Christopher. "John Buchan's Novels about Scotland," in Joachim Schwend and Horst W. Drescher, eds., *Studies in Scottish Fiction,* 45–55.

WILLIAM BUCHAN

Kumari, 1955

Mukherjee, Sujit. *Forster and Further,* 234–37.

SHAN F. BULLOCK

Robert Thorne: The Story of a London Clerk, 1907

Carey, John. *The Intellectuals and the Masses,* 60–62.

EDWARD BULWER-LYTTON

The Caxtons, 1849

Reed, John R. *Victorian Will,* 238–41.

Eugene Aram, 1832

Cloy, John. "Two Altered Endings: Dickens and Bulwer-Lytton." *Univ of Mississippi Stud in Engl* 10 (1992), 170–72.
Drexler, Peter. *Literatur, Recht, Kriminalität,* 144–47.

The Last Days of Pompeii, 1834

Göbel, Walter. "Entertaining Knowledge: Systemreferenz in Bulwers *Last Days of Pompeii.*" *Germanisch-Romanische Monatsschrift* 40 (1990), 399–406.
Heilman, Robert Bechtold. *The Workings of Fiction,* 173–78.
Reed, John R. *Victorian Will,* 234–38.

Lucretia; or, The Children of the Night, 1846

Ciolkowski, Laura. "The Woman (In) Question: Gender, Politics, and Edward Bulwer-Lytton's *Lucretia.*" *Novel* 26 (1992), 80–95.

My Novel, 1853

Reed, John R. *Victorian Will,* 240–44.

Paul Clifford, 1830

Drexler, Peter. *Literatur, Recht, Kriminalität,* 140–44.

Pelham, 1828

Bernstein, Carol L. *The Celebration of Scandal,* 83–85, 108–12.

Kissel, Wolfgang. "Englischer Gentleman und russischer 'Mann von Ehre': Zu Puškins Rezeption des Gesellschaftsromans *Pelham; or, the Adventures of a Gentleman* von Lord Bulwer-Lytton." *Zeitschrift für Slavische Philologie* 51:1 (1991), 60–85.

Oakley, J. W. "The Reform of Honor in Bulwer's *Pelham.*" *Nineteenth-Cent Lit* 47 (1992), 49–71.

A Strange Story, 1862

Basham, Diana. *The Trial of Woman,* 178–80.

Reed, John R. *Victorian Will,* 232–34.

Zanoni, 1842

Christensen, Allan C. "Bulwer, Bloch, Bussotti and the Filial Muse: Recalled and Foreseen Sources of Inspiration." *Mosaic* 26:3 (1993), 37–41.

Geary, Robert F. *The Supernatural in Gothic Fiction,* 116–18.

Reed, John R. *Victorian Will,* 227–29.

JOHN BUNYAN

The Life and Death of Mr. Badman, 1680

Sim, Stuart. "'Safe for Those for Whom it is to be Safe': Salvation and Damnation in Bunyan's Fiction," in Anne Lawrence et al., eds., *John Bunyan and His England,* 150–51, 154–56.

Smith, Nigel. "Bunyan and the Language of the Body in Seventeenth-Century England," in Anne Lawrence et al., eds., *John Bunyan and His England,* 167.

The Pilgrim's Progress, 1678

Aguirre, Manuel. "The Evolution of Dreams." *Neohelicon* 17:2 (1990), 9–26.

Alblas, Jacques B. H. "The Reception of *The Pilgrim's Progress* in Holland during the Eighteenth and Nineteenth Centuries," in M. van Os and G. J. Schutte, eds., *Bunyan in England and Abroad,* 121–30.

Breen, Margaret Soenser. "The Sexed Pilgrim's Progress." *Stud in Engl Lit, 1500–1900* 32 (1992), 443–58.

Campbell, Julie. "Pilgrim's Progress/Regress/Stasis: Some Thoughts on the Treatment of the Quest in Bunyan's *Pilgrim's Progress* and Beckett's *Mercier and Camier." Compar Lit Stud* 30 (1993), 137–52.

Graham, Elspeth. "Authority, Resistance and Loss: Gendered Difference in the Writings of John Bunyan and Hannah Allen," in Anne Lawrence et al., eds., *John Bunyan and His England,* 125–28.

Haskin, Dayton. "Bunyan's Scriptural Acts," in Robert G. Collmer, ed., *Bunyan in Our Time,* 61–92.

Johnson, Barbara A. "Falling into Allegory: The 'Apology' to *The Pilgrim's Progress* and Bunyan's Scriptural Methodology," in Robert G. Collmer, ed., *Bunyan in Our Time,* 113–37.

Kaufmann, U. Milo. "*The Pilgrim's Progress* and *The Pilgrim's Regress:* John Bunyan and C. S. Lewis on the Shape of the Christian Quest," in Robert G. Collmer, ed., *Bunyan in Our Time,* 186–99.

Keeble, N. H. " 'Here is her Glory, even to be under Him': The Feminine in the Thought and Work of John Bunyan," in Anne Lawrence et al., eds., *John Bunyan and His England,* 135–45.

Kiely, Robert. "Angelic Discourse or Unstable Allegory? The Play of the Literal and Figurative in Augustine's *Confessions, The Little Flowers of St. Francis,* and Bunyan's *Pilgrim's Progress." Stanford Lit R* 5 (1988), 121–30.

Knótt, John R. *Discourses of Martyrdom,* 199–215.

MacDonald, Ruth K. *Christian's Children,* 1–99.

MacIntyre, Wendell P. "John Bunyan's 'Celestial City' and Oliver Cromwell's 'Ideal Society.' " *Revista Alicantina de Estudios Ingleses* 3 (1990), 77–88.

Miller, J. Hillis. *Victorian Subjects,* 229–35.

Owens, W. R. "The Reception of *The Pilgrim's Progress* in England," in M. van Os and G. J. Schutte, eds., *Bunyan in England and Abroad,* 91–102.

Reed, John R. *Victorian Will,* 248–50.

Ross, Aileen M. "Paradise Regained: The Development of John Bunyan's Millenarianism," in M. van Os and G. J. Schutte, eds., *Bunyan in England and Abroad,* 73–87.

Schellenberg, Betty A. "Sociability and the Sequel: Rewriting Hero and Journey in *The Pilgrim's Progress,* Part II." *Stud in the Novel* 23 (1991), 312–21.

Sim, Stuart. " 'Safe for Those for Whom it is to be Safe': Salvation and Damnation in Bunyan's Fiction," in Anne Lawrence et al., eds., *John Bunyan and His England,* 152–54, 158–60.

Smith, Herbert W. "Bunyan and Dante: Puritan Mechanick Preacher and Medieval Scholar-Poet (A Comparative Study of the Men and Their Masterpieces)." *Durham Univ J* 84 (1992), 215–26.

Smith, Nigel. "Bunyan and the Language of the Body in Seventeenth-Century England," in Anne Lawrence et al., eds., *John Bunyan and His England,* 166–67, 169, 171–72.

Stranahan, Brainerd P. "Bunyan's Satire and Its Biblical Sources," in Robert G. Collmer, ed., *Bunyan in Our Time,* 35–60.

Stratton, Jon. *Writing Sites,* 74–78.

Swaim, Kathleen M. "Christian's 'Christian Behaviour' to his Family in *Pilgrim's Progress.*" *Rel and Lit* 21:3 (1989), 1–13.

Swaim, Kathleen M. "Mercy and the Feminine Heroic in the Second Part of *Pilgrim's Progress.*" *Stud in Engl Lit, 1500–1900* 30 (1990), 387–406.

Walton, George W. "Bunyan's Proverbial Language," in Robert G. Collmer, ed., *Bunyan in Our Time,* 7–34.

KATHARINE BURDEKIN

Proud Man, 1934

Patai, Daphne. "Imagining Reality: The Utopian Fiction of Katharine Burdekin," in Angela Ingram and Daphne Patai, eds., *Rediscovering Forgotten Radicals,* 231–36.

Swastika Night, 1937

Pagetti, Carlo. "In the Year of Our Lord Hitler 720: Katharine Burdekin's *Swastika Night.*" *Science-Fiction Stud* 17 (1990), 360–67.

Patai, Daphne. "Imagining Reality: The Utopian Fiction of Katharine Burdekin," in Angela Ingram and Daphne Patai, eds., *Rediscovering Forgotten Radicals,* 236–39.

Russell, Elizabeth. "Katherine Burdekin's *Swastika Night:* The Search for Truths and Texts." *Foundation* 55 (1992), 36–42.

Russell, Elizabeth. "The Loss of the Feminine Principle in Charlotte Haldane's *Man's World* and Katherine Burdekin's *Swastika Night,*" in Lucie Armitt, ed., *Where No Man Has Gone Before,* 21–28.

ANTHONY BURGESS

Abba Abba, 1977

Stinson, John J. *Anthony Burgess Revisited,* 133–36.

Any Old Iron, 1989

Stinson, John J. *Anthony Burgess Revisited,* 127–32.

Beard's Roman Women, 1976

Stinson, John J. *Anthony Burgess Revisited,* 132–34.

Beds in the East, 1959

Stinson, John J. *Anthony Burgess Revisited,* 32–33.

A Clockwork Orange, 1962

Gorra, Michael. "The World of *A Clockwork Orange.*" *Gettysburg R* 3 (1990), 630–43.

Kopper, Edward A., Jr. "Joyce's *Ulysses* and Burgess' *A Clockwork Orange:* A Note." *Notes on Mod Irish Lit* 1 (1989), 12–13.

Stinson, John J. *Anthony Burgess Revisited,* 52–60.

The Clockwork Testament, 1974

> Stinson, John J. *Anthony Burgess Revisited,* 95–98.

Devil of a State, 1961

> Stinson, John J. *Anthony Burgess Revisited,* 34–36.

The Doctor Is Sick, 1960

> Stinson, John J. *Anthony Burgess Revisited,* 68–71.

Earthly Powers, 1980

> Stinson, John J. *Anthony Burgess Revisited,* 119–27.

The End of the World News, 1982

> Scanlan, Margaret. *Traces of Another Time,* 175–96.
> Stinson, John J. *Anthony Burgess Revisited,* 136–37.

Enderby, 1968

> Stinson, John J. *Anthony Burgess Revisited,* 92–95.

Enderby's Dark Lady, 1984

> Stinson, John J. *Anthony Burgess Revisited,* 98–103.

The Eve of St. Venus, 1964

> Stinson, John J. *Anthony Burgess Revisited,* 80–81.

Honey for the Bears, 1963

> Stinson, John J. *Anthony Burgess Revisited,* 36–40.

The Kingdom of the Wicked, 1985

> Stinson, John J. *Anthony Burgess Revisited,* 138–39.

The Long Day Wanes, 1965

> Stinson, John J. *Anthony Burgess Revisited,* 28–30, 32–34.

Man of Nazareth, 1979

> Stinson, John J. *Anthony Burgess Revisited,* 137–38.

MF, 1971

> Cassola, Arnold. "*MF:* A Glossary of Anthony Burgess's Castitan Language." *Engl Lang Notes* 26:4 (1989), 72–78.
> Stinson, John J. *Anthony Burgess Revisited,* 103–10.

Napoleon Symphony, 1974

> Stinson, John J. *Anthony Burgess Revisited,* 110–18.

1985, 1978

> Stinson, John J. *Anthony Burgess Revisited,* 60–63.

Nothing Like the Sun, 1964

> Stinson, John J. *Anthony Burgess Revisited,* 88–92, 98–103.

One Hand Clapping, 1961

> Stinson, John J. *Anthony Burgess Revisited,* 71–74.

The Pianoplayers, 1986

    Stinson, John J. *Anthony Burgess Revisited,* 13–15.

The Right to an Answer, 1960

    Stinson, John J. *Anthony Burgess Revisited,* 65–68.

Tremor of Intent, 1966

    Stinson, John J. *Anthony Burgess Revisited,* 40–46.
    Woodman, Thomas. *Faithful Fictions,* 117–18, 145–46.

A Vision of Battlements, 1965

    Stinson, John J. *Anthony Burgess Revisited,* 83–88.

The Wanting Seed, 1962

    Stinson, John J. *Anthony Burgess Revisited,* 47–52.

The Worm and the Ring, 1961

    Stinson, John J. *Anthony Burgess Revisited,* 74–80.

FRANCES HODGSON BURNETT

A Little Princess, 1905

    Wall, Barbara. *The Narrator's Voice,* 169–75.

Sara Crewe, 1888

    Wall, Barbara. *The Narrator's Voice,* 169–74.

The Secret Garden, 1911

    Bixler, Phyllis. "Gardens, Houses, and Nurturant Power in *The Secret Garden,*" in James Holt McGavran, Jr., ed., *Romanticism and Children's Literature,* 208–23.
    Wall, Barbara. *The Narrator's Voice,* 175–77.

FANNY BURNEY

Camilla, 1796

    McMaster, Juliet. "The Body inside the Skin: The Medical Model of Character in the Eighteenth-Century Novel." *Eighteenth-Cent Fiction* 4 (1992), 298–300.
    McMaster, Juliet. *The Index of the Mind,* 29–31.
    McMaster, Juliet. "The Silent Angel: Impediments to Female Expression in Frances Burney's Novels." *Stud in the Novel* 21 (1989), 242–47.
    Mei, Huang. *Transforming the Cinderella Dream,* 50–52.
    Rogers, Katharine M. *Frances Burney,* 67–107.

Cecilia, 1782

    Campbell, D. Grant. "Fashionable Suicide: Conspicuous Consumption and the Collapse of Credit in Frances Burney's *Cecilia.*" *Stud in Eighteenth-Cent Culture* 20 (1990), 131–42.

Kraft, Elizabeth. *Character & Consciousness,* 147–53.

McMaster, Juliet. "The Silent Angel: Impediments to Female Expression in Frances Burney's Novels." *Stud in the Novel* 21 (1989), 240–42.

Rogers, Katharine M. *Frances Burney,* 41–66.

Ross, Deborah. *The Excellence of Falsehood,* 147–65.

Simons, Judy. "Fanny Burney: The Tactics of Subversion," in Dale Spender, ed., *Living by the Pen,* 130–33.

Evelina, 1778

Baldwin, Louis. *One Woman's Liberation,* 36–42, 167–85.

Campbell, Gina. "Bringing Belmont to Justice: Burney's Quest for Paternal Recognition in *Evelina.*" *Eighteenth-Cent Fiction* 3 (1991), 321–40.

Campbell, Gina. "How to Read Like a Gentleman: Burney's Instruction to Her Critics in *Evelina.*" *ELH* 57 (1990), 557–82.

Cutting-Gray, Joanne. "Writing Innocence: Fanny Burney's *Evelina.*" *Tulsa Stud in Women's Lit* 9 (1990), 43–55.

David, Gail. *Female Heroism,* 59–82.

Doody, Margaret Anne. "Beyond *Evelina:* The Individual Novel and the Community of Literature." *Eighteenth-Cent Fiction* 3 (1991), 359–71.

Dowling, William C. "*Evelina* and the Genealogy of Literary Shame." *Eighteenth-Cent Life* 16:3 (1992), 208–15.

Fraiman, Susan. *Unbecoming Women,* 29–58.

Georgia, Jennifer. "The Joys of Social Intercourse: Men, Women, and Conversation in the Eighteenth Century," in Kevin L. Cope, ed., *Compendious Conversations,* 253–55.

Glendening, John. "Young Fanny Burney and the Mentor." *The Age of Johnson* 4 (1991), 299–308.

Greenfield, Susan C. "'Oh Dear Resemblance of Thy Murdered Mother': Female Authorship in *Evelina.*" *Eighteenth-Cent Fiction* 3 (1991), 301–20.

Hall, K. G. *The Exalted Heroine,* 110–22.

Hatch, Ronald B. "'Lordship and Bondage': Women Novelists of the Eighteenth Century." *REAL: Yrbk of Res in Engl and Am Lit* 8 (1991/92), 239–40.

Hilliard, Raymond F. "Laughter Echoing from Mouth to Mouth: Symbolic Cannibalism and Gender in *Evelina.*" *Eighteenth-Cent Life* 17:1 (1993), 46–58.

Hutner, Heidi. "Evelina and the Problem of the Female Grotesque." *Genre* 23 (1990), 191–203.

Kraft, Elizabeth. *Character & Consciousness,* 143–45.

McMaster, Juliet. "The Silent Angel: Impediments to Female Expression in Frances Burney's Novels." *Stud in the Novel* 21 (1989), 235–40.

Mei, Huang. *Transforming the Cinderella Dream,* 31–53.

Oakleaf, David. "The Name of the Father: Social Identity and the Ambition of *Evelina.*" *Eighteenth-Cent Fiction* 3 (1991), 341–58.

Pawl, Amy J. "'And What Other Name May I Claim?': Names and Their

Owners in Frances Burney's *Evelina.*" *Eighteenth-Cent Fiction* 3 (1991), 283–99.

Probyn, Clive T. *English Fiction,* 175–79.

Rogers, Katharine M. *Frances Burney,* 25–40.

Schaffer, Julie. "Not Subordinate: Empowering Women in the Marriage Plot—The Novels of Frances Burney, Maria Edgeworth, and Jane Austen." *Criticism* 34 (1992), 57–61.

Simons, Judy. "Fanny Burney: The Tactics of Subversion," in Dale Spender, ed., *Living by the Pen,* 129–33.

Spencer, Jane. " 'Of Use to Her Daughter': Maternal Authority and Early Women Novelists," in Dale Spender, ed., *Living by the Pen,* 205–6.

Spender, Dale. "A Vindication of the Writing Woman," in Dale Spender, ed., *Living by the Pen,* 17–19.

Tucker, Irene. "Writing Home: *Evelina,* the Epistolary Novel and the Paradox of Property." *ELH* 60 (1993), 421–35.

Yeazell, Ruth Bernard. *Fictions of Modesty,* 122–42.

The Wanderer, 1814

McMaster, Juliet. "The Silent Angel: Impediments to Female Expression in Frances Burney's Novels." *Stud in the Novel* 21 (1989), 247–50.

Mei, Huang. *Transforming the Cinderella Dream,* 50–52.

Rogers, Katharine M. *Frances Burney,* 131–66.

Ross, Deborah. *The Excellence of Falsehood,* 147–65.

Simons, Judy. "Fanny Burney: The Tactics of Subversion," in Dale Spender, ed., *Living by the Pen,* 130–35.

SAMUEL BUTLER

Erewhon, 1872

Raby, Peter. *Samuel Butler,* 115–32.

Reed, John R. *Victorian Will,* 340–42.

Erewhon Revisited, 1901

Marroni, Francesco. "*Erewhon Revisited:* il ritorno del Figlio del Sole," in Carlo Pagetti, ed., *Nel tempo del sogno,* 37–53.

Raby, Peter. *Samuel Butler,* 276–84.

The Way of All Flesh, 1903

Auerbach, Emily. *Maestros, Dilettantes, and Philistines,* 120–23.

Ganz, Margaret. *Humor, Irony, and the Realm of Madness,* 141–83.

Guest, David. "Acquired Characters: Cultural versus Biological Determinism in Butler's *The Way of All Flesh.*" *Engl Lit in Transition* 34 (1991), 283–92.

Raby, Peter. *Samuel Butler,* 15–23, 25–34, 207–9, 295–99.

Reed, John R. *Victorian Will,* 342–44.

A. S. BYATT

Possession, 1990

> Hulbert, Ann. "The Great Ventriloquist: A. S. Byatt's *Possession: A Romance,*" in Robert E. Hosmer, Jr., ed., *Contemporary British Women Writers,* 55–61.
> Rossen, Janice. *The University in Modern Fiction,* 144–49, 153–55.
> Yelin, Louise. "Cultural Cartography: A. S. Byatt's *Possession* and the Politics of Victorian Studies." *Victorian Newsl* 81 (1992), 38–41.

Shadow of a Sun, 1964

> Taylor, D. J. *A Vain Conceit,* 60–62.

Still Life, 1985

> Buschini, Marie-Pascale. "Attrait du Sud et mise en abyme du processus de création dans *Still Life* de A. S. Byatt." *Cycnos* 7 (1991), 97–111.
> Cosslett, Tess. "Childbirth from the Woman's Point of View in British Women's Fiction: Enid Bagnold's *The Squire* and A. S. Byatt's *Still Life.*" *Tulsa Stud in Women's Lit* 8 (1989), 263–83.
> Rossen, Janice. *The University in Modern Fiction,* 48–51, 116–18.
> Taylor, D. J. *A Vain Conceit,* 62–65.

The Virgin in the Garden, 1978

> Rossen, Janice. *The University in Modern Fiction,* 49–51.

MONA CAIRD

The Wing of Azrael, 1889

> Ardis, Ann L. *New Women, New Novels,* 68–72.

ARTHUR CALDER-MARSHALL

Pie in the Sky, 1937

> Croft, Andy. *Red Letter Days,* 262–65.

SARAH CAMPION

Duet for Female Voices, 1936

> Brothers, Barbara. "British Women Write the Story of the Nazis: A Conspiracy of Silence," in Angela Ingram and Daphne Patai, eds., *Rediscovering Forgotten Radicals,* 253–55.

If She Is Wise, 1935

> Brothers, Barbara. "British Women Write the Story of the Nazis: A Conspiracy of Silence," in Angela Ingram and Daphne Patai, eds., *Rediscovering Forgotten Radicals,* 252–53.

LEWIS CARROLL

Alice's Adventures in Wonderland, 1865

Antoch, Robert F. "*Alice in Wonderland:* A Dream of Reality." *Jabberwocky* 17 (1988), 23–29.

Conroy, Mark. "A Tale of Two Alices in Wonderland." *Lit and Psych* 37:3 (1991), 29–41.

Corsetti, Jean-Paul. "Gel ou métamorphose des fées: réflexion sur l'esthétique de Lewis Carroll," in *La Littérature Fantastique,* 121–35.

Docherty, John. "Dantean Allusions in Wonderland." *Jabberwocky* 19:1–2 (1990), 13–16.

Docherty, John. "Neoplatonism and a Nursery Rhyme." *Jabberwocky* 19:1–2 (1990), 17–18.

Docherty, John. "A Note on Bill the Lizard and His Two Friends." *Jabberwocky* 18 (1989), 37–39.

Duffy, Maureen. "The Illustration of Peter Newell and John Tenniel in Lewis Carroll's *Alice's Adventures in Wonderland.*" *Jabberwocky* 21 (1992), 59–64.

Gilbert, Pamela K. "Alice's Ab-surd-ity: Demon in Wonderland." *Victorian Newsl* 83 (1993), 17–22.

Gilead, Sarah. "Magic Abjured: Closure in Children's Fantasy Fiction." *PMLA* 106 (1991), 282–84.

Hadomi, Leah, and Robert Elbaz. "*Alice in Wonderland* and Utopia." *Orbis Litterarum* 45 (1990), 136–53.

Hancher, Michael. "Alice's Audiences," in James Holt McGavran, Jr., ed., *Romanticism and Children's Literature,* 190–202.

Honig, Edith Lazaros. *Breaking the Angelic Image,* 75–86.

Kelly, Richard. *Lewis Carroll,* 14–16, 51–57, 70–92, 110–28.

Knight, Peter J. "Lewis Carroll and the Rise of Feminism." *Jabberwocky* 21 (1992), 79–84.

Lee, Vicky. "An Investigation into the Neuro-psychological poisoning of the Hatter in *Alice's Adventures in Wonderland.*" *Jabberwocky* 21 (1992), 101–3.

Madden, Fred. "'Alice, Who are you?': Charles Mackay and *Alice's Adventures in Wonderland.*" *Jabberwocky* 17 (1988), 35–36.

Maiden, Jeffery, Gary Graham, and Nancy Fox. "A Tale in a Tail-Rhyme." *Jabberwocky* 18 (1989), 32–36.

Mandelker, Amy. "The Mushroom and the Egg: Lewis Carroll's *Alice* as an Otherworldly Introduction to Semiotics." *Canadian-Am Slavic Stud* 22 (1988), 101–14.

O'Connor, Michael. "The Adult-Child and the Child-Adult." *Jabberwocky* 21 (1992), 69–77.

Pennington, John. "Alice at the Back of the North Wind, Or the Metafictions of Lewis Carroll and George MacDonald." *Extrapolation* 33 (1992), 66–71.

Petersen, Robert C. "To Begin at the Beginning: 'Tis the Voise of Alice. I Heard Him Declare." *Jabberwocky* 21:2 (1992), 39–50.

Reinstein, P. Gila. *Alice in Context,* 169–216.

Schoenburg, Nadine. "A Look at How Alice's Playing in the Looking Glass Reflects Back on Her." *Neohelicon* 20:1 (1993), 201–14.

Steig, Michael. *Stories of Reading,* 105–23.

Stratton, Jon. *Writing Sites,* 168–73.

Susina, Jan. "Educating Alice: The Lessons of *Wonderland.*" *Jabberwocky* 18 (1989), 3–9.

Thomas, Ronald R. *Dreams of Authority,* 55–61.

Wall, Barbara. *The Narrator's Voice,* 97–110.

Wallace, Richard. *The Agony of Lewis Carroll,* 37–44, 56–57, 162–64.

Sylvie and Bruno, 1889

Kelly, Richard. *Lewis Carroll,* 129–45.

Wall, Barbara. *The Narrator's Voice,* 106–8.

Wallace, Richard. *The Agony of Lewis Carroll,* 37, 60–68, 78–82.

Sylvie and Bruno Concluded, 1893

Kelly, Richard. *Lewis Carroll,* 129–45.

Through the Looking-Glass, 1871

Corsetti, Jean-Paul. "Gel ou métamorphose des fées: réflexion sur l'esthétique de Lewis Carroll," in *La Littérature Fantastique,* 121–35.

Gilead, Sarah. "Magic Abjured: Closure in Children's Fantasy Fiction." *PMLA* 106 (1991), 282–84.

Hancher, Michael. "Alice's Audiences," in James Holt McGavran, Jr., ed., *Romanticism and Children's Literature,* 192–202.

Imholtz, August A., Jr. "King's Cross Loss." *Jabberwocky* 21:1 (1991/92), 22–23.

Kelly, Richard. *Lewis Carroll,* 57–63, 92–106, 114–28.

O'Connor, Michael. "The Adult-Child and the Child-Adult." *Jabberwocky* 21 (1992), 69–77.

Pennington, John. "Alice at the Back of the North Wind, Or the Metafictions of Lewis Carroll and George MacDonald." *Extrapolation* 33 (1992), 66–71.

Reinstein, P. Gila. *Alice in Context,* 169–216.

Riddle, Brian. "Musings on Humpty Dumpty." *Jabberwocky* 18 (1989), 40–41.

Schoenburg, Nadine. "A Look at How Alice's Playing in the Looking Glass Reflects Back on Her." *Neohelicon* 20:1 (1993), 201–14.

Wall, Barbara. *The Narrator's Voice,* 103–6.

Wallace, Richard. *The Agony of Lewis Carroll,* 35–37, 57–60.

SALLY CARSON

The Prisoner, 1936

Brothers, Barbara. "British Women Write the Story of the Nazis: A Conspiracy of Silence," in Angela Ingram and Daphne Patai, eds., *Rediscovering Forgotten Radicals,* 256–57.

A Traveller Came By, 1938

> Brothers, Barbara. "British Women Write the Story of the Nazis: A Conspiracy of Silence," in Angela Ingram and Daphne Patai, eds., *Rediscovering Forgotten Radicals,* 257–58.

ANGELA CARTER

Heroes and Villains, 1969

> Kenyon, Olga. *Writing Women,* 21–22.

The Infernal Desire Machines of Doctor Hoffmann, 1972

> Manlove, Colin. " 'In the Demythologizing Business': Angela Carter's *The Infernal Desire Machines of Dr. Hoffmann* (1972)," in Kath Filmer, ed., *Twentieth-Century Fantasists,* 148–58.
> Robinson, Sally. *Engendering the Subject,* 98–117.
> Schmidt, Ricarda. "The Journey of the Subject in Angela Carter's Fiction." *Textual Practice* 3 (1989), 56–61.

The Magic Toyshop, 1967

> Kenyon, Olga. *Writing Women,* 18–19.
> Mills, Sara, Lynne Pearce, Sue Spaull, and Elaine Millard. *Feminist Readings,* 133–41, 170–80.

Nights at the Circus, 1984

> Humm, Maggie. *Border Traffic,* 54–57.
> Kendrick, Walter. "The Real Magic of Angela Carter," in Robert E. Hosmer, Jr., ed., *Contemporary British Women Writers,* 75–80.
> Kenyon, Olga. *Writing Women,* 19–21, 26–28.
> Powrie, Phil. "Angela Carter/Chantal Chawaf: Rewriting the Domestic." *New Comparison* 11 (1991), 127–35.
> Punter, David. "Essential Imaginings: The Novels of Angela Carter and Russell Hoban," in James Acheson, ed. *The British and Irish Novel,* 143–48.
> Robinson, Sally. *Engendering the Subject,* 122–32.
> Schmidt, Ricarda. "The Journey of the Subject in Angela Carter's Fiction." *Textual Practice* 3 (1989), 67–73.

The Passion of New Eve, 1977

> Kenyon, Olga. *Writing Women,* 23–25.
> Rubenstein, Roberta. "Intersexions: Gender Metamorphosis in Angela Carter's *The Passion of New Eve* and Lois Gould's *A Sea-Change.*" *Tulsa Stud in Women's Lit* 12 (1993), 104–16.
> Schmidt, Ricarda. "The Journey of the Subject in Angela Carter's Fiction." *Textual Practice* 3 (1989), 61–67.

JOYCE CARY

Castle Corner, 1938

> Emprin, Jacques. "Joyce Cary's *Castle Corner:* A Big House Novel?," in Jacqueline Genet, ed., *The Big House in Ireland,* 131–41.

Except the Lord, 1953

> Holmesland, Oddvar. "Joyce Cary: A Metaphysical Novelist." *Engl Stud* 72 (1991), 264–66.

Herself Surprised, 1941

> Holmesland, Oddvar. "Joyce Cary: A Metaphysical Novelist." *Engl Stud* 72 (1991), 262–64.

The Horse's Mouth, 1944

> Holmesland, Oddvar. "Joyce Cary: A Metaphysical Novelist." *Engl Stud* 72 (1991), 262–64.
> Waldeck, Peter B. *Weighing Delight and Dole,* 195–211.

Mister Johnson, 1939

> Holmesland, Oddvar. "Joyce Cary: A Metaphysical Novelist." *Engl Stud* 72 (1991), 258–62.

The Moonlight, 1946

> Fenwick, Julie. "Women, Sex, and Culture in *The Moonlight:* Joyce Cary's Response to D. H. Lawrence." *Ariel* 24:2 (1993), 27–40.

Not Honour More, 1955

> Holmesland, Oddvar. "Joyce Cary: A Metaphysical Novelist." *Engl Stud* 72 (1991), 264–66.

Prisoner of Grace, 1952

> Holmesland, Oddvar. "Joyce Cary: A Metaphysical Novelist." *Engl Stud* 72 (1991), 264–66.

To Be a Pilgrim, 1942

> Harvie, Christopher. *The Centre of Things,* 193–96.
> Holmesland, Oddvar. "Joyce Cary: A Metaphysical Novelist." *Engl Stud* 72 (1991), 262–64.

MARGARET CAVENDISH

Sociable Letters, 1664

> Donovan, Josephine. "Women and the Rise of the Novel: A Feminist-Marxist Theory." *Signs* 16 (1991), 455–58.

ROBIN CHAPMAN

The Duchess's Diary, 1985

> Friedman, Edward H. "Voices Within: Robin Chapman's *The Duchess's Diary* and the Intertextual Conundrum of *Don Quixote.*" *RLA: Romance Languages Annual* 2 (1990), 400–405.

MARY CHARLTON

Rosella, 1799

> Huber, Werner. "Forgotten Novels of the Romantic Era, Part II: Mary Charlton, *Rosella* (1799)," in Günter Ahrends and Hans-Jürgen Diller, eds., *English Romantic Prose,* 39–49.

BRUCE CHATWIN

On the Black Hill, 1983

> Castay, Marie-Thérèse. "*On the Black Hill* de Bruce Chatwin et le monde des marches galloises." *Caliban* 27 (1990), 35–46.

GEORGE CHESNEY

The Dilemma, 1876

> Paxton, Nancy L. "Mobilizing Chivalry: Rape in British Novels about the Indian Uprising of 1857." *Victorian Stud* 36 (1992), 13–16.

G. K. CHESTERTON

The Club of Queer Trades, 1905

> Scheick, William J. "Ethical Romance and the Detecting Reader: The Example of *The Club of Queer Trades,*" in Ronald G. Walker and June M. Frazer, eds., *The Cunning Craft,* 86–97.

The Return of Don Quixote, 1927

> Woodman, Thomas. *Faithful Fictions,* 99–100.

ERSKINE CHILDERS

The Riddle of the Sands, 1903

> Seed, David. "The Adventure of Spying: Erskine Childers's *The Riddle of the Sands,*" in Clive Bloom, ed., *Spy Thrillers,* 28–41.
> Stafford, David. *The Silent Game,* 33–35.
> Trotter, David. "The Politics of Adventure in the Early British Spy Novel," in Wesley K. Wark, ed., *Spy Fiction,* 40–42.

MARY CHOLMONDELEY

Red Pottage, 1899

> Ardis, Ann L. *New Women, New Novels,* 128–33.
> Rainwater, Catherine, and William J. Scheick. "Aliens in the Garden: The Re-Vision of Mary Cholmondeley's *Red Pottage.*" *Philol Q* 71 (1992), 101–16.

AGATHA CHRISTIE

Appointment with Death, 1938

> Gerald, Michael C. *The Poisonous Pen,* 14–15, 160–62.
> Light, Alison. *Forever England,* 102–4.

The Body in the Library, 1942

> Gill, Gillian. *Agatha Christie,* 188–98.

Cards on the Table, 1936

> Gill, Gillian. *Agatha Christie,* 135–48.

Death on the Nile, 1937

> Gerald, Michael C. *The Poisonous Pen,* 179–80.

Giants' Bread, 1930

> Gill, Gillian. *Agatha Christie,* 91–96.

The Moving Finger, 1942

> Paul, Robert S. *Whatever Happened to Sherlock Homes?,* 233–35.

The Murder of Roger Ackroyd, 1926

> Gesuato, Sara. "Textually Interesting Aspects of Agatha Christie's *The Murder of Roger Ackroyd.*" *Versus* 57 (1990), 29–56.
> Lovitt, Carl R. "Controlling Discourse in Detective Fiction: Or, Caring Very Much Who Killed Roger Ackroyd," in Ronald G. Walker and June M. Frazer, eds., *The Cunning Craft,* 68–85.

The Mysterious Affair at Styles, 1920

> Gerald, Michael C. *The Poisonous Pen,* 50–53.
> Gill, Gillian. *Agatha Christie,* 33–64.
> Light, Alison. *Forever England,* 66–67.

Nemesis, 1971

> Gill, Gillian. *Agatha Christie,* 196–201.

The Pale Horse, 1961

> Gerald, Michael C. *The Poisonous Pen,* 30–32, 194–95.

The Rose and the Yew Tree, 1947

> Gill, Gillian. *Agatha Christie,* 156–74.

The Secret of Chimneys, 1925

> Gill, Gillian. *Agatha Christie,* 74–90.

Ten Little Niggers, 1939

> Light, Alison. *Forever England,* 98–99.

Unfinished Portrait, 1934

> Gill, Gillian. *Agatha Christie,* 100–108.

JOHN CHRISTOPHER

The Death of Grass, 1956

    Ruddick, Nicholas. *Ultimate Island,* 143–46.

The World in Winter, 1962

    Ruddick, Nicholas. *Ultimate Island,* 146–48.

A Wrinkle in the Skin, 1965

    Ruddick, Nicholas. *Ultimate Island,* 149–51.

JANE HUME CLAPPERTON

Margaret Dunmore; or, A Socialist Home, 1888

    Waters, Chris. "New Women and Socialist-Feminist Fiction: The Novels of Isabella Ford and Katharine Bruce Glasier," in Angela Ingram and Daphne Patai, eds., *Rediscovering Forgotten Radicals,* 29–30.

ARTHUR C. CLARKE

Childhood's End, 1953

    Abrash, Merritt. "Utopia Subverted: Unstated Messages in *Childhood's End." Extrapolation* 30 (1989), 372–79.

    Malmgren, Carl D. *Worlds Apart,* 69–71.

    Waugh, Robert H. "The Lament of the Midwives: Arthur C. Clarke and the Tradition." *Extrapolation* 31 (1990), 36–52.

The City and the Stars, 1956

    Greven-Borde, Hélène. "Utopie et science-fiction: le discours des bâtisseurs de cités." *Etudes Anglaises* 41 (1988), 282–85.

Rendezvous with Rama, 1973

    Feeley, Gregory. "Partners in Plunder: Or, Rendezvous with Manna." *Foundation* 49 (1990), 58–63.

    Malmgren, Carl D. *Worlds Apart,* 104–11.

2001: A Space Odyssey, 1968

    Goizet, Annette. "*2001–2010:* les odyssés de l'espace d'Arthur C. Clarke." *Etudes Anglaises* 41 (1988), 328–33.

2010: Odyssey Two, 1982

    Goizet, Annette. "*2001–2010:* les odyssés de l'espace d'Arthur C. Clarke." *Etudes Anglaises* 41 (1988), 328–33.

JOHN CLELAND

Fanny Hill, 1748

    Bell, Ian A. *Literature and Crime,* 144–46.

    Kahn, Madeleine. *Narrative Transvestism,* 154–60.

    Kibbie, Ann Louise. "Sentimental Properties: *Pamela* and *Memoirs of a Woman of Pleasure." ELH* 58 (1991), 569–76.

Probyn, Clive T. *English Fiction*, 80–83.

Simmons, Philip E. "John Cleland's *Memoirs of a Woman of Pleasure:* Literary Voyeurism and the Technique of Novelistic Transgression." *Eighteenth-Cent Fiction* 3 (1990), 43–63.

Trumbach, Randolph. "Modern Prostitution and Gender in *Fanny Hill:* Libertine and Domesticated Fantasy," in G. S. Rousseau and Roy Porter, eds., *Sexual Underworlds*, 69–85.

Turner, James Grantham. "'Illustrious Depravity' and the Erotic Sublime." *The Age of Johnson* 2 (1989), 1–38.

Yeazell, Ruth Bernard. *Fictions of Modesty*, 102–21.

ISABEL COLEGATE

The Shooting Party, 1980

Averitt, Brett T. "The Strange Clarity of Distance: History, Myth, and Imagination in the Novels of Isabel Colegate," in Robert E. Hosmer, Jr., ed., *Contemporary British Women Writers*, 88–100.

WILKIE COLLINS

Antonina, 1850

Heller, Tamar. *Dead Secrets*, 48–57.

Armadale, 1866

Milbank, Alison. *Daughters of the House*, 37–46.

Peters, Catherine. *The King of Inventors*, 266–68, 272–74.

Reed, John R. *Victorian Will*, 291–93.

Thoms, Peter. *The Windings of the Labyrinth*, 114–38.

Tutor, Jonathan Craig. "Lydia Gwilt: Wilkie Collins's Satanic, Sirenic Psychotic." *Univ of Mississippi Stud in Engl* 10 (1992), 37–52.

Zeitz, Lisa M., and Peter Thoms. "Collins's Use of the Strasbourg Clock in *Armadale.*" *Nineteenth-Cent Lit* 45 (1991), 495–503.

Basil, 1852

Heller, Tamar. *Dead Secrets*, 58–81.

Peters, Catherine. *The King of Inventors*, 116–21.

Thoms, Peter. *The Windings of the Labyrinth*, 16–31.

The Black Robe, 1881

Peters, Catherine. *The King of Inventors*, 396–98.

The Dead Secret, 1857

Thoms, Peter. *The Windings of the Labyrinth*, 44–50.

The Fallen Leaves, 1879

Peters, Catherine. *The King of Inventors*, 385–88.

Hide and Seek, 1854

Milbank, Alison. *Daughters of the House*, 54–57.

Thoms, Peter. *The Windings of the Labyrinth*, 31–44.

The Law and the Lady, 1875

> Peters, Catherine. *The King of Inventors,* 370–77.

Man and Wife, 1870

> Peters, Catherine. *The King of Inventors,* 314–23.

The Moonstone, 1868

> Crooks, Robert. "Reopening the Mysteries: Colonialist Logic and Cultural Difference in *The Moonstone* and *The Horse Latitudes." LIT* 4 (1993), 220–26.
>
> Heller, Tamar. *Dead Secrets,* 142–63.
>
> Kayman, Martin A. *From Bow Street to Baker Street,* 193–209.
>
> Knezevic, Borislav. "(Sub)merging Metonymies: *The Moonstone." Studia Romanica et Anglica Zagrabiensia* 35 (1990), 3–21.
>
> Milbank, Alison. *Daughters of the House,* 57–64.
>
> Nayder, Lillian. "Robinson Crusoe and Friday in Victorian Britain: 'Discipline,' 'Dialogue,' and Collins's Critique of Empire in *The Moonstone." Dickens Stud Annual* 21 (1992), 213–27.
>
> Paul, Robert S. *Whatever Happened to Sherlock Homes?,* 40–43.
>
> Peters, Catherine. *The King of Inventors,* 303–11.
>
> Reed, John R. *Victorian Will,* 293–95.
>
> Roy, Ashish. "The Fabulous Imperialist Semiotic of Wilkie Collins's *The Moonstone." New Liter Hist* 24 (1993), 657–77.
>
> Thomas, Ronald R. *Dreams of Authority,* 201–28.
>
> Thomas, Ronald R. "Minding the Body Politic: The Romance of Science and the Revision of History in Victorian Detective Fiction." *Victorian Lit and Culture* 19 (1991), 235–42.
>
> Thoms, Peter. *The Windings of the Labyrinth,* 139–66.

The New Magdalen, 1873

> Peters, Catherine. *The King of Inventors,* 337–40.

No Name, 1862

> David, Deirdre. "Rewriting the Male Plot in Wilkie Collins's *No Name:* Captain Wragge Orders an Omelette and Mrs. Wragge Goes into Custody," in Laura Claridge and Elizabeth Langland, eds., *Out of Bounds,* 186–96.
>
> Horne, Lewis. "Magdalen's Peril." *Dickens Stud Annual* 20 (1991), 281–93.
>
> Huskey, Melynda. "*No Name:* Embodying the Sensation Heroine." *Victorian Newsl* 82 (1992), 5–12.
>
> Litvak, Joseph. *Caught in the Act,* 134–37.
>
> Milbank, Alison. *Daughters of the House,* 25–37.
>
> Peters, Catherine. *The King of Inventors,* 240–56.
>
> Thoms, Peter. *The Windings of the Labyrinth,* 87–111.

The Woman in White, 1860

Auerbach, Emily. *Maestros, Dilettantes, and Philistines,* 65–68.

Cvetkovich, Ann. "Ghostlier Determinations: The Economy of Sensation and *The Woman in White.*" *Novel* 23 (1989), 24–43.

Cvetkovich, Ann. *Mixed Feelings,* 71–96.

Donaghy, Mary, and Pamela Perkins. "A Man's Resolution: Narrative Strategies in Wilkie Collins' *The Woman in White.*" *Stud in the Novel* 22 (1990), 392–401.

Drexler, Peter. *Literatur, Recht, Kriminalität,* 173–76.

Elam, Diane. "White Narratology: Gender and Reference in Wilkie Collins's *The Woman in White,*" in Lloyd Davis, ed., *Virginal Sexuality,* 50–63.

Heller, Tamar. *Dead Secrets,* 110–41.

Hendershot, Cyndy. "A Sensation Novel's Appropriation of the Terror-Gothic: Wilkie Collins's *The Woman in White.*" *Clues* 13:2 (1992), 127–32.

Litvak, Joseph. *Caught in the Act,* 128–35.

Milbank, Alison. *Daughters of the House,* 63–79.

Miller, D. A. "*Cage aux folles:* Sensation and Gender in Wilkie Collins's *The Woman in White,*" in Elaine Showalter, ed., *Speaking of Gender,* 187–213.

Nayder, Lillian. "Agents of Empire in *The Woman in White.*" *Victorian Newsl* 83 (1993), 1–6.

Peters, Catherine. *The King of Inventors,* 212–25.

Reed, John R. *Victorian Will,* 288–90.

Sutherland, John. "Wilkie Collins and the Origin of the Sensation Novel." *Dickens Stud Annual* 20 (1991), 246–57.

Taylor, Jenny Bourne. "Psychology and Sensation: The Narrative of Moral Management in *The Woman in White.*" *Crit Survey* 2:1 (1990), 49–56.

Thoms, Peter. *The Windings of the Labyrinth,* 55–86.

GERTRUDE COLMORE

Suffragette Sally, 1911

Peterson, Shirley. "The Politics of Moral Crusade: Gertrude Colmore's *Suffragette Sally,*" in Angela Ingram and Daphne Patai, eds., *Rediscovering Forgotten Radicals,* 103–15.

IVY COMPTON-BURNETT

Daughters and Sons, 1937

Gentile, Kathy Justice. *Ivy Compton-Burnett,* 98–99.

Kiernan, Robert F. *Frivolity Unbound,* 133–40.

Dolores, 1911

Gentile, Kathy Justice. *Ivy Compton-Burnett,* 30–38.

Elders and Betters, 1944

Gentile, Kathy Justice. *Ivy Compton-Burnett,* 59–64.

A Family and a Fortune, 1939

Bellringer, Alan W. "I. Compton-Burnett's *A Family and a Fortune:* The Note of Sadness." *Durham Univ J* 84 (1992), 103–9.
Gentile, Kathy Justice. *Ivy Compton-Burnett,* 83–87.
Kiernan, Robert F. *Frivolity Unbound,* 140–47.

A Father and His Fate, 1957

Gentile, Kathy Justice. *Ivy Compton-Burnett,* 99–101.
Ross, Marlon B. "Contented Spinsters: Governessing and the Limits of Discursive Desire in the Fiction of I. Compton-Burnett," in Laura L. Doan, ed., *Old Maids,* 39–49.

A God and His Gifts, 1963

Crecy, Susan. "Ivy Compton-Burnett: Family as Nightmare," in Mark Lilly, ed., *Lesbian and Gay Writing,* 13–22.
Gentile, Kathy Justice. *Ivy Compton-Burnett,* 110–15.
Ross, Marlon B. "Contented Spinsters: Governessing and the Limits of Discursive Desire in the Fiction of I. Compton-Burnett," in Laura L. Doan, ed., *Old Maids,* 55–56.

A House and Its Head, 1935

Gentile, Kathy Justice. *Ivy Compton-Burnett,* 68–75.
Ross, Marlon B. "Contented Spinsters: Governessing and the Limits of Discursive Desire in the Fiction of I. Compton-Burnett," in Laura L. Doan, ed., *Old Maids,* 52–54.

The Last and the First, 1971

Crecy, Susan. "Ivy Compton-Burnett: Family as Nightmare," in Mark Lilly, ed., *Lesbian and Gay Writing,* 13–22.
Gentile, Kathy Justice. *Ivy Compton-Burnett,* 115–19.

Manservant and Maidservant, 1947

Gentile, Kathy Justice. *Ivy Compton-Burnett,* 75–83.

Men and Wives, 1931

Gentile, Kathy Justice. *Ivy Compton-Burnett,* 54–59.
Manthey, Jürgen. "Komödie des kommunikativen Handelns: Zu Ivy Compton-Burnetts Roman *Männer und Frauen.*" *Merkur* 41:11 (1987), 994–97.

The Mighty and Their Fall, 1961

Crecy, Susan. "Ivy Compton-Burnett: Family as Nightmare," in Mark Lilly, ed., *Lesbian and Gay Writing,* 13–22.

More Women Than Men, 1933

Gentile, Kathy Justice. *Ivy Compton-Burnett,* 44–46.

Hendriksen, John. "Ivy Compton-Burnett's *More Women Than Men:* A Study in Morbid Psychology." *Durham Univ J* 84 (1992), 95–101.

Kiernan, Robert F. *Frivolity Unbound,* 126–33.

Parents and Children, 1941

Ross, Marlon B. "Contented Spinsters: Governessing and the Limits of Discursive Desire in the Fiction of I. Compton-Burnett," in Laura L. Doan, ed., *Old Maids,* 56–63.

Pastors and Masters, 1925

Bellringer, A. W. "I. Compton-Burnett's *Pastors and Masters:* A 1920's Experiment." *Engl Stud* 72 (1991), 246–55.

Gentile, Kathy Justice. *Ivy Compton-Burnett,* 38–44.

Two Worlds and Their Ways, 1949

Gentile, Kathy Justice. *Ivy Compton-Burnett,* 104–10.

BARBARA COMYNS

Our Spoons Came From Woolworths, 1950

Baker, Niamh. *Happily Ever After?,* 50–53.

WILLIAM CONGREVE

Incognita, 1692

Aercke, Kristiaan P. "Congreve's *Incognita:* Romance, Novel, Drama?" *Eighteenth-Cent Fiction* 2 (1990), 293–308.

Probyn, Clive T. *English Fiction,* 1–2.

JOSEPH CONRAD

Almayer's Folly, 1895

Bennett, Carl D. *Joseph Conrad,* 42–44.

Halperin, John. *Novelists in their Youth,* 142–50.

Hampson, Robert. *Joseph Conrad,* 11–31.

Hawthorn, Jeremy. *Joseph Conrad,* 88–90.

Hervouet, Yves. *The French Face,* 19–23.

Humphries, Reynold. "The Discourse of Colonialism: Its Meaning and Relevance for Conrad's Fiction." *Conradiana* 21 (1989), 117–31.

Krajka, Wieslaw. *Isolation and Ethos,* 34–40.

Maisonnat, Claude. "La question de la langue dans *Almayer's Folly* de Joseph Conrad." *Etudes Anglaises* 43 (1990), 270–82.

Nadelhaft, Ruth L. *Joseph Conrad,* 13–27.

Putnam, Walter C., III. *L'Aventure littéraire,* 73–86.

Rising, Catharine. *Darkness at Heart,* 15–17, 27–28, 34–35, 40–41.

Spittles, Brian. *Joseph Conrad,* 5–6, 160–61.

Watts, Cedric. *Joseph Conrad,* 56–60.

Watts, Cedric. *A Preface to Conrad,* 27–30, 122–24.

Willy, Todd G. "Almayer's Folly and the Imperatives of Conradian Atavism." *Conradiana* 24 (1992), 3–18.

The Arrow of Gold, 1919

Campbell, Elizabeth. "Auto-mythology in *The Arrow of Gold:* Conrad's Folly or Conrad's Letter to a Friend?" *Conradiana* 25 (1993), 115–40.

Hampson, Robert. *Joseph Conrad,* 252–71.

Nadelhaft, Ruth L. *Joseph Conrad,* 119–28.

Röder-Bolton, Gerlinde. "Conrad, Goethe and the King of Ultima Thule." *Conradiana* 24 (1992), 41–44.

Chance, 1913

Hampson, Robert. *Joseph Conrad,* 196–231.

Hampson, Robert. " 'Topographical Mysteries': Conrad and London," in Gene M. Moore, ed., *Conrad's Cities,* 171–74.

Hawthorn, Jeremy. *Joseph Conrad,* 133–54.

Krajka, Wieslaw. *Isolation and Ethos,* 5–7, 9–11, 54–56, 153–55, 178–80.

Lothe, Jakob. *Conrad's Narrative Method,* 34–44.

McLauchlan, Juliet. "Conrad's 'Decivilized' Cities," in Gene M. Moore, ed., *Conrad's Cities,* 69–75.

Nadelhaft, Ruth L. *Joseph Conrad,* 109–19.

Watts, Cedric. *Joseph Conrad,* 115–22.

Lord Jim, 1900

Bennett, Carl D. *Joseph Conrad,* 61–75.

Benson, Donald R. "Constructing an Ethereal Cosmos: Late Classical Physics and *Lord Jim.*" *Conradiana* 23 (1991), 133–46.

Bohlmann, Otto. *Conrad's Existentialism,* 48–71, 109–12, 114–18, 124–26, 153–57, 162–69, 171–76.

Bonney, William. "Politics, Perception, and Gender in Conrad's *Lord Jim* and Greene's *The Quiet American.*" *Conradiana* 23 (1991), 99–118.

Born, Daniel. "Echoes of Kipling in Marlow's 'Privileged Man.' " *Conradiana* 24 (1992), 100–113.

Clayton, John J. *Gestures of Healing,* 75–79.

DeMille, Barbara. "Cruel Illusions: Nietzsche, Conrad, Hardy, and the 'Shadowy Ideal.' " *Stud in Engl Lit, 1500–1900* 30 (1990), 697–713.

Ducharme, Robert. "The Power of Culture in *Lord Jim.*" *Conradiana* 22 (1990), 3–22.

Faris, Wendy B. "The 'Dehumanization' of the Arts: J. M. W. Turner, Joseph Conrad, and the Advent of Modernism." *Compar Lit* 41 (1989), 305–25.

Halperin, John. *Novelists in their Youth,* 143–45.

Hampson, Robert. *Joseph Conrad,* 116–36.

Heilman, Robert Bechtold. *The Workings of Fiction,* 70–78.

Henricksen, Bruce. *Nomadic Voices,* 81–109.

Hervouet, Yves. *The French Face*, 64–76.

Kelleher, V. M. K. "A Third Voice: The Dialectical Structure of *Lord Jim.*" *Unisa Engl Stud* 25:1 (1987), 24–28.

Krajka, Wieslaw. *Isolation and Ethos*, 17–19, 24–26, 79–85, 93–98, 100–105, 150–55, 166–68, 181–83, 190–200.

Lothe, Jakob. *Conrad's Narrative Method*, 39–41, 133–74.

Mongia, Padmini. "Narrative Strategy and Imperialism in Conrad's *Lord Jim.*" *Stud in the Novel* 24 (1992), 173–83.

Murawski, John. "Conrad's *Lord Jim.*" *Explicator* 48 (1990), 266–68.

Nadelhaft, Ruth L. *Joseph Conrad*, 36–38, 50–57.

Osa, Osayimwense. "The Quitclaim of Okonkwo and Lord Jim." *Creative Forum* 1:3 (1988), 9–18.

Putnam, Walter C., III. *L'Aventure littéraire*, 161–85.

Reilly, Jim. *Joseph Conrad*, 36–37.

Rising, Catharine. *Darkness at Heart*, 50–64.

Sabol, C. Ruth. "Semantic Analysis and Fictive Worlds in Ford and Conrad." *Liter and Linguistic Computing* 6 (1991), 97–103.

Scheick, William J. *Fictional Structure & Ethics*, 138–47.

Schwarz, Daniel R. *The Transformation*, 222–41.

Seeley, Tracy. "Conrad's Modernist Romance: *Lord Jim.*" *ELH* 59 (1992), 495–509.

Stevenson, Randall. *Modernist Fiction*, 22–26, 188–90.

Walch, Günter. "Conrad's Hamlets: Intertextuality and the Process of History." *Zeitschrift für Anglistik und Amerikanistik* 38 (1990), 306–13.

Watts, Cedric. *Joseph Conrad*, 74–84.

Watts, Cedric. *A Preface to Conrad*, 131–33, 137–39.

Wollaeger, Mark A. *Joseph Conrad*, 78–119.

The Nigger of the "Narcissus," 1897

Bennett, Carl D. *Joseph Conrad*, 49–55.

Hampson, Robert. *Joseph Conrad*, 101–6.

Hampson, Robert. " 'Topographical Mysteries': Conrad and London," in Gene M. Moore, ed., *Conrad's Cities*, 160–61.

Hawthorn, Jeremy. *Joseph Conrad*, 69–79, 101–28.

Henricksen, Bruce. *Nomadic Voices*, 23–46.

Hervouet, Yves. *The French Face*, 39–49, 137–40.

Krajka, Wieslaw. *Isolation and Ethos*, 5–7, 9–12, 116–18, 129–33, 135–37, 144–49, 151–53, 156–62, 170–73.

Livingston, Robert Eric. "Seeing Through Reading: Class, Race and Literary Authority in Joseph Conrad's *The Nigger of the 'Narcissus.'*" *Novel* 26 (1993), 133–50.

Lothe, Jakob. *Conrad's Narrative Method*, 87–101.

Nadelhaft, Ruth L. *Joseph Conrad*, 37–41.

Onions, John. *English Fiction and Drama*, 24–25.

Putnam, Walter C., III. *L'Aventure littéraire*, 96–113.

Reilly, Jim. *Joseph Conrad*, 38–57.

Rising, Catharine. *Darkness at Heart*, 65–76.

Spittles, Brian. *Joseph Conrad,* 11–12, 16–17, 161–62, 166–67.

Watts, Cedric. "Conrad and the Myth of the Monstrous Town," in Gene M. Moore, ed., *Conrad's Cities,* 18–21.

Watts, Cedric. *Joseph Conrad,* 65–73.

Nostromo, 1904

Berthoud, Jacques. "The Modernization of Sulaco," in Gene M. Moore, ed., *Conrad's Cities,* 139–57.

Billy, Ted. "A Curious Case of Influence: *Nostromo* and *Alien(s)*." *Conradiana* 21 (1989), 147–56.

Bivona, Daniel. "Conrad's Bureaucrats: Agency, Bureaucracy and the Problem of Intention." *Novel* 26 (1993), 159–64.

Bohlmann, Otto. *Conrad's Existentialism,* 127–31, 170–84.

Bradshaw, Graham. "Mythos, Ethos, and the Heart of Conrad's Darkness." *Engl Stud* 72 (1991), 160–72.

Cawthra, Gillian. *Cultural Climate and Linguistic Style,* 36–41, 77–89.

Das Gupta, Aditi. "Joseph Conrad and the Decline of Liberalism: An Approach to *Nostromo* and *Heart of Darkness,*" in Jasodhara Bagchi, ed., *Literature, Society and Ideology,* 73–80.

Demory, Pamela H. "*Nostromo:* Making History." *Texas Stud in Lit and Lang* 35 (1993), 316–42.

Desforges, Michel. "Conrad's Napoleonic Interests: A Note on Historical Sources for *Nostromo.*" *Conradiana* 24 (1992), 135–36.

Elam, Diane. *Romancing the Postmodern,* 80–101.

Hampson, Robert. *Joseph Conrad,* 137–58.

Hawthorn, Jeremy. *Joseph Conrad,* 203–17.

Hays, Peter L., and Pamela Demory. "*Nostromo* and *The Great Gatsby.*" *Etudes Anglaises* 41 (1988), 405–16.

Henricksen, Bruce. *Nomadic Voices,* 97–99, 109–36.

Hervouet, Yves. *The French Face,* 83–95.

Krajka, Wieslaw. *Isolation and Ethos,* 11–15, 99–102, 255–68.

Lessay, Franck. "*Nostromo:* le roman du *nunc stans.*" *Etudes Anglaises* 45 (1992), 433–40.

Lothe, Jakob. *Conrad's Narrative Method,* 175–225.

McLauchlan, Juliet. "Conrad's 'Decivilized' Cities," in Gene M. Moore, ed., *Conrad's Cities,* 75–84.

Nadelhaft, Ruth L. *Joseph Conrad,* 81–83, 88–96.

Phillips, K. J. *Dying Gods in Twentieth-Century Fiction,* 108–18.

Reilly, Jim. *Shadowtime,* 135–37, 143–49, 162–65.

Rising, Catharine. *Darkness at Heart,* 89–109.

Spittles, Brian. *How to Study a Joseph Conrad Novel,* 47–63.

Spittles, Brian. *Joseph Conrad,* 39–40, 93–114.

Talib, I. S. "Conrad's *Nostromo* and the Reader's Understanding of Anachronic Narratives." *J of Narrative Technique* 20 (1990), 1–17.

Toker, Leona. *Eloquent Reticence,* 43–58.

Toker, Leona. "Parallel Experience in Conrad's *Nostromo.*" *Conradiana* 21 (1989), 183–200.

Visser, Nicholas. "Crowds and Politics in *Nostromo*." *Mosaic* 23:2 (1990), 1–14.

Ward, David Allen. "'An Ideal Conception': Conrad's *Nostromo* and the Problem of Identity." *Engl Lit in Transition* 35 (1992), 288–97.

Watts, Cedric. *Joseph Conrad*, 96–103.

Watts, Cedric. *Literature and Money*, 76–80.

Watts, Cedric. *A Preface to Conrad*, 140–75.

Watts, Cedric. "The Truth of Fiction." *Crit Survey* 2:1 (1990), 70–81.

Wollaeger, Mark A. *Joseph Conrad*, 122–42, 155–69.

The Rescue, 1920

Bennett, Carl D. *Joseph Conrad*, 128–39.

Halperin, John. *Novelists in their Youth*, 143–45.

Hawthorn, Jeremy. *Joseph Conrad*, 79–88, 93–99.

Krajka, Wieslaw. *Isolation and Ethos*, 6–9, 141–43, 159–62, 182–84.

McLauchlan, Juliet. "Conrad's 'Decivilized' Cities," in Gene M. Moore, ed., *Conrad's Cities*, 66–69.

Meyers, Jeffrey. "Conrad and Music." *Conradiana* 23 (1991), 186–93.

Nadelhaft, Ruth L. *Joseph Conrad*, 128–33.

The Rover, 1923

Hampson, Robert. *Joseph Conrad*, 272–81.

La Bossière, Camille R. "Pop Conrad and Child's Play: A Context for *The Rover*." *Dalhousie R* 71 (1991), 5–16.

Rising, Catharine. *Darkness at Heart*, 155–61.

The Secret Agent, 1907

Bennett, Carl D. *Joseph Conrad*, 98–106.

Bivona, Daniel. "Conrad's Bureaucrats: Agency, Bureaucracy and the Problem of Intention." *Novel* 26 (1993), 164–69.

Bloom, Clive. "The Spy Thriller: A Genre Under Cover?," in Clive Bloom, ed., *Spy Thrillers*, 5–7.

Bohlmann, Otto. *Conrad's Existentialism*, 75–78, 119–22, 177–80.

English, James F. "Anarchy in the Flesh: Conrad's 'Counterrevolutionary' Modernism and the *Witz* of the Political Unconscious." *Mod Fiction Stud* 38 (1992), 616–28.

Epstein, Hugh. "A Pier-Glass in the Cavern: The Construction of London in *The Secret Agent*," in Gene M. Moore, ed., *Conrad's Cities*, 175–96.

Erdinast-Vulcan, Daphna. "'Sudden Holes in Space and Time': Conrad's Anarchist Aesthetics in *The Secret Agent*," in Gene M. Moore, ed., *Conrad's Cities*, 207–21.

Hampson, Robert. *Joseph Conrad*, 158–66.

Hampson, Robert. "'Topographical Mysteries': Conrad and London," in Gene M. Moore, ed., *Conrad's Cities*, 168–71.

Harpham, Geoffrey Galt. "Abroad Only by a Fiction: Creation, Irony, and Necessity in Conrad's *The Secret Agent*." *Representations* 37 (1992), 79–101.

Hawthorn, Jeremy. *Joseph Conrad*, 69–79, 91–93.

Hervouet, Yves. *The French Face*, 97–101.

Knowles, Owen. "Fishy Business in Conrad's *The Secret Agent.*" *Notes and Queries* 235 (1990), 433–34.

Krajka, Wieslaw. *Isolation and Ethos*, 69–71, 233–45.

Lee, A. Robert. "Cracked Bells and Really Intelligent Detonators: Dislocation in Conrad's *The Secret Agent*," in Clive Bloom, ed., *Spy Thrillers*, 12–26.

Lothe, Jakob. *Conrad's Narrative Method*, 226–62.

Nadelhaft, Ruth L. *Joseph Conrad*, 92–101.

Ray, Martin. "The Landscape of *The Secret Agent*," in Gene M. Moore, ed., *Conrad's Cities*, 197–206.

Reilly, Jim. *Joseph Conrad*, 58–75.

Rising, Catharine. *Darkness at Heart*, 109–18.

Schneidau, Herbert N. *Waking Giants*, 103–35.

Schwarz, Daniel R. *The Transformation*, 17–19.

Shaffer, Brian W. *The Blinding Torch*, 70–78.

Spittles, Brian. *How to Study a Joseph Conrad Novel*, 64–84.

Spittles, Brian. *Joseph Conrad*, 34–37, 117–39, 176–79.

Stevenson, Randall. *Modernist Fiction*, 119–22.

Watts, Cedric. "Conrad and the Myth of the Monstrous Town," in Gene M. Moore, ed., *Conrad's Cities*, 25–30.

Watts, Cedric. *Joseph Conrad*, 104–7.

Watts, Cedric. "*The Wild Duck* and *The Secret Agent.*" *Conradiana* 25 (1993), 47–51.

Wollaeger, Mark A. *Joseph Conrad*, 142–55, 160–65.

Suspense, 1925

Moore, Gene M. "In Defense of *Suspense.*" *Conradiana* 25 (1993), 99–111.

Mursia, Ugo. "Notes on Conrad's Italian Novel: *Suspense*," in Gene M. Moore, ed., *Conrad's Cities*, 269–81.

Under Western Eyes, 1911

Bennett, Carl D. *Joseph Conrad*, 107–13.

Bohlmann, Otto. *Conrad's Existentialism*, 22–26, 82–84, 169–71, 184–90.

Carabine, Keith. " 'The Figure Behind the Veil': Conrad and Razumov in *Under Western Eyes*," in David R. Smith, ed., *Joseph Conrad's "Under Western Eyes*," 1–26.

Carabine, Keith. "From *Razumov* to *Under Western Eyes.*" *Conradiana* 25 (1993), 3–26.

Davis, Roderick. "Crossing the Dark Roadway: Razumov on the Boulevard des Philosophes," in David R. Smith, ed., *Joseph Conrad's "Under Western Eyes*," 155–71.

Hampson, Robert. *Joseph Conrad*, 167–91.

Hawthorn, Jeremy. *Joseph Conrad*, 236–59.

Hay, Eloise Knapp. "*Under Western Eyes* and the Missing Center," in David R. Smith, ed., *Joseph Conrad's "Under Western Eyes*," 121–51.

Henricksen, Bruce. *Nomadic Voices*, 65–67, 137–60.

Hepburn, Allan. "Above Suspicion: Audience and Deception in *Under Western Eyes*." *Stud in the Novel* 24 (1992), 282–96.

Higdon, David Leon. "'Complete. But Uncorrected': The Typescript of Conrad's *Under Western Eyes*," in David R. Smith, ed., *Joseph Conrad's "Under Western Eyes*," 83–110.

Horsley, Lee. *Political Fiction*, 56–60, 90–122.

Kirschner, Paul. "Topodialogic Narrative in *Under Western Eyes* and the Rasoumoffs of 'La Petite Russie,'" in Gene M. Moore, ed., *Conrad's Cities*, 223–54.

Krajka, Wieslaw. *Isolation and Ethos*, 88–90, 245–53.

Lothe, Jakob. *Conrad's Narrative Method*, 263–93.

Lovely, Deborah. "'But I Digress': The Teacher in *Under Western Eyes*." *West Virginia Univ Philol Papers* 36 (1990), 30–37.

Moore, Gene M. "Conrad's *Under Western Eyes*." *Explicator* 49 (1991), 103–4.

Nadelhaft, Ruth L. *Joseph Conrad*, 102–8.

Paccaud, Josiane. "Conrad's Technique of Free Indirect Discourse in *Under Western Eyes*." *Conradiana* 22 (1990), 45–62.

Paccaud, Josiane. "Hypertextuality in Joseph Conrad's *Under Western Eyes*." *Cahiers Victoriens et Edouardiens* 29 (1989), 73–81.

Pendleton, Robert. "Arabesques of Influence: The Repressed Conradian Masterplot in the Novels of Graham Greene." *Conradiana* 25 (1993), 87–94.

Putnam, Walter C., III. *L'Aventure littéraire*, 203–15.

Rado, Lisa. "Walking Through Phantoms: Irony, Skepticism, and Razumov's Self-Delusion in *Under Western Eyes*." *Conradiana* 24 (1992), 83–98.

Rising, Catharine. *Darkness at Heart*, 121–33.

Smith, David R. "The Hidden Narrative: The *K* in Conrad," in David R. Smith, ed., *Joseph Conrad's "Under Western Eyes*," 39–72.

Spittles, Brian. *Joseph Conrad*, 168–70.

Watts, Cedric. *Joseph Conrad*, 109–14.

Wollaeger, Mark A. *Joseph Conrad*, 170–92.

Victory, 1915

Bennett, Carl D. *Joseph Conrad*, 116–22.

Bohlmann, Otto. *Conrad's Existentialism*, 84–86, 88–92, 122–28, 134–37, 139–53.

Collits, Terry. "Imperialism, Marxism, Conrad: A Political Reading of *Victory*." *Textual Practice* 3 (1989), 303–22.

Hampson, Robert. *Joseph Conrad*, 231–50.

Hampson, Robert. "'Topographical Mysteries': Conrad and London," in Gene M. Moore, ed., *Conrad's Cities*, 171–74.

Hervouet, Yves. *The French Face*, 122–35.

Howison, Patricia M. "'The Baseless Fabric of This Vision': Expectation, Illusion, and Dream in Conrad's *Victory*." *Conradiana* 22 (1990), 163–82.

Krajka, Wieslaw. *Isolation and Ethos,* 44–48, 54–56.
Orel, Harold. *Popular Fiction in England,* 117–23.
Rising, Catharine. *Darkness at Heart,* 137–48.
Spittles, Brian. *How to Study a Joseph Conrad Novel,* 85–103.
Spittles, Brian. *Joseph Conrad,* 110–12, 145–59.
Watts, Cedric. *Joseph Conrad,* 122–24.

JOSEPH CONRAD AND FORD MADOX FORD

The Inheritors, 1901

Hoffmann, Charles G. *Ford Madox Ford,* 5–7.
Watts, Cedric. *Joseph Conrad,* 92–93.

Romance, 1903

Hervouet, Yves. *The French Face,* 77–78.
Hoffmann, Charles G. *Ford Madox Ford,* 7–10.
Watts, Cedric. *Joseph Conrad,* 92–93.

SUSAN MARY COOPER

The Dark Is Rising, 1965

Goodrich, Peter. "Magical Medievalism and the Fairy Tale in Susan Cooper's *The Dark Is Rising.*" *The Lion and the Unicorn* 12:2 (1988), 165–77.

SAMUEL RUTHERFORD CROCKETT

The Lilac Sunbonnet, 1894

Letley, Emma. *From Galt to Douglas Brown,* 244–51.

CHARLOTTE DACRE

The Confessions of the Nun of St Omer, 1805

Miles, Robert. *Gothic Writing,* 100–103.

The Passions, 1811

Miles, Robert. *Gothic Writing,* 67–69.

Zofloya, 1806

Miles, Robert. *Gothic Writing,* 179–88.

WARWICK DEEPING

Sorrell and Son, 1925

Bracco, Rosa Maria. *'Betwixt and Between,'* 40–43.

DANIEL DEFOE

Captain Singleton, 1720

Faller, Lincoln B. *Crime and Defoe,* 52–55, 96–102.
Hammond, J. R. *A Defoe Companion,* 86–94.
Merrett, Robert James. "Natural History and the Eighteenth-Century English Novel." *Eighteenth-Cent Stud* 25 (1991–92), 158–60.

Colonel Jacque, 1722

Détis, Elisabeth. "*Colonel Jack* et l'image du gentleman: identification et différenciation." *Bull de la Société d'Etudes Anglo-Américaines des XVIIe et XVIIIe Siècles* 32 (1991), 57–66.
Faller, Lincoln B. *Crime and Defoe,* 52–55, 58–61, 92–100, 165–69, 211–15.
Hammond, J. R. *A Defoe Companion,* 118–26.
Hentzi, Gary. "'An Itch of Gaming': The South Sea Bubble and the Novels of Daniel Defoe." *Eighteenth-Cent Life* 17:1 (1993), 37–42.
Probyn, Clive T. *English Fiction,* 46–50.
Uphaus, Robert W. *The Idea of the Novel,* 55–58.

A Journal of the Plague Year, 1722

Flynn, Carol Houlihan. *The Body in Swift and Defoe,* 8–36, 139–48.
Hammond, J. R. *A Defoe Companion,* 106–17.
Hentzi, Gary. "Sublime Moments and Social Authority in *Robinson Crusoe* and *A Journal of the Plague Year.*" *Eighteenth-Cent Stud* 26 (1993), 419–34.
Hopes, Jeffrey. "Les contradictions de Defoe: providence, stratégies et discours didactiques dans *A Journal of the Plague Year.*" *Etudes Anglaises* 46 (1993), 129–39.
Leavy, Barbara Fass. *To Blight with Plague,* 21–39, 55–59.
Mayer, Robert. "The Reception of *A Journal of the Plague Year* and the Nexus of Fiction and History in the Novel." *ELH* 57 (1990), 529–50.
Moore, Benjamin. "Governing Discourses: Problems of Narrative Authority in *A Journal of the Plague Year.*" *Eighteenth Cent* 33 (1992), 133–44.
Probyn, Clive T. *English Fiction,* 44–46.
Stephanson, Raymond. "The Plague Narratives of Defoe and Camus: Illness as Metaphor." *Mod Lang Q* 48 (1987), 224–41.
Wainwright, V. L. "Lending to the Lord: Defoe's Rhetorical Design in *A Journal of the Plague Year.*" *British J for Eighteenth-Cent Stud* 13 (1990), 59–71.

The Memoirs of a Cavalier, 1720

Hammond, J. R. *A Defoe Companion,* 80–85.

Moll Flanders, 1722

Backscheider, Paula R. "*Moll Flanders,*" 21–99.
Bell, Ian A. *Literature and Crime,* 140–42.
Bender, John. "The Novel and the Rise of the Penitentiary: Narrative and

Ideology in Defoe, Gay, Hogarth, and Fielding," in H. George Hahn, ed., *The Country Myth*, 104–10.

Boardman, Michael M. *Narrative Innovation*, 28–30.

Brink, André. "Mutants of the Picaresque: *Moll Flanders* and *A Sport of Nature*." *J of Liter Stud* 6 (1990), 261–74.

Butler, Mary. "'Onomaphobia' and Personal Identity in *Moll Flanders*." *Stud in the Novel* 22 (1990), 377–88.

Faller, Lincoln B. *Crime and Defoe*, 36–39, 47–50, 52–56, 89–95, 104–6, 118–33, 142–65, 208–11.

Flynn, Carol Houlihan. *The Body in Swift and Defoe*, 61–76.

Hammond, J. R. *A Defoe Companion*, 95–105.

Hampsey, John C. "Defoe's *Moll Flanders:* The Realism of the Spoken Word." *Greyfriar* 30 (1989–90), 35–42.

Heilman, Robert Bechtold. *The Workings of Fiction*, 34–37.

Hentzi, Gary. "Holes in the Heart: *Moll Flanders, Roxana,* and 'Agreeable Crime.'" *Boundary 2* 18:1 (1991), 174–200.

Hentzi, Gary. "'An Itch of Gaming': The South Sea Bubble and the Novels of Daniel Defoe." *Eighteenth-Cent Life* 17:1 (1993), 37–42.

Hodge, Robert. *Literature as Discourse*, 96–100.

Kayman, Martin A. *From Bow Street to Baker Street*, 49–50.

Krebs, Jean-Daniel. "La pícara, l'aventurière, la pionnière: Fonctions de l'héroïne picaresque à travers les figures de Justina, Courage et Moll." *Arcadia* 24 (1989), 239–52.

Langford, Larry L. "Retelling Moll's Story: The Editor's Preface to *Moll Flanders*." *J of Narrative Technique* 22 (1992), 164–76.

Nelson, T. G. A. "Incest in the Early Novel and Related Genres." *Eighteenth-Cent Life* 16:1 (1992), 144–48.

Nicoletta, Daniela. *Vibrazione e risonanza*, 53–62.

Oakleaf, David. "Marks, Stamps, and Representations: Character in Eighteenth-Century Fiction." *Stud in the Novel* 23 (1991), 305–8.

Page, Norman. *Speech in the English Novel*, 46–48.

Price, John Valdimir. "Patterns of Sexual Behavior in Some Eighteenth-Century Novels," in H. George Hahn, ed., *The Country Myth*, 125–37.

Probyn, Clive T. *English Fiction*, 37–41.

Rietz, John. "Criminal Ms-Representation: Moll Flanders and Female Criminal Biography." *Stud in the Novel* 23 (1991), 183–93.

Scheuermann, Mona. *Her Bread to Earn*, 13–35.

Troy, Mark. "The Blank Page of Daniel Defoe." *Orbis Litterarum* 46 (1991), 1-12.

Uphaus, Robert W. *The Idea of the Novel*, 58–65.

Varey, Simon. *Space and the Eighteenth-Century English Novel*, 142–47.

Robinson Crusoe, 1719

Adriani, Maurilio. "L'isola di Robinson." *Città di Vita* 44 (1989), 155–58.

Armstrong, Dianne. "The Myth of Cronus: Cannibal and Sign in *Robinson Crusoe*." *Eighteenth-Cent Fiction* 4 (1992), 207–20.

Bender, John. "The Novel and the Rise of the Penitentiary: Narrative and

Ideology in Defoe, Gay, Hogarth, and Fielding," in H. George Hahn, ed., *The Country Myth*, 110–14.

Boardman, Michael M. *Narrative Innovation*, 30–31, 34–36.

Braverman, Richard. *Plots and Counterplots*, 248–71.

Bull, J. A. *The Framework of Fiction*, 71–77.

Cope, Kevin L. "Defoe, Berkeley, and Mackenzie and the Social Contract of Genre." *Stud on Voltaire and the Eighteenth Cent* 264 (1989), 937–40.

Cro, Stelio. *The Noble Savage*, 93–103.

Dahl, Erhard. "Der Wertkomplex 'Arbeit' in den englischen Kinderbuchausgaben des *Robinson Crusoe* zwischen 1719 und 1860," in Harro Segeberg, ed., *Vom Wert der Arbeit*, 30–39.

Dupas, Jean-Claude. "Robinson Crusoe, nom de nom." *Bull de la Société d'Etudes Anglo-Américaines des XVIIe et XVIIIe Siècles* 33 (1991), 53–60.

Erlebach, Peter. *Theorie und Praxis des Romaneingangs*, 141–46.

Fiérobe, Claude. "*Robinson Crusoe* ou les voies du possible." *Etudes Anglaises* 45 (1992), 3–13.

Flynn, Carol Houlihan. *The Body in Swift and Defoe*, 149–59.

Foster, James O. "*Robinson Crusoe* and the Uses of the Imagination." *JEGP* 91 (1992), 179–202.

Gliserman, Martin J. "*Robinson Crusoe:* The Vicissitudes of Greed—Cannibalism to Capitalism." *Am Imago* 47 (1990), 197–225.

Hammond, J. R. *A Defoe Companion*, 67–79.

Loxley, Diana. *Problematic Shores*, 3–11, 34–48, 141–50.

Maher, Susan Naramore. "Confronting Authority: J. M. Coetzee's *Foe* and the Remaking of *Robinson Crusoe*." *Intl Fiction R* 18 (1991), 34–40.

Michel-Michot, Paulette. "The Myth of Innocence: *Robinson Crusoe, The Coral Island* and *Lord of the Flies*," in Jeanne Delbaere, ed., *William Golding*, 41–44.

Novak, Maximillian E. "Robinson Crusoe's Song on the 'Country Life' and Defoe's Knowledge of Music." *Notes and Queries* 237 (1992), 40–42.

Peterson, Brent O. "Wezel and the Genre of *Robinson Crusoe*." *Lessing Yrbk* 20 (1988), 183–204.

Plake, Klaus. "Aufklärung und innerweltliche Askese," in Harro Segeberg, ed., *Vom Wert der Arbeit*, 11–20.

Probyn, Clive T. *English Fiction*, 30–36.

Schonhorn, Manuel. *Defoe's Politics*, 141–64.

Stevenson, John Allen. *The British Novel*, 5–20.

Stratton, Jon. *Writing Sites*, 99–100, 154–58, 164–67.

Thomas, Ronald R. *Dreams of Authority*, 139–41.

Troy, Mark. "The Blank Page of Daniel Defoe." *Orbis Litterarum* 46 (1991), 1–12.

Varey, Simon. *Space and the Eighteenth-Century English Novel*, 148–55.

Vesterman, William. "Mastering the Free Spirit: Status and Contract in Some Fictional Polities." *Eighteenth-Cent Life* 16:3 (1992), 186–90.

Watts, Cedric. *Literature and Money*, 81–94.

Roxana, 1724

Bell, Ian A. *Literature and Crime,* 142–44.

Boardman, Michael M. *Narrative Innovation,* 20–58.

Burke, Helen. "*Roxana,* Corruption, and the Progressive Myth." *Genre* 23 (1990), 103–19.

Faller, Lincoln B. *Crime and Defoe,* 46–50, 54–56, 66–69, 90–94, 100–104, 215–44.

Flanders, W. Austin. "Urban Life and the Early Novel," in H. George Hahn, ed., *The Country Myth,* 57–58.

Flynn, Carol Houlihan. *The Body in Swift and Defoe,* 76–87.

Hammond, J. R. *A Defoe Companion,* 127–35.

Hentzi, Gary. "Holes in the Heart: *Moll Flanders, Roxana,* and 'Agreeable Crime.'" *Boundary 2* 18:1 (1991), 174–200.

Jacobsen, Susan L. "A Dialogue of Commerce: Defoe's Roxana as Mistress and Entrepreneur," in Kevin L. Cope, ed., *Compendious Conversations,* 218–31.

Kahn, Madeleine. *Narrative Transvestism,* 57–102.

New, Melvyn. *Telling New Lies,* 37–39, 72–73.

Oakleaf, David. "Marks, Stamps, and Representations: Character in Eighteenth-Century Fiction." *Stud in the Novel* 23 (1991), 305–8.

Probyn, Clive T. *English Fiction,* 41–44.

Richetti, John. "The Public Sphere and the Eighteenth-Century Novel: Social Criticism and Narrative Enactment." *Eighteenth-Cent Life* 16:3 (1992), 121–22.

Scheuermann, Mona. *Her Bread to Earn,* 35–59.

Soulier-Detis, Elisabeth. "Colliers, gants et manchon: Les Pulsions dévoilées." *Bull de la Société d'Etudes Anglo-Américaines des XVIIe et XVIIIe Siècles* 28 (1989), 145–62.

WALTER DE LA MARE

The Three Mulla-Mulgars, 1910

Bentinck, A. "Tolkien and De la Mare: The Fantastic Secondary Worlds of *The Hobbit* and *The Three Mulla-Mulgars.*" *Mythlore* 15:3 (1989), 39–43.

THOMAS DELONEY

Jack of Newbury, 1597

Erlebach, Peter. *Theorie und Praxis des Romaneingangs,* 131–36.

Linton, Joan Pong. "*Jack of Newbury* and Drake in California: Narratives of English Cloth and Manhood." *ELH* 59 (1992), 23–45.

CHARLES DICKENS

Barnaby Rudge, 1841

Ackroyd, Peter. *Dickens,* 324–28, 342–45.

Ackroyd, Peter. *Introduction to Dickens,* 70–77.

Alexander, Doris. *Creating Characters,* 130–32.

Buckley, Jerome H. " 'Quoth the Raven': The Role of Grip in *Barnaby Rudge.*" *Dickens Stud Annual* 21 (1992), 27–33.

Case, Alison. "Against Scott: The Antihistory of Dickens's *Barnaby Rudge.*" *CLIO* 19 (1990), 127–45.

Chittick, Kathryn. *Dickens and the 1830s,* 166–70, 172–76.

Crawford, Iain. " 'Nature . . . Drenched in Blood': *Barnaby Rudge* and Wordsworth's 'The Idiot Boy.' " *Dickens Q* 8 (1991), 29–37.

Drexler, Peter. *Literatur, Recht, Kriminalität,* 148–50.

Flynn, Judith. "The Sexual Politics of *Barnaby Rudge.*" *Engl Stud in Canada* 16 (1990), 55–70.

Golden, Morris. *Dickens Imagining Himself,* 21–52.

Hollington, Michael. "Monstrous Faces: Physiognomy in *Barnaby Rudge.*" *Dickens Q* 8 (1991), 6–14.

Ingham, Patricia. *Dickens, Women and Language,* 73–77, 80–82.

McKnight, Natalie. *Idiots, Madmen,* 81–91.

Stuart, Barbara L. "The Centaur in *Barnaby Rudge.*" *Dickens Q* 8 (1991), 29–37.

Bleak House, 1853

Ackroyd, Peter. *Dickens,* 642–49, 672–75.

Ackroyd, Peter. *Introduction to Dickens,* 122–28.

Alexander, Doris. *Creating Characters,* 35–48, 49–57, 59–67, 69–76.

Arms, G. D. "Reassembling *Bleak House:* 'Is there *three* of 'em?' " *Lit and Psych* 39:1–2 (1993), 84–95.

Armstrong, Frances. *Dickens and the Concept of Home,* 93–108.

Bernstein, Carol L. *The Celebration of Scandal,* 120–21, 179–83.

Boasberg, James E. "Chancery as Megalosaurus: Lawyers, Courts, and Society in *Bleak House.*" *Univ of Hartford Stud in Lit* 21 (1989), 38–60.

Boheemen, Christine van. *The Novel as Family Romance,* 101–31.

Booth, Alison. "*Middlemarch, Bleak House,* and Gender in the Nineteenth-Century Novel Course," in Kathleen Blake, ed., *Approaches,* 129–37.

Briganti, Chiara. "The Monstrous Actress: Esther Summerson's Spectral Name." *Dickens Stud Annual* 19 (1990), 205–27.

Carey, John. *The Violent Effigy,* 174–88.

Chaudhuri, Brahma. "Dickens's Serial Structure in *Bleak House.*" *Dickensian* 86 (1990), 67–81.

Cohan, Steven. "Figures beyond the Text: A Theory of Readable Character in the Novel," in Mark Spilka and Caroline McCracken-Flesher, eds., *Why the Novel Matters,* 120–23.

Collins, Philip. "Some Narrative Devices in *Bleak House*." *Dickens Stud Annual* 19 (1990), 125–45.

Cowles, David L. "Methods of Inquiry, Modes of Evidence: Perception, Self-Deception, and Truth in *Bleak House*." *Dickensian* 87 (1991), 153–63.

Cummings, Katherine. *Telling Tales*, 191–229.

Cvetkovich, Ann. *Mixed Feelings*, 51–55.

Danahay, Martin A. "Housekeeping and Hegemony in *Bleak House*." *Stud in the Novel* 23 (1991), 416–29.

Davies, James A. *The Textual Life*, 86–94.

Drexler, Peter. *Literatur, Recht, Kriminalität*, 178–79.

Erlebach, Peter. *Theorie und Praxis des Romaneingangs*, 226–29.

Feinberg, Monica. "Family Plot: The Bleak House of Victorian Romance." *Victorian Newsl* 76 (1989), 5–17.

Friedman, Stanley. "*Bleak House* and Bulwer-Lytton's Not So Bad As We Seem." *Dickens Q* 9 (1992), 25–28.

Gaughan, Richard T. "Their Places are a Blank: The Two Narrators in *Bleak House*." *Dickens Stud Annual* 21 (1992), 79–92.

Gaye, Mamadou. "La Solitude urbaine dans quelques œuvres de Dickens: *Bleak House* et *Hard Times*." *Bridges* 3 (1991), 55–67.

Ginsburg, Michal Peled. "The Case Against Plot in *Bleak House* and *Our Mutual Friend*." *ELH* 59 (1992), 179–86.

Golden, Morris. *Dickens Imagining Himself*, 125–62.

Goodman, Marcia Renee. " 'I'll Follow the Other': Tracing the (M)other in *Bleak House*." *Dickens Stud Annual* 19 (1990), 147–66.

Gottfried, Barbara. "Fathers and Suitors: Narratives of Desire in *Bleak House*." *Dickens Stud Annual* 19 (1990), 169–200.

Gurney, Michael S. "Disease as Device: The Role of Smallpox in *Bleak House*." *Lit and Medicine* 9 (1990), 79–91.

Herst, Beth F. *The Dickens Hero*, 67–89.

Hochberg, Shifra. "The Influence of *King Lear* on *Bleak House*." *Dickensian* 89 (1993), 45–48.

Hochberg, Shifra. "Onomastics, Topicality, and Dickens's Use of Etymology in *Bleak House*." *Dickensian* 86 (1990), 85–86.

Holbrook, David. "Some Plot Inconsistencies in *Bleak House*." *English* 39:165 (1990), 209–14.

Hopkins, Sandra. " 'Wooman, Lovely Wooman': Four Dickens Heroines and the Critics," in Sally Minogue, ed., *Problems for Feminist Criticism*, 126–32.

Ingham, Patricia. *Dickens, Women and Language*, 20–22, 81–84, 93–104, 106–9, 125–30.

Jaffe, Audrey. *Vanishing Points*, 128–49.

Jolly, Diane L. "The Nature of Esther." *Dickensian* 86 (1990), 29–39.

Lawson, R. Bland. "The 'Condition of England Question': *Past and Present* and *Bleak House*." *Victorian Newsl* 79 (1991), 24–27.

Malone, Cynthia Northcutt. " 'Flight' and 'Pursuit': Fugitive Identity in *Bleak House*." *Dickens Stud Annual* 19 (1990), 107–21.

Marshall, Brenda. "Dickens and Another Modernity: The Eruption of the Real." *Lit and Psych* 37:4 (1991), 37–43.

Maxwell, Richard. *The Mysteries*, 160–90.

Milbank, Alison. *Daughters of the House*, 80–101.

Miller, J. Hillis. *Victorian Subjects*, 179–99.

Misenheimer, Carolyn, and James B. Misenheimer. "Structural Unities: Paired Parallel Chapters in Dickens's *Bleak House*." *Dickensian* 85 (1989), 140–49.

Morris, Pam. *"Bleak House,"* 1–89.

Morris, Pam. *Dickens's Class Consciousness*, 81–99.

Muir, Kenneth. *"Bleak House* Revisited." *Aligarh Crit Miscellany* 2:1 (1989), 85–100.

Newcomb, Mildred. *The Imagined World*, 10–12, 27–31, 52–55, 77–79, 103–5, 117–20, 130–43, 155–57.

Newsom, Robert. *"Villette* and *Bleak House:* Authorizing Women." *Nineteenth-Cent Lit* 46 (1991), 54–81.

Newton, Ruth, and Naomi Lebowitz. *Dickens, Manzoni, Zola, and James*, 11–13, 17–19, 30–34, 72–78, 96–102, 109–16, 144–50.

Nicholls, Maria. "Lady Dedlock's Sin." *Dickensian* 89 (1993), 39–44.

Page, Norman. *"Bleak House,"* 27–91.

Page, Norman. *Speech in the English Novel*, 161–68.

Peltason, Timothy. "Esther's Will." *ELH* 59 (1992), 671–90.

Pendleton, Robert W. "The Detective's Languishing Forefinger: Narrative Guides in *Bleak House* and *Little Dorrit*." *Dickens Q* 7 (1990), 312–19.

Pritchard, Allan. "The Urban Gothic of *Bleak House*." *Nineteenth-Cent Lit* 45 (1991), 432–52.

Raizada, Harish. "Symbolism and Imagery in *Bleak House*." *Aligarh J of Engl Stud* 13 (1988), 224–41.

Reed, John R. *Victorian Will*, 255–66.

Ryals, Clyde de L. *A World of Possibilities*, 76–93.

Sadrin, Anny. "Charlotte Dickens: The Female Narrator of *Bleak House*." *Dickens Q* 9 (1992), 47–56.

Sadrin, Anny. *Dickens ou le roman-théâtre*, 54–89.

Schad, John. *The Reader*, 17–19, 26–28, 46–48, 116–20.

Schwarzbach, F. S. *"Bleak House:* The Social Pathology of Urban Life." *Lit and Medicine* 9 (1990), 93–102.

Selby, Keith. *How to Study a Charles Dickens Novel*, 57–79.

Smalley, R. Ann. "Crossing the Gulfs: The Importance of the Master-Servant Relationship in Dickens's *Bleak House*." *Dickensian* 85 (1989), 151–60.

Steig, Michael. *Stories of Reading*, 64–77.

Storey, Graham. *Charles Dickens: "Bleak House,"* 16–93.

Thorpe, Douglas. " 'I Never Knew My Lady Swoon Before': Lady Dedlock and the Revival of the Victorian Fainting Woman." *Dickens Stud Annual* 20 (1991), 103–22.

Tillotson, Kathleen. *"Bleak House* at a Séance." *Dickensian* 84 (1988), 2–5.

Tindall, Gillian. *Countries of the Mind,* 130–33.

Toker, Leona. *Eloquent Reticence,* 61–83.

Tropp, Martin. *Images of Fear,* 68–74.

Tuss, Alex J., SM. *The Inward Revolution,* 53–73.

Ware, Michele S. " 'True Legitimacy': The Myth of the Foundling in *Bleak House.*" *Stud in the Novel* 22 (1990), 1–9.

West, Gilian. "*Bleak House:* Esther's Illness." *Engl Stud* 73 (1992), 30–34.

West, Gilian. "The 'Glaring Fault' in the Structure of *Bleak House.*" *Dickensian* 89 (1993), 36–38.

West, Gilian. "Some Inconsistencies in *Bleak House.*" *Dickensian* 87 (1991), 164–65.

White, Allon. *Carnival, Hysteria, and Writing,* 88–110.

Whitehead, Gwen. "The First Fictional English Detective." *Round Table of the South Central Coll Engl Assoc* 27:3 (1987), 1–3.

Wright, Kay Hetherly. "The Grotesque and Urban Chaos in *Bleak House.*" *Dickens Stud Annual* 21 (1992), 97–109.

The Chimes, 1844

Ackroyd, Peter. *Introduction to Dickens,* 96–98.

Allingham, Philip V. "Dickens' Christmas Books: Names and Motifs." *Engl Lang Notes* 29:4 (1992), 60–64.

Maxwell, Richard. *The Mysteries,* 154–58.

A Christmas Carol, 1843

Ackroyd, Peter. *Dickens,* 407–15.

Ackroyd, Peter. *Introduction to Dickens,* 93–96.

Armstrong, Frances. *Dickens and the Concept of Home,* 39–40, 89–90.

Buckwald, Craig. "Stalking the Figurative Oyster: The Excursive Ideal in *A Christmas Carol.*" *Stud in Short Fiction* 27 (1990), 1–14.

Burleson, Donald R. "Dickens's *A Christmas Carol.*" *Explicator* 50 (1992), 211–12.

Butterworth, R. D. "*A Christmas Carol* and the Masque." *Stud in Short Fiction* 30 (1993), 63–69.

Davies, James A. *The Textual Life,* 75–86.

Davis, Paul. "Retelling *A Christmas Carol:* Text and Culture-Text." *Am Scholar* 59:1 (1990), 109–15.

Harvie, Christopher. *The Centre of Things,* 18–20.

O'Connor, Michael. "The Adult-Child and the Child-Adult." *Jabberwocky* 21 (1992), 69–77.

Thomas, Ronald R. *Dreams of Authority,* 61–69.

David Copperfield, 1850

Ackroyd, Peter. *Dickens,* 78–80, 601–8.

Ackroyd, Peter. *Introduction to Dickens,* 114–21.

Alexander, Doris. *Creating Characters,* 77–88, 89–98, 99–105, 107–13.

Armstrong, Frances. *Dickens and the Concept of Home,* 56–59, 79–84.

Auerbach, Nina. "Performing Suffering: From Dickens to David." *Browning Inst Stud* 18 (1990), 15–22.

Basch, Françoise. "Réflexion sur le sentiment et le 'genre' dans deux romans victoriens: Charles Dickens, *David Copperfield* et George Eliot, *Le Moulin sur la Floss,"* in Ellen Constans, ed., *Le Roman sentimental,* 131–42.

Butler, Gerald J. *Love and Reading,* 88–97, 159–63.

Carey, John. *The Violent Effigy,* 126–28, 131–35, 137–39, 169–72.

Chaston, Joel D. "Crusoe, Crocodiles, and Cookery Books: *David Copperfield* and the Affective Power of Reading Fiction." *Univ of Mississippi Stud in Engl* 9 (1991), 141–51.

D'Arcy, Chantal Cornut-Gentille. "Books, Pens and Pencils: The Trials of a Victorian Youth." *Revista Alicantina de Estudios Ingleses* 2 (1989), 21–29.

Eigner, Edwin M. *The Dickens Pantomime,* 30–32, 49–55, 61–65, 74–90, 94–102, 104–8, 116–21, 125–28, 133–39, 146–52, 159–67.

Foltinek, Herbert. "Unsicherheit, die nach Gewißheit strebt: Der Verlust des kirschroten Bandes in *David Copperfield." Germanisch-Romanische Monatsschrift* 40 (1990), 278–302.

Golden, Morris. *Dickens Imagining Himself,* 87–124.

Herst, Beth F. *The Dickens Hero,* 43–66.

Hochman, Baruch, and Ilja Wachs. "Straw People, Hollow Men, and the Postmodernist Hall of Dissipating Mirrors: The Case of *David Copperfield." Style* 24 (1990), 392–406. (Also in John V. Knapp, ed., *Literary Character,* 44–58.)

Hollington, Michael. "Dickens and Australia." *Cahiers Victoriens et Edouardiens* 33 (1991), 23–26.

Hopkins, Sandra. " 'Wooman, Lovely Wooman': Four Dickens Heroines and the Critics," in Sally Minogue, ed., *Problems for Feminist Criticism,* 121–25, 132–37.

Ingham, Patricia. *Dickens, Women and Language,* 39–41, 44–48, 54–62, 65–68.

Jaffe, Audrey. *Vanishing Points,* 116–28.

Kellogg, David. " 'My Most Unwilling Hand': The Mixed Motivations of *David Copperfield." Dickens Stud Annual* 20 (1991), 57–71.

Langland, Elizabeth. "Nobody's Angels: Domestic Ideology and Middle-Class Women in the Victorian Novel." *PMLA* 107 (1992), 298–99.

Lund, Michael. *Reading Thackeray,* 72–77.

Marsden, Malcolm M. "Dickens' Mr. Micawber and Mark Twain's Colonel Sellers: The Genesis of an American Comic." *Dickens Stud Annual* 21 (1992), 63–76.

Miller, J. Hillis. *Victorian Subjects,* 97–101.

Morgan, Nicholas H. *Secret Journeys,* 59–78.

Morris, Pam. *Dickens's Class Consciousness,* 63–79.

Newcomb, Mildred. *The Imagined World,* 93–95, 153–55.

Newton, Ruth, and Naomi Lebowitz. *Dickens, Manzoni, Zola, and James,* 66–67, 125–28, 152–58, 180–82, 187–92.

Ortiz, Gloria. *The Dandy and the "Señorito,"* 37–40.

Palmer, William. "Dickens and Shipwreck." *Dickens Stud Annual* 18 (1989), 59–70.

Reed, John R. *Victorian Will,* 252–56.

Rogers, Philip. "A Tolstoyan Reading of *David Copperfield.*" *Compar Lit* 42 (1990), 1–27.

Sadrin, Anny. *Dickens ou le roman-théâtre,* 109–29.

Schad, John. *The Reader,* 31–35, 114–16.

Schaumburger, Nancy E. "Partners in Pathology: David, Dora, and Steerforth." *Dickensian* 84 (1988), 155–59.

Scheuerle, William H. "Cries of the Children in the Novels of Charles Dickens," in Sara Munson Deats and Lagretta Tallent Lenker, eds., *The Aching Hearth,* 152–53.

Schroeder, Natalie E., and Ronald A. Schroeder. "Betsey Trotwood and Jane Murdstone: Dickensian Doubles." *Stud in the Novel* 21 (1989), 268–77.

Simon, Irène. "*David Copperfield:* A Künstlerroman?" *R of Engl Stud* 43 (1992), 40–56.

Steig, Michael. *Stories of Reading,* 130–43.

Storey, Graham. "*David Copperfield,*" 23–102.

Thomas, Ronald R. *Dreams of Authority,* 136–39.

Tick, Stanley. "Dickens, Dickens, Micawber . . . and Bakhtin." *Victorian Newsl* 79 (1991), 34–37.

Wilkes, David M. "Dickens's *David Copperfield.*" *Explicator* 51 (1993), 157–59.

Woodfield, Malcolm J. "The Endless Memorial: Dickens and Memory/Writing/History." *Dickens Stud Annual* 20 (1991), 75–97.

Dombey and Son, 1848

Ackroyd, Peter. *Dickens,* 520–26.

Ackroyd, Peter. *Introduction to Dickens,* 106–13.

Alexander, Doris. *Creating Characters,* 5–33.

Armstrong, Frances. *Dickens and the Concept of Home,* 61–67, 76–79.

Auerbach, Emily. *Maestros, Dilettantes, and Philistines,* 82–85.

Baumgarten, Murray. "Railway/Reading/Time: *Dombey & Son* and the Industrial World." *Dickens Stud Annual* 19 (1990), 65–87.

Carey, John. *The Violent Effigy,* 105–7.

Cervetti, Nancy. "Dickens and Eliot in Dialogue: Empty Space, Angels and Maggie Tulliver." *Victorian Newsl* 80 (1991), 18–23.

Currie, Richard. "Doubles, Self-Attack, and Murderous Rage in Florence Dombey." *Dickens Stud Annual* 21 (1992), 113–26.

Dentith, Simon. "How Popular was *Dombey and Son?*" *Dickensian* 88 (1992), 69–80.

Eigner, Edwin M. *The Dickens Pantomime,* 28–30, 72–73, 110–12.

Greenstein, Michael. "Measuring Time in *Dombey and Son.*" *Dickens Q* 9 (1992), 151–57.

Hill, Nancy Klenk. "*Dombey and Son:* Parable for the Age." *Dickens Q* 8 (1991), 169–76.

Hollington, Michael. "Dickens and Australia." *Cahiers Victoriens et Edouardiens* 33 (1991), 20–23.

Horne, Lewis. "The Way of Resentment in *Dombey and Son.*" *Mod Lang Q* 51 (1990), 44–62.

Ingham, Patricia. *Dickens, Women and Language,* 74–89, 92–98, 100–110.

Jaffe, Audrey. *Vanishing Points,* 71–111.

Joseph, Gerhard. "*Dombey,* Change, and the Changeling." *Dickens Stud Annual* 18 (1989), 179–94.

Loesberg, Jonathan. "Deconstruction, Historicism, and Overdetermination: Dislocations of the Marriage Plots in *Robert Elsmere* and *Dombey and Son.*" *Victorian Stud* 33 (1990), 456–64.

McCarthy, Patrick J. "*Dombey and Son:* Language and the Roots of Meaning." *Dickens Stud Annual* 19 (1990), 91–104.

McCombie, Frank. "Sexual Repression in *Dombey and Son.*" *Dickensian* 88 (1992), 25–37.

MacKay, Carol Hanbery. "Controlling Death and Sex: Magnification v. the Rhetoric of Rules in Dickens and Thackeray," in Regina Barreca, ed., *Sex and Death,* 124–25.

McKnight, Natalie. *Idiots, Madmen,* 95–108.

Marks, Patricia. "'On Tuesday Last, at St. George's . . .': The Dandaical Wedding in Dickens." *Victorian Newsl* 78 (1990), 11–12.

Marsh, Joss Lutz. "Good Mrs. Brown's Connections: Sexuality and Story-Telling in *Dealings with the Firm of Dombey and Son.*" *ELH* 58 (1991), 405–23.

Moglen, Helene. "Theorizing Fiction/Fictionalizing Theory: The Case of *Dombey and Son.*" *Victorian Stud* 35 (1992), 159–80.

Newcomb, Mildred. *The Imagined World,* 109–12, 114–17, 121–24.

Newsom, Robert. "Embodying Dombey: Whole and in Part." *Dickens Stud Annual* 18 (1989), 197–215.

Nord, Deborah Epstein. "The Urban Peripatetic: Spectator, Streetwalker, Woman Writer." *Nineteenth-Cent Lit* 46 (1991), 360–64.

Rajan, Rajeswari Sunder. "'The Shadow of that Expatriated Prince': The Exorbitant Native of *Dombey and Son.*" *Victorian Lit and Culture* 19 (1991), 85–102.

Schacht, Paul. "Dickens and the Uses of Nature." *Victorian Stud* 34 (1990), 85–93.

Selby, Keith. *How to Study a Charles Dickens Novel,* 100–127.

Sheridan, Daniel. "The Unreadable *Dombey.*" *Dickens Q* 6 (1989), 142–49.

Squires, Michael. "Lawrence, Dickens, and the English Novel," in Michael Squires and Keith Cushman, eds., *The Challenge of D. H. Lawrence,* 42–55, 57–59.

Tindall, Gillian. *Countries of the Mind,* 63–66.

Waters, Catherine. "Ambiguous Intimacy: Brother and Sister Relationships in *Dombey and Son.*" *Dickensian* 84 (1988), 9–26.

Great Expectations, 1861

Ackroyd, Peter. *Dickens,* 898–902.

Ackroyd, Peter. *Introduction to Dickens,* 157–63.

Alexander, Doris. *Creating Characters,* 125–37.

Allingham, Philip V. "Patterns of Deception in *Huckleberry Finn* and *Great Expectations.*" *Nineteenth-Cent Lit* 46 (1992), 447–72.

Armstrong, Frances. *Dickens and the Concept of Home,* 131–39.

Beatty, C. J. P. "Charles Dickens's *Great Expectations* (1860–1) and the Probable Source of the Expression 'Brought Up By Hand.'" *Notes and Queries* 38 (1991), 315.

Berman, Jeffrey. *Narcissism and the Novel,* 125–47.

Bradbury, Nicola. *Charles Dickens' "Great Expectations,"* 29–115.

Brooks-Davies, Douglas. *Charles Dickens: "Great Expectations,"* 15–127.

Burgan, Mary. "Bringing Up By Hand: Dickens and the Feeding of Children." *Mosaic* 24:3–4 (1991), 70–87.

Carey, John. *The Violent Effigy,* 51–53, 131–34.

Cheadle, Brian. "Sentiment and Resentment in *Great Expectations.*" *Dickens Stud Annual* 20 (1991), 149–71.

Cloy, John. "Two Altered Endings: Dickens and Bulwer-Lytton." *Univ of Mississippi Stud in Engl* 10 (1992), 170–72.

Cohen, William A. "Manual Conduct in *Great Expectations.*" *ELH* 60 (1993), 217–52.

Cunningham, John. "The Figure of the Wedding Feast in *Great Expectations.*" *Dickens Q* 10 (1993), 87–90.

Davies, James A. *The Textual Life,* 94–102.

DeBona, Guerric, OSB. "Doing Time; Undoing Time: Plot Mutation in David Lean's *Great Expectations.*" *Lit/Film Q* 20 (1992), 77–85.

Edgecombe, Rodney Stenning. "Dickens, Hunt and the 'Dramatic Criticism' in *Great Expectations:* A Note." *Dickensian* 88 (1992), 25–37.

Filmer, Kath. "The Spectre of the Self in *Frankenstein* and *Great Expectations,*" in Kath Filmer, ed., *The Victorian Fantasists,* 172–82.

Friedman, Stanley. "Ridley's *Tales of the Genii* and Dickens's *Great Expectations.*" *Nineteenth-Cent Lit* 44 (1989), 215–18.

Giddings, Robert. "Great Misrepresentations: Dickens and Film." *Crit Survey* 3 (1991), 305–12.

Golden, Morris. *Dickens Imagining Himself,* 163–93.

Herst, Beth F. *The Dickens Hero,* 117–38.

Hollington, Michael. "Dickens and Australia." *Cahiers Victoriens et Edouardiens* 33 (1991), 26–31.

Hornback, Bert G. *"Great Expectations": A Novel of Friendship.*

Houston, Gail Turley. "'Pip' and 'Property': The (Re)Production of the Self in *Great Expectations.*" *Stud in the Novel* 24 (1992), 13–23.

Johnston, Judith. "Women and Violence in Dickens' *Great Expectations.*" *Sydney Stud in Engl* 18 (1992–93), 93–110.

Kusnetz, Ella. "'This Leaf of My Life': Writing and Play in *Great Expectations.*" *Dickens Q* 10 (1993), 91–103, 146–59.

Litvak, Joseph. *Caught in the Act,* 123–28.

McFarlane, Brian. "David Lean's *Great Expectations:* Meeting Two Challenges." *Lit/Film Q* 20 (1992), 68–76.

Maxwell, Richard. *The Mysteries,* 276–81.

Meckier, Jerome. "Charles Dickens's *Great Expectations:* A Defense of the Second Ending." *Stud in the Novel* 25 (1993), 28–54.

Meckier, Jerome. "Dating the Action in *Great Expectations:* A New Chronology." *Dickens Stud Annual* 21 (1992), 157–90.

Meckier, Jerome. "Dickens, *Great Expectations,* and the Dartmouth College Notes." *Papers on Lang & Lit* 28 (1992), 111–31.

Milbank, Alison. *Daughters of the House,* 121–39.

Morgan, Nicholas H. *Secret Journeys,* 101–22.

Morris, Pam. *Dickens's Class Consciousness,* 103–18.

Newcomb, Mildred. *The Imagined World,* 19–23, 38–40, 143–45, 161–64.

Ortiz, Gloria. *The Dandy and the "Señorito,"* 41–44.

Phelan, James. *Reading People,* 116–31.

Polhemus, Robert M. *Erotic Faith,* 137–67.

Raphael, Linda. "A Re-vision of Miss Havisham: Her Expectations and Our Responses." *Stud in the Novel* 21 (1989), 400–410.

Sadrin, Anny. *Dickens ou le roman-théâtre,* 130–38.

Schaumburger, Nancy E. "The 'Time Machine' of *Great Expectations:* Pip, Magwitch and Developmental Time." *Dickensian* 89 (1993), 32–35.

Selby, Keith. *How to Study a Charles Dickens Novel,* 31–56.

Stein, Robert A. "Repetitions During Pip's Closure." *Dickens Stud Annual* 21 (1992), 143–54.

Tharaud, Barry. "*Great Expectations* as Literature and Film." *Dickensian* 87 (1991), 102–8.

Thomas, Ronald R. *Dreams of Authority,* 169–89.

Wiesenfarth, Joseph. *Gothic Manners,* 83–100.

Hard Times, 1854

Ackroyd, Peter. *Dickens,* 698–711.

Ackroyd, Peter. *Introduction to Dickens,* 129–34.

Allingham, Philip. "Mr. Dickens Enters Literature 12: Or, *Hard Times* in the British Columbia Classroom." *Update* 31:3 (1989), 17–19.

Allingham, Philip V. "Theme, Form, and the Naming of Names in *Hard Times For These Times.*" *Dickensian* 87 (1991), 17–30.

Alton, Anne Hiebert. "Education in Victorian Fact and Fiction: Kay-Shuttleworth and Dickens's *Hard Times.*" *Dickens Q* 9 (1992), 67–78.

Armstrong, Frances. *Dickens and the Concept of Home,* 105–7.

Beauchamp, Gorman. "Mechanomorphism in *Hard Times.*" *Stud in the Liter Imagination* 22:1 (1989), 61–77.

Butterworth, R. D. "Dickens the Novelist: The Preston Strike and *Hard Times.*" *Dickensian* 88 (1992), 91–101.

Carr, Jean Ferguson. "Writing as a Woman: Dickens, *Hard Times,* and Feminine Discourses." *Dickens Stud Annual* 18 (1989), 161–74.

Cowles, David L. "Having it Both Ways: Gender and Paradox in *Hard Times.*" *Dickens Q* 8 (1991), 79–84.

Erlebach, Peter. *Theorie und Praxis des Romaneingangs,* 208–12.

Friedman, Stanley. "Sad Stephen and Troubled Louisa: Paired Protagonists in *Hard Times.*" *Dickens Q* 7 (1990), 254–61.

Gaye, Mamadou. "La Solitude urbaine dans quelques œuvres de Dickens: *Bleak House* et *Hard Times.*" *Bridges* 3 (1991), 55–67.

Harvie, Christopher. *The Centre of Things,* 46–49.

Herst, Beth F. *The Dickens Hero,* 67–89.

Hochberg, Shifra. "Mrs Sparsit's Coriolanian Eyebrows and Dickensian Approach to Topicality." *Dickensian* 87 (1991), 32–35.

Hollington, Michael. "Physiognomy in *Hard Times.*" *Dickens Q* 9 (1992), 58–66.

Horne, Felicity. "Character and Theme in *Hard Times.*" *CRUX* 22:3 (1988), 56–61.

Ingham, Patricia. *Dickens, Women and Language,* 93–97, 99–103, 106–10.

Kearns, Katherine. "A Tropology of Realism in *Hard Times.*" *ELH* 59 (1992), 857–78.

Laurence, Patricia Ondek. *The Reading of Silence,* 79–82.

Law, Joe K. "'The One Thing Needful': Biblical Allusion and the Social Gospel in *Hard Times.*" *Conf of Coll Teachers of Engl Stud* 56 (1991), 76–82.

Litvak, Joseph. *Caught in the Act,* 117–23.

Manlove, Colin. "Charles Kingsley, H. G. Wells, and the Machine in Victorian Fiction." *Nineteenth-Cent Lit* 48 (1993), 221–24.

Mills, Alice. "Happy Endings in *Hard Times* and *Granny's Wonderful Chair,*" in Kath Filmer, ed., *The Victorian Fantasists,* 184–94.

Newcomb, Mildred. *The Imagined World,* 60–62, 107–9, 124–28, 177–79.

Nussbaum, Martha C. "The Literary Imagination in Public Life." *New Liter Hist* 22 (1991), 877–910.

Palmer, William. "Dickens and Shipwreck." *Dickens Stud Annual* 18 (1989), 70–75.

Pettit, Alexander. "Sympathetic Criminality in the Mid-Victorian Novel." *Dickens Stud Annual* 19 (1990), 282–96.

Samuelian, Kristin Flieger. "Being Rid of Women: Middle-Class Ideology in *Hard Times.*" *Victorian Newsl* 82 (1992), 58–61.

Schacht, Paul. "Dickens and the Uses of Nature." *Victorian Stud* 34 (1990), 80–85.

Selby, Keith. *How to Study a Charles Dickens Novel,* 10–30.

Simpson, Margaret. "*Hard Times* and Circus Times." *Dickens Q* 10 (1993), 131–44.

Smith, Grahame. "Comic Subversion and *Hard Times.*" *Dickens Stud Annual* 18 (1989), 145–60.

Smith, Grahame. "'O reason not the need': *King Lear, Hard Times* and Utilitarian Values." *Dickensian* 86 (1990), 164–70.

Weber, Jean Jacques. *Critical Analysis of Fiction,* 107–19.

The Haunted Man, 1847

Allingham, Philip V. "Dickens' Christmas Books: Names and Motifs."
  Engl Lang Notes 29:4 (1992), 67–68.
Moncrieff, Scott. "Remembrance of Wrongs Past in *The Haunted Man.*"
  Stud in Short Fiction 28 (1991), 535–41.

Little Dorrit, 1857

Ackroyd, Peter. *Dickens,* 742–58.
Ackroyd, Peter. *Introduction to Dickens,* 135–42.
Alexander, Doris. "Benevolent Sage or Blundering Booby?" *Dickens Q* 8
  (1991), 120–26.
Alexander, Doris. *Creating Characters,* 115–23.
Bernstein, Carol L. *The Celebration of Scandal,* 156–61.
Carey, John. *The Violent Effigy,* 189–205.
Castronovo, David. *The English Gentleman,* 65–69.
Childers, Joseph W. "History, Totality, Opposition: The New Historicism
  and *Little Dorrit.*" *Dickens Q* 6 (1989), 150–57.
Crawford, Iain. " 'Machinery in Motion': Time in *Little Dorrit.*" *Dicken-
  sian* 84 (1988), 30–40.
Crosby, Christina. *The Ends of History,* 69–109.
Currie, Richard A. " 'As if she had done him a wrong': Hidden Rage and
  Object Protection in Dickens's Amy Dorrit." *Engl Stud* 72 (1991), 368–
  75.
Daleski, H. M. "Large, Loose, Baggy Monsters and *Little Dorrit.*" *Dick-
  ens Stud Annual* 21 (1992), 131–42.
Davies, James A. *The Textual Life,* 131–50.
Dentith, Simon. *A Rhetoric of the Real,* 92–115.
Dvorak, Wilfred P. "The Misunderstood Pancks: Money and the Rhetoric
  of Disguise in *Little Dorrit.*" *Stud in the Novel* 23 (1991), 339–46.
Easson, Angus. "A Novel Scarcely Historical? Time and History in Dick-
  ens's *Little Dorrit,*" in Angus Easson, ed., *History and the Novel,* 27–
  40.
Eigner, Edwin M. *The Dickens Pantomime,* 30–32, 173–75.
Fields, Darin E. " 'Two Spheres of Action and Suffering': Empire and Dec-
  adence in *Little Dorrit.*" *Dickens Q* 7 (1990), 379–83.
Flahiff, F. T. " 'Mysteriously Come Together': Dickens, Chaucer, and *Little
  Dorrit.*" *Univ of Toronto Q* 61 (1991/92), 250–66.
Greenstein, Michael. "Liminality in *Little Dorrit.*" *Dickens Q* 7 (1990),
  275–82.
Hardinge, Emma. "Identity, Self and Shadow in *Little Dorrit.*" *Sydney Stud
  in Engl* 18 (1992–93), 111–28.
Hardy, Barbara. "The Talkative Woman in Shakespeare, Dickens and
  George Eliot," in Sally Minogue, ed., *Problems for Feminist Criticism,*
  37–39.
Herst, Beth F. *The Dickens Hero,* 90–106.
Horne, Lewis. "*Little Dorrit* and the Region of Despair." *Dalhousie R* 69
  (1989–90), 533–46.

Ingham, Patricia. *Dickens, Women and Language,* 59–61, 120–24.

Kiely, Robert. "Charles Dickens: The Lives of Some Important Nobodies," in Laurence S. Lockridge et al., eds., *Nineteenth-Century Lives,* 69–81.

Leavis, L. R. "Dickens and Hawthorne: *Little Dorrit* and *The House of the Seven Gables.*" *Engl Stud* 72 (1991), 414–20.

McKnight, Natalie. *Idiots, Madmen,* 111–26.

Manning, Sylvia. "Social Criticism and Textual Subversion in *Little Dorrit.*" *Dickens Stud Annual* 20 (1991), 127–46.

Marks, Patricia. "'On Tuesday Last, at St. George's . . .': The Dandaical Wedding in Dickens." *Victorian Newsl* 78 (1990), 12–13.

Maxwell, Richard. *The Mysteries,* 270–75.

Metz, Nancy Aycock. "The Blighted Tree and the Book of Fate: Female Models of Storytelling in *Little Dorrit.*" *Dickens Stud Annual* 18 (1989), 221–40.

Metz, Nancy Aycock. "*Little Dorrit*'s London: Babylon Revisited." *Victorian Stud* 33 (1990), 465–86.

Milbank, Alison. *Daughters of the House,* 102–20.

Morgan, Nicholas H. *Secret Journeys,* 79–100.

Newcomb, Mildred. *The Imagined World,* 31–33, 55–60, 148–50, 157–60.

Newton, Ruth, and Naomi Lebowitz. *Dickens, Manzoni, Zola, and James,* 114–15, 130–34.

Pendleton, Robert W. "The Detective's Languishing Forefinger: Narrative Guides in *Bleak House* and *Little Dorrit.*" *Dickens Q* 7 (1990), 371–78.

Philpotts, Trey. "Dickens, Patent Reform, and the Inventor: Daniel Doyce and the Question of Topicality." *Dickens Q* 9 (1992), 158–68.

Reed, John R. *Victorian Will,* 267–71.

Rosenberg, Brian. "Character and Contradiction in Dickens." *Nineteenth-Cent Lit* 47 (1992), 149–63.

Rotkin, Charlotte. *Deception in Dickens' "Little Dorrit,"* 7–138.

Sutherland, Kathryn. "A Guide through the Labyrinth: Dickens's *Little Dorrit* as Hypertext." *Liter and Linguistic Computing* 5 (1990), 305–9.

Winter, Sarah. "Domestic Fictions: Feminine Deference and Maternal Shadow Labor in Dickens's *Little Dorrit.*" *Dickens Stud Annual* 18 (1989), 243–53.

Yeazell, Ruth Bernard. "Do It or Dorrit." *Novel* 25 (1991), 33–49.

Martin Chuzzlewit, 1844

Ackroyd, Peter. *Dickens,* 390–403.

Ackroyd, Peter. *Introduction to Dickens,* 86–92.

Allingham, Philip V. "The Names of Dickens's American Originals in *Martin Chuzzlewit.*" *Dickens Q* 7 (1990), 329–36.

Armstrong, Frances. *Dickens and the Concept of Home,* 71–75.

Davies, James A. *The Textual Life,* 32–47.

Edgecombe, R. S. "Locution and Authority in *Martin Chuzzlewit.*" *Engl Stud* 74 (1993), 143–53.

Eigner, Edwin M. *The Dickens Pantomime,* 110–12.

Golden, Morris. *Dickens Imagining Himself,* 53–85.

Golden, Morris. "Politics, Class, and *Martin Chuzzlewit.*" *Dickens Q* 10 (1993), 17–31.

Hardy, Barbara. "The Talkative Woman in Shakespeare, Dickens and George Eliot," in Sally Minogue, ed., *Problems for Feminist Criticism,* 26–28, 36–37.

Heineman, Helen K. *Three Victorians in the New World,* 149–73.

Hollington, Michael. "The Live Hieroglyphic: *Physiologie* and Physiognomy in *Martin Chuzzlewit.*" *Dickens Q* 10 (1993), 57–67.

Kiely, Robert. "Charles Dickens: The Lives of Some Important Nobodies," in Laurence S. Lockridge et al., eds., *Nineteenth-Century Lives,* 59–62, 64–68.

Lougy, Robert E. "Repressive and Expressive Forms: The Bodies of Comedy and Desire in *Martin Chuzzlewit.*" *Dickens Stud Annual* 21 (1992), 37–57.

Maxwell, Richard. *The Mysteries,* 126–49.

Meckier, Jerome. "Hannibal Chollop's Offensiveness: Natty Bumppo and Chapters 33–34 of *Martin Chuzzlewit.*" *Dickens Q* 10 (1993), 33–54.

Meckier, Jerome. *Innocent Abroad,* 8–15, 22–36, 55–58, 113–20.

Metz, Nancy Aycock. "Dickens, *Punch* and Pecksniff." *Dickens Q* 10 (1993), 6–16.

Miller, J. Hillis. *Victorian Subjects,* 112–14.

Morris, Pam. *Dickens's Class Consciousness,* 39–58.

Newton, Ruth, and Naomi Lebowitz. *Dickens, Manzoni, Zola, and James,* 71–79, 107–12, 129–31.

Page, Norman. *Speech in the English Novel,* 159–61.

Schad, John. *The Reader,* 74–77, 80–82.

Selby, Keith. *How to Study a Charles Dickens Novel,* 80–99.

Steig, Michael. *Stories of Reading,* 146–48.

Summers, Anne. "The Mysterious Demise of Sarah Gamp: The Domiciliary Nurse and Her Detractors, c. 1830–1860." *Victorian Stud* 32 (1989), 365–82.

The Mystery of Edwin Drood, 1870

Ackroyd, Peter. *Dickens,* 1048–57.

Ackroyd, Peter. *Introduction to Dickens,* 171–77.

Alexander, Doris. *Creating Characters,* 148–50.

Alexander, Doris. "Solving the Mysteries of the Mind in *Edwin Drood.*" *Dickens Q* 9 (1992), 125–30.

Auerbach, Emily. *Maestros, Dilettantes, and Philistines,* 88–89.

Davies, James A. *The Textual Life,* 119–30.

Fisher, Benjamin Franklin, IV. "Sunshine and Shadow in *The Mystery of Edwin Drood.*" *Mystery FANcier* 11:4 (1989), 11–28.

Fleissner, Robert F. "Drood Renominated." *Names* 40 (1992), 117–21.

Forsyte, Charles. "Charles Dickens Junior, Harold Macmillan, and *Edwin Drood.*" *Notes and Queries* 235 (1990), 35–36.

Forsyte, Charles. "Dickens and Dick Datchery." *Dickensian* 87 (1991), 50–57.

Forsyte, Charles. "How did Drood Die?" *Dickensian* 84 (1988), 81–95.

Fusco, Richard. "Entrapment, Flight and Death: A Recurring Motif in Dickens with Plot and Interpretive Consequences for *Edwin Drood.*" *Essays in Arts and Sciences* 20 (1991), 68–84.

Herst, Beth F. *The Dickens Hero,* 161–84.

Lund, Michael. *Reading Thackeray,* 133–46.

Maxwell, Richard. *The Mysteries,* 304–8, 310–19.

Newcomb, Mildred. *The Imagined World,* 24–26, 62–70.

Reece, Benny R. *The Mystery of Edwin Drood Solved,* 1–49.

Schaumburger, Nancy E. "The 'Gritty Stages' of Life: Psychological Time in *The Mystery of Edwin Drood.*" *Dickensian* 86 (1990), 158–63. (Also in *Univ of Mississippi Stud in Engl* 8 [1990], 155–66.)

Smith, Allan Lloyd. "The Phantoms of *Drood* and *Rebecca:* The Uncanny Reencountered through Abraham and Torok's 'Cryptonymy.'" *Poetics Today* 13 (1992), 295–300.

Thacker, John. *"Edwin Drood,"* 13–140.

Thomas, Ronald R. *Dreams of Authority,* 219–39.

Nicholas Nickleby, 1839

Ackroyd, Peter. *Dickens,* 253–64.

Ackroyd, Peter. *Introduction to Dickens,* 55–61.

Auerbach, Emily. *Maestros, Dilettantes, and Philistines,* 76–78.

Chittick, Kathryn. *Dickens and the 1830s,* 118–20, 134–39.

Cipar, Mary Cleopha. "Picaresque Characteristics in *Nicholas Nickleby.*" *Dickensian* 84 (1988), 43–46.

Colatosti, Camille. "Male versus Female Self-Denial: The Subversive Potential of the Feminine Ideal in the Fiction of Dickens." *Dickens Stud Annual* 19 (1990), 8–20.

Eigner, Edwin M. *The Dickens Pantomime,* 17–19, 26–29, 73–75, 145–48.

Erlebach, Peter. *Theorie und Praxis des Romaneingangs,* 206–7.

Ganz, Margaret. *Humor, Irony, and the Realm of Madness,* 65–99.

Hardy, Barbara. "The Talkative Woman in Shakespeare, Dickens and George Eliot," in Sally Minogue, ed., *Problems for Feminist Criticism,* 23–26, 34–36.

Holway, Tatiana M. "The Game of Speculation: Economics and Representation." *Dickens Q* 9 (1992), 107–11.

Litvak, Joseph. *Caught in the Act,* 111–19.

McKnight, Natalie. *Idiots, Madmen,* 69–79.

Marks, Patricia. "'On Tuesday Last, at St. George's . . .': The Dandaical Wedding in Dickens." *Victorian Newsl* 78 (1990), 10–11.

Schad, John. *The Reader,* 34–38.

Schlicke, Paul. "Crummles Once More." *Dickensian* 86 (1990), 3–16.

The Old Curiosity Shop, 1841

Ackroyd, Peter. *Dickens,* 309–22.

Ackroyd, Peter. *Introduction to Dickens,* 62–69.

Armstrong, Frances. *Dickens and the Concept of Home,* 51–54, 72–74.

Armstrong, Frances. "Gender and Miniaturization: Games of Littleness in Nineteenth-Century Fiction." *Engl Stud in Canada* 16 (1990), 407–11.

Auerbach, Emily. *Maestros, Dilettantes, and Philistines,* 76–78.

Bertinetti, Roberto. "Vivere in un'allegoria: *La bottega dell'antiquario* di Charles Dickens." *Il Lettore di Provincia* 23 (1991), 63–73.

Brattin, Joel J. "Some Old Curiosities from *The Old Curiosity Shop* Manuscript." *Dickens Q* 7 (1990), 218–32.

Carey, John. *The Violent Effigy,* 24–28, 139–41.

Chittick, Kathryn. *Dickens and the 1830s,* 148–51.

Conlon, John J. "Private Sphinx and Public Sphynx: Riddle and Revelation in *The Old Curiosity Shop." Dickens Q* 7 (1990), 234–36.

David, Deirdre. "Children of Empire: Victorian Imperialism and Sexual Politics in Dickens and Kipling," in Antony H. Harrison and Beverly Taylor, eds., *Gender and Discourse,* 124–33.

Dvorak, Wilfred P. "Charles Dickens's *The Old Curiosity Shop:* The Triumph of Compassion." *Papers on Lang & Lit* 28 (1992), 52–70.

Feinberg, Monica L. "Reading *Curiosity:* Does Dick's Shop Deliver?" *Dickens Q* 7 (1990), 200–211.

Georgas, Marilyn. "Little Nell and the Art of Holy Dying: Dickens and Jeremy Taylor." *Dickens Stud Annual* 20 (1991), 35–54.

Gitter, Elisabeth G. "Laura Bridgman and Little Nell." *Dickens Q* 8 (1991), 75–78.

Hodgell, Pat. "Charles Dickens' *Old Curiosity Shop:* The Gothic Novel in Transition." *Riverside Q* 8:3 (1990), 152–69.

Horton, Susan R. "Swivellers and Snivellers: Competing Epistemologies in *The Old Curiosity Shop." Dickens Q* 7 (1990), 212–16.

Ingham, Patricia. *Dickens, Women and Language,* 33–35.

Jaffe, Audrey. *Vanishing Points,* 45–70.

Lapointe, Adriane. "Little Nell Once More: Absent Fathers in *The Old Curiosity Shop." Dickens Stud Annual* 18 (1989), 19–35.

McCarthy, Patrick J. "The Curious Road to Death's Nell." *Dickens Stud Annual* 20 (1991), 17–31.

MacKay, Carol Hanbery. "Controlling Death and Sex: Magnification v. the Rhetoric of Rules in Dickens and Thackeray," in Regina Barreca, ed., *Sex and Death,* 125–27.

Maxwell, Richard. *The Mysteries,* 96–125.

Möller, Joachim. "Spiegel der Seele: Charakterporträts bei Dickens am Beispiel von *The Old Curiosity Shop." Literatur in Wissenschaft und Unterricht* 23 (1990), 337–45.

Morgan, Nicholas H. *Secret Journeys,* 31–57.

Newcomb, Mildred. *The Imagined World,* 47–50.

Peters, Ross. "Imaginative Transformation and Unity in *The Old Curiosity Shop." AUMLA* 78 (1992), 41–61.

Pettersson, Torsten. "'Impostors and Deceptions': The Social Side of *The Old Curiosity Shop." Studia Neophilologica* 64 (1992), 81–86.

Reed, John R. *Victorian Will,* 249–51.

Schad, John. *The Reader,* 142–44.

Schiefelbein, Michael. "Little Nell, Catholicism, and Dickens's Investigation of Death." *Dickens Q* 9 (1992), 115–24.

Schlicke, Paul. "The True Pathos of *The Old Curiosity Shop.*" *Dickens Q* 7 (1990), 189–98.

Wallace, Anne D. *Walking, Literature, and English Culture,* 222–29.

Westland, Ella. "Little Nell and the Marchioness: Some Functions of Fairy Tale in *The Old Curiosity Shop.*" *Dickens Q* 8 (1991), 68–74.

Oliver Twist, 1838

Ackroyd, Peter. *Dickens,* 218–33.

Ackroyd, Peter. *Introduction to Dickens,* 46–54.

Andrade, Mary Anne. "Wake into Dream." *Dickensian* 86 (1990), 17–27.

Baldridge, Cates. "The Instabilities of Inheritance in *Oliver Twist.*" *Stud in the Novel* 25 (1993), 184–94.

Bernstein, Stephen. "*Oliver* Twisted: Narrative and Doubling in Dickens's Second Novel." *Victorian Newsl* 79 (1991), 27–33.

Brantlinger, Patrick. "How Oliver Twist Learned to Read, and What He Read." *Bucknell R* 34:2 (1990), 59–79.

Bull, J. A. *The Framework of Fiction,* 129–40.

Chittick, Kathryn. *Dickens and the 1830s,* 74–79, 84–90, 119–29.

Dunn, Richard J. *"Oliver Twist,"* 31–103.

Edwards, Simon. "Anorexia Nervosa vs. the Fleshpots of London: Rose and Nancy in *Oliver Twist.*" *Dickens Stud Annual* 19 (1990), 49–63.

Eigner, Edwin M. *The Dickens Pantomime,* 111–13.

Erlebach, Peter. *Theorie und Praxis des Romaneingangs,* 202–5.

Hollington, Michael. "Dickens and Cruikshank as Physiognomers in *Oliver Twist.*" *Dickens Q* 7 (1990), 243–54.

Houston, Gail Turley. "Broadsides at the Board: Collations of *Pickwick Papers* and *Oliver Twist.*" *Stud in Engl Lit, 1500–1900* 31 (1991), 735–52.

Ingham, Patricia. *Dickens, Women and Language,* 39–41, 44–46.

Johae, Antony. "Hallucination in *Oliver Twist* and *Crime and Punishment.*" *New Comparison* 9 (1990), 128–38.

Jordan, John O. "The Purloined Handkerchief." *Dickens Stud Annual* 18 (1989), 1–15.

Maxwell, Richard. *The Mysteries,* 72–95.

Miller, J. Hillis. *Victorian Subjects,* 31–48.

Montgomery, Martin, Alan Durant, Nigel Fabb, Tom Furniss, and Sara Mills. *Ways of Reading,* 29–31.

Morris, Virginia B. *Double Jeopardy,* 56–60.

Newcomb, Mildred. *The Imagined World,* 43–47.

Nord, Deborah Epstein. "The Urban Peripatetic: Spectator, Streetwalker, Woman Writer." *Nineteenth-Cent Lit* 46 (1991), 358–60.

Paroissien, David. "Oliver Twist and the Contours of Early Victorian England." *Victorian Newsl* 83 (1993), 14–17.

Petterson, Torsten. "Enough to Have Bodies? Two Incongruities in *Oliver Twist.*" *Orbis Litterarum* 45 (1990), 341–50.

Reed, John R. "Authorized Punishment in Dickens's Fiction." *Stud in the Novel* 24 (1992), 116–17.

Scheuerle, William H. "Cries of the Children in the Novels of Charles Dickens," in Sara Munson Deats and Lagretta Tallent Lenker, eds., *The Aching Hearth*, 155–61.

Tindall, Gillian. *Countries of the Mind*, 127–30.

Vega-Ritter, Max. "Loi, Innocence et Crime dans *Oliver Twist*." *Cahiers Victoriens et Edouardiens* 29 (1989), 15–39.

Our Mutual Friend, 1865

Ackroyd, Peter. *Dickens*, 940–59.

Ackroyd, Peter. *Introduction to Dickens*, 164–70.

Alexander, Doris. *Creating Characters*, 107–13.

Armstrong, Frances. *Dickens and the Concept of Home*, 139–51.

Armstrong, Frances. "Gender and Miniaturization: Games of Littleness in Nineteenth-Century Fiction." *Engl Stud in Canada* 16 (1990), 406–11.

Bernstein, Carol L. *The Celebration of Scandal*, 192–206.

Butler, Lance St. John. *Victorian Doubt*, 37–40.

Carey, John. *The Violent Effigy*, 74–76, 108–11.

Cerny, Lothar. "'All my work'? Wirkungsbedingungen der Mimesis in *Our Mutual Friend*." *Anglia* 108 (1990), 75–95.

Davies, James A. *The Textual Life*, 47–56, 102–9, 111–19, 151–63.

Dvorak, Wilfred P. "Dickens and Popular Culture: Silas Wegg's Ballads in *Our Mutual Friend*." *Dickensian* 86 (1990), 142–55.

Eigner, Edwin M. *The Dickens Pantomime*, 30–32, 173–77.

Gaughan, Richard T. "Prospecting for Meaning in *Our Mutual Friend*." *Dickens Stud Annual* 19 (1990), 231–44.

Ginsburg, Michal Peled. "The Case Against Plot in *Bleak House* and *Our Mutual Friend*." *ELH* 59 (1992), 179–94.

Golden, Morris. *Dickens Imagining Himself*, 195–229.

Greenstein, Michael. "Mutuality in *Our Mutual Friend*." *Dickens Q* 8 (1991), 127–33.

Herst, Beth F. *The Dickens Hero*, 107–16, 151–60.

Hopkins, Sandra. "'Wooman, Lovely Wooman': Four Dickens Heroines and the Critics," in Sally Minogue, ed., *Problems for Feminist Criticism*, 137–40.

Ingham, Patricia. *Dickens, Women and Language*, 19–20, 81–84.

Jaffe, Audrey. *Vanishing Points*, 150–66.

Mackay, Carol Hanbery. "The Encapsulated Romantic: John Harmon and the Boundaries of Victorian Soliloquy." *Dickens Stud Annual* 18 (1989), 255–72.

Marks, Patricia. "'On Tuesday Last, at St. George's . . .': The Dandaical Wedding in Dickens." *Victorian Newsl* 78 (1990), 13–14.

Maxwell, Richard. *The Mysteries*, 281–88.

Miller, J. Hillis. *Victorian Subjects*, 69–77.

Morris, Pam. *Dickens's Class Consciousness*, 120–38.

Newcomb, Mildred. *The Imagined World,* 40–43.

Newton, Ruth, and Naomi Lebowitz. *Dickens, Manzoni, Zola, and James,* 134–35, 142–43, 150–51, 182–83.

O'Donnell, Patrick. *Echo Chambers,* 27–63.

O'Donnell, Patrick. "'A Speeches of Chaff': Ventriloquy and Expression in *Our Mutual Friend.*" *Dickens Stud Annual* 19 (1990), 247–74.

Ortiz, Gloria. *The Dandy and the "Señorito,"* 113–14.

Page, Norman. *Speech in the English Novel,* 105–12, 148–52.

Palmer, William. "Dickens and Shipwreck." *Dickens Stud Annual* 18 (1989), 82–89.

Poovey, Mary. "Reading History in Literature: Speculation and Virtue in *Our Mutual Friend,*" in Janet Levarrie Smarr, ed., *Historical Criticism,* 42–72.

Reed, John R. "Authorized Punishment in Dickens's Fiction." *Stud in the Novel* 24 (1992), 120–28.

Reed, John R. *Victorian Will,* 272–74.

Robson, John M. "Crime in *Our Mutual Friend,*" in M. L. Friedland, ed., *Rough Justice,* 114–36.

Sadrin, Anny. *Dickens ou le roman-théâtre,* 139–52.

Schad, John. *The Reader,* 70–71, 77–78, 86–87, 105–6, 174–75.

Smith, Peter. "The Aestheticist Argument of *Our Mutual Friend.*" *Cambridge Q* 18 (1989), 363–82.

Spencer, Jamieson. "Charles Dickens in School: One Teacher's Report Card." *Dickensian* 86 (1990), 105–14.

Tuss, Alex J., SM. *The Inward Revolution,* 111–26.

Worthington, Pepper. "The Religious Issues of Materialism, Love, and God in Dickens' Last Novel, *Our Mutual Friend* (1865)." *Mount Olive R* 5 (1991), 61–73.

The Pickwick Papers, 1837

Ackroyd, Peter. *Dickens,* 190–200.

Ackroyd, Peter. *Introduction to Dickens,* 38–45.

Chittick, Kathryn. *Dickens and the 1830s,* 61–71, 75–80.

Clayton, Jay. "Dickens and the Genealogy of Postmodernism." *Nineteenth-Cent Lit* 46 (1991), 192–95.

Davies, James A. *The Textual Life,* 22–31.

Edgecombe, Rodney Stenning. "Comic Hypotheses in *The Pickwick Papers.*" *Dickens Q* 7 (1990), 359–70.

Ganz, Margaret. *Humor, Irony, and the Realm of Madness,* 25–64.

Houston, Gail Turley. "Broadsides at the Board: Collations of *Pickwick Papers* and *Oliver Twist.*" *Stud in Engl Lit, 1500–1900* 31 (1991), 735–52.

Kincaid, James R. "Fattening Up on Pickwick." *Novel* 25 (1992), 235–44.

Lansdown, Richard. "*The Pickwick Papers:* Something Nobler than a Novel?" *Crit R* (Melbourne) 31 (1991), 75–91.

Morris, Pam. *Dickens's Class Consciousness,* 26–37.

Page, Norman. *Speech in the English Novel,* 144–48.

Potau, Mercedes. "Notes on Parallels between *The Pickwick Papers* and *Don Quixote.*" *Dickens Q* 10 (1993), 105–9.

Roberts, Doreen. "*The Pickwick Papers* and the Sex War." *Dickens Q* 7 (1990), 299–310.

Schlicke, Paul. "The Showman of the *Pickwick Papers.*" *Dickens Stud Annual* 20 (1991), 1–13.

A Tale of Two Cities, 1859

Ackroyd, Peter. *Dickens,* 858–73.

Ackroyd, Peter. *Introduction to Dickens,* 143–49.

Allingham, Philip. "*A Tale of Two Cities:* A Model of the Integration of History and Literature." *BCETA Professional J* July 1991, 35–43.

Baldridge, Cates. "Alternatives to Bourgeois Individualism in *A Tale of Two Cities.*" *Stud in Engl Lit, 1500–1900* 30 (1990), 633–53.

Barnes, Christopher J. "Pasternak, Dickens, and the Novel Tradition." *Forum for Mod Lang Stud* 26 (1990), 326–41.

Collins, Irene. "Charles Dickens and the French Revolution." *Lit & Hist* 2nd ser. 1:1 (1990), 40–55.

Court, Franklin E. "*A Tale of Two Cities:* Dickens, Revolution,, and the 'Other' C D." *Victorian Newsl* 80 (1991), 14–18.

Eigner, Edwin M. *The Dickens Pantomime,* 105–7, 115–17.

Forsyte, Charles. "*A Tale of Two Cities:* A New Source." *Etudes Anglaises* 43 (1990), 298–302.

Glancy, Ruth. "*A Tale of Two Cities,*" 31–119.

Herst, Beth F. *The Dickens Hero,* 143–51.

Knezevic, Borislav. "A Study of Aggression: *A Tale of Two Cities.*" *Studia Romanica et Anglica Zagrabiensia* 36–37 (1991–92), 251–70.

Lloyd, Tom. "Language, Love and Identity: *A Tale of Two Cities.*" *Dickensian* 88 (1992), 154–67.

Morris, Virginia B. *Double Jeopardy,* 67–71.

Nelson, Harland S. "Shadow and Substance in *A Tale of Two Cities.*" *Dickensian* 84 (1988), 97–105.

Palmer, William. "Dickens and Shipwreck." *Dickens Stud Annual* 18 (1989), 75–82.

Sadrin, Anny. *Dickens ou le roman-théâtre,* 90–105, 153–57.

Schad, John. *The Reader,* 38–39, 42–44, 132–33, 165–66, 181–83.

Sørensen, Knud. "Carlyle and Dickens on the French Revolution: A Stylistic Study," in Anders Iversen, ed., *The Impact of the French Revolution,* 141–44.

Stewart, Garrett. "Leaving History: Dickens, Gance, Blanchot." *Yale J of Criticism* 2 (1989), 145–90.

Tuss, Alex J., SM. *The Inward Revolution,* 76–88.

BENJAMIN DISRAELI

Coningsby, 1844

Brantlinger, Patrick. "Nations and Novels: Disraeli, George Eliot, and Orientalism." *Victorian Stud* 35 (1992), 263–66.

Harvie, Christopher. *The Centre of Things,* 34–37, 39–46.

Lessenich, Rolf P. "Synagogue, Church, and Young England: The Jewish Contribution to British Civilization in Benjamin Disraeli's Trilogy," in Franz Link, ed., *Jewish Life and Suffering*, 33–46.

Prawer, S. S. *Israel at Vanity Fair*, 140–45.

Endymion, 1880

Harvie, Christopher. *The Centre of Things*, 111–13.

Lothair, 1870

Basham, Diana. *The Trial of Woman*, 209–11.

Harvie, Christopher. *The Centre of Things*, 98–100.

Sybil, 1845

Harvie, Christopher. *The Centre of Things*, 8–12, 39–46.

Lessenich, Rolf P. "Synagogue, Church, and Young England: The Jewish Contribution to British Civilization in Benjamin Disraeli's Trilogy," in Franz Link, ed., *Jewish Life and Suffering*, 33–46.

Prawer, S. S. *Israel at Vanity Fair*, 142–46.

Roy, Parama. "*Sybil:* The Two Nations and the Manorial Ideal." *Victorians Inst J* 17 (1989), 63–75.

Tancred, 1847

Auerbach, Emily. *Maestros, Dilettantes, and Philistines*, 59–60.

Brantlinger, Patrick. "Nations and Novels: Disraeli, George Eliot, and Orientalism." *Victorian Stud* 35 (1992), 266–68.

Lessenich, Rolf P. "Synagogue, Church, and Young England: The Jewish Contribution to British Civilization in Benjamin Disraeli's Trilogy," in Franz Link, ed., *Jewish Life and Suffering*, 33–46.

Venetia, 1837

Basham, Diana. *The Trial of Woman*, 32–37.

Vivian Grey, 1826–1827

Weintraub, Stanley. "Disraeli and Wilde's Dorian Gray." *Cahiers Victoriens et Edouardiens* 36 (1992), 23–26.

The Young Duke, 1831

Bernstein, Carol L. *The Celebration of Scandal*, 93–97, 101–4.

GERTRUDE DIX

The Image-Breakers, 1900

Ardis, Ann. " 'The Journey from Fantasy to Politics': The Representation of Socialism and Feminism in *Gloriana* and *The Image-Breakers*," in Angela Ingram and Daphne Patai, eds., *Rediscovering Forgotten Radicals*, 48–54.

FLORENCE DIXIE

Gloriana; or, The Revolution of 1900, 1890

Ardis, Ann. "'The Journey from Fantasy to Politics': The Representation of Socialism and Feminism in *Gloriana* and *The Image-Breakers,*" in Angela Ingram and Daphne Patai, eds., *Rediscovering Forgotten Radicals,* 44–48, 52–54.

Ardis, Ann L. *New Women, New Novels,* 119–22.

ELLA HEPWORTH DIXON

The Story of a Modern Woman, 1894

Ardis, Ann L. *New Women, New Novels,* 110–12.

NORMAN DOUGLAS

South Wind, 1917

Orel, Harold. *Popular Fiction in England,* 65–77.

ARTHUR CONAN DOYLE

The Hound of the Baskervilles, 1902

Frank, Lawrence. "Reading the Gravel Page: Lyell, Darwin, and Conan Doyle." *Nineteenth-Cent Lit* 44 (1989), 364–87.

Levitt, Mark E. "The Vatican File." *Baker Street J* 41 (1991), 212–14.

The Sign of the Four, 1890

Thomas, Ronald R. "Minding the Body Politic: The Romance of Science and the Revision of History in Victorian Detective Fiction." *Victorian Lit and Culture* 19 (1991), 242–52.

Verrico, Rose May. "Detective Fiction and the Quest Hero." *Clues* 14:1 (1993), 135–41, 148–52.

A Study in Scarlet, 1887

Anderson, L. M. "Jefferson Hope as Tragic Revenger." *Baker Street J* 39 (1989), 135–43.

Caldwell, Patrice. "Detecting the Art of *A Study in Scarlet.*" *Univ of Mississippi Stud in Engl* 6 (1988), 173–79.

Hutton, Lloyd A. "Sherlock Holmes and the Resident Doctor." *Baker Street J* 41 (1991), 77–81.

Jeffers, H. Paul. "'You Have Been in Peshawar, I Perceive.'" *Baker Street J* 41 (1991), 82–84.

Klis, Oliver. "*A Study in Scarlet:* Doyle und sein Vorbild Gaboriau." *Die Horen* 34:2 (1989), 134–39.

Leps, Marie-Christine. *Apprehending the Criminal,* 200–203.

Loader, Colin. "Conan Doyle's *A Study in Scarlet:* A Study in Irony." *CLIO* 19 (1990), 147–59.

Moss, Robert A. "Brains and Attics." *Baker Street J* 41 (1991), 93–95.
Stetak, Ruthann H. "Jefferson Hope: A Fairly Good Dispenser." *Baker Street J* 39 (1989), 144–47.

MARGARET DRABBLE

The Garrick Year, 1964

Myer, Valerie Grosvenor. *Margaret Drabble,* 30–34.
Salzmann-Brunner, Brigitte. *Amanuenses to the Present,* 107–17.

The Ice Age, 1977

Myer, Valerie Grosvenor. *Margaret Drabble,* 104–23.

Jerusalem the Golden, 1967

Myer, Valerie Grosvenor. *Margaret Drabble,* 49–56.
Salzmann-Brunner, Brigitte. *Amanuenses to the Present,* 84–106.
Stovel, Nora Forster. "'A Great Kick at Misery': Lawrence's and Drabble's Rebellion Against the Fatalism of Bennett," in Keith Cushman and Dennis Jackson, eds., *D. H. Lawrence's Literary Inheritors,* 131–54.

The Middle Ground, 1980

Campbell, Jane. "'Both a Joke and a Victory': Humor as Narrative Strategy in Margaret Drabble's Fiction." *Contemp Lit* 32 (1991), 87–89.
Cunningham, Gail. "Patchwork and Patterns: The Condition of England in Margaret Drabble's Later Novels," in James Acheson, ed. *The British and Irish Novel,* 130–37.
Greene, Gayle. "Feminist Fiction and the Uses of Memory." *Signs* 16 (1991), 311–14.
Myer, Valerie Grosvenor. *Margaret Drabble,* 125–40.
Salzmann-Brunner, Brigitte. *Amanuenses to the Present,* 164–78.

The Millstone, 1965

Cosslett, Tess. "Childbirth on the National Health: Issues of Class, Race, and Gender Identity in Two Post-War British Novels." *Women's Stud* 19 (1991), 100–108.
Cunningham, Gail. "Patchwork and Patterns: The Condition of England in Margaret Drabble's Later Novels," in James Acheson, ed. *The British and Irish Novel,* 127–29.
Jain, Sangeeta. "'Women No Longer Swing in the Ancient Orbits': Margaret Drabble's *The Millstone* and *The Realms of Gold,*" in Sushila Singh, ed., *Feminism and Recent Fiction,* 189–91.
Myer, Valerie Grosvenor. *Margaret Drabble,* 35–47.
Salzmann-Brunner, Brigitte. *Amanuenses to the Present,* 134–42.

A Natural Curiosity, 1989

Campbell, Jane. "'Both a Joke and a Victory': Humor as Narrative Strategy in Margaret Drabble's Fiction." *Contemp Lit* 32 (1991), 78–97.
Cunningham, Gail. "Patchwork and Patterns: The Condition of England

in Margaret Drabble's Later Novels," in James Acheson, ed. *The British and Irish Novel,* 139–41.

Myer, Valerie Grosvenor. *Margaret Drabble,* 153–63.

Rubenstein, Roberta. "Severed Heads, Primal Crimes, Narrative Revisions: Margaret Drabble's *A Natural Curiosity." Critique* (Washington, DC) 33 (1992), 95–105.

The Needle's Eye, 1972

Friedman, Lawrence S. "Puritan Self-Fashioning in *The Needle's Eye." Coll Lang Assoc J* 34 (1991), 426–35.

Myer, Valerie Grosvenor. *Margaret Drabble,* 72–84.

Salzmann-Brunner, Brigitte. *Amanuenses to the Present,* 143–54.

The Radiant Way, 1987

Bromberg, Pamela S. "Margaret Drabble's *The Radiant Way:* Feminist Metafiction." *Novel* 24 (1990), 5–23.

Campbell, Jane. "'Both a Joke and a Victory': Humor as Narrative Strategy in Margaret Drabble's Fiction." *Contemp Lit* 32 (1991), 92–93.

Cunningham, Gail. "Patchwork and Patterns: The Condition of England in Margaret Drabble's Later Novels," in James Acheson, ed. *The British and Irish Novel,* 135–39.

Goss, Marjorie Hill. "Murder and Martyrdom in Margaret Drabble's *The Radiant Way." Notes on Contemp Lit* 19:3 (1989), 2.

Greene, Gayle. *Changing the Story,* 214–22.

Massie, Allan. *The Novel Today,* 20–22.

Myer, Valerie Grosvenor. *Margaret Drabble,* 141–51.

Taylor, D. J. *A Vain Conceit,* 51–55.

Realms of Gold, 1975

Campbell, Jane. "'Both a Joke and a Victory': Humor as Narrative Strategy in Margaret Drabble's Fiction." *Contemp Lit* 32 (1991), 90–92.

Jain, Sangeeta. "'Women No Longer Swing in the Ancient Orbits': Margaret Drabble's *The Millstone* and *The Realms of Gold,*" in Sushila Singh, ed., *Feminism and Recent Fiction,* 191–94.

Myer, Valerie Grosvenor. *Margaret Drabble,* 86–102.

Salzmann-Brunner, Brigitte. *Amanuenses to the Present,* 155–63.

A Summer Bird-Cage, 1963

Campbell, Jane. "'Both a Joke and a Victory': Humor as Narrative Strategy in Margaret Drabble's Fiction." *Contemp Lit* 32 (1991), 85–86.

Levin, Amy K. *The Suppressed Sister,* 111–17.

Myer, Valerie Grosvenor. *Margaret Drabble,* 21–28.

Salzmann-Brunner, Brigitte. *Amanuenses to the Present,* 84–106.

The Waterfall, 1969

Bergmann, Harriet F. "'A Piercing Virtue': Emily Dickinson in Margaret Drabble's *The Waterfall." Mod Fiction Stud* 36 (1990), 181–93.

Greene, Gayle. *Changing the Story,* 130–47.

Myer, Valerie Grosvenor. *Margaret Drabble,* 59–70.

Salzmann-Brunner, Brigitte. *Amanuenses to the Present,* 118–33.
Shurbutt, S. B. "Margaret Drabble's *The Waterfall:* The Writer as Fiction, or Overcoming the Dilemma of Female Authorship." *Women's Stud* 16 (1989), 283–91.

DAPHNE DU MAURIER

Frenchman's Creek, 1941

Light, Alison. *Forever England,* 179–80.
Shallcross, Martyn. *The Private World,* 86–90.

The House on the Strand, 1969

Whissen, Thomas Reed. *The Devil's Advocates,* 78–80.

I'll Never Be Young Again, 1932

Light, Alison. *Forever England,* 168–70.

Jamaica Inn, 1936

Light, Alison. *Forever England,* 171–77.
Shallcross, Martyn. *The Private World,* 46–57.

The Loving Spirit, 1931

Light, Alison. *Forever England,* 166–68.
Shallcross, Martyn. *The Private World,* 42–45.

Rebecca, 1938

Light, Alison. *Forever England,* 157–58, 163–64, 177–79, 188–91.
Shallcross, Martyn. *The Private World,* 59–84.
Smith, Allan Lloyd. "The Phantoms of *Drood* and *Rebecca:* The Uncanny Reencountered through Abraham and Torok's 'Cryptonymy.'" *Poetics Today* 13 (1992), 300–306.

GEORGE DU MAURIER

Peter Ibbetson, 1891

Reed, John R. *Victorian Will,* 372–74.

Trilby, 1894

Auerbach, Emily. *Maestros, Dilettantes, and Philistines,* 68–72.

MAUREEN DUFFY

Change, 1987

Brimstone, Lyndie. "'Keepers of History': The Novels of Maureen Duffy," in Mark Lilly, ed., *Lesbian and Gay Writing,* 43–44.

Gor Saga, 1981

Brimstone, Lyndie. "'Keepers of History': The Novels of Maureen Duffy," in Mark Lilly, ed., *Lesbian and Gay Writing,* 36–38.
Newman, Jenny. "Mary and the Monster: Mary Shelley's *Frankenstein* and

Maureen Duffy's *Gor Saga*," in Lucie Armitt, ed., *Where No Man Has Gone Before*, 85–96.

Sizemore, Christine W. "Neanderthals, Human Gorillas and Their Fathers: Crossing Scientific Boundaries in Doris Lessing's *The Fifth Child* and Maureen Duffy's *Gor Saga*." *Doris Lessing Newsl* 15:1 (1993), 3, 7, 10, 14.

Housespy, 1978

Brimstone, Lyndie. " 'Keepers of History': The Novels of Maureen Duffy," in Mark Lilly, ed., *Lesbian and Gay Writing*, 35–36.

I Want to Go to Moscow, 1973

Brimstone, Lyndie. " 'Keepers of History': The Novels of Maureen Duffy," in Mark Lilly, ed., *Lesbian and Gay Writing*, 33–34.

Londoners, 1983

Brimstone, Lyndie. " 'Keepers of History': The Novels of Maureen Duffy," in Mark Lilly, ed., *Lesbian and Gay Writing*, 40–43.

Love Child, 1971

Brimstone, Lyndie. " 'Keepers of History': The Novels of Maureen Duffy," in Mark Lilly, ed., *Lesbian and Gay Writing*, 32–33.

The Microcosm, 1966

Brimstone, Lyndie. " 'Keepers of History': The Novels of Maureen Duffy," in Mark Lilly, ed., *Lesbian and Gay Writing*, 28–30.

The Paradox Players, 1967

Brimstone, Lyndie. " 'Keepers of History': The Novels of Maureen Duffy," in Mark Lilly, ed., *Lesbian and Gay Writing*, 30–31.

Scarborough Fear, 1982

Brimstone, Lyndie. " 'Keepers of History': The Novels of Maureen Duffy," in Mark Lilly, ed., *Lesbian and Gay Writing*, 38–40.

The Single Eye, 1964

Brimstone, Lyndie. " 'Keepers of History': The Novels of Maureen Duffy," in Mark Lilly, ed., *Lesbian and Gay Writing*, 27–28.

That's How It Was, 1962

Brimstone, Lyndie. " 'Keepers of History': The Novels of Maureen Duffy," in Mark Lilly, ed., *Lesbian and Gay Writing*, 25–27.

Wounds, 1969

Brimstone, Lyndie. " 'Keepers of History': The Novels of Maureen Duffy," in Mark Lilly, ed., *Lesbian and Gay Writing*, 31–32.

LAWRENCE DURRELL

The Alexandria Quartet, 1961

Alexander, Marguerite. *Flights from Realism,* 74–82.

Alexandre-Garner, Corinne. "The Triangle of Love, Incest, and Writing," in Michael H. Begnal, ed., *On Miracle Ground,* 52–57.

Bergonzi, Bernard. *Wartime and Aftermath,* 119–22.

Boone, Joseph A. "Mappings of Male Desire in Durrell's *Alexandria Quartet:* Homoerotic Negotiations in the Colonial Narrative," in Laura Claridge and Elizabeth Langland, eds., *Out of Bounds,* 316–66.

Bowen, Roger. "Closing the 'Toybox': Orientalism and Empire in the *Alexandria Quartet." Stud in the Liter Imagination* 24:1 (1991), 9–17.

Briganti, Chiara. "Lawrence Durrell and the Vanishing Author," in Michael H. Begnal, ed., *On Miracle Ground,* 41–51.

Fertile, Candace. "Joshua Samuel Scobie: A Celebration of Life," in Betsy Nichols et al., eds., *Selected Essays,* 50–59.

Fertile, Candace. "The Role of the Writer in Lawrence Durrell's Fiction," in Michael H. Begnal, ed., *On Miracle Ground,* 64–69.

Kellman, Steven G. "Sailing to Alexandria: The Reader in/of Durrell's Byzantine *Quartet,"* in Frank L. Kersnowski, ed., *Into the Labyrinth,* 117–23.

Kostkowska, Justyna. "Physics and the *Alexandria Quartet* by Lawrence Durrell." *Zagadnienia Rodzajów Literackich* 32:2 (1989), 83–96.

Nambiar, C. Ravindran. "The Resonance of India in the Novels of Durrell." *Liter Criterion* 27:1–2 (1992), 44–47.

Nichols, James R. "The Risen Angels in Durrell's Fallen Women: The Fortunate Fall and Calvinism in Lawrence Durrell's *Quincunx* and *The Alexandria Quartet,"* in Michael H. Begnal, ed., *On Miracle Ground,* 179–86.

Peirce, Carol. "Durrell's Festive Comedy: 'Very Reverent Sport,'" in Betsy Nichols et al., eds., *Selected Essays,* 22–38.

Peirce, Carol. "'One other gaudy night': Lawrence Durrell's Elizabethan *Quartet,"* in Frank L. Kersnowski, ed., *Into the Labyrinth,* 101–14.

Peirce, Carol. "That 'one book there, a Plutarch': Of *Isis* and *Osiris* in *The Alexandria Quartet,"* in Michael H. Begnal, ed., *On Miracle Ground,* 79–91.

Robillard, Douglas, Jr. "The Alchemist of *The Alexandria Quartet." Cauda Pavonis* 8:2 (1989), 7–9.

Woods, David M. "Love and Meaning in *The Alexandria Quartet:* Some Tantric Perspectives," in Michael H. Begnal, ed., *On Miracle Ground,* 93–111.

The Avignon Quintet, 1974–1985

Alexandre-Garner, Corinne. "The Triangle of Love, Incest, and Writing," in Michael H. Begnal, ed., *On Miracle Ground,* 57–61.

Begnal, Michael. *"The Avignon Quintet:* Durrell Meets Pursewarden

Meets Lewis Carroll." *Stud in the Liter Imagination* 24:1 (1991), 119–24.

Begnal, Michael H. "The Mystery of the Templars in *The Avignon Quintet,*" in Michael H. Begnal, ed., *On Miracle Ground,* 155–64.

Closter, Susan Vander. "Writer as Painter in Lawrence Durrell's *Avignon Quintet,*" in Michael H. Begnal, ed., *On Miracle Ground,* 166–77.

Fertile, Candace. "The Role of the Writer in Lawrence Durrell's Fiction," in Michael H. Begnal, ed., *On Miracle Ground,* 69–70, 73–75.

Gibaldi, Ann. "Entropy in Durrell's *Avignon Quintet:* Theme and Structure in *Sebastian* and *Quinx.*" *Stud in the Liter Imagination* 24:1 (1991), 101–6.

Godshalk, William L. "Lawrence Durrell's Game in *The Avignon Quintet,*" in Michael H. Begnal, ed., *On Miracle Ground,* 187–99.

Kaczvinsky, Donald P. "Classical and Medieval Sources for Lawrence Durrell's *Livia.*" *Notes on Contemp Lit* 23:2 (1993), 11–12.

Nambiar, C. Ravindran. "The Resonance of India in the Novels of Durrell." *Liter Criterion* 27:1–2 (1992), 47–49.

Olson, Danel. "Sex and Comedy in Lawrence Durrell's *Avignon Quintet,*" in Betsy Nichols et al., eds., *Selected Essays,* 92–101.

Balthazar, 1958

Godshalk, William. "*Balthazar:* A Comedy of Surrogation," in Betsy Nichols et al., eds., *Selected Essays,* 81–90.

The Black Book, 1938

Christensen, Peter G. "Social and Anti-Social Comedy in Lawrence Durrell's Early Work," in Betsy Nichols et al., eds., *Selected Essays,* 115–20.

Fertile, Candace. "The Role of the Writer in Lawrence Durrell's Fiction," in Michael H. Begnal, ed., *On Miracle Ground,* 63–64.

MacNiven, Ian S. "Lawerence and Durrell: 'ON THE SAME TRAM,'" in Keith Cushman and Dennis Jackson, eds., *D. H. Lawrence's Literary Inheritors,* 63–66.

MacNiven, Ian S. "Pied Piper of Death: Method and Theme in the Early Novels," in Michael H. Begnal, ed., *On Miracle Ground,* 34–39.

The Dark Labyrinth, 1947

Dickson, Gregory. "The Narrator in *The Dark Labyrinth,*" in Frank L. Kersnowski, ed., *Into the Labyrinth,* 63–72.

Livia, 1978

Kersnowski, Frank. "B is for Babylon and Banana Peel," in Betsy Nichols et al., eds., *Selected Essays,* 61–70.

Raper, Julius Rowan. "The Philosopher's Stone and Durrell's Psychological Vision in *Monsieur* and *Livia.*" *Twentieth Cent Lit* 36 (1990), 419–32.

Monsieur; or, The Prince of Darkness, 1974

> Fertile, Candace. "The Role of the Writer in Lawrence Durrell's Fiction," in Michael H. Begnal, ed., *On Miracle Ground,* 70–71.
>
> Raper, Julius Rowan. "The Philosopher's Stone and Durrell's Psychological Vision in *Monsieur* and *Livia.*" *Twentieth Cent Lit* 36 (1990), 419–32.
>
> Spinks, C. W. "Durrell's *Monsieur:* Gnosis, Trickster, and the Othering Side," in Betsy Nichols et al., eds., *Selected Essays,* 121–31.

Mountolive, 1958

> Hollahan, Eugene. "Who Wrote *Mountolive?* The Same One Who Wrote 'Swann in Love,'" in Michael H. Begnal, ed., *On Miracle Ground,* 113–29.

Nunquam, 1970

> Kaczvinsky, Donald P. "'The True Birth of Free Man': Culture and Civilization in *Tunc-Nunquam,*" in Michael H. Begnal, ed., *On Miracle Ground,* 140–51.
>
> Kersnowski, Frank. "Authorial Conscience in *Tunc* and *Nunquam,*" in Michael H. Begnal, ed., *On Miracle Ground,* 133–38.
>
> Thomas, Gordon K. "Black Parody: The 'Gothic Frankensteinery' of *Nunquam,*" in Betsy Nichols et al., eds., *Selected Essays,* 71–80.

Panic Spring, 1937

> MacNiven, Ian S. "Pied Piper of Death: Method and Theme in the Early Novels," in Michael H. Begnal, ed., *On Miracle Ground,* 29–34.

Pied Piper of Lovers, 1935

> MacNiven, Ian S. "Pied Piper of Death: Method and Theme in the Early Novels," in Michael H. Begnal, ed., *On Miracle Ground,* 25–28.

The Revolt of Aphrodite, 1970

> Christensen, Peter G. "The Hazards of Intellectual Burglary in Durrell's *The Revolt of Aphrodite.*" *Stud in the Liter Imagination* 24:1 (1991), 41–54.
>
> Kaczvinsky, Donald P. "'The True Birth of Free Man': Culture and Civilization in *Tunc-Nunquam,*" in Michael H. Begnal, ed., *On Miracle Ground,* 140–51.

Sebastian; or, Ruling Passions, 1983

> Raper, Julius Rowan. "Durrell's *Sebastian:* The Novel of Transferences." *Stud in the Liter Imagination* 24:1 (1991), 109–17.

Tunc, 1968

> Kaczvinsky, Donald P. "'The True Birth of Free Man': Culture and Civilization in *Tunc-Nunquam,*" in Michael H. Begnal, ed., *On Miracle Ground,* 140–51.
>
> Kersnowski, Frank. "Authorial Conscience in *Tunc* and *Nunquam,*" in Michael H. Begnal, ed., *On Miracle Ground,* 133–38.

MARIA EDGEWORTH

The Absentee, 1812

> Dunleavy, Janet Egleson. "Maria Edgeworth and the Novel of Manners," in Bege K. Bowers and Barbara Brothers, eds., *Reading and Writing,* 61–63.

Belinda, 1801

> Dunleavy, Janet Egleson. "Maria Edgeworth and the Novel of Manners," in Bege K. Bowers and Barbara Brothers, eds., *Reading and Writing,* 56–60.
>
> Perry, Ruth. "Colonizing the Breast: Sexuality and Maternity in Eighteenth-Century England." *Eighteenth-Cent Life* 16:1 (1992), 205–6.
>
> Schaffer, Julie. "Not Subordinate: Empowering Women in the Marriage Plot—The Novels of Frances Burney, Maria Edgeworth, and Jane Austen." *Criticism* 34 (1992), 61–64.

Castle Rackrent, 1800

> Dunleavy, Janet Egleson. "Maria Edgeworth and the Novel of Manners," in Bege K. Bowers and Barbara Brothers, eds., *Reading and Writing,* 52–56.
>
> Le Gros, Bernard. "Maria Edgeworth: *Castle Rackrent,*" in Jacqueline Genet, ed., *The Big House in Ireland,* 61–70.
>
> McCormack, W. J. "Setting and Ideology: with Reference to the Fiction of Maria Edgeworth," in Otto Rauchbauer, ed., *Ancestral Voices,* 43–48.
>
> Saito, Yasushi. "Looking for Mr Good-Landlord: *Castle Rackrent* and the Union." *Shiron* 30 (1991), 1–14.
>
> Weekes, Ann Owens. *Irish Women Writers,* 36–59.

Helen, 1834

> Ackley, Katherine Anne. "Violence Against Women in the Novels of Early British Women Writers," in Dale Spender, ed., *Living by the Pen,* 221–23.
>
> Dunleavy, Janet Egleson. "Maria Edgeworth and the Novel of Manners," in Bege K. Bowers and Barbara Brothers, eds., *Reading and Writing,* 63–65.

Patronage, 1814

> McCormack, W. J. "Setting and Ideology: with Reference to the Fiction of Maria Edgeworth," in Otto Rauchbauer, ed., *Ancestral Voices,* 53–56.

GEORGE ELIOT

Adam Bede, 1859

> Adams, James Eli. "Gyp's Tale: On Sympathy, Silence, and Realism in *Adam Bede.*" *Dickens Stud Annual* 20 (1991), 227–39.
>
> Alley, Henry. "George Eliot and the Ambiguity of Murder." *Stud in the Novel* 25 (1993), 60–62.

Auerbach, Emily. *Maestros, Dilettantes, and Philistines,* 149–53.

Booth, Alison. *Greatness Engendered,* 126–28.

Brady, Kristin. *George Eliot,* 84–93.

Brown, Monika. "Dutch Painters and British Novel-Readers: *Adam Bede* in the Context of Victorian Cultural Literacy." *Victorians Inst J* 18 (1990), 113–29.

Carroll, Alicia. "Tried by Earthly Fires: Hetty Wesley, Hetty Sorrel, and *Adam Bede.*" *Nineteenth-Cent Lit* 44 (1989), 218–24.

Connors, Patricia E. "Arthurian Legend as a Source for George Eliot's *Adam Bede.*" *Round Table of the South Central Coll Engl Assoc* 28:2 (1989), 4–7.

Dale, Peter Allan. *In Pursuit of a Scientific Culture,* 89–94.

Dillon, Steven. "George Eliot and the Feminine Gift." *Stud in Engl Lit, 1500–1900* 32 (1992), 708–13.

Gunn, Daniel P. "Dutch Painting and the Simple Truth in *Adam Bede.*" *Stud in the Novel* 24 (1992), 366–77.

Haight, Gordon S. *George Eliot's Originals,* 9–13, 107–10.

Handley, Graham. *George Eliot's Midlands,* 41–43, 48–50, 60–63, 96–100, 113–16, 160–65, 177–82, 225–29.

Handley, Graham. *State of the Art George Eliot,* 25–28, 52–55, 70–74.

Hardy, Barbara. "The Talkative Woman in Shakespeare, Dickens and George Eliot," in Sally Minogue, ed., *Problems for Feminist Criticism,* 32–34.

Huggins, Cynthia. "*Adam Bede:* Author, Narrator and Narrative." *George Eliot R* 23 (1992), 35–38.

Johnstone, Peggy Fitzhugh. "Self-Disorder and Aggression in *Adam Bede:* A Kohutian Analysis." *Mosaic* 22:4 (1989), 59–70.

Klein, William H. "The Triumph of Spirit over Law: Free Will versus Determinism in *Adam Bede.*" *George Eliot Fellowship R* 21 (1990), 80–89.

Krueger, Christine L. *The Reader's Repentance,* 251–63.

Lovesey, Oliver. *The Clerical Character,* 36–47.

McMaster, Juliet. *The Index of the Mind,* 19–20.

McSweeney, Kerry. *George Eliot,* 62–74.

Mitchell, Judith. "George Eliot and the Problematic of Female Beauty." *Mod Lang Stud* 20:3 (1990), 17–20.

Morris, Virginia B. *Double Jeopardy,* 75–81.

Neetens, Wim. *Writing and Democracy,* 24–32.

Norbelie, Barbro Almqvist. '*Oppressive Narrowness,*' 84–111.

Page, Norman. *Speech in the English Novel,* 134–37.

Pettit, Alexander. "Sympathetic Criminality in the Mid-Victorian Novel." *Dickens Stud Annual* 19 (1990), 282–96.

Wallace, Anne D. *Walking, Literature, and English Culture,* 202–4.

Daniel Deronda, 1876

Alley, Henry. "George Eliot and the Ambiguity of Murder." *Stud in the Novel* 25 (1993), 66–71.

Auerbach, Emily. *Maestros, Dilettantes, and Philistines,* 165–78.

Boardman, Michael M. *Narrative Innovation,* 105–10, 120–45.

Bodenheimer, Rosemarie. "Ambition and Its Audiences: George Eliot's Performing Figures." *Victorian Stud* 34 (1990), 25–31.

Booth, Alison. *Greatness Engendered,* 236–64, 275–84.

Brady, Kristin. *George Eliot,* 174–90.

Brantlinger, Patrick. "Nations and Novels: Disraeli, George Eliot, and Orientalism." *Victorian Stud* 35 (1992), 268–73.

Butler, Lance St. John. *Victorian Doubt,* 134–59.

Crosby, Christina. *The Ends of History,* 12–43.

Cvetkovich, Ann. *Mixed Feelings,* 128–64.

Dale, Peter Allan. *In Pursuit of a Scientific Culture,* 150–63.

DeMaria, Joanne Long. "The Wondrous Marriages of *Daniel Deronda:* Gender, Work, and Love." *Stud in the Novel* 22 (1990), 403–15.

Elam, Diane. *Romancing the Postmodern,* 134–36.

Garg, Kiran. "The Common Yearning of Womanhood: The Images of Women in the Novels of George Eliot." *Panjab Univ Res Bull* 21:2 (1990), 87–94.

Goldberg, S. L. *Agents and Lives,* 118–49.

Gray, Beryl. *George Eliot and Music,* 100–119.

Haight, Gordon S. *George Eliot's Originals,* 68–77.

Handley, Graham. *State of the Art George Eliot,* 25–27, 30–32, 37–39, 100–102.

Harrison, James. "The Root of the Matter with *Daniel Deronda.*" *Philol Q* 68 (1989), 509–22.

Hirsch, Marianne. *The Mother/Daughter Plot,* 68–88.

Hochberg, Shifra. "Onomastics and the German Literary Ancestry of Daniel Deronda's Mother." *Engl Lang Notes* 28:1 (1990), 46–50.

Lessenich, Rolf. "Jew, Artist, Providential Leader: Neoromantic Aspects in George Eliot's *Daniel Deronda.*" *Literaturwissenschaftliches Jahrbuch im Auftrage der Görres-Gesellschaft* 30 (1989), 123–40.

Levin, Amy K. *The Suppressed Sister,* 89–92.

Linehan, Katherine Bailey. "Mixed Politics: The Critique of Imperialism in *Daniel Deronda.*" *Texas Stud in Lit and Lang* 34 (1992), 323–44.

Litvak, Joseph. *Caught in the Act,* 147–94.

Liu, Joyce. "Pregnant Movements in the Past: History and the Narrative in George Eliot's *Daniel Deronda.*" *Fu Jen Stud* 23 (1990), 116–35.

Lovesey, Oliver. *The Clerical Character,* 98–114.

McSweeney, Kerry. *George Eliot,* 133–41.

Martin, Carol A. "Contemporary Critics and Judaism in *Daniel Deronda.*" *Victorian Periodicals R* 21:3 (1988), 90–107.

Meyer, Susan. " 'Safely to Their Own Borders': Proto-Zionism, Feminism, and Nationalism in *Daniel Deronda.*" *ELH* 60 (1993), 733–56.

Morris, Virginia B. *Double Jeopardy,* 81–87.

Reilly, Jim. *Shadowtime,* 122–32.

Rosenman, Ellen. "The House and the Home: Money, Women and the Family in the *Banker's Magazine* and *Daniel Deronda.*" *Women's Stud* 17 (1990), 179–90.

Rowe, Margaret Moan. "Melting Outlines in *Daniel Deronda.*" *Stud in the Novel* 22 (1990), 10–17.

Shelston, Alan. "Were They Beautiful?: *Far from the Madding Crowd* and *Daniel Deronda.*" *Thomas Hardy J* 8:2 (1992), 65–67.

Sorensen, Katherine M. "Daniel Deronda & George Eliot's Ministers." *Victorians Inst J* 19 (1991), 89–106.

Stewart, Garrett. "'Beckoning Death': *Daniel Deronda* and the Plotting of Reading," in Regina Barreca, ed., *Sex and Death,* 69–100.

Tucker, John L. "Prophecy, Originality, and Authorship in *Daniel Deronda.*" *Essays in Lit* (Macomb) 17 (1990), 190–201.

Tuss, Alex J., SM. *The Inward Revolution,* 142–58.

Vrettos, Athena. "From Neurosis to Narrative: The Private Life of the Nerves in *Villette* and *Daniel Deronda.*" *Victorian Stud* 33 (1990), 560–79.

Weber, Jean Jacques. *Critical Analysis of Fiction,* 50–52.

Weisser, Susan Ostrov. "Gwendolen's Hidden Wound: Sexual Possibilities and Impossibilities in *Daniel Deronda.*" *Mod Lang Stud* 20:3 (1990), 3–12.

Williams, Meg Harris, and Margot Waddell. *The Chamber of Maiden Thought,* 159–69.

Wolstenholme, Susan. *Gothic (Re)Visions,* 105–26.

Felix Holt, 1866

Blin-Hetherington, Lynn. "Mrs. Transome or the Absence of Pardon." *Mythes, Croyances et Religions dans le Monde Anglo-Saxon* 7 (1989), 50–60.

Booth, Alison. *Greatness Engendered,* 204–37.

Booth, Alison. "Not All Men Are Selfish and Cruel: *Felix Holt* as a Feminist Novel," in Antony H. Harrison and Beverly Taylor, eds., *Gender and Discourse,* 143–58.

Brady, Kristin. *George Eliot,* 135–49.

Drexler, Peter. *Literatur, Recht, Kriminalität,* 153–56.

Glage, Liselotte. "Was ist radikal an George Eliots Roman *Felix Holt, the Radical?*," in Gregory Claeys and Liselotte Glage, eds., *Radikalismus in Literatur und Gesellschaft,* 219–42.

Handley, Graham. *George Eliot's Midlands,* 5–8, 30–33, 92–96, 122–26, 133–38, 210–14, 233–35.

Handley, Graham. *State of the Art George Eliot,* 9–11.

Harvie, Christopher. *The Centre of Things,* 57–60, 78–82.

Krueger, Christine L. *The Reader's Repentance,* 285–306.

Lovesey, Oliver. *The Clerical Character,* 76–83.

McSweeney, Kerry. *George Eliot,* 120–24.

Mahanta, Aparna. "Women, Marriage and Vocation: A Feminist Approach to the Novels of George Eliot," in Jasodhara Bagchi, ed., *Literature, Society and Ideology,* 224–27.

Neetens, Wim. *Writing and Democracy,* 32–35.

Thompson, Andrew. "George Eliot, Dante, and Moral Choice in *Felix Holt, the Radical.*" *Mod Lang R* 86 (1991), 553–66.

Wilt, Judith. "Felix Holt, the Killer: A Reconstruction." *Victorian Stud* 35 (1991), 51–67.

Middlemarch, 1872

Alley, Henry. "George Eliot and the Ambiguity of Murder." *Stud in the Novel* 25 (1993), 63–66.

Auerbach, Emily. *Maestros, Dilettantes, and Philistines,* 158–65.

Bernstein, Carol L. *The Celebration of Scandal,* 177–79.

Black, Michael. "A Bit of Both: George Eliot & D. H. Lawrence." *Crit R* (Melbourne) 29 (1989), 90–103.

Blythe, David-Everett. "Eliot's *Middlemarch.*" *Explicator* 48 (1989), 22–23.

Boardman, Michael M. *Narrative Innovation,* 114–20.

Bodenheimer, Rosemary. "George Eliot and the Power of Evil-Speaking." *Dickens Stud Annual* 20 (1991), 214–21.

Booth, Alison. *Greatness Engendered,* 40–43, 105–8, 126–28, 151–53, 157–61, 163–67.

Booth, Alison. "*Middlemarch, Bleak House,* and Gender in the Nineteenth-Century Novel Course," in Kathleen Blake, ed., *Approaches,* 129–37.

Bowers, Bege K. "George Eliot's *Middlemarch* and the 'Text' of the Novel of Manners," in Bege K. Bowers and Barbara Brothers, eds., *Reading and Writing,* 105–17.

Brady, Kristin. *George Eliot,* 159–74.

Bystrom, Valerie, and Michael Kischner. "Really Reading *Middlemarch* in a Community College," in Kathleen Blake, ed., *Approaches,* 129–37.

Campbell, Elizabeth A. "Relative Truths: Character in *Middlemarch,*" in Kathleen Blake, ed., *Approaches,* 154–61.

Carlisle, Janice. "Reading *Middlemarch,* Then and Now," in Kathleen Blake, ed., *Approaches,* 98–108.

Dale, Peter Allan. *In Pursuit of a Scientific Culture,* 136–50.

Dillon, Steven. "George Eliot and the Feminine Gift." *Stud in Engl Lit, 1500–1900* 32 (1992), 713–19.

Durey, Jill Felicity. "Intermodality in the Novels of George Eliot, Lev Tolstoy and Gustave Flaubert." *Revue de Littérature Comparée* 66 (1992), 185, 187–88, 190–91.

Ermarth, Elizabeth Deeds. "Teaching *Middlemarch* as Narrative," in Kathleen Blake, ed., *Approaches,* 30–38.

Feinberg, Monica L. "Scenes of Marital Life: The Middle March of Extratextual Reading." *Victorian Newsl* 77 (1990), 16–26.

Furst, Lilian R. *Through the Lens of the Reader,* 111–12, 141–43.

Garg, Kiran. "The Common Yearning of Womanhood: The Images of Women in the Novels of George Eliot." *Panjab Univ Res Bull* 21:2 (1990), 87–94.

Gould, Carol S. "Plato, George Eliot, and Moral Narcissism." *Philos and Lit* 14 (1990), 24–37.

Graver, Suzanne. "'Incarnate History': The Feminisms of *Middlemarch*," in Kathleen Blake, ed., *Approaches*, 64–74.

Gray, Beryl. *George Eliot and Music*, 79–99.

Greiner, Walter. "'Shapen After the Average': Zur Macht der Mediokrität in George Eliots *Middlemarch*." *Zeitschrift für Anglistik und Amerikanistik* 41 (1993), 40–53.

Haight, Gordon S. *George Eliot's Originals*, 22–37, 38–57, 58–67.

Handley, Graham. *George Eliot's Midlands*, 34–39, 80–85, 126–31, 138–44, 190–99, 214–20.

Handley, Graham. *State of the Art George Eliot*, 15–17, 36–40, 56–60, 68–77, 87–91, 97–104.

Hasan, Noorul. "*Middlemarch, Tess*, and the Marriage Question," in Jasodhara Bagchi, ed., *Literature, Society and Ideology*, 233–43.

Havely, Cicely Palser. "Authorization in *Middlemarch*." *Essays in Criticism* 40 (1990), 303–20.

Heilman, Robert Bechtold. *The Workings of Fiction*, 117–23.

Hochberg, Shifra. "The Vista from Dorothea's Boudoir Window and a Coleridgian Source." *Engl Lang Notes* 29:3 (1992), 41–45.

Hochman, Baruch. "Recon/Decon/Structing *Middlemarch*," in Kathleen Blake, ed., *Approaches*, 39–50.

Johnston, Judith. "*Middlemarch*: Medieval Discourse and Will Ladislaw." *Sydney Stud in Engl* 15 (1989–90), 125–39.

Johnston, Judith. "*Middlemarch*'s Dorothea Brooke and Medieval Hagiography." *George Eliot R* 23 (1992), 40–45.

Jumeau, Alain. "Les premiers chemins de fer, la réalité et la fiction: Fanny Kemble (*Record of a Girlhood*), Samuel Smiles (*Lives of the Engineers*) et George Eliot (*Middlemarch*)." *Etudes Anglaises* 43 (1990), 409–12.

Leng, Andrew. "Dorothea Brooke's Awakening Consciousness and the Pre-Raphaelite Aesthetic in *Middlemarch*." *AUMLA* 75 (1991), 52–62.

Levin, Amy K. *The Suppressed Sister*, 83–89.

Litvak, Joseph. *Caught in the Act*, 147–49.

Logan, Peter M. "Conceiving the Body: Realism and Medicine in *Middlemarch*." *Hist of the Human Sciences* 4 (1991), 197–222.

Lops, Marina. "Femminile, flusso e forma in George Eliot," in A. Arru and M. T. Chialant, eds., *Il racconto delle donne*, 206–12.

Lorenz, Paul H. "Technology and Development: Opposition to the Railway in *Middlemarch*." *George Eliot Fellowship R* 22 (1991), 21–23.

Lovesey, Oliver. *The Clerical Character*, 84–97.

McClure, Laura. "On Knowing Greek: George Eliot and the Classical Tradition." *Classical and Mod Lit* 13 (1993), 139–56.

McCormack, Kathleen. "*Middlemarch*: Dorothea's Husbands in the Vatican Museums." *Victorians Inst J* 20 (1992), 75–87.

McGhee, Richard D. "'To Be Wise Herself': The Widowing of Dorothea Brooke in George Eliot's *Middlemarch*," in JoAnna Stephens Mink and Janet Doubler Ward, eds., *Joinings and Disjoinings*, 77–95.

McMaster, Juliet. "'A Microscope Directed on a Water-Drop': Chapter 19," in Kathleen Blake, ed., *Approaches,* 109–16.

McMaster, Juliet. "Will Ladislaw and Other Italians with White Mice." *Victorian R* 16:2 (1990), 1–7.

McSweeney, Kerry. *George Eliot,* 124–30.

Martin, Carol A. "Reading *Middlemarch* in Installments as Victorian Readers Did," in Kathleen Blake, ed., *Approaches,* 39–50.

Matus, Jill L. "The Iconography of Motherhood: Word and Image in *Middlemarch.*" *Engl Stud in Canada* 17 (1991), 283–98.

Matus, Jill L. "Saint Teresa, Hysteria, and *Middlemarch.*" *J of the Hist of Sexuality* 1:2 (1990), 215–40.

Miller, J. Hillis. "Teaching *Middlemarch:* Close Reading and Theory," in Kathleen Blake, ed., *Approaches,* 51–63.

Miller, J. Hillis. *Victorian Subjects,* 81–84, 229–35.

Mitchell, Judith. "George Eliot and the Problematic of Female Beauty." *Mod Lang Stud* 20:3 (1990), 23–26.

Moldstad, David. "Old Age in *Middlemarch,*" in Kathleen Blake, ed., *Approaches,* 123–28.

Mooneyham, Laura. "Closure and Escape: The Questionable Comedy of George Eliot's *Middlemarch.*" *Genre* 24 (1991), 137–52.

Moring, Meg M. "George Eliot's Scrupulous Research: The Facts Behind Eliot's Use of the *Keepsake* in *Middlemarch.*" *Victorian Periodicals R* 26 (1993), 19–23.

Morris, Timothy. "The Dialogic Universe of *Middlemarch.*" *Stud in the Novel* 22 (1990), 282–95.

Moseley, Merritt. "A Fuller Sort of Companionship: Defending Old-Fashioned Qualities," in Kathleen Blake, ed., *Approaches,* 75–84.

Neale, Catherine. "Torpedoes, Tapirs and Tortoises: Scientific Discourse in *Middlemarch.*" *Crit Survey* 2:1 (1990), 57–62.

Nicholes, Joseph. "Dorothea in the Moated Grange: Millais's *Mariana* and the *Middlemarch* Window-Scenes." *Victorians Inst J* 20 (1992), 93–119.

Nicholes, Joseph. "Vertical Context in *Middlemarch:* George Eliot's Civil War of the Soul." *Nineteenth-Cent Lit* 45 (1990), 144–75.

Novy, Marianne. "*Middlemarch* and George Eliot's Female (Re)Vision of Shakespeare." *JEGP* 90 (1991), 61–78.

Phelan, James. *Reading People,* 198–202.

Ralph, Phyllis C. *Victorian Transformations,* 146–58.

Rampton, David. "The Doctors' Plot: Some Classic Nineteenth-Century Novels Revisited." *Mod Lang Stud* 22:4 (1992), 63–66.

Reed, John R. *Victorian Will,* 322–27.

Reilly, Jim. *Shadowtime,* 45–51, 120–22.

Rudnik-Smalbraak, Marijke. "The One and Another: George Eliot's Dialogic Incarnations." *Neophilologus* 77 (1993), 504–6.

Scholes, Robert. "The Novel as Ethical Paradigm?," in Mark Spilka and Caroline McCracken-Flesher, eds., *Why the Novel Matters,* 209–14.

Tambling, Jeremy. "*Middlemarch,* Realism and the Birth of the Clinic." *ELH* 57 (1990), 939–58.

Thomas, Jeanie. "A Novel 'Written for Grown-Up People': *Middlemarch* in the Undergraduate Classroom," in Kathleen Blake, ed., *Approaches*, 162–70.

Tick, Stanley. " 'The Very Nature of a Conclusion,' " in Kathleen Blake, ed., *Approaches*, 146–53.

Tindall, Gillian. *Countries of the Mind*, 174–76.

Tucker, John L. "George Eliot's Reflexive Text: Three Tonalities in the Narrative Voice of *Middlemarch*." *Stud in Engl Lit, 1500–1900* 31 (1991), 773–88.

VanArsdel, Rosemary T. "*Middlemarch* and the Modern American Student: Making the Cultural Leap," in Kathleen Blake, ed., *Approaches*, 138–45.

Warhol, Robyn R. "Before We Go in Depth: A Narratological Approach," in Kathleen Blake, ed., *Approaches*, 138–45.

Watts, Cedric. *Literature and Money*, 74–76.

Weber, Jean Jacques. *Critical Analysis of Fiction*, 49–63.

Wiesenfarth, Joseph. *Gothic Manners*, 103–19.

Wright, T. R. *George Eliot's "Middlemarch,"* 25–92.

The Mill on the Floss, 1860

Auerbach, Emily. *Maestros, Dilettantes, and Philistines*, 154–58.

Bodenheimer, Rosemary. "George Eliot and the Power of Evil-Speaking." *Dickens Stud Annual* 20 (1991), 212–14.

Booth, Alison. *Greatness Engendered*, 143–52.

Brady, Kristin. *George Eliot*, 94–106.

Carlisle, Janice. "The Mirror in *The Mill on the Floss*: Toward a Reading of Autobiography as Discourse." *Stud in the Liter Imagination* 23:2 (1990), 177–96.

Cervetti, Nancy. "Dickens and Eliot in Dialogue: Empty Space, Angels and Maggie Tulliver." *Victorian Newsl* 80 (1991), 18–23.

Cohen, Paula Marantz. *The Daughter's Dilemma*, 115–49.

Dale, Peter Allan. *In Pursuit of a Scientific Culture*, 94–101.

David, Gail. *Female Heroism*, 199–221.

De Jong, Mary G. "Different Voices: Moral Conflict in *Jane Eyre, The Mill on the Floss,* and *Romola*." *CEA Critic* 51:2–3 (1989), 58–60.

Dillon, Steven. "George Eliot and the Feminine Gift." *Stud in Engl Lit, 1500–1900* 32 (1992), 708–13.

Durey, Jill Felicity. "Intermodality in the Novels of George Eliot, Lev Tolstoy and Gustave Flaubert." *Revue de Littérature Comparée* 66 (1992), 179–81, 184–85, 188, 190–91.

Elam, Diane. *Romancing the Postmodern*, 128–33.

Fludernik, Monika. "Subversive Irony: Reflectorization, Trustworthy Narration and Dead-Pan Narrative in *The Mill on the Floss*." *REAL: Yrbk of Res in Engl and Am Lit* 8 (1991/92), 157–82.

Fraiman, Susan. "*The Mill on the Floss*, the Critics, and the *Bildungsroman*." *PMLA* 108 (1993), 136–47.

Fraiman, Susan. *Unbecoming Women*, 121–41.

Garg, Kiran. "The Common Yearning of Womanhood: The Images of Women in the Novels of George Eliot." *Panjab Univ Res Bull* 21:2 (1990), 87–94.

Goldberg, S. L. *Agents and Lives*, 151–85.

Gray, Beryl. *George Eliot and Music*, 14–78.

Haight, Gordon S. *George Eliot's Originals*, 13–18.

Handley, Graham. *George Eliot's Midlands*, 18–28, 72–76, 116–21, 146–51, 171–74, 182–89, 229–32.

Handley, Graham. *State of the Art George Eliot*, 24–26, 96–98, 102–4.

Honig, Edith Lazaros. *Breaking the Angelic Image*, 67–70.

Johnstone, Peggy Ruth Fitzhugh. "Narcissistic Rage in *The Mill on the Floss*." *Lit and Psych* 36:1–2 (1990), 90–107.

Landa, José Angel Garcia. "The Chains of Semiosis: Semiotics, Marxism, and the Female Stereotypes in *The Mill on the Floss*." *Papers on Lang & Lit* 27 (1991), 32–49.

Law, Jules. "Water Rights and the 'crossing o' breeds': Chiastic Exchange in *The Mill on the Floss*," in Linda M. Shires, ed., *Rewriting the Victorians*, 52–66.

Levin, Amy K. *The Suppressed Sister*, 80–83.

Lops, Marina. "Femminile, flusso e forma in George Eliot," in A. Arru and M. T. Chialant, eds., *Il racconto delle donne*, 199–206.

Lovesey, Oliver. *The Clerical Character*, 56–66.

Ludwig, Mark. "George Eliot and the Trauma of Loss." *Essays in Lit* (Macomb) 19 (1992), 209–12.

Lumpkin, Ramona. "(Re)Visions of Virtue: Elizabeth Gaskell's *Moorland Cottage* and George Eliot's *The Mill on the Floss*." *Stud in the Novel* 23 (1991), 432–40.

MacKay, Carol Hanbery. "Controlling Death and Sex: Magnification v. the Rhetoric of Rules in Dickens and Thackeray," in Regina Barreca, ed., *Sex and Death*, 122–23.

McSweeney, Kerry. *George Eliot*, 88–97.

Mahanta, Aparna. "Women, Marriage and Vocation: A Feminist Approach to the Novels of George Eliot," in Jasodhara Bagchi, ed., *Literature, Society and Ideology*, 222–24.

Miller, J. Hillis. *Victorian Subjects*, 292–99.

Mitchell, Judith. "George Eliot and the Problematic of Female Beauty." *Mod Lang Stud* 20:3 (1990), 20–23.

Norbelie, Barbro Almqvist. *'Oppressive Narrowness,'* 112–40.

Ortiz, Gloria. *The Dandy and the "Señorito,"* 40–41.

Philip, Ranjini. "Maggie, Tom and Oedipus: A Lacanian Reading of *The Mill on the Floss*." *Victorian Newsl* 82 (1992), 35–39.

Polhemus, Robert M. *Erotic Faith*, 168–95.

Postlethwaite, Diana. "Of Maggie, Mothers, Monsters, and Madonnas: Diving Deep in *The Mill on the Floss*." *Women's Stud* 20 (1992), 303–16.

Ralph, Phyllis C. *Victorian Transformations*, 133–46.

Reed, John R. *Victorian Will*, 318–22.

Smith, Jonathan. "The 'Wonderful Geological Story': Uniformitarianism and *The Mill on the Floss.*" *Papers on Lang & Lit* 27 (1991), 430–51.

Romola, 1863

Alley, Henry. "George Eliot and the Ambiguity of Murder." *Stud in the Novel* 25 (1993), 62–63.

Booth, Alison. *Greatness Engendered,* 168–203.

Brady, Kristin. *George Eliot,* 119–35.

Carpenter, Mary Wilson. "The Trouble with Romola," in Thais Morgan, ed., *Victorian Sages,* 105–28.

Cottereau, Serge. "Le *Romola* de George Eliot: trop d'histoire, ou trop peu?" *Caliban* 28 (1991), 101–5.

De Jong, Mary G. "Different Voices: Moral Conflict in *Jane Eyre, The Mill on the Floss,* and *Romola.*" *CEA Critic* 51:2–3 (1989), 60–63.

Elam, Diane. *Romancing the Postmodern,* 117–20.

Fraser, Hilary. *The Victorians and Renaissance Italy,* 206–10.

Handley, Graham. *State of the Art George Eliot,* 55–59, 97–99.

Krueger, Christine L. *The Reader's Repentance,* 262–85.

Lops, Marina. "Femminile, flusso e forma in George Eliot," in A. Arru and M. T. Chialant, eds., *Il racconto delle donne,* 206–12.

Lovesey, Oliver. *The Clerical Character,* 67–76.

McClure, Laura. "On Knowing Greek: George Eliot and the Classical Tradition." *Classical and Mod Lit* 13 (1993), 139–56.

McSweeney, Kerry. *George Eliot,* 98–105.

Mahanta, Aparna. "Women, Marriage and Vocation: A Feminist Approach to the Novels of George Eliot," in Jasodhara Bagchi, ed., *Literature, Society and Ideology,* 229–31.

Reed, John R. *Victorian Will,* 314–18.

Reilly, Jim. *Shadowtime,* 99–104, 110–21.

Winnett, Susan. "Coming Unstrung: Women, Men, Narrative, and Principles of Pleasure." *PMLA* 105 (1990), 512–15.

Woodring, Carl. *Nature into Art,* 118–19.

Scenes of Clerical Life, 1858

Auerbach, Emily. *Maestros, Dilettantes, and Philistines,* 143–49.

Bennett, J. W. "The Apprenticeship of George Eliot: Characterization as Case Study in 'Janet's Repentance.'" *Lit and Medicine* 9 (1990), 50–66.

Booth, Alison. *Greatness Engendered,* 117–20.

Brady, Kristin. *George Eliot,* 60–80.

Haight, Gordon S. *George Eliot's Originals,* 3–9, 105–7.

Handley, Graham. *George Eliot's Midlands,* 54–60.

Handley, Graham. *State of the Art George Eliot,* 34–36, 95–97.

Jumeau, Alain. "Images de la femme dans les *Scenes of Clerical Life* de George Eliot." *Cahiers Victoriens et Edouardiens* 31 (1990), 51–60.

Kidd, Millie M. "In Defense of Latimer: A Study of Narrative Technique in George Eliot's 'The Lifted Veil.'" *Victorian Newsl* 79 (1991), 37–40.

Krueger, Christine L. *The Reader's Repentance,* 243–51.

Lovesey, Oliver. *The Clerical Character,* 21–35.

Ludwig, Mark. "George Eliot and the Trauma of Loss." *Essays in Lit* (Macomb) 19 (1992), 205–9.

McCann, J. Clinton, Jr. "Disease and Cure in 'Janet's Repentance': George Eliot's Change of Mind." *Lit and Medicine* 9 (1990), 69–77.

McSweeney, Kerry. *George Eliot*, 55–61.

Morris, Virginia B. *Double Jeopardy*, 72–75.

Norbelie, Barbro Almqvist. *'Oppressive Narrowness,'* 58–83.

Williams, Meg Harris, and Margot Waddell. *The Chamber of Maiden Thought*, 150–53.

Silas Marner, 1861

Auerbach, Emily. *Maestros, Dilettantes, and Philistines*, 153–54.

Barrat, Alain. "George Eliot's Mixed Vision of Human Progress in *Silas Marner:* A Pessimistic Reading of the Novel." *Cahiers Victoriens et Edouardiens* 35 (1992), 193–200.

Boardman, Michael M. *Narrative Innovation*, 110–12.

Bonaparte, Felicia. "Carrying the Word of the Lord to the Gentiles: *Silas Marner* and the Translation of Scripture into a Secular Text." *Rel and Lit* 23:2 (1991), 39–58.

Booth, Alison. *Greatness Engendered*, 171–74.

Brady, Kristin. *George Eliot*, 108–18.

Buyniak, Victor O. "Eliot and Kraszewski: A Literary Connection?" *Selecta* 10 (1989), 30–36.

Dawson, Terence. " 'Light Enough to Trusten By': Structure and Experience in *Silas Marner.*" *Mod Lang R* 88 (1993), 26–45.

Handley, Graham. *George Eliot's Midlands*, 120–22, 155–60, 208–10.

Handley, Graham. *State of the Art George Eliot*, 98–100.

Heilman, Robert Bechtold. *The Workings of Fiction*, 230–40.

Lovesey, Oliver. *The Clerical Character*, 47–55.

McSweeney, Kerry. *George Eliot*, 62–69, 74–79.

Reed, John R. *Victorian Will*, 313–15.

Reilly, Jim. *Shadowtime*, 95–97.

Williams, Meg Harris, and Margot Waddell. *The Chamber of Maiden Thought*, 153–58.

Woodring, Carl. *Nature into Art*, 119–21.

SUSAN ERTZ

Charmed Circle, 1957

Baker, Niamh. *Happily Ever After?*, 59–61.

LEONORA EYLES

Margaret Protests, 1919

Joannou, Maroula. " 'The Woman in the Little House': Leonora Eyles and Socialist Feminism," in Angela Ingram and Daphne Patai, eds., *Rediscovering Forgotten Radicals*, 86–95.

F. W. FARRAR

Eric, or Little by Little, 1858

Bristow, Joseph. *Empire Boys,* 70–74.

J. G. FARRELL

The Siege of Krishnapur, 1973

Rao, A. V. Krishna. "History and the Art of Fiction: J. G. Farrell's Example—*The Siege of Krishnapur.*" *Liter Criterion* 23:3 (1988), 38–47.

The Singapore Grip, 1978

Hartveit, Lars. "The 'Jolting Passage over the Switched Points of History' and the Experience of Dislocation in J. G. Farrell's *The Singapore Grip.*" *Engl Stud* 70 (1989), 566–80.

Troubles, 1970

Cichofi, Anna. "History in J. G. Farrell's *Troubles.*" *Anglica Wratislaviensia* 19 (1991), 33–47.

Hartveit, Lars. "The Carnivalistic Impulse in J. G. Farrell's *Troubles.*" *Engl Stud* 73 (1992), 444–57.

MacPhail, Fiona. "Major and Majestic: J. G. Farrell's *Troubles,*" in Jacqueline Genet, ed., *The Big House in Ireland,* 243–52.

Scanlan, Margaret. *Traces of Another Time,* 50–60.

ELIZA FENWICK

Secresy; or, The Ruin on the Rock, 1795

Grundy, Isobel. "'A novel in a series of letters by a lady': Richardson and Some Richardsonian Novels," in Margaret Anne Doody and Peter Sabor, eds., *Samuel Richardson,* 233–35.

SUSAN FERRIER

Destiny, 1831

Fletcher, Loraine. "Great Expectations: Wealth and Inheritance in the Novels of Susan Ferrier." *Scottish Liter J* 16:2 (1989), 69–76.

The Inheritance, 1824

Fletcher, Loraine. "Great Expectations: Wealth and Inheritance in the Novels of Susan Ferrier." *Scottish Liter J* 16:2 (1989), 64–69.

Marriage, 1818

Fletcher, Loraine. "Great Expectations: Wealth and Inheritance in the Novels of Susan Ferrier." *Scottish Liter J* 16:2 (1989), 62–64.

Letley, Emma. *From Galt to Douglas Brown,* 56–58.

HENRY FIELDING

Amelia, 1752

Bell, Ian A. *Literature and Crime,* 216–27.

Bender, John. "The Novel and the Rise of the Penitentiary: Narrative and Ideology in Defoe, Gay, Hogarth, and Fielding," in H. George Hahn, ed., *The Country Myth,* 117–18.

Butler, Gerald J. *Henry Fielding,* 115–19.

Doody, Margaret A. "Work and Working People in Fielding's Novels." *The Age of Johnson* 4 (1991), 231–34.

Flanders, W. Austin. "Urban Life and the Early Novel," in H. George Hahn, ed., *The Country Myth,* 60–61.

Hall, K. G. *The Exalted Heroine,* 62–73.

Hilliard, Raymond F. "Desire and the Structure of Eighteenth-Century Fiction," in H. George Hahn, ed., *The Country Myth,* 170–73.

Hudson, Nicholas. "Signs, Interpretations, and the Collapse of Meaning in *Tom Jones* and *Amelia.*" *Engl Stud in Canada* 16 (1990), 28–32.

Probyn, Clive T. *English Fiction,* 100–104.

Scheuermann, Mona. "Henry Fielding's Images of Women." *The Age of Johnson* 3 (1990), 234–36, 240–43, 248–49, 254–69.

Scheuermann, Mona. *Her Bread to Earn,* 116–25.

Varey, Simon. *Space and the Eighteenth-Century English Novel,* 176–80.

Wanko, Cheryl. "Characterization and the Reader's Quandary in Fielding's *Amelia.*" *JEGP* 90 (1991), 505–23.

Jonathan Wild, 1743

Baird, John D. "Criminal Elements: Fielding's *Jonathan Wild,*" in M. L. Friedland, ed., *Rough Justice,* 76–92.

Bender, John. "The Novel and the Rise of the Penitentiary: Narrative and Ideology in Defoe, Gay, Hogarth, and Fielding," in H. George Hahn, ed., *The Country Myth,* 117–18.

Doody, Margaret A. "Work and Working People in Fielding's Novels." *The Age of Johnson* 4 (1991), 239–48.

Golden, Morris. "Public Context and Imagining Self in *Joseph Andrews* and *Jonathan Wild.*" *JEGP* 88 (1989), 500–509.

Kayman, Martin A. *From Bow Street to Baker Street,* 51–53.

Probyn, Clive T. *English Fiction,* 100–104.

Wilputte, Earla A. "The Autodiegetic Power of Mrs Heartfree in Henry Fielding's *Jonathan Wild.*" *Durham Univ J* 84 (1992), 229–34.

Joseph Andrews, 1742

Adams, Percy G. "The Coach and the Inn," in H. George Hahn, ed., *The Country Myth,* 201–5.

Bartolomeo, Joseph B. "Interpolated Tales as Allegories of Reading: *Joseph Andrews.*" *Stud in the Novel* 23 (1991), 405–14.

Bell, Ian A. *Literature and Crime,* 199–208.

Butler, Gerald J. *Henry Fielding,* 49–57.

Butler, Gerald J. *Love and Reading,* 35–37.

Costa, Astrid Masetti Lobo. "Up and Down Stairways: Escher, Bakhtin, and *Joseph Andrews.*" *Stud in Engl Lit, 1500–1900* 31 (1991), 553–66.
Doody, Margaret A. "Work and Working People in Fielding's Novels." *The Age of Johnson* 4 (1991), 218–22.
Duncan, Jeffrey L. "The Rural Ideal in Eighteenth-Century Fiction," in H. George Hahn, ed., *The Country Myth*, 256–58.
Dupas, Jean-Claude. "Récit aventureux ou espaces de la fiction dans *Joseph Andrews.*" *Bull de la Société d'Etudes Anglo-Américaines des XVIIe et XVIIIe Siècles* 31 (1990), 43–69.
Erlebach, Peter. *Theorie und Praxis des Romaneingangs*, 146–50.
Fishelov, David. "Types of Character, Characteristics of Type," in John V. Knapp, ed., *Literary Character*, 79–81, 84–85.
Flanders, W. Austin. "Urban Life and the Early Novel," in H. George Hahn, ed., *The Country Myth*, 58–59.
Frank, Judith. "Literacy, Desire, and the Novel: From *Shamela* to *Joseph Andrews.*" *Yale J of Criticism* 6:2 (1993), 157–71.
Golden, Morris. "Public Context and Imagining Self in *Joseph Andrews* and *Jonathan Wild.*" *JEGP* 88 (1989), 487–500.
Goubert, Pierre. "Le Double Jeu de l'auteur comique dans certaines scènes de *Joseph Andrews.*" *Bull de la Société d'Etudes Anglo-Américaines des XVIIe et XVIIIe Siècles* 31 (1990), 71–81.
Haspel, Jane Seay. "Sex and Moral Purpose in *Joseph Andrews.*" *Lit/Film Q* 19 (1991), 122–26.
Hicks, Stephen. "Bridging the Great Cognitive Divide: A Discourse Analysis of *Joseph Andrews* and *Waverley.*" *Lang Q* 28:1–2 (1990), 13–21.
Klein, Jürgen. "Romantheorie und Romanstruktur in Henry Fieldings *Joseph Andrews.*" *Anglia* 109 (1991), 377–409.
Knight, Charles A. "*Joseph Andrews* and the Failure of Authority." *Eighteenth-Cent Fiction* 4 (1992), 109–24.
Kraft, Elizabeth. "Public Nurturance and Private Civility: The Transposition of Values in Eighteenth-Century Fiction." *Stud in Eighteenth-Cent Culture* 22 (1992), 186–87.
Kropf, Carl R. "Dialogical Engagement in *Joseph Andrews* and the Community of Narrative Agencies," in Kevin L. Cope, ed., *Compendious Conversations*, 206–16.
Leduc, Guyonne. "Vertus et vertu dans *Joseph Andrews.*" *Bull de la Société d'Etudes Anglo-Américaines des XVIIe et XVIIIe Siècles* 31 (1990), 83–108.
Madelin, Hervé. "Savoir, ignorance et vertu dans *Joseph Andrews.*" *Bull de la Société d'Etudes Anglo-Américaines des XVIIe et XVIIIe Siècles* 31 (1990), 109–22.
Ogee, Frédéric. "Form and Fiction: Fielding and Hogarth's 'Line of Beauty.'" *Stud on Voltaire and the Eighteenth Cent* 264 (1989), 1077–80.
Orange, Michael. "Prudes, Lusciousness and *Joseph Andrews.*" *Sydney Stud in Engl* 17 (1991–92), 46–66.
Price, John Valdimir. "Patterns of Sexual Behavior in Some Eighteenth-Century Novels," in H. George Hahn, ed., *The Country Myth*, 125–37.

Probyn, Clive T. *English Fiction,* 79–92.

Punter, David. *The Romantic Unconscious,* 69–71.

Ruml, Treadwell, II. "Joseph Andrews as Exemplary Gentleman." *Stud in Eighteenth-Cent Culture* 22 (1992), 195–205.

Scheuermann, Mona. "Henry Fielding's Images of Women." *The Age of Johnson* 3 (1990), 236–37.

Soupel, Serge. "Le couvert et le découvert: *Joseph Andrews* paradoxal." *Etudes Anglaises* 44 (1991), 15–30.

Stephanson, Raymond. "'Silenc'd by Authority' in *Joseph Andrews:* Power, Submission, and Mutuality in 'The History of Two Friends.'" *Stud in the Novel* 24 (1992), 1–10.

Varey, Simon. *"Joseph Andrews,"* 23–105.

Shamela, 1741

Frank, Judith. "Literacy, Desire, and the Novel: From *Shamela* to J*oseph Andrews." Yale J of Criticism* 6:2 (1993), 157–71.

Nickel, Terri. *"Pamela* as Fetish: Masculine Anxiety in Henry Fielding's *Shamela* and James Parry's *The True Anti-Pamela." Stud in Eighteenth-Cent Culture* 22 (1992), 38–42.

Oakleaf, David. "Marks, Stamps, and Representations: Character in Eighteenth-Century Fiction." *Stud in the Novel* 23 (1991), 300.

Tom Jones, 1749

Bell, Ian A. *Literature and Crime,* 208–13.

Bevis, Richard. "Fielding's Normative Authors: *Tom Jones* and the Rehearsal Play." *Philol Q* 69 (1990), 55–68.

Boheemen, Christine van. *The Novel as Family Romance,* 44–133.

Butler, Gerald J. *Henry Fielding,* 81–113.

Butler, Gerald J. *Love and Reading,* 37–38, 155–59.

Campbell, Jill. *"Tom Jones,* Jacobitism, and Gender: History and Fiction at the Ghosting Hour." *Genre* 23 (1990), 161–88.

Chibka, Robert L. "Taking 'The SERIOUS' Seriously: The Introductory Chapters of *Tom Jones." Eighteenth Cent* 31 (1990), 23–39.

DeRitter, Jones. "'How came this Muff Here?' A Note on *Tom Jones." Engl Lang Notes* 26:4 (1989), 41–46.

Doody, Margaret A. "Work and Working People in Fielding's Novels." *The Age of Johnson* 4 (1991), 222–35.

Erlebach, Peter. *Theorie und Praxis des Romaneingangs,* 150–61.

Evans, James E. "Blifil as Tartuffe: The Dialogic Comedy of *Tom Jones." Compar Lit Stud* 27 (1990), 101–11.

Flanders, W. Austin. "Urban Life and the Early Novel," in H. George Hahn, ed., *The Country Myth,* 60.

Goscilo, Margaret Bozenna. *The Bastard Hero,* 54–66.

Hudson, Nicholas. "Signs, Interpretations, and the Collapse of Meaning in *Tom Jones* and *Amelia." Engl Stud in Canada* 16 (1990), 17–28.

Jacques, Eileen. "Fielding's *Tom Jones* and the *Nicomachean Ethics." Engl Lang Notes* 30:1 (1992), 20–30.

Kraft, Elizabeth. *Character & Consciousness,* 65–74, 78–82.

Kropf, Carl R. "Judgment and Character, Evidence and the Law in *Tom Jones.*" *Stud in the Novel* 21 (1989), 357–65.

Mace, Nancy A. "Henry Fielding's Classical Learning." *Mod Philology* 88 (1991), 255–60.

McNeil, David. *The Grotesque Depiction of War,* 116–67.

Merrett, Robert James. "Natural History and the Eighteenth-Century English Novel." *Eighteenth-Cent Stud* 25 (1991–92), 160–61.

Nelson, T. G. A. "Incest in the Early Novel and Related Genres." *Eighteenth-Cent Life* 16:1 (1992), 153–59.

New, Melvyn. *Telling New Lies,* 40–42.

Ogee, Frédéric. "Form and Fiction: Fielding and Hogarth's 'Line of Beauty.'" *Stud on Voltaire and the Eighteenth Cent* 264 (1989), 1077–80.

Ortiz, Ricardo L. "Fielding's 'Orientalist' Moment: Historical Fiction and Historical Knowledge in *Tom Jones.*" *Stud in Engl Lit, 1500–1900* 33 (1993), 609–24.

Page, Norman. *Speech in the English Novel,* 122–26.

Paulson, Ronald. "The Pilgrimage and the Family: Structures in the Novels of Fielding and Smollett," in H. George Hahn, ed., *The Country Myth,* 181–98.

Polhemus, Robert M. *Erotic Faith,* 50–52.

Probyn, Clive T. *English Fiction,* 92–100.

Reilly, Patrick. *"Tom Jones,"* 27–134.

Richetti, John. "The Old Order and the New Novel of the Mid-Eighteenth Century: Narrative Authority in Fielding and Smollett." *Eighteenth-Cent Fiction* 2 (1990), 183–93.

Scheuermann, Mona. "Henry Fielding's Images of Women." *The Age of Johnson* 3 (1990), 232–34, 237–40, 244–48, 250–54, 269–76.

Scheuermann, Mona. *Her Bread to Earn,* 97–115.

Soulier-Detis, Elisabeth. "Colliers, gants et manchon: Les Pulsions dévoilées." *Bull de la Société d'Etudes Anglo-Américaines des XVIIe et XVIIIe Siècles* 28 (1989), 145–62.

Stevenson, John Allen. *The British Novel,* 46–66.

Stewart, Maaja A. "Ingratitude in *Tom Jones.*" *JEGP* 89 (1990), 512–32.

Toker, Leona. *Eloquent Reticence,* 105–26.

Unsworth, John. *"Tom Jones:* The Comedy of Knowledge." *Mod Lang Q* 48 (1987), 242–53.

Varey, Simon. *Space and the Eighteenth-Century English Novel,* 161–77.

SARAH FIELDING

The Countess of Dellwyn, 1759

Lanser, Susan Sniader. *Fictions of Authority,* 49–50.

The Cry, 1754

Hunter, J. Paul. "Novels and History and Northrop Frye." *Eighteenth-Cent Stud* 24 (1990–91), 233–37.

David Simple, 1744–1753

> Hall, K. G. *The Exalted Heroine,* 54–61.
> Hatch, Ronald B. "'Lordship and Bondage': Women Novelists of the Eighteenth Century." *REAL: Yrbk of Res in Engl and Am Lit* 8 (1991/92), 235.
> McMaster, Juliet. *The Index of the Mind,* 27–28.
> Skinner, Gillian. "'The price of a tear': Economic Sense and Sensibility in Sarah Fielding's *David Simple.*" *Lit & Hist* 1:1 (1992), 16–26.
> Woodward, Carolyn. "Sarah Fielding's Self-Destructing Utopia: *The Adventures of David Simple,*" in Dale Spender, ed., *Living by the Pen,* 65–79.

EVA FIGES

Nelly's Version, 1977

> Hassam, Andrew. *Writing and Reality,* 122–24, 126–29.

RONALD FIRBANK

Concerning the Eccentricities of Cardinal Pirelli, 1926

> Kiernan, Robert F. *Frivolity Unbound,* 60–65.
> Woodman, Thomas. *Faithful Fictions,* 68–69.

The Flower Beneath the Foot, 1923

> Kiernan, Robert F. *Frivolity Unbound,* 50–55.

Sorrow in Sunlight, 1925

> Kiernan, Robert F. *Frivolity Unbound,* 55–60.

PENELOPE FITZGERALD

At Freddie's, 1982

> Sudrann, Jean. "'Magic or Miracles': The Fallen World of Penelope Fitzgerald's Novels," in Robert E. Hosmer, Jr., ed., *Contemporary British Women Writers,* 112–16.

The Beginning of Spring, 1988

> Sudrann, Jean. "'Magic or Miracles': The Fallen World of Penelope Fitzgerald's Novels," in Robert E. Hosmer, Jr., ed., *Contemporary British Women Writers,* 120–23.

Human Voices, 1980

> Sudrann, Jean. "'Magic or Miracles': The Fallen World of Penelope Fitzgerald's Novels," in Robert E. Hosmer, Jr., ed., *Contemporary British Women Writers,* 117–19.

Innocence, 1986

Sudrann, Jean. "'Magic or Miracles': The Fallen World of Penelope Fitzgerald's Novels," in Robert E. Hosmer, Jr., ed., *Contemporary British Women Writers,* 107–11.

FORD MADOX FORD

The Benefactor, 1905

Hoffmann, Charles G. *Ford Madox Ford,* 13–16.

A Call, 1910

Hoffmann, Charles G. *Ford Madox Ford,* 29–34.

The *Fifth Queen* Trilogy, 1962

Hoffmann, Charles G. *Ford Madox Ford,* 16–21.

The Good Soldier, 1915

Adams, James T. "Discrepancies in the Time-Scheme of *The Good Soldier.*" *Engl Lit in Transition* 34 (1991), 153–63.

Eggenschwiler, David. "'Shuttlecocks': Kipling in *The Good Soldier.*" *Engl Lang Notes* 30:1 (1992), 51–54.

Goodheart, Eugene. *Desire and Its Discontents,* 79–84.

Hoffmann, Charles G. *Ford Madox Ford,* 30–34, 47–66.

Imhof, Rüdiger. "Ford Madox Ford und der englischsprachige Roman des Zwanzigsten Jarhunderts." *Literatur in Wissenschaft und Unterricht* 24 (1991), 277–80.

Knowles, Sebastian D. G. *A Purgatorial Flame,* 194–97.

Meyer, Eric. "'The Nature of a Text': Ford and Conrad in Plato's Pharmacy." *Mod Fiction Stud* 36 (1990), 506–12.

Nicholls, Peter. "Apes and Familiars: Modernism, Mimesis and the Work of Wyndham Lewis." *Textual Practice* 6 (1992), 425–26.

Nigro, Frank G. "Who Framed *The Good Soldier?* Dowell's Story in Search of a Form." *Stud in the Novel* 24 (1992), 381–90.

Orel, Harold. *Popular Fiction in England,* 125–33.

Poole, Roger. "The Real Plot Line of Ford Madox Ford's *The Good Soldier:* An Essay in Applied Deconstruction." *Textual Practice* 4 (1990), 390–427.

Sabol, C. Ruth. "Reliable Narration in *The Good Soldier,*" in Rosanne G. Potter, ed., *Literary Computing and Literary, Criticism,* 207–23.

Sabol, C. Ruth. "Semantic Analysis and Fictive Worlds in Ford and Conrad." *Liter and Linguistic Computing* 6 (1991), 97–103.

Scott, James B. "Coincidence or Irony? Ford's Use of August 4th in *The Good Soldier.*" *Engl Lang Notes* 30:4 (1993), 53–57.

Stevenson, Randall. *Modernist Fiction,* 25–27, 95–98.

The "Half-Moon," 1909

Hoffmann, Charles G. *Ford Madox Ford,* 26–28.

Henry for Hugh, 1934

> Hoffmann, Charles G. *Ford Madox Ford,* 110–14.

Ladies Whose Bright Eyes, 1911

> Hoffmann, Charles G. *Ford Madox Ford,* 36–39.
> Scott, James B. "Ford Madox Ford and 'The Mystery That Comforteth':
> Romance as an Escape from Positivism." *Engl Stud in Canada* 18 (1992),
> 310–13.

Last Post, 1928

> Hoffmann, Charles G. *Ford Madox Ford,* 92–98.

A Man Could Stand Up—, 1926

> Hoffmann, Charles G. *Ford Madox Ford,* 87–92.

The Marsden Case, 1923

> Hoffmann, Charles G. *Ford Madox Ford,* 67–69.

Mr. Apollo, 1908

> Hoffmann, Charles G. *Ford Madox Ford,* 24–26.
> Scott, James B. "Ford Madox Ford and 'The Mystery That Comforteth':
> Romance as an Escape from Positivism." *Engl Stud in Canada* 18 (1992),
> 303–8.

Mr. Fleight, 1913

> Hoffmann, Charles G. *Ford Madox Ford,* 42–45.

The New Humpty-Dumpty, 1912

> Hoffmann, Charles G. *Ford Madox Ford,* 40–42.

No More Parades, 1925

> Hibberd, Dominic. *The First World War,* 162–65.
> Hoffmann, Charles G. *Ford Madox Ford,* 81–87.

Parade's End, 1950

> Hoffmann, Charles G. *Ford Madox Ford,* 67–103.
> Knowles, Sebastian D. G. *A Purgatorial Flame,* 207–9.
> MacKay, Carol. "The Relation of *Parade's End* to the Misanthrope Tra-
> dition." *Focus on Robert Graves and His Contemporaries* 1:12 (1991),
> 18–24.
> Meyer, Eric. "Ford's War and (Post) Modern Memory: *Parade's End* and
> National Allegory." *Criticism* 32 (1990), 81–97.
> Onions, John. *English Fiction and Drama,* 116–34.
> Wiesenfarth, Joseph. *Gothic Manners,* 161–84.

The Portrait, 1910

> Hoffmann, Charles G. *Ford Madox Ford,* 28–29.

The Rash Act, 1933

> Hoffmann, Charles G. *Ford Madox Ford,* 112–14.

Some Do Not, 1924

Hoffmann, Charles G. *Ford Madox Ford,* 73–81, 89–100.

The Young Lovell, 1913

Scott, James B. "Ford Madox Ford and 'The Mystery That Comforteth': Romance as an Escape from Positivism." *Engl Stud in Canada* 18 (1992), 308–9.

ISABELLA FORD

Miss Blake of Monkshalton, 1890

Waters, Chris. "New Women and Socialist-Feminist Fiction: The Novels of Isabella Ford and Katharine Bruce Glasier," in Angela Ingram and Daphne Patai, eds., *Rediscovering Forgotten Radicals,* 30–32.

Mr. Elliott, 1901

Waters, Chris. "New Women and Socialist-Feminist Fiction: The Novels of Isabella Ford and Katharine Bruce Glasier," in Angela Ingram and Daphne Patai, eds., *Rediscovering Forgotten Radicals,* 38–40.

On the Threshold, 1895

Waters, Chris. "New Women and Socialist-Feminist Fiction: The Novels of Isabella Ford and Katharine Bruce Glasier," in Angela Ingram and Daphne Patai, eds., *Rediscovering Forgotten Radicals,* 34–36.

E. M. FORSTER

Howards End, 1910

Born, Daniel. "Private Gardens, Public Swamps: *Howards End* and the Revaluation of Liberal Guilt." *Novel* 25 (1992), 141–59.

Castronovo, David. *The English Gentleman,* 119–21.

Daniels, Molly A. *The Prophetic Novel,* 45–47.

DiBattista, Maria. *First Love,* 61–64.

Dorsey, Shelly. "Austen, Forster, and Economics." *Persuasions* 12 (1990), 54–59.

Duckworth, Alistair M. *"Howards End,"* 27–139.

Land, Stephen K. *Challenge and Conventionality,* 141–68.

Langland, Elizabeth. "Gesturing toward an Open Space: Gender, Form, and Language in E. M. Forster's *Howards End,*" in Laura Claridge and Elizabeth Langland, eds., *Out of Bounds,* 252–67.

Olson, Jeane N. "E. M. Forster's Prophetic Vision of the Modern Family in *Howards End.*" *Texas Stud in Lit and Lang* 35 (1993), 347–60.

Schneidau, Herbert N. *Waking Giants,* 64–98.

Schwarz, Daniel R. *The Transformation of the English Novel,* 127–29.

Tindall, Gillian. *Countries of the Mind,* 67–70, 87–89.

Trodd, Anthea. *A Reader's Guide,* 33–37.

Watts, Cedric. *Literature and Money,* 152–63.

The Longest Journey, 1907

Castronovo, David. *The English Gentleman,* 117–19.

Harrison, Bernard. *Inconvenient Fictions,* 98–102.

Land, Stephen K. *Challenge and Conventionality,* 67–101.

Nelson, Scott R. "Narrative Inversion: The Textual Construction of Homosexuality in E. M. Forster's Novels." *Style* 26 (1992), 310–20.

Rahman, Tariq. *"Maurice* and *The Longest Journey:* A Study of E. M.
Forster's Deviation from the Representation of Male Homosexuality in
Literature." *Stud in Engl Lit* (Tokyo) English Nr. 1990, 57–75.

Rahman, Tariq. "The Under-Plot in E. M. Forster's *The Longest Journey."
Durham Univ J* 83 (1991), 59–67.

Richards, Jeffrey. *Happiest Days,* 168–81.

Rossen, Janice. *The University in Modern Fiction,* 103–9.

Schwarz, Daniel R. *The Transformation of the English Novel,* 124–25.

Maurice, 1971

Harned, Jon. "Becoming Gay in E. M. Forster's *Maurice." Papers on Lang
& Lit* 29 (1993), 49–66.

Land, Stephen K. *Challenge and Conventionality,* 177–88.

Nelson, Scott R. "Narrative Inversion: The Textual Construction of Homosexuality in E. M. Forster's Novels." *Style* 26 (1992), 315–20.

Rahman, Tariq. *"Maurice* and *The Longest Journey:* A Study of E. M.
Forster's Deviation from the Representation of Male Homosexuality in
Literature." *Stud in Engl Lit* (Tokyo) English Nr. 1990, 57–75.

Rahman, Tariq. "A Study of Alienation in E. M. Forster's *Maurice." Durham Univ J* 82 (1990), 81–87.

Schwarz, Daniel R. *The Transformation of the English Novel,* 129–30.

Stape, J. H. "Comparing Mythologies: Forster's *Maurice* and Pater's *Marius." Engl Lit in Transition* 33 (1990), 141–52.

Summers, Claude J. *Gay Fictions,* 84–103.

A Passage to India, 1924

Armstrong, Paul B. "Reading India: E. M. Forster and the Politics of Interpretation." *Twentieth Cent Lit* 38 (1992), 365–82.

Bacchiega, Franca. *"Passaggio in India* di E. M. Forster." *Città di Vita* 44
(1989), 265–80.

Barratt, Robert. "Marabar: The Caves of Deconstruction." *J of Narrative
Technique* 23 (1993), 127–34.

Clayton, John J. *Gestures of Healing,* 109–11.

Daniels, Molly A. *The Prophetic Novel,* 1–132.

Doherty, Gerald. "White Circles/Black Holes: Worlds of Difference in *A
Passage to India." Orbis Litterarum* 46 (1991), 105–22.

Doloff, Steven. "Forster's Use of Names in *A Passage to India." Engl Lang
Notes* 28:4 (1991), 61–62.

Fernández, Francisco. *"A Passage to India:* El lenguaje artístico y sim-
bólico de E. M. Forster." *Revista Alicantina de Estudios Ingleses* 1
(1988), 33–79.

Fincham, Gail. "Arches and Echoes: Framing Devices in *A Passage to India*." *Pretexts* 2:1 (1990), 52–67.

Ganguly, Adwaita P. *India: Mystic, Complex and Real—A Detailed Study of E. M. Forster's "A Passage to India."*

Heath, Jeffrey. "A Voluntary Surrender: Imperialism and Imagination in *A Passage to India*." *Univ of Toronto Q* 59 (1989/90), 287–307.

Italia, Paul G. "Under the Rules of Time: Story and Plot in E. M. Forster's *A Passage to India*." *Engl Lang Notes* 27:3 (1990), 58–62.

Land, Stephen K. *Challenge and Conventionality*, 189–217.

Lindley, Arthur. "Raj as Romance/Raj as Parody: Lean's and Forster's *Passage to India*." *Lit/Film Q* 20 (1992), 61–66.

McClure, John A. "Late Imperial Romance." *Raritan* 10:4 (1991), 124–30.

Moffat, Wendy. "*A Passage to India* and the Limits of Certainty." *J of Narrative Technique* 20 (1990), 331–39.

Montgomery, Martin, Alan Durant, Nigel Fabb, Tom Furniss, and Sara Mills. *Ways of Reading*, 197–201.

Mukherjee, Sujit. *Forster and Further*, 59–61.

Nagarajan, M. S. "Homeward to One's Self: Passages to India." *Liter Criterion* 27:1–2 (1992), 84–89.

Panda, Ram Narayan. "*A Passage to India* and *Heart of Darkness:* Into the Belly of the Whale." *Panjab Univ Res Bull* 21:2 (1990), 105–11.

Pether, Penelope. "E. M. Forster's *A Passage to India:* A Passage to the Patria?" *Sydney Stud in Engl* 17 (1991–92), 88–120.

Phillips, K. J. *Dying Gods in Twentieth-Century Fiction*, 118–33.

Phillips, K. J. "Hindu Avatars, Moslem Martyrs, and Primitive Dying Gods in E. M. Forster's *A Passage to India*." *J of Mod Lit* 15:1 (1988), 121–40.

Potter, Nicholas. "*A Passage to India:* The Crisis of 'Reasonable Form.'" *Durham Univ J* 83 (1991), 209–13.

Procter, Margaret. "Possibilities of Completion: The Endings of *A Passage to India* and *Women in Love*." *Engl Lit in Transition* 34 (1991), 261–78.

Rahman, Tariq. "Syed Ross Masood and E. M. Forster's *A Passage to India*." *ANQ* 4:2 (1991), 79–81.

Restuccia, Frances L. "'A Cave of My Own': E. M. Forster and Sexual Politics." *Raritan* 9:2 (1989), 110–28.

Schneidau, Herbert N. *Waking Giants*, 98–100.

Schwarz, Daniel R. *The Transformation of the English Novel*, 130–35.

Sharpe, Jenny. *Allegories of Empire*, 113–35.

Toker, Leona. *Eloquent Reticence*, 129–51.

A Room with a View, 1908

Harris, Janice H. "Lawrence and the Edwardian Feminists," in Michael Squires and Keith Cushman, eds., *The Challenge of D. H. Lawrence*, 64–66.

Higdon, David Leon. "Opus 3 or Opus 111 in Forster's *A Room with a View?*" *Engl Lang Notes* 28:4 (1991), 57–59.

Katz, Susan. "Writing for 'Monie': The Legacy of the Spinster to E. M. Forster," in Laura L. Doan, ed., *Old Maids*, 77–83.

Land, Stephen K. *Challenge and Conventionality*, 115–36.

Rahman, Tariq. "The Double-Plot in E. M. Forster's *A Room with a View.*" *Cahiers Victoriens et Edouardiens* 33 (1991), 43–60.

Schwarz, Daniel R. *The Transformation of the English Novel*, 125–27.

Wagner, Philip C., Jr. "Phaeton, Persephone, and *A Room with a View.*" *Compar Lit Stud* 27 (1990), 275–83.

Where Angels Fear to Tread, 1905

Harrison, Bernard. *Inconvenient Fictions*, 108–22.

Katz, Susan. "Writing for 'Monie': The Legacy of the Spinster to E. M. Forster," in Laura L. Doan, ed., *Old Maids*, 70–76.

Land, Stephen K. *Challenge and Conventionality*, 45–66.

Schwarz, Daniel R. *The Transformation of the English Novel*, 122–24.

Tindall, Gillian. *Countries of the Mind*, 178–80.

MARGARET FORSTER

Private Papers, 1986

Hassam, Andrew. *Writing and Reality*, 85–89.

FREDERICK FORSYTH

The Dogs of War, 1974

Moroz, Grzegorz. "Frederick Forsyth, *The Dogs of War:* Is Africa Presented in This Novel Real or Fictitious?" *Africana Bull* 37 (1991), 59–70.

JOHN FOWLES

The Collector, 1963

Aubrey, James R. *John Fowles*, 86–94.

Butler, Lance St. John. "John Fowles and the Fiction of Freedom," in James Acheson, ed., *The British and Irish Novel*, 62–70.

Cooper, Pamela. *The Fictions of John Fowles*, 19–49.

Costa, Dominique. "Narrative Voice and Focalization: The Presentation of the Different Selves in John Fowles' *The Collector,*" in Philip Shaw and Peter Stockwell, eds., *Subjectivity and Literature*, 113–19.

Costello, Jacqueline A. "The Prison-House of Culture: John Fowles' *The Collector.*" *Recovering Lit* 17 (1989/90), 19–31.

Garard, Charles. *Point of View in Fiction and Film*, 25–50.

Hassam, Andrew. *Writing and Reality*, 81–85.

Magistrale, Anthony. "Art Versus Madness in Stephen King's *Misery,*" in Donald E. Morse et al., eds., *The Celebration of the Fantastic*, 271–74.

Salami, Mahmoud. *John Fowles's Fiction*, 46–72.

Sander, Hans-Jochen. "Power Relations and Their Representation in John Fowles' Novels." *REAL: Yrbk of Res in Engl and Am Lit* 8 (1991/92), 144–46.

Vincent-Durroux, Laurence. "Points de vue et changements de points de vue dans *The Collector* de John Fowles." *Bull de l'ACLA* 11:1 (1989), 65–70.

Daniel Martin, 1977

Aubrey, James R. *John Fowles,* 117–24.

Butler, Lance St. John. "John Fowles and the Fiction of Freedom," in James Acheson, ed., *The British and Irish Novel,* 67–69, 72–74.

Cooper, Pamela. *The Fictions of John Fowles,* 194–204.

Costello, Jacqueline. "When Worlds Collide: Freedom, Freud, and Jung in John Fowles's *Daniel Martin." Univ of Hartford Stud in Lit* 22:1 (1990), 31–43.

Lee, Alison. *Realism and Power,* 119–25.

Lorenz, Paul H. "Epiphany among the Ruins: Etruscan Places in John Fowles's *Daniel Martin." Texas R* 11:1–2 (1990), 78–86.

Salami, Mahmoud. *John Fowles's Fiction,* 159–90.

Vieth, Lynne S. "The Re-humanization of Art: Pictorial Aesthetics in John Fowles's *The Ebony Tower* and *Daniel Martin." Mod Fiction Stud* 37 (1991), 217–31.

The French Lieutenant's Woman, 1969

Alexander, Marguerite. *Flights from Realism,* 127–32.

Aubrey, James R. *John Fowles,* 102–9.

Aubrey, James R. "The Pre-Raphaelite 'pack of satyrs' in John Fowles's *The French Lieutenant's Woman." Nineteenth-Cent Prose* 18:1 (1990/91), 32–36.

Begiebing, Robert J. *Toward a New Synthesis,* 41–45.

Billi, Mirella. "Dialogismo testuale e parodia in *The French Lieutenant's Woman* di John Fowles." *Rivista di Letterature Moderne e Comparate* 41:3 (1988), 165–80.

Booker, M. Keith. "What We Have Instead of God: Sexuality, Textuality and Infinity in *The French Lieutenant's Woman." Novel* 24 (1991), 178–97.

Butler, Lance St. John. "John Fowles and the Fiction of Freedom," in James Acheson, ed., *The British and Irish Novel,* 62–64.

Cohan, Steven. "Figures beyond the Text: A Theory of Readable Character in the Novel," in Mark Spilka and Caroline McCracken-Flesher, eds., *Why the Novel Matters,* 132–36.

Cooper, Pamela. *The Fictions of John Fowles,* 103–41.

Garard, Charles. *Point of View in Fiction and Film,* 89–117.

Goscilo, Margaret Bozenna. "John Fowles's Pre-Raphaelite Woman: Interart Strategies and Gender Politics." *Mosaic* 26:2 (1993), 63–81.

McKee, Alison L. "She Had Eyes a Man Could Drown In: Narrative, Desire, and the Female Gaze in *The French Lieutenant's Woman." Lit/Film Q* 20 (1992), 146–54.

Maggitti, Vincenzo. "Dis/adattamento: *The French Lieutenant's Woman*," in Donatello Izzo, ed., *Il racconto allo specchio*, 123–47.

Phelan, James. *Reading People*, 83–105.

Rutelli, Romana. "Le consonanze empatiche." *Strumenti Critici* 6 (1991), 433–40.

Salami, Mahmoud. *John Fowles's Fiction*, 105–34.

Weber, Jean Jacques. *Critical Analysis of Fiction*, 142–59.

Wiesenfarth, Joseph. *Gothic Manners*, 194–97.

A Maggot, 1985

Aubrey, James R. *John Fowles*, 129–35.

Begiebing, Robert J. *Toward a New Synthesis*, 45–50.

Chouleur, Jacques. "John Fowles et les Shakers." *Mythes, Croyances et Religions dans le Monde Anglo-Saxon* 7 (1989), 61–71.

Cooper, Pamela. *The Fictions of John Fowles*, 212–22.

Gauthier, Dominique. "Le Sourire du Kouros, ou: La Grèce, le beau et le vrai dans *The Magus* de John Fowles." *Cycnos* 7 (1991), 85–95.

Holmes, Frederick M. "History, Fiction, and the Dialogic Imagination: John Fowles's *A Maggot*." *Contemp Lit* 32 (1991), 229–42.

Monnin, Pierre E. "Cumulative Strangeness Without and Within *A Maggot* by J. Fowles," in Margaret Bridges, ed., *On Srangeness*, 151–62.

Reed, John R. *Victorian Will*, 414–17.

Salami, Mahmoud. *John Fowles's Fiction*, 215–52.

Sander, Hans-Jochen. "Power Relations and Their Representation in John Fowles' Novels." *REAL: Yrbk of Res in Engl and Am Lit* 8 (1991/92), 149–55.

Weber, Jean Jacques. *Critical Analysis of Fiction*, 121–38.

The Magus, 1966

Alexander, Marguerite. *Flights from Realism*, 169–75.

Aubrey, James R. *John Fowles*, 94–101.

Begiebing, Robert J. *Toward a New Synthesis*, 21–41.

Boccia, Michael. "Feminism in *The Magus* by John Fowles." *New Hampshire Coll J* 6:1 (1989), 59–70.

Butler, Lance St. John. "John Fowles and the Fiction of Freedom," in James Acheson, ed., *The British and Irish Novel*, 62–70.

Cooper, Pamela. *The Fictions of John Fowles*, 51–101.

Garard, Charles. *Point of View in Fiction and Film*, 55–80.

Kane, Richard C. "Didactic Demons in Contemporary British Fiction." *Univ of Mississippi Stud in Engl* 8 (1990), 49–56.

Lee, Alison. *Realism and Power*, 87–94.

Lengeler, Rainer. "Das Bild Deutschlands im englischen Roman der Nachkriegszeit." *Archiv für das Studium der neueren Sprachen und Literaturen* 229 (1992), 31–35.

Salami, Mahmoud. *John Fowles's Fiction*, 73–104.

Sander, Hans-Jochen. "Power Relations and Their Representation in John Fowles' Novels." *REAL: Yrbk of Res in Engl and Am Lit* 8 (1991/92), 146–49.

Mantissa, 1982

Aubrey, James R. *John Fowles,* 124–29.

Cooper, Pamela. *The Fictions of John Fowles,* 205–12.

Salami, Mahmoud. *John Fowles's Fiction,* 191–214.

Sertori, Daniela Carpi. "Parodia come fine dell'illusione mimetica in *Mantissa* di John Fowles." *Lingua e Stile* 25 (1990), 297–303.

Wilson, Raymond J., III. "Fowles's Allegory of Literary Invention: *Mantissa* and Contemporary Theory." *Twentieth Cent Lit* 36 (1990), 61–70.

DICK FRANCIS

Proof, 1985

Wilhelm, Albert E. "Fathers and Sons in Dick Francis' *Proof.*" *Critique* 32 (1991), 169–78.

GILBERT FRANKAU

Peter Jackson, 1920

Bracco, Rosa Maria. *'Betwixt and Between,'* 16–20.

THOMAS FROST

Paul the Poacher, 1848

Drexler, Peter. *Literatur, Recht, Kriminalität,* 137–40.

JOHN GALSWORTHY

The Forsyte Saga, 1922

Ru, Yi-ling. *The Family Novel,* 28–31, 89–110.

The Man of Property, 1906

Strahan, Linda. "What's in a Name? Richardson's Roger Solmes and Galsworthy's Soames Forsyte." *Univ of Mississippi Stud in Engl* 8 (1990), 155–66.

Trodd, Anthea. *A Reader's Guide,* 55–57.

JOHN GALT

Annals of the Parish, 1821

Campbell, Ian. "The Bible, the Kirk and Scottish Literature," in David F. Wright et al., eds., *The Bible in Scottish Life and Literature,* 113–17.

Divine, Ann Roberts. "The Changing Village: Loss of Community in John Galt's *Annals of the Parish.*" *Stud in Scottish Lit* 25 (1990), 121–33.

Letley, Emma. *From Galt to Douglas Brown,* 67–70.

The Ayrshire Legatees, 1820–1821

> Datta, Kitty. "The Theme of Indian Fortunes in English Fiction from Mackenzie to Thackeray: Between Confrontation and Evasions," in Jasodhara Bagchi, ed., *Literature, Society and Ideology,* 257–59.
> Letley, Emma. *From Galt to Douglas Brown,* 58–62.
> Manning, Susan. *The Puritan-Provincial Vision,* 151–53.

The Entail, 1822

> Letley, Emma. *From Galt to Douglas Brown,* 79–85.

The Last of the Lairds, 1826

> Letley, Emma. *From Galt to Douglas Brown,* 76–79.

The Member, 1832

> Datta, Kitty. "The Theme of Indian Fortunes in English Fiction from Mackenzie to Thackeray: Between Confrontation and Evasions," in Jasodhara Bagchi, ed., *Literature, Society and Ideology,* 261–63.
> Harvie, Christopher. *The Centre of Things,* 33–35.

Ringan Gilhaize, 1823

> Letley, Emma. *From Galt to Douglas Brown,* 40–46.

Sir Andrew Wylie, 1822

> Letley, Emma. *From Galt to Douglas Brown,* 63–66.

ALAN GARNER

The Owl Service, 1967

> Filmer, Kath. "Atseinian O Ddyddian Gynt: Welsh Myth and Culture in Contemporary Fantasy," in Kath Filmer, ed., *Twentieth-Century Fantasists,* 115–20.

GEORGE GASCOIGNE

The Adventures of Master F. J., 1573

> Bloomfield, Josephine. "Gascoigne's *Master F. J.* as a Renaissance Proto-Novel: The Birth of the Judicious Editor as Narrator." *Essays in Lit* (Macomb) 19 (1992), 163–70.

ELIZABETH GASKELL

Cousin Phillis, 1865

> Brown, Pearl L. "The Pastoral and Anti-Pastoral in Elizabeth Gaskell's *Cousin Phillis.*" *Victorian Newsl* 82 (1992), 22–27.
> Craik, Wendy. "Lore and Learning in *Cousin Phillis,* I." *Gaskell Soc J* 3 (1989), 68–80.
> Prasad, Nityanand. *Fission and Fusion,* 165–79.

Recchio, Thomas E. "A Victorian Version of the Fall: Mrs Gaskell's *Cousin Phillis* and the Domestication of Myth." *Gaskell Soc J* 5 (1991), 37–50.

Spencer, Jane. *Elizabeth Gaskell,* 126–30.

Cranford, 1853

Bowes, Vincent J. "The Issue of Centrality in Elizabeth Gaskell's *Cranford.*" *Dalhousie R* 69 (1989), 366–72.

Buchanan, Laurie. "Marriages of Partnership: Elizabeth Gaskell and the Victorian Androgynous Ideal," in JoAnna Stephens Mink and Janet Doubler Ward, eds., *Joinings and Disjoinings,* 99–100.

Carse, Wendy K. "A Penchant for Narrative: 'Mary Smith' in Elizabeth Gaskell's *Cranford.*" *J of Narrative Technique* 20 (1990), 318–29.

Davis, Deanna L. "Feminist Critics and Literary Mothers: Daughters Reading Elizabeth Gaskell." *Signs* 17 (1992), 528–29.

Gillooly, Eileen. "Humor as Daughterly Defense in *Cranford.*" *ELH* 59 (1992), 883–906.

Kucich, John. "Transgression and Sexual Difference in Elizabeth Gaskell's Novels." *Texas Stud in Lit and Lang* 32 (1990), 189–210.

Langland, Elizabeth. "Nobody's Angels: Domestic Ideology and Middle-Class Women in the Victorian Novel." *PMLA* 107 (1992), 299–300.

Lanser, Susan Sniader. *Fictions of Authority,* 241–47.

Levin, Amy K. *The Suppressed Sister,* 57–63.

Prasad, Nityanand. *Fission and Fusion,* 59–80.

Spencer, Jane. *Elizabeth Gaskell,* 75–87.

Wittenberg, Judith Bryant. "Re-Vision and Transformation: *Deephaven* and *Cranford.*" *Colby Q* 27 (1991), 121–30.

Mary Barton, 1848

Beck, Rudolf. " 'Romance' und 'Truth': Mrs. Gaskells Schwierigkeiten beim Schreiben der Wahrheit." *Anglia* 108 (1990), 51–74.

Bull, J. A. *The Framework of Fiction,* 141–45.

Davis, Deanna L. "Feminist Critics and Literary Mothers: Daughters Reading Elizabeth Gaskell." *Signs* 17 (1992), 522–23.

Drexler, Peter. *Literatur, Recht, Kriminalität,* 166–67.

Harvie, Christopher. *The Centre of Things,* 22–24.

Krueger, Christine L. *The Reader's Repentance,* 169–80.

Kucich, John. "Transgression and Sexual Difference in Elizabeth Gaskell's Novels." *Texas Stud in Lit and Lang* 32 (1990), 189–210.

Pollard, Arthur. "Faith and Family: Fundamental Values in *Mary Barton.*" *Gaskell Soc J* 3 (1989), 1–5.

Prasad, Nityanand. *Fission and Fusion,* 1–26.

Shelston, Alan. "Elizabeth Gaskell's Manchester, I." *Gaskell Soc J* 3 (1989), 46–67.

Spencer, Jane. *Elizabeth Gaskell,* 32–50.

Stone, Marjorie. "Bakhtinian Polyphony in *Mary Barton:* Class, Gender, and the Textual Voice." *Dickens Stud Annual* 20 (1991), 175–96.

Wheeler, Michael. "Two Tales of Manchester Life." *Gaskell Soc J* 3 (1989), 6–28.

Moorland Cottage, 1850

Lumpkin, Ramona. "(Re)Visions of Virtue: Elizabeth Gaskell's *Moorland Cottage* and George Eliot's *The Mill on the Floss.*" *Stud in the Novel* 23 (1991), 432–40.

My Lady Ludlow, 1859

Krueger, Christine L. "The 'female paternalist' as Historian: Elizabeth Gaskell's *My Lady Ludlow,*" in Linda M. Shires, ed., *Rewriting the Victorians,* 166–80.

Wright, Edgar. "*My Lady Ludlow:* Forms of Social Change and Forms of Fiction, I." *Gaskell Soc J* 3 (1989), 29–41.

North and South, 1855

Buchanan, Laurie. "Marriages of Partnership: Elizabeth Gaskell and the Victorian Androgynous Ideal," in JoAnna Stephens Mink and Janet Doubler Ward, eds., *Joinings and Disjoinings,* 100–106.

Butler, Lance St. John. *Victorian Doubt,* 49–51.

Davis, Deanna L. "Feminist Critics and Literary Mothers: Daughters Reading Elizabeth Gaskell." *Signs* 17 (1992), 523–25.

Defromont, Françoise. "Amour, machine dans *North and South.*" *Cahiers Victoriens et Edouardiens* 31 (1990), 93–100.

Heyns, Michiel. "The Steam-hammer and the Sugar-tongs: Sexuality and Power in Elizabeth Gaskell's *North and South.*" *Engl Stud in Africa* 32 (1989), 79–94.

Krueger, Christine L. *The Reader's Repentance,* 205–20.

Kucich, John. "Transgression and Sexual Difference in Elizabeth Gaskell's Novels." *Texas Stud in Lit and Lang* 32 (1990), 189–210.

Minogue, Sally. "Gender and Class in *Villette* and *North and South,*" in Sally Minogue, ed., *Problems for Feminist Criticism,* 75–79.

Nord, Deborah Epstein. "The Urban Peripatetic: Spectator, Streetwalker, Woman Writer." *Nineteenth-Cent Lit* 46 (1991), 368–75.

Page, Norman. *Speech in the English Novel,* 68–70.

Prasad, Nityanand. *Fission and Fusion,* 83–122.

Spencer, Jane. *Elizabeth Gaskell,* 75–79, 87–95.

Stevenson, Catherine Barnes. "'What Must Not Be Said': *North and South* and the Problem of Women's Work." *Victorian Lit and Culture* 19 (1991), 67–80.

Tindall, Gillian. *Countries of the Mind,* 104–6.

Vann, J. Don. "Dickens, Charles Lever and Mrs. Gaskell." *Victorian Periodicals R* 22:2 (1989), 64–71.

Watts, Cedric. *Literature and Money,* 146–52.

Ruth, 1853

David, Gail. *Female Heroism in the Pastoral,* 171–99.

Frantz, Andrea Breemer. *Redemption and Madness,* 36–41.

Krueger, Christine L. *The Reader's Repentance,* 186–205.

Prasad, Nityanand. *Fission and Fusion,* 29–55.

Schor, Hilary. "The Plot of the Beautiful Ignoramus: *Ruth* and the Tradition of the Fallen Woman," in Regina Barreca, ed., *Sex and Death,* 158–72.

Spencer, Jane. *Elizabeth Gaskell,* 21–24, 51–65.

Sylvia's Lovers, 1863

Krueger, Christine L. *The Reader's Repentance,* 228–32.

Kucich, John. "Transgression and Sexual Difference in Elizabeth Gaskell's Novels." *Texas Stud in Lit and Lang* 32 (1990), 189–210.

Prasad, Nityanand. *Fission and Fusion,* 127–62.

Spencer, Jane. *Elizabeth Gaskell,* 96–115.

Wives and Daughters, 1866

Buchanan, Laurie. "Marriages of Partnership: Elizabeth Gaskell and the Victorian Androgynous Ideal," in JoAnna Stephens Mink and Janet Doubler Ward, eds., *Joinings and Disjoinings,* 104–7.

Buchanan, Laurie. "Mothers and Daughters in Elizabeth Gaskell's *Wives and Daughters:* In a Woman's World." *Midwest Q* 31 (1990), 499–513.

Davis, Deanna L. "Feminist Critics and Literary Mothers: Daughters Reading Elizabeth Gaskell." *Signs* 17 (1992), 525–28.

Langland, Elizabeth. "Nobody's Angels: Domestic Ideology and Middle-Class Women in the Victorian Novel." *PMLA* 107 (1992), 300–301.

Levin, Amy K. *The Suppressed Sister,* 63–70.

Prasad, Nityanand. *Fission and Fusion,* 182–211.

Reddy, Maureen T. "Men, Women, and Manners in *Wives and Daughters,*" in Bege K. Bowers and Barbara Brothers, eds., *Reading and Writing,* 67–85.

Spencer, Jane. *Elizabeth Gaskell,* 130–40.

Unsworth, Anna. "Some Social Themes in *Wives and Daughters,* II: The Social Values of the 1860s and 'Old England' Compared." *Gaskell Soc J* 5 (1991), 51–61.

Yarrow, Dorothy F. "*Mansfield Park* and *Wives and Daughters.*" *Gaskell Soc Newsl* 12 (1991), 4–5.

Yeazell, Ruth Bernard. *Fictions of Modesty,* 194–216.

WILLIAM ALEXANDER GERHARDIE

Futility, 1922

Sell, Roger D. "Gerhardie's Chekhovian Doubt." *Essays in Criticism* 4:1 (1991), 28–50.

GEORGE GISSING

Born in Exile, 1892

Cleto, Fabio. "The Biological Drama: Darwinian Ethics in George Gissing's Fiction." *Gissing J* 28:3 (1992), 9–12.

Deledalle-Rhodes, Janice. "La dramatisation du conflit entre la science et la religion dans *Born in Exile* de George Gissing." *Mythes, Croyances et Religions dans le Monde Anglo-Saxon* 7 (1989), 85–98.

Demos, 1886

Carey, John. *The Intellectuals and the Masses,* 110–12.

Neetens, Wim. *Writing and Democracy,* 69–81.

Smith, Diane M. "Narrative Subversion in the Naturalist Novel: Three Novels of the 1880s." *Compar Lit Stud* 29 (1992), 163–69.

The Emancipated, 1890

Federico, Annette. *Masculine Identity,* 29–44.

In the Year of Jubilee, 1894

Bernstein, Carol L. *The Celebration of Scandal,* 133–41.

Federico, Annette. *Masculine Identity,* 29–35, 44–54.

Harman, Barbara Leah. "Going Public: Female Emancipation in George Gissing's *In the Year of Jubilee." Texas Stud in Lit and Lang* 34 (1992), 347–71.

The Nether World, 1889

Bernstein, Carol L. *The Celebration of Scandal,* 48–49, 53–56, 65–69.

Henkle, Roger. "Morrison, Gissing, and the Stark Reality." *Novel* 25 (1992), 312–19.

New Grub Street, 1891

Cawthra, Gillian. *Cultural Climate and Linguistic Style,* 31–36, 52–65.

Cleto, Fabio. "The Biological Drama: Darwinian Ethics in George Gissing's Fiction." *Gissing J* 28:3 (1992), 4–9.

Halperin, John. *Novelists in their Youth,* 107–10.

Pittock, Murray G. H. *Spectrum of Decadence,* 117–21.

The Odd Women, 1893

Ardis, Ann L. *New Women, New Novels,* 87–90.

Federico, Annette. *Masculine Identity,* 76–82, 90–100.

Gibson, Mark. "Odd Women and Male Vision: Men's Views of Women in *The Odd Women." Gissing Newsl* 26:2 (1990), 2–19.

Halperin, John. *Novelists in their Youth,* 107–27.

Neetens, Wim. *Writing and Democracy,* 106–9.

Perry, Carolyn J. "A Voice of the Past: Ruskin's Pervasive Presence in Gissing's *The Odd Women." Publs of the Missouri Philol Assoc* 13 (1988), 63–70.

The Private Papers of Henry Ryecroft, 1903

Allen, M. D. "Lawrence of Arabia and *Ryecroft." Gissing Newsl* 26:4 (1990), 11–15.

Kropholler, P. F. "Notes on *The Private Papers of Henry Ryecroft." Gissing Newsl* 26:1 (1990), 27–30.

Thyrza, 1887

Bernstein, Carol L. *The Celebration of Scandal,* 62–64, 72–78.

The Unclassed, 1884

> Bernstein, Carol L. *The Celebration of Scandal,* 59–61.
> Harsh, Constance D. "Gissing's *The Unclassed* and the Perils of Naturalism." *ELH* 59 (1992), 911–34.
> Scheick, William J. *Fictional Structure & Ethics,* 47–73.

The Whirlpool, 1897

> Bernstein, Carol L. *The Celebration of Scandal,* 129–32.
> Cleto, Fabio. "The Biological Drama: Darwinian Ethics in George Gissing's Fiction." *Gissing J* 28:4 (1992), 11–20.
> Federico, Annette. *Masculine Identity,* 99–101, 102–11, 119–29.
> Greenslade, William. "Women and the Disease of Civilization: George Gissing's *The Whirlpool.*" *Victorian Stud* 32 (1989), 507–23.

Workers in the Dawn, 1880

> Bernstein, Carol L. *The Celebration of Scandal,* 56–59.
> Halperin, John. *Novelists in their Youth,* 116–25.

KATHARINE BRUCE GLASIER

Aimée Furniss, Scholar, 1896

> Waters, Chris. "New Women and Socialist-Feminist Fiction: The Novels of Isabella Ford and Katharine Bruce Glasier," in Angela Ingram and Daphne Patai, eds., *Rediscovering Forgotten Radicals,* 36–38.

Husband and Brother, 1894

> Waters, Chris. "New Women and Socialist-Feminist Fiction: The Novels of Isabella Ford and Katharine Bruce Glasier," in Angela Ingram and Daphne Patai, eds., *Rediscovering Forgotten Radicals,* 32–33.

Marget, 1902–1903

> Waters, Chris. "New Women and Socialist-Feminist Fiction: The Novels of Isabella Ford and Katharine Bruce Glasier," in Angela Ingram and Daphne Patai, eds., *Rediscovering Forgotten Radicals,* 38–40.

FRANCIS GODWIN

The Man in the Moon, 1638

> Pleithner, Regina. "Zwei Mondreisen des 17. Jahrhunderts: *Voyages imaginaires* oder Reisenutopien?," in Regina Pleithner, ed., *Reisen des Barock,* 75–87.

WILLIAM GODWIN

Caleb Williams, 1794

> Aguirre, Manuel. *The Closed Space,* 104–6.
> Barker, Gerard A. "The Narrative Mode of *Caleb Williams:* Problems and Resolutions." *Stud in the Novel* 25 (1993), 1–12.

Bode, Christoph. "Godwin's *Caleb Williams* and the Fiction of 'Things as They Are,'" in Günter Ahrends and Hans-Jürgen Diller, eds., *English Romantic Prose*, 95–112.

Clemit, Pamela. *The Godwinian Novel*, 35–69.

Damrosch, Leo. *Fictions of Reality*, 216–41.

Dentith, Simon. *A Rhetoric of the Real*, 48–49, 50–52.

Drexler, Peter. *Literatur, Recht, Kriminalität*, 137–40.

Ferguson, Frances. *Solitude and the Sublime*, 98–105.

Geary, Robert F. *The Supernatural in Gothic Fiction*, 90–92.

Graham, Kenneth W. "Narrative and Ideology in Godwin's *Caleb Williams*." *Eighteenth-Cent Fiction* 2 (1990), 215–28.

Graham, Kenneth W. *The Politics of Narrative*, 13–168.

Graham, Kenneth W. "The Two Endings of *Caleb Williams*: Politics and Aesthetics in a Revolutionary Novel." *Stud on Voltaire and the Eighteenth Cent* 265 (1989), 1238.

Manning, Susan. *The Puritan-Provincial Vision*, 72–76.

May, Marilyn. "Publish and Perish: William Godwin, Mary Shelley, and the Public Appetite for Scandal." *Papers on Lang & Lit* 26 (1990), 491–92, 496–502.

Paul, Robert S. *Whatever Happened to Sherlock Homes?*, 59–61.

Scheuermann, Mona. *Her Bread to Earn*, 144–48.

Smith, Ken Edward. "William Godwin: Social Critique in *Caleb Williams*." *Stud on Voltaire and the Eighteenth Cent* 263 (1989), 337–41.

Uphaus, Robert W. *The Idea of the Novel*, 35–37.

Fleetwood, 1805

Bruhm, Steven. "William Godwin's *Fleetwood:* The Epistemology of the Tortured Body." *Eighteenth-Cent Life* 16:2 (1992), 25–41.

Mellor, Anne K. *Mary Shelley*, 108–10.

Imogen, 1784

Clemit, Pamela. *The Godwinian Novel*, 13–34.

Clemit, Pamela. "*A Pastoral Romance, From the Ancient British:* Godwin's Rewriting of *Comus*." *Eighteenth-Cent Fiction* 3 (1991), 217–39.

Mandeville, 1817

Clemit, Pamela. *The Godwinian Novel*, 96–102.

St. Leon, 1799

Clemit, Pamela. *The Godwinian Novel*, 88–95.

Geary, Robert F. *The Supernatural in Gothic Fiction*, 69–80.

Magnier, Mireille. "Saint Leon, alchemiste et philanthrope (1799)." *Mythes, Croyances et Religions dans le Monde Anglo-Saxon* 9 (1991), 93–102.

Roberts, Marie. "Science and Irrationality in William Godwin's *St. Leon*." *Stud on Voltaire and the Eighteenth Cent* 264 (1989), 1196–99.

Scheuermann, Mona. *Her Bread to Earn*, 148–52.

LOUIS GOLDING

Mr. Emmanuel, 1939

    Croft, Andy. *Red Letter Days,* 331–33.

WILLIAM GOLDING

Close Quarters, 1987

    Boyd, S. J. *The Novels of William Golding,* 178–98.

    Friedman, Lawrence S. *William Golding,* 149–53.

    Gindin, James. "The Historical Imagination in William Golding's Later Fiction," in James Acheson, ed., *The British and Irish Novel,* 119–21.

    Stape, J. H. "'Fiction in the Wild, Modern Manner': Metanarrative Gesture in William Golding's *To the End of the Earth* Trilogy." *Twentieth Cent Lit* 38 (1992), 226–38.

Darkness Visible, 1979

    Boyd, S. J. *The Novels of William Golding,* 125–53.

    Dickson, L. L. *The Modern Allegories,* 109–17.

    Fiddes, Paul S. *Freedom and Limit,* 223–24, 228–30.

    Friedman, Lawrence S. *William Golding,* 122–38.

    Gindin, James. "The Historical Imagination in William Golding's Later Fiction," in James Acheson, ed., *The British and Irish Novel,* 112–14.

    Granofsky, Ronald. "'Man at an extremity': Elemental Trauma and Revelation in the Fiction of William Golding." *Mod Lang Stud* 20:2 (1990), 60–62.

    Schreurs, Willy. "*Darkness Visible:* The Choice between Good and Evil," in Jeanne Delbaere, ed., *William Golding,* 133–45.

    Tebbutt, Glorie. "Reading and Righting: Metafiction and Metaphysics in William Golding's *Darkness Visible.*" *Twentieth Cent Lit* 39 (1993), 47–57.

    Tiger, Virginia. "William Golding's Darkness Visible: Namings, Numberings, and Narrative Strategies." *Style* 24 (1990), 284–99.

Fire Down Below, 1989

    Boyd, S. J. *The Novels of William Golding,* 178–98.

    Friedman, Lawrence S. *William Golding,* 153–58.

    Gindin, James. "The Historical Imagination in William Golding's Later Fiction," in James Acheson, ed., *The British and Irish Novel,* 121–23.

    Stape, J. H. "'Fiction in the Wild, Modern Manner': Metanarrative Gesture in William Golding's *To the End of the Earth* Trilogy." *Twentieth Cent Lit* 38 (1992), 226–38.

Free Fall, 1959

    Bande, Usha. "Why Does Miss Pringle Hate Sammy? A Note on *Free Fall.*" *Aligarh J of Engl Stud* 13 (1988), 242–45.

    Boyd, S. J. *The Novels of William Golding,* 63–82.

    Delbaere, Jeanne. "From the Cellar to the Rock: A Recurrent Pattern in

William Golding's Novels," in Jeanne Delbaere, ed., *William Golding,*
7–9.

Delbaere, Jeanne. "Time as Structural Device in *Free Fall,*" in Jeanne Delbaere, ed., *William Golding,* 92–106.

Dickson, L. L. *The Modern Allegories,* 58–75.

Diericks, Jean. "The Theme of the Fall in the Novels of William Golding," in Jeanne Delbaere, ed., *William Golding,* 21–24.

Erlebach, Peter. *Theorie und Praxis des Romaneingangs,* 288–95.

Fiddes, Paul S. *Freedom and Limit,* 217–20.

Friedman, Lawrence S. *William Golding,* 67–85.

Granofsky, Ronald. "'Man at an extremity': Elemental Trauma and Revelation in the Fiction of William Golding." *Mod Lang Stud* 20:2 (1990), 54–56.

Kamm, Jürgen. "Narrative Cross-References as a Structural Device in William Golding's *Free Fall.*" *Anglia* 107 (1989), 89–92.

The Inheritors, 1955

Adriaens, Mark. "Style in *The Inheritors,*" in Jeanne Delbaere, ed., *William Golding,* 45–60.

Boyd, S. J. *The Novels of William Golding,* 24–45.

Delbaere, Jeanne. "Lok-Like-Log: Structure and Imagery in *The Inheritors,*" in Jeanne Delbaere, ed., *William Golding,* 61–73.

Dickson, L. L. *The Modern Allegories,* 27–41.

Diericks, Jean. "The Theme of the Fall in the Novels of William Golding," in Jeanne Delbaere, ed., *William Golding,* 15–18.

Fiddes, Paul S. *Freedom and Limit,* 220–23.

François, Pierre. "The Rule of Oa in *The Inheritors,*" in Jeanne Delbaere, ed., *William Golding,* 74–83.

Friedman, Lawrence S. *William Golding,* 33–50.

Ruddick, Nicholas. *Ultimate Island,* 77–82.

Lord of the Flies, 1954

Bergonzi, Bernard. *Wartime and Aftermath,* 190–93.

Boyd, S. J. *The Novels of William Golding,* 1–23.

Delbaere, Jeanne. "From the Cellar to the Rock: A Recurrent Pattern in William Golding's Novels," in Jeanne Delbaere, ed., *William Golding,* 3–5.

Delbaere, Jeanne. "Rhythm and Expansion in *Lord of the Flies,*" in Jeanne Delbaere, ed., *William Golding,* 25–34.

Dickson, L. L. *The Modern Allegories,* 12–26.

Diericks, Jean. "The Theme of the Fall in the Novels of William Golding," in Jeanne Delbaere, ed., *William Golding,* 12–15.

Fitzgerald, John F., and John R. Kayser. "Golding's *Lord of the Flies:* Pride as Original Sin." *Stud in the Novel* 24 (1992), 78–85.

Friedman, Lawrence S. *William Golding,* 19–32.

Michel-Michot, Paulette. "The Myth of Innocence: *Robinson Crusoe, The*

Coral Island and *Lord of the Flies,*" in Jeanne Delbaere, ed., *William Golding,* 35–44.

Reilly, Patrick. *"Lord of the Flies,"* 25–125.

The Paper Men, 1984

Boyd, S. J. *The Novels of William Golding,* 199–214.

D'Amelio, Nadia. "No Inheritors in *The Paper Men,*" in Jeanne Delbaere, ed., *William Golding,* 152–65.

Delbaere, Jeanne. "The Artist as Clown of God in *The Paper Men,*" in Jeanne Delbaere, ed., *William Golding,* 166–75.

Dickson, L. L. *The Modern Allegories,* 127–33.

Fiddes, Paul S. *Freedom and Limit,* 231–34.

Friedman, Lawrence S. *William Golding,* 159–71.

Gindin, James. "The Historical Imagination in William Golding's Later Fiction," in James Acheson, ed., *The British and Irish Novel,* 114–16.

Simon, Irène. "Vision or Dream? The Supernatural Design in *The Paper Men,*" in Jeanne Delbaere, ed., *William Golding,* 176–85.

Pincher Martin, 1956

Alexander, Marguerite. *Flights from Realism,* 49–54.

Boyd, S. J. *The Novels of William Golding,* 46–62.

Delbaere, Jeanne. "The Chinese-Box Structure of *Pincher Martin,*" in Jeanne Delbaere, ed., *William Golding,* 84–91.

Delbaere, Jeanne. "From the Cellar to the Rock: A Recurrent Pattern in William Golding's Novels," in Jeanne Delbaere, ed., *William Golding,* 5–7.

Dickson, L. L. *The Modern Allegories,* 42–57.

Diericks, Jean. "The Theme of the Fall in the Novels of William Golding," in Jeanne Delbaere, ed., *William Golding,* 18–21.

Friedman, Lawrence S. *William Golding,* 51–66.

Granofsky, Ronald. "'Man at an extremity': Elemental Trauma and Revelation in the Fiction of William Golding." *Mod Lang Stud* 20:2 (1990), 52–54.

Sertori, Daniela Carpi. "Il racconto del sogno: *Bruno's Dream* di Iris Murdoch e *Pincher Martin* di William Golding." *Lingua e Stile* 24 (1989), 457–65.

Sugimura, Yasunori. "Hallucination and Plotmaking Principle in *Pincher Martin* by William Golding." *Stud in Engl Lit* (Tokyo) 1989:21–36.

The Pyramid, 1967

Boyd, S. J. *The Novels of William Golding,* 106–24.

Dickson, L. L. *The Modern Allegories,* 96–108.

Friedman, Lawrence S. *William Golding,* 105–15.

Gindin, James. "The Historical Imagination in William Golding's Later Fiction," in James Acheson, ed., *The British and Irish Novel,* 110–13.

Maufort, Marc. "Golding's Stilbourne: Symbolic Space in *The Pyramid,*" in Jeanne Delbaere, ed., *William Golding,* 125–32.

Rites of Passage, 1980

Boyd, S. J. *The Novels of William Golding,* 154–77.

Dickson, L. L. *The Modern Allegories,* 117–27.

Friedman, Lawrence S. *William Golding,* 140–49.

Gindin, James. "The Historical Imagination in William Golding's Later Fiction," in James Acheson, ed., *The British and Irish Novel,* 116–19.

Hassam, Andrew. *Writing and Reality,* 103–9.

Rao, V. V. Subba. "Sin and Shame: A Note on Colley's Fall in Golding's *Rites of Passage." Liter Endeavour* 9 (1987–88), 71–78.

Servotte, Herman. "The Sound of Silence in the Sea Trilogy," in Jeanne Delbaere, ed., *William Golding,* 186–93.

Simon, Irène. "The Theatre Motif in *Rites of Passage,"* in Jeanne Delbaere, ed., *William Golding,* 146–51.

Stape, J. H. " 'Fiction in the Wild, Modern Manner': Metanarrative Gesture in William Golding's *To the End of the Earth* Trilogy." *Twentieth Cent Lit* 38 (1992), 226–38.

The Spire, 1964

Bande, Usha. "Jocelin's Glorified Self: A Horneyan Interpretation of Golding's *The Spire." Notes on Contemp Lit* 21:5 (1991), 9–10.

Boyd, S. J. *The Novels of William Golding,* 83–105.

Delbaere, Jeanne. "The Evil Plant in *The Spire,"* in Jeanne Delbaere, ed., *William Golding,* 107–14.

Delbaere, Jeanne. "From the Cellar to the Rock: A Recurrent Pattern in William Golding's Novels," in Jeanne Delbaere, ed., *William Golding,* 9–11.

Dickson, L. L. *The Modern Allegories,* 76–95.

Fiddes, Paul S. *Freedom and Limit,* 211–14.

Friedman, Lawrence S. *William Golding,* 86–103.

Granofsky, Ronald. " 'Man at an extremity': Elemental Trauma and Revelation in the Fiction of William Golding." *Mod Lang Stud* 20:2 (1990), 56–60.

OLIVER GOLDSMITH

The Vicar of Wakefield, 1766

Boardman, Michael M. *Narrative Innovation,* 63–75.

Bony, Alain. *"The Vicar of Wakefield* as a Philosophic Tale: A Generic Approach." *Zagadnienia Rodzajów Literackich* 32:2 (1989), 31–41.

Brooks, Christopher K. "Marriage in Goldsmith: The Single Woman, Feminine Space, and 'Virtue,' " in JoAnna Stephens Mink and Janet Doubler Ward, eds., *Joinings and Disjoinings,* 27–32.

Derry, Stephen. "Jane Austen's Use of *The Vicar of Wakefield* in *Pride and Prejudice." Engl Lang Notes* 28:3 (1991), 25–27.

Dixon, Peter. *Oliver Goldsmith Revisited,* 75–96.

Duncan, Jeffrey L. "The Rural Ideal in Eighteenth-Century Fiction," in H. George Hahn, ed., *The Country Myth,* 261–64.

Emprin, Ginette. "Lieux Indéfinis et Temps Multiple dans *The Vicar of Wakefield.*" *Etudes Irlandaises* 14:1 (1989), 25–31.

Haggerty, George E. "Satire and Sentiment in *The Vicar of Wakefield.*" *Eighteenth Cent* 32 (1991), 25–37.

Hall, K. G. *The Exalted Heroine,* 74–89.

Kane, Baydallaye. "Du statut des lois dans *The Vicar of Wakefield.*" *Bull de la Société d'Etudes Anglo-Américaines des XVIIe et XVIIIe Siècles* 33 (1991), 111–18.

Mullan, John. *Sentiment and Sociability,* 136–42.

Probyn, Clive T. *English Fiction,* 157–60.

Taylor, Richard C. "Goldsmith's First Vicar." *R of Engl Stud* 41 (1990), 191–99.

MARY GORDON

The Company of Women, 1980

Seabury, Marcia Bundy. "Of Belief and Unbelief: The Novels of Mary Gordon." *Christianity and Lit* 40 (1990), 43–44.

Final Payments, 1978

Seabury, Marcia Bundy. "Of Belief and Unbelief: The Novels of Mary Gordon." *Christianity and Lit* 40 (1990), 39–42.

Men and Angels, 1985

Seabury, Marcia Bundy. "Of Belief and Unbelief: The Novels of Mary Gordon." *Christianity and Lit* 40 (1990), 45–48.

The Other Side, 1989

Seabury, Marcia Bundy. "Of Belief and Unbelief: The Novels of Mary Gordon." *Christianity and Lit* 40 (1990), 48–53.

KENNETH GRAHAME

The Wind in the Willows, 1908

DeForest, Mary. "*The Wind in the Willows:* A Tale for Two Readers." *Classical and Mod Lit* 10 (1989), 81–87.

Moore, John David. "Pottering About in the Garden: Kenneth Grahame's Version of Pastoral in *The Wind in the Willows.*" *J of the Midwest Mod Lang Assoc* 23:1 (1990), 45–59.

Philip, Neil. "*The Wind in the Willows:* The Vitality of a Classic," in Gillian Avery and Julia Briggs, eds., *Children and Their Books,* 299–316.

Steig, Michael. *Stories of Reading,* 79–104.

Wall, Barbara. *The Narrator's Voice,* 138–42.

SARAH GRAND

The Beth Book, 1897

Neetens, Wim. *Writing and Democracy,* 109–17.

The Heavenly Twins, 1893

> Bounell, Marilyn. "The Legacy of Sarah Grand's *The Heavenly Twins:* A Review Essay." *Engl Lit in Transition* 36 (1993), 467–77.

JAMES GRANT

First Love and Last Love: A Tale of the Indian Mutiny, 1868

> Paxton, Nancy L. "Mobilizing Chivalry: Rape in British Novels about the Indian Uprising of 1857." *Victorian Stud* 36 (1992), 10–13.

The Romance of War, or The Highlanders in Spain, 1846

> Dendle, Brian J. *"The Romance of War, or The Highlanders in Spain:* The Peninsular War and the British Novel." *Anales de Literatura Española* 7 (1991), 49–64.

RICHARD GRAVES

Plexippus, or The Aspiring Plebeian, 1790

> Tournebize, Cassilde. *"Plexippus* (1790) de Richard Graves: l'illusion d'avoir découvert le roman historique." *Caliban* 28 (1991), 71–77.

The Spiritual Quixote, 1773

> Hall, K. G. *The Exalted Heroine,* 90–109.
> Tournebize, Cassilde. "Ambiguïté de la satire du méthodisme dans le *Spiritual Quixote* (1773), de Richard Graves." *Caliban* 29 (1992), 39–47.

ALASDAIR GRAY

Lanark, 1981

> Lee, Alison. *Realism and Power,* 99–114.

HENRY GREEN

Back, 1946

> Doan, Laura L. "Recuperating the Postwar Moment: Green's *Back* and Bacon's *Three Studies for Figures at the Base of a Crucifixion." Mosaic* 23:3 (1990), 113–24. (Also in Evelyn J. Hinz, ed., *Troops versus Tropes,* 113–24.)
> Gindin, James. *British Fiction,* 147–49.
> Klass, Sabine von. *Die Romane Henry Greens,* 87–112.

Blindness, 1926

> Gindin, James. *British Fiction,* 148–50.
> Klass, Sabine von. *Die Romane Henry Greens,* 147–48.

Caught, 1943

> Bergonzi, Bernard. *Wartime and Aftermath*, 31–34.
> Klass, Sabine von. *Die Romane Henry Greens*, 154–57.
> Munton, Alan. *English Fiction*, 44–47.

Concluding, 1948

> Facknitz, Mark A. R. "The Edge of Night: Figures of Change in Henry Green's *Concluding*." *Twentieth Cent Lit* 36 (1990), 10–21.
> Gorra, Michael. *The English Novel*, 48–51.
> Klass, Sabine von. *Die Romane Henry Greens*, 113–45.

Doting, 1952

> Gindin, James. *British Fiction*, 147–49.
> Klass, Sabine von. *Die Romane Henry Greens*, 158–61.
> Page, Norman. *Speech in the English Novel*, 138–41.

Living, 1929

> Gindin, James. *British Fiction*, 136–38, 148–52.
> Gorra, Michael. *The English Novel*, 30–36.
> Klass, Sabine von. *Die Romane Henry Greens*, 149–51.

Loving, 1945

> Gindin, James. *British Fiction*, 144–46.
> Gorra, Michael. *The English Novel*, 40–46.
> Klass, Sabine von. *Die Romane Henry Greens*, 49–86.
> MacPhail, Fiona. "A Shadowless Castle of Treasures: Kinalty Castle in Henry Green's *Loving*," in Jacqueline Genet, ed., *The Big House in Ireland*, 233–40.

Nothing, 1950

> Klass, Sabine von. *Die Romane Henry Greens*, 158–61.

Party Going, 1939

> Ames, Christopher. *The Life of the Party*, 202–20.
> Gindin, James. *British Fiction*, 136–38, 141–44.
> Gorra, Michael. *The English Novel*, 36–40.
> Klass, Sabine von. *Die Romane Henry Greens*, 152–54.

GRAHAM GREENE

Brighton Rock, 1938

> Adamson, Judith. *Graham Greene*, 25–27, 40–42.
> Antor, Heinz. "Graham Greene as a Catholic Novelist," in Peter Erlebach and Thomas Michael Stein, eds., *Graham Greene in Perspective*, 97–102.
> Carey, John. *The Intellectuals and the Masses*, 83–85.
> Choi, Jae-Suck. *Greene and Unamuno*, 35–62.
> Diemert, Brian. "Ida Arnold and the Detective Story: Reading *Brighton Rock*." *Twentieth Cent Lit* 38 (1992), 386–401.

Friedman, Alan Warren. " 'The Dangerous Edge': Beginning with Death," in Jeffrey Meyers, ed., *Graham Greene*, 142–46.

Gorra, Michael. *The English Novel*, 124–28.

Malamet, Elliott. "Graham Greene and the Hounds of *Brighton Rock*." *Mod Fiction Stud* 37 (1991), 689–702.

Miller, R. H. *Understanding Graham Greene*, 33–51.

Monnier, Jean-Yves. " 'Knowing' in *Brighton Rock*," in Peter Erlebach and Thomas Michael Stein, eds., *Graham Greene in Perspective*, 31–40.

Nehring, Neil. "Revolt into Style: Graham Greene Meets the Sex Pistols." *PMLA* 106 (1991), 223–36.

Sharma, S. K. *Graham Greene*, 80–90.

Williams, Trevor L. "History and Theology: The Case for Pinkie in Greene's *Brighton Rock*." *Stud in the Novel* 24 (1992), 67–75.

A Burnt-Out Case, 1961

Adamson, Judith. *Graham Greene*, 193–95.

Antor, Heinz. "Graham Greene as a Catholic Novelist," in Peter Erlebach and Thomas Michael Stein, eds., *Graham Greene in Perspective*, 106–9, 114–17.

Choi, Jae-Suck. *Greene and Unamuno*, 159–84.

Miller, R. H. *Understanding Graham Greene*, 90–94.

Pisano, Frank. "Greene's *A Burnt-Out Case*." *Explicator* 49 (1991), 177–80.

Sharma, S. K. *Graham Greene*, 148–60.

The Comedians, 1966

Adamson, Judith. *Graham Greene*, 148–50, 153–59.

Barrett, Dorothea L. L. "Communism and Catholicism in *The Comedians*," in Peter Erlebach and Thomas Michael Stein, eds., *Graham Greene in Perspective*, 119–30.

Gorra, Michael. *The English Novel*, 146–51.

Miller, R. H. *Understanding Graham Greene*, 116–23.

Sharma, S. K. *Graham Greene*, 163–71.

Doctor Fisher of Geneva, 1980

Miller, R. H. *Understanding Graham Greene*, 144–48.

Sharma, S. K. *Graham Greene*, 197–204.

The End of the Affair, 1951

Bergonzi, Bernard. *Wartime and Aftermath*, 88–90.

Choi, Jae-Suck. *Greene and Unamuno*, 131–55.

Erlebach, Peter. *Theorie und Praxis des Romaneingangs*, 283–88.

Gorra, Michael. *The English Novel*, 138–41.

Miller, R. H. *Understanding Graham Greene*, 81–89.

Piroëlle, Ann. "Graham Greene: Fiction and Film," in Peter Erlebach and Thomas Michael Stein, eds., *Graham Greene in Perspective*, 82–85.

Sharma, S. K. *Graham Greene*, 124–38.

Smith, Rowland. "A People's War in Greeneland: Heroic Virtue and Communal Effort in the Wartime Tales," in Jeffrey Meyers, ed., *Graham Greene*, 120–22.

England Made Me, 1935

Brown, Tony. "Fact and Fiction in the 1930s: A Reading of Graham Greene's *England Made Me*." *Essays in Graham Greene* 2 (1990), 35–57.

Gorra, Michael. *The English Novel*, 119–21.

Hoskins, Robert. "'Those Dreadful Clothes': *The Meaning of Modern Sculpture* and the Genesis of Greene's *England Made Me*." *South Atlantic R* 57:2 (1992), 73–90.

Miller, R. H. *Understanding Graham Greene*, 24–32.

Sharma, S. K. *Graham Greene*, 62–70.

A Gun for Sale, 1936

Adamson, Judith. *Graham Greene*, 36–42.

Panek, LeRoy L. "*A Gun for Sale:* Greene's First Thriller." *Essays in Graham Greene* 2 (1990), 127–41.

The Heart of the Matter, 1948

Adamson, Judith. *Graham Greene*, 79–90.

Antor, Heinz. "Graham Greene as a Catholic Novelist," in Peter Erlebach and Thomas Michael Stein, eds., *Graham Greene in Perspective*, 112–14.

Chace, William M. "Spies and God's Spies: Greene's Espionage Fiction," in Jeffrey Meyers, ed., *Graham Greene*, 156–58, 161–63.

Choi, Jae-Suck. *Greene and Unamuno*, 97–126.

Fraser, Robert. "Sinners and Saints: Graham Greene and George Barker." *Essays in Graham Greene* 2 (1990), 1–19.

Freis, Richard. "Scobie's World." *Rel & Lit* 24:3 (1992), 57–76.

Gorra, Michael. *The English Novel*, 133–38.

Hollahan, Eugene. "'Of Course the Whole Thing Was Couéism': *The Heart of the Matter* as a Critique of Emile Coué's Psychotherapy." *Stud in the Novel* 21 (1989), 320–30.

Miller, R. H. *Understanding Graham Greene*, 68–81.

Page, Norman. *Speech in the English Novel*, 127–30.

Sharma, S. K. *Graham Greene*, 100–118.

Smith, Rowland. "A People's War in Greeneland: Heroic Virtue and Communal Effort in the Wartime Tales," in Jeffrey Meyers, ed., *Graham Greene*, 118–20.

The Honorary Consul, 1973

Adamson, Judith. *Graham Greene*, 173–79.

Böker, Uwe. "'Mixed up and Caught up': Dimension of Political Experience in *The Quiet American* and *The Honorary Consul*," in Peter Erlebach and Thomas Michael Stein, eds., *Graham Greene in Perspective*, 145–47.

Malamet, Elliott. "'Art in a Police Station': Detection, Fatherhood, and

Textual Influence in Greene's *The Honorary Consul.*" *Texas Stud in Lit and Lang* 34 (1992), 106–24.

Miller, R. H. *Understanding Graham Greene,* 130–40.

Piroëlle, Ann. "Graham Greene: Fiction and Film," in Peter Erlebach and Thomas Michael Stein, eds., *Graham Greene in Perspective,* 80–82.

Sharma, S. K. *Graham Greene,* 180–87.

Weber, Jean Jacques. *Critical Analysis of Fiction,* 83–92.

Wood, Nigel. "Graham Greene and the Image of the Novelist," in Peter Erlebach and Thomas Michael Stein, eds., *Graham Greene in Perspective,* 67–72.

Woodman, Thomas. *Faithful Fictions,* 91–93.

The Human Factor, 1978

Adamson, Judith. *Graham Greene,* 195–97.

Antor, Heinz. "Graham Greene as a Catholic Novelist," in Peter Erlebach and Thomas Michael Stein, eds., *Graham Greene in Perspective,* 105–6.

Chace, William M. "Spies and God's Spies: Greene's Espionage Fiction," in Jeffrey Meyers, ed., *Graham Greene,* 171–74.

Miller, R. H. *Understanding Graham Greene,* 140–44.

Miller, Robert H. "Destructive Innocents and the Getting of Wisdom: Greene's Post-War Spies." *Essays in Graham Greene* 2 (1990), 93–96.

Scanlan, Margaret. *Traces of Another Time,* 101–9.

Schöneich, Christoph. "Der Leser als Agent: Literarische Anspielungen in Graham Greenes *The Human Factor.*" *Archiv für das Studium der neueren Sprachen und Literaturen* 227 (1990), 282–98.

Shapiro, Henry L. "Morality and Ambivalence in *The Human Factor.*" *Essays in Graham Greene* 2 (1990), 99–109.

Sharma, S. K. *Graham Greene,* 188–97.

Stafford, David. *The Silent Game,* 192–93.

Stein, Thomas Michael. " 'Watertight boxes': Ben Nicholson's 'Painting 1937' and Graham Greene's Novel *The Human Factor,*" in Peter Erlebach and Thomas Michael Stein, eds., *Graham Greene in Perspective,* 175–87.

It's a Battlefield, 1934

Miller, R. H. *Understanding Graham Greene,* 16–34.

Sharma, S. K. *Graham Greene,* 52–62.

The Man Within, 1929

Sharma, S. K. *Graham Greene,* 46–52.

The Ministry of Fear, 1943

Adamson, Judith. *Graham Greene,* 72–74.

Smith, Rowland. "A People's War in Greeneland: Heroic Virtue and Communal Effort in the Wartime Tales," in Jeffrey Meyers, ed., *Graham Greene,* 115–19, 122–27.

Stafford, David. *The Silent Game,* 143–45.

Monsignor Quixote, 1982

Adamson, Judith. *Graham Greene*, 187–92.

Champagne, Roland A. "The Charm of *Monsignor Quixote:* Graham Greene's Art of Laughter." *Essays in Graham Greene* 2 (1990), 143–50.

Choi, Jae-Suck. *Greene and Unamuno*, 187–99.

Desmond, John F. "The Heart of (the) Matter: The Mystery of the Real in *Monsignor Quixote.*" *Rel and Lit* 22:1 (1990), 59–76.

Gorra, Michael. *The English Novel*, 153–55.

Holderness, Graham. " 'Knight-errant of Faith'?: *Monsignor Quixote* as 'Catholic Fiction.' " *Lit & Theology* 7 (1993), 259–81.

Müller, Wolfgang. "Graham Greene's *Monsignor Quixote:* An Intertextual Analysis," in Peter Erlebach and Thomas Michael Stein, eds., *Graham Greene in Perspective,* 161–74.

O'Prey, Paul. " 'Taking sides': Faith, Action and Indifference in the Novels of Graham Greene," in Peter Erlebach and Thomas Michael Stein, eds., *Graham Greene in Perspective,* 156–59.

Whitehouse, J. C. W. "Grammars of Assent and Dissent in Graham Greene and Brian Moore." *Renascence* 42 (1990), 157–71.

Our Man in Havana, 1958

Adamson, Judith. *Graham Greene*, 142–45.

Chace, William M. "Spies and God's Spies: Greene's Espionage Fiction," in Jeffrey Meyers, ed., *Graham Greene,* 168–71.

Miller, R. H. *Understanding Graham Greene,* 113–16.

Miller, Robert H. "Destructive Innocents and the Getting of Wisdom: Greene's Post-War Spies." *Essays in Graham Greene* 2 (1990), 92–93.

Smyth, Denis. "*Our Man in Havana,* Their Man in Madrid: Literary Invention in Espionage Fact and Fiction," in Wesley K. Wark, ed., *Spy Fiction,* 117–32.

Stafford, David. *The Silent Game,* 188–90.

The Power and the Glory, 1940

Adamson, Judith. *Graham Greene*, 58–63.

Antor, Heinz. "Graham Greene as a Catholic Novelist," in Peter Erlebach and Thomas Michael Stein, eds., *Graham Greene in Perspective,* 104–5.

Choi, Jae-Suck. *Greene and Unamuno*, 65–93.

De Caro, Frank. "Proverbs in Graham Greene's *The Power and the Glory:* Framing Thematic Concerns in a Modern Novel." *Proverbium* 6 (1989), 1–7.

Diephouse, Daniel. "The Sense of Ends in Graham Greene and *The Power and the Glory.*" *J of Narrative Technique* 20 (1990), 22–39.

Erlebach, Peter. "Major Themes and Structural Ways of Arguing Meaning in Graham Greene's Novels of the 1940s and 1950s," in Peter Erlebach and Thomas Michael Stein, eds., *Graham Greene in Perspective,* 23–30.

Friedman, Alan Warren. " 'The Dangerous Edge': Beginning with Death," in Jeffrey Meyers, ed., *Graham Greene,* 145–47.

Gorra, Michael. *The English Novel,* 128–33.

Miller, R. H. *Understanding Graham Greene,* 54–67.
Sharma, S. K. *Graham Greene,* 90–100.
Woodman, Thomas. *Faithful Fictions,* 101–4.

The Quiet American, 1955

Adamson, Judith. *Graham Greene,* 128–36.
Böker, Uwe. "'Mixed up and Caught up': Dimension of Political Experience in *The Quiet American* and *The Honorary Consul,*" in Peter Erlebach and Thomas Michael Stein, eds., *Graham Greene in Perspective,* 140–45.
Bonney, William. "Politics, Perception, and Gender in Conrad's *Lord Jim* and Greene's *The Quiet American.*" *Conradiana* 23 (1991), 99–118.
Chace, William M. "Spies and God's Spies: Greene's Espionage Fiction," in Jeffrey Meyers, ed., *Graham Greene,* 166–68.
Gorra, Michael. *The English Novel,* 141–46.
Miller, R. H. *Understanding Graham Greene,* 106–13.
Miller, Robert H. "Destructive Innocents and the Getting of Wisdom: Greene's Post-War Spies." *Essays in Graham Greene* 2 (1990), 91–92.
Pendleton, Robert. "Arabesques of Influence: The Repressed Conradian Masterplot in the Novels of Graham Greene." *Conradiana* 25 (1993), 87–94.
Sharma, S. K. *Graham Greene,* 138–48.

Stamboul Train, 1932

Gorra, Michael. *The English Novel,* 108–10.

The Tenth Man, 1985

Wolfe, Peter. "The Coward and the Cheat: A Reading of *The Tenth Man.*" *Essays in Graham Greene* 2 (1990), 113–26.

The Third Man, 1950

Adamson, Judith. *Graham Greene,* 91–94.
Chace, William M. "Spies and God's Spies: Greene's Espionage Fiction," in Jeffrey Meyers, ed., *Graham Greene,* 164–65.
Kalson, Albert E. "Raymond Chandler's *Long Goodbye* to Graham Greene's *The Third Man.*" *Essays in Graham Greene* 2 (1990), 23–33.
Miller, R. H. *Understanding Graham Greene,* 104–6.
Miller, Robert H. "Destructive Innocents and the Getting of Wisdom: Greene's Post-War Spies." *Essays in Graham Greene* 2 (1990), 90–91.
Piroëlle, Ann. "Graham Greene: Fiction and Film," in Peter Erlebach and Thomas Michael Stein, eds., *Graham Greene in Perspective,* 85–90.

Travels with My Aunt, 1969

Hartveit, Lars. "The Author as Picaro in *Travels with My Aunt.*" *Essays in Graham Greene* 2 (1990), 63–84.
Miller, R. H. *Understanding Graham Greene,* 126–30.
Schulz, Volker. "'Passing the Border': The Two Worlds of *Travels With My*

Aunt," in Peter Erlebach and Thomas Michael Stein, eds., *Graham Greene in Perspective*, 41–58.

Sharma, S. K. *Graham Greene*, 171–79.

ROBERT GREENE

The Card of Fancy, 1584

Heilman, Robert Bechtold. *The Workings of Fiction*, 187–204.

Mamillia, 1580

Lucas, Caroline. *Writing for Women*, 77–84.

Myrror of Modestie, 1584

Lucas, Caroline. *Writing for Women*, 84–86.

Pandosto, 1588

Margolies, David. "Picaresque Irony in Nashe and Greene." *New Comparison* 11 (1991), 45–48.

Penelope's Web, 1587

Lucas, Caroline. *Writing for Women*, 91–94.

Philomela, 1592

Lucas, Caroline. *Writing for Women*, 86–91.

FRANK GRIFFIN

October Day, 1939

Croft, Andy. *Red Letter Days*, 309–11.

NEIL GUNN

The Key of the Chest, 1945

Pick, J. B. "A Neglected Major Novel: Neil Gunn's *The Key of the Chest.*" *Scottish Liter J* 17:1 (1990), 35–45.

HENRY RIDER HAGGARD

Eric Brighteyes, 1898

Orel, Harold. "Adapting the Conventions of the Historical Romance: Rider Haggard's *Eric Brighteyes.*" *Engl Lit in Transition* 36 (1993), 50–57.

King Solomon's Mines, 1885

Bristow, Joseph. *Empire Boys*, 127–39.

Scheick, William J. "Adolescent Pornography and Imperialism in Haggard's *King Solomon's Mines.*" *Engl Lit in Transition* 34 (1991), 19–29.

She, 1887

> Basham, Diana. *The Trial of Woman,* 186–95.
> Bristow, Joseph. *Empire Boys,* 133–46.

CHARLOTTE HALDANE

Man's World, 1926

> Russell, Elizabeth. "The Loss of the Feminine Principle in Charlotte Haldane's *Man's World* and Katherine Burdekin's *Swastika Night,*" in Lucie Armitt, ed., *Where No Man Has Gone Before,* 15–28.
> Squier, Susan. "Sexual Biopolitics in *Man's World:* The Writings of Charlotte Haldane," in Angela Ingram and Daphne Patai, eds., *Rediscovering Forgotten Radicals,* 236–39.

MARGUERITE RADCLYFFE HALL

The Unlit Lamp, 1924

> Brimstone, Lyndie. "Towards a New Cartography: Radclyffe Hall, Virginia Woolf and the Working of Common Land," in Elaine Hobby and Chris White, eds., *What Lesbians Do in Books,* 90–92, 97–99.
> Brown, Penny. *The Poison at the Source,* 53–65.

The Well of Loneliness, 1928

> Brimstone, Lyndie. "Towards a New Cartography: Radclyffe Hall, Virginia Woolf and the Working of Common Land," in Elaine Hobby and Chris White, eds., *What Lesbians Do in Books,* 96–99, 101–2.
> Brown, Penny. *The Poison at the Source,* 66–79.
> O'Rourke, Rebecca. *Reflecting on "The Well of Loneliness,"* 1–144.
> Tylee, Claire M. *The Great War,* 169–80.

BRUCE HAMILTON

Traitor's Way, 1938

> Croft, Andy. *Red Letter Days,* 194–96.

ELIZABETH HAMILTON

The Cottagers of Glenburnie, 1808

> Campbell, Ian. "Glenburnie Revisited," in Joachim Schwend et al., eds., *Literatur im Kontext,* 71–89.

Memoirs of Modern Philosophers, 1800

> Ty, Eleanor. "Female Philosophy Refunctioned: Elizabeth Hamilton's Parodic Novel." *Ariel* 22:4 (1991), 111–26.

MARY AGNES HAMILTON

Dead Yesterday, 1916

Tylee, Claire M. *The Great War,* 108–12.

PATRICK HAMILTON

Impromptu in Moribundia, 1939

Croft, Andy. *Red Letter Days,* 293–95.

The Plains of Cement, 1934

Croft, Andy. *Red Letter Days,* 145–47.

Slaves of Solitude, 1947

Gindin, James. *British Fiction,* 78–80.

JAMES HANLEY

No Directions, 1943

Bergonzi, Bernard. *Wartime and Aftermath,* 29–31.

THOMAS HARDY

Desperate Remedies, 1871

Brady, Kristin. "Textual Hysteria: Hardy's Narrator on Women," in Margaret R. Higonnet, ed., *The Sense of Sex,* 90–94.

DiBattista, Maria. *First Love,* 243–45.

Halperin, John. *Novelists in their Youth,* 81–84, 86–94.

Hands, Timothy. *Thomas Hardy,* 39–43.

Ingham, Patricia. *Thomas Hardy,* 14–22, 26–28, 32–34, 56–58.

Pinion, F. B. *Hardy the Writer,* 94–97.

Riesen, Beat. *Thomas Hardy's Minor Novels,* 49–60.

Roberts, Patrick. "Patterns of Relationship in *Desperate Remedies.*" *Thomas Hardy J* 8:2 (1992), 50–57.

Wright, T. R. *Hardy and the Erotic,* 37–43.

Far from the Madding Crowd, 1874

Berger, Sheila. *Thomas Hardy and Visual Structures,* 44–46, 65–66, 80–90.

Bronfen, Elisabeth. "Pay as You Go: Exchanges of Bodies and Signs," in Margaret R. Higonnet, ed., *The Sense of Sex,* 66–74.

Collins, Deborah L. *Thomas Hardy and His God,* 104–7.

Federico, Annette. *Masculine Identity,* 55–68.

Garson, Marjorie. *Hardy's Fables of Integrity,* 25–53.

Goode, John. "Hardy and Marxism," in Dale Kramer, ed., *Critical Essays,* 27–28.

Goss, Michael. "Aspects of Time in *Far from the Madding Crowd*." *Thomas Hardy J* 6:3 (1990), 43–53.

Hands, Timothy. *Thomas Hardy,* 44–46, 49–51, 63–65, 82–84, 92–95.

Ingham, Patricia. *Thomas Hardy,* 16–18, 22–25, 30–32.

Krasner, James. *The Entangled Eye,* 88–90.

Mistichelli, William. "Androgyny, Survival, and Fulfillment in Thomas Hardy's *Far from the Madding Crowd." Mod Lang Stud* 18:3 (1988), 53–64.

Morgan, William W. "Gender and Silence in Thomas Hardy's Texts," in Antony H. Harrison and Beverly Taylor, eds., *Gender and Discourse,* 169–75.

Ogden, Daryl. "Bathsheba's Visual Estate: Female Spectatorship in *Far From the Madding Crowd." J of Narrative Technique* 23 (1993), 1–13.

Pinion, F. B. *Hardy the Writer,* 18–20, 28–33.

Polhemus, Robert M. *Erotic Faith,* 223–50.

Sasaki, Toru. "On Boldwood's Retina: A 'Moment of Vision' in *Far from the Madding Crowd* and Its Possible Relation to *Middlemarch." Thomas Hardy J* 8:3 (1992), 57–60.

Schwarz, Daniel R. *The Transformation of the English Novel,* 31–33, 52–55.

Sheard, Robert F. "Triangles, Love, and Isolation in Hardy's *Far from the Madding Crowd." Thomas Hardy Yrbk* 19 (1991), 13–16.

Shelston, Alan. "Were They Beautiful?: *Far from the Madding Crowd* and *Daniel Deronda." Thomas Hardy J* 8:2 (1992), 65–67.

Shires, Linda M. "Narrative, Gender, and Power in *Far from the Madding Crowd." Novel* 24 (1991), 162–76. (Also in Margaret R. Higonnet, ed., *The Sense of Sex,* 49–64.)

Swann, Charles. "*Far From the Madding Crowd:* How Good a Shepherd Is Gabriel Oak?" *Notes and Queries* 237 (1992), 189.

Williams, Merryn. *A Preface to Hardy,* 89–91.

Wright, T. R. *Hardy and the Erotic,* 50–54.

The Hand of Ethelberta, 1876

Boumelha, Penny. "'A Complicated Position for a Woman': *The Hand of Ethelberta,"* in Margaret R. Higonnet, ed., *The Sense of Sex,* 242–58.

Goode, John. "Hardy and Marxism," in Dale Kramer, ed., *Critical Essays,* 28–29.

Hands, Timothy. *Thomas Hardy,* 55–57.

Mistichelli, William J. "The Comedy of Survival in Thomas Hardy's *The Hand of Ethelberta." Mod Lang Stud* 22:4 (1992), 88–103.

Riesen, Beat. *Thomas Hardy's Minor Novels,* 85–95.

Wright, T. R. *Hardy and the Erotic,* 54–57.

Jude the Obscure, 1895

Adelman, Gary. *"Jude the Obscure,"* 29–115.

Auerbach, Emily. *Maestros, Dilettantes, and Philistines,* 132–35.

Berger, Sheila. *Thomas Hardy and Visual Structures,* 38–39, 143–46, 166–77.

Berman, Jeffrey. "Infanticide and Object Loss in *Jude the Obscure*," in Vera J. Camden, ed., *Compromise Formations*, 155–81.

Berman, Jeffrey. *Narcissism and the Novel*, 176–98.

Brady, Kristin. "Textual Hysteria: Hardy's Narrator on Women," in Margaret R. Higonnet, ed., *The Sense of Sex*, 94–99.

Chapman, Raymond. *The Language of Thomas Hardy*, 63–66, 122–24, 128–30.

Collins, Deborah L. *Thomas Hardy and His God*, 136–42.

Dale, Peter Allan. *In Pursuit of a Scientific Culture*, 257–72.

Davis, William A., Jr. "Hardy, Sir Francis Jeune, and Divorce by 'False Pretences' in *Jude the Obscure*." *Thomas Hardy J* 9:1 (1993), 62–73.

Dellamora, Richard. "Male Relations in Thomas Hardy's *Jude the Obscure*." *Papers on Lang & Lit* 27 (1991), 453–71.

DeMille, Barbara. "Cruel Illusions: Nietzsche, Conrad, Hardy, and the 'Shadowy Ideal.'" *Stud in Engl Lit, 1500–1900* 30 (1990), 697–713.

DiBattista, Maria. *First Love*, 59–64, 93–111.

Draper, Ronald P. "Hardy's Comic Tragedy: *Jude the Obscure*," in Dale Kramer, ed., *Critical Essays*, 243–54.

Federico, Annette. *Masculine Identity*, 102–19.

Freeman, Janet H. "Highways and Cornfields: Space and Time in the Narration of *Jude the Obscure*." *Colby Q* 27 (1991), 161–73.

Garson, Marjorie. *Hardy's Fables of Integrity*, 152–79.

Goode, John. "Hardy and Marxism," in Dale Kramer, ed., *Critical Essays*, 33–34.

Gordon, Jan B. "Gossip and the Letter: Ideologies of 'Restoration' in *Jude the Obscure*." *Lore and Lang* 8:1 (1989), 45–80.

Hands, Timothy. *Thomas Hardy*, 69–71, 76–78, 94–96.

Heilman, Robert Bechtold. *The Workings of Fiction*, 179–83, 265–79.

Ingham, Patricia. *Thomas Hardy*, 75–82.

Kelly, Mary Ann. "Individuation and Consummation in Hardy's *Jude the Obscure*: The Lure of the Void." *Victorian Newsl* 82 (1992), 62–64.

Kincaid, James R. "Girl-watching, Child-beating, and Other Exercises for Readers of *Jude the Obscure*," in Margaret R. Higonnet, ed., *The Sense of Sex*, 132–46.

Langland, Elizabeth. "Becoming a Man in *Jude the Obscure*," in Margaret R. Higonnet, ed., *The Sense of Sex*, 32–46.

LeVay, John. "Hardy's *Jude the Obscure*." *Explicator* 49 (1991), 219–22.

McNees, Eleanor. "Reverse Typology in *Jude the Obscure*." *Christianity and Lit* 39 (1989), 35–46.

Mallet, Phillip. "Sexual Ideology and Narrative Form in *Jude the Obscure*." *English* 38:162 (1989), 211–23.

Miller, J. Hillis. *Tropes, Parables, Performatives*, 65–67.

Pinion, F. B. *Hardy the Writer*, 123–26, 152–68.

Rivinus, Timothy M. "Tragedy of the Commonplace: The Impact of Addiction on Families in the Fiction of Thomas Hardy." *Lit and Medicine* 11 (1992), 257–60.

Rossen, Janice. *The University in Modern Fiction*, 11–21, 28–31.

Scheick, William J. *Fictional Structure & Ethics*, 92–117.

Schwarz, Daniel R. *The Transformation of the English Novel*, 44–47, 63–66.

Simpson, Anne B. "Sue Bridehead Revisited." *Victorian Lit and Culture* 19 (1991), 55–65.

Steig, Michael. *Stories of Reading*, 151–56, 184–97.

Tindall, Gillian. *Countries of the Mind*, 28–31.

Watts, Cedric. *Thomas Hardy: "Jude the Obscure,"* 22–120.

Wiesenfarth, Joseph. *Gothic Manners*, 141–60.

Williams, Merryn. *A Preface to Hardy*, 75–80, 98–100.

Wright, T. R. *Hardy and the Erotic*, 120–31.

Wright, Terence. "Space, Time, and Paradox: The Sense of History in Hardy's Last Novels," in Angus Easson, ed., *History and the Novel*, 46–52.

A Laodicean, 1881

Austin, Linda M. "Hardy's Laodicean Narrative." *Mod Fiction Stud* 35 (1989), 211–21.

Berger, Sheila. *Thomas Hardy and Visual Structures*, 66–67.

Hands, Timothy. *Thomas Hardy*, 56–61, 81–83.

Pinion, F. B. *Hardy the Writer*, 224–26.

Riesen, Beat. *Thomas Hardy's Minor Novels*, 105–17.

Wright, T. R. *Hardy and the Erotic*, 65–68.

The Mayor of Casterbridge, 1886

Adamson, Jane. "Who and What is Henchard? Hardy, Character and Moral Inquiry." *Crit R* (Melbourne) 31 (1991), 47–74.

Agovi, K. E. *Novels of Social Change*, 20–40.

Auerbach, Emily. *Maestros, Dilettantes, and Philistines*, 129–31.

Baer, Florence E. "Folklore and *The Mayor of Casterbridge*." *Thomas Hardy Yrbk* 19 (1991), 34–41.

Berger, Sheila. *Thomas Hardy and Visual Structures*, 71–72, 109–11, 119–20.

Chapman, Raymond. *The Language of Thomas Hardy*, 98–100, 103–5, 122–24.

Chapman, Raymond. "The Reader as Listener: Dialect and Relationships in *The Mayor of Casterbridge*," in Leo Hickey, ed., *The Pragmatics of Style*, 159–87.

Collins, Deborah L. *Thomas Hardy and His God*, 116–21.

Davis, Karen. "A Deaf Ear to Essence: Music and Hardy's *The Mayor of Casterbridge*." *JEGP* 89 (1990), 181–201.

Davis, W. Eugene. "Of Furmity, Mothers and Sons in *The Mayor of Casterbridge*." *Thomas Hardy Yrbk* 19 (1991), 31–32.

Dessner, Lawrence Jay. "Space, Time, and Coincidence in Hardy." *Stud in the Novel* 24 (1992), 158–69.

Erlebach, Peter. *Theorie und Praxis des Romaneingangs*, 220–25.

Garson, Marjorie. *Hardy's Fables of Integrity*, 94–129.

Goode, John. "Hardy and Marxism," in Dale Kramer, ed., *Critical Essays,* 31–32.

Hands, Timothy. *Thomas Hardy,* 41–43.

Heilman, Robert Bechtold. *The Workings of Fiction,* 241–59, 280–89.

Ingersoll, Earl. "Writing and Memory in *The Mayor of Casterbridge.*" *Engl Lit in Transition* 33 (1990), 299–308.

Ingersoll, Earl G. "Troping and the Machine in Thomas Hardy's *The Mayor of Casterbridge.*" *Univ of Hartford Stud in Lit* 22:2–3 (1990), 59–66.

King, Jeannette. "*The Mayor of Casterbridge:* Talking About Character." *Thomas Hardy J* 8:3 (1992), 42–46.

Krasner, James. *The Entangled Eye,* 106–7.

Langbaum, Robert. "The Minimisation of Sexuality in *The Mayor of Casterbridge.*" *Thomas Hardy J* 8:1 (1992), 20–31.

Overing, Gillian R. "Patterning, Time and Nietzsche's 'Spirit of Revenge' in *Beowulf* and *The Mayor of Casterbridge.*" *Univ of Mississippi Stud in Engl* 7 (1989), 41–49.

Pinion, F. B. *Hardy the Writer,* 33–36, 268–73, 338–40.

Reed, John R. *Victorian Will,* 351–53.

Rivinus, Timothy M. "Tragedy of the Commonplace: The Impact of Addiction on Families in the Fiction of Thomas Hardy." *Lit and Medicine* 11 (1992), 244–49.

Room, Adrian. "The Case for Casterbridge: Thomas Hardy as Placename Creator." *Names* 37 (1989), 1–14.

Schwarz, Daniel R. *The Transformation of the English Novel,* 37–42, 56–59.

Tindall, Gillian. *Countries of the Mind,* 22–24.

Williams, Merryn. *A Preface to Hardy,* 101–15.

Wright, T. R. *Hardy and the Erotic,* 72–80.

A Pair of Blue Eyes, 1873

Berger, Sheila. *Thomas Hardy and Visual Structures,* 58–59, 135–36.

Dale, Peter Allan. *In Pursuit of a Scientific Culture,* 234–35.

Devereux, Jo. "Thomas Hardy's *A Pair of Blue Eyes:* The Heroine as Text." *Victorian Newsl* 81 (1992), 20–22.

Halperin, John. *Jane Austen's Lovers,* 130–39.

Ingham, Patricia. *Thomas Hardy,* 16–20, 41–44, 48–52, 57–60.

McClure, Paul. "A Note on the Cliff Scene in Hardy's *A Pair of Blue Eyes.*" *Durham Univ J* 83 (1991), 53.

Pinion, F. B. *Hardy the Writer,* 82–84, 216–19.

Riesen, Beat. *Thomas Hardy's Minor Novels,* 71–84.

Rimmer, Mary. "Club Laws: Chess and the Construction of Gender in *A Pair of Blue Eyes,*" in Margaret R. Higonnet, ed., *The Sense of Sex,* 203–15.

Wright, T. R. *Hardy and the Erotic,* 45–48.

Wright, Terence. "Space, Time, and Paradox: The Sense of History in

Hardy's Last Novels," in Angus Easson, ed., *History and the Novel*, 43–44.

The Return of the Native, 1878

Agovi, K. E. *Novels of Social Change*, 1–20.

Berger, Sheila. *Thomas Hardy and Visual Structures*, 26–27, 57–58, 75–79, 112–15, 188–89.

Chapman, Raymond. *The Language of Thomas Hardy*, 157–63.

Collins, Deborah L. *Thomas Hardy and His God*, 109–14.

Dale, Peter A. "Thomas Hardy and the Best Consummation Possible," in John Christie and Sally Shuttleworth, eds., *Nature Transfigured*, 209–11.

Dale, Peter Allan. *In Pursuit of a Scientific Culture*, 273–77.

Davis, William A., Jr. "Clough's *Amours De Voyage* and Hardy's *The Return of the Native:* A Probable Source." *Engl Lang Notes* 31:1 (1993), 47–54.

DiBattista, Maria. *First Love*, 46–50, 71–89.

Erlebach, Peter. *Theorie und Praxis des Romaneingangs*, 229–33.

Garson, Marjorie. *Hardy's Fables of Integrity*, 54–93.

Hands, Timothy. *Thomas Hardy*, 60–66, 89–91, 120–22.

Hawkins, Desmond. "The Birds of Egdon Heath." *Thomas Hardy J* 7:3 (1991), 86–87.

Heilman, Robert Bechtold. *The Workings of Fiction*, 291–306.

Jewell, John. "Hardy's *The Return of the Native.*" *Explicator* 49 (1991), 159–62.

Krasner, James. *The Entangled Eye*, 80–82, 86–87, 96–99.

Manford, Alan. "Emma Hardy's Helping Hand," in Dale Kramer, ed., *Critical Essays*, 108–17.

Mitchell, Giles. "Narcissism and Death Wish in *The Return of the Native:* An Analysis of Eustacia Vye's Suicide." *Panjab Univ Res Bull* 21:1 (1990), 3–16.

Mitchell, Judith. "Hardy's Female Reader," in Margaret R. Higonnet, ed., *The Sense of Sex*, 177–78, 180–82.

Pinion, F. B. *Hardy the Writer*, 84–88, 117–21.

Reed, John R. *Victorian Will*, 349–51.

Schwarz, Daniel R. *The Transformation of the English Novel*, 34–37, 55–56.

Trezise, Simon. "Ways of Learning in *The Return of the Native.*" *Thomas Hardy J* 7:2 (1991), 56–64.

Wallace, Anne D. *Walking, Literature, and English Culture*, 245–47.

Ward, Paul. "The Incident at the Well in *The Return of the Native.*" *Thomas Hardy Yrbk* 19 (1991), 46–48.

Wike, Jonathan. "The World as Text in Hardy's Fiction." *Nineteenth-Cent Lit* 47 (1993), 455–71.

Williams, Merryn. *A Preface to Hardy*, 91–93.

Wright, T. R. *Hardy and the Erotic*, 57–62.

Tess of the d'Urbervilles, 1891

Ardis, Ann L. *New Women, New Novels,* 72–79.

Auerbach, Emily. *Maestros, Dilettantes, and Philistines,* 131–32.

Basham, Diana. *The Trial of Woman,* 148–57.

Berger, Sheila. *Thomas Hardy and Visual Structures,* 7–8, 15–16, 24–25, 59–60, 74–75, 118–19, 141–43, 159–61, 177–86.

Bernstein, Susan David. "Confessing and Editing: The Politics of Purity in Hardy's *Tess,*" in Lloyd Davis, ed., *Virginal Sexuality,* 159–78.

Blank, Paula C. "*Tess of the D'Urbervilles:* The English Novel and the Foreign Plot." *Mid-Hudson Lang Stud* 12:1 (1989), 62–71.

Bronfen, Elisabeth. "Pay as You Go: Exchanges of Bodies and Signs," in Margaret R. Higonnet, ed., *The Sense of Sex,* 74–84.

Buckley, Jerome H. "Tess and the d'Urbervilles." *Victorians Inst J* 20 (1992), 1–11.

Bull, J. A. *The Framework of Fiction,* 172–78.

Butler, Lance St. John. *Victorian Doubt,* 206–16.

Campbell, Elizabeth. "*Tess of the D'Urbervilles:* Misfortune Is a Woman." *Victorian Newsl* 76 (1989), 1–5.

Casagrande, Peter J. "*Tess of the d'Urbervilles,*" 25–112.

Chapman, Raymond. *The Language of Thomas Hardy,* 131–34.

Collins, Deborah L. *Thomas Hardy and His God,* 126–36.

Dale, Peter A. "Thomas Hardy and the Best Consummation Possible," in John Christie and Sally Shuttleworth, eds., *Nature Transfigured,* 211–13.

Dale, Peter Allan. *In Pursuit of a Scientific Culture,* 245–57.

Davis, William A., Jr. "'But he can be prosecuted for this': Legal and Sociological Backgrounds of the Mock Marriage in Hardy's Serial *Tess.*" *Colby Lib Q* 25 (1989), 28–39.

Davis, William A., Jr. "Hardy and the 'Deserted Wife' Question: The Failure of the Law in *Tess of the d'Urbervilles.*" *Colby Q* 29 (1993), 5–18.

DiBattista, Maria. *First Love,* 66–68, 93–95.

Ebbatson, Roger. "The Plutonic Master: Hardy and the Steam Threshing-Machine." *Crit Survey* 2:1 (1990), 63–69.

Federico, Annette. *Masculine Identity,* 31–35, 57–59.

Fleissner, Robert F. "Tess of the d'Urbervilles and George Turberville." *Names* 37 (1989), 65–67.

Garson, Marjorie. *Hardy's Fables of Integrity,* 130–51.

Goode, John. "Hardy and Marxism," in Dale Kramer, ed., *Critical Essays,* 34–35.

Greenslade, William. "The Lure of Pedigree in *Tess of the d'Urbervilles.*" *Thomas Hardy J* 7:3 (1991), 103–14.

Handley, Graham. *Thomas Hardy: "Tess of the d'Urbervilles,"* 15–115.

Hands, Timothy. *Thomas Hardy,* 46–48, 66–69, 71–75, 92–95, 111–14.

Hasan, Noorul. "*Middlemarch, Tess,* and the Marriage Question," in Jasodhara Bagchi, ed., *Literature, Society and Ideology,* 233–43.

Heilman, Robert Bechtold. *The Workings of Fiction,* 143–44, 150–61.

Higonnet, Margaret R. "Fictions of Feminine Voice: Antiphony and Silence in Hardy's *Tess of the D'Urbervilles,*" in Laura Claridge and Elizabeth Langland, eds., *Out of Bounds,* 197–218.

Higonnet, Margaret R. "A Woman's Story: Tess and the Problem of Voice," in Margaret R. Higonnet, ed., *The Sense of Sex,* 14–28.

Ingham, Patricia. *Thomas Hardy,* 71–74, 79–81, 86–89.

Johnson, Trevor. "Hardy, Leopardi, and *Tess of the d'Urbervilles.*" *Thomas Hardy J* 9:2 (1993), 51–53.

Kincaid, James. "'You Did Not Come': Absence, Death and Eroticism in *Tess,*" in Regina Barreca, ed., *Sex and Death,* 9–30.

Kramer, Dale. *Thomas Hardy: "Tess of the d'Urbervilles,"* 33–98.

Krasner, James. *The Entangled Eye,* 82–89, 91–94.

Kucich, John. "Moral Authority in the Late Novels: The Gendering of Art," in Margaret R. Higonnet, ed., *The Sense of Sex,* 229–30, 234–37.

Lee, So-young. "An Essay on Tess's Androgynous Vision: Hardy's Yin-Yang Principle in *Tess of the D'Urbervilles.*" *J of Engl Lang and Lit* 35 (1989), 651–69.

Mason, D. G. "Hardy and Zola: A Comparative Study of *Tess* and *Abbé Mouret.*" *Thomas Hardy J* 7:3 (1991), 89–101.

Mills, Sara, Lynne Pearce, Sue Spaull, and Elaine Millard. *Feminist Readings,* 28–30, 36–38, 40–45.

Montgomery, Martin, Alan Durant, Nigel Fabb, Tom Furniss, and Sara Mills. *Ways of Reading,* 159–61.

Morgan, William W. "Gender and Silence in Thomas Hardy's Texts," in Antony H. Harrison and Beverly Taylor, eds., *Gender and Discourse,* 175–78.

Moring, Meg M. "The Dark Glass: Mirroring and Sacrifice in Shakespeare's *Othello* and Hardy's *Tess of the D'Urbervilles.*" *Conf of Coll Teachers of Engl Stud* 56 (1991), 12–18.

Morris, Virginia B. *Double Jeopardy,* 127–42.

Morrison, Ronald D. "Reading and Restoration in *Tess of the d'Urbervilles.*" *Victorian Newsl* 82 (1992), 27–34.

Nemesvari, Richard. "An Unpleasant Story Told in a Very Unpleasant Way: Hardy's Challenge to His Audience in *Tess of the d'Urbervilles.*" *Thomas Hardy Yrbk* 19 (1991), 54–57.

Nunokawa, Jeff. "*Tess,* Tourism, and the Spectacle of the Woman," in Linda M. Shires, ed., *Rewriting the Victorians,* 70–83.

Parker, Lynn. "'Pure Woman' and Tragic Heroine? Conflicting Myths in Hardy's *Tess of the D'Urbervilles.*" *Stud in the Novel* 24 (1992), 273–80.

Pettit, Charles P. C. "Hardy's Concept of Purity in *Tess of the d'Urbervilles.*" *Thomas Hardy J* 7:3 (1991), 49–56.

Pinion, F. B. *Hardy the Writer,* 37–39, 88–93, 94–111, 121–23.

Ramel, Annie. "'Poor wounded name': le nom blessé dans *Tess of the d'Urbervilles.*" *Etudes Anglaises* 44 (1991), 385–97.

Reed, John R. *Victorian Will,* 345–48.

Reichman, Brunilda Tempel. "The Concurrence of the Spatio-Temporal and Psychological Planes in *Tess of the D'Urbervilles* and *Mrs. Dallo-way." Ilha do Desterro* 24:2 (1990), 21–26.

Reitz, Bernhard. " 'The Fiction of Sex and New Woman'? Zur Themati-sierung von Emanzipation, Melodrama und Tragödie in Thomas Hardys *Tess of the D'Urbervilles,"* in Therese Fischer-Seidel, ed., *Frauen und Frauendarstellung,* 273–94.

Rivinus, Timothy M. "Tragedy of the Commonplace: The Impact of Ad-diction on Families in the Fiction of Thomas Hardy." *Lit and Medicine* 11 (1992), 250–57.

Sadoff, Dianne Fallon. "Looking at Tess: The Female Figure in Two Nar-rative Media," in Margaret R. Higonnet, ed., *The Sense of Sex,* 149–69.

Scherzinger, Karen. "The Problem of the Pure Woman: South African Pas-toralism and Female Rites of Passage." *J of the Dept of Engl* (Calcutta) 29:2 (1991), 29–35.

Schoenburg, Nadine. "The Supernatural in *Tess." Thomas Hardy Yrbk* 19 (1991), 49–52.

Schwarz, Daniel R. *The Transformation of the English Novel,* 42–44, 63–66.

Tindall, Gillian. *Countries of the Mind,* 25–28.

Vorhees, Duane Leroy. "Hardy, *Tess,* and Psychic Scotoma." *J of Engl Lang and Lit* 35 (1989), 671–75.

Wallace, Anne D. *Walking, Literature, and English Culture,* 242–45.

Williams, Merryn. *A Preface to Hardy,* 95–98, 194–96.

Wright, T. R. *Hardy and the Erotic,* 106–19.

Wright, Terence. "Space, Time, and Paradox: The Sense of History in Hardy's Last Novels," in Angus Easson, ed., *History and the Novel,* 44–46.

The Trumpet-Major, 1880

Hands, Timothy. *Thomas Hardy,* 109–11.

Nemesvari, Richard. "The Anti-Comedy of *The Trumpet-Major." Victo-rian Newsl* 77 (1990), 8–13.

Riesen, Beat. *Thomas Hardy's Minor Novels,* 97–104.

Wright, T. R. *Hardy and the Erotic,* 62–65.

Wright, Terence. "Space, Time, and Paradox: The Sense of History in Hardy's Last Novels," in Angus Easson, ed., *History and the Novel,* 41–43.

Two on a Tower, 1882

Beech, Martin. "Hardy's Astronomy: An Examination of *Two on a Tower." Thomas Hardy Yrbk* 19 (1991), 18–28.

Hands, Timothy. *Thomas Hardy,* 55–57, 60–62, 130–32.

Ingham, Patricia. *Thomas Hardy,* 49–54.

Pinion, F. B. *Hardy the Writer,* 41–55.

Riesen, Beat. *Thomas Hardy's Minor Novels,* 119–30.

Wright, T. R. *Hardy and the Erotic,* 68–71.

Under the Greenwood Tree, 1872

Auerbach, Emily. *Maestros, Dilettantes, and Philistines*, 124–27.

D'Agnillo, Renzo. "Music and Metaphor in *Under the Greenwood Tree*." *Thomas Hardy J* 9:2 (1993), 39–48.

Garson, Marjorie. *Hardy's Fables of Integrity*, 6–24.

Hands, Timothy. *Thomas Hardy*, 102–5.

Irvin, Glenn. "Hardy's Comic Archetype: *Under the Greenwood Tree*." *Thomas Hardy J* 6:3 (1990), 54–58.

Riesen, Beat. *Thomas Hardy's Minor Novels*, 61–69.

Schwarz, Daniel R. *The Transformation of the English Novel*, 33–34.

The Well-Beloved, 1892

Berman, Jeffrey. *Narcissism and the Novel*, 196–98.

Brady, Kristin. "Textual Hysteria: Hardy's Narrator on Women," in Margaret R. Higonnet, ed., *The Sense of Sex*, 99–102.

Bulaila, Abdul Aziz M. " 'The clay but not the potter': Love and Marriage in *The Well-Beloved*." *Thomas Hardy J* 9:2 (1993), 61–70.

Dale, Peter A. "Thomas Hardy and the Best Consummation Possible," in John Christie and Sally Shuttleworth, eds., *Nature Transfigured*, 213–19.

DiBattista, Maria. *First Love*, 246–48.

Federico, Annette. *Masculine Identity*, 76–90.

Hudson, Glenda A. *Sibling Love and Incest*, 28–31.

Ingham, Patricia. *Thomas Hardy*, 96–107.

Kucich, John. "Moral Authority in the Late Novels: The Gendering of Art," in Margaret R. Higonnet, ed., *The Sense of Sex*, 224–29, 231–34.

Page, Norman. "*The Well-Beloved* and Other Hardyan Fantasies." *Thomas Hardy J* 8:3 (1992), 75–83.

Pinion, F. B. *Hardy the Writer*, 169–86, 234–36.

Reilly, Jim. *Shadowtime*, 56–59.

Riesen, Beat. *Thomas Hardy's Minor Novels*, 131–37.

Wright, T. R. *Hardy and the Erotic*, 132–42.

The Woodlanders, 1887

Agovi, K. E. *Novels of Social Change*, 40–58.

Berger, Sheila. *Thomas Hardy and Visual Structures*, 56–58, 69–70, 108–9.

Butler, Lance St. John. *Victorian Doubt*, 184–88.

Federico, Annette. *Masculine Identity*, 55–62, 70–75.

Glance, Jonathan C. "The Problem of the Man-Trap in Hardy's *The Woodlanders*." *Victorian Newsl* 78 (1990), 26–28.

Higgins, Lesley. "Pastoral Meets Melodrama in *The Woodlanders*." *Thomas Hardy J* 6:2 (1990), 111–24.

Ingham, Patricia. *Thomas Hardy*, 68–71, 79–84.

Kiely, Robert. "The Menace of Solitude: The Politics and Aesthetics of Exclusion in *The Woodlanders*," in Margaret R. Higonnet, ed., *The Sense of Sex*, 188–201.

Krasner, James. *The Entangled Eye*, 76–77, 90–91, 95–96.

Manford, Alan. "Emma Hardy's Helping Hand," in Dale Kramer, ed., *Critical Essays*, 108–17.

Morrison, Ronald D. "Love and Evolution in Thomas Hardy's *The Woodlanders*." *Kentucky Philol R* 6 (1991), 32–37.

Pinion, F. B. *Hardy the Writer*, 63–79, 229–31.

Schwarz, Daniel R. *The Transformation of the English Novel*, 39–42, 59–61.

Skilling, M. R. "Investigations into the Country of *The Woodlanders*." *Thomas Hardy J* 8:3 (1992), 62–67.

Stewart, Ralph. "Hardy's *Woodlanders*." *Explicator* 48 (1990), 195–96.

Williams, Merryn. *A Preface to Hardy*, 93–95.

Wright, T. R. *Hardy and the Erotic*, 80–88.

ROBERT HARLING

The Enormous Shadow, 1955

Bloom, Clive. "The Spy Thriller: A Genre Under Cover?," in Clive Bloom, ed., *Spy Thrillers*, 8–10.

L. P. HARTLEY

Eustace and Hilda, 1947

Bergonzi, Bernard. *Wartime and Aftermath*, 113–15.

Gindin, James. *British Fiction*, 182–85.

Petersen, Robert C. "The Expanding Symbol as Narrative Device in the *Eustace and Hilda* Trilogy of L. P. Hartley." *Essays in Lit* (Macomb) 17 (1990), 43–50.

The Go-Between, 1953

Gindin, James. *British Fiction*, 179–82.

MacArthur, Fiona. "Miscommunication, Language Development, and Enculturation in L. P. Hartley's *The Go-Between*." *Style* 24 (1990), 103–11.

The Hireling, 1957

Gindin, James. *British Fiction*, 185–87.

The Shrimp and the Anemone, 1944

Gindin, James. *British Fiction*, 182–85.

The Sixth Heaven, 1946

Gindin, James. *British Fiction*, 182–85.

JOHN MACDOUGALL HAY

Gillespie, 1914

Burns, John. "*Gillespie*: Facing the Elemental," in Joachim Schwend and Horst W. Drescher, eds., *Studies in Scottish Fiction*, 83–98.

ELIZA HAYWOOD

Betsy Thoughtless, 1751

> Ackley, Katherine Anne. "Violence Against Women in the Novels of Early British Women Writers," in Dale Spender, ed., *Living by the Pen,* 215–21.
> Ross, Deborah. *The Excellence of Falsehood,* 69–93.

Fantomina, 1724

> Ballaster, Ros. "Preparatives to Love: Seduction as Fiction in the Works of Eliza Haywood," in Dale Spender, ed., *Living by the Pen,* 59–63.
> Craft, Catherine A. "Reworking Male Models: Aphra Behn's *Fair Vow-Breaker,* Eliza Haywood's *Fantomina,* and Charlotte Lennox's *Female Quixote." Mod Lang R* 86 (1991), 828–32.

Love in Excess, 1719–1720

> Williamson, Marilyn L. *Raising Their Voices,* 229–30.

MARY HEARNE

The Female Deserter, 1719

> Williamson, Marilyn L. *Raising Their Voices,* 226–28.

The Lover's Week, 1718

> Williamson, Marilyn L. *Raising Their Voices,* 224–26.

G. A. HENTY

Rujub the Juggler, 1893

> Paxton, Nancy L. "Mobilizing Chivalry: Rape in British Novels about the Indian Uprising of 1857." *Victorian Stud* 36 (1992), 21–22.

RAYNER HEPPENSTALL

The Pier, 1986

> Hassam, Andrew. *Writing and Reality,* 51–60.

AIDAN HIGGINS

Balcony of Europe, 1972

> O'Neill, Patrick. "Aidan Higgins," in Rüdiger Imhof, ed., *Contemporary Irish Novelists,* 100–104.

Bornholm Night-Ferry, 1983

> O'Neill, Patrick. "Aidan Higgins," in Rüdiger Imhof, ed., *Contemporary Irish Novelists,* 105–7.

Langrishe, Go Down, 1966

> Kreilkamp, Vera. "Reinventing a Form: The Big House in Aidan Higgins' *Langrishe, Go Down,*" in Otto Rauchbauer, ed., *Ancestral Voices,* 207–18.
>
> O'Neill, Patrick. "Aidan Higgins," in Rüdiger Imhof, ed., *Contemporary Irish Novelists,* 96–99.

HEADON HILL

The Spies of the Wight, 1899

> Trotter, David. "The Politics of Adventure in the Early British Spy Novel," in Wesley K. Wark, ed., *Spy Fiction,* 39–42.

SUSAN HILL

A Change for the Better, 1969

> Hofer, Ernest H. "Enclosed Structures, Disclosed Lives: The Fictions of Susan Hill," in Robert E. Hosmer, Jr., ed., *Contemporary British Women Writers,* 130–32.

I'm the King of the Castle, 1970

> Hofer, Ernest H. "Enclosed Structures, Disclosed Lives: The Fictions of Susan Hill," in Robert E. Hosmer, Jr., ed., *Contemporary British Women Writers,* 132–34.

Strange Meeting, 1971

> Hofer, Ernest H. "Enclosed Structures, Disclosed Lives: The Fictions of Susan Hill," in Robert E. Hosmer, Jr., ed., *Contemporary British Women Writers,* 134–39.

JACK HILTON

Champion, 1938

> Croft, Andy. *Red Letter Days,* 250–52.

JAMES HILTON

Goodbye, Mr. Chips, 1933

> Richards, Jeffrey. *Happiest Days,* 252–64.

DESMOND HOGAN

A Curious Street, 1984

> D'Haen, Theo. "Desmond Hogan and Ireland's Postmodern Past," in Joris Duytschaever and Geert Lernout, eds., *History and Violence,* 79–84.

JAMES HOGG

The Brownie of Bodsbeck, 1818

> Letley, Emma. *From Galt to Douglas Brown,* 28–34.

The Private Memoirs and Confessions of a Justified Sinner, 1824

> Arnaud, Pierre. "Les réverbérations de l'angoisse dans *The Private Memoirs & Confessions of a Justified Sinner:* du narcissisme de Hogg au narcissisme du texte," in Christian La Cassagnère, ed., *Visages de l'angoisse,* 231–47.
>
> Campbell, Ian. "James Hogg and the Bible," in David F. Wright et al., eds., *The Bible in Scottish Life and Literature,* 101–7.
>
> Groves, David. "The Frontispiece to James Hogg's *Confessions." Notes and Queries* 235 (1990), 421–22.
>
> Groves, David. "'W-M B-E, A Great Original': William Blake, The Grave, and James Hogg's *Confessions." Scottish Liter J* 18:2 (1991), 27–40.
>
> Hutton, Clarke. "Kierkegaard, Antinomianism, and James Hogg's *Private Memoirs and Confessions of a Justified Sinner." Scottish Liter J* 20:1 (1993), 37–46.
>
> Jones, Douglas. "Double Jeopardy and the Chameleon Art in James Hogg's *Justified Sinner." Stud in Scottish Lit* 23 (1988), 164–81.
>
> Kayman, Martin A. *From Bow Street to Baker Street,* 152–59.
>
> Letley, Emma. *From Galt to Douglas Brown,* 22–27.
>
> Manning, Susan. *The Puritan-Provincial Vision,* 80–84.
>
> Marigny, Jean. "Le double et la mise en abyme dans les *Mémoires privés et confessions d'un pécheur justifié* de James Hogg (1824)," in *La Littérature Fantastique,* 90–101.
>
> Petrie, David. "Mis-taken Signs: The Reception of James Hogg's *Justified Sinner* in the Context of Scottish Calvinist Controversy." *Quaderni di Lingue e Letterature* 15 (1990), 175–86.
>
> Rubenstein, Jill. "Confession, Damnation and the Dissolution of Identity in Novels by James Hogg and Harold Frederic." *Stud in Hogg and His World* 1 (1990), 103–13.
>
> Rutelli, Romana. *Il desiderio del diverso,* 87–142.
>
> Steig, Michael. *Stories of Reading,* 128–30.

The Three Perils of Man, 1822

> DeGroot, H. B. "The Imperilled Reader in *The Three Perils of Man." Stud in Hogg and His World* 1 (1990), 114–25.

The Three Perils of Woman, 1823

> Groves, David. "*The Three Perils of Woman* and the Edinburgh Prostitution Scandal of 1823." *Stud in Hogg and His World* 2 (1991), 95–102.
>
> Hasler, Antony J. "*The Three Perils of Woman* and John Wilson's Lights and Shadows of Scottish Life." *Stud in Hogg and His World* 1 (1990), 30–45.

Letley, Emma. "Some Literary Uses of Scots in *The Three Perils of Woman*." *Stud in Hogg and His World* 1 (1990), 46–56.

Mack, Douglas. "Gatty's Illness in *The Three Perils of Woman*." *Stud in Hogg and His World* 1 (1990), 133–35.

DAVID HOLBROOK

Flesh Wounds, 1966

Munton, Alan. *English Fiction,* 68–71.

THOMAS HOLCROFT

Anna St. Ives, 1792

Scheuermann, Mona. *Her Bread to Earn,* 134–44.

ETHEL CARNIE HOLDSWORTH

Miss Nobody, 1913

Fox, Pamela A. "Ethel Carnie Holdsworth's 'Revolt of the Gentle': Romance and the Politics of Resistance in Working-Class Women's Writing," in Angela Ingram and Daphne Patai, eds., *Rediscovering Forgotten Radicals,* 61–65.

This Slavery, 1925

Fox, Pamela A. "Ethel Carnie Holdsworth's 'Revolt of the Gentle': Romance and the Politics of Resistance in Working-Class Women's Writing," in Angela Ingram and Daphne Patai, eds., *Rediscovering Forgotten Radicals,* 65–72.

W. S. HOLNUT

Olympia's Journal, 1895

Ardis, Ann L. *New Women, New Novels,* 149–52.

WINIFRED HOLTBY

South Riding, 1936

Baurley, George L. "Winifred Holtby's *South Riding* through German Eyes: Interpreted for the Use of the English and Especially for Yorkshire Folk." *Trans of the Yorkshire Dialect Soc* 17:88 (1989), 48–55.

Gindin, James. *British Fiction,* 64–66.

GEOFFREY HOUSEHOLD

Rogue Male, 1939

Hayes, Michael J. "The Story of an Encounter: Geoffrey Household's *Rogue Male*," in Clive Bloom, ed., *Spy Thrillers,* 73–85.

Stafford, David. *The Silent Game,* 145–47.

ELIZABETH JANE HOWARD

After Julius, 1965

Levin, Amy K. *The Suppressed Sister,* 108–11.

The Beautiful Visit, 1950

Baker, Niamh. *Happily Ever After?,* 146–48.

The Long View, 1956

Lassner, Phyllis. "The Quiet Revolution: World War II and the English Domestic Novel." *Mosaic* 23:3 (1990), 90–92. (Also in Evelyn J. Hinz, ed., *Troops versus Tropes,* 90–92.)

FRED HOYLE

Ossian's Ride, 1959

Carter, Ian. *Ancient Cultures of Conceit,* 130–32.

WILLIAM HENRY HUDSON

A Crystal Age, 1887

Miller, David. *W. H. Hudson,* 115–23.

Green Mansions, 1904

Miller, David. *W. H. Hudson,* 136–63.

The Purple Land, 1885

Miller, David. *W. H. Hudson,* 106–14.

RICHARD HUGHES

The Fox in the Attic, 1961

Schaffeld, Norbert. *Die Darstellung des nationalsozialistischen Deutschland,* 43–63, 72–79.

The Human Predicament, 1961–

Lengeler, Rainer. "Das Bild Deutschlands im englischen Roman der Nachkriegszeit." *Archiv für das Studium der neueren Sprachen und Literaturen* 229 (1992), 25–26, 35–40.

The Wooden Shepherdess, 1973

Schaffeld, Norbert. *Die Darstellung des nationalsozialistischen Deutschland,* 63–71, 79–87, 113–19.

THOMAS HUGHES

Tom Brown's School Days, 1857

Bristow, Joseph. *Empire Boys,* 53–64.
Nelson, Claudia. "Sex and the Single Boy: Ideals of Manliness and Sexuality in Victorian Literature for Boys." *Victorian Stud* 32 (1989), 535–40.
Richards, Jeffrey. *Happiest Days,* 23–65.
Tuss, Alex J., SM. *The Inward Revolution,* 26–29.
Wall, Barbara. *The Narrator's Voice,* 52–55.

E. M. HULL

The Sheik, 1919

Trotter, David. "A Horse Is Being Beaten: Modernism and Popular Fiction," in Kevin J. H. Dettmar, ed., *Rereading the New,* 207–16.

A. S. M. HUTCHINSON

If Winter Comes, 1921

Bracco, Rosa Maria. *'Betwixt and Between,'* 20–21.

ALDOUS HUXLEY

Ape and Essence, 1949

Deery, June. "Technology and Gender in Aldous Huxley's Alternative (?) Worlds." *Extrapolation* 33 (1992), 265–67.

Brave New World, 1932

Carey, John. *The Intellectuals and the Masses,* 86–89.
Combs, James. "Towards 2084: Continuing the Orwellian Tradition," in Robert L. Savage et al., eds., *The Orwellian Moment,* 167–70.
Deery, June. "Technology and Gender in Aldous Huxley's Alternative (?) Worlds." *Extrapolation* 33 (1992), 258–65.
Hankins, June Chase. "Making Use of the Literacy Debate: Literacy, Citizenship, and *Brave New World." CEA Critic* 53:1 (1990), 40–49.
Hoyles, John. *The Literary Underground,* 122–25.
Rindisbacher, Hans J. *The Smell of Books,* 230–33.
Seehase, I. "Karel Capeks Umgang mit Huxleys *Brave New World." Zeitschrift für Slawistik* 35 (1990), 56–65.
Strau, Dietrich. "*Brave New World:* Gedanken zum Phänomen einer Verdrängung," in Joachim Schwend et al., eds., *Literatur im Kontext,* 237–46.

Island, 1962

> Beauchamp, Gorman. *"Island:* Aldous Huxley's Psychedelic Utopia." *Utopian Stud* 1:1 (1990), 59–72.
> Deery, June. "Technology and Gender in Aldous Huxley's Alternative (?) Worlds." *Extrapolation* 33 (1992), 267–71.

ELIZABETH INCHBALD

Nature and Art, 1796

> Rogers, Katharine M. "Elizabeth Inchbald: Not Such a Simple Story," in Dale Spender, ed., *Living by the Pen,* 87–90.
> Scheuermann, Mona. *Her Bread to Earn,* 169–75.

A Simple Story, 1791

> Hatch, Ronald B. "'Lordship and Bondage': Women Novelists of the Eighteenth Century." *REAL: Yrbk of Res in Engl and Am Lit* 8 (1991/92), 237–39.
> Rogers, Katharine M. "Elizabeth Inchbald: Not Such a Simple Story," in Dale Spender, ed., *Living by the Pen,* 82–90.
> Spencer, Jane. "'Of Use to Her Daughter': Maternal Authority and Early Women Novelists," in Dale Spender, ed., *Living by the Pen,* 205–6.

CHRISTOPHER ISHERWOOD

All the Conspirators, 1928

> Schwerdt, Lisa M. *Isherwood's Fiction,* 22–35.
> Wade, Stephen. *Christopher Isherwood,* 18–24.

Down There on a Visit, 1962

> Schwerdt, Lisa M. *Isherwood's Fiction,* 135–60.
> Summers, Claude J. *Gay Fictions,* 198–99.
> Wade, Stephen. *Christopher Isherwood,* 72–76.

Goodbye to Berlin, 1939

> Mizejewski, Linda. *Divine Decadence,* 37–84.
> Schaffeld, Norbert. *Die Darstellung des nationalsozialistischen Deutschland,* 98–106, 178–82.
> Schwerdt, Lisa M. *Isherwood's Fiction,* 77–94.
> Tindall, Gillian. *Countries of the Mind,* 160–62.
> Wade, Stephen. *Christopher Isherwood,* 49–60.

Lions and Shadows, 1938

> Schwerdt, Lisa M. *Isherwood's Fiction,* 72–77.
> Wade, Stephen. *Christopher Isherwood,* 5–8.

A Meeting by the River, 1967

> Schwerdt, Lisa M. *Isherwood's Fiction,* 177–86.
> Wade, Stephen. *Christopher Isherwood,* 86–89.

The Memorial, 1932

> Schwerdt, Lisa M. *Isherwood's Fiction*, 35–48.
> Wade, Stephen. *Christopher Isherwood*, 24–29.

Mr. Norris Changes Trains, 1935

> Croft, Andy. *Red Letter Days*, 328–30.
> Schaffeld, Norbert. *Die Darstellung des nationalsozialistischen Deutschland*, 88–98.
> Schwerdt, Lisa M. *Isherwood's Fiction*, 56–72.
> Wade, Stephen. *Christopher Isherwood*, 41–46.

Prater Violet, 1946

> Poznar, Walter. "Christopher Isherwood's *Prater Violet:* The Power of Illusion." *North Dakota Q* 56:1 (1988), 186–93.
> Schwerdt, Lisa M. *Isherwood's Fiction*, 94–109.
> Wade, Stephen. *Christopher Isherwood*, 30–39.

A Single Man, 1964

> Schwerdt, Lisa M. *Isherwood's Fiction*, 162–77.
> Summers, Claude J. *Gay Fictions*, 199–214.
> Wade, Stephen. *Christopher Isherwood*, 93–102.

The World in the Evening, 1954

> Schwerdt, Lisa M. *Isherwood's Fiction*, 119–35.
> Summers, Claude J. *Gay Fictions*, 196–98.
> Wade, Stephen. *Christopher Isherwood*, 69–73.

P. D. JAMES

The Black Tower, 1975

> Paul, Robert S. *Whatever Happened to Sherlock Homes?*, 219–24.

A Taste for Death, 1986

> Paul, Robert S. *Whatever Happened to Sherlock Homes?*, 224–26.

An Unsuitable Job for a Woman, 1973

> Paul, Robert S. *Whatever Happened to Sherlock Homes?*, 216–18.
> Rossen, Janice. *The University in Modern Fiction*, 26–28.

MARGARET STORM JAMESON

A Cup of Tea for Mr. Thorgill, 1957

> Gindin, James. *British Fiction*, 210–12.

RICHARD JEFFERIES

After London, 1885

> Strugnell, John. "Richard Jefferies' Vision of England," in Kath Filmer, ed., *The Victorian Fantasists*, 195–203.

Amaryllis at the Fair, 1887

> Krasner, James. *The Entangled Eye,* 142–49.

Bevis, 1882

> Wall, Barbara. *The Narrator's Voice,* 118–23.

ELIZABETH JENKINS

Dr. Gully, 1972

> MacKillop, Ian. "Elizabeth Jenkins: Perhaps the History Woman," in Clive Bloom, ed., *Twentieth-Century Suspense,* 231–36.

Harriet, 1934

> MacKillop, Ian. "Elizabeth Jenkins: Perhaps the History Woman," in Clive Bloom, ed., *Twentieth-Century Suspense,* 231–36.

The Tortoise and the Hare, 1954

> Baker, Niamh. *Happily Ever After?,* 94–98, 127–29.
> MacKillop, Ian. "Elizabeth Jenkins: Perhaps the History Woman," in Clive Bloom, ed., *Twentieth-Century Suspense,* 227–31.

B. S. JOHNSON

Trawl, 1966

> Hassam, Andrew. *Writing and Reality,* 109–12.

SAMUEL JOHNSON

Rasselas, 1759

> Boardman, Michael M. *Narrative Innovation,* 64–67.
> Braverman, Richard. "The Narrative Architecture of *Rasselas." The Age of Johnson* 3 (1990), 91–107.
> Brooks, Christopher. "Nekayah's Courage and Female Wisdom." *Coll Lang Assoc J* 36 (1992), 52–72.
> DeMaria, Robert, Jr. *The Life of Samuel Johnson,* 204–12.
> Erlebach, Peter. *Theorie und Praxis des Romaneingangs,* 173–80.
> Finch, G. J. "Reason, Imagination and Will in 'Rasselas' and 'The Vanity of Human Wishes.'" *English* 38:162 (1989), 195–209.
> Greene, Donald. *Samuel Johnson,* 99–104, 140–49.
> Henson, Eithne. *"The Fictions of Romantick Chivalry,"* 128–37.
> Hewitt, Regina. "Time in *Rasselas:* Johnson's Use of Locke's Concept." *Stud in Eighteenth-Cent Culture* 19 (1989), 267–74.
> Hilliard, Raymond F. "Desire and the Structure of Eighteenth-Century Fiction," in H. George Hahn, ed., *The Country Myth,* 167–68.
> Hudson, Nicholas. "'Open' and 'Enclosed' Readings of *Rasselas." Eighteenth Cent* 31 (1990), 47–65.

Hudson, Nicholas. "Three Steps to Perfection: *Rasselas* and the Philosophy of Richard Hooker." *Eighteenth-Cent Life* 14:3 (1990), 29–37.

Jain, Nalini. *The Mind's Extensive View*, 109–13.

Potkay, Adam. "The Spirit of Ending in Johnson and Hume." *Eighteenth-Cent Life* 16:3 (1992), 153–64.

Powell, J. Enoch. "Rasselas." *Johnson Soc Trans* 1989/1990: 30–40.

Rogers, Pat. "Johnson and the Art of Flying." *Notes and Queries* 238 (1993), 329–30.

Scherwatzky, Steven. "Johnson, Rasselas, and the Politics of Empire." *Eighteenth-Cent Life* 16:3 (1992), 103–12.

Tomarken, Edward. *Johnson, "Rasselas," and the Choice of Criticism*, 3–106.

Tomarken, Edward. "Perspectivism: The Methodological Implications of 'The History of Imlac' in *Rasselas*." *The Age of Johnson* 2 (1989), 262–80.

JENNIFER JOHNSTON

The Captains and the Kings, 1972

Kamm, Jürgen. "Jennifer Johnston," in Rüdiger Imhof, ed., *Contemporary Irish Novelists*, 126–40.

Lubbers, Klaus. " 'This White Elephant of a Place': Jennifer Johnston's Uses of the Big House," in Otto Rauchbauer, ed., *Ancestral Voices*, 223–26.

The Christmas Tree, 1981

Kamm, Jürgen. "Jennifer Johnston," in Rüdiger Imhof, ed., *Contemporary Irish Novelists*, 137–40.

Weekes, Ann Owens. *Irish Women Writers*, 203–7.

Fool's Sanctuary, 1987

Kamm, Jürgen. "Jennifer Johnston," in Rüdiger Imhof, ed., *Contemporary Irish Novelists*, 128–40.

Lubbers, Klaus. " 'This White Elephant of a Place': Jennifer Johnston's Uses of the Big House," in Otto Rauchbauer, ed., *Ancestral Voices*, 234–37.

The Gates, 1973

Kamm, Jürgen. "Jennifer Johnston," in Rüdiger Imhof, ed., *Contemporary Irish Novelists*, 127–40.

Lubbers, Klaus. " 'This White Elephant of a Place': Jennifer Johnston's Uses of the Big House," in Otto Rauchbauer, ed., *Ancestral Voices*, 226–29.

How Many Miles to Babylon?, 1974

Kamm, Jürgen. "Jennifer Johnston," in Rüdiger Imhof, ed., *Contemporary Irish Novelists*, 129–40.

Lubbers, Klaus. " 'This White Elephant of a Place': Jennifer Johnston's

Uses of the Big House," in Otto Rauchbauer, ed., *Ancestral Voices*, 229–31.

Weekes, Ann Owens. *Irish Women Writers*, 195–97.

The Old Jest, 1979

Kamm, Jürgen. "Jennifer Johnston," in Rüdiger Imhof, ed., *Contemporary Irish Novelists*, 128–40.

Lubbers, Klaus. "'This White Elephant of a Place': Jennifer Johnston's Uses of the Big House," in Otto Rauchbauer, ed., *Ancestral Voices*, 231–34.

Weekes, Ann Owens. *Irish Women Writers*, 199–203.

The Railway Station Man, 1984

Kamm, Jürgen. "Jennifer Johnston," in Rüdiger Imhof, ed., *Contemporary Irish Novelists*, 131–40.

Weekes, Ann Owens. *Irish Women Writers*, 207–11.

Shadows on Our Skin, 1977

Kamm, Jürgen. "Jennifer Johnston," in Rüdiger Imhof, ed., *Contemporary Irish Novelists*, 130–40.

Weekes, Ann Owens. *Irish Women Writers*, 197–99.

EDITH JOHNSTONE

A Sunless Heart, 1894

Ardis, Ann L. *New Women, New Novels*, 135–38.

GWYNETH A. JONES

Divine Endurance, 1989

Jones, Gwyneth. "The Profession of Science Fiction, 38: Riddles in the Dark." *Foundation* 43 (1988), 50–59.

The Hidden Ones, 1988

Jones, Gwyneth. "Writing Science Fiction for the Teenage Reader," in Lucie Armitt, ed., *Where No Man Has Gone Before*, 173–77.

LEWIS JONES

Cwmardy, 1937

Bell, Ian. "Lewis Grassic Gibbon's Revolutionary Romanticism," in Joachim Schwend and Horst W. Drescher, eds., *Studies in Scottish Fiction*, 258–64.

We Live, 1939

Bell, Ian. "Lewis Grassic Gibbon's Revolutionary Romanticism," in Joachim Schwend and Horst W. Drescher, eds., *Studies in Scottish Fiction*, 258–64.

JAMES JOYCE

Finnegans Wake, 1939

Alexander, James D. "*Finnegans Wake:* Imitating Sources." *J of Irish Lit* 21:2 (1992), 24–38.

Altieri, Charles. "*Finnegans Wake* as Modernist Historiography," in Mark Spilka and Caroline McCracken-Flesher, eds., *Why the Novel Matters,* 256–68.

Ames, Christopher. *The Life of the Party,* 68–80.

Anspaugh, Kelly. "Death on the Missisliffi: *Huckleberry Finn* in *Finnegans Wake.*" *Colby Q* 28 (1992), 144–53.

Astro, Alan. *Understanding Samuel Beckett,* 27–30.

Attridge, Derek. "Finnegans Awake: The Dream of Interpretation." *James Joyce Q* 27 (1989), 11–26.

Attridge, Derek. "Reading Joyce," in Derek Attridge, ed., *The Cambridge Companion,* 10–23.

Aubert, Jacques. "From History to *Mémoires:* Joyce's Chateaubriand as Celtic Palampcestor." *Joyce Stud Annual 1991,* 177–200.

Aubert, Jacques. "Riverrun," in Derek Attridge and Daniel Ferrer, eds., *Post-structuralist Joyce,* 69–77.

Beja, Morris. *James Joyce,* 88–93, 119–22.

Beja, Morris. *Joyce, the Artist Manqué, and Indeterminacy,* 18–20.

Benstock, Bernard. "The Anti-Schematics of *Finnegans Wake.*" *Joyce Stud Annual 1990,* 96–116.

Benstock, Bernard. "Cataloguing in *Finnegans Wake:* Counting Counties," in Vincent J. Cheng and Timothy Martin, eds., *Joyce in Context,* 259–68.

Benstock, Shari. "Apostrophizing the Feminine in *Finnegans Wake.*" *Mod Fiction Stud* 35 (1989), 587–613.

Berressem, Hanjo. "The Letter! The Litter! The Defilements of the Signifier in *Finnegans Wake,*" in Geert Lernout, ed., *"Finnegans Wake,"* 139–64.

Booker, M. Keith. "*Finnegans Wake* and *The Satanic Verses:* Two Modern Myths of the Fall." *Critique* (Washington, DC) 32 (1991), 190–205.

Brasil, Assis. *Joyce e Faulkner,* 96–105.

Brivic, Sheldon. "The Terror and Pity of Love: ALP's Soliloquy." *James Joyce Q* 29 (1991), 145–68.

Brown, Dennis. *Intertextual Dynamics,* 125–32, 158–65.

Brown, Richard. *James Joyce,* 98–121.

Brownstein, Marilyn L. "Against Mediation: The Rule of the Postmodern in the *Phaedrus* and *Finnegans Wake,*" in Christine van Boheemen, ed., *Joyce, Modernity, and its Mediation,* 79–96.

Brownstein, Marilyn. "The Preservation of Tenderness: A Confusion of Tongues in *Ulysses* and *Finnegans Wake,*" in Susan Stanford Friedman, ed., *Joyce,* 245–56.

Cheng, Vincent J. "The General and the Sepoy: Imperialism and Power in the Museyroom," in Patrick A. McCarthy, ed., *Critical Essays*, 258–67.

Cheng, Vincent J. "'Goddinpotty': James Joyce and the Language of Excrement," in Rosa Maria Bollettieri Bosinelli et al., eds., *The Languages of Joyce*, 90–98.

Cheng, Vincent J. "Joyce and Ford Madox Ford," in Vincent J. Cheng and Timothy Martin, eds., *Joyce in Context*, 62–69.

Cheng, Vincent J. "White Horse, Dark Horse: Joyce's Allhorse of Another Color." *Joyce Stud Annual 1991*, 110–28.

Clark, Hilary. *The Fictional Encyclopedia*, 47–82.

Clark, Hilary. "Networking in *Finnegans Wake*." *James Joyce Q* 27 (1990), 745–57.

Cumpiano, Marion. "Joyce's *Finnegans Wake*." *Explicator* 48 (1989), 48–50.

Deane, Seamus. "Joyce the Irishman," in Derek Attridge, ed., *The Cambridge Companion*, 50–53.

Deane, Vincent. "HCE and the Fall of Pelagius," in Geert Lernout, ed., *"Finnegans Wake,"* 109–23.

Devlin, Kimberly J. *Wandering and Return in "Finnegans Wake,"* 3–181.

Eco, Umberto. "Joyce, Semiosis and Semiotics," in Rosa Maria Bollettieri Bosinelli et al., eds., *The Languages of Joyce*, 22–25, 32–37.

Erlebach, Peter. *Theorie und Praxis des Romaneingangs*, 270–83.

Froula, Christine. "Mothers of Invention/Doaters of Inversion: Narcissan Scenes in *Finnegans Wake*," in Susan Stanford Friedman, ed., *Joyce*, 283–303.

Frumkin, Robert. "James Joyce and the Masques of Ben Jonson." *J of Irish Lit* 21:2 (1992), 21–23.

Gillespie, Michael Patrick. "When Is a Man not a Man?: Deconstructive and Reconstructive Impulses in *Finnegans Wake*." *Intl Fiction R* 18 (1991), 1–14.

Gordon, John. "The Golden Ass in *Finnegans Wake*." *Notes on Mod Irish Lit* 3 (1991), 45–48.

Gordon, John. "Joyce's *Finnegans Wake*." *Explicator* 50 (1992), 96–98.

Griffin, Robert. "Vico, Joyce, and the Matrix of Worldly Appearance." *Rivista di Letterature Moderne e Comparate* 40:2 (1989), 123–38.

Harper, Margaret Mills. *The Aristocracy of Art*, 50–52, 142–52.

Hart, Clive. "*Finnegans Wake* in Adjusted Perspective," in Patrick A. McCarthy, ed., *Critical Essays*, 15–31.

Hayman, David. "I Think Her Pretty: Reflections of the Familiar in Joyce's Notebook VI.B.5." *Joyce Stud Annual 1990*, 43–60.

Hayman, David. "Reading Joyce's Notebooks?! *Finnegans Wake* From Within," in Geert Lernout, ed., *"Finnegans Wake,"* 7–22.

Hayman, David. *The "Wake" in Transit*, 18–199.

Heath, Stephen. "Ambiviolences: Notes for Reading Joyce," in Derek Attridge and Daniel Ferrer, eds., *Post-structuralist Joyce*, 31–62.

Henke, Suzette. "Anna the 'Allmaziful': Toward the Evolution of a Feminine Discourse," in Diana A. Ben-Merre and Maureen Murphy, eds., *James Joyce,* 37–46.

Herr, Cheryl. "'After the Lessions of Experience I Speak from Inspiration': The Sermon in *Finnegans Wake* 111, ii," in Diana A. Ben-Merre and Maureen Murphy, eds., *James Joyce,* 59–66.

Hofheinz, Thomas. "'Group drinkards maaks grope thinkards': Narrative in the 'Norwegian Captain' Episode of *Finnegans Wake.*" *James Joyce Q* 29 (1992), 643–55.

Hofheinz, Thomas C. "Vico, Natural Law Philosophy, and Joyce's Ireland." *Joyce Stud Annual 1993,* 55–97.

Hogan, Patrick Colm. "Joyce's Miltonic Pamtomomiom and the Paradox Lust of *Finnegans Wake.*" *James Joyce Q* 27 (1990), 815–33.

Jacquet, Claude. "In the buginning is the woid: James Joyce and Genetic Criticism," in Geert Lernout, ed., *"Finnegans Wake,"* 23–35.

Jones, Ellen Carol. "Textual Mater: Writing the Mother in Joyce," in Susan Stanford Friedman, ed., *Joyce,* 257–61.

Kemeny, Tomaso. "Mallarmé, Wagner and Joyce's Sublime," in Tomaso Kemeny, ed., *Differences Similar,* 81–83.

Kenner, Hugh. "Shem the Textman," in Rosa Maria Bollettieri Bosinelli et al., eds., *The Languages of Joyce,* 146–48, 150–54.

Levitt, Morton P. "The New Midrash: *Finnegans Wake.*" *Joyce Stud Annual 1992,* 57–76.

Lewis, Janet E. "*The Cat and the Devil* and *Finnegans Wake.*" *James Joyce Q* 29 (1992), 805–13.

Lindquist, Vern. "Sir Edward Sullivan's *Book of Kells* and Joyce's *Finnegans Wake.*" *Eire-Ireland* 27:4 (1992), 78–90.

Long, Charles. "*Finnegans Wake:* Some Strange Tristan Influences." *Canadian J of Irish Stud* 15:1 (1989), 23–33.

Long, Charles. "Joyce's 'Missymissy,' Cocteau's 'Eternal Cycle,' and Claudel's 'Ysé.'" *Claudel Stud* 15:1 (1988), 33–37.

Long, Charles. "Missymissy the Seductress: Taughterly and Cistern and Brothelly Love." *Canadian J of Irish Stud* 16:2 (1990), 47–56.

Lowe-Evans, Mary. "'The Commonest of All Cases': Birth Control on Trial in the *Wake.*" *James Joyce Q* 27 (1990), 803–13.

Lowe-Evans, Mary. *Crimes Against Fecundity,* 76–79, 80–99.

McCarthy, Patrick A. "The Last Epistle of *Finnegans Wake.*" *James Joyce Q* 27 (1990), 725–32.

McCormack, W. J. "*Finnegans Wake* and Irish Literary History," in Joris Duytschaever and Geert Lernout, eds., *History and Violence,* 111–35.

McGee, Patrick. "Reading Authority: Feminism and Joyce." *Mod Fiction Stud* 35 (1989), 421–36.

Mahaffey, Vicki. "'Minxing marrage and making loof': Anti-Oedipal Reading." *James Joyce Q* 30 (1993), 228–35.

Martin, Timothy. *Joyce and Wagner,* 70–76, 97–106, 113–41, 159–62.

Martin, Timothy P. "Joyce, Wagner, and the Wandering Jew." *Compar Lit* 42 (1990), 65–70.

Melchiori, Giorgio. "The Languages of Joyce," in Rosa Maria Bollettieri Bosinelli et al., eds., *The Languages of Joyce,* 15–18.

Milesi, Laurent. "Metaphors of the Quest in *Finnegans Wake,*" in Geert Lernout, ed., *"Finnegans Wake,"* 79–104.

Milesi, Laurent. "The Perversions of 'Aerse' and the Anglo-Irish Middle Voice in *Finnegans Wake." Joyce Stud Annual 1993,* 98–118.

Milesi, Laurent. "Toward a Female Grammar of Sexuality: The De/Re-composition of 'Storiella as she is syung.'" *Mod Fiction Stud* 35 (1989), 569–85.

Myers, Peter. *The Sound of "Finnegans Wake,"* 1–181.

Norris, Margot. *"Finnegans Wake,"* in Derek Attridge, ed., *The Cambridge Companion,* 161–82.

Norris, Margot. *Joyce's Web,* 68–94.

Norris, Margot. "The Politics of Childhood in 'The Mime of Mick, Nick, and the Maggies.'" *Joyce Stud Annual 1990,* 61–95.

Norris, Margot. "The Postmodernization of *Finnegans Wake* Reconsidered," in Kevin J. H. Dettmar, ed., *Rereading the New,* 343–60.

O'Neill, Patrick. *The Comedy of Entropy,* 295–301.

Peterson, Laura. "The Bygmester, His Geamatron, and the Triumphs of the Craftygild: *Finnegans Wake* and the Art of Freemasonry." *James Joyce Q* 27 (1990), 777–91.

Peterson, Richard F. *James Joyce Revisited,* 81–104.

Polhemus, Robert M. *Erotic Faith,* 251–78.

Rabaté, Jean-Michel. *James Joyce, Authorized Reader,* 56–59, 116–31, 132–49, 179–84, 190–92.

Rabaté, Jean-Michel. *Joyce upon the Void,* 69–214.

Rabaté, Jean-Michel. "Lapsus ex machina," in Derek Attridge and Daniel Ferrer, eds., *Post-structuralist Joyce,* 79–99.

Reichert, Klaus. "Towards the Sublime," in Rosa Maria Bollettieri Bosinelli et al., eds., *The Languages of Joyce,* 223–28.

Reichert, Klaus. "Vico's Method and its Relation to Joyce's," in Geert Lernout, ed., *"Finnegans Wake,"* 47–59.

Robinson, Marian. "Funny Funereels: Single Combat in *Finnegans Wake* and the *Táin Bó Cuailnge." Eire-Ireland* 26:3 (1991), 96–106.

Robinson, Marian. "The Girl in the Mirror." *J of Mod Lit* 15:1 (1988), 158–61.

Rose, Danis, and John O'Hanlon. "A Nice Beginning: On the *Ulysses/ Finnegans Wake* Interface," in Geert Lernout, ed., *"Finnegans Wake,"* 165–73.

Roughley, Alan. "ALP's 'Sein' und 'Zeit': Questions of *Finnegans Wake's* Being and Language in a Philosophical Context," in Geert Lernout, ed., *"Finnegans Wake,"* 125–38.

Roughley, Alan. *James Joyce and Critical Theory,* 36–41, 60–67, 98–104, 120–22, 251–64.

Roughley, Alan R. " 'Untitled,' " in Rosa Maria Bollettieri Bosinelli et al., eds., *The Languages of Joyce,* 257–64.

Ruge, Elisabeth, Reinhard Schäfer, and Dirk Vanderbeke. "Digressions of the Book for AlleMannen," in Geert Lernout, ed., *"Finnegans Wake,"* 37–45.

Sailer, Susan Shaw. "Conjunctions: Commentary and Text in *Finnegans Wake* II.2." *James Joyce Q* 27 (1990), 793–801.

Sailer, Susan Shaw. "A Methodology of Reading *Finnegans Wake.*" *Twentieth Cent Lit* 35 (1989), 195–202.

Sailer, Susan Shaw. "St. Patrick at the Wake." *Notes on Mod Irish Lit* 2 (1990), 34–41.

Schaffer, Talia. "Letters to Biddy: About That Original Hen." *James Joyce Q* 29 (1992), 623–42.

Schiff, Dan. "James Joyce and Cartoons," in Vincent J. Cheng and Timothy Martin, eds., *Joyce in Context*, 201–18.

Schork, R. J. " 'All the Sinkts in the Colander': *Finnegans Wake*, 1939." *Eire-Ireland* 24:4 (1989), 121–28.

Schork, R. J. "Awake, Phoenician Too Frequent." *James Joyce Q* 27 (1990), 767–74.

Schork, R. J. "Barnum at the *Wake.*" *James Joyce Q* 27 (1990), 767–74.

Schork, R. J. " 'Nodebinding Ayes': Milton, Blindness, and Egypt in the *Wake.*" *James Joyce Q* 30 (1992), 69–81.

Schork, R. J. "Sheep, Goats, and the *Figura Etymologica* in *Finnegans Wake.*" *JEGP* 92 (1993), 200–211.

Schork, R. J. "*Simplex Mendaciis:* Horace in the Works of James Joyce." *Classical and Mod Lit* 10 (1990), 336–42.

Scott, Bonnie Kime. " 'The Look in the Throat of a Stricken Animal': Joyce as Met by Djuna Barnes." *Joyce Stud Annual 1991*, 153–76.

Segall, Jeffrey. *Joyce in America*, 101–3, 128–30, 162–64.

Senn, Fritz. "Linguistic Dissatisfaction in the *Wake,*" in Rosa Maria Bollettieri Bosinelli et al., eds., *The Languages of Joyce*, 211–22.

Senn, Fritz. "Vexations of Group Reading: 'transluding from the other man,' " in Geert Lernout, ed., *"Finnegans Wake,"* 61–78.

Simpkins, Scott. "The Agency of the Title: *Finnegans Wake.*" *James Joyce Q* 27 (1990), 735–42.

Simpkins, Scott. "Reeling in the Signs: Unlimited Semiosis and the Agenda of Literary Semiotics." *Versus* 55–56 (1990), 153–73.

Skrabanek, Petr. "*Finnegans Wake:* Night Joyce of a Thousand Tiers," in Augustine Martin, ed., *James Joyce*, 229–40.

Sorlin, Evelyne. "Le Forficule et l'Oreille dans *Finnegans Wake.*" *Etudes Irlandaises* 14:1 (1989), 89–101.

Stevenson, Randall. *Modernist Fiction*, 172–74, 193–96.

Tardits, Annie. "Joyce in Babylonia," in Rosa Maria Bollettieri Bosinelli et al., eds., *The Languages of Joyce*, 229–31, 237–42, 245–47.

Theall, Donald F. "The Hieroglyphs of Engined Egypsians: Machines, Media, and Modes of Communication in *Finnegans Wake.*" *Joyce Stud Annual 1991*, 129–52.

Vanderbeke, Dirk. "Physics, Rhetoric, and the Language of *Finnegans Wake,*" in Rosa Maria Bollettieri Bosinelli et al., eds., *The Languages of Joyce*, 249–56.

Wales, Katie. *The Language of James Joyce,* 1–4, 27–29, 31–33, 133–57.

Walton, James. " 'a chiliad of perihelygangs.' " *James Joyce Q* 30 (1993), 459–63.

Wang, Jennie. "The Player's Song of *Finnegans Wake:* Translating Sound Sense." *J of Narrative Technique* 21 (1991), 212–22.

Weir, Lorraine. *Writing Joyce,* 54–104.

A Portrait of the Artist as a Young Man, 1917

Alexander, Marguerite. *Flights from Realism,* 24–28.

Bair, Deirdre. *"A Portrait of the Artist as a Young Man,"* in Augustine Martin, ed., *James Joyce,* 83–98.

Beja, Morris. *James Joyce,* 28–31, 40–43, 59–62.

Beja, Morris. *Joyce, the Artist Manqué, and Indeterminacy,* 7–9.

Bendelli, Giuliana. "Configurations in *A Portrait,*" in Tomaso Kemeny, ed., *Differences Similar,* 7–13.

Boheemen, Christine van. *The Novel as Family Romance,* 14–17, 153–56.

Brown, Dennis. *Intertextual Dynamics,* 54–60.

Brown, Richard. *James Joyce,* 29–60.

Brunsdale, Mitzi M. *James Joyce,* 52–104, 201–19.

Canavesi, Angelo. " 'Music, when soft voices die': Shelley and Joyce," in Tomaso Kemeny, ed., *Differences Similar,* 15–17.

Castle, Gregory. "The Book of Youth: Reading Joyce's Bildungsroman." *Genre* 22 (1989), 21–38.

Cawthra, Gillian. *Cultural Climate and Linguistic Style,* 46–51, 66–76.

Cervo, Nathan. "Joyce's *A Portrait of the Artist as a Young Man.*" *Explicator* 49 (1991), 114–16.

Chi, Ch'iu-lang. "Esthetics of Mystical Understanding: Joyce, Hopkins, and Tsung-ping." *Tamkang R* 20:1 (1989), 89–109.

Cixous, Hélène. "Reaching the Point of Wheat: Or, A Portrait of the Artist as a Maturing Woman." *Remate de Males* 9 (1989), 39–54.

Clayton, Jay. "A Portrait of the Romantic Poet as a Young Modernist: Literary History as Textual Unconscious," in Susan Stanford Friedman, ed., *Joyce,* 121–27.

Clayton, John J. *Gestures of Healing,* 71–73.

Comens, Bruce. "Narrative Nets and Lyric Flights in Joyce's *A Portrait.*" *James Joyce Q* 29 (1992), 297–312.

Corti, Claudia. " 'Contrahit orator, variant in carmine vates': Allusioni e intrusioni poetiche nel *Portrait* di Joyce." *Rivista di Letterature Moderne e Comparate* 42 (1989), 275–95.

Cotta Ramusino, Elena. "Seamus Heaney's 'Station Island' and James Joyce's *A Portrait of the Artist as a Young Man:* A Case of Intertextuality," in Tomaso Kemeny, ed., *Differences Similar,* 19–23.

Crooks, Robert. "Triptych Vision: Voyeurism and Screen Memories in Joyce's *Portrait.*" *Mod Fiction Stud* 38 (1992), 377–400.

Crump, Ian. "Refining Himself out of Existence: The Evolution of Joyce's Aesthetic Theory and the Drafts of *A Portrait,*" in Vincent J. Cheng and Timothy Martin, eds., *Joyce in Context,* 223–29, 234–35.

Deidda, Antioco. "Queens With Prize-bulls," in Tomaso Kemeny, ed., *Differences Similar,* 25–27.

DiBattista, Maria. *First Love,* 12–14, 170–72.

Doyle, Laura. "Races and Chains: The Sexuo-Racial Matrix in *Ulysses,*" in Susan Stanford Friedman, ed., *Joyce,* 163–67.

Elbarbary, Samir. "The Image of the Goat in *Portrait of the Artist as a Young Man.*" *Coll Lit* 16 (1989), 261–73.

Empric, Julienne H. "The Mediation of the Woman and the Interpretation of the Artist in Joyce's *Portrait,*" in Diana A. Ben-Merre and Maureen Murphy, eds., *James Joyce,* 11–15.

Finney, Brian. "Suture in Literary Analysis." *LIT* 2 (1990), 131–44.

Flood, Jeanne A. "The Sow That Eats Her Farrow: Gender and Politics," in Diana A. Ben-Merre and Maureen Murphy, eds., *James Joyce,* 69–76.

Friedman, Susan Stanford. "The Return of the Repressed in Joyce: (Self)Censorship and the Making of a Modernist," in Rosa Maria Bollettieri Bosinelli et al., eds., *The Languages of Joyce,* 60–67.

Friedman, Susan Stanford. "(Self)Censorship and the Making of Joyce's Modernism," in Susan Stanford Friedman, ed., *Joyce,* 25–27, 29–44, 47–50, 53–55.

Froula, Christine. "Mothers of Invention/Doaters of Inversion: Narcissan Scenes in *Finnegans Wake,*" in Susan Stanford Friedman, ed., *Joyce,* 289–92.

Frumkin, Robert. "James Joyce and the Masques of Ben Jonson." *J of Irish Lit* 21:2 (1992), 3–10.

Gabler, Hans Walter. "Joyce's Text in Progress," in Derek Attridge, ed., *The Cambridge Companion,* 220–23.

Giobbi, Giuliana. "Pavese and Joyce: Exile, Myth and the Past." *J of European Stud* 81 (1991), 43–53.

Goldberg, S. L. *Agents and Lives,* 64–75.

Greene, Gayle. *Changing the Story,* 152–56.

Harkness, Marguerite. *"A Portrait of the Artist as a Young Man,"* 21–111.

Harper, Margaret Mills. *The Aristocracy of Art,* 2–7, 9–18, 20–61, 65–67, 116–20.

Hawkins, Hunt. "Joyce as a Colonial Writer." *Coll Lang Assoc J* 35 (1992), 406–10.

Herzberger, David, and M. Carmen Rodríguez-Margenot. "Luis Goytisolo's *Antagonía:* A Portrait of the Artist as a Young Man." *Revista Canadiense de Estudios Hispánicos* 13:1 (1988), 79–92.

Höfele, Andreas. "Daedalus-Laokoon: Künstlerbild und autobiographische Fiktion bei James Joyce und Malcolm Lowry." *Anglia* 109 (1991), 410–29.

Kearney, Colbert. "Stephen's Green: The Image of Ireland in Joyce's *Portrait,*" in Augustine Martin, ed., *James Joyce,* 101–20.

Kemeny, Tomaso. "Mallarmé, Wagner and Joyce's Sublime," in Tomaso Kemeny, ed., *Differences Similar,* 81–84.

Kittay, Jeffrey. "On Notation." *Lang & Communication* 10 (1990), 149–65.

Klein, Jürgen. *Literaturtheorie,* 182–95.

Lawrence, Karen. "Joyce and Feminism," in Derek Attridge, ed., *The Cambridge Companion,* 246–48.

Loucks, James F. " 'What an Awful Power, Stephen': Simony and Joyce's Medieval Sources in *A Portrait." Papers on Lang & Lit* 28 (1992), 133–48.

Lowe-Evans, Mary. *Crimes Against Fecundity,* 33–36, 47–50.

Lowe-Evans, Mary. "Joyce's *Portrait of the Artist as a Young Man." Explicator* 48 (1990), 275–77.

Lowe-Evans, Mary. "Sex and Confession in the Joyce Canon: Some Historical Parallels." *J of Mod Lit* 16 (1990), 563–76.

McArthur, Murray. *Stolen Writings,* 59–64.

McDonald, Michael Bruce. "The Strength and Sorrow of Young Stephen: Toward a Reading of the Dialectic of Harmony and Dissonance in Joyce's *Portrait." Twentieth Cent Lit* 37 (1991), 361–83.

McGowan, John. "From Pater to Wilde to Joyce: Modernist Epiphany and the Soulful Self." *Texas Stud in Lit and Lang* 32 (1990), 436–42.

McMichael, James. *"Ulysses" and Justice,* 90–92, 118–21, 141–45.

Manganiello, Dominic. "Through a Cracked Looking Glass: *The Picture of Dorian Gray* and *A Portrait of the Artist as a Young Man,"* in Diana A. Ben-Merre and Maureen Murphy, eds., *James Joyce,* 89–94.

Martin, Timothy. *Joyce and Wagner,* 33–38, 40–46.

Mathews, Carolyn L. "Joyce's *A Portrait of the Artist as a Young Man." Explicator* 50 (1991), 38–40.

Melchiori, Giorgio. "The Languages of Joyce," in Rosa Maria Bollettieri Bosinelli et al., eds., *The Languages of Joyce,* 11–15.

Moreiras, Alberto. "Pharmaconomy: Stephen and the Daedalids," in Susan Stanford Friedman, ed., *Joyce,* 62–70.

Neefs, Jacques. "Ecrits de formation: *L'Education sentimentale* de 1845 et le *Portrait." Revue des Lettres Modernes* 953–958 (1990), 85–99.

Norris, Margot. *Joyce's Web,* 52–67.

O'Gorman, Kathleen. "The Performativity of Utterance in *A Portrait of the Artist as a Young Man." James Joyce Q* 30 (1993), 419–25.

O'Grady, Thomas B. "Conception, Gestation, and Reproduction: Stephen's Dream of Parnell." *James Joyce Q* 27 (1990), 293–99.

Pearce, Richard. *The Politics of Narration,* 37–48.

Pearce, Richard. "Simon's Irish Rose: Famine Songs, Blackfaced Minstrels, and Woman's Repression in *A Portrait,"* in Susan Stanford Friedman, ed., *Joyce,* 128–46.

Peterson, Richard F. *James Joyce Revisited,* 37–55.

Petruso, Thomas F. *Life Made Real,* 40–42, 45–47, 60–62, 76–78.

Potts, Willard. "Stephen Dedalus and 'Irrland's Split Little Pea.' " *James Joyce Q* 27 (1990), 559–74.

Restuccia, Frances L. *Joyce and the Law of the Father,* 9–14.

Riquelme, John Paul. "*Stephen Hero, Dubliners,* and *A Portrait of the Ar-*

tist as a Young Man: Styles of Realism and Fantasy," in Derek Attridge, ed., *The Cambridge Companion,* 116–22.

Robinson, David W. " 'What kind of a name is that?': Joyce's Critique of Names and Naming in *A Portrait." James Joyce Q* 27 (1990), 325–34.

Roughley, Alan. *James Joyce and Critical Theory,* 86–91.

Sacchetto, Alberto. "*A Portrait of the Artist as a Young Man* di James Joyce: la formazione di Stephen Dedalus e il processo di individuazione junghiano." *Quaderni di Lingue e Letterature* 16 (1991), 211–25.

Scanlan, Margaret. *Traces of Another Time,* 28–32.

Schneidau, Herbert N. *Waking Giants,* 11–13.

Scholes, Robert. *In Search of James Joyce,* 7–15, 52–58, 63–69, 70–81.

Schork, R. J. "Ayala's Joycean 'Portrait': A.M.D.G." *Compar Lit Stud* 26:1 (1989), 50–70.

Schwarz, Daniel R. *The Transformation of the English Novel,* 242–46, 249–53.

Scott, Bonnie Kime. "Hanna and Francis Sheehy-Skeffington: Reformers in the Company of Joyce," in Diana A. Ben-Merre and Maureen Murphy, eds., *James Joyce,* 77–84.

Segall, Jeffrey. *Joyce in America,* 58–60, 151–54.

Senn, Fritz. "Entering the Lists: Sampling Early Catalogues," in Vincent J. Cheng and Timothy Martin, eds., *Joyce in Context,* 243–46.

Shepard, Alan. "From Aristotle to Keats: Stephen's Search for 'The Good Life' in *A Portrait of the Artist as a Young Man." Engl Stud* 74 (1993), 105–12.

Singer, Thomas C. "Riddles, Silence, and Wonder: Joyce and Wittgenstein Encountering the Limits of Language." *ELH* 57 (1990), 459–83.

Suzuki, Takashi. "Cathleens in Yeats and Joyce: Love's Bitter Mystery," in Takashi Suzuki and Tsuyoshi Mukai, eds., *Arthurian and Other Studies,* 65–68.

Thomas, Calvin. "Stephen in Process/Stephen on Trial: The Anxiety of Production in Joyce's *Portrait." Novel* 23 (1990), 282–302.

Thomas, Ronald R. *Dreams of Authority,* 260–79.

Wachtel, Albert. *The Cracked Lookingglas,* 63–96.

Wales, Katie. *The Language of James Joyce,* 8–10, 12–15, 32–36, 55–66.

Walters, Mark. "The Personal Pronouns in the Opening Section of *Portrait of the Artist* and the Establishment." *Word & Image* 7 (1991), 311–13.

Watt, Stephen. *Joyce, O'Casey, and the Irish Popular Theater,* 116–18, 131–33.

Weir, Lorraine. *Writing Joyce,* 13–28.

Wilde, Dana. "A Note on Stephen's Shapeless Thoughts from Swedenborg in *A Portrait of the Artist." J of Mod Lit* 16:1 (1989), 179–81.

Stephen Hero, 1944

Bair, Deirdre. "*A Portrait of the Artist as a Young Man,*" in Augustine Martin, ed., *James Joyce,* 88–90.

Crump, Ian. "Refining Himself out of Existence: The Evolution of Joyce's

Aesthetic Theory and the Drafts of *A Portrait*," in Vincent J. Cheng and Timothy Martin, eds., *Joyce in Context,* 223–27, 230–34.

Friedman, Susan Stanford. "The Return of the Repressed in Joyce: (Self)Censorship and the Making of a Modernist," in Rosa Maria Bollettieri Bosinelli et al., eds., *The Languages of Joyce,* 60–67.

Friedman, Susan Stanford. "(Self)Censorship and the Making of Joyce's Modernism," in Susan Stanford Friedman, ed., *Joyce,* 25–27, 29–44, 47–49.

Gabler, Hans Walter. "Joyce's Text in Progress," in Derek Attridge, ed., *The Cambridge Companion,* 219–21.

Harper, Margaret Mills. *The Aristocracy of Art,* 1–6, 56–59.

Klein, Jürgen. *Literaturtheorie,* 171–81.

Manganiello, Dominic. "The Politics of the Unpolitical in Joyce's Fictions." *James Joyce Q* 29 (1992), 241–56.

Melchiori, Giorgio. "The Languages of Joyce," in Rosa Maria Bollettieri Bosinelli et al., eds., *The Languages of Joyce,* 2–4, 11–16.

Norris, Margot. *Joyce's Web,* 44–67.

Peterson, Richard F. *James Joyce Revisited,* 18–19, 37–39.

Reichert, Klaus. "The European Background of Joyce's Writing," in Derek Attridge, ed., *The Cambridge Companion,* 62–66.

Riquelme, John Paul. "*Stephen Hero, Dubliners,* and *A Portrait of the Artist as a Young Man:* Styles of Realism and Fantasy," in Derek Attridge, ed., *The Cambridge Companion,* 103–16.

Scholes, Robert. *In Search of James Joyce,* 63–67.

Scott, Bonnie Kime. "Hanna and Francis Sheehy-Skeffington: Reformers in the Company of Joyce," in Diana A. Ben-Merre and Maureen Murphy, eds., *James Joyce,* 77–84.

Tardits, Annie. "Joyce in Babylonia," in Rosa Maria Bollettieri Bosinelli et al., eds., *The Languages of Joyce,* 235–37.

Wales, Katie. *The Language of James Joyce,* 8–9, 12–14, 55–58.

Ulysses, 1922

Alexander, Marguerite. *Flights from Realism,* 28–32.

Ames, Christopher. *The Life of the Party,* 57–68.

Ames, Christopher. "The Modernist Canon Narrative: Woolf's *Between the Acts* and Joyce's 'Oxen of the Sun.'" *Twentieth Cent Lit* 37 (1991), 390–403.

Amiran, Eyal. "Bloom and Disraeli: On the Side of the Angels?" *Engl Lang Notes* 27:3 (1990), 53–56.

Amiran, Eyal. "Proofs of Origin: Stephen's Intertextual Art in *Ulysses*." *James Joyce Q* 29 (1992), 775–86.

Amiran, Eyal. "Rhetorics of Simulation and the 1984 *Ulysses*." *Stud in the Novel* 22 (1990), 142–46.

Arnold, Bruce. *The Scandal of "Ulysses,"* 1–247.

Arnold, David Scott. *Liminal Readings,* 64–86.

Attridge, Derek. "Molly's Flow: The Writing of 'Penelope' and the Question of Women's Language." *Mod Fiction Stud* 35 (1989), 543–62.

Barry, David. "Peninsular Art: A Context for a Comparative Study of Goethe and Joyce." *Compar Lit Stud* 29 (1992), 380–94.

Battaglia, Rosemarie A. "Joyce, Stephen, Bloom." *Notes on Mod Irish Lit* 2 (1990), 25–28.

Bazargan, Susan. "Monologue as Dialogue: Molly Bloom's 'History' as Myriorama." *Works and Days* 10 (1987), 63–77.

Beja, Morris. *James Joyce*, 17–20, 63–70, 73–78, 82–87, 93–99.

Beja, Morris. *Joyce, the Artist Manqué, and Indeterminacy*, 9–12, 16–18, 20–23.

Bell, Robert H. *Jocoserious Joyce: The Fate of Folly in "Ulysses."*

Benstock, Bernard. "Decoding in the Dark in 'Oxen of the Sun.'" *James Joyce Q* 28 (1991), 637–42.

Benstock, Bernard. *Narrative Con/Texts in "Ulysses."*

Benstock, Shari. "*Traduire* Joyce," in Daniel Ferrer et al., eds., *"Ulysse" à l'article*, 207–20.

Bentley, Joseph. "The Stylistics of Regression in *Ulysses*," in Diana A. Ben-Merre and Maureen Murphy, eds., *James Joyce*, 31–35.

Bergonzi, Bernard. *Wartime and Aftermath*, 180–82.

Bersani. Leo. *The Culture of Redemption*, 155–78.

Bialas, Zbigniew. "Fundamentals of Life as Archetypes in Homer's *Odyssey* and Joyce's *Ulysses*." *Anglica Wratislaviensia* 18 (1990), 23–33.

Boheemen, Christine van. "'The Language of Flow': Joyce's Dispossession of the Feminine in *Ulysses*," in Christine van Boheemen, ed., *Joyce, Modernity, and its Mediation*, 63–77.

Boheemen, Christine van. *The Novel as Family Romance*, 132–88.

Booker, M. Keith. "From the Sublime to the Ridiculous: Dante's Beatrice and Joyce's Bella Cohen." *James Joyce Q* 29 (1992), 357–66.

Booker, M. Keith. "Joyce, Planck, Einstein, and Heisenberg: A Relativistic Quantum Mechanical Discussion of *Ulysses*." *James Joyce Q* 27 (1990), 577–85.

Boone, Joseph A. "Representing Interiority: Spaces of Sexuality in *Ulysses*," in Rosa Maria Bollettieri Bosinelli et al., eds., *The Languages of Joyce*, 69–83.

Boone, Joseph A. "Staging Sexuality: Repression, Representation, and 'Interior' States in *Ulysses*," in Susan Stanford Friedman, ed., *Joyce*, 190–221.

Bormanis, John. "'in the first bloom of her new motherhood': the Appropriation of the Maternal and the Representation of Mothering in *Ulysses*." *James Joyce Q* 29 (1992), 593–604.

Bowen, Zack. *"Ulysses" as a Comic Novel*, 17–131.

Brancoli, Cristina, Laura Fabbri, Elisabetta Innocenti, Sibilla Mischi, Paola Pugliatti, Rita Romanelli, and Antonella Santerini. "In the Wake of 'Cyclops': A Genetic Approach to *Ulysses* Manuscripts," in Tomaso Kemeny, ed., *Differences Similar*, 49–76.

Brasil, Assis. *Joyce e Faulkner*, 59–95.

Briric, Sheldon. "The Veil of Signs: Perception as Language in Joyce's *Ulysses*." *ELH* 57 (1990), 737–53.

Brockman, William S. "The New Bloom in 'Eumaeus': The Emendations of *Ulysses: A Critical and Synoptic Edition.*" *James Joyce Q* 28 (1990), 153–66.

Brown, Dennis. *Intertextual Dynamics,* 89–97, 101–3.

Brown, Richard. *James Joyce,* 62–96.

Brown, Richard. "Post-Genetic and Post-Intentionalist Considerations for the Hyper-Criticism of the 'Circe' Episode of Joyce's *Ulysses:* 'Everything' in 'Circe,' " in Daniel Ferrer et al., eds., *"Ulysse" à l'article,* 143–59.

Brownstein, Marilyn. "The Preservation of Tenderness: A Confusion of Tongues in *Ulysses* and *Finnegans Wake,*" in Susan Stanford Friedman, ed., *Joyce,* 225–29, 235–49.

Brüggemann, Heinz. "Bewegtes Sehen und literarisches Verfahren: James Joyce, *Ulysses* und der Kubismus." *Neue Rundschau* 102:3 (1991), 146–59.

Brunazzi, Elizabeth. "La Narration de l'autogenèse dans *La Tentation de Saint Antoine* et dans *Ulysses.*" *Revue des Lettres Modernes* 953–958 (1990), 123–31.

Buckley, William K. *Senses' Tender,* 53–60.

Buning, Marius. "History and Modernity in Joyce's *Ulysses,*" in Christine van Boheemen, ed., *Joyce, Modernity, and its Mediation,* 127–37.

Burnham, Michelle. " 'Dark Lady and Fair Man': The Love Triangle in Shakespeare's Sonnets and *Ulysses.*" *Stud in the Novel* 22 (1990), 43–53.

Byrnes, Robert. "Bloom's Sexual Tropes: Stigmata of the 'Degenerate' Jew." *James Joyce Q* 27 (1990), 303–22.

Callow, Heather Cook. "Joyce's Female Voices in *Ulysses.*" *J of Narrative Technique* 22 (1992), 151–61.

Callow, Heather Cook. " 'Marion of the Bountiful Bosoms': Molly Bloom and the Nightmare of History." *Twentieth Cent Lit* 36 (1990), 464–75.

Card, James Van Dyck. "Molly Bloom, Soprano." *James Joyce Q* 27 (1990), 595–601.

Carey, John. *The Intellectuals and the Masses,* 19–21.

Carpentier, Martha Celeste. "Eleusinian Archetype and Ritual in 'Eumaeus' and 'Ithaca.' " *James Joyce Q* 28 (1990), 221–37.

Castle, Gregory. " 'I am almosting it': History, Nature, and the Will to Power in 'Proteus.' " *James Joyce Q* 29 (1992), 281–94.

Channel-Purdy, Marilyn. " 'Circe' and Thomas Otway's *The Souldier's Fortune.*" *James Joyce Q* 28 (1991), 651–55.

Cheng, Vincent J. " 'Goddinpotty': James Joyce and the Language of Excrement," in Rosa Maria Bollettieri Bosinelli et al., eds., *The Languages of Joyce,* 88–93.

Cheng, Vincent J. "White Horse, Dark Horse: Joyce's Allhorse of Another Color." *Joyce Stud Annual 1991,* 101–10.

Cheyette, Bryan. " 'Jewgreek is greekjew': The Disturbing Ambivalence of Joyce's Semitic Discourse in *Ulysses.*" *Joyce Stud Annual 1992,* 32–56.

Chin, Sheon-Joo. "The Death of Rudy: James Joyce's Use of the Doctrine of Prenatal Influence in *Ulysses.*" *J of Engl Lang and Lit* 35 (1989), 115–30.

Chinitz, David. "All the Dishevelled Wandering Stars: Astronomical Symbolism in 'Ithaca.'" *Twentieth Cent Lit* 37 (1991), 432–40.

Corti, Claudia. "'Circe': Il comico onirico di Joyce." *Rivista di Letterature Moderne e Comparate* 39 (1986), 45–64.

Crumb, Michael. "*Sweets of Sin:* Joyce's *Ulysses* and Swinburne's 'Dolores.'" *James Joyce Q* 28 (1990), 239–45.

Culleton, Claire A. "Naming and Gender in James Joyce's Fiction." *Names* 39 (1991), 306–16.

Dasenbrock, Reed Way. *Imitating the Italians,* 128–31, 134–43, 193–206.

Dervin, Daniel. "Bloom Again? Questions of Aggression and Psychoanalytic Reconstruction." *Am Imago* 47 (1990), 249–63.

Dettmar, Kevin J. H. "'Working in Accord with Obstacles': A Postmodern Perspective on Joyce's 'Mythical Method,'" in Kevin J. H. Dettmar, ed., *Rereading the New,* 278–92.

Devlin, Kimberly J. "Castration and its Discontents: A Lacanian Approach to *Ulysses.*" *James Joyce Q* 29 (1991), 117–40.

Devlin, Kimberly J. "Pretending in 'Penelope': Masquerade, Mimicry, and Molly Bloom." *Novel* 25 (1991), 71–89.

DiBattista, Maria. *First Love,* 37–39, 53–57, 167–69, 173–201.

Doherty, Lillian E. "Joyce's Penelope and Homer's: Feminist Reconsiderations." *Classical and Mod Lit* 10 (1990), 343–49.

Domenichelli, Mario. "*Ulysses* as Trauerarbeit: Amor Matris," in Tomaso Kemeny, ed., *Differences Similar,* 29–35.

Donoghue, Denis. "Is There a Case Against *Ulysses?,*" in Vincent J. Cheng and Timothy Martin, eds., *Joyce in Context,* 30–36.

Doody, Terrence. "*Don Quixote, Ulysses,* and the Idea of Realism," in Mark Spilka and Caroline McCracken-Flesher, eds., *Why the Novel Matters,* 76–80, 82–85, 90–92.

Doyle, Laura. "Races and Chains: The Sexuo-Racial Matrix in *Ulysses,*" in Susan Stanford Friedman, ed., *Joyce,* 149–89.

Duffy, Andrew Enda. "Parnellism and Rebellion: The Irish War of Independence and Revisions of the Heroic in *Ulysses.*" *James Joyce Q* 28 (1990), 179–94.

Ellman, Maud. "The Ghosts of *Ulysses,*" in Augustine Martin, ed., *James Joyce,* 193–218. (Also in Rosa Maria Bollettieri Bosinelli et al., eds., *The Languages of Joyce,* 103–18.)

Ferrer, Daniel. "Circe, Regret and Regression," in Derek Attridge and Daniel Ferrer, eds., *Post-structuralist Joyce,* 127–42.

Ferrer, Daniel. "Introduction: A l'article . . . ," in Daniel Ferrer et al., eds., *"Ulysse" à l'article,* 7–35.

Fishelov, David. "Types of Character, Characteristics of Type," in John V. Knapp, ed., *Literary Character,* 85–88.

Forbes, Robert P. "Eliade, Joyce, and the Terror of History." *Cross Currents* 36 (1986), 179–92.

Ford, Charles. "Dante's Other Brush: *Ulysses* and the Irish Revolution." *James Joyce Q* 29 (1992), 751–60.

Fox, Cheryl. "Absolutely: Redefining the Word Known to All Men." *James Joyce Q* 29 (1992), 799–804.

Friedman, Susan Stanford. "The Return of the Repressed in Joyce: (Self)Censorship and the Making of a Modernist," in Rosa Maria Bollettieri Bosinelli et al., eds., *The Languages of Joyce*, 65–67.

Friedman, Susan Stanford. "(Self)Censorship and the Making of Joyce's Modernism," in Susan Stanford Friedman, ed., *Joyce*, 7–11, 50–55.

Froula, Christine. "History's Nightmare, Fiction's Dream: Joyce and the Psychohistory of *Ulysses.*" *James Joyce Q* 28 (1991), 857–70.

Frumkin, Robert. "James Joyce and the Masques of Ben Jonson." *J of Irish Lit* 21:2 (1992), 10–21.

Frumkin, Robert. "*Ulysses:* Stephen's Parable of the Plums." *Colby Q* 28 (1992), 5–18.

Fuller, David. *James Joyce's "Ulysses,"* 31–100.

Gabler, Hans Walter. "Joyce's Text in Progress," in Derek Attridge, ed., *The Cambridge Companion*, 223–33.

Galef, David. "The Fashion Show in *Ulysses.*" *Twentieth Cent Lit* 37 (1991), 420–29.

Garcia-Leon, Rafael I. "'Threemaster': A Note on the Last Lines of the Telemachia of *Ulysses.*" *Notes on Mod Irish Lit* 3 (1991), 49–51.

Garnier, Marie-Dominique. "*Ulysse* à l'aveuglette: le clin et la lisse," in Daniel Ferrer et al., eds., *"Ulysse" à l'article*, 195–206.

Garvey, Johanna X. K. "'A Voice Bubbling Up': *Mrs Dalloway* in Dialogue with *Ulysses*," in Vara Neverow-Turk and Mark Hussey, eds., *Virginia Woolf*, 299–306.

Garvey, Johanna X. K. "Woolf and Joyce: Reading and Re/Vision," in Vincent J. Cheng and Timothy Martin, eds., *Joyce in Context*, 40–51.

Gatti-Taylor, Marisa. "It Loses Something in Translation: Italian and French Profanity in Joyce's *Ulysses*," in Christine van Boheemen, ed., *Joyce, Modernity, and its Mediation*, 141–49.

Gibb, Robert. "Cloacal Obsession: Food, Sex, and Death in *Lestrygonians.*" *J of Evolutionary Psych* 10 (1989), 268–73.

Gibson, Andrew. "'History, All That': Revival Historiography and Literary Strategy in the 'Cyclops' Episode in *Ulysses*," in Angus Easson, ed., *History and the Novel*, 53–69.

Gilbert, Inger. "Text into Origin: Apprenticeship of Joyce as Artificer, Rilke as Prodigal Son." *Compar Lit Stud* 26 (1989), 304–20.

Gillespie, Michael Patrick. "Certitude and Circularity: The Search for *Ulysses.*" *Stud in the Novel* 22 (1990), 216–28.

Giovannangeli, J. L. "L'Idée de Nation dans 'Le Cyclope' et 'Nestor.'" *Etudes Irlandaises* 15:2 (1990), 21–34.

Giovannangeli, Jean-Louis. "Des mots à la dérive: l'incomplétude du sens dans *Ulysses*," in Daniel Ferrer et al., eds., *"Ulysse" à l'article*, 255–67.

Giovannangeli, Jean-Louis. "Du Sol au Livre: Joyce entre engagement et retrait." *Etudes Irlandaises* 17:2 (1992), 37–47.

Gordon, John. "Haines and the Black Panther." *James Joyce Q* 27 (1990), 587–93.

Gordon, John. "Love in Bloom, by Stephen Dedalus." *James Joyce Q* 27 (1990), 241–54.

Gordon, John. "Obeying the Boss in 'Oxen in the Sun.'" *ELH* 58 (1991), 233–56.

Hardy, Barbara. "Joyce and Homer: Seeing Double," in Augustine Martin, ed., *James Joyce*, 169–89.

Harper, Margaret Mills. *The Aristocracy of Art*, 117–41, 143–50.

Hart, Clive. "Gaps and Cracks in *Ulysses*." *James Joyce Q* 30 (1993), 427–36.

Hart, Clive. "The Rhythm of *Ulysses*," in Augustine Martin, ed., *James Joyce*, 153–66.

Harty, John. "'Grave Morrice' (*Ulysses* 2.155): The Morris Dances." *Notes on Mod Irish Lit* 2 (1990), 29–33.

Henderson, Diana E. "Joyce's Modernist Woman: Whose Last Word?" *Mod Fiction Stud* 35 (1989), 517–27.

Henke, Suzette. "Re-visioning Joyce's Masculine Signature," in Vincent J. Cheng and Timothy Martin, eds., *Joyce in Context*, 138–49.

Herman, David. "*Ulysses* and Vacuous Pluralism." *Philos and Lit* 17 (1993), 65–74.

Herring, Phillip. "Joyce's Sourcebooks for *Ulysses* in the Manuscripts," in Daniel Ferrer et al., eds., *"Ulysse" à l'article*, 269–74.

Herring, Phillip F. "James Joyce and Gift Exchange," in Rosa Maria Bollettieri Bosinelli et al., eds., *The Languages of Joyce*, 178–82, 188–90.

Higgins, Michael. "A Note on 'time or setdown' in *Ulysses*." *Notes and Queries* 234 (1989), 200–201.

Hogan, Patrick Colm. "Influxes of Influence, Agonists Hurl Odyssean Mythpuns and Crackquips, Aristotelian Designs Thought Likely." *Univ of Hartford Stud in Lit* 21 (1989), 26–36.

Hogan, Patrick Colm. "Molly Bloom's Lacanian Firtree: Law, Ambiguity, and the Limits of Paradise." *James Joyce Q* 29 (1991), 103–15.

Hong, Duk-Seon. "James Joyce's Use of History in *Ulysses*." *J of Engl Lang and Lit* 36 (1990), 679–90.

Huss, Roger. "Masculinité et fémininité dans *Madame Bovary* et *Ulysses*." *Revue des Lettres Modernes* 953–958 (1990), 102–22.

Jackson, Tony E. "'Cyclops,' 'Nausicaa,' and Joyce's Imaginary Irish Couple." *James Joyce Q* 29 (1991), 63–81.

Janusko, Robert. "Grave Beauty: Newman in 'Oxen.'" *James Joyce Q* 28 (1991), 617–20.

Janusko, Robert. "More on J. A. Dowie (& Son)." *James Joyce Q* 29 (1992), 607–12.

Janusko, Robert. "Yet another Anthology for the 'Oxen': Murison's Selections." *Joyce Stud Annual 1990*, 117–31.

Johnson, Jeri. "'Beyond the Veil': *Ulysses*, Feminism, and the Figure of Woman," in Christine van Boheemen, ed., *Joyce, Modernity, and its Mediation*, 201–28.

Jones, Ellen Carol. "Textual Mater: Writing the Mother in Joyce," in Susan Stanford Friedman, ed., *Joyce,* 264–66, 269–71, 276–78, 280–81.

Jordan, Richard Douglas. *The Quiet Hero,* 146–78.

Kadlec, David. "Joyce's 'Penelope' and Woman Suffrage." *Works and Days* 20 (1992), 43–59.

Kemeny, Tomaso. "Mallarmé, Wagner and Joyce's Sublime," in Tomaso Kemeny, ed., *Differences Similar,* 84–86.

Kennelly, Brendan. "Joyce's Humanism," in Augustine Martin, ed., *James Joyce,* 327–32.

Kimball, Jean. "Autobiography as Epic: Freud's Three-Time Scheme in *Ulysses." Texas Stud in Lit and Lang* 31 (1989), 475–91.

King, Debra W. "Just Can't Find the Words: How Expression Is Achieved." *Philos and Rhetoric* 24:1 (1991), 54–72.

Klein, Scott W. "Speech Lent by Males: Gender, Identity, and the Example of Stephen's Shakespeare." *James Joyce Q* 30 (1993), 439–48.

Kopper, Edward A., Jr. "Joyce's *Ulysses* and Burgess' *A Clockwork Orange:* A Note." *Notes on Mod Irish Lit* 1 (1989), 12–13.

Krysinski, Wladimir. "Subjectivities in *Ulysses* and Before." *Discours Social/Social Discourse* 2:1–2 (1989), 3–12.

Kumar, Udaya. *The Joycean Labyrinth,* 50–154.

Kurjiaka, Susan. "The Hypnagogic State in *Ulysses." Mount Olive R* 3 (1989), 50–58.

Lamos, Colleen R. "Cheating on the Father: Joyce and Gender Justice in *Ulysses,*" in Vincent J. Cheng and Timothy Martin, eds., *Joyce in Context,* 91–98.

Lang, Frederick K. *"Ulysses" and the Irish God,* 15–279.

Laroque, François. " 'Calypso': le carnaval des lettres," in Daniel Ferrer et al., eds., *"Ulysse" à l'article,* 61–82.

Law, Jules David. " 'Pity They Can't See Themselves': Assessing the 'Subject' of Pornography in 'Nausicaa.' " *James Joyce Q* 27 (1990), 219–38.

Lawrence, Karen. "Joyce and Feminism," in Derek Attridge, ed., *The Cambridge Companion,* 237–43, 248–54.

Lawrence, Karen R. " 'Beggaring Description': Politics and Style in Joyce's 'Eumaeus.' " *Mod Fiction Stud* 38 (1992), 355–74.

Leonard, Garry M. "Joyce and Lacan: The Twin Narratives of History and His[$]tory in the 'Nestor' Chapter of *Ulysses,*" in Vincent J. Cheng and Timothy Martin, eds., *Joyce in Context,* 170–80.

Leonard, Garry M. "The Virgin Mary and the Urge in Gerty: The Packaging of Desire in the 'Nausicaa' Chapter of *Ulysses." Univ of Hartford Stud in Lit* 23:1 (1991), 3–19.

Leonard, Garry M. "Women on the Market: Commodity Culture, 'Femininity,' and 'Those Lovely Seaside Girls' in Joyce's *Ulysses." Joyce Stud Annual 1991,* 27–68.

Levine, Jennifer. *"Ulysses,"* in Derek Attridge, ed., *The Cambridge Companion,* 131–58.

Levitt, Annette Shandler. "The Pattern out of the Wallpaper: Luce Irigaray and Molly Bloom." *Mod Fiction Stud* 35 (1989), 507–16.

Lind, L. R. "The Uses of Homer." *Classical and Mod Lit* 10:1 (1989), 7–20.

Linguanti, Elsa. "Rhetoric and Literature: 'Inventio' and the 'Ithaca' Episode in Joyce's *Ulysses,*" in Tomaso Kemeny, ed., *Differences Similar,* 37–41.

Losey, Jay. "Joyce's 'New Realism' in *Ulysses.*" *Notes on Mod Irish Lit* 2 (1990), 19–24.

Lowe-Evans, Mary. *Crimes Against Fecundity,* 53–74.

Lowe-Evans, Mary. "Sex and Confession in the Joyce Canon: Some Historical Parallels." *J of Mod Lit* 16 (1990), 563–76.

Lyotard, Jean François. "Going Back to the Return," in Rosa Maria Bollettieri Bosinelli et al., eds., *The Languages of Joyce,* 193–96, 200–210.

McArthur, Murray. *Stolen Writings,* 65–146.

McCarthy, Patrick A. *"Ulysses": Portals of Discovery,* 25–112.

McCormick, Kathleen. " 'First Steps' in 'Wandering Rocks': Students' Differences, Literary Transactions, and Pleasures." *Reader* 20 (1988), 48–67.

McCormick, Kathleen. "Psychoanalytic and Ideological Pleasures in Reading Joyce." *LIT* 2 (1990), 27–39.

McHale, Brian. "Constructing (Post) Modernism: The Case of *Ulysses.*" *Style* 24 (1990), 1–15.

McMichael, James. " 'James Joyce Speaks.' " *Kenyon R* 11:3 (1989), 27–40.

McMichael, James. *"Ulysses" and Justice,* 34–194.

Major, David. "The Satirizing Superpowers Stephen Dedalus and Zarathustra." *Colby Q* 28 (1992), 115–21.

Manganiello, Dominic. "The Politics of the Unpolitical in Joyce's Fictions." *James Joyce Q* 29 (1992), 247–56.

Martella, Giuseppe. "Allusions to *Hamlet* in 'Circe,' " in Tomaso Kemeny, ed., *Differences Similar,* 43–48.

Martella, Giuseppe. "The Order of Myth in *Ulysses.*" *Lingua e Stile* 25 (1990), 289–96.

Martin, Timothy. *Joyce and Wagner,* 42–46, 64–70, 83–85, 155–59.

Martin, Timothy P. "Joyce, Wagner, and the Wandering Jew." *Compar Lit* 42 (1990), 49–65.

Mayo, Wendell. "Joyce's *Ulysses.*" *Explicator* 50 (1992), 164–65.

Melchiori, Giorgio. "The Languages of Joyce," in Rosa Maria Bollettieri Bosinelli et al., eds., *The Languages of Joyce,* 4–6, 11–15.

Merritt, Robert. "Faith and Betrayal: The Potato in *Ulysses.*" *James Joyce Q* 28 (1990), 269–76.

Mikics, David. "History and the Rhetoric of the Artist in 'Aeolus.' " *James Joyce Q* 27 (1990), 533–52.

Milesi, Laurent. "The Signs the Si-ren Seal: Textual Strategies in Joyce's 'Sirens,' " in Daniel Ferrer et al., eds., *"Ulysse" à l'article,* 127–41.

Miller, Nicholas A. "Beyond Recognition: Reading the Unconscious in the 'Ithaca' Episode of *Ulysses.*" *James Joyce Q* 30 (1993), 209–18.

Moreiras, Alberto. "Pharmaconomy: Stephen and the Daedalids," in Susan Stanford Friedman, ed., *Joyce,* 71–82.

Morse, Donald E. "'More Real Than Reality': An Introduction to the Fantastic in Irish Literature and the Arts," in Donald E. Morse and Csilla Bertha, eds., *More Real Than Reality,* 4–10.

Morse, Donald E. "Source Book or Book of Conduct: Changing Perspectives on Reading Joyce's *Ulysses.*" *Hungarian Stud in Engl* 21 (1990), 67–71.

Moshenberg, Daniel. "What shouts in the street: 1904, 1922, 1990." *James Joyce Q* 28 (1991), 809–18.

Nadel, Ira B. " 'Circe': Textual Method and Textual Meaning." *Stud in the Novel* 22 (1990), 163–76.

Nadel, Ira B. "Joyce and Expressionism." *J of Mod Lit* 16:1 (1989), 141–60.

Nair, Mark. "Joyce's *Ulysses.*" *Explicator* 50 (1992), 237–38.

Neeper, L. Layne. " 'The Very Worst Hour of the Day': Betrayal and Bloom in Joyce's 'Lestrygonians.' " *Eire-Ireland* 28:1 (1993), 107–20.

Newman, Robert D. " 'Eumaeus' as Sacrificial Narrative." *James Joyce Q* 30 (1993), 451–57.

Newman, Robert D. "Narrative Transgression and Restoration: Hermetic Messengers in *Ulysses.*" *James Joyce Q* 29 (1992), 315–32.

Norris, Margot. *Joyce's Web,* 119–80.

O'Connor, Theresa. "Demythologizing Nationalism: Joyce's Dialogized Grail Myth," in Vincent J. Cheng and Timothy Martin, eds., *Joyce in Context,* 100–117.

O'Donnell, Patrick. *Echo Chambers,* 64–92.

Osteen, Mark. "The Intertextual Economy in 'Scylla and Charybdis.' " *James Joyce Q* 28 (1990), 197–206.

Osteen, Mark. "Narrative Gifts: 'Cyclops' and the Economy of Excess." *Joyce Stud Annual 1990,* 162–96.

Pearce, Richard. *The Politics of Narration,* 60–70.

Pearce, Richard. "Who Comes First, Joyce or Woolf?," in Vara Neverow-Turk and Mark Hussey, eds., *Virginia Woolf,* 59–67.

Peterson, Richard F. *James Joyce Revisited,* 8–11, 58–82.

Petruso, Thomas F. *Life Made Real,* 39–44, 47–49, 61–66, 74–82, 96–104.

Pillai, A. S. D. "Spatial Form in Modern Fiction: A Reading of *Ulysses* and *The Waves.*" *Aligarh J of Engl Stud* 14:1 (1989), 108–22.

Piwinski, David J. "Tomatoes as 'Love Apples' in *Ulysses.*" *ANQ* 4:4 (1991), 199–89.

Platt, L. H. "The Buckeen and the Dogsbody: Aspects of History and Culture in 'Telemachus.' " *James Joyce Q* 27 (1989), 77–85.

Platt, L. H. "The Voice of Esau: Culture and Nationalism in 'Scylla and Charybdis.' " *James Joyce Q* 29 (1992), 737–49.

Polhemus, Robert M. *Erotic Faith,* 253–56, 263–68.

Pott, Hans-Georg. *Neue Theorie des Romans,* 163–207.

Power, Mary. "Molly Bloom and Mary Anderson: The Inside Story," in

Christine van Boheemen, ed., *Joyce, Modernity, and its Mediation*, 113–18.

Pugliatti, Paola. "The New *Ulysses* between Philology, Semiotics and Textual Genetics." *Dispositio* 12:30–32 (1987), 113–40.

Quick, Jonathan. "Molly Bloom's Mother." *ELH* 57 (1990), 223–39.

Rabaté, Jean-Michel. "Ce qu'aurait montré le silence des Sirènes," in Daniel Ferrer et al., eds., *"Ulysse" à l'article*, 109–25.

Rabaté, Jean-Michel. *James Joyce, Authorized Reader*, 50–56, 59–115, 150–79.

Rabaté, Jean-Michel. *Joyce upon the Void*, 43–68.

Rea, Joanne E. "Tramways and Death: Joycean Echoes in Camus' 'Entre oui et non.'" *Romance Notes* 29 (1989), 213–16.

Restuccia, Frances L. *Joyce and the Law of the Father*, 34–41, 47–49, 65–72, 76–90, 92–94, 103–11, 135–37, 141–52, 165–72.

Roughley, Alan. *James Joyce and Critical Theory*, 94–98, 201–6, 233–47, 264–70.

Ryu, Ju-Hyun. "Author and His Experience: Scylla and Charybdis in *Ulysses*." *J of Engl Lang and Lit* 35 (1989), 445–62.

Salado, Régis. "Monologues antérieurs: Propositions pour la lecture des formes de monologue intérieur dans *Ulysses*," in Daniel Ferrer et al., eds., *"Ulysse" à l'article*, 161–91.

Salvadori, Mario, and Myron Schwartzman. "Musemathematics: The Literary Use of Science and Mathematics in Joyce's *Ulysses*." *James Joyce Q* 29 (1992), 339–54.

Sarbu, Aladár. "The Fantastic in James Joyce's *Ulysses*: Representational Strategies in 'Circe' and 'Penelope,'" in Donald E. Morse and Csilla Bertha, eds., *More Real Than Reality*, 219–28.

Sayers, William. "A Schoolmaster's June Day Walk Round the City: Joyce and Strindberg's Albert Blom." *Studia Neophilologica* 61 (1989), 183–92.

Scafi, Roberta. "*Ulysses* e *Doktor Faustus*: Di due tendenze del romanzo moderno." *Rivista di Letterature Moderne e Comparate* 40 (1987), 251–72.

Schlossman, Beryl. "Figures Transfigured: Madonnas of Modernism, Altars of the Sublime," in Daniel Ferrer et al., eds., *"Ulysse" à l'article*, 221–54.

Schlossman, Beryl. "Retrospective Beginnings." *James Joyce Q* 29 (1991), 87–100.

Schneidau, Herbert N. *Waking Giants*, 8–20.

Schneider, Ulrich. "Mediatization in 'Aeolus' and 'Oxen of the Sun,'" in Christine van Boheemen, ed., *Joyce, Modernity, and its Mediation*, 15–21.

Scholes, Robert. *In Search of James Joyce*, 117–28, 201–5.

Schrand, Thomas G. "Authority and Catechesis: Narrative and Knowledge in *Ulysses*." *James Joyce Q* 28 (1990), 209–20.

Schwarz, Daniel R. *The Transformation of the English Novel*, 242–57.

Scott, Bonnie Kime. "Joyce and Michelet: Why Watch Molly Menstruate?," in Vincent J. Cheng and Timothy Martin, eds., *Joyce in Context,* 122–34.

Scott, Bonnie Kime. "Riding the 'vicociclometer': Women and Cycles of History in Joyce." *James Joyce Q* 28 (1991), 829–38.

Segall, Jeffrey. *Joyce in America,* 11–188.

Segall, Jeffrey. "Thirteen Ways of Looking at an Ad-Canvasser: Bloom and the Politics of Joyce Criticism." *Joyce Stud Annual 1991,* 69–85.

Seidl, Michael. "The Pathology of the Everyday: Uses of Madness in *Mrs. Dalloway* and *Ulysses,*" in Vara Neverow-Turk and Mark Hussey, eds., *Virginia Woolf,* 52–58.

Senn, Fritz. "AnaCalypso," in Daniel Ferrer et al., eds., *"Ulysse" à l'article,* 83–108.

Senn, Fritz. "Anagnostic Probes," in Christine van Boheemen, ed., *Joyce, Modernity, and its Mediation,* 37–61.

Senn, Fritz. "Entering the Lists: Sampling Early Catalogues," in Vincent J. Cheng and Timothy Martin, eds., *Joyce in Context,* 247–57.

Senn, Fritz. "History As Text in Reverse." *James Joyce Q* 28 (1991), 765–74.

Senn, Fritz. "In Quest of *a nisus formativus Joyceanus.*" *Joyce Stud Annual 1990,* 26–42.

Senn, Fritz. "Inherent Delicacy: Eumaean Questions." *Stud in the Novel* 22 (1990), 179–86.

Senn, Fritz. "Intellectual Nodality of the Lisible: *Genus Omne.*" *Revue des Lettres Modernes* 953–958 (1990), 173–88.

Senn, Fritz. "Protean Inglossabilities: 'To No End Gathered,' " in Christine van Boheemen, ed., *Joyce, Modernity, and its Mediation,* 151–76.

Senn, Fritz. " 'A Rump and Dozen.' " *Notes on Mod Irish Lit* 1 (1989), 4–6.

Shaffer, Brian W. *The Blinding Torch,* 103–20.

Shaffer, Brian W. "Joyce and Freud: Discontent and Its Civilizations," in Vincent J. Cheng and Timothy Martin, eds., *Joyce in Context,* 74–81.

Shanahan, Dennis M. "The Eucharistic Aesthetics of the Passion: The Testament of Blood in *Ulysses.*" *James Joyce Q* 27 (1990), 373–84.

Shloss, Carol. "Molly's Resistance to the Union: Marriage and Colonialism in Dublin, 1904." *Mod Fiction Stud* 35 (1989), 529–40.

Sisk, John P. "Taking History Personally." *Antioch R* 46 (1988), 428–37.

Smith, Craig. "Twilight in Dublin: A Look at Joyce's 'Nausicaa.' " *James Joyce Q* 28 (1991), 631–35.

Smith, Craig S. "Joyce's *Ulysses:* Dimensions of the Sacred at Sandymount." *Engl Lang Notes* 27:4 (1990), 57–61.

Smith, Craig S. "Joyce's *Ulysses,* 13.633." *Explicator* 50 (1991), 37–38.

Smith, Craig S., and M. C. Bisch. "Joyce's *Ulysses* 11.1–4." *Explicator* 48 (1990), 206.

Smith, Craig S., and Matthew L. Jockers. "Joyce's *Ulysses.*" *Explicator* 50 (1992), 235–36.

Smith, Craig Stanley. "Eros in the 'Nausicaa' of Homer and Joyce." *Researcher* (Jackson State Univ.) 13:3 (1990), 53–61.

Steinberg, Erwin R. "'Persecuted . . . sold . . . in Morocco like slaves.'" *James Joyce Q* 29 (1992), 615–21.

Stevens, Cristina M. T. "The Mock-Hero in Joyce's *Ulysses.*" *Estudos Anglo-Americanos* 12–13 (1988–89), 144–49.

Stevenson, Randall. *Modernist Fiction*, 46–53, 100–102, 159–63.

Tagopoulos, Constance V. "Joyce and Homer: Return, Disguise, and Recognition in 'Ithaca,'" in Vincent J. Cheng and Timothy Martin, eds., *Joyce in Context*, 184–98.

Tardits, Annie. "Joyce in Babylonia," in Rosa Maria Bollettieri Bosinelli et al., eds., *The Languages of Joyce*, 229–40, 243–47.

Temple-Thurston, Barbara. "The Reader as Absentminded Beggar: Recovering South Africa in *Ulysses.*" *James Joyce Q* 28 (1990), 247–55.

Theoharis, Theoharis Constantine. *Joyce's "Ulysses,"* 1–209.

Thomas, Brook. *"Ulysses* on Trial: Some Supplementary Reading." *Criticism* 33 (1991), 371–93.

Topia, André. "Le laboratoire bloomien," in Daniel Ferrer et al., eds., *"Ulysse" à l'article*, 37–60.

Topia, André. "The Matrix and the Echo: Intertextuality in *Ulysses,*" in Derek Attridge and Daniel Ferrer, eds., *Post-structuralist Joyce*, 103–24.

Tymoczko, Maria. "Symbolic Structures in *Ulysses* from Early Irish Literature," in Diana A. Ben-Merre and Maureen Murphy, eds., *James Joyce*, 17–27.

Valente, Joseph. "Who Made the Tune: Becoming-Woman in 'Sirens.'" *James Joyce Q* 30 (1993), 191–207.

Villanueva, Darío. "Valle-Inclán and James Joyce: *Ulysses* to *Luces de Bohemia.*" *Revue de Littérature Comparée* 65 (1991), 45–59.

Voelker, Joe, and Thomas Arner. "Bloomian Pantomime: J. A. Dowie and the 'Messianic Scene.'" *James Joyce Q* 27 (1990), 283–90.

Wachtel, Albert. *The Cracked Lookingglas*, 97–141.

Wales, Katie. *The Language of James Joyce*, 27–29, 68–132.

Watt, Stephen. *Joyce, O'Casey, and the Irish Popular Theater,* 21–23, 27–30, 35–37, 41–44, 90–94, 100–115, 121–25, 131–42.

Weir, David. "Sophomore Plum(p)s for Old Man Moses." *James Joyce Q* 28 (1991), 657–61.

Weir, Lorraine. *Writing Joyce*, 29–53.

Wetherill, Michael. "La Notion d'avant-texte: Perspectives modernes et moyenâgeuses." *Neuphilologische Mitteilungen* 89:1 (1988), 18–32.

Wicke, Jennifer. "'Who's She When She's At Home?': Molly Bloom and the Work of Consumption." *James Joyce Q* 28 (1991), 749–62.

Wilcox, Joan Parisi. "Joyce, Euclid, and 'Ithaca.'" *James Joyce Q* 28 (1991), 643–48.

Williams, Trevor. "'Conmeeism' and the Universe of Discourse in 'Wandering Rocks.'" *James Joyce Q* 29 (1992), 267–78.

Williams, Trevor L. "'As It Was in the Beginning': The Struggle for History in the 'Nestor' Episode of *Ulysses.*" *Canadian J of Irish Stud* 16:2 (1990), 36–46.

Williams, Trevor L. "Demystifying the Power of the Given: The 'Tele-machus' Episode of *Ulysses.*" *'Twentieth Cent Lit* 37 (1991), 38–51.

Williams, Trevor L. " 'Hungry man is an angry man': A Marxist Reading of Consumption in Joyce's *Ulysses.*" *Mosaic* 26:1 (1993), 87–107.

Wollaeger, Mark A. "Bloom's Coronation and the Subjection of the Sub-ject." *James Joyce Q* 28 (1991), 799–807.

Wollaeger, Mark A. "Posters, Modernism, Cosmopolitanism: *Ulysses* and World War I Recruiting Posters in Ireland." *Yale J of Criticism* 6:2 (1993), 87–124.

Wright, David G. *Ironies of "Ulysses,"* 1–148.

Zacchi, Romana. "Quoting Words and Worlds: Discourse Strategies in *Ulysses.*" *James Joyce Q* 27 (1989), 101–8.

Ziarek, Ewa. " 'Circe': Joyce's *Argumentum ad Feminam.*" *James Joyce Q* 30 (1992), 51–66.

PATRICK KAVANAGH

Tarry Flynn, 1948

Jacquin, Danielle. "L'étudiant d'*At Swim-Two-Birds* et le paysan de *Tarry Flynn* sur les chemins de la liberté." *Etudes Irlandaises* 15:1 (1990), 85–95.

SHEILA KAYE-SMITH

The End of the House of Alard, 1923

Bracco, Rosa Maria. *'Betwixt and Between,'* 30–31.

Joanna Godden, 1921

Bracco, Rosa Maria. *'Betwixt and Between,'* 29–30.

ROBERT KEABLE

Simon Called Peter, 1921

Bracco, Rosa Maria. *'Betwixt and Between,'* 23–25.

MOLLY KEANE

Full House, 1986

Elliot, Maurice. "Molly Keane's Big Houses," in Jacqueline Genet, ed., *The Big House in Ireland,* 191–92.

Good Behaviour, 1981

Adams, Alice. "Coming Apart at the Seams: *Good Behavior* as an Anti Comedy of Manners." *J of Irish Lit* 20:3 (1991), 27–35.

Elliot, Maurice. "Molly Keane's Big Houses," in Jacqueline Genet, ed., *The Big House in Ireland,* 198–202.

Imhof, Rüdiger. "Molly Keane, *Good Behaviour, Time After Time,* and *Loving and Giving,*" in Otto Rauchbauer, ed., *Ancestral Voices,* 196–99.

Weekes, Ann Owens. *Irish Women Writers,* 156–73.

Loving and Giving, 1988

Elliot, Maurice. "Molly Keane's Big Houses," in Jacqueline Genet, ed., *The Big House in Ireland,* 202–6.

Imhof, Rüdiger. "Molly Keane, *Good Behaviour, Time After Time,* and *Loving and Giving,*" in Otto Rauchbauer, ed., *Ancestral Voices,* 201–2.

Time After Time, 1983

Deane, Paul. "The Big House Revisited: Molly Keane's *Time after Time.*" *Notes on Mod Irish Lit* 3 (1991), 37–44.

Imhof, Rüdiger. "Molly Keane, *Good Behaviour, Time After Time,* and *Loving and Giving,*" in Otto Rauchbauer, ed., *Ancestral Voices,* 199–201.

Two Days in Aragon, 1985

Elliot, Maurice. "Molly Keane's Big Houses," in Jacqueline Genet, ed., *The Big House in Ireland,* 195–98.

Young Entry, 1989

Elliot, Maurice. "Molly Keane's Big Houses," in Jacqueline Genet, ed., *The Big House in Ireland,* 193–94.

MARGARET KENNEDY

The Constant Nymph, 1924

Bracco, Rosa Maria. *'Betwixt and Between,'* 27–28.

BENEDICT KIELY

Nothing Happens in Carmincross, 1985

Casey, Daniel J. "Benedict Kiely," in Rüdiger Imhof, ed., *Contemporary Irish Novelists,* 25–28.

CHARLES KINGSLEY

Alton Locke, 1850

Drexler, Peter. *Literatur, Recht, Kriminalität,* 153–56.

Harvie, Christopher. *The Centre of Things,* 22–25.

Haynes, Roslynn D. "Dream Allegory in Charles Kingsley and Olive Schreiner," in Kath Filmer, ed., *The Victorian Fantasists,* 155–61.

Rauch, Alan. "The Tailor Transformed: Kingsley's *Alton Locke* and the Notion of Change." *Stud in the Novel* 25 (1993), 196–210.

Reed, John R. *Victorian Will,* 281–83.

Sharma, S. K. *Charles Kingsley,* 54–73.

Hereward the Wake, 1866

Sharma, S. K. *Charles Kingsley,* 142–54.

Hypatia, 1853

Myer, Valerie Grosvenor. "Charles Kingsley's *Hypatia:* A Seminal Novel." *Notes and Queries* 237 (1992), 179–80.

Sharma, S. K. *Charles Kingsley,* 75–96.

Two Years Ago, 1857

Sharma, S. K. *Charles Kingsley,* 112–28.

The Water-Babies, 1863

Manlove, Colin. "Charles Kingsley, H. G. Wells, and the Machine in Victorian Fiction." *Nineteenth-Cent Lit* 48 (1993), 216–22.

Manlove, Colin. "MacDonald and Kingsley: A Victorian Contrast," in William Raeper, ed., *The Gold Thread,* 140–59.

Sharma, S. K. *Charles Kingsley,* 130–40.

Uffelman, Larry, and Patrick Scott. "Kingsley's Serial Novels, II: *The Water-Babies." Victorian Periodicals R* 19:4 (1986), 122–31.

Wall, Barbara. *The Narrator's Voice,* 56–60.

Westward Ho!, 1855

Sharma, S. K. *Charles Kingsley,* 98–110.

Yeast, 1848

Goetsch, Paul. "Das Verhältnis von Dame und Mann im englischen Roman von Kingsley bis Lawrence: Zur Zählebigkeit und Überwindung von Normen und Vorurteilen," in Titus Heydenreich and Egert Pöhlmann, eds., *Liebesroman—Liebe im Roman,* 102–4.

Sharma, S. K. *Charles Kingsley,* 25–50.

Tuss, Alex J., SM. *The Inward Revolution,* 21–23.

RUDYARD KIPLING

Kim, 1901

Belliappa, K. C. *The Image of India,* 89–110.

Belliappa, K. C. "The Meaning of Rudyard Kipling's *Kim." J of Commonwealth Lit* 26:1 (1991), 151–57.

Bristow, Joseph. *Empire Boys,* 195–213.

Crook, Nora. *Kipling's Myths,* 1–3.

David, Deirdre. "Children of Empire: Victorian Imperialism and Sexual Politics in Dickens and Kipling," in Antony H. Harrison and Beverly Taylor, eds., *Gender and Discourse,* 133–39.

Leenerts, Cynthia A. "Kipling's Vision of Law in *Kim." Liter Criterion* 25:4 (1990), 48–61.

Lohman, W. J., Jr. *The Culture Shocks,* 263–79.

Mukherjee, Sujit. *Forster and Further,* 172–74.

Paffard, Mark. *Kipling's Indian Fiction,* 80–91.

Seymour-Smith, Martin. *Rudyard Kipling*, 300–304.
Stafford, David. *The Silent Game*, 5–6.
Sullivan, Zohreh T. *Narratives of Empire*, 145–80.
Trodd, Anthea. *A Reader's Guide*, 26–29.

The Light That Failed, 1890

Arata, Stephen D. "A Universal Foreignness: Kipling in the Fin-de-Siècle." *Engl Lit in Transition* 36 (1993), 27–34.
Crook, Nora. *Kipling's Myths*, 14–15, 152–53, 174–75.
Lohman, W. J., Jr. *The Culture Shocks*, 233–47.
Paffard, Mark. *Kipling's Indian Fiction*, 113–15.
Seymour-Smith, Martin. *Rudyard Kipling*, 171–92.

The Naulakha, 1892

Belliappa, K. C. *The Image of India*, 110–12.
Seymour-Smith, Martin. *Rudyard Kipling*, 149–50, 200–206.

Stalky & Co., 1899

Bristow, Joseph. *Empire Boys*, 174–80.
Orel, Harold. *Popular Fiction in England*, 137–40.
Richards, Jeffrey. *Happiest Days*, 146–64.
Rossen, Janice. *The University in Modern Fiction*, 109–12.
Seymour-Smith, Martin. *Rudyard Kipling*, 269–78.

ARTHUR KOESTLER

Arrival and Departure, 1943

Hoyles, John. *The Literary Underground*, 129–32.
Schaffeld, Norbert. *Die Darstellung des nationalsozialistischen Deutschland*, 213–29.

Darkness at Noon, 1940

Bergonzi, Bernard. *Wartime and Aftermath*, 11–13, 96–97.
Hoyles, John. *The Literary Underground*, 125–29.
Sutherland, Robert. "Eternity in *Darkness at Noon* and the *Consolation of Philosophy*." *Classical and Mod Lit* 13 (1992), 31–43.

LADY CAROLINE LAMB

Glenarvon, 1816

Graham, Peter W. "Fictive Biography in 1816: The Case of *Glenarvon*." *Byron J* 19 (19991), 53–68.

PHILIP LARKIN

A Girl in Winter, 1947

Bergonzi, Bernard. *Wartime and Aftermath*, 102–4.

Jill, 1946

Bergonzi, Bernard. *Wartime and Aftermath*, 102–4.
Rossen, Janice. *The University in Modern Fiction*, 65–69.

D. H. LAWRENCE

Aaron's Rod, 1922

Bell, Michael. *D. H. Lawrence*, 139–46.
Cowan, James C. *D. H. Lawrence and the Trembling Balance*, 70–72.
Doherty, Gerald. "One Vast Hermeneutic Sentence: The Total Lawrentian Text." *PMLA* 106 (1991), 1139–41.
Dorbad, Leo J. *Sexually Balanced Relationships*, 115–19.
Holbrook, David. *Where D. H. Lawrence Was Wrong*, 276–82.
Humma, John B. *Metaphor and Meaning*, 7–15.
Hyde, Virginia. *The Risen Adam*, 119–41.
Mensch, Barbara. *D. H. Lawrence*, 119–69.
Nielsen, Inge Padkær, and Karsten Hvidtfelt Nielsen. "The Modernism of D. H. Lawrence and the Discourses of Decadence: Sexuality and Tradition in *The Trespasser, Fantasia of the Unconscious,* and *Aaron's Rod.*" *Arcadia* 25 (1990), 283–86.
Pinkney, Tony. *D. H. Lawrence*, 106–23.
Pluto, Anne Elezabeth. "Blutbrüderschaft." *Paunch* 63–64 (1990), 98–102.
Widmer, Kingsley. *Defiant Desire*, 52–55.

John Thomas and Lady Jane, 1972

Holbrook, David. *Where D. H. Lawrence Was Wrong*, 323–35.
Storch, Margaret. *Sons and Adversaries*, 187–89.
Widmer, Kingsley. *Defiant Desire*, 86–90.

Kangaroo, 1923

Bell, Michael. *D. H. Lawrence*, 146–61.
Darroch, Robert. "D. H. Lawrence's Australia." *Overland* 113 (1988), 34–38.
Doherty, Gerald. "One Vast Hermeneutic Sentence: The Total Lawrentian Text." *PMLA* 106 (1991), 1139–41.
Dommergues, André. "*Kangaroo,* stratégie de rupture." *Etudes Lawrenciennes* 3 (1988), 139–52.
Dorbad, Leo J. *Sexually Balanced Relationships*, 119–23.
Holbrook, David. *Where D. H. Lawrence Was Wrong*, 283–92.
Horsley, Lee. *Political Fiction*, 59–61, 123–64.
Humma, John B. *Metaphor and Meaning*, 29–44.
Mensch, Barbara. *D. H. Lawrence*, 171–205.
Padhi, Babhu. *D. H. Lawrence*, 31–36.
Pinkney, Tony. *D. H. Lawrence*, 112–23.
Pluto, Anne Elezabeth. "Blutbrüderschaft." *Paunch* 63–64 (1990), 102–7.

Rylance, Rick. "Lawrence's Politics," in Keith Brown, ed., *Rethinking Lawrence,* 170–72.

Storch, Margaret. *Sons and Adversaries,* 15–16.

Tylee, Claire M. *The Great War,* 231–33.

Van Herk, Aritha. "Crow B(e)ars and Kangaroos of the Future: The Post-Colonial Ga(s)p." *World Lit Written in Engl* 30:2 (1990), 42–54.

Widmer, Kingsley. *Defiant Desire,* 55–58.

Lady Chatterley's Lover, 1928

Balbert, Peter. "From *Lady Chatterley's Lover* to *The Deer Park:* Lawrence, Mailer, and the Dialectic of Erotic Risk." *Stud in the Novel* 22 (1990), 72–79.

Bell, Michael. *D. H. Lawrence,* 208–25.

Buckley, William K. *Senses' Tender,* 43–50.

Butler, Gerald J. *Love and Reading,* 85–87.

Castronovo, David. *The English Gentleman,* 121–23.

Cowan, James C. *D. H. Lawrence and the Trembling Balance,* 74–81, 212–36.

Cowan, James C. "The Fall of John Thomas." *Lit and Medicine* 11 (1992), 271–78.

Doherty, Gerald. "One Vast Hermeneutic Sentence: The Total Lawrentian Text." *PMLA* 106 (1991), 1141–43.

Dorbad, Leo J. *Sexually Balanced Relationships,* 129–39.

Edwards, Duane. "D. H. Lawrence and the Problem of Submission." *Southern Hum R* 25 (1991), 207–14.

Efron, Arthur. " 'The Way Our Sympathy Flows and Recoils': Lawrence's Last Theory of the Novel." *Paunch* 63–64 (1990), 71–80.

Fjågesund, Peter. "D. H. Lawrence, Knut Hamsun and Pan." *Engl Stud* 72 (1991), 421–25.

Goetsch, Paul. "Das Verhältnis von Dame und Mann im englischen Roman von Kingsley bis Lawrence: Zur Zählebigkeit und Überwindung von Normen und Vorurteilen," in Titus Heydenreich and Egert Pöhlmann, eds., *Liebesroman—Liebe im Roman,* 109–16.

Holbrook, David. *Where D. H. Lawrence Was Wrong,* 213–53, 335–53.

Humma, John B. *Metaphor and Meaning,* 85–99.

Iido, Takeo. "Lawrence's Pagan Gods and Christianity." *D. H. Lawrence R* 23 (1991), 185–89.

Jackson, Dennis. "Chapter Making in *Lady Chatterley's Lover.*" *Texas Stud in Lit and Lang* 35 (1993), 363–80.

Kalnins, Mara. "Lawrence's Men and Women: Complements and Opposites," in Sally Minogue, ed., *Problems for Feminist Criticism,* 171–76.

King, Debra W. "Just Can't Find the Words: How Expression Is Achieved." *Philos and Rhetoric* 24:1 (1991), 54–72.

Krasner, James. *The Entangled Eye,* 168–69.

Masina, Léa. "*O Amante de Lady Chatterley:* Um Romance Atípico e Tumultuado." *Minas Gerais, Suplemento Literário* 24 (1991), 11–13.

Matthews, Betty A. "*Lady Chatterley's Lover:* The Courage of Tenderness." *Publs of the Arkansas Philol Assoc* 15:2 (1989), 43–60.

Messenger, Nigel. *How to Study a D. H. Lawrence Novel,* 105–31.

Pinkney, Tony. *D. H. Lawrence,* 134–47.

Pluto, Anne Elezabeth. "Blutbrüderschaft." *Paunch* 63–64 (1990), 115–18.

Polhemus, Robert M. *Erotic Faith,* 279–306.

Rowley, Stephen. "The Sight-Touch Metaphor in *Lady Chatterley's Lover.*" *Etudes Lawrenciennes* 3 (1988), 179–88.

Rylance, Rick. "Lawrence's Politics," in Keith Brown, ed., *Rethinking Lawrence,* 172–78.

Sklenicka, Carol. *D. H. Lawrence and the Child,* 169–71.

Spilka, Mark. "Lawrence and the Clitoris," in Michael Squires and Keith Cushman, eds., *The Challenge of D. H. Lawrence,* 178–86.

Spilka, Mark. *Renewing the Normative D. H. Lawrence,* 9–13, 39–41, 63–69, 70–72, 83–85, 87–89, 160–69, 174–76, 180–84, 188–90, 195–97.

Sproles, Karyn Z. "D. H. Lawrence and the Pre-Raphaelites: Love Among the Ruins." *D. H. Lawrence R* 22 (1990), 303–5.

Stewart, Jack F. "Primordial Affinities: Lawrence, Van Gogh and the Miners." *Mosaic* 24:1 (1991), 107–10.

Storch, Margaret. *Sons and Adversaries,* 187–89.

Swift, Jennifer. "The Body and Transcendence of Two Wastelands: *Lady Chatterley's Lover* and *The Waste Land.*" *Paunch* 63–64 (1990), 141–68.

Widmer, Kingsley. *Defiant Desire,* 70–99.

The Lost Girl, 1920

Balbert, Peter. "Ten Men and a Sacred Prostitute: The Psychology of Sex in *The Lost Girl.*" *Twentieth Cent Lit* 36 (1990), 381–400.

Bell, Michael. *D. H. Lawrence,* 136–39.

Cowan, James C. *D. H. Lawrence and the Trembling Balance,* 96–101.

Fowler, Roger. "*The Lost Girl:* Discourse and Focalization," in Keith Brown, ed., *Rethinking Lawrence,* 53–65.

Pluto, Anne Elezabeth. "Blutbrüderschaft." *Paunch* 63–64 (1990), 97.

Siegel, Carol. *Lawrence among the Women,* 99–100, 103–4, 171–72.

Stovel, Nora Forster. "'A Great Kick at Misery': Lawrence's and Drabble's Rebellion Against the Fatalism of Bennett," in Keith Cushman and Dennis Jackson, eds., *D. H. Lawrence's Literary Inheritors,* 131–54.

Widmer, Kingsley. *Defiant Desire,* 28–30.

Mr. Noon, 1984

Ingersoll, Earl. "Lawrence in the Tyrol: Psychic Geography in *Women in Love* and *Mr Noon.*" *Forum for Mod Lang Stud* 26:1 (1990), 1–12.

Ingersoll, Earl G. "D. H. Lawrence's *Mr Noon* as a Postmodern Text." *Mod Lang R* 85 (1990), 304–9.

Ingersoll, Earl G. "The Progress Towards Marriage in D. H. Lawrence's *Mr Noon.*" *Dutch Q R of Anglo-American Letters* 19 (1989), 294–306.

Ingersoll, Earl G. "The Theme of Friendship and the Genesis of D. H. Lawrence's *Mr. Noon.*" *Durham Univ J* 83 (1991), 69–73.

Lodge, David. "Lawrence, Dostoevsky, Bakhtin: Lawrence and Dialogic Fiction," in Keith Brown, ed., *Rethinking Lawrence*, 105–7.

Preston, Peter. "*Mr Noon* and Lawrence's Quarrel with Tolstoy." *Etudes Lawrenciennes* 3 (1988), 109–23.

Widmer, Kingsley. *Defiant Desire*, 30–31.

The Plumed Serpent, 1926

Bayley, John. "Lawrence's Comedy, and the War of Superiorities," in Keith Brown, ed., *Rethinking Lawrence*, 3–4, 10–11.

Bell, Michael. *D. H. Lawrence*, 165–207.

Bell, Michael. "Sentimental Primitivism in D. H. Lawrence's *The Plumed Serpent*," in Winfried Herget, ed., *Sentimentality in Modern Literature*, 109–37.

Christensen, Peter G. "The 'Dark Gods' and Modern Society: *Maiden Castle* and *The Plumed Serpent*," in Denis Lane, ed., *In the Spirit of Powys*, 157–77.

Christensen, Peter G. "Katherine Anne Porter's 'Flowering Judas' and D. H. Lawrence's *The Plumed Serpent:* Contrasting Visions of Women in the Mexican Revolution." *South Atlantic R* 56:1 (1991), 35–45.

Christensen, Peter G. "Revolution in Drieu La Rochelle's *The Man on Horseback* and D. H. Lawrence's *The Plumed Serpent*." *Revue de Littérature Comparée* 66 (1992), 397–405.

Cowan, James C. *D. H. Lawrence and the Trembling Balance*, 185–211.

Doherty, Gerald. "One Vast Hermeneutic Sentence: The Total Lawrentian Text." *PMLA* 106 (1991), 1139–41.

Dorbad, Leo J. *Sexually Balanced Relationships*, 123–27.

Edwards, Duane. "Erich Neumann and the Shadow Problem in *The Plumed Serpent*." *D. H. Lawrence R* 23 (1991), 129–39.

García Ramírez, Fernando. "D. H. Lawrence y la religión de la serpiente." *Vuelta* 15:172 (1991), 35–36.

Holbrook, David. *Where D. H. Lawrence Was Wrong*, 293–311.

Humma, John B. *Metaphor and Meaning*, 62–76.

Hyde, Virginia. *The Risen Adam*, 14–22, 173–206.

Iido, Takeo. "Lawrence's Pagan Gods and Christianity." *D. H. Lawrence R* 23 (1991), 183–84.

Kushigian, Nancy. *Pictures and Fictions*, 154–56.

Martz, Louis. "*Quetzalcoatl:* The Early Version of *The Plumed Serpent*." *D. H. Lawrence R* 22 (1990), 286–98.

Mensch, Barbara. *D. H. Lawrence*, 207–52.

Padhi, Babhu. *D. H. Lawrence*, 196–200.

Phillips, K. J. *Dying Gods in Twentieth-Century Fiction*, 139–48.

Pichardie, Jean-Paul. "Le Mexique: *Ordo ab chao*." *Etudes Lawrenciennes* 3 (1988), 163–69.

Pinkney, Tony. *D. H. Lawrence*, 147–62.

Pluto, Anne Elezabeth. "Blutbrüderschaft." *Paunch* 63–64 (1990), 107–15.

Shaffer, Brian W. *The Blinding Torch*, 123–29, 133–36.

Sicker, Philip. "Lawrence's *Auto da fé:* The Grand Inquisitor in *The Plumed Serpent.*" *Compar Lit Stud* 29 (1992), 417–38.

Sklenicka, Carol. *D. H. Lawrence and the Child,* 154–55.

Smith, Evans Lansing. *Rape and Revelation,* 52–55.

Spilka, Mark. *Renewing the Normative D. H. Lawrence,* 215–19, 225–30.

Storch, Margaret. *Sons and Adversaries,* 157–78.

Talbot, Lynn K. "Did Baroja Influence Lawrence? A Reading of *César O Nada* and *The Plumed Serpent.*" *D. H. Lawrence R* 22 (1990), 39–49.

Vichy, Thérèse. "Le Mexique dans *The Plumed Serpent.*" *Cycnos* 7 (1991), 41–50.

Widmer, Kingsley. *Defiant Desire,* 58–60.

The Rainbow, 1915

Adelman, Gary. *Snow of Fire,* 17–50.

Bell, Michael. *D. H. Lawrence,* 51–96, 97–102.

Bonds, Diane S. *Language and the Self,* 53–75.

Booth, Wayne C. "Confessions of a Lukewarm Lawrentian," in Michael Squires and Keith Cushman, eds., *The Challenge of D. H. Lawrence,* 21–25.

Bull, J. A. *The Framework of Fiction,* 178–79.

Christensen, Peter G. "Problems in Characterization in D. H. Lawrence's *The Rainbow.*" *AUMLA* 77 (1992), 78–95.

Cowan, James C. *D. H. Lawrence and the Trembling Balance,* 18–21, 58–60.

Davis, Jane. "Envoi: The Genie in the Second-Hand Shop," in Keith Brown, ed., *Rethinking Lawrence,* 181–83.

DiBattista, Maria. *First Love,* 115–39.

Doherty, Gerald. "The Metaphorical Imperative: From Trope to Narrative in *The Rainbow.*" *South Central R* 6:1 (1989), 46–61.

Doherty, Gerald. "One Vast Hermeneutic Sentence: The Total Lawrentian Text." *PMLA* 106 (1991), 1137–39.

Dorbad, Leo J. *Sexually Balanced Relationships,* 59–89.

Edwards, Duane. *"The Rainbow,"* 25–106.

Galbraith, Mary. "Feeling Moments in the Work of D. H. Lawrence." *Paunch* 63–64 (1990), 24–27.

Gomez, Joseph A. "The Elusive Gold at the End of *The Rainbow:* Russell's Adaptation of Lawrence's Novel." *Lit/Film Q* 18 (1990), 134–36.

Goodheart, Eugene. *Desire and Its Discontents,* 63–67.

Harding, Adrian. "Self-Parody and Ethical Satire in *The Rainbow.*" *Etudes Lawrenciennes* 6 (1991), 31–38.

Harris, Janice H. "Lawrence and the Edwardian Feminists," in Michael Squires and Keith Cushman, eds., *The Challenge of D. H. Lawrence,* 66–75.

Hoerner, Dennis. "Ursula, Anton, and the 'Sons of God': Armor and Core in *The Rainbow*'s Third Generation." *Paunch* 63–64 (1990), 173–98.

Holbrook, David. *Where D. H. Lawrence Was Wrong,* 131–83.

Hyde, Virginia. *The Risen Adam,* 1–8, 73–99, 101–3, 108–10.

Ingram, Allan. *The Language of D. H. Lawrence*, 5–10, 21–24, 53–56, 85–93, 98–102, 119–37.

Janik, Del Ivan. "A Cumbrian *Rainbow:* Melvyn Bragg's Tallentire Trilogy," in Keith Cushman and Dennis Jackson, eds., *D. H. Lawrence's Literary Inheritors*, 73–87.

Kalnins, Mara. "Lawrence's Men and Women: Complements and Opposites," in Sally Minogue, ed., *Problems for Feminist Criticism*, 147–55.

Kelsey, Nigel. *D. H. Lawrence*, 121–40.

Krasner, James. *The Entangled Eye*, 157–63.

Kushigian, Nancy. *Pictures and Fictions*, 75–148.

Messenger, Nigel. *How to Study a D. H. Lawrence Novel*, 53–77.

Miliaras, Barbara A. "The Collapse of Agrarian Order and the Death of Thomas Brangwen in D. H. Lawrence's *The Rainbow.*" *Etudes Lawrenciennes* 3 (1988), 65–77.

Miller, Donna R. " 'This Pulsing, Frictional To—and Fro': The Function(s) of Lexico-Grammatical Reiteration in D. H. Lawrence." *Lingua e Stile* 24 (1989), 467–81.

Padhi, Babhu. *D. H. Lawrence*, 108–36, 159–62.

Pinkney, Tony. *D. H. Lawrence*, 60–78.

Pluto, Anne Elezabeth. "Blutbrüderschaft." *Paunch* 63–64 (1990), 88–89.

Robbins, Ross. " 'By this he knew she wept': A Note on Lawrence and Meredith." *R of Engl Stud* 44 (1993), 389–92.

Scherr, Barry J. "The 'Fecund Darkness' of *The Rainbow.*" *Recovering Lit* 18 (1991/92), 8–27.

Schwarz, Daniel R. *The Transformation of the English Novel*, 94–115.

Siegel, Carol. *Lawrence among the Women*, 15–17, 133–35, 147–48.

Sklenicka, Carol. *D. H. Lawrence and the Child*, 5–7, 56–145.

Smith, Evans Lansing. *Rape and Revelation*, 44–49.

Squires, Michael. "Lawrence, Dickens, and the English Novel," in Michael Squires and Keith Cushman, eds., *The Challenge of D. H. Lawrence*, 45–51.

Stevenson, Randall. *Modernist Fiction*, 30–34, 143–51.

Storch, Margaret. *Sons and Adversaries*, 19–20, 128–29.

Tartera, Nicole. "Lydia, Anna, Ursula, ou de l'Exil Extérieur à l'Exil Intérieur." *Cahiers Victoriens et Edouardiens* 32 (1990), 81–91.

Templeton, Wayne. *States of Estrangement*, 107–65.

Tytell, John. *Passionate Lives*, 38–46.

Widmer, Kingsley. *Defiant Desire*, 17–21.

Woodman, Leonora. "D. H. Lawrence and the Hermetic Tradition." *Cauda Pavonis* 8:2 (1989), 1–6.

Sons and Lovers, 1913

Baron, Helen. "Lawrence's *Sons and Lovers* versus Garnett's." *Essays in Criticism* 42 (1992), 265–78.

Barron, Janet. "Equality Puzzle: Lawrence and Feminism," in Keith Brown, ed., *Rethinking Lawrence*, 15–16, 19–20.

Bell, Michael. *D. H. Lawrence*, 36–50.

Berman, Jeffrey. *Narcissism and the Novel,* 199–223.

Black, Michael. *D. H. Lawrence,* 123–44.

Black, Michael. *D. H. Lawrence: "Sons and Lovers,"* 1–108.

Bonds, Diane S. *Language and the Self,* 29–52.

Bull, J. A. *The Framework of Fiction,* 178–82.

Cawthra, Gillian. *Cultural Climate and Linguistic Style,* 41–46, 52–65.

Cowan, James C. *D. H. Lawrence and the Trembling Balance,* 54–58.

Delany, Paul. "*Sons and Lovers:* The Morel Marriage as a War of Position." *D. H. Lawrence R* 21 (1989), 153–64.

Doherty, Gerald. "One Vast Hermeneutic Sentence: The Total Lawrentian Text." *PMLA* 106 (1991), 1137.

Dorbad, Leo J. *Sexually Balanced Relationships,* 43–58.

Eggert, Paul. "Opening Up the Text: The Case of *Sons and Lovers*," in Keith Brown, ed., *Rethinking Lawrence,* 38–51.

Erlebach, Peter. *Theorie und Praxis des Romaneingangs,* 253–60.

Farr, Judith. "D. H. Lawrence's Mother as Sleeping Beauty: The 'Still Queen' of His Poems and Fictions." *Mod Fiction Stud* 36 (1990), 202–4.

Fiddes, Paul S. *Freedom and Limit,* 154–57, 164–66.

Finney, Brian. *D. H. Lawrence,* 5–116.

Galbraith, Mary. "Feeling Moments in the Work of D. H. Lawrence." *Paunch* 63–64 (1990), 18–23.

Haegert, John. "D. H. Lawrence and the Aesthetics of Transgression." *Mod Philology* 88 (1990), 5–10.

Hilton, Enid. "Alice Dax: D. H. Lawrence's Clara in *Sons and Lovers*." *D. H. Lawrence R* 22 (1990), 274–85.

Hinz, Evelyn J., and John J. Teunissen. " 'They Thought of Sons and Lovers': D. H. Lawrence and Thomas Wolfe." *Southern Q* 29:3 (1991), 77–89.

Holbrook, David. *Where D. H. Lawrence Was Wrong,* 60–77.

Ingram, Allan. *The Language of D. H. Lawrence,* 20–25, 34–44, 53–55, 81–85.

Kelsey, Nigel. *D. H. Lawrence,* 71–120.

Kiely, Robert. "Out on Strike: The Language and Power of the Working Class in Lawrence's Fiction," in Michael Squires and Keith Cushman, eds., *The Challenge of D. H. Lawrence,* 91–95.

Kushigian, Nancy. *Pictures and Fictions,* 35–71.

Martínez, José Mateo. "Lawrence y la naturaleza: Una empatía sinestésica." *Revista Alicantina de Estudios Ingleses* 1 (1988), 139–51.

Messenger, Nigel. *How to Study a D. H. Lawrence Novel,* 24–52.

Padhi, Babhu. *D. H. Lawrence,* 95–108, 149–57.

Perez, Carlos A. "Husbands and Wives, Sons and Lovers: Intimate Conflict in the Fiction of D. H. Lawrence," in Sara Munson Deats and Lagretta Tallent Lenker, eds., *The Aching Hearth,* 175–86.

Pinkney, Tony. *D. H. Lawrence,* 27–51.

Pittock, Malcolm. "*Sons and Lovers:* The Price of Betrayal," in Keith Brown, ed., *Rethinking Lawrence,* 120–31.

Pluto, Anne Elezabeth. "Blutbrüderschaft." *Paunch* 63–64 (1990), 87–88.

Pons, Xavier. " 'Baptism of fire': The Oedipal Element in D. H. Lawrence's *Sons and Lovers.*" *Cahiers Victoriens et Edouardiens* 32 (1990), 101–9.

Saje, Natasha. "*Hamlet*, D. H. Lawrence, and *Sons and Lovers.*" *Dalhousie R* 71 (1991), 334–45.

Schneidau, Herbert N. *Waking Giants*, 137–43.

Schwarz, Daniel R. *The Transformation of the English Novel*, 68–93.

Siegel, Carol. *Lawrence among the Women*, 75–76, 157–58.

Sklenicka, Carol. *D. H. Lawrence and the Child*, 36–55.

Spilka, Mark. *Renewing the Normative D. H. Lawrence*, 27–30, 34–42, 54–59.

Sproles, Karyn Z. "D. H. Lawrence and the Pre-Raphaelites: Love Among the Ruins." *D. H. Lawrence R* 22 (1990), 300–301.

Sproles, Karyn Z. "D. H. Lawrence and the Schizoid State: Reading *Sons and Lovers* through *The White Peacock.*" *Paunch* 63–64 (1990), 51–67.

Steig, Michael. *Stories of Reading*, 196–200.

Stewart, Jack F. "Primordial Affinities: Lawrence, Van Gogh and the Miners." *Mosaic* 24:1 (1991), 98–107.

Storch, Margaret. *Sons and Adversaries*, 97–107, 112–14, 120–23.

Templeton, Wayne. *States of Estrangement*, 58–106.

Vega-Ritter, Max. "*Sons and Lovers*: roman de l'immolation." *Cahiers Victoriens et Edouardiens* 32 (1990), 111–24.

Vichy, Thérèse. "Les Formes du temps dans *Sons and Lovers.*" *Etudes Lawrenciennes* 3 (1988), 23–39.

Widmer, Kingsley. *Defiant Desire*, 13–15.

The Trespasser, 1912

Atkins, A. R. "Recognising the 'Stranger' in D. H. Lawrence's *The Trespasser.*" *Cambridge Q* 20 (1991), 1–20.

Bell, Michael. *D. H. Lawrence*, 25–36.

Black, Michael. *D. H. Lawrence*, 36–39.

Cowan, James C. *D. H. Lawrence and the Trembling Balance*, 51–54.

Nielsen, Inge Padkær, and Karsten Hvidtfelt Nielsen. "The Modernism of D. H. Lawrence and the Discourses of Decadence: Sexuality and Tradition in *The Trespasser, Fantasia of the Unconscious*, and *Aaron's Rod.*" *Arcadia* 25 (1990), 273–78.

Pinkney, Tony. *D. H. Lawrence*, 54–60.

Templeton, Wayne. *States of Estrangement*, 15–57.

Widmer, Kingsley. *Defiant Desire*, 11–12, 42–43.

The White Peacock, 1911

Bell, Michael. *D. H. Lawrence*, 14–24.

Black, Michael. "A Bit of Both: George Eliot & D. H. Lawrence." *Crit R* (Melbourne) 29 (1989), 103–9.

Black, Michael. *D. H. Lawrence*, 26–36, 69–73.

Delany, Paul. "D. H. Lawrence and Deep Ecology." *CEA Critic* 55:2 (1993), 31–33.

Hawthorn, Jeremy. "Lawrence and Working-Class Fiction," in Keith Brown, ed., *Rethinking Lawrence*, 68–69,, 74–75.

Holbrook, David. *Where D. H. Lawrence Was Wrong*, 45–60.

Iido, Takeo. "Lawrence's Pagan Gods and Christianity." *D. H. Lawrence R* 23 (1991), 180–82.

Ingram, Allan. *The Language of D. H. Lawrence*, 27–34.

Kushigian, Nancy. *Pictures and Fictions*, 9–31.

Padhi, Babhu. *D. H. Lawrence*, 11–15, 17–25.

Pinkney, Tony. *D. H. Lawrence*, 12–27.

Siegel, Carol. *Lawrence among the Women*, 56–65.

Sproles, Karyn Z. "D. H. Lawrence and the Schizoid State: Reading *Sons and Lovers* through *The White Peacock*." *Paunch* 63–64 (1990), 39–67.

Sproles, Karyn Z. "Shooting *The White Peacock*: Victorian Art and Feminine Sexuality in D. H. Lawrence's First Novel." *Criticism* 34 (1992), 237–57.

Storch, Margaret. "The Lacerated Male: Ambivalent Images of Women in *The White Peacock*." *D. H. Lawrence R* 21 (1989), 117–34.

Storch, Margaret. *Sons and Adversaries*, 45–64.

Widmer, Kingsley. *Defiant Desire*, 11–12.

Women in Love, 1920

Adelman, Gary. *Snow of Fire*, 51–120.

Agovi, K. E. *Novels of Social Change*, 201–37.

Bell, Michael. *D. H. Lawrence*, 97–132.

Bell, Michael. "Sentimental Primitivism in D. H. Lawrence's *The Plumed Serpent*," in Winfried Herget, ed., *Sentimentality in Modern Literature*, 118–19.

Bonds, Diane S. *Language and the Self*, 77–109.

Booth, Wayne C. "Confessions of a Lukewarm Lawrentian," in Michael Squires and Keith Cushman, eds., *The Challenge of D. H. Lawrence*, 10–20.

Cowan, James C. *D. H. Lawrence and the Trembling Balance*, 60–70.

Davis, Jane. "Envoi: The Genie in the Second-Hand Shop," in Keith Brown, ed., *Rethinking Lawrence*, 183–88.

Delany, Paul. "D. H. Lawrence and Deep Ecology." *CEA Critic* 55:2 (1993), 33–39.

DiBattista, Maria. *First Love*, 143–64.

Doherty, Gerald. "The Art of Leaping: Metaphor Unbound in D. H. Lawrence's *Women in Love*." *Style* 26 (1992), 50–63.

Doherty, Gerald. "One Vast Hermeneutic Sentence: The Total Lawrentian Text." *PMLA* 106 (1991), 1137–39.

Dorbad, Leo J. *Sexually Balanced Relationships*, 89–112.

Eldred, Janet M. "Plot and Subplot in *Women in Love*." *J of Narrative Technique* 20 (1990), 284–93.

Fernihough, Anne. *D. H. Lawrence*, 25–29, 49–54, 145–53.

Fiddes, Paul S. *Freedom and Limit*, 148–51.

Fleishman, Avrom. "Lawrence and Bakhtin: Where Pluralism Ends and Dialogism Begins," in Keith Brown, ed., *Rethinking Lawrence*, 110–17.

Fourtina, Hervé. "La Perversion dans *Women in Love*." *Etudes Lawrenciennes* 4 (1989), 71–86.

Galbraith, Mary. "Feeling Moments in the Work of D. H. Lawrence." *Paunch* 63–64 (1990), 27–38.

Goodheart, Eugene. *Desire and Its Discontents*, 67–78.

Gouirand, Jacqueline. "Les Chemins de l'écriture: Les Chapitres 'Man to Man' et 'Gladiatorial' des avant-textes à la version finale de *Women in Love*." *Etudes Lawrenciennes* 3 (1988), 79–97.

Gouirand, Jacqueline. "Gerald et Birkin, du 'Prologue' à la version définitive de *Women in Love*." *Etudes Lawrenciennes* 5 (1990), 29–50.

Gouirand, Jacqueline. "L'Imagerie thématique des avant-textes à la version publiée de *Women in Love*." *Etudes Lawrenciennes* 4 (1989), 37–52.

Haegert, John. "D. H. Lawrence and the Aesthetics of Transgression." *Mod Philology* 88 (1990), 10–13.

Heilman, Robert Bechtold. *The Workings of Fiction*, 131–37.

Holbrook, David. *Where D. H. Lawrence Was Wrong*, 184–240.

Humma, John B. "Lawrence in Another Light: *Women in Love* and Existentialism." *Stud in the Novel* 24 (192), 392–407.

Hyde, Virginia. *The Risen Adam*, 101–18.

Ingram, Allan. *The Language of D. H. Lawrence*, 61–65, 109–18.

Kalnins, Mara. "Lawrence's Men and Women: Complements and Opposites," in Sally Minogue, ed., *Problems for Feminist Criticism*, 155–62.

Katz-Roy, Ginette. "Les Arts plastiques et la mode dans *Women in Love*." *Etudes Lawrenciennes* 4 (1989), 53–70.

Katz-Roy, Ginette. "Le dialogue avec les avant-gardes dans *Women in Love*." *Etudes Lawrenciennes* 5 (1990), 51–75.

Kelsey, Nigel. *D. H. Lawrence*, 141–80.

Kiely, Robert. "Out on Strike: The Language and Power of the Working Class in Lawrence's Fiction," in Michael Squires and Keith Cushman, eds., *The Challenge of D. H. Lawrence*, 99–102.

Krasner, James. *The Entangled Eye*, 166–68.

Kushigian, Nancy. *Pictures and Fictions*, 152–53.

Levy, Eric P. "Lawrence's Psychology of Void and Center in *Women in Love*." *D. H. Lawrence R* 23 (1991), 5–19.

Lodge, David. "Lawrence, Dostoevsky, Bakhtin: Lawrence and Dialogic Fiction," in Keith Brown, ed., *Rethinking Lawrence*, 97–101.

Mensch, Barbara. *D. H. Lawrence*, 71–118.

Messenger, Nigel. *How to Study a D. H. Lawrence Novel*, 78–104.

Mills, Howard W. "Stylistic Revision of *Women in Love* (The Prologue/The Wedding Chapter)." *Etudes Lawrenciennes* 3 (1988), 99–108.

Paccaud-Huguet, Josiane. "Structure perverse et écriture dans *Women in Love*." *Etudes Anglaises* 46 (1993), 32–46.

Padhi, Babhu. *D. H. Lawrence*, 136–46, 163–85.

Parker, David. "Into the Ideological Unknown: *Women in Love.*" *Crit R* (Melbourne) 30 (1990), 3–24.

Pichardie, Jean-Paul. "*Women in Love* dans l'œuvre romanesque de D. H. Lawrence." *Etudes Lawrenciennes* 5 (1990), 21–27.

Pichardie, Jean-Paul. "*Women in Love:* Structures." *Etudes Lawrenciennes* 4 (1989), 7–19.

Pinkney, Tony. *D. H. Lawrence,* 79–99.

Pluto, Anne Elezabeth. "Blutbrüderschaft." *Paunch* 63–64 (1990), 89–97.

Procter, Margaret. "Possibilities of Completion: The Endings of *A Passage to India* and *Women in Love.*" *Engl Lit in Transition* 34 (1991), 261–78.

Rihoit, Catherine. "D'une quête féminine de la connaissance dans *Women in Love.*" *Etudes Lawrenciennes* 4 (1989), 87–104.

Robins, Ross. "From a Study of *Women in Love:* 'Moony.'" *Spectrum* 31 (1989), 7–11.

Ross, Charles L. "*Women in Love,*" 23–137.

Scherr, Barry J. "The 'Body of Darkness' of *Women in Love.*" *Recovering Lit* 18 (1991/92), 29–40.

Scherr, Barry J. "Lawrence's 'Dark Flood': A Platonic Interpretation of 'Excurse.'" *Paunch* 63–64 (1990), 209–35.

Siegel, Carol. *Lawrence among the Women,* 68–70, 101–7, 141–42, 151–52.

Sinzelle, Claude. "Du poulpe à la rose dans 'Moony.'" *Etudes Lawrenciennes* 5 (1990), 77–96.

Sklenicka, Carol. *D. H. Lawrence and the Child,* 146–53.

Smith, Evans Lansing. *Rape and Revelation,* 49–52.

Spilka, Mark. *Renewing the Normative D. H. Lawrence,* 59–65, 100–103, 105–9, 147–51.

Sproles, Karyn Z. "D. H. Lawrence and the Pre-Raphaelites: Love Among the Ruins." *D. H. Lawrence R* 22 (1990), 301–3.

Squires, Michael. "Lawrence, Dickens, and the English Novel," in Michael Squires and Keith Cushman, eds., *The Challenge of D. H. Lawrence,* 51–57.

Stevenson, Randall. *Modernist Fiction,* 30–34, 114–17, 148–51.

Stewart, Jack F. "Dialects of Knowing in *Women in Love.*" *Twentieth Cent Lit* 37 (1991), 59–74.

Storch, Margaret. *Sons and Adversaries,* 110–20.

Swift, John N. "Repetition, Consummation, and 'This Eternal Unrelief,'" in Michael Squires and Keith Cushman, eds., *The Challenge of D. H. Lawrence,* 121–28.

Templeton, Wayne. *States of Estrangement,* 166–305.

Topia, André. "Dialogisme et relativisme dans *Women in Love.*" *Etudes Lawrenciennes* 4 (1989), 21–36.

Trotter, David. "A Horse Is Being Beaten: Modernism and Popular Fiction," in Kevin J. H. Dettmar, ed., *Rereading the New,* 194–202, 211–16.

Tytell, John. *Passionate Lives,* 51–57.

Vichy, Thérèse. "Liberté et création dans *Women in Love.*" *Etudes Lawrenciennes* 5 (1990), 7–19.

Vitoux, Pierre. "Le fleuve souterrain dans *Women in Love.*" *Etudes Anglaises* 42 (1989), 13–26.

Widmer, Kingsley. *Defiant Desire*, 21–28, 45–48.

JOHN LE CARRÉ

Call for the Dead, 1961

Beene, LynnDianne. *John le Carré*, 28–36.

Bradbury, Richard. "Reading John le Carré," in Clive Bloom, ed., *Spy Thrillers*, 130–33.

Seed, David. "The Well-Wrought Structures of John le Carré's Early Fiction," in Clive Bloom, ed., *Spy Thrillers*, 142–45.

The Honourable Schoolboy, 1977

Beene, LynnDianne. *John le Carré*, 100–105.

The Little Drummer Girl, 1983

Beene, LynnDianne. *John le Carré*, 112–22.

Hayes, Michael J. "Are You Telling Me Lies David? The Work of John le Carré," in Clive Bloom, ed., *Spy Thrillers*, 125–26.

The Looking-Glass War, 1965

Beene, LynnDianne. *John le Carré*, 60–65.

Halperin, John. *Jane Austen's Lovers*, 217–19.

Hayes, Michael J. "Are You Telling Me Lies David? The Work of John le Carré," in Clive Bloom, ed., *Spy Thrillers*, 120–21.

Seed, David. "The Well-Wrought Structures of John le Carré's Early Fiction," in Clive Bloom, ed., *Spy Thrillers*, 152–55.

A Murder of Quality, 1962

Beene, LynnDianne. *John le Carré*, 36–45.

Bradbury, Richard. "Reading John le Carré," in Clive Bloom, ed., *Spy Thrillers*, 133–35.

Halperin, John. *Jane Austen's Lovers*, 217–19.

Seed, David. "The Well-Wrought Structures of John le Carré's Early Fiction," in Clive Bloom, ed., *Spy Thrillers*, 145–47.

The Naive and Sentimental Lover, 1971

Beene, LynnDianne. *John le Carré*, 77–87.

Dubois, Betty Lou. "Regular Adverbs of Manner in Le Carré's *Naive and Sentimental Lover:* Shamus Demanded Testily, but Sandra Returned Peevishly, While Sal Waited Patiently, and Cassidy Retorted Churlishly." *Southwest J of Ling* 9:2 (1990), 43–62.

A Perfect Spy, 1986

Barley, Tony. " 'Loving and Lying': Multiple Identity in John le Carré's *A Perfect Spy,*" in Ian A. Bell and Graham Daldry, eds., *Watching the Detectives*, 152–69.

Beene, LynnDianne. *John le Carré,* 122–28.

Daleski, H. M. *"A Perfect Spy* and a Great Tradition." *J of Narrative Technique* 20 (1990), 56–64.

Griffiths, Gwen. "Individual and Societal Entropy in le Carré's *A Perfect Spy." Critique* (Washington, DC) 31 (1990), 112-23.

Hayes, Michael J. "Are You Telling Me Lies David? The Work of John le Carré," in Clive Bloom, ed., *Spy Thrillers,* 126–28.

Loe, Thomas. "The Double Plot in John Le Carré's *A Perfect Spy." Notes on Contemp Lit* 18:4 (1988), 5–7.

The Russia House, 1989

Beene, LynnDianne. *John le Carré,* 128–34.

The Secret Pilgrim, 1991

Beene, LynnDianne. *John le Carré,* 134–37.

A Small Town in Germany, 1968

Beene, LynnDianne. *John le Carré,* 65–70.

Halperin, John. *Jane Austen's Lovers,* 216–23.

Hayes, Michael J. "Are You Telling Me Lies David? The Work of John le Carré," in Clive Bloom, ed., *Spy Thrillers,* 121–23.

Seed, David. "The Well-Wrought Structures of John le Carré's Early Fiction," in Clive Bloom, ed., *Spy Thrillers,* 155–58.

Smiley's People, 1980

Beene, LynnDianne. *John le Carré,* 105–11.

The Spy Who Came in from the Cold, 1963

Beene, LynnDianne. *John le Carré,* 49–59.

Hayes, Michael J. "Are You Telling Me Lies David? The Work of John le Carré," in Clive Bloom, ed., *Spy Thrillers,* 116–20.

Martin, B. K. "Le Carré's *The Spy Who Came In From The Cold:* A Structuralist Reading." *Sydney Stud in Engl* 14 (1988–89), 72–88.

Seed, David. "The Well-Wrought Structures of John le Carré's Early Fiction," in Clive Bloom, ed., *Spy Thrillers,* 147–52.

Stafford, David. *The Silent Game,* 197–98, 199–2009.

Tinker, Tailor, Soldier, Spy, 1974

Beene, LynnDianne. *John le Carré,* 96–100.

Halperin, John. *Jane Austen's Lovers,* 232–37.

Lasseter, Victor. *"Tinker, Tailor, Soldier, Spy:* A Story of Modern Love." *Critique* (Washington, DC) 31 (1990), 101-11.

Scanlan, Margaret. *Traces of Another Time,* 98–100.

SOPHIA LEE

The Recess, 1785

DeLamotte, Eugenia C. *Perils of the Night,* 168–73.

JOSEPH SHERIDAN LEFANU

Carmilla, 1872

Bhalla, Alok. *Politics of Atrocity and Lust,* 26–34.

Bhalla, Alok. "Politics of Atrocity and Lust: Folklore of Vampirism and the Tales of Byron, Polidori, Prest and Le Fanu," in Jasodhara Bagchi, ed., *Literature, Society and Ideology,* 144–51.

Cornwell, Neil. *The Literary Fantastic,* 90–92.

Geary, Robert F. *The Supernatural in Gothic Fiction,* 111–13.

Girard, Gaid. "Les écrits de Laura: analyse de *Carmilla,* de J. S. LeFanu," in Roger Bozzetto et al., eds., *Eros,* 21–33.

McCormack, W. J. *Dissolute Characters,* 148–53, 155–58.

Stoddart, Helen. " 'The Precautions of Nervous People Are Infectious': Sheridan Le Fanu's Symptomatic Gothic." *Mod Lang R* 86 (1991), 19–34.

Tracy, Robert. "Loving You All Ways: Vamps, Vampires, Necrophiles and Necrofilles in Nineteenth-Century Fiction," in Regina Barreca, ed., *Sex and Death,* 40–42.

Checkmate, 1871

McCormack, W. J. *Dissolute Characters,* 163–68.

Guy Deverell, 1865

McCormack, W. J. *Dissolute Characters,* 71–75.

The House by the Churchyard, 1863

McCormack, W. J. *Dissolute Characters,* 34–44.

The Rose and the Key, 1871

Milbank, Alison. *Daughters of the House,* 165–69.

Uncle Silas, 1864

Cornwell, Neil. *The Literary Fantastic,* 92–94.

Howes, Marjorie. "Misalliance and Anglo-Irish Tradition in Le Fanu's *Uncle Silas.*" *Nineteenth-Cent Lit* 47 (1992), 164–86.

Lozes, Jean. "Le Fanu's Houses," in Jacqueline Genet, ed., *The Big House in Ireland,* 104–8.

McCormack, W. J. *Dissolute Characters,* 27–30, 66–69, 88–91.

Milbank, Alison. *Daughters of the House,* 174–97.

Wylder's Hand, 1864

McCormack, W. J. *Dissolute Characters,* 60–66.

Milbank, Alison. *Daughters of the House,* 169–73.

ROSAMOND LEHMANN

The Ballad and the Source, 1944

Siegel, Ruth. *Rosamond Lehmann,* 135–49.

Simons, Judy. *Rosamond Lehmann,* 93–113.

Dusty Answer, 1927

> Brown, Penny. *The Poison at the Source,* 86–102.
> Gindin, James. *British Fiction,* 100–102.
> Rossen, Janice. *The University in Modern Fiction,* 114–16.
> Siegel, Ruth. *Rosamond Lehmann,* 61–78.
> Simons, Judy. *Rosamond Lehmann,* 38–54.

The Echoing Grove, 1953

> Alexander, Marguerite. *Flights from Realism,* 70–74.
> Gindin, James. *British Fiction,* 86–89, 93–99, 102–4.
> Siegel, Ruth. *Rosamond Lehmann,* 152–68.
> Simons, Judy. *Rosamond Lehmann,* 114–29.

Invitation to the Waltz, 1932

> Brown, Penny. *The Poison at the Source,* 102–9.
> Siegel, Ruth. *Rosamond Lehmann,* 91–103.
> Simons, Judy. *Rosamond Lehmann,* 60–76.

A Note in Music, 1930

> Siegel, Ruth. *Rosamond Lehmann,* 79–90.
> Simons, Judy. *Rosamond Lehmann,* 38–40, 54–59.

A Sea-Grape Tree, 1976

> Siegel, Ruth. *Rosamond Lehmann,* 168–73.
> Simons, Judy. *Rosamond Lehmann,* 18–19, 133–35.

The Weather in the Streets, 1936

> Brown, Penny. *The Poison at the Source,* 109–19.
> Gindin, James. *British Fiction,* 86–89, 91–93, 103–5.
> Montgomery, Martin, Alan Durant, Nigel Fabb, Tom Furniss, and Sara Mills. *Ways of Reading,* 187–89.
> Siegel, Ruth. *Rosamond Lehmann,* 105–15.
> Simons, Judy. *Rosamond Lehmann,* 77–92.

CHARLOTTE LENNOX

The Female Quixote, 1752

> Craft, Catherine A. "Reworking Male Models: Aphra Behn's *Fair Vow-Breaker,* Eliza Haywood's *Fantomina,* and Charlotte Lennox's *Female Quixote." Mod Lang R* 86 (1991), 832–38.
> Gallagher, Catherine. "Nobody's Story: Gender, Property, and the Rise of the Novel." *Mod Lang Q* 53 (1992), 270–74.
> Henson, Eithne. *"The Fictions of Romantick Chivalry,"* 137–40.
> Kraft, Elizabeth. *Character & Consciousness,* 83–88, 92–99.
> Marshall, David. "Writing Masters and 'Masculine Exercises' in *The Female Quixote." Eighteenth-Cent Fiction* 5 (1993), 105–35.
> Ross, Deborah. *The Excellence of Falsehood,* 94–109.
> Schaffer, Julie. "Not Subordinate: Empowering Women in the Marriage

Plot—The Novels of Frances Burney, Maria Edgeworth, and Jane Austen." *Criticism* 34 (1992), 53–54.

Thomson, Helen. "Charlotte Lennox's *The Female Quixote:* A Novel Interrogation," in Dale Spender, ed., *Living by the Pen*, 113–25.

Uphaus, Robert W. *The Idea of the Novel*, 7–9.

The Life of Harriot Stuart, 1751

Howard, Susan K. "Identifying the Criminal in Charlotte Lennox's *The Life of Harriot Stuart.*" *Eighteenth-Cent Fiction* 5 (1993), 137–52.

Ross, Deborah. *The Excellence of Falsehood*, 69–93.

DORIS LESSING

Briefing for a Descent into Hell, 1971

Bazin, Nancy Topping. "Madness, Mysticism, and Fantasy: Shifting Perspectives in the Novels of Doris Lessing, Bessie Head, and Nadine Gordimer." *Extrapolation* 33 (1992), 79–80.

King, Jeannette. *Doris Lessing*, 55–68.

Kramer, Reinhold. "Im/maculate: Some Instances of Gnostic Science Fiction," in Nicholas Ruddick, ed., *State of the Fantastic*, 49–51.

Malekin, Peter. " 'What Dreams May Come?': Relativity of Perception in Doris Lessing's *Briefing for a Descent into Hell*," in Donald E. Morse et al., eds., *The Celebration of the Fantastic*, 73–78.

Maslen, Elizabeth. "Narrators and Readers in Three Novels." *Doris Lessing Newsl* 10:2 (1986), 5.

Myles, Anita. *Doris Lessing*, 10–12, 69–70, 82–84.

Pickering, Jean. *Understanding Doris Lessing*, 125–31.

Smith, Evans Lansing. *Rape and Revelation*, 101–3.

Canopus in Argos, 1979–1983

Auberlen, Eckhard. "Great Creating Nature and the Human Experiment in *The Golden Notebook* and *Canopus in Argos.*" *Doris Lessing Newsl* 13:1 (1989), 12–15.

Bertelsen, Eve. "The Quest and the Quotidian: Doris Lessing in South Africa," in Claire Sprague, ed., *In Pursuit of Doris Lessing*, 53–54.

King, Jeannette. *Doris Lessing*, 69–92.

Monteith, Moira. "Doris Lessing and the Politics of Violence," in Lucie Armitt, ed., *Where No Man Has Gone Before*, 72–79.

Children of Violence, 1952–1969

Bertelsen, Eve. "The Quest and the Quotidian: Doris Lessing in South Africa," in Claire Sprague, ed., *In Pursuit of Doris Lessing*, 47–49.

Cartwright, John F. "Bound and Free: The Paradox of the Quest in Doris Lessing's *Children of Violence.*" *Commonwealth Novel in Engl* 4:1 (1991), 46–61.

King, Jeannette. *Doris Lessing*, 14–35.

Myles, Anita. *Doris Lessing*, 7–9, 15–16.

Pickering, Jean. *Understanding Doris Lessing,* 38–88.
Robinson, Sally. *Engendering the Subject,* 29–47, 55–75.

The Fifth Child, 1988

Dean, Sharon L. "Lessing's *The Fifth Child.*" *Explicator* 50 (1992), 120–22.
Pickering, Jean. *Understanding Doris Lessing,* 191–95.
Pifer, Ellen. "*The Fifth Child:* Lessing's Subversion of the Pastoral," in Donald E. Morse et al., eds., *The Celebration of the Fantastic,* 123–31.
Sizemore, Christine W. "Neanderthals, Human Gorillas and Their Fathers: Crossing Scientific Boundaries in Doris Lessing's *The Fifth Child* and Maureen Duffy's *Gor Saga.*" *Doris Lessing Newsl* 15:1 (1993), 3, 7, 10, 14.

The Four-Gated City, 1969

Gohlman, Susan Ashley. *Starting Over,* 69–131.
Hanson, Clare. "Doris Lessing in Pursuit of the English, or, No Small, Personal Voice," in Claire Sprague, ed., *In Pursuit of Doris Lessing,* 64–66.
Harris, Jocelyn. "Doris Lessing's Beautiful Impossible Blueprints," in James Acheson, ed., *The British and Irish Novel,* 32–33, 37–38, 40–41.
King, Jeannette. *Doris Lessing,* 25–35.
Myles, Anita. *Doris Lessing,* 9–13, 15–17, 62–65, 80–84.
Pickering, Jean. *Understanding Doris Lessing,* 72–88.

The Golden Notebook, 1962

Alexander, Marguerite. *Flights from Realism,* 87–93.
Auberlen, Eckhard. "Great Creating Nature and the Human Experiment in *The Golden Notebook* and *Canopus in Argos.*" *Doris Lessing Newsl* 13:1 (1989), 12–15.
Bertelsen, Eve. "*The Golden Notebook:* The African Background," in Corey Kaplan and Ellen Cronan Rose, eds., *Approaches,* 30–36.
Bertelsen, Eve. "The Quest and the Quotidian: Doris Lessing in South Africa," in Claire Sprague, ed., *In Pursuit of Doris Lessing,* 49–52.
Brown, Sandra. "'Where words, patterns, order, dissolve': *The Golden Notebook* as Fugue," in Corey Kaplan and Ellen Cronan Rose, eds., *Approaches,* 121–26.
Cederstrom, Lorelei. "The Principal Archetypal Elements of *The Golden Notebook,*" in Corey Kaplan and Ellen Cronan Rose, eds., *Approaches,* 50–56.
Dentith, Simon. "*The Golden Notebook* and the End of History." *Lit & Hist* 1:2 (1992), 55–64.
Eykman, Christoph. *Der Intellektuelle,* 181–87.
Fishburn, Katherine. "*The Golden Notebook:* A Challenge to the Teaching Establishment," in Corey Kaplan and Ellen Cronan Rose, eds., *Approaches,* 127–31.
Greene, Gayle. *Changing the Story,* 105–29.

Greene, Gayle. "Feminist Fiction and the Uses of Memory." *Signs* 16 (1991), 308–10.

Hanson, Clare. "Doris Lessing in Pursuit of the English, or, No Small, Personal Voice," in Claire Sprague, ed., *In Pursuit of Doris Lessing*, 66–68.

Harris, Jocelyn. "Doris Lessing's Beautiful Impossible Blueprints," in James Acheson, ed., *The British and Irish Novel*, 32–39, 41–43.

Hassam, Andrew. *Writing and Reality*, 72–74, 139–47.

Hileman, Sharon. "*The Golden Notebook* and Undergraduates: Strategies for Involving Students," in Corey Kaplan and Ellen Cronan Rose, eds., *Approaches*, 95–100.

Hite, Molly. "*The Golden Notebook* in a Graduate Seminar on Contemporary Experimental Fiction," in Corey Kaplan and Ellen Cronan Rose, eds., *Approaches*, 84–89.

Humm, Maggie. *Border Traffic*, 50–54.

Hynes, Joseph. "A Sixties Book for All Seasons," in Corey Kaplan and Ellen Cronan Rose, eds., *Approaches*, 65–71.

King, Jeannette. *Doris Lessing*, 36–54.

Knapp, Mona. "*The Golden Notebook:* A Feminist Context for the Classroom," in Corey Kaplan and Ellen Cronan Rose, eds., *Approaches*, 108–14.

Lightfoot, Marjorie. "*The Golden Notebook* as a Modernist Novel," in Corey Kaplan and Ellen Cronan Rose, eds., *Approaches*, 58–64.

Myles, Anita. *Doris Lessing*, 7–8, 15–18, 28–32, 58–62, 100–102.

Pickering, Jean. "Philosophical Contexts for *The Golden Notebook*," in Corey Kaplan and Ellen Cronan Rose, eds., *Approaches*, 43–49.

Pickering, Jean. *Understanding Doris Lessing*, 90–122.

Rubenstein, Roberta. "*The Golden Notebook* in an Introductory Women's Studies Course," in Corey Kaplan and Ellen Cronan Rose, eds., *Approaches*, 72–77.

Saxton, Ruth. "*The Golden Notebook* and Creative Writing Majors," in Corey Kaplan and Ellen Cronan Rose, eds., *Approaches*, 90–94.

Seligman, Dee. "In Pursuit of Doris Lessing," in Corey Kaplan and Ellen Cronan Rose, eds., *Approaches*, 21–29.

Spilka, Mark. *Renewing the Normative D. H. Lawrence*, 127–45.

Sprague, Claire. "*The Golden Notebook:* In Whose or What Great Tradition?," in Corey Kaplan and Ellen Cronan Rose, eds., *Approaches*, 78–83.

Sprague, Claire. "Lessing's *The Grass Is Singing, Retreat to Innocence, The Golden Notebook* and Eliot's *The Waste Land.*" *Explicator* 50 (1992), 177–80.

Stern, Frederick C. "Politics and *The Golden Notebook*," in Corey Kaplan and Ellen Cronan Rose, eds., *Approaches*, 37–42.

Tiger, Virginia. "Illusions of Actuality: First-Person Pronoun in *The Golden Notebook*," in Corey Kaplan and Ellen Cronan Rose, eds., *Approaches*, 101–7.

Wilson, Sharon R. *"The Golden Notebook's* Inner Film," in Corey Kaplan and Ellen Cronan Rose, eds., *Approaches,* 115–20.

The Good Terrorist, 1985

DiSalvo, Jacqueline. "The Intertextuality of Doris Lessing's *The Good Terrorist* and Milton's *Samson Agonistes." Doris Lessing Newsl* 12:1 (1988), 3–4.

Hanson, Clare. "Doris Lessing in Pursuit of the English, or, No Small, Personal Voice," in Claire Sprague, ed., *In Pursuit of Doris Lessing,* 70–72.

Hidalgo, Pilar. *"The Good Terrorist:* Lessing's Tract for the Times." *Doris Lessing Newsl* 11:1 (1987), 7–8.

King, Jeannette. *Doris Lessing,* 93–106.

Pickering, Jean. *Understanding Doris Lessing,* 185–90.

Scanlan, Margaret. "Language and the Politics of Despair in Doris Lessing's *The Good Terrorist." Novel* 23 (1990), 182–96.

Scott, Virginia. "Doris Lessing's Modern Alice in Wonderland: *The Good Terrorist* as Fantasy." *Intl Fiction R* 16 (1989), 123–27.

The Grass Is Singing, 1950

Bertelsen, Eve. "The Quest and the Quotidian: Doris Lessing in South Africa," in Claire Sprague, ed., *In Pursuit of Doris Lessing,* 43–45.

Geoffroy, Alain. "Dreams in Doris Lessing's *The Grass Is Singing." Commonwealth Essays and Stud* 11:2 (1989), 110–20.

Hanley, Lynne. "Writing Across the Color Bar: Apartheid and Desire." *Massachusetts R* 32 (1991), 495–506.

Hunter, Eva. "Marriage or Death: A Reading of Doris Lessing's *The Grass Is Singing,"* in Cherry Clayton, ed., *Women and Writing in South Africa,* 139–61.

Jacob, Susan. "Sharers in a Common Hell: The Colonial Text in Schreiner, Conrad and Lessing." *Liter Criterion* 23:4 (1988), 88–91.

King, Jeannette. *Doris Lessing,* 1–13.

Maslen, Elizabeth. "Narrators and Readers in Three Novels." *Doris Lessing Newsl* 10:2 (1986), 4–5.

Myles, Anita. *Doris Lessing,* 1–5, 21–23.

Pickering, Jean. *Understanding Doris Lessing,* 18–37.

Landlocked, 1965

Pickering, Jean. *Understanding Doris Lessing,* 63–72.

The Making of the Representative for Planet 8, 1982

King, Jeannette. *Doris Lessing,* 81–86.

Pickering, Jean. *Understanding Doris Lessing,* 168–72.

The Marriages between Zones Three, Four, and Five, 1980

Armitt, Lucie. "Your Word Is My Command: The Structures of Language and Power in Women's Science Fiction," in Lucie Armitt, ed., *Where No Man Has Gone Before,* 123–30.

Barr, Marleen. "Working at Loving: The Postseparatist Feminist Utopia," in Roger Bozzetto et al., eds., *Eros,* 183–85.

Colakis, Marianthe. "Doris Lessing's New Cupid and Psyche: A Platonic Myth Retold." *Classical and Mod Lit* 12 (1992), 153–60.

Peel, Ellen. "Leaving the Self Behind in *Marriages.*" *Doris Lessing Newsl* 11:2 (1987), 3, 10.

Pickering, Jean. *Understanding Doris Lessing,* 150–58.

Sheiner, Marcy. "Thematic Consistency in the Work of Doris Lessing: The Marriage Between Martha Quest and Zones Three, Four, and Five." *Doris Lessing Newsl* 11:2 (1987), 4, 14.

Martha Quest, 1952

Bazin, Nancy Topping. "Madness, Mysticism, and Fantasy: Shifting Perspectives in the Novels of Doris Lessing, Bessie Head, and Nadine Gordimer." *Extrapolation* 33 (1992), 73–75, 78–79.

Daymond, M. J. "*Martha Quest:* The Self and Its Spatial Metaphors," in Cherry Clayton, ed., *Women and Writing in South Africa,* 163–81.

King, Jeannette. *Doris Lessing,* 14–25.

Pickering, Jean. *Understanding Doris Lessing,* 40–48.

Sheiner, Marcy. "Thematic Consistency in the Work of Doris Lessing: The Marriage Between Martha Quest and Zones Three, Four, and Five." *Doris Lessing Newsl* 11:2 (1987), 4, 14.

The Memoirs of a Survivor, 1974

Chown, Linda E. *Narrative Authority and Homeostasis,* 265–93, 299–329.

Conboy, Sheila C. "The Limits of Transcendental Experience in Doris Lessing's *The Memoirs of a Survivor.*" *Mod Lang Stud* 20:1 (1990), 67–76.

Matheson, Sue. "Lessing on Stage: An Examination of Theatrical Metaphor and Architectural Motif in *The Memoirs of a Survivor.*" *Doris Lessing Newsl* 10:2 (1986), 8–9.

Myles, Anita. *Doris Lessing,* 12–13, 80–85.

Pickering, Jean. *Understanding Doris Lessing,* 135–40.

Singer, Sandra. "Unleashing Human Potentialities: Doris Lessing's *The Memoirs of a Survivor.*" *Text & Context* 1:1 (1986), 79–95.

Wright, Derek. "The Space in Time: Doris Lessing's *Memoirs of a Survivor.*" *Intl Fiction R* 18 (1991), 86–90.

A Proper Marriage, 1954

Greene, Gayle. "Feminist Fiction and the Uses of Memory." *Signs* 16 (1991), 302–3.

Pickering, Jean. *Understanding Doris Lessing,* 48–57.

Robinson, Sally. *Engendering the Subject,* 39–42, 60–63.

A Ripple from the Storm, 1958

Pickering, Jean. *Understanding Doris Lessing,* 57–63.

The Sentimental Agents, 1983

King, Jeannette. *Doris Lessing,* 86–92.
Maslen, Elizabeth. "Narrators and Readers in Three Novels." *Doris Lessing Newsl* 10:2 (1986), 5–6.
Pickering, Jean. *Understanding Doris Lessing,* 172–77.

Shikasta, 1979

Hanley, Lynne. "Writing Across the Color Bar: Apartheid and Desire." *Massachusetts R* 32 (1991), 495–506.
Hanley, Lynne. *Writing War,* 116–25.
King, Jeannette. *Doris Lessing,* 72–81.
Monteith, Moira. "Doris Lessing and the Politics of Violence," in Lucie Armitt, ed., *Where No Man Has Gone Before,* 72–79.
Myles, Anita. *Doris Lessing,* 13–15, 32–33, 89–95.
Perrakis, Phyllis Sternberg. "The Marriage of Inner and Outer Space in Doris Lessing's *Shikasta.*" *Science-Fiction Stud* 17 (1990), 221–35.
Pickering, Jean. *Understanding Doris Lessing,* 143–50.

The Sirian Experiments, 1981

Monteith, Moira. "Doris Lessing and the Politics of Violence," in Lucie Armitt, ed., *Where No Man Has Gone Before,* 73–79.
Mosièr, M. Patricia. "A Sufi Model for the Teacher/Disciple Relationship in *The Sirian Experiments.*" *Extrapolation* 32 (1991), 209–21.
Myles, Anita. *Doris Lessing,* 14–15, 92–96.
Pickering, Jean. *Understanding Doris Lessing,* 158–68.

The Summer Before the Dark, 1973

Bouson, J. Brooks. *The Empathic Reader,* 121–37.
Chown, Linda E. *Narrative Authority and Homeostasis,* 72–106, 120–62.
Greene, Gayle. "Feminist Fiction and the Uses of Memory." *Signs* 16 (1991), 310–11.
Harris, Jocelyn. "Doris Lessing's Beautiful Impossible Blueprints," in James Acheson, ed., *The British and Irish Novel,* 37–39.
Myles, Anita. *Doris Lessing,* 11–13.
Pickering, Jean. *Understanding Doris Lessing,* 131–35.
Stout, Janis P. "A Quest of One's Own: Doris Lessing's *The Summer Before the Dark.*" *Ariel* 21:2 (1990), 5–17.
Wellington, Charmaine. "Mary Finchley in *The Summer Before the Dark:* A Present Absence." *Doris Lessing Newsl* 12:2 (1989), 6–7, 13.

CHARLES LEVER

The Martins of Cro' Martin, 1856

Morash, Christopher. "Reflecting Absent Interiors: The Big-House Novels of Charles Lever," in Otto Rauchbauer, ed., *Ancestral Voices,* 67–74.

GEORGE HENRY LEWES

Ranthorpe, 1847

    Chittick, Kathryn. *Dickens and the 1830s,* 6–8.

C. S. LEWIS

The Chronicles of Narnia

Byfield, Virginia. "The Success of the Narnia Stories." *Chesterton R* 17 (1991), 420–21.

Caldecott, Leonie. "Narnia—A Taste of Paradise." *Chesterton R* 17 (1991), 415–18.

Christopher, Joe R. "J. R. R. Tolkien, Narnian Exile." *Mythlore* 15:1 (1988), 37–45; 15:2 (1988), 17–31.

Daigle, Marsha Ann. "Dante's *Divine Comedy* and C. S. Lewis's *Narnia Chronicles." Christianity & Lit* 34:4 (1985), 41–57.

Edwards, Sara Dudley, OP. "The Theological Dimensions of the Narnia Stories." *Chesterton R* 17 (1991), 429–35.

Filmer, Kath. *The Fiction of C. S. Lewis,* 43–52.

Jones, Karla Faust. "Girls in Narnia: Hindered or Human?" *Mythlore* 13:3 (1987), 15–19.

Kern, Raimund B. "Von der Wirklichkeit zum Phantastischen und zurück: Natur und Kultur in den Narnia-Büchern von C. S. Lewis." *Inklings* 8 (1990), 71–101.

Kreeft, Peter. *C. S. Lewis,* 54–56.

Lindskoog, Kathryn. "The First Chronicle of Narnia: The Restoring of Names." *Mythlore* 12:4 (1986), 43–46, 63.

McPherson, Joseph W. "The Narnia Lesson." *Chesterton R* 17 (1991), 421–23.

Manguel, Alberto. "The Narnia Stories." *Chesterton R* 17 (1991), 423–24.

Manlove, Colin. "'Caught Up into the Larger Pattern': Images and Narrative Structures in C. S. Lewis's Fiction," in Peter J. Schakel and Charles A. Huttar, eds., *Word and Story,* 271–72, 274–75.

Manlove, Colin. *"The Chronicles of Narnia,"* 25–115.

Matheson, Sue. "C. S. Lewis and the Lion: Primitivism and Archetype in *The Chronicles of Narnia." Mythlore* 15:1 (1988), 13–18.

Murrin, Michael. "The Multiple Worlds of the Narnia Stories," in Peter J. Schakel and Charles A. Huttar, eds., *Word and Story,* 232–55.

Patterson, Nancy-Lou. "Always Winter and Never Christmas: Symbols of Time in Lewis' *Chronicles of Narnia." Mythlore* 18:1 (1991), 10–14.

Pietrusz, Jim. "Rites of Passage: The Chronicles of Narnia and the Seven Sacraments." *Mythlore* 14:4 (1988), 61–63.

Riga, Frank P. "Mortals Call Their History Fable: Narnia and the Use of Fairy Tale." *Children's Lit Assoc Q* 14:1 (1989), 26–30.

Saunders, Betty. "The Harsh Morality of the Narnia Stories." *Chesterton R* 17 (1991), 413–15.

Tixier, Eliane. "Chesterton's Paradox and Lewis's Fantasy." *Chesterton R* 17 (1991), 424–29.

The Horse and His Boy, 1954

Holbrook, David. *The Skeleton in the Wardrobe,* 185–87.
Patterson, Nancy-Lou. "The Bolt of Tash: The Figure of Satan in C. S. Lewis' *The Horse and His Boy* and *The Last Battle.*" *Mythlore* 16:4 (1990), 23–26.

The Last Battle, 1956

Filmer, Kath. *The Fiction of C. S. Lewis,* 48–51, 84–86.
Holbrook, David. *The Skeleton in the Wardrobe,* 188–217.
Patterson, Nancy-Lou. "The Bolt of Tash: The Figure of Satan in C. S. Lewis' *The Horse and His Boy* and *The Last Battle.*" *Mythlore* 16:4 (1990), 23–26.

The Lion, the Witch, and the Wardrobe, 1950

Holbrook, David. *The Skeleton in the Wardrobe,* 27–61.
McLaughlin, Sara. "On Reading *The Lion, the Witch, and the Wardrobe* to a Four-Year-Old." *Chesterton R* 17 (1991), 418–19.
Nicholson, Mervyn. "Magic Food, Compulsive Eating, and Power Poetics," in Lilian R. Furst and Peter W. Graham, eds., *Disorderly Eaters,* 55–59.

The Magician's Nephew, 1955

Holbrook, David. *The Skeleton in the Wardrobe,* 145–61.

Out of the Silent Planet, 1938

Boenig, Robert. "Critical and Fictional Pairings in C. S. Lewis," in Bruce L. Edwards, ed., *The Taste of the Pineapple,* 143–46.
Downing, David C. *Planets in Peril,* 34–156.
Flieger, Verlyn. "The Sound of Silence: Lnguage and Experience in *Out of the Silent Planet,*" in Peter J. Schakel and Charles A. Huttar, eds., *Word and Story,* 42–57.
Kreeft, Peter. *C. S. Lewis,* 49–53.
Lake, David. "Wells, *The First Men in the Moon,* and Lewis's Ransom Trilogy," in Kath Filmer, ed., *Twentieth-Century Fantasists,* 26–27.
Lobdell, Jared C. "C. S. Lewis's Ransom Stories and Their Eighteenth-Century Ancestry," in Peter J. Schakel and Charles A. Huttar, eds., *Word and Story,* 213–19, 225–27.
Loney, Douglas. "Humpty Dumpty in the Heavens: Perspective in *Out of the Silent Planet.*" *Mythlore* 16:2 (1989), 14–20.
Lutton, Jeannette Hume. "The Feast of Reason: *Out of the Silent Planet* as the Book of Hnau." *Mythlore* 13:1 (1986), 37–41, 50.
Manlove, Colin. "'Caught Up into the Larger Pattern': Images and Narrative Structures in C. S. Lewis's Fiction," in Peter J. Schakel and Charles A. Huttar, eds., *Word and Story,* 263–74.
Musacchio, George. "Warfaring Christian." *Mythlore* 14:3 (1988), 31–33.

Rawls, Melanie. *"Herland* and *Out of the Silent Planet." Mythlore* 13:2 (1986), 51–54.

Riga, Frank. "The Platonic Imagery of George MacDonald and C. S. Lewis: The Allegory of the Cave Transfigured," in Roderick McGillis, ed., *For the Childlike,* 115–19.

Vonarburg, Elisabeth. "The Reproduction of the Body in Space," in Nicholas Ruddick, ed., *State of the Fantastic,* 60–62.

Wolfe, Gregory. "Essential Speech: Language and Myth in the Ransom Trilogy," in Peter J. Schakel and Charles A. Huttar, eds., *Word and Story,* 58–75.

Perelandra, 1943

Buning, Marius. *"Perelandra* Revisited in the Light of Modern Allegorical Theory," in Peter J. Schakel and Charles A. Huttar, eds., *Word and Story,* 277–98.

Campbell, David C., and Dale E. Hess. "Olympian Detachment: A Critical Look at the World of C. S. Lewis's Characters." *Stud in the Liter Imagination* 22:2 (1989), 211–15.

Downing, David C. *Planets in Peril,* 34–156.

Filmer, Kath. *The Fiction of C. S. Lewis,* 96–99.

Glover, Donald E. "Bent Language in *Perelandra:* The Storyteller's Temptation," in Peter J. Schakel and Charles A. Huttar, eds., *Word and Story,* 171–81.

Holbrook, David. *The Skeleton in the Wardrobe,* 244–50.

Kreeft, Peter. *C. S. Lewis,* 49–53.

Lake, David. "Wells, *The First Men in the Moon,* and Lewis's Ransom Trilogy," in Kath Filmer, ed., *Twentieth-Century Fantasists,* 27–29.

Lobdell, Jared C. "C. S. Lewis's Ransom Stories and Their Eighteenth-Century Ancestry," in Peter J. Schakel and Charles A. Huttar, eds., *Word and Story,* 219–27.

Logan, Darlene. "Battle Strategy in *Perelandra: Beowulf* Revisited." *Mythlore* 9:3 (1982), 19, 21.

Manlove, Colin. "'Caught Up into the Larger Pattern': Images and Narrative Structures in C. S. Lewis's Fiction," in Peter J. Schakel and Charles A. Huttar, eds., *Word and Story,* 263–75.

Musacchio, George. "Warfaring Christian." *Mythlore* 14:3 (1988), 31–33.

Wolfe, Gregory. "Essential Speech: Language and Myth in the Ransom Trilogy," in Peter J. Schakel and Charles A. Huttar, eds., *Word and Story,* 58–75.

Prince Caspian, 1951

Holbrook, David. *The Skeleton in the Wardrobe,* 131–44.

The Silver Chair, 1953

Holbrook, David. *The Skeleton in the Wardrobe,* 176–83.

Simmons, Courtney Lynn, and Joe Simmons. *"The Silver Chair* and Plato's Allegory of the Cave: The Archetype of Spiritual Liberation." *Mythlore* 17:4 (1991), 12–15.

That Hideous Strength, 1945

Arbuckle, Nan. "That Hidden Strength: C. S. Lewis' Merlin as Modern Grail," in Jeanie Watson and Maureen Fries, eds., *The Figure of Merlin,* 79–96.

Campbell, David C., and Dale E. Hess. "Olympian Detachment: A Critical Look at the World of C. S. Lewis's Characters." *Stud in the Liter Imagination* 22:2 (1989), 201–9.

Carter, Ian. *Ancient Cultures of Conceit,* 85–87.

Downing, David C. *Planets in Peril,* 34–156.

Filmer, Kath. *The Fiction of C. S. Lewis,* 24–27, 34–36, 69–76.

Holbrook, David. *The Skeleton in the Wardrobe,* 221–32.

Kreeft, Peter. *C. S. Lewis,* 56–59.

Lake, David. "Wells, *The First Men in the Moon,* and Lewis's Ransom Trilogy," in Kath Filmer, ed., *Twentieth-Century Fantasists,* 29–33.

Lane, Dorothy F. "Resurrecting the 'Ancient Unities': The Incarnation of Myth and the Legend of Logres in C. S. Lewis' *That Hideous Strength.*" *Mythlore* 16:3 (1990), 9–14.

Lobdell, Jared C. "C. S. Lewis's Ransom Stories and Their Eighteenth-Century Ancestry," in Peter J. Schakel and Charles A. Huttar, eds., *Word and Story,* 225–29.

McClatchey, Joe. "The Affair of Jane's Dreams: Reading *That Hideous Strength* as Iconographic Art," in Bruce L. Edwards, ed., *The Taste of the Pineapple,* 166–85.

Manlove, Colin. "'Caught Up into the Larger Pattern': Images and Narrative Structures in C. S. Lewis's Fiction," in Peter J. Schakel and Charles A. Huttar, eds., *Word and Story,* 261–65, 269–73.

Musacchio, George. "Warfaring Christian." *Mythlore* 14:3 (1988), 31–33.

Patterson, Nancy-Lou. "'Some Kind of Company': The Sacred Community in *That Hideous Strength.*" *Mythlore* 13:1 (1986), 8–19.

Wolfe, Gregory. "Essential Speech: Language and Myth in the Ransom Trilogy," in Peter J. Schakel and Charles A. Huttar, eds., *Word and Story,* 58–75.

Till We Have Faces, 1956

Bartlett, Sally A. "Humanistic Psychology in C. S. Lewis's *Till We Have Faces:* A Feministic Critique." *Stud in the Liter Imagination* 22:2 (1989), 185–98.

Campbell, David C., and Dale E. Hess. "Olympian Detachment: A Critical Look at the World of C. S. Lewis's Characters." *Stud in the Liter Imagination* 22:2 (1989), 209–11.

Donaldson, Mara E. "Orual's Story and the Art of Retelling: A Study of *Till We Have Faces,*" in Peter J. Schakel and Charles A. Huttar, eds., *Word and Story,* 157–70.

Filmer, Kath. *The Fiction of C. S. Lewis,* 39–42, 112–20.

Filmer, Kath. "Neither Here Nor There: The Spirit of Place in George MacDonald's *Lilith* and Lewis' *Till We Have Faces.*" *Mythlore* 16:1 (1989), 9–12.

Holbrook, David. *The Skeleton in the Wardrobe,* 261–67.

Holyer, Robert. "The Epistemology of C. S. Lewis's *Till We Have Faces,*" in Cynthia Marshall, ed., *Essays on C. S. Lewis and George MacDonald,* 53–80.

Kreeft, Peter. *C. S. Lewis,* 53–54.

Manlove, Colin. "'Caught Up into the Larger Pattern': Images and Narrative Structures in C. S. Lewis's Fiction," in Peter J. Schakel and Charles A. Huttar, eds., *Word and Story,* 262–65, 272–76.

Medcalf, Stephen. "Language and Self-Consciousness: The Making and Breaking of C. S. Lewis's Personae," in Peter J. Schakel and Charles A. Huttar, eds., *Word and Story,* 133–35.

The Voyage of the "Dawn Treader," 1952

Filmer, Kath. *The Fiction of C. S. Lewis,* 45–47.

Holbrook, David. *The Skeleton in the Wardrobe,* 163–75.

Manlove, Colin. "'Caught Up into the Larger Pattern': Images and Narrative Structures in C. S. Lewis's Fiction," in Peter J. Schakel and Charles A. Huttar, eds., *Word and Story,* 263–66.

CECIL DAY LEWIS

The Beast Must Die, 1938

Gindin, James. *British Fiction,* 159–61.

MATTHEW GREGORY LEWIS

The Monk, 1796

Albertazzi, Silvia. *Il sogno gotico,* 51–69.

Conger, Syndy M. "Sensibility Restored: Radcliffe's Answer to Lewis's *The Monk,*" in Kenneth W. Graham, ed., *Gothic Fictions,* 113–49.

Fiérobe, Claude. "Eros médusé," in Roger Bozzetto et al., eds., *Eros,* 10–11.

Geary, Robert F. "M. G. Lewis and Later Gothic Fiction: The Numinous Dissipated," in Nicholas Ruddick, ed., *State of the Fantastic,* 75–78.

Geary, Robert F. *The Supernatural in Gothic Fiction,* 60–69.

Haggerty, George E. *Gothic Fiction,* 24–27.

Hennlein, Elmar. *Religion und Phantastik,* 35–36, 42–43.

Hilliard, Raymond F. "Desire and the Structure of Eighteenth-Century Fiction," in H. George Hahn, ed., *The Country Myth,* 174–76.

Jones, Wendy. "Stories of Desire in *The Monk.*" *ELH* 57 (1990), 129–46.

Kauhl, Gudrun. "On the Release from Monkish Fetters: Matthew Lewis Reconsidered." *Dutch Q R of Anglo-American Letters* 19 (1989), 264–80.

MacDonald, D. L. "The Erotic Sublime: The Marvellous in *The Monk.*" *Engl Stud in Canada* 18 (1992), 273–84.

Marigny, Jean. "*The Monk* de M. G. Lewis et la pensée révolutionaire." *Cycnos* 5 (1989), 105–12.

Miles, Robert. *Gothic Writing*, 160–74.
Napier, Elizabeth R. *The Failure of Gothic*, 112–32.
Polhemus, Robert M. *Erotic Faith*, 20–25.

WYNDHAM LEWIS

The Apes of God, 1930

Ayers, David. *Wyndham Lewis and Western Man*, 146–56.
Brown, Dennis. *Intertextual Dynamics*, 145–51.
Edwards, Paul. "Augustan and Related Allusions in *The Apes of God*."
   Enemy News 24 (1987), 17–21.
Schenker, Daniel. *Wyndham Lewis*, 70–83.

The Childermass, 1928

Ayers, David. *Wyndham Lewis and Western Man*, 99–133.
Bergonzi, Bernard. *Wartime and Aftermath*, 130–33.
Brown, Dennis. *Intertextual Dynamics*, 111–18.
Schenker, Daniel. *Wyndham Lewis*, 126–58.

The Human Age, 1955

Schenker, Daniel. *Wyndham Lewis*, 159–91.

Mrs. Dukes' Million, 1977

Quéme, Anne. "*Mrs Duke's Millions:* A Mystery." *Enemy News* 27 (1988),
   12–16.
Schenker, Daniel. *Wyndham Lewis*, 22–27.

The Revenge for Love, 1937

Ayers, David. *Wyndham Lewis and Western Man*, 157–85.
Manthey, Jürgen. "Eingeredete Gewalt: Wyndham Lewis' Roman *Rache
   für Liebe*." *Merkur* 43:3 (1989), 241–46.
Schenker, Daniel. *Wyndham Lewis*, 160–65.

Self Condemned, 1954

Brown, Dennis. *Intertextual Dynamics*, 171–78.
Schenker, Daniel. *Wyndham Lewis*, 165–68.

Snooty Baronet, 1932

Dasenbrock, Reed Way. "Lewis's Sources for the Persian Settings of
   Snooty Baronet." *Enemy News* 22 (1986), 42–49.
Schenker, Daniel. *Wyndham Lewis*, 86–93.

Tarr, 1918

Ayers, David. *Wyndham Lewis and Western Man*, 139–46.
Brown, Dennis. *Intertextual Dynamics*, 67–73.
Bürger, Peter. "Modernity and the Avantgarde in Wyndham Lewis's *Tarr*."
   News From Nowhere 7 (1989), 9–17.
Bürger, Peter. "Subjektauflösung und verhärtetes Ich: Moderne und
   Avant-garde in Wyndham Lewis' Künstlerroman *Tarr*," in Manfred
   Pfister, ed., *Die Modernisierung des Ich*, 286–92.

Michel, Walter. "On the Genesis of *Tarr.*" *Enemy News* 22 (1986), 38–41.

Myrthen, Toby. "Wyndham Lewis: Between Nietzsche and Derrida." *Engl Stud in Canada* 16 (1990), 349–52.

Nicholls, Peter. "Apes and Familiars: Modernism, Mimesis and the Work of Wyndham Lewis." *Textual Practice* 6 (1992), 421–24, 426–34.

Orel, Harold. *Popular Fiction in England,* 147–51.

Quéma, Anne. "Beresin, Cairn, and Tarr." *Enemy News* 29 (1989), 4–10.

Quéma, Anne. "*Tarr* and the Vortex." *Enemy News* 26 (1988), 15–19.

Schenker, Daniel. *Wyndham Lewis,* 27–32, 39–48.

Sheppard, Richard W. "Wyndham Lewis's *Tarr:* An (Anti–)Vorticist Novel?" *JEGP* 88 (1989), 510–30.

Verstl, Ina. "*Tarr*—a Joke Too Deep for Laughter? The Comic, the Body and Gender." *Enemy News* 33 (1991), 4–9.

DAVID LINDSAY

A Voyage to Arcturus, 1920

Punter, David. *The Romantic Unconscious,* 109–10.

JACK LINDSAY

1649, 1938

Croft, Andy. *Red Letter Days,* 208–10.

ELIZA LINTON

In Haste and at Leisure, 1895

Ardis, Ann L. *New Women, New Novels,* 96–98.

PENELOPE LIVELY

Moon Tiger, 1987

Dukes, Thomas. "Desire Satisfied: War and Love in *The Heat of the Day* and *Moon Tiger.*" *War, Lit, and the Arts* 3:1 (1991), 75–97.

DAVID LODGE

The British Museum Is Falling Down, 1965

Levine, Robert T. "The 'Dangerous Quest': Echoes of *The Aspern Papers* in Lodge's *The British Museum Is Falling Down.*" *Comparatist* 13 (1989), 53–59.

Changing Places, 1975

Acheson, James. "The Small Worlds of Malcolm Bradbury and David Lodge," in James Acheson, ed., *The British and Irish Novel,* 86–88.

Ahrends, Rüdiger. "Satirical Norm and Narrative Technique in the Mod-

ern University Novel: David Lodge's *Changing Places* and *Small World*,"
in Joachim Schwend et al., eds., *Literatur im Kontext*, 280–85.

Kühn, Thomas. "Kommunikationsmedien und menschliche Verständigung in David Lodges Roman *Changing Places*." *Literatur in Wissenschaft und Unterricht* 22 (1989), 299–311.

Ommundsen, Wenche. "Sin, Sex, and Semiology: Metafictional Bliss and Anxiety in the Novels of David Lodge." *AUMLA* 73 (1990), 126–27.

Rossen, Janice. *The University in Modern Fiction*, 150–53.

How Far Can You Go?, 1980

Acheson, James. "The Small Worlds of Malcolm Bradbury and David Lodge," in James Acheson, ed., *The British and Irish Novel*, 85–87.

Ommundsen, Wenche. "Sin, Sex, and Semiology: Metafictional Bliss and Anxiety in the Novels of David Lodge." *AUMLA* 73 (1990), 127–33.

Woodman, Thomas. *Faithful Fictions*, 91–94, 125–27, 156–58.

Nice Work, 1988

Acheson, James. "The Small Worlds of Malcolm Bradbury and David Lodge," in James Acheson, ed., *The British and Irish Novel*, 89–91.

Carter, Ian. *Ancient Cultures of Conceit*, 254–56.

Taylor, D. J. *A Vain Conceit*, 39–41.

Watts, Cedric. *Literature and Money*, 149–52.

The Picturegoers, 1960

Ommundsen, Wenche. "Sin, Sex, and Semiology: Metafictional Bliss and Anxiety in the Novels of David Lodge." *AUMLA* 73 (1990), 124–26.

Small World, 1984

Acheson, James. "The Small Worlds of Malcolm Bradbury and David Lodge," in James Acheson, ed., *The British and Irish Novel*, 88–89.

Ahrends, Rüdiger. "Satirical Norm and Narrative Technique in the Modern University Novel: David Lodge's *Changing Places* and *Small World*," in Joachim Schwend et al., eds., *Literatur im Kontext*, 286–94.

Alexander, Marguerite. *Flights from Realism*, 118–23.

Holmes, Frederick M. "The Reader as Discoverer in David Lodge's *Small World*." *Critique* (Washington, DC) 32 (1990), 47–57.

Laing, Stuart. "The Three Small Worlds of David Lodge." *Crit Survey* 3 (1991), 324–30.

Maceda Gilbert, María Teresa. "*Small World* . . . y baldío." *Revista Alicantina de Estudios Ingleses* 2 (1989), 83–90.

Ommundsen, Wenche. "Sin, Sex, and Semiology: Metafictional Bliss and Anxiety in the Novels of David Lodge." *AUMLA* 73 (1990), 133–39.

Rossen, Janice. *The University in Modern Fiction*, 149–53.

Wolf, Werner. "Literaturtheorie in der Literatur: David Lodges *Small World* als kritische Auseinandersetzung mit dem Dekonstruktivismus." *Arbeiten aus Anglistik und Amerikanistik* 14:1 (1989), 19–37.

THOMAS LODGE

Rosalynde, 1590

Conlon, Raymond. "Lodge's *Rosalind.*" *Explicator* 50 (1991), 7–9.

MALCOLM LOWRY

Dark as the Grave Wherein My Friend Is Laid, 1968

Barnes, Jim. *Fiction of Malcolm Lowry,* 117–20.
Petruso, Thomas F. *Life Made Real,* 115–18.
Sugars, Cynthia. "The Road to Renewal: *Dark as the Grave* and the Rite of Initiation," in Sherrill Grace, ed., *Swinging the Maelstrom,* 149–59.

Lunar Caustic, 1968

Falk, David. "The Drunken Boat: Malcolm Lowry's *Lunar Caustic.*" *Univ of Mississippi Stud in Engl* 7 (1989), 207–20.
Newton, Norman. "The Loxodromic Curve: A Study of *Lunar Caustic* by Malcolm Lowry." *Canadian Lit* 126 (1990), 65–84.

October Ferry to Gabriola, 1970

Doyen, Victor. "From Innocent Story to Charon's Boat: Reading the 'October Ferry' Manuscripts," in Sherrill Grace, ed., *Swinging the Maelstrom,* 163–96.

Ultramarine, 1933

Shaffer, Brian W. *The Blinding Torch,* 153–60.
Williams, Mark. "Muscular Aesthete: Malcolm Lowry and 1930s English Literary Culture." *J of Commonwealth Lit* 24:1 (1989), 73–85.

Under the Volcano, 1947

Alexander, Marguerite. *Flights from Realism,* 46–49.
Asals, Frederick. "Lowry's Use of Indian Sources in *Under the Volcano.*" *J of Mod Lit* 16 (1989), 113–40.
Asals, Frederick. "Revision and Illusion in *Under the Volcano,*" in Sherrill Grace, ed., *Swinging the Maelstrom,* 93–110.
Barnes, Jim. *Fiction of Malcolm Lowry,* 11–94, 97–116.
Bergonzi, Bernard. *Wartime and Aftermath,* 180–82.
Binns, Ronald. "Filming *Under the Volcano,*" in Sue Vice, ed., *Malcolm Lowry,* 108–23.
Bromley, Roger. "Removing the Landmarks: Malcolm Lowry and the Politics of Cultural Change," in Paul Tiessen, ed., *Apparently Incongruous Parts,* 149–62.
Costa, Richard Hauer. "The Grisly Graphics of Malcolm Lowry," in Paul Tiessen, ed., *Apparently Incongruous Parts,* 71–78.
Hadfield, Duncan. "*Under the Volcano*'s 'Central' Symbols: Trees, Towers and Their Variants," in Paul Tiessen, ed., *Apparently Incongruous Parts,* 80–104.
Heilman, Robert Bechtold. *The Workings of Fiction,* 330–38.

Höfele, Andreas. "Daedalus-Laokoon: Künstlerbild und autobiographische Fiktion bei James Joyce und Malcolm Lowry." *Anglia* 109 (1991), 410–29.

Jewison, D. B. "The Uses of Intertextuality in *Under the Volcano,*" in Sherrill Grace, ed., *Swinging the Maelstrom,* 136–44.

Kim, Suzanne. "Le récit piégé de *Under the Volcano.*" *Etudes Anglaises* 43 (1990), 55–73.

Kums, Guido. "Dovetailing in Depth: *The Waste Land* and *Under the Volcano.*" *New Comparison* 5 (1988), 150–61.

Lengeler, Rainer. "Das Bild Deutschlands im englischen Roman der Nachkriegszeit." *Archiv für das Studium der neueren Sprachen und Literaturen* 229 (1992), 28–31.

MacGregor, Catherine. "Conspiring with the Addict: Yvonne's Co-dependency in *Under the Volcano.*" *Mosaic* 24:3–4 (1991), 145–62.

Miró, Micheline. "Masques et mascarades: les représentations de l'homme-dieu dans *Under the Volcano.*" *Etudes Anglaises* 43 (1990), 169–80.

Mulholland, Joan. "The Consul as Communicator: The Voice under the Volcano," in Sherrill Grace, ed., *Swinging the Maelstrom,* 112–21.

O'Donnell, Patrick. *Echo Chambers,* 116–53.

O'Kill, Brian. "The Role of Language in Lowry's Fiction," in Paul Tiessen, ed., *Apparently Incongruous Parts,* 177–86.

Orr, John. "Doubling and Modernism in *Under the Volcano,*" in Sue Vice, ed., *Malcolm Lowry,* 18–33.

Petruso, Thomas F. *Life Made Real,* 96–115.

Rosenwasser, David. "'Folded Upon Itself, A Burning Castle': The End(s) of the Word in *Under the Volcano.*" *Essays in Lit* (Macomb) 17 (1990), 222–31.

Sage, Victor. "The Art of Sinking in Prose: Charles Jackson, Joyce and *Under the Volcano,*" in Sue Vice, ed., *Malcolm Lowry,* 35–49.

Schulz-Keil, Wieland. "The 67th Reading: *Under the Volcano* and Its Screenplays," in Paul Tiessen, ed., *Apparently Incongruous Parts,* 129–41.

Sepcic, Visnja. "Malcolm Lowry's *Under the Volcano* and the Romantic Tradition." *Studia Romanica et Anglica Zagrabiensia* 34 (1989), 149–65.

Shaffer, Brian W. *The Blinding Torch,* 123–25, 130–33, 136–41, 143–47, 149–59.

Smith, Evans Lansing. *Rape and Revelation,* 83–88.

Suter, Anthony. "Wagner under the Volcano." *Caliban* 27 (1990), 125–35.

Thomas, Hilda. "Praxis as Prophylaxis: A Political Reading of *Under the Volcano,*" in Sherrill Grace, ed., *Swinging the Maelstrom,* 82–92.

Vice, Sue. "Fear of Perfection, Love of Death and the Bottle," in Sue Vice, ed., *Malcolm Lowry,* 92–105.

Vice, Sue. "The *Volcano* of a Postmodern Lowry," in Sherrill Grace, ed., *Swinging the Maelstrom,* 123–33.

Walker, Ronald G. "'The Weight of the Past': Toward a Chronology of *Under the Volcano,*" in Paul Tiessen, ed., *Apparently Incongruous Parts,* 55–69.

Walker, Ronald G., and Leigh Holt. "The Pattern of Faustian Despair: Marlowe's Hero and *Under the Volcano*," in Paul Tiessen, ed., *Apparently Incongruous Parts*, 110–26.

JOHN LYLY

Euphues, 1578

Bates, Catherine. "'A Large Occasion of Discourse': John Lyly and the Art of Civil Conversation." *R of Engl Stud* 42:168 (1991), 469–86.
Erlebach, Peter. *Theorie und Praxis des Romaneingangs*, 112–19.
Lucas, Caroline. *Writing for Women*, 44–47.

ALEXANDER MCARTHUR AND H. KINGSLEY LONG

No Mean City, 1935

Whyte, Christopher. "Imagining the City: The Glasgow Novel," in Joachim Schwend and Horst W. Drescher, eds., *Studies in Scottish Fiction*, 322–25.

ROSE MACAULAY

Non-Combatants and Others, 1916

Boxwell, D. A. "The (M)Other Battle of World War One: The Maternal Politics of Pacifism in Rose Macaulay's *Non-Combatants and Others*." *Tulsa Stud in Women's Lit* 12 (1993), 89–97.
Tylee, Claire M. *The Great War*, 112–18.

The World My Wilderness, 1950

Humm, Maggie. *Border Traffic*, 42–44.
Lassner, Phyllis. "Reimagining the Arts of War: Language and History in Elizabeth Bowen's *The Heat of the Day* and Rose Macaulay's *The World My Wilderness*." *Perspectives on Contemp Lit* 14 (1988), 30–37.

GEORGE MACDONALD

Adela Cathcart, 1864

Honig, Edith Lazaros. *Breaking the Angelic Image*, 48–50.

Alec Forbes of Howglen, 1865

Letley, Emma. *From Galt to Douglas Brown*, 109–11.
Robb, David S. *George MacDonald*, 42–50, 63–64.
Robb, David S. "George MacDonald's Scottish Novels," in William Raeper, ed., *The Gold Thread*, 24–29.

At the Back of the North Wind, 1871

> McGillis, Roderick. "Language and Secret Knowledge in *At the Back of the North Wind,*" in Roderick McGillis, ed., *For the Childlike,* 145–59.
>
> Manlove, Colin. "MacDonald and Kingsley: A Victorian Contrast," in William Raeper, ed., *The Gold Thread,* 152–58.
>
> Pennington, John. "Alice at the Back of the North Wind, Or the Metafictions of Lewis Carroll and George MacDonald." *Extrapolation* 33 (1992), 62–66.
>
> Raeper, William. "Diamond and Kilmeny: MacDonald, Hogg, and the Scottish Folk Tradition," in Roderick McGillis, ed., *For the Childlike,* 133–36.
>
> Riga, Frank. "The Platonic Imagery of George MacDonald and C. S. Lewis: The Allegory of the Cave Transfigured," in Roderick McGillis, ed., *For the Childlike,* 120–21.
>
> Riga, Frank P. "From Time to Eternity: MacDonald's Doorway Between," in Cynthia Marshall, ed., *Essays on C. S. Lewis and George MacDonald,* 83–99.
>
> Robb, David S. *George MacDonald,* 123–28.
>
> Smith, Lesley. "Old Wine in New Bottles: Aspects of Prophecy in George MacDonald's *At the Back of the North Wind,*" in Roderick McGillis, ed., *For the Childlike,* 161–67.

Castle Warlock, 1882

> Robb, David S. *George MacDonald,* 59–62.

David Elginbrod, 1863

> Letley, Emma. *From Galt to Douglas Brown,* 93–105.
>
> Robb, David S. "George MacDonald's Scottish Novels," in William Raeper, ed., *The Gold Thread,* 22–24.

The Golden Key, 1867

> Honig, Edith Lazaros. *Breaking the Angelic Image,* 86–92.

Lilith, 1895

> Cusick, Edmund. "MacDonald and Jung," in William Raeper, ed., *The Gold Thread,* 68–71.
>
> Filmer, Kath. "La Belle Dame sans merci: Cultural Criticism and Mythopoeic Imagination in George MacDonald's *Lilith.*" *Mythlore* 15:4 (1989), 17–20.
>
> Filmer, Kath. "*La Belle Dame Sans Merci:* Cultural Criticism and Mythopoeic Vision in *Lilith,*" in Kath Filmer, ed., *The Victorian Fantasists,* 90–102.
>
> Filmer, Kath. "Neither Here Nor There: The Spirit of Place in George MacDonald's *Lilith* and Lewis' *Till We Have Faces.*" *Mythlore* 16:1 (1989), 9–12.
>
> McGillis, Roderick F. "*Phantastes* and *Lilith:* Femininity and Freedom," in William Raeper, ed., *The Gold Thread,* 31–54.

O'Sullivan, Maurice. " 'Subtly of Herself Contemplative': The Legends of Lilith." *Stud in the Hum* 20 (1993), 15–17.

Pittock, Murray G. H. *Spectrum of Decadence*, 114–15.

Reed, John R. *Victorian Will*, 367–71.

Riga, Frank. "The Platonic Imagery of George MacDonald and C. S. Lewis: The Allegory of the Cave Transfigured," in Roderick McGillis, ed., *For the Childlike*, 121–22.

Robb, David S. *George MacDonald*, 94–108.

Malcolm, 1875

Letley, Emma. *From Galt to Douglas Brown*, 111–17.

Robb, David S. *George MacDonald*, 67–75.

Robb, David S. "George MacDonald's Scottish Novels," in William Raeper, ed., *The Gold Thread*, 21–22.

Phantastes, 1858

McGillis, Roderick. "The Community of the Centre: Structure and Theme in *Phantastes*," in Roderick McGillis, ed., *For the Childlike*, 51–63.

McGillis, Roderick F. "*Phantastes* and *Lilith:* Femininity and Freedom," in William Raeper, ed., *The Gold Thread*, 31–45.

Manlove, Colin. "MacDonald and Kingsley: A Victorian Contrast," in William Raeper, ed., *The Gold Thread*, 147–49.

Muirhead, Graeme A. "Meta-Phantastes: A Self-Referential Faerie Romance for Men and Women." *Scottish Liter J* 19:2 (1992), 36–48.

Palusci, Oriana. " 'The road into Fairy-Land': *Phantastes* di George MacDonald," in Carlo Pagetti, ed., *Nel tempo del sogno*, 13–34.

Pennington, John. "*Phantastes* as Metafiction: George MacDonald's Self-Reflexive Myth." *Mythlore* 14:3 (1988), 26–29.

Robb, David S. *George MacDonald*, 77–94.

The Princess and Curdie, 1883

Sigman, Joseph. "The Diamond in the Ashes: A Jungian Reading of the 'Princess' Books," in Roderick McGillis, ed., *For the Childlike*, 187–93.

The Princess and the Goblin, 1872

Honig, Edith Lazaros. *Breaking the Angelic Image*, 18–20, 126–29.

Patterson, Nancy-Lou. "*Kore* Motifs in *The Princess and the Goblin*," in Roderick McGillis, ed., *For the Childlike*, 169–82.

Robb, David S. *George MacDonald*, 114–23.

Sigman, Joseph. "The Diamond in the Ashes: A Jungian Reading of the 'Princess' Books," in Roderick McGillis, ed., *For the Childlike*, 183–87.

Steig, Michael. *Stories of Reading*, 206–11.

Robert Falconer, 1868

Letley, Emma. *From Galt to Douglas Brown*, 105–11.

Robb, David S. *George MacDonald*, 65–67.

Salted with Fire, 1897

Letley, Emma. *From Galt to Douglas Brown*, 126–28.

Sir Gibbie, 1879

Letley, Emma. *From Galt to Douglas Brown,* 118–26.

Thomas Wingfold, Curate, 1876

Cusick, Edmund. "MacDonald and Jung," in William Raeper, ed., *The Gold Thread,* 72–74.

Wilfrid Cumbermede, 1872

Cusick, Edmund. "MacDonald and Jung," in William Raeper, ed., *The Gold Thread,* 74–75.

Durie, Catherine. "George MacDonald and C. S. Lewis," in William Raeper, ed., *The Gold Thread,* 176–84.

TOM MACDONALD

The Albannach, 1932

Monnickendam, Andrew. "Through the Glass Bleakly: Fionn Mac Colla's View of the Gaelic World in *The Albannach,*" in Joachim Schwend and Horst W. Drescher, eds., *Studies in Scottish Fiction,* 303–14.

Whyte, Christopher. "Imagining the City: The Glasgow Novel," in Joachim Schwend and Horst W. Drescher, eds., *Studies in Scottish Fiction,* 330–32.

IAN MCEWAN

The Cement Garden, 1978

Wicht, Wolfgang. "Ian McEwan: *Der Zementgarten.*" *Weimarer Beiträge* 36 (1990), 1146–56.

The Child in Time, 1987

Massie, Allan. *The Novel Today,* 49–52.

Taylor, D. J. *A Vain Conceit,* 58–59.

JOHN MCGAHERN

Amongst Women, 1990

Gitzen, Julian. "Wheels along the Shannon: The Fiction of John McGahern." *J of Irish Lit* 20:3 (1991), 42–44.

Quinn, Antoinette. "A Prayer for My Daughters: Patriarchy in *Amongst Women.*" *Canadian J of Irish Stud* 17:1 (1991), 79–90.

The Barracks, 1963

Brown, Terence. "Redeeming the Time: The Novels of John McGahern and John Banville," in James Acheson, ed., *The British and Irish Novel,* 161–62.

Gitzen, Julian. "Wheels along the Shannon: The Fiction of John McGahern." *J of Irish Lit* 20:3 (1991), 37–38.

Kamm, Jürgen. "John McGahern," in Rüdiger Imhof, ed., *Contemporary Irish Novelists*, 176–80.

The Dark, 1965

Brown, Terence. "Redeeming the Time: The Novels of John McGahern and John Banville," in James Acheson, ed., *The British and Irish Novel*, 160–61.

Gitzen, Julian. "Wheels along the Shannon: The Fiction of John Mc-Gahern." *J of Irish Lit* 20:3 (1991), 38–39.

Kamm, Jürgen. "John McGahern," in Rüdiger Imhof, ed., *Contemporary Irish Novelists*, 180–83.

The Leavetaking, 1974

Brown, Terence. "Redeeming the Time: The Novels of John McGahern and John Banville," in James Acheson, ed., *The British and Irish Novel*, 161–63.

Gitzen, Julian. "Wheels along the Shannon: The Fiction of John Mc-Gahern." *J of Irish Lit* 20:3 (1991), 39–41.

Kamm, Jürgen. "John McGahern," in Rüdiger Imhof, ed., *Contemporary Irish Novelists*, 183–85.

Killeen, Terence. "Versions of Exile: A Reading of *The Leavetaking*." *Canadian J of Irish Stud* 17:1 (1991), 69–79.

The Pornographer, 1979

Brown, Terence. "Redeeming the Time: The Novels of John McGahern and John Banville," in James Acheson, ed., *The British and Irish Novel*, 161–62.

Gitzen, Julian. "Wheels along the Shannon: The Fiction of John Mc-Gahern." *J of Irish Lit* 20:3 (1991), 41–42.

Kamm, Jürgen. "John McGahern," in Rüdiger Imhof, ed., *Contemporary Irish Novelists*, 185–89.

Lloyd, Richard. "Memory Becoming Imagination: The Novels of John McGahern." *J of Irish Lit* 18:3 (1989), 39–44.

ARTHUR MACHEN

The Great God Pan, 1894

Owens, Jill Tedford. "Arthur Machen's Supernaturalism: The Decadent Variety." *Univ of Mississippi Stud in Engl* 8 (1990), 117–25.

The Hill of Dreams, 1907

Joshi, S. T. *The Weird Tale*, 29–31.

The Secret Glory, 1922

Joshi, S. T. *The Weird Tale*, 18–20.

WILLIAM MCILVANNEY

The Big Man, 1985

> Dixon, Keith. "Writing on the Borderline: The Works of William Mc-
> Ilvanney." *Stud in Scottish Lit* 24 (1989), 147–57.

Docherty, 1975

> Dixon, Keith. "Writing on the Borderline: The Works of William Mc-
> Ilvanney." *Stud in Scottish Lit* 24 (1989), 147–57.

Laidlaw, 1977

> Dentith, Simon. "'This Shitty Urban Machine Humanised': The Urban
> Crime Novel and the Novels of William McIlvanney," in Ian A. Bell and
> Graham Daldry, eds., *Watching the Detectives,* 31–35.

The Papers of Tony Veitch, 1983

> Dentith, Simon. "'This Shitty Urban Machine Humanised': The Urban
> Crime Novel and the Novels of William McIlvanney," in Ian A. Bell and
> Graham Daldry, eds., *Watching the Detectives,* 31–35.

COMPTON MACKENZIE

The Early Life and Adventures of Sylvia Scarlett, 1918

> Orel, Harold. *Popular Fiction in England,* 91–103.

The Four Winds of Love, 1937–1945

> Ross, Ian. "Boxing Compton Mackenzie's Compass: A Turn Round *The
> Four Winds of Love,"* in Joachim Schwend and Horst W. Drescher, eds.,
> *Studies in Scottish Fiction,* 101–14.

Water on the Brain, 1933

> Stafford, David. *The Silent Game,* 87–89.

HENRY MACKENZIE

Julia de Roubigné, 1777

> Michasiw, Kim Ian. "Imitation and Ideology: Henry Mackenzie's Rous-
> seau." *Eighteenth-Cent Fiction* 5 (1993), 153–76.
> Mullan, John. *Sentiment and Sociability,* 131–34.

The Man of Feeling, 1771

> Burling, William J. "A 'sickly sort of refinement': The Problem of Senti-
> mentalism in Mackenzie's *The Man of Feeling." Stud in Scottish Lit* 23
> (1988), 136–47.
> Datta, Kitty. "The Theme of Indian Fortunes in English Fiction from
> Mackenzie to Thackeray: Between Confrontation and Evasions," in
> Jasodhara Bagchi, ed., *Literature, Society and Ideology,* 252–54.
> Hagstrum, Jean H. *Eros and Vision,* 58–59.

Mullan, John. *Sentiment and Sociability,* 118–22.
Probyn, Clive T. *English Fiction,* 160–65.

The Man of the World, 1773

Probyn, Clive T. *English Fiction,* 164–65.

ELIZABETH MACKINTOSH

The Daughter of Time, 1951

Stewart, Ralph. "Richard III, Josephine Tey, and Some Uses of Rhetoric." *Clues* 12:1 (1991), 91–99.

THOMAS MALORY

Le Morte Darthur, 1485

Adderley, C. M. "Malory's Portrayal of Sir Lancelot." *Lang Q* 29:1–2 (1991), 47–65.

Archibald, Elizabeth. "Malory's Ideal of Fellowship." *R of Engl Stud* 43 (1992), 311–28.

Brewer, Derek. "Hauberk and Helm in Malory's *Le Morte Darthur,*" in Takashi Suzuki and Tsuyoshi Mukai, eds., *Arthurian and Other Studies,* 87–93.

Canfield, J. Douglas. *Word as Bond in English Literature,* 179–90.

Cochran, Rebecca. "William Morris: Arthurian Innovator," in Debra N. Mancoff, ed., *The Arthurian Revival,* 80–95.

Couch, Julie Nelson. "With Due Respect: The Royal Court in Malory's 'The Poisoned Apple' and 'The Fair Maid of Astolat,'" in D. Thomas Hanks, Jr., ed., *Sir Thomas Malory,* 63–76.

Drewes, Jeanne. "The Sense of Hidden Identity in Malory's *Morte Darthur,*" in D. Thomas Hanks, Jr., ed., *Sir Thomas Malory,* 17–23.

Edwards, Elizabeth. "Amnesia and Remembrance in Malory's *Morte Darthur.*" *Paragraph* 13:2 (1990), 132–46.

Erlebach, Peter. *Theorie und Praxis des Romaneingangs,* 102–7.

Field, P. J. C. "Hunting, Hawking, and Textual Criticism in Malory's *Morte Darthur,*" in Takashi Suzuki and Tsuyoshi Mukai, eds., *Arthurian and Other Studies,* 95–105.

Field, P. J. C. *The Life and Times of Sir Thomas Malory,* 1–11, 24–26, 32–35, 80–82, 123–27, 142–47, 170–74.

Firmin, Sally. "Deep and Wide: Malory's 'Marvelous Forest,'" in D. Thomas Hanks, Jr., ed., *Sir Thomas Malory,* 26–41.

Goodman, Jennifer R. *The Legend of Arthur,* 46–66.

Grimm, Kevin T. "Knightly Love and the Narrative Structure of Malory's Tale Seven." *Arthurian Interpretations* 3:2 (1989), 76–95.

Hanks, D. Thomas, Jr. "Malory, the *Mort[e]s,* and the Confrontation in Guinevere's Chamber," in D. Thomas Hanks, Jr., ed., *Sir Thomas Malory,* 63–76.

Hendrix, Howard V. *The Ecstasy of Catastrophe,* 47–79.

Heng, Geraldine. "Enchanted Ground: The Feminine Subtext in Malory," in Keith Busby and Erik Kooper, eds., *Courtly Literature,* 283–300.

Hoffman, Donald L. "Malory's Tragic Merlin." *Quondam et Futurus* 1:2 (1991), 15–31.

Hood, Gwenyth E. "Medieval Love-Madness and Divine Love." *Mythlore* 16:3 (1990), 20–28, 34.

Jember, Gregory K. "Chaucer and Malory: Signs of the Times," in Takashi Suzuki and Tsuyoshi Mukai, eds., *Arthurian and Other Studies,* 136–42.

Kayman, Martin A. *From Bow Street to Baker Street,* 24–27.

Kennedy, Beverly. *Knighthood in the "Morte Darthur,"* 1–353.

Kennedy, Beverly. "Notions of Adventure in Malory's *Morte Darthur." Arthurian Interpretations* 3:2 (1989), 38–59.

Kennedy, Edward Donald. "Malory's 'Noble Tale of Sir Launcelot du Lake,' the Vulgate *Lancelot,* and the Post-Vulgate *Roman du Graal,"* in Takashi Suzuki and Tsuyoshi Mukai, eds., *Arthurian and Other Studies,* 107–29.

Kooistra, Lorraine Janzen. "Beardsley's Reading of Malory's *Morte Darthur:* Images of a Decadent World." *Mosaic* 23:1 (1999), 55–72.

Lynch, Andrew. "Good Name and Narrative in Malory." *Nottingham Medieval Stud* 24 (1990), 141–51.

MacBain, Danielle Morgan. "The Tristramization of Malory's Lancelot." *Engl Stud* 74 (1993), 57–65.

McCarthy, Terrence. "Did Morgan le Fay Have a Lover?" *Medium Ævum* 60 (1991), 284–89.

McCarthy, Terrence. *An Introduction,* 1–46, 49–155.

McGuiness, David. "Purple Hearts and Coronets: Caring for Wounds in Malory." *Arthurian Interpretations* 4:1 (1989), 43–54.

Moran, Virginia. "Malory/Guenevere: Sexuality as Deconstruction." *Quondam et Futurus* 1:2 (1991), 70–76.

Morgan, Jeffery L. "Malory's Double Ending: The Duplicitous Death and Departing," in D. Thomas Hanks, Jr., ed., *Sir Thomas Malory,* 91–105.

Mukai, Tsuyoshi. "De Worde's Displacement of Malory's Secularization," in Takashi Suzuki and Tsuyoshi Mukai, eds., *Arthurian and Other Studies,* 179–87.

Noguchi, Shunichi. "Malorian Knights: Their Humility and Patience." *In Geardagum* 10 (1989), 19–27.

Salda, Michael N. "Reconsidering Vinaver's Sources for Malory's 'Tristram.'" *Mod Philology* 88 (1991), 373–81.

Thornton, Ginger. "The Weakening of the King: Arthur's Disintegration in *The Book of Sir Tristram de Lyones,"* in D. Thomas Hanks, Jr., ed., *Sir Thomas Malory,* 3–14.

Thornton, Ginger, and Krista May. "Malory as Feminist? The Role of Percival's Sister in the Grail Quest," in D. Thomas Hanks, Jr., ed., *Sir Thomas Malory,* 43–52.

Waldron, Peter. "'Vertuouse Love' and Adulterous Lovers: Coming to Terms with Malory," in D. Thomas Hanks, Jr., ed., *Sir Thomas Malory,* 54–61.

Welsh, Andrew. "Lancelot at the Crossroads in Malory and Steinbeck."
Philol Q 70 (1991), 485–500.

Withrington, John. "Caxton, Malory, and The Roman War in the *Morte Darthur.*" *Stud in Philology* 89 (1992), 350–66.

MARY DELARIVIERE MANLEY

The Adventures of Rivella, 1714

Donovan, Josephine. "Women and the Rise of the Novel: A Feminist-Marxist Theory." *Signs* 16 (1991), 458–60.

Ross, Deborah. *The Excellence of Falsehood,* 55–60.

Williamson, Marilyn L. *Raising Their Voices,* 219–21.

The New Atalantis, 1709

Bell, Ian A. *Literature and Crime,* 138–39.

Nelson, T. G. A. "Incest in the Early Novel and Related Genres." *Eighteenth-Cent Life* 16:1 (1992), 149–50.

Ross, Deborah. *The Excellence of Falsehood,* 40–55.

Williamson, Marilyn L. *Raising Their Voices,* 221–24.

FREDERIC MANNING

The Middle Parts of Fortune, 1929

Coleman, Verna. *The Last Exquisite,* 2–5, 164–75.

Hibberd, Dominic. *The First World War,* 114–18.

Onions, John. *English Fiction and Drama,* 150–63.

OLIVIA MANNING

Artist Among the Missing, 1945

Baker, Niamh. *Happily Ever After?,* 102–4.

The Balkan Trilogy, 1960

Munton, Alan. *English Fiction,* 99–108.

The Doves of Venus, 1955

Baker, Niamh. *Happily Ever After?,* 119–21.

ROSEMARY MANNING

The Chinese Garden, 1962

Griffin, Gabriele. "*The Chinese Garden:* A Cautionary Tale," in Elaine Hobby and Chris White, eds., *What Lesbians Do in Books,* 134–46.

FREDERICK MARRYAT

Masterman Ready, 1841–1842

Bristow, Joseph. *Empire Boys,* 93–103.
Loxley, Diana. *Problematic Shores,* 95–98, 108–14, 116–26.
Wall, Barbara. *The Narrator's Voice,* 45–48.

RICHARD MARSH

The Beetle, 1897

Hurley, Kelly. " 'The Inner Chambers of All Nameless Sin': *The Beetle,*
Gothic Female Sexuality, and Oriental Barbarism," in Lloyd Davis, ed.,
Virginal Sexuality, 193–213.

CHARLES ROBERT MATURIN

Fatal Revenge, 1807

Magnier, Mireille. "Le Moine Schemoli et la famille Montorio." *Mythes,
Croyances et Religions dans le Monde Anglo-Saxon* 6 (1988), 59–70.

Melmoth the Wanderer, 1820

Aguirre, Manuel. *The Closed Space,* 116–18.
Cornwell, Neil. *The Literary Fantastic,* 75–78.
DeLamotte, Eugenia C. *Perils of the Night,* 60–64.
Fiérobe, Claude. "Irish Homes in the Work of C. R. Maturin," in Jac-
queline Genet, ed., *The Big House in Ireland,* 80–82.
Haggerty, George E. *Gothic Fiction,* 27–33.
Hennlein, Elmar. *Religion und Phantastik,* 37–39, 65–66, 120–21.
Napier, Elizabeth R. *The Failure of Gothic,* 46–48.
Vuillemin, Marie-Christine. "Melmoth the Wanderer: An English Rep-
resentation of Faust." *Mythes, Croyances et Religions dans le Monde
Anglo-Saxon* 7 (1989), 143–49.

The Milesian Chief, 1812

Fiérobe, Claude. "Irish Homes in the Work of C. R. Maturin," in Jacqueline Genet, ed., *The Big House in Ireland,* 75–79.
Leerssen, J. Th. "Fiction Poetics and Cultural Stereotype: Local Colour
in Scott, Morgan, and Maturin." *Mod Lang R* 86 (1991), 278–79.

The Wild Irish Boy, 1808

Fiérobe, Claude. "Irish Homes in the Work of C. R. Maturin," in Jacqueline Genet, ed., *The Big House in Ireland,* 72–79.
Leerssen, J. Th. "Fiction Poetics and Cultural Stereotype: Local Colour
in Scott, Morgan, and Maturin." *Mod Lang R* 86 (1991), 276–78.

WILLIAM SOMERSET MAUGHAM

Cakes and Ale, 1930

> Halperin, John. *Novelists in their Youth,* 233–37.
> Raphael, Frederic. *Somerset Maugham,* 54–58.

Liza of Lambeth, 1897

> Halperin, John. *Novelists in their Youth,* 224–26.
> Raphael, Frederic. *Somerset Maugham,* 10–13.

The Moon and Sixpence, 1919

> Halperin, John. *Novelists in their Youth,* 231–33.

Of Human Bondage, 1915

> Dobrinsky, Joseph. "Les non-dits de la psychologie amoureuse dans *Of Human Bondage.*" *Etudes Anglaises* 41 (1988), 37–47.
> Fleissner, Robert F. *A Rose by Another Name,* 103–15.
> Halperin, John. *Novelists in their Youth,* 208–12, 226–31.
> Noll-Wiemann, Renate. "Maughams *Of Human Bondage* und die Tradition des Entwicklungsromans," in Heinz-Joachim Müllenbrock and Alfons Klein, eds., *Themen in englischsprachiger Literatur,* 321–42.

The Painted Veil, 1925

> Raphael, Frederic. *Somerset Maugham,* 44–46.

The Razor's Edge, 1944

> Halperin, John. *Novelists in their Youth,* 237–42.
> Raphael, Frederic. *Somerset Maugham,* 76–79.
> Whissen, Thomas Reed. *The Devil's Advocates,* 21–22.

FLORA MACDONALD MAYOR

The Third Miss Symons, 1913

> Brown, Penny. *The Poison at the Source,* 214–16.

GEORGE MEREDITH

Beauchamp's Career, 1875

> Harvie, Christopher. *The Centre of Things,* 105–11.
> Reed, John R. *Victorian Will,* 330–32.

Diana of the Crossways, 1885

> Bernstein, Carol L. *The Celebration of Scandal,* 165–67.
> Boumelha, Penny. " 'The Rattling of her Discourse and the Flapping of her Dress': Meredith Writing the 'Women of the Future,' " in Susan Sellers, ed., *Feminist Criticism,* 197–207.
> McGlamery, Gayla. "In His Beginning, His Ends: The 'Preface' to Meredith's *Diana of the Crossways.*" *Stud in the Novel* 23 (1991), 470–86.

Marsh, Joss Lutz. "'Bibliolatry' and 'Bible-Smashing': G. W. Foote, George Meredith, and the Heretic Trope of the Book." *Victorian Stud* 34 (1991), 330–34.

Reed, John R. *Victorian Will*, 337–39.

The Egoist, 1879

Brown, Alanna Kathleen. "The Self and the Other: George Meredith's *The Egoist*," in Katherine Anne Ackley, ed., *Women and Violence in Literature*, 105–38.

Cawthra, Gillian. *Cultural Climate and Linguistic Style*, 26–31, 77–89.

Craig, Randall. "Promising Marriage: *The Egoist*, Don Juan, and the Problem of Language." *ELH* 56 (1989), 897–919.

Dale, Peter Allan. *In Pursuit of a Scientific Culture*, 208–12.

McWhirter, David. "Imagining a Distance: Feminism and Comedy in Meredith's *The Egoist*." *Genre* 22 (1989), 263–83.

Marsh, Joss Lutz. "'Bibliolatry' and 'Bible-Smashing': G. W. Foote, George Meredith, and the Heretic Trope of the Book." *Victorian Stud* 34 (1991), 327–30.

Reed, John R. *Victorian Will*, 335–37.

Schabert, Ina. "*A Literature of the Other:* Die Tradition des *Male Feminism* und George Meredith, *The Egoist*," in Therese Fischer-Seidel, ed., *Frauen und Frauendarstellung*, 235–56.

Wallace, Anne D. *Walking, Literature, and English Culture*, 210–13.

Lord Ormont and His Aminta, 1894

McMaster, Graham. "All for Love: The Imperial Moment in *Lord Ormont and His Aminta*." *Shiron* 30 (1991), 35–55.

One of Our Conquerors, 1891

McGlamery, Gayla S. "'The Malady Afflicting England': *One of Our Conquerors* as Cautionary Tale." *Nineteenth-Cent Lit* 46 (1991), 327–50.

The Ordeal of Richard Feveral, 1859

Halperin, John. *Jane Austen's Lovers*, 48–56.

Horne, Lewis. "Sir Austin, His Devil, and the Well-Designed World." *Stud in the Novel* 24 (192), 35–46.

Marsh, Joss Lutz. "'Bibliolatry' and 'Bible-Smashing': G. W. Foote, George Meredith, and the Heretic Trope of the Book." *Victorian Stud* 34 (1991), 326–27.

Rhoda Fleming, 1865

Marsh, Joss Lutz. "'Bibliolatry' and 'Bible-Smashing': G. W. Foote, George Meredith, and the Heretic Trope of the Book." *Victorian Stud* 34 (1991), 326–27.

Sandra Belloni, 1886

Auerbach, Emily. *Maestros, Dilettantes, and Philistines*, 61–65.

Vittoria, 1867

Auerbach, Emily. *Maestros, Dilettantes, and Philistines*, 61–65.

BETTY MILLER

On the Side of the Angels, 1945

Lassner, Phyllis. "The Quiet Revolution: World War II and the English Domestic Novel." *Mosaic* 23:3 (1990), 93–95. (Also in Evelyn J. Hinz, ed., *Troops versus Tropes,* 93–95.)

A. A. MILNE

Winnie-the-Pooh, 1926

Wall, Barbara. *The Narrator's Voice,* 180–85.

JAMES LESLIE MITCHELL

Grey Granite, 1934

Bell, Ian. "Lewis Grassic Gibbon's Revolutionary Romanticism," in Joachim Schwend and Horst W. Drescher, eds., *Studies in Scottish Fiction,* 264–69.

A Scots Quair, 1932–1934

Bell, Ian. "Lewis Grassic Gibbon's Revolutionary Romanticism," in Joachim Schwend and Horst W. Drescher, eds., *Studies in Scottish Fiction,* 257–69.

Campbell, Ian. *Lewis Grassic Gibbon,* 58–116.

Dixon, Keith. "Rough Edges: The Feminist Representation of Women in the Writing of Lewis Grassic Gibbon," in Joachim Schwend and Horst W. Drescher, eds., *Studies in Scottish Fiction,* 293–99.

Gindin, James. *British Fiction,* 66–73.

Harvie, Christopher. *The Centre of Things,* 183–86.

NAOMI MITCHISON

The Blood of the Martyrs, 1939

Murray, Isobel. "Human Relations: An Outline of Some Major Themes in Naomi Mitchison's Adult Fiction," in Joachim Schwend and Horst W. Drescher, eds., *Studies in Scottish Fiction,* 250–51.

The Bull Calves, 1947

Gifford, Douglas. "Forgiving the Past: Naomi Mitchison's *The Bull Calves,*" in Joachim Schwend and Horst W. Drescher, eds., *Studies in Scottish Fiction,* 221–40.

Cloud Cuckoo Land, 1925

Murray, Isobel. "Human Relations: An Outline of Some Major Themes in Naomi Mitchison's Adult Fiction," in Joachim Schwend and Horst W. Drescher, eds., *Studies in Scottish Fiction,* 248–49.

The Conquered, 1923

> Murray, Isobel. "Human Relations: An Outline of Some Major Themes in Naomi Mitchison's Adult Fiction," in Joachim Schwend and Horst W. Drescher, eds., *Studies in Scottish Fiction,* 245–47.

Lobsters on the Agenda, 1952

> Murray, Isobel. "Human Relations: An Outline of Some Major Themes in Naomi Mitchison's Adult Fiction," in Joachim Schwend and Horst W. Drescher, eds., *Studies in Scottish Fiction,* 252–53.

NICHOLAS MONSARRAT

The Cruel Sea, 1951

> Munton, Alan. *English Fiction,* 77–80.

GEORGE MOORE

The Brook Kerith, 1916

> Orel, Harold. *Popular Fiction in England,* 49–63.
> Orel, Harold. "A Reassessment of George Moore's Achievement in *The Brook Kerith.*" *Engl Lit in Transition* 34 (1991), 167–80.

A Drama in Muslin, 1886

> Goetsch, Paul. "The Country House in George Moore's *A Drama in Muslin,*" in Otto Rauchbauer, ed., *Ancestral Voices,* 79–91.
> Noël, Jean. "George Moore's *Drama in Muslin,*" in Jacqueline Genet, ed., *The Big House in Ireland,* 113–26.

Esther Waters, 1894

> Cirillo, Nancy R. "A Girl Need Never Go Wrong, Or, The Female Servant as Ideological Image in Germinie Lacerteux and Esther Waters." *Compar Lit Stud* 28 (1991), 68–71, 79–87.
> Federico, Annette. "Subjectivity and Story in George Moore's *Esther Waters.*" *Engl Lit in Transition* 36 (1993), 141–53.

The Lake, 1905

> Gonzalez, Alexander G. "The Symbolism of Paralysis in George Moore's *The Lake.*" *Canadian J of Irish Stud* 15:2 (1989), 30–38.

HANNAH MORE

Coelebs in Search of a Wife, 1809

> Krueger, Christine L. *The Reader's Repentance,* 117–24.

CHARLES MORGAN

The Fountain, 1932

> Bracco, Rosa Maria. *'Betwixt and Between,'* 65–66.

SYDNEY MORGAN

Florence Macarthy, 1818

Newcomer, James. *Lady Morgan the Novelist,* 47–58.

The Missionary, 1811

Newcomer, James. *Lady Morgan the Novelist,* 30–31.

The Novice of St. Dominick, 1805

Newcomer, James. *Lady Morgan the Novelist,* 26–30.

The O'Briens and the O'Flaherties, 1827

Brihault, Jean. "Lady Morgan, Mother of the Irish Historical Novel?" *Etudes Irlandaises* 18:1 (1993), 31–36.
Leerssen, J. Th. "Fiction Poetics and Cultural Stereotype: Local Colour in Scott, Morgan, and Maturin." *Mod Lang R* 86 (1991), 279–81.
Newcomer, James. *Lady Morgan the Novelist,* 59–65.

O'Donnel, 1814

Newcomer, James. *Lady Morgan the Novelist,* 40–46.

The Princess, 1833

Newcomer, James. *Lady Morgan the Novelist,* 73–79.

St. Clair, 1802

Newcomer, James. *Lady Morgan the Novelist,* 22–26.

The Wild Irish Girl, 1806

Leerssen, J. Th. "Fiction Poetics and Cultural Stereotype: Local Colour in Scott, Morgan, and Maturin." *Mod Lang R* 86 (1991), 275–78.
Newcomer, James. *Lady Morgan the Novelist,* 28–30, 32–39.

WILLIAM MORRIS

A Dream of John Ball, 1888

Guy, Josephine M. *The British Avant-Garde,* 131–33.
Holzman, Michael. "The Encouragement and Warning of History: William Morris's *A Dream of John Ball,*" in Florence S. Boos and Carole G. Silver, eds., *Socialism and . . . William Morris,* 98–116.
Salmon, Nicholas. "The Revision of *A Dream of John Ball.*" *J of the William Morris Soc* 10:2 (1993), 15–17.

News from Nowhere, 1890

Belsey, Andrew. "Getting Somewhere: Rhetoric and Politics in *News from Nowhere.*" *Textual Practice* 5 (1991), 337–51.
Boos, Florence S., and William Boos. "*News from Nowhere* and Victorian Socialist-Feminism." *Nineteenth-Cent Contexts* 14 (1990), 3–28.
Coleman, Roger. "Design and Technology in Nowhere." *J of the William Morris Soc* 9:2 (1991), 28–39.

Dentith, Simon. *A Rhetoric of the Real,* 119–44.

Donaldson, Laura. "Boffin in Paradise, or the Artistry of Reversal in *News from Nowhere,"* in Florence S. Boos and Carole G. Silver, eds., *Socialism and . . . William Morris,* 26–37.

Fellman, Michael. "Bloody Sunday and *News from Nowhere." J of the William Morris Soc* 8:4 (1990), 9–17.

Francis, Anne Cranny. "The Education of Desire: Utopian Fiction and Feminist Fantasy," in Kath Filmer, ed., *The Victorian Fantasists,* 48–58.

Holm, Jan. "The Old Grumbler at Runnymede." *J of the William Morris Soc* 10:2 (1993), 17–21.

LeMire, Eugene D. "Mind in Morris's Englands." *J of the William Morris Soc* 9:2 (1991), 2–10.

Litton, Alfred G. "'A Great Resource to Us': America and William Morris's Vision in *News from Nowhere." Nineteenth-Cent Prose* 17:2 (1990), 15–23.

Ludlow, Gregory. "Imagining the Future: Mercier's *L'An 2440* and Morris' *News from Nowhere." Compar Lit Stud* 29 (1992), 20–37.

Lutchmansingh, Lawrence D. "Archaeological Socialism: Utopia and Art in William Morris," in Florence S. Boos and Carole G. Silver, eds., *Socialism and . . . William Morris,* 22–25.

MacDonald, Alexander. "Bellamy, Morris, and the Great Victorian Debate," in Florence S. Boos and Carole G. Silver, eds., *Socialism and . . . William Morris,* 78–87.

MacDonald, Alexander. "The Liveliness of *News from Nowhere:* Structure, Language and Allusion." *J of the William Morris Soc* 10:2 (1993), 22–26.

McMaster, Rowland. "Tensions in Paradise: Anarchism, Civilization, and Pleasure in Morris's *News from Nowhere." Engl Stud in Canada* 17 (1991), 73–85.

Marsh, Jan. "*News from Nowhere* as Erotic Dream." *J of the William Morris Soc* 8:4 (1990), 19–23.

Mineo, Ady. "Eros Unbound: Sexual Identities in *News from Nowhere." J of the William Morris Soc* 9:4 (1992), 8–13.

Neetens, Wim. *Writing and Democracy,* 138–45.

Parrinder, Patrick. "News from the Land of No News." *Foundation* 51 (1991), 29–36.

Pinkney, Tony. "Postmodern Space and Morris's Utopia." *News From Nowhere* 9 (1991), 33–48.

Sander, Hans-Jochen. "*News from Nowhere* (1890): William Morris' kommunistische Zukunftsvision als utopischer Diskurs neuen Typs." *Wissenschaftliche Zeitschrift der Friedrich-Schiller-Universität Jena (Gesellschafts- und Sprachwissenschaftliche Reihe)* 38:1 (1989), 98–103.

Sargent, Lyman Tower. "William Morris and the Anarchist Tradition," in Florence S. Boos and Carole G. Silver, eds., *Socialism and . . . William Morris,* 68–71.

Shaw, Christopher. "William Morris and the Division of Labour: The Idea of Work in *News from Nowhere." J of the William Morris Soc* 9:3 (1991), 19–29.

Suvin, Darko. "Counter-Projects: William Morris and the Science Fiction of the 1880s," in Florence S. Boos and Carole G. Silver, eds., *Socialism and . . . William Morris,* 92–97.

Talbot, Norman. "A Guest in the Future: *News from Nowhere,"* in Florence S. Boos and Carole G. Silver, eds., *Socialism and . . . William Morris,* 38–60.

Walle, Alf H. "William Morris' *News from Nowhere:* Socialist Theory in an Age of Flux." *Zeitschrift für Anglistik und Amerikanistik* 38 (1990), 230–32.

Watts, Cedric. *Literature and Money,* 184–89.

The Water of the Wondrous Isles, 1897

Silver, Carole G. "Socialism Internalized: The Last Romances of William Morris," in Florence S. Boos and Carole G. Silver, eds., *Socialism and . . . William Morris,* 124–26.

Talbot, Norman. "Heroine as Hero: Morris's Case Against Quest-Romance," in Kath Filmer, ed., *The Victorian Fantasists,* 25–43.

The Wood Beyond the World, 1894

Mendelson, Michael. *"The Wood Beyond the World* and the Politics of Desire." *Essays in Lit* (Macomb) 18 (1991), 211–31.

Silver, Carole G. "Socialism Internalized: The Last Romances of William Morris," in Florence S. Boos and Carole G. Silver, eds., *Socialism and . . . William Morris,* 122–24.

ARTHUR MORRISON

A Child of the Jago, 1896

Henkle, Roger. "Morrison, Gissing, and the Stark Reality." *Novel* 25 (1992), 306–12.

Neetens, Wim. *Writing and Democracy,* 98–103.

Pittock, Murray G. H. *Spectrum of Decadence,* 104–6.

PENELOPE MORTIMER

Daddy's Gone A-Hunting, 1958

Salzmann-Brunner, Brigitte. *Amanuenses to the Present,* 14–25.

The Handyman, 1983

Salzmann-Brunner, Brigitte. *Amanuenses to the Present,* 55–66.

The Home, 1971

Salzmann-Brunner, Brigitte. *Amanuenses to the Present,* 39–54.

My Friend Says It's Bullet-Proof, 1967

Salzmann-Brunner, Brigitte. *Amanuenses to the Present,* 67–78.

The Pumpkin Eater, 1962

> Salzmann-Brunner, Brigitte. *Amanuenses to the Present,* 26–38.

RALPH HALE MOTTRAM

The Spanish Farm Trilogy, 1927

> Onions, John. *English Fiction and Drama,* 99–109.

EDWIN MUIR

Poor Tom, 1942

> Whyte, Christopher. "Imagining the City: The Glasgow Novel," in Joachim Schwend and Horst W. Drescher, eds., *Studies in Scottish Fiction,* 319–22.

WILLA MUIR

Imagined Corners, 1931

> Robb, David S. "The Published Novels of Willa Muir," in Joachim Schwend and Horst W. Drescher, eds., *Studies in Scottish Fiction,* 149–55.

Mrs. Ritchie, 1933

> Robb, David S. "The Published Novels of Willa Muir," in Joachim Schwend and Horst W. Drescher, eds., *Studies in Scottish Fiction,* 149–55.

DINAH MARIA MULOCK

Hannah, 1871

> Gullette, Margaret Morganroth. "The Puzzling Case of the Deceased Wife's Sister: Nineteenth-Century England Deals with a Second-Chance Plot." *Representations* 31 (1990), 147–50.

IRIS MURDOCH

An Accidental Man, 1971

> Fletcher, John. "Rough Magic and Moral Toughness: Iris Murdoch's Fictional Universe," in James Acheson, ed., *The British and Irish Novel,* 21–22.

The Bell, 1958

> Mettler, Darlene D. *Sound and Sense,* 23–43.
> Sinha, A. K. "Iris Murdoch: The Feminist Perspective," in Sushila Singh, ed., *Feminism and Recent Fiction,* 178–80.

The Black Prince, 1973

Mettler, Darlene D. *Sound and Sense,* 89–102.
Vahali, Diamond Oberoi. "Inter-Textuality, Self-Reflexivity and Self-Consciousness in Murdoch's *The Black Prince.*" *Panjab Univ Res Bull* 21:2 (1990), 53–57.

The Book and the Brotherhood, 1987

Bove, Cheryl. "New Directions: Iris Murdoch's Latest Women," in Lindsey Tucker, ed., *Critical Essays,* 193–94.
Fiddes, Paul S. *Freedom and Limit,* 189–91.
Ramanathan, Suguna. *Iris Murdoch,* 173–203.

Bruno's Dream, 1969

Sertori, Daniela Carpi. "Il racconto del sogno: *Bruno's Dream* di Iris Murdoch e *Pincher Martin* di William Golding." *Lingua e Stile* 24 (1989), 457–65.

A Fairly Honourable Defeat, 1970

Fletcher, John. "Rough Magic and Moral Toughness: Iris Murdoch's Fictional Universe," in James Acheson, ed., *The British and Irish Novel,* 20–21.
Mettler, Darlene D. *Sound and Sense,* 77–88.

The Flight from the Enchanter, 1956

Rice, Thomas Jackson. "The Reader's *Flight from the Enchanter,*" in Lindsey Tucker, ed., *Critical Essays,* 75–82.

The Good Apprentice, 1985

Ramanathan, Suguna. *Iris Murdoch,* 147–72.

Henry and Cato, 1976

Mettler, Darlene D. *Sound and Sense,* 10–12.
Ramanathan, Suguna. *Iris Murdoch,* 39–66.

The Message to the Planet, 1989

Bove, Cheryl. "New Directions: Iris Murdoch's Latest Women," in Lindsey Tucker, ed., *Critical Essays,* 194–96.
Ramanathan, Suguna. *Iris Murdoch,* 204–22.

The Nice and the Good, 1968

Mettler, Darlene D. *Sound and Sense,* 61–76.

Nuns and Soldiers, 1980

Hank, Gary S. "Moral Transcendence in Iris Murdoch's *Nuns and Soldiers:* Apropos of Theocentric Ethics." *Christianity and Lit* 40 (1991), 137–55.
Mettler, Darlene D. *Sound and Sense,* 117–33.
Ramanathan, Suguna. *Iris Murdoch,* 97–121.
Sinha, A. K. "Iris Murdoch: The Feminist Perspective," in Sushila Singh, ed., *Feminism and Recent Fiction,* 183–85.

The Philosopher's Pupil, 1983

> Mettler, Darlene D. *Sound and Sense,* 135–55.
> Ramanathan, Suguna. *Iris Murdoch,* 122–46.

The Red and the Green, 1965

> Scanlan, Margaret. *Traces of Another Time,* 23–39.

The Sea, the Sea, 1978

> Alexander, Marguerite. *Flights from Realism,* 175–82.
> Fletcher, John. "Rough Magic and Moral Toughness: Iris Murdoch's Fictional Universe," in James Acheson, ed., *The British and Irish Novel,* 27–28.
> Mettler, Darlene D. *Sound and Sense,* 103–15.
> Ramanathan, Suguna. *Iris Murdoch,* 67–96.
> Sinha, A. K. "Iris Murdoch: The Feminist Perspective," in Sushila Singh, ed., *Feminism and Recent Fiction,* 182–83.

A Severed Head, 1961

> Arnold, David Scott. *Liminal Readings,* 87–116.
> Fletcher, John. "Rough Magic and Moral Toughness: Iris Murdoch's Fictional Universe," in James Acheson, ed., *The British and Irish Novel,* 18–19.
> Kane, Richard C. "Didactic Demons in Contemporary British Fiction." *Univ of Mississippi Stud in Engl* 8 (1990), 39–44.
> Mettler, Darlene D. *Sound and Sense,* 13–19, 77–80.
> Turner, Jack. "Murdoch vs. Freud in *A Severed Head* and Other Novels." *Lit and Psych* 36:1–2 (1990), 110–19.

A Time of the Angels, 1966

> Mettler, Darlene D. *Sound and Sense,* 45–59.

Under the Net, 1954

> Backus, Guy. *Iris Murdoch,* 47–51.
> Bergonzi, Bernard. *Wartime and Aftermath,* 193–95.
> Hooks, Susan Luck. "Development of Identity: Iris Murdoch's *Under the Net." Notes on Contemp Lit* 23:4 (1993), 6–8.
> O'Connor, Patricia J. "Iris Murdoch: Philosophical Novelist." *New Comparison* 8 (1989), 168–75.

The Unicorn, 1963

> Backus, Guy. *Iris Murdoch,* 117–325.
> Cosenza, Joseph A. "Murdoch's *The Unicorn." Explicator* 50 (1992), 175–77.
> Decap, Roger. "Mythe et modernité: *The Unicorn* d'Iris Murdoch." *Caliban* 27 (1990), 83–96.
> Sinha, A. K. "Iris Murdoch: The Feminist Perspective," in Sushila Singh, ed., *Feminism and Recent Fiction,* 180–81.

A Word Child, 1975

Fletcher, John. "Rough Magic and Moral Toughness: Iris Murdoch's Fictional Universe," in James Acheson, ed., *The British and Irish Novel,* 22–26.

Howard, Catherine E. "'Only Connect': Logical Aesthetic of Fragmentation in *A Word Child.*" *Twentieth Cent Lit* 38 (1992), 54–64.

LEOPOLD HAMILTON MYERS

The Near and the Far, 1929

Belliappa, K. C. *The Image of India,* 135–86.

Belliappa, K. C. "India in L. H. Myers's *The Near and the Far.*" *Liter Criterion* 27:1–2 (1992), 50–65.

V. S. NAIPAUL

A Bend in the River, 1979

Duyck, Rudy. "V. S. Naipaul and John Donne: The Morning After." *J of Commonwealth Lit* 24:1 (1989), 155–61.

Fersch, Annabelle F. "V. S. Naipaul's *A Bend in the River* and the Art of Re-Reading." *Commonwealth Novel in Engl* 4:1 (1991), 69–76.

Kamra, Shashi. *The Novels of V. S. Naipaul,* 116–26, 133–45.

King, Bruce. *V. S. Naipaul,* 117–35.

Weiss, Timothy F. *On the Margins,* 184–93.

The Enigma of Arrival, 1987

Brunton, Roseanne. "The Death Motif in V. S. Naipaul's *The Enigma of Arrival:* The Fusion of Autobiography and Novel as the Enigma of Life-and-Death." *World Lit Written in Engl* 29:2 (1989), 69–82.

Goss, Marjorie Hill. "*The Enigma of Arrival:* Novel as Palimpsest." *Publs of the Arkansas Philol Assoc* 16:1 (1990), 31–39.

Kamra, Shashi. *The Novels of V. S. Naipaul,* 165–72.

King, Bruce. *V. S. Naipaul,* 138–49.

McWatt, Mark. "The West Indian Writer and the Self: Recent 'Fictional Autobiography' by Naipaul and Harris." *J of West Indian Lit* 3:1 (1989), 16–27.

Massie, Allan. *The Novel Today,* 34–36.

Valls-Russell, Janice. "From the Outside In: V. S. Naipaul in Rural England." *Caliban* 27 (1990), 137–47.

Wegner, Hart L. "Glory in the Seasons: The Magical Vision of Landscape." *West Virginia Univ Philol Papers* 37 (1991), 1–8.

Weiss, Timothy F. *On the Margins,* 194–214.

Guerillas, 1975

Bryan, Violet H. "The Sense of Place in Naipaul's *A House for Mr. Biswas* and *Guerillas.*" *Coll Lang Assoc J* 33 (1989), 31–35.

Hassan, Dolly Zulakha. *V. S. Naipaul,* 268–77.

Kamra, Shashi. *The Novels of V. S. Naipaul,* 116–33.

King, Bruce. *V. S. Naipaul,* 99–115.

Kortenaar, Neil ten. "Writers and Readers, the Written and the Read: V. S. Naipaul and *Guerillas." Contemp Lit* 31 (1990), 324–33.

Lolla, Maria Grazia. "V. S. Naipaul's Poetics of Reality: 'The Killings in Trinidad' and *Guerillas." Caribana* 1 (1990), 41–50.

Weiss, Timothy F. *On the Margins,* 177–84.

A House for Mr. Biswas, 1961

Bryan, Violet H. "The Sense of Place in Naipaul's *A House for Mr. Biswas* and *Guerillas." Coll Lang Assoc J* 33 (1989), 26–35.

Golüke, Guido. "Moerasnotities: In het voetspoor van Naipauls *Biswas." Maatstaf* 36:2 (1988), 57–76.

Hassan, Dolly Zulakha. *V. S. Naipaul,* 147–70.

Kamra, Shashi. *The Novels of V. S. Naipaul,* 82–101.

King, Bruce. *V. S. Naipaul,* 36–52, 153–55.

Riley, Geoffrey. "Echoes of Wells in Naipaul's *A House for Mr Biswas." Notes and Queries* 234 (1989), 208–9.

Prickett, Stephen. "Centring the Margins: Postmodernism and Fantasy," in Kath Filmer, ed., *Twentieth-Century Fantasists,* 186–87.

Tsomondo, Thorell. "Metaphor, Metonymy and Houses: Figures of Construction in *A House for Mr. Biswas." World Lit Written in Engl* 29:2 (1989), 83–94.

Tsomondo, Thorell. "Speech and Writing: A Matter of Presence and Absence in *A House for Mr Biswas." Kunapipi* 10:3 (1988), 18–28.

Weiss, Timothy F. *On the Margins,* 46–64.

Miguel Street, 1959

Hassan, Dolly Zulakha. *V. S. Naipaul,* 108–16.

King, Bruce. *V. S. Naipaul,* 17–28.

Weiss, Timothy F. *On the Margins,* 23–31.

The Mimic Men, 1967

Hassan, Dolly Zulakha. *V. S. Naipaul,* 251–63.

Kamra, Shashi. *The Novels of V. S. Naipaul,* 50–59, 70–80.

King, Bruce. *V. S. Naipaul,* 66–80, 153–55.

Weiss, Timothy F. *On the Margins,* 92–104.

Mr. Stone and the Knights Companion, 1963

Kamra, Shashi. *The Novels of V. S. Naipaul,* 82–91, 101–14.

King, Bruce. *V. S. Naipaul,* 56–61.

Weiss, Timothy F. *On the Margins,* 104–10.

The Mystic Masseur, 1957

Hassan, Dolly Zulakha. *V. S. Naipaul,* 117–26.

Kamra, Shashi. *The Novels of V. S. Naipaul,* 50–64, 77–80.

King, Bruce. *V. S. Naipaul,* 28–31.

Weiss, Timothy F. *On the Margins,* 37–45.

The Suffrage of Elvira, 1958

>   Hassan, Dolly Zulakha. *V. S. Naipaul,* 126–36.
>   Kamra, Shashi. *The Novels of V. S. Naipaul,* 50–59, 64–70.
>   King, Bruce. *V. S. Naipaul,* 31–35.
>   Weiss, Timothy F. *On the Margins,* 31–37.

THOMAS NASHE

The Unfortunate Traveller, 1594

>   Erlebach, Peter. *Theorie und Praxis des Romaneingangs,* 127–31.
>   Hutson, Lorna. *Thomas Nashe in Context,* 215–44.
>   Jacobs, Naomi. *The Character of Truth,* 4–6.
>   Margolies, David. "Picaresque Irony in Nashe and Greene." *New Comparison* 11 (1991), 41–42, 45, 48.

JOHN MASON NEALE

Theodora Phranza, 1879

>   Litvack, Leon B. "*Theodora Phranza:* Or, Neale's Fears Realized." *Victorian R* 15:2 (1989), 1–14.

ROBERT NYE

The Voyage of the Destiny, 1982

>   Hassam, Andrew. *Writing and Reality,* 106–11.

EDNA O'BRIEN

Casualties of Peace, 1966

>   Salmon, Mary. "Edna O'Brien," in Rüdiger Imhof, ed., *Contemporary Irish Novelists,* 147–48.

The Country Girls, 1960

>   Salmon, Mary. "Edna O'Brien," in Rüdiger Imhof, ed., *Contemporary Irish Novelists,* 143–45.

Girls in Their Married Bliss, 1964

>   Salmon, Mary. "Edna O'Brien," in Rüdiger Imhof, ed., *Contemporary Irish Novelists,* 145–47.

Johnny I Hardly Knew You, 1977

>   Salmon, Mary. "Edna O'Brien," in Rüdiger Imhof, ed., *Contemporary Irish Novelists,* 151–52.

Night, 1972

>   Salmon, Mary. "Edna O'Brien," in Rüdiger Imhof, ed., *Contemporary Irish Novelists,* 149–50.

FLANN O'BRIEN

At Swim-Two-Birds, 1939

> Alexander, Marguerite. *Flights from Realism,* 36–40.
> Asbee, Sue. *Flann O'Brien,* 19–50.
> Devlin, Joseph. "The Politics of Comedy in *At Swim-Two-Birds.*" *Eire-Ireland* 27:4 (1992), 91–105.
> Gallagher, Monique. "Deux versions modernes de la Légende de Suibhne: *At Swim-Two-Birds* de Flann O'Brien et *Sweeney Astray* de Seamus Heaney." *Etudes Irlandaises* 17:1 (1992), 47–60.
> Gallagher, Monique. *Flann O'Brien,* 8–12, 20–23.
> Gallagher, Monique. "Reflecting Mirrors in Flann O'Brien's *At Swim-Two-Birds.*" *J of Narrative Technique* 22 (1992), 128–35.
> Henry, P. L. "The Structure of Flann O'Brien's *At Swim-Two-Birds.*" *Irish Univ R* 20:1 (1990), 35–40.
> Jacquin, Danielle. "L'étudiant d'*At Swim-Two-Birds* et le paysan de *Tarry Flynn* sur les chemins de la liberté." *Etudes Irlandaises* 15:1 (1990), 85–95.
> O'Grady, Thomas B. "*At Swim-Two-Birds* and the Bardic Schools." *Eire-Ireland* 24:3 (1989), 65–77.
> Shea, Thomas F. *Flann O'Brien's Exorbitant Novels,* 35–37, 46–48, 50–112.

The Dalkey Archive, 1964

> Asbee, Sue. *Flann O'Brien,* 96–109.
> Shea, Thomas F. "The Craft of Seeming Pedestrian: Flann O'Brien's *The Hard Life.*" *Colby Lib Q* 25 (1989), 258–66.
> Shea, Thomas F. "Irony atop Peripeteia: Flann O'Brien's Indian Giving." *Notes on Mod Irish Lit* 1 (1989), 13–21.
> Shea, Thomas F. *Flann O'Brien's Exorbitant Novels,* 152–67.

The Hard Life, 1961

> Asbee, Sue. *Flann O'Brien,* 84–95.
> Shea, Thomas F. *Flann O'Brien's Exorbitant Novels,* 142–52.

The Poor Mouth, 1941

> Asbee, Sue. *Flann O'Brien,* 71–83.

The Third Policeman, 1967

> Asbee, Sue. *Flann O'Brien,* 51–70.
> Booker, M. Keith. "Science, Philosophy, and *The Third Policeman:* Flann O'Brien and the Epistemology of Futility." *South Atlantic R* 56:4 (1991), 37–52.
> Shea, Thomas F. *Flann O'Brien's Exorbitant Novels,* 113–41.
> Tigges, Wim. *An Anatomy of Literary Nonsense,* 205–16.

KATE O'BRIEN

The Ante-Room, 1934

Dalsimer, Adele M. *Kate O'Brien,* 21–32.
Weekes, Ann Owens. *Irish Women Writers,* 117–20.

As Music and Splendour, 1958

Baker, Niamh. *Happily Ever After?,* 79–81, 154–56.
Dalsimer, Adele M. *Kate O'Brien,* 112–23.

The Flower of May, 1953

Dalsimer, Adele M. *Kate O'Brien,* 99–111.

The Land of Spices, 1941

Dalsimer, Adele M. *Kate O'Brien,* 59–72.
Weekes, Ann Owens. *Irish Women Writers,* 120–32.

The Last of Summer, 1943

Dalsimer, Adele M. *Kate O'Brien,* 73–85.

Mary Lavelle, 1936

Dalsimer, Adele M. *Kate O'Brien,* 33–46.
Quiello, Rose. "'Disturbed Desires': The Hysteric in Kate O'Brien's *Mary Lavelle.*" *Eire-Ireland* 25:1 (1990), 46–57.

Pray for the Wanderer, 1938

Dalsimer, Adele M. *Kate O'Brien,* 47–58.

That Lady, 1946

Dalsimer, Adele M. *Kate O'Brien,* 86–98.

Without My Cloak, 1931

Dalsimer, Adele M. *Kate O'Brien,* 5–20.
Favre, Noël. "Symbolisme, sommaire d'irréalité: le personnage de Molly Considine dans *Without My Cloak.*" *Etudes Irlandaises* 17:2 (1992), 67–78.
Weekes, Ann Owens. *Irish Women Writers,* 112–17.

PEADER O'DONNELL

The Big Windows, 1955

Gonzalez, Alexander G. "Intricacies of Glen Life at the Turn of the Century: The Broad Appeal of Peader O'Donnell's *The Big Windows.*" *J of Irish Lit* 20:3 (1991), 19–26.

JULIA O'FAOLAIN

The Irish Signorina, 1984

Imhof, Rüdiger. "Julia O'Faolain," in Rüdiger Imhof, ed., *Contemporary Irish Novelists,* 170–72.

No Country for Young Men, 1980

    Imhof, Rüdiger. "Julia O'Faolain," in Rüdiger Imhof, ed., *Contemporary Irish Novelists,* 164–67.

    Moore, Thomas R. "Triangles and Entrapment: Julia O'Faolain's *No Country for Young Men.*" *Colby Q* 27 (1991), 9–16.

    VanDale, Laura B. "Women Across Time: Sister Judith Remembers." *Colby Q* 27 (1991), 17–26.

    Weekes, Ann Owens. *Irish Women Writers,* 179–90.

The Obedient Wife, 1982

    Imhof, Rüdiger. "Julia O'Faolain," in Rüdiger Imhof, ed., *Contemporary Irish Novelists,* 168–70.

Women in the Wall, 1975

    Imhof, Rüdiger. "Julia O'Faolain," in Rüdiger Imhof, ed., *Contemporary Irish Novelists,* 163–64.

SEAN O'FAOLAIN

Bird Alone, 1936

    Bonaccorso, Richard. *Sean O'Faolain's Irish Vision,* 63–65.

Come Back to Erin, 1940

    Bonaccorso, Richard. *Sean O'Faolain's Irish Vision,* 51–52, 126–27.

A Nest of Simple Folk, 1933

    Bonaccorso, Richard. *Sean O'Faolain's Irish Vision,* 103–8.

    Sampson, Denis. "The Big House in Seán O'Faoláin's Fiction," in Jacqueline Genet, ed., *The Big House in Ireland,* 180–81.

LIAM O'FLAHERTY

The Assassin, 1928

    Friberg, Hedda. "Women in Three Works by Liam O'Flaherty: In Search of an Egalitarian Impulse," in Birgit Bramsbäck, ed., *Homage to Ireland,* 45–61.

Insurrection, 1950

    Klaus, H. Gustav. " 'Carry the Wild Rose of Insurrection': Liam O'Flaherty's Novel on the Easter Rising." *Etudes Irlandaises* 14:1 (1989), 117–25.

The Martyr, 1933

    Friberg, Hedda. "Women in Three Works by Liam O'Flaherty: In Search of an Egalitarian Impulse," in Birgit Bramsbäck, ed., *Homage to Ireland,* 45–61.

MARGARET OLIPHANT

A Beleaguered City, 1880

    Basham, Diana. *The Trial of Woman,* 166–69.

Miss Marjoribanks, 1866

    O'Mealy, Joseph H. "Mrs. Oliphant, Miss Marjoribanks, and the Victorian Canon." *Victorian Newsl* 82 (1992), 44–49.

The Perpetual Curate, 1864

    O'Mealy, Joseph H. "Scenes of Professional Life: Mrs. Oliphant and the New Victorian Clergyman." *Stud in the Novel* 23 (1991), 251–59.

Salem Chapel, 1863

    O'Mealy, Joseph H. "Scenes of Professional Life: Mrs. Oliphant and the New Victorian Clergyman." *Stud in the Novel* 23 (1991), 249–51.

AMELIA OPIE

Adeline Mowbray; or, Mother and Daughter, 1801

    Spencer, Jane. " 'Of Use to Her Daughter': Maternal Authority and Early Women Novelists," in Dale Spender, ed., *Living by the Pen,* 208–10.

GEORGE ORWELL

Burmese Days, 1934

    Ingle, Stephen. *George Orwell,* 8–11.
    Meyers, Valerie. *George Orwell,* 43–59.
    Mukherjee, Sujit. *Forster and Further,* 34–40.
    Page, Norman. *Speech in the English Novel,* 82–83.
    Rai, Alok. *Orwell and the Politics of Despair,* 32–38.

A Clergyman's Daughter, 1935

    Ingle, Stephen. *George Orwell,* 28–31.
    Meyers, Valerie. *George Orwell,* 60–73.

Coming Up for Air, 1939

    Knowles, Sebastian D. G. *A Purgatorial Flame,* 63–65.
    Meyers, Valerie. *George Orwell,* 87–100.
    Rodden, John. *The Politics of Literary Reputation,* 43–46.
    Tindall, Gillian. *Countries of the Mind,* 70–72, 101–3.

Down and Out in Paris and London, 1933

    Ingle, Stephen. *George Orwell,* 25–28.
    Rai, Alok. *Orwell and the Politics of Despair,* 53–55.
    Rodden, John. *The Politics of Literary Reputation,* 175–80.

Homage to Catalonia, 1938

Dentith, Simon. *A Rhetoric of the Real,* 161–69.
Ingle, Stephen. *George Orwell,* 54–56, 68–72.
Meyers, Valerie. *George Orwell,* 14–17.
Rai, Alok. *Orwell and the Politics of Despair,* 81–83.
Rodden, John. *The Politics of Literary Reputation,* 73–78, 80–88.

Keep the Aspidistra Flying, 1936

Ingle, Stephen. *George Orwell,* 31–35.
Meyers, Valerie. *George Orwell,* 74–86.
Rai, Alok. *Orwell and the Politics of Despair,* 38–40, 55–57.
Tindall, Gillian. *Countries of the Mind,* 150–52.

Nineteen Eighty-Four, 1948

Aguirre, Manuel. *The Closed Space,* 177–80.
Argyros, Alexander J. "Chaos versus Contingency Theory: Epistemological Issues in Orwell's *1984.*" *Mosaic* 26:1 (1993), 109–20.
Bergonzi, Bernard. *Wartime and Aftermath,* 99–101.
Bouchard, Guy. "*1984*—Le pouvoir des codes et le code du pouvoir," in Guy Bouchard et al., *Orwell et "1984,"* 81–199.
Combs, James. "Towards 2084: Continuing the Orwellian Tradition," in Robert L. Savage et al., eds., *The Orwellian Moment,* 157–71.
Cooper, Thomas W. "Fictional *1984* and Factual 1984: Ethical Questions Regarding the Control of Consciousness by Mass Media," in Robert L. Savage et al., eds., *The Orwellian Moment,* 83–104.
Cory, Mark E. "Dark Utopia: *1984* and its German Contemporaries," in Robert L. Savage et al., eds., *The Orwellian Moment,* 69–80.
Crick, Bernard. *Essays on Politics and Literature,* 133–65.
Eckstein, Arthur. "*1984* and George Orwell's Other View of Capitalism." *Modern Age* 29:1 (1985), 11–19.
Folks, Jeffrey J. "Orwell on the Environment: Fifty Years Later." *CEA Critic* 54:3 (1992), 56–63.
Friedenberg, Edgar Z. "George Orwell's Neglected Prophecy." *Dalhousie R* 69 (1989), 270–75.
Gray, W. Russel. " 'That Frightful Torrent of Trash': Crime/Detective Fiction and *Nineteen Eighty-Four,*" in Jonathan Rose, ed., *The Revised Orwell,* 123–27.
Harris, Mason. "The Psychology of Power in Tolkien's *The Lord of the Rings,* Orwell's *1984* and Le Guin's *A Wizard of Earthsea.*" *Mythlore* 15:1 (1988), 46–56.
Harvie, Christopher. *The Centre of Things,* 196–200, 224–26.
Hoyles, John. *The Literary Underground,* 136–40.
Ingersoll, Earl G. "The Decentering of Tragic Narrative in George Orwell's *Nineteen Eighty-Four.*" *Stud in the Hum* 16 (1989), 69–82.
Ingle, Stephen. *George Orwell,* 95–106, 116–18.
Kies, Daniel. "Fourteen Types of Passivity: Suppressing Agency in *Nineteen Eighty-Four,*" in Jonathan Rose, ed., *The Revised Orwell,* 47–60.

Lonoff, Sue. "Composing *Nineteen Eighty-Four:* The Art of Nightmare," in Jonathan Rose, ed., *The Revised Orwell*, 25–41.

Matthews, Kenneth. " 'Guardian of the Human Spirit': The Moral Foundation of *Nineteen Eighty-Four.*" *Christianity and Lit* 40 (1991), 157–66.

Meyers, Valerie. *George Orwell*, 114–39.

Nelson, John S. "Orwell's Political Myths and Ours," in Robert L. Savage et al., eds., *The Orwellian Moment*, 11–39.

New, Melvyn. *Telling New Lies*, 108–33.

Newsinger, John. *"Nineteen Eighty-Four* since the Collapse of Communism." *Foundation* 56 (1992), 75–83.

Phelan, James. *Reading People*, 28–43.

Porter, Laurence M. "Psychomachia versus Socialism in *Nineteen Eighty-Four:* A Psychoanalytical View," in Jonathan Rose, ed., *The Revised Orwell*, 61–72.

Rai, Alok. *Orwell and the Politics of Despair*, 116–22, 133–49.

Rocque, André. "L'institution orwellienne," in Guy Bouchard et al., *Orwell et "1984,"* 211–73.

Rodden, John. *The Politics of Literary Reputation*, 119–21, 193–95, 199–211, 288–301.

Rodden, John. "Varieties of Literary Experience: *1984* and George Orwell's 'Prophetic Visions.' " *Zeitschrift für Anglistik und Amerikanistik* 38 (1990), 209–20. [Also in *Engl Stud in Africa* 33 (1990), 111–25.]

Rogers, Richard A. "*1984* to *Brazil:* From the Pessimism of Reality to the Hope of Dreams." *Text and Performance Q* 10:1 (1990), 34–46.

Rose, Jonathan. "The Invisible Sources of *Nineteen Eighty-Four,*" in Jonathan Rose, ed., *The Revised Orwell*, 131–46.

Ruelland, Jacques G. "George Orwell, conscience politique de notre temps," in Guy Bouchard et al., *Orwell et "1984,"* 15–60.

Zuckert, Michael P. "Orwell's Hopes, Orwell's Fears: *1984* as a Theory of Totalitarianism," in Robert L. Savage et al., eds., *The Orwellian Moment*, 45–64.

Zwerdling, Alex. "Rethinking the Modernist Legacy in *Nineteen Eighty-Four,*" in Jonathan Rose, ed., *The Revised Orwell*, 13–23.

The Road to Wigan Pier, 1937

Ingle, Stephen. *George Orwell*, 46–54.

Meyers, Valerie. *George Orwell*, 10–14.

Rai, Alok. *Orwell and the Politics of Despair*, 67–78.

Rodden, John. *The Politics of Literary Reputation*, 43–46.

ROBERT PALTOCK

Peter Wilkins, 1750

Crook, Nora. "*Peter Wilkins:* A Romantic Cult Book," in Philip W. Martin and Robin Jarvis, eds., *Reviewing Romanticism*, 86–95.

MOLLIE PANTER-DOWNES

One Fine Day, 1946

Lassner, Phyllis. "The Quiet Revolution: World War II and the English Domestic Novel." *Mosaic* 23:3 (1990), 97–99. (Also in Evelyn J. Hinz, ed., *Troops versus Tropes,* 97–99.)

WALTER HORATIO PATER

Gaston de Latour, 1896

Reed, John R. *Victorian Will,* 380–82.

Marius the Epicurean, 1885

Adams, James Eli. "Gentleman, Dandy, Priest: Manliness and Social Authority in Pater's Aestheticism." *ELH* 59 (1992), 441–62.

Cawthra, Gillian. *Cultural Climate and Linguistic Style,* 21–26, 66–76.

Guy, Josephine M. *The British Avant-Garde,* 102–5.

Inman, Billie Andrew. "Freud, Pater, and God," in Ann B. Dobie, ed., *Explorations,* 100–116.

Ryals, Clyde de L. *A World of Possibilities,* 114–30.

Stape, J. H. "Comparing Mythologies: Forster's *Maurice* and Pater's *Marius.*" *Engl Lit in Transition* 33 (1990), 141–52.

THOMAS LOVE PEACOCK

Crotchet Castle, 1831

McKay, Margaret. *Peacock's Progress,* 82–87, 98–106, 133–42.

Gryll Grange, 1860

Auerbach, Emily. *Maestros, Dilettantes, and Philistines,* 113–15.

McKay, Margaret. *Peacock's Progress,* 48–52, 87–88, 106–14, 142–54.

Headlong Hall, 1816

Kiernan, Robert F. *Frivolity Unbound,* 20–29.

McKay, Margaret. *Peacock's Progress,* 34–36, 54–60, 91–93.

Maid Marian, 1822

McKay, Margaret. *Peacock's Progress,* 75–78, 129–32.

Melincourt, 1817

McKay, Margaret. *Peacock's Progress,* 61–67, 94–98, 121–25.

The Misfortunes of Elphin, 1829

McKay, Margaret. *Peacock's Progress,* 78–82.

Nightmare Abbey, 1818

Cunningham, Mark. " 'Fatout! who am I?': A Model for the Honourable Mr. Listless in Thomas Love Peacock's *Nightmare Abbey.*" *Engl Lang Notes* 30:1 (1992), 43–45.

Kiernan, Robert F. *Frivolity Unbound,* 29–37.
McKay, Margaret. *Peacock's Progress,* 37–39, 67–75, 125–29.
Wright, Julia M. "Peacock's Early Parody of Thomas Moore in *Nightmare Abbey.*" *Engl Lang Notes* 30:4 (1993), 31–37.

MERVYN PEAKE

Gormenghast, 1950

Gardiner-Scott, Tanya J. *Mervyn Peake,* 99–172.

Titus Alone, 1959

Gardiner-Scott, Tanya J. *Mervyn Peake,* 173–271.

Titus Groan, 1946

Gardiner-Scott, Tanya J. *Mervyn Peake,* 5–98.

HAROLD PINTER

The Dwarfs, 1990

Gillen, Francis. "Between Fluidity and Fixity: Harold Pinter's Novel *The Dwarfs.*" *Pinter R* 1990: 50–60.
Gillen, Francis. " 'To Lay Bare': Pinter, Shakespeare, and *The Dwarfs,* " in Lois Gordon, ed., *Harold Pinter,* 189–99.

JAMES PLUNKETT

Farewell Companions, 1977

Achilles, Jochen. "James Plunkett," in Rüdiger Imhof, ed., *Contemporary Irish Novelists,* 53–56.

Strumpet City, 1969

Achilles, Jochen. "James Plunkett," in Rüdiger Imhof, ed., *Contemporary Irish Novelists,* 49–53.
Newsinger, John. "The Priest in the Irish Novel: James Plunkett's *Strumpet City.*" *Etudes Irlandaises* 14:2 (1989), 65–76.

ANTHONY POWELL

The Acceptance World, 1955

Gorra, Michael. *The English Novel,* 79–81, 87–89.
McEwan, Neil. *Anthony Powell,* 46–49, 85–87.
Selig, Robert L. *Time and Anthony Powell,* 37–38, 41–43, 64–66, 85–89.

Afternoon Men, 1931

Gorra, Michael. *The English Novel,* 60–67.
McEwan, Neil. *Anthony Powell,* 16–22.

Agents and Patients, 1936

>   McEwan, Neil. *Anthony Powell,* 31–35.

At Lady Molly's, 1957

>   McEwan, Neil. *Anthony Powell,* 48–51.
>   Selig, Robert L. *Time and Anthony Powell,* 63–64, 73–74, 91–97.

Books Do Furnish a Room, 1971

>   McEwan, Neil. *Anthony Powell,* 65–67.
>   Selig, Robert L. *Time and Anthony Powell,* 129–36.

A Buyer's Market, 1952

>   Gorra, Michael. *The English Novel,* 84–86.
>   McEwan, Neil. *Anthony Powell,* 44–49, 103–5.
>   Selig, Robert L. *Time and Anthony Powell,* 33–34, 43–44, 60–62, 80–85.

Casanova's Chinese Restaurant, 1960

>   McEwan, Neil. *Anthony Powell,* 52–55.
>   Selig, Robert L. *Time and Anthony Powell,* 48–49, 56–59, 98–103.

A Dance to the Music of Time, 1951–1975

>   Bergonzi, Bernard. *Wartime and Aftermath,* 124–28.
>   Bruce, Donald William. "Anthony Powell: The Reversals and Renewals of Time." *Contemp R* 256 (1990), 309–14; 257 (1990), 40–44.
>   Facknitz, Mark A. R. "Self-Effacement as Revelation: Narration and Art in Anthony Powell's *Dance to the Music of Time.*" *J of Mod Lit* 15 (1989), 519–29.
>   Felber, Lynette. "The Fictional Narrator as Historian: Ironic Detachment and the Project of History in Anthony Powell's *A Dance to the Music of Time.*" *CLIO* 22 (1992), 21–35.
>   Gorra, Michael. *The English Novel,* 71–107.
>   Knowles, Sebastian D. G. *A Purgatorial Flame,* 207–13.
>   McEwan, Neil. *Anthony Powell,* 40–115.
>   McSweeney, Kerry. "The Silver-Grey Discourse of *The Music of Time.*" *Engl Stud in Canada* 18 (1992), 43–57.
>   Massie, Allan. *The Novel Today,* 9–11.
>   Munton, Alan. *English Fiction,* 80–82.
>   Rifelj, Carol de Dobay. *Reading the Other,* 163–227.

The Fisher King, 1986

>   McEwan, Neil. *Anthony Powell,* 126–38.

From a View to a Death, 1933

>   McEwan, Neil. *Anthony Powell,* 28–31.

Hearing Secret Harmonies, 1975

>   McEwan, Neil. *Anthony Powell,* 70–75.
>   Selig, Robert L. *Time and Anthony Powell,* 146–54.

The Kindly Ones, 1962

> McEwan, Neil. *Anthony Powell*, 54–56.
> Selig, Robert L. *Time and Anthony Powell*, 44–48, 103–9.

The Military Philosophers, 1968

> McEwan, Neil. *Anthony Powell*, 60–64.
> Selig, Robert L. *Time and Anthony Powell*, 123–27.

A Question of Upbringing, 1951

> Gorra, Michael. *The English Novel*, 74–77.
> McEwan, Neil. *Anthony Powell*, 40–47.
> Selig, Robert L. *Time and Anthony Powell*, 75–79.

The Soldier's Art, 1966

> McEwan, Neil. *Anthony Powell*, 58–61.
> Selig, Robert L. *Time and Anthony Powell*, 117–23.

Temporary Kings, 1973

> McEwan, Neil. *Anthony Powell*, 67–70, 123–25.
> Selig, Robert L. *Time and Anthony Powell*, 136–46.

The Valley of Bones, 1964

> McEwan, Neil. *Anthony Powell*, 55–58.
> Selig, Robert L. *Time and Anthony Powell*, 110–17.

Venusberg, 1932

> McEwan, Neil. *Anthony Powell*, 22–28.

What's Become of Waring, 1939

> Gorra, Michael. *The English Novel*, 69–80.
> McEwan, Neil. *Anthony Powell*, 35–40.

JOHN COWPER POWYS

After My Fashion, 1980

> Knight, G. Wilson. *Visions & Vices*, 59–62.

A Glastonbury Romance, 1932

> Jones, Ben. "The 'mysterious word Esplumeoir' and Polyphonic Structure in *A Glastonbury Romance*," in Denis Lane, ed., *In the Spirit of Powys*, 71–83.
> Knight, G. Wilson. *Visions & Vices*, 46–51.
> Maxwell, Richard. "The Lie of the Land, or, Plot and Autochthony in John Cowper Powys," in Denis Lane, ed., *In the Spirit of Powys*, 194–201.
> Southwick, A. Thomas. "Rituals of Return," in Denis Lane, ed., *In the Spirit of Powys*, 94–96, 100–103.

Maiden Castle, 1936

> Christensen, Peter G. "The 'Dark Gods' and Modern Society: *Maiden Castle* and *The Plumed Serpent*," in Denis Lane, ed., *In the Spirit of Powys*, 157–61, 165–71, 174–77.

Moran, Margaret. "Animating Fictions in *Maiden Castle*," in Denis Lane, ed., *In the Spirit of Powys*, 180–92.

Owen Glendower, 1940

Knight, G. Wilson. *Visions & Vices*, 93–97.

Porius, 1951

Ballin, Michael. "Porius and the Cauldron of Rebirth," in Denis Lane, ed., *In the Spirit of Powys*, 214–34.

Maxwell, Richard. "The Lie of the Land, or, Plot and Autochthony in John Cowper Powys," in Denis Lane, ed., *In the Spirit of Powys*, 202–11.

Rodmoor, 1916

Knight, G. Wilson. *Visions & Vices*, 61–63.

Weymouth Sands, 1935

Fawkner, H. W. "The Battered Center: John Cowper Powys and Nonbeing," in Denis Lane, ed., *In the Spirit of Powys*, 150–55.

Low, Anthony. "Dry Sand and Wet Sand: Margins and Thresholds in *Weymouth Sands*," in Denis Lane, ed., *In the Spirit of Powys*, 112–33.

Wolf Solent, 1929

Christensen, Peter G. "Jason's Poems in *Wolf Solent*," in Belinda Humfrey, ed., *John Cowper Powys's "Wolf Solent*," 143–57.

Coates, Carole. "Gerda and Christie," in Belinda Humfrey, ed., *John Cowper Powys's "Wolf Solent*," 159–71.

Diffey, T. J. "Not in the Light of Truth: Philosophy and Poetry in *Wolf Solent*," in Belinda Humfrey, ed., *John Cowper Powys's "Wolf Solent*," 69–85.

Easingwood, Peter. "The Face on the Waterloo Steps," in Belinda Humfrey, ed., *John Cowper Powys's "Wolf Solent*," 55–67.

Fawkner, H. W. "The Battered Center: John Cowper Powys and Nonbeing," in Denis Lane, ed., *In the Spirit of Powys*, 142–45.

Hallett, Tony. "Ramsguard to Black Sod: The Setting of *Wolf Solent*." *Powys R* 6:4 (1989), 23–30.

Hodgson, John. " 'A Victim of Self-Vivisection': John Cowper Powys and *Wolf Solent*," in Belinda Humfrey, ed., *John Cowper Powys's "Wolf Solent*," 31–53.

Hughes, Ian. "Allusion, Illusion, and Reality: Fact and Fiction in *Wolf Solent*," in Belinda Humfrey, ed., *John Cowper Powys's "Wolf Solent*," 103–15.

Humfrey, Belinda. " 'Let Our Crooked Smokes Climb . . . from Our Blessed Altars!': *Wolf Solent*—Designs, Writing, Achievement," in Belinda Humfrey, ed., *John Cowper Powys's "Wolf Solent*," 1–30.

Jones, Ben. "The Look of the Other in *Wolf Solent*," in Belinda Humfrey, ed., *John Cowper Powys's "Wolf Solent*," 131–41.

Lane, Denis. "The Elemental Image in *Wolf Solent*," in Denis Lane, ed., *In the Spirit of Powys*, 55–69.

Lock, Charles. "*Wolf Solent:* Myth and Narrative," in Belinda Humfrey, ed., *John Cowper Powys's "Wolf Solent,"* 117–30.

Lukacher, Ned. "Notre-homme-des-fleurs: *Wolf Solent*'s Metaphoric Legends," in Belinda Humfrey, ed., *John Cowper Powys's "Wolf Solent,"* 87–102.

Moran, Margaret. "Creative Lies," in Belinda Humfrey, ed., *John Cowper Powys's "Wolf Solent,"* 191–214.

Samway, Patrick, SJ. "Meditative Thoughts on *Wolf Solent* as Ineffable History," in Denis Lane, ed., *In the Spirit of Powys,* 43–54.

Smith, Penny. "*Wolf Solent:* Exploring the Limits of the Will," in Belinda Humfrey, ed., *John Cowper Powys's "Wolf Solent,"* 215–25.

Tombs, Elizabeth. "*Wolf Solent:* Prodding the Female Substance of the Earth," in Belinda Humfrey, ed., *John Cowper Powys's "Wolf Solent,"* 173–90.

THEODORE FRANCIS POWYS

Innocent Birds, 1926

Williams, John. "T. F. Powys: Absence and Exile in *Innocent Birds.*" *Powys R* 8:2 (1991), 3–10.

Unclay, 1931

Gunnell, Bryn. "T. F. Powys's *Unclay,* or the Unconditional Gift." *Durham Univ J* 85 (1993), 95–103.

CHRISTOPHER PRIEST

The Inverted World, 1974

Greven-Borde, Hélène. "Utopie et science-fiction: le discours des bâtisseurs de cités." *Etudes Anglaises* 41 (1988), 285–86.

J. B. PRIESTLEY

Angel Pavement, 1930

Tindall, Gillian. *Countries of the Mind,* 141–44.

Bright Day, 1946

Tindall, Gillian. *Countries of the Mind,* 110–13.

Daylight on Saturday, 1943

Munton, Alan. *English Fiction,* 47–49.

The Good Companions, 1929

Bracco, Rosa Maria. '*Betwixt and Between,*' 60–62.
Gindin, James. *British Fiction,* 47–49.

They Walk in the City, 1964

Gindin, James. *British Fiction,* 45–48, 50–53, 55–57.

BARBARA PYM

An Academic Question, 1986

>   Weld, Annette. *Barbara Pym and the Novel of Manners,* 180–82.
>   Wyatt-Brown, Anne M. *Barbara Pym,* 120–23.

Crampton Hodnet, 1985

>   Doan, Laura L. "Pym's Singular Interest: The Self as Spinster," in Laura L. Doan, ed., *Old Maids,* 141–46.
>   Holt, Hazel. *A Lot to Ask,* 96–97.
>   Liddell, Robert. *A Mind at Ease,* 22–24.
>   Weld, Annette. *Barbara Pym and the Novel of Manners,* 75–81.
>   Wyatt-Brown, Anne M. *Barbara Pym,* 50–58.

Excellent Women, 1952

>   Griffin, Barbara. "Private Space and Self-Definition in Barbara Pym's *Excellent Women." Essays in Lit* (Macomb) 19 (1992), 132–42.
>   Holt, Hazel. *A Lot to Ask,* 147–54.
>   Kennard, Jean E. "Barbara Pym and Romantic Love." *Contemp Lit* 34:1 (1993), 53–57.
>   Liddell, Robert. *A Mind at Ease,* 38–47.
>   Weld, Annette. *Barbara Pym and the Novel of Manners,* 82–95.
>   Wyatt-Brown, Anne M. *Barbara Pym,* 71–77.

A Few Green Leaves, 1980

>   Gordon, Joan. "Cozy Heroines: Quotidian Bravery in Barbara Pym's Novels." *Essays in Lit* (Macomb) 16 (1989), 231–33.
>   Holt, Hazel. *A Lot to Ask,* 267–68, 272–74.
>   Liddell, Robert. *A Mind at Ease,* 134–43.
>   Rubenstein, Jill. "Comedy and Consolation in the Novels of Barbara Pym." *Renascence* 42 (1990), 177–78.
>   Weld, Annette. *Barbara Pym and the Novel of Manners,* 195–200.
>   Wyatt-Brown, Anne M. *Barbara Pym,* 142–50.

A Glass of Blessings, 1958

>   Baker, Niamh. *Happily Ever After?,* 69–70, 111–12.
>   Halperin, John. *Jane Austen's Lovers,* 207–9.
>   Holt, Hazel. *A Lot to Ask,* 180–81.
>   Liddell, Robert. *A Mind at Ease,* 69–78.
>   Rubenstein, Jill. "Comedy and Consolation in the Novels of Barbara Pym." *Renascence* 42 (1990), 181–83.
>   Weld, Annette. *Barbara Pym and the Novel of Manners,* 105–19.
>   Wyatt-Brown, Anne M. *Barbara Pym,* 91–98.

Jane and Prudence, 1953

>   Baker, Niamh. *Happily Ever After?,* 27–28, 48–49.
>   Brothers, Barbara. "Love, Marriage, and Manners in the Novels of Barbara Pym," in Bege K. Bowers and Barbara Brothers, eds., *Reading and Writing,* 160–69.

Gordon, Joan. "Cozy Heroines: Quotidian Bravery in Barbara Pym's Novels." *Essays in Lit* (Macomb) 16 (1989), 224–26.

Halperin, John. *Jane Austen's Lovers*, 201–5.

Holt, Hazel. *A Lot to Ask*, 164–67, 200–201.

Liddell, Robert. *A Mind at Ease*, 48–58.

Rubenstein, Jill. "Comedy and Consolation in the Novels of Barbara Pym." *Renascence* 42 (1990), 178–81.

Weld, Annette. *Barbara Pym and the Novel of Manners*, 94–105.

Wyatt-Brown, Anne M. *Barbara Pym*, 77–82, 88–91.

Less Than Angels, 1955

Halperin, John. *Jane Austen's Lovers*, 205–7.

Holt, Hazel. *A Lot to Ask*, 168–71.

Liddell, Robert. *A Mind at Ease*, 59–68.

Weld, Annette. *Barbara Pym and the Novel of Manners*, 119–35.

Wyatt-Brown, Anne M. *Barbara Pym*, 85–91.

No Fond Return of Love, 1961

Holt, Hazel. *A Lot to Ask*, 181–84.

Liddell, Robert. *A Mind at Ease*, 79–88.

Weld, Annette. *Barbara Pym and the Novel of Manners*, 135–48.

Wyatt-Brown, Anne M. *Barbara Pym*, 98–104.

Quartet in Autumn, 1977

Gordon, Joan. "Cozy Heroines: Quotidian Bravery in Barbara Pym's Novels." *Essays in Lit* (Macomb) 16 (1989), 226–29.

Holt, Hazel. *A Lot to Ask*, 252–56, 258–61.

Kennard, Jean E. "Barbara Pym and Romantic Love." *Contemp Lit* 34:1 (1993), 58–59.

Liddell, Robert. *A Mind at Ease*, 122–33.

Weld, Annette. *Barbara Pym and the Novel of Manners*, 184–92.

Wyatt-Brown, Anne M. *Barbara Pym*, 123–27, 129–36.

Some Tame Gazelle, 1950

Baker, Niamh. *Happily Ever After?*, 67–68.

Holt, Hazel. *A Lot to Ask*, 143–45, 151–57, 266–67.

Levin, Amy K. *The Suppressed Sister*, 98–103.

Liddell, Robert. *A Mind at Ease*, 11–20.

Weld, Annette. *Barbara Pym and the Novel of Manners*, 56–71.

Wyatt-Brown, Anne M. *Barbara Pym*, 42–46, 65–75.

The Sweet Dove Died, 1978

Gordon, Joan. "Cozy Heroines: Quotidian Bravery in Barbara Pym's Novels." *Essays in Lit* (Macomb) 16 (1989), 229–31.

Halperin, John. *Jane Austen's Lovers*, 209–12.

Holt, Hazel. *A Lot to Ask*, 221–25, 264–66, 270–73.

Liddell, Robert. *A Mind at Ease*, 109–21.

Weld, Annette. *Barbara Pym and the Novel of Manners*, 171–80.

Wyatt-Brown, Anne M. *Barbara Pym*, 114–20.

An Unsuitable Attachment, 1982

> Holt, Hazel. *A Lot to Ask,* 189–202.
> Levin, Amy K. *The Suppressed Sister,* 103–7.
> Liddell, Robert. *A Mind at Ease,* 89–97.
> Weld, Annette. *Barbara Pym and the Novel of Manners,* 149–71.
> Wyatt-Brown, Anne M. *Barbara Pym,* 105–14.

ANN QUIN

Passages, 1969

> Hassam, Andrew. *Writing and Reality,* 93–99.

Three, 1966

> Hassam, Andrew. *Writing and Reality,* 132–38, 149–51.

ANN RADCLIFFE

The Castles of Athlin and Dunbayne, 1789

> Miles, Robert. *Gothic Writing,* 134–37.

Gaston de Blondeville, 1826

> Magnier, Mireille. "Croyances médiévales dans *Gaston de Blondeville* (1826)." *Mythes, Croyances et Religions dans le Monde Anglo-Saxon* 7 (1989), 125–32.

The Italian, 1797

> Aguirre, Manuel. *The Closed Space,* 109.
> Bruce, Donald Williams. "Ann Radcliffe and the Extended Imagination." *Contemp R* 258 (1991), 300–308.
> Conger, Syndy M. "Sensibility Restored: Radcliffe's Answer to Lewis's *The Monk,*" in Kenneth W. Graham, ed., *Gothic Fictions,* 113–49.
> Geary, Robert F. *The Supernatural in Gothic Fiction,* 50–58.
> Greenfield, Susan C. "Veiled Desire: Mother-Daughter Love and Sexual Imagery in Ann Radcliffe's *The Italian.*" *Eighteenth Cent* 33 (1992), 73–86.
> Howells, Coral Ann. "The Pleasure of the Woman's Text: Ann Radcliffe's Subtle Transgressions in *The Mysteries of Udolpho* and *The Italian,*" in Kenneth W. Graham, ed., *Gothic Fictions,* 151–62.
> Magnier, Mireille. "Le Moine Schemoli et la famille Montorio." *Mythes, Croyances et Religions dans le Monde Anglo-Saxon* 6 (1988), 59–70.
> Miles, Robert. *Gothic Writing,* 171–79.
> Napier, Elizabeth R. *The Failure of Gothic,* 133–46.
> Ross, Deborah. *The Excellence of Falsehood,* 147–65.
> Snyder, William C. "Mother Nature's Other Natures: Landscape in Women's Writing, 1770–1830." *Women's Stud* 21 (1992), 155–60.
> Wolstenholme, Susan. *Gothic (Re)Visions,* 15–36.

The Mysteries of Udolpho, 1794

Aguirre, Manuel. *The Closed Space,* 106–9.

Albertazzi, Silvia. *Il sogno gotico,* 33–49.

Bruce, Donald Williams. "Ann Radcliffe and the Extended Imagination." *Contemp R* 258 (1991), 300–308.

Clery, E. J. "The Politics of the Gothic Heroine in the 1790s," in Philip W. Martin and Robin Jarvis, eds., *Reviewing Romanticism,* 71–76.

David, Gail. *Female Heroism in the Pastoral,* 82–110.

DeLamotte, Eugenia C. *Perils of the Night,* 11–13, 29–34.

Duckworth, Alistair M. "Fiction and Some Uses of the Country House Setting from Richardson to Scott," in H. George Hahn, ed., *The Country Myth,* 236–39.

Erlebach, Peter. *Theorie und Praxis des Romaneingangs,* 180–85.

Geary, Robert F. *The Supernatural in Gothic Fiction,* 42–50.

Graham, Kenneth W. "Emily's Demon Lover: The Gothic Revolution and *The Mysteries of Udolpho,*" in Kenneth W. Graham, ed., *Gothic Fictions,* 163–71.

Haggerty, George E. *Gothic Fiction,* 21–24.

Hagstrum, Jean H. *Eros and Vision,* 171–75.

Hatch, Ronald B. "'Lordship and Bondage': Women Novelists of the Eighteenth Century." *REAL: Yrbk of Res in Engl and Am Lit* 8 (1991/92), 235–36.

Heller, Tamar. *Dead Secrets,* 19–25.

Howells, Coral Ann. "The Pleasure of the Woman's Text: Ann Radcliffe's Subtle Transgressions in *The Mysteries of Udolpho* and *The Italian,*" in Kenneth W. Graham, ed., *Gothic Fictions,* 151–62.

Madoff, Mark S. "Inside, Outside, and the Gothic Locked-Room Mystery," in Kenneth W. Graham, ed., *Gothic Fictions,* 49–62.

Miles, Robert. *Gothic Writing,* 76–80.

Napier, Elizabeth R. *The Failure of Gothic,* 100–111.

Roberts, Bette B. "The Horrid Novels: *The Mysteries of Udolpho* and *Northanger Abbey,*" in Kenneth W. Graham, ed., *Gothic Fictions,* 89–111.

Taylor, Michael. "Reluctant Romancers: Self-Consciousness and Derogation in Prose Romances." *Engl Stud in Canada* 17 (1991), 95–97.

The Romance of the Forest, 1791

Miles, Robert. *Gothic Writing,* 131–34, 137–42.

A Sicilian Romance, 1790

Heller, Tamar. *Dead Secrets,* 17–19.

Miles, Robert. *Gothic Writing,* 136–39.

HERBERT READ

The Green Child, 1935

Brown, Richard E. "Worlds of Darkness, Light and Half-Light in *The Green Child.*" *Extrapolation* 31 (1990), 170–86.

CLARA REEVE

The Old English Baron, 1778

Aguirre, Manuel. *The Closed Space,* 93–95.
Geary, Robert F. *The Supernatural in Gothic Fiction,* 32–40.
Miles, Robert. *Gothic Writing,* 109–11.

JEAN RHYS

After Leaving Mr. Mackenzie, 1931

Emery, Mary Lou. *Jean Rhys at "World's End,"* 122–43.
Howells, Coral Ann. *Jean Rhys,* 53–67.
Le Gallez, Paula. *The Rhys Woman,* 54–81.
Naipaul, V. S. "Without a Dog's Chance: *After Leaving Mr. Mackenzie,"*
   in Pierrette M. Frickey, ed., *Critical Perspectives,* 54–58.
Nebeker, Helen E. "The Artist Emerging," in Pierrette M. Frickey, ed.,
   Critical Perspectives, 148–57.
Vincent, Nathalie. "Indices de personne et jeu énonciatif: les voix de Jean
   Rhys." *Caliban* 30 (1993), 77–81.

Good Morning, Midnight, 1939

Bowlby, Rachel. *Still Crazy After All These Years,* 34–57.
Emery, Mary Lou. *Jean Rhys at "World's End,"* 144–72.
Horner, Avril, and Sue Zlosnik. *Landscapes of Desire,* 133–48.
Howells, Coral Ann. *Jean Rhys,* 92–103.
Le Gallez, Paula. *The Rhys Woman,* 114–40.
Vincent, Nathalie. "Indices de personne et jeu énonciatif: les voix de Jean
   Rhys." *Caliban* 30 (1993), 69–77.

Quartet, 1928

Emery, Mary Lou. *Jean Rhys at "World's End,"* 105–21.
Howells, Coral Ann. *Jean Rhys,* 42–52.
Le Gallez, Paula. *The Rhys Woman,* 22–53.
Staley, Thomas F. "The Emergence of a Form: Style and Consciousness in
   Jean Rhys's *Quartet,"* in Pierrette M. Frickey, ed., *Critical Perspectives,*
   129–46.
Vincent, Nathalie. "Indices de personne et jeu énonciatif: les voix de Jean
   Rhys." *Caliban* 30 (1993), 77–81.

Voyage in the Dark, 1934

Emery, Mary Lou. *Jean Rhys at "World's End,"* 63–81, 85–104.
Horner, Avril, and Sue Zlosnik. *Landscapes of Desire,* 148–61.
Howells, Coral Ann. *Jean Rhys,* 68–91.
James, Louis. "Sun Fire—Painted Fire: Jean Rhys as a Caribbean Nov-
   elist," in Pierrette M. Frickey, ed., *Critical Perspectives,* 121–25.
Le Gallez, Paula. *The Rhys Woman,* 82–113.
Morris, Mervyn. "Oh, Give the Girl a Chance: Jean Rhys and *Voyage in
   the Dark." J of West Indian Lit* 3:2 (1989), 1–8.

Wide Saragasso Sea, 1966

Barber-Williams, Patricia. "Jean Rhys and Her French West Indian Counterpart." *J of West Indian Lit* 3:2 (1989), 9–19.

Bender, Todd K. "Jean Rhys and the Genius of Impressionism," in Pierrette M. Frickey, ed., *Critical Perspectives,* 75–84.

Carrera Suárez, Isabel, and Esther Álvarez López. "Social and Personal Selves: Race, Gender and Otherness in Rhys's 'Let Them Call It Jazz' and *Wide Saragasso Sea.*" *Dutch Q R of Anglo-American Letters* 20 (1990), 154–62.

Cliff, Michelle. "Caliban's Daughter: The Tempest and the Teapot." *Frontiers* 12:2 (1991), 36–51.

Curtis, Jan. "The Secret of *Wide Saragasso Sea.*" *Critique* (Washington, DC) 31 (1990), 185–95.

Delourme, Chantal. "La mémoire fécondée. Réflexions sur l'intertextualité: *Jane Eyre, Wide Saragasso Sea.*" *Etudes Anglaises* 42 (1989), 257–68.

Dole, Carol M. "The Nature World in *Jane Eyre* and *Wide Saragasso Sea.*" *West Virginia Univ Philol Papers* 37 (1991), 60–66.

Emery, Mary Lou. *Jean Rhys at "World's End,"* 35–62.

García Rayego, Rosa María. "Apuntes sobre la evolución del punto de vista en la ficción de Jean Rhys: *Wide Saragasso Sea.*" *Revista Alicantina de Estudios Ingleses* 3 (1990), 49–55.

Gregg, Veronica M. "Symbolic Imagery and Mirroring Techniques in *Wide Saragasso Sea,*" in Pierrette M. Frickey, ed., *Critical Perspectives,* 158–65.

Hallidy, Gregory H. "Antoinette's First Dream: The Birth-Fantasy in Jean Rhys' *Wide Saragasso Sea.*" *Notes on Contemp Lit* 21:1 (1991), 8–9.

Hearne, John. "The Wide Saragasso Sea: A West Indian Reflection," in Pierrette M. Frickey, ed., *Critical Perspectives,* 186–93.

Horner, Avril, and Sue Zlosnik. *Landscapes of Desire,* 161–80.

Howells, Coral Ann. *Jean Rhys,* 104–23.

Humm, Maggie. *Border Traffic,* 66–70, 76–81, 83–93.

James, Louis. "Sun Fire—Painted Fire: Jean Rhys as a Caribbean Novelist," in Pierrette M. Frickey, ed., *Critical Perspectives,* 126–27.

Koenen, Anne. "The Fantastic as Feminine Mode: *Wide Saragasso Sea.*" *Jean Rhys R* 4:1 (1990), 15–27.

Lawson, Lori. "Mirror and Madness: A Lacanian Analysis of the Feminine Subject in *Wide Saragasso Sea.*" *Jean Rhys R* 4:2 (1991), 19–27.

Le Gallez, Paula. *The Rhys Woman,* 141–75.

Loe, Thomas. "Patterns of the Zombie in Jean Rhys's *Wide Saragasso Sea.*" *World Lit Written in Engl* 31:1 (1991), 34–42.

Luengo, Anthony. "*Wide Saragasso Sea* and the Gothic Mode," in Pierrette M. Frickey, ed., *Critical Perspectives,* 166–75.

Mellown, Elgin W. "Character and Themes in the Novels of Jean Rhys," in Pierrette M. Frickey, ed., *Critical Perspectives,* 112–16.

Mills, Sara, Lynne Pearce, Sue Spaull, and Elaine Millard. *Feminist Readings,* 94–109.

Olaussen, Maria. "Jean Rhys's Construction of Blackness as Escape from White Femininity in *Wide Saragasso Sea." Ariel* 24:2 (1993), 65–81.

Ramchand, Kenneth. *"Wide Saragasso Sea,"* in Pierrette M. Frickey, ed., *Critical Perspectives,* 194–205.

Robinson, Jeffrey. "Gender, Myth and the White West Indian: Rhys's *Wide Saragasso Sea* and Drayton's *Christopher." Commonwealth Essays and Stud* 13:2 (1991), 22–30.

Robinson, Jeffrey. "The Gorgon's Eye: Visual Imagery and Death in Wide Saragasso Sea and Another Life." *J of West Indian Lit* 4:2 (1990), 46–64.

Starks, Lisa S. "Altars to Attics: The Madwoman's Point of View," in Sara Munson Deats and Lagretta Tallent Lenker, eds., *The Aching Hearth,* 105–16.

Thorpe, Michael. " 'The Other Side': *Wide Saragasso Sea* and *Jane Eyre,"* in Pierrette M. Frickey, ed., *Critical Perspectives,* 178–84.

Vincent, Nathalie. "Indices de personne et jeu énonciatif: les voix de Jean Rhys." *Caliban* 30 (1993), 71–77.

DOROTHY RICHARDSON

Pilgrimage, 1915–1967

Breen, Jennifer. *In Her Own Write,* 15–17.

Brown, Penny. *The Poison at the Source,* 151–213.

Fromm, Gloria G. "Being Old: The Example of Dorothy Richardson," in Anne M. Wyatt-Brown and Janice Rossen, eds., *Aging and Gender,* 258–70.

Levy, Anita. "Gendered Labor, the Woman Writer and Dorothy Richardson." *Novel* 25 (1991), 58–70.

Radford, Jean. "Coming to Terms: Dorothy Richardson, Modernism, and Women." *News From Nowhere* 7 (1989), 28–35.

Stevenson, Randall. *Modernist Fiction,* 36–43.

Trodd, Anthea. *A Reader's Guide,* 74–76.

Würzbach, Natascha. "Subjective Presentation of Characters from the Perspective of Miriam's Experience in Dorothy Richardson's Novel *Pilgrimage:* A Contribution to the Analysis of Constructivist Narrative," in Reingard M. Nischik and Barbara Korte, eds., *Modes of Narrative,* 278–302.

SAMUEL RICHARDSON

Clarissa, 1748

Aikins, Janet E. "Richardson's 'Speaking Pictures,' " in Margaret Anne Doody and Peter Sabor, eds., *Samuel Richardson,* 146–48, 156–63.

Boardman, Michael M. *Narrative Innovation,* 33–36.

Brooks, Christopher. "The Family and 'Familiar' in *Clarissa:* Dictators and Scribes." *Coll Lang Assoc J* 36 (1993), 440–57.

Bull, J. A. *The Framework of Fiction,* 78–82.

Butler, Gerald J. *Henry Fielding,* 63–77.

Cohen, Paula Marantz. "The Anorexic Syndrome and the Nineteenth-Century Domestic Novel," in Lilian R. Furst and Peter W. Graham, eds., *Disorderly Eaters,* 131–33.

Cohen, Paula Marantz. *The Daughter's Dilemma,* 35–58.

Copeland, Edward. "Remapping London: *Clarissa* and the Woman in the Window," in Margaret Anne Doody and Peter Sabor, eds., *Samuel Richardson,* 51–69.

Cox, Stephen. "Sensibility as Argument," in Syndy McMillen Conger, ed., *Sensibility in Transformation,* 70–72.

Cummings, Katherine. *Telling Tales,* 90–156.

Duggan, Margaret. "Gesture and Physical Attitude in Two Novels by Samuel Richardson." *Stud on Voltaire and the Eighteenth Cent* 265 (1989), 1608–10.

Dussinger, John A. "Truth and Storytelling in *Clarissa,*" in Margaret Anne Doody and Peter Sabor, eds., *Samuel Richardson,* 40–50.

Erickson, Robert A. "'Written in the Heart': *Clarissa* and Scripture." *Eighteenth-Cent Fiction* 2 (1989), 17–52.

Erlebach, Peter. *Theorie und Praxis des Romaneingangs,* 161–68.

Fasick, Laura. "The Edible Woman: Eating and Breast-Feeding in the Novels of Samuel Richardson." *South Atlantic R* 58:1 (1993), 23–27.

Fasick, Laura. "Sentiment, Authority, and the Female Body in the Novels of Samuel Richardson." *Essays in Lit* (Macomb) 19 (1992), 196–201.

Ferguson, Frances. "Rape and the Rise of the Novel," in R. Howard Bloch and Frances Ferguson, eds., *Misogyny, Misandry, and Misanthropy,* 98–110.

Flanders, W. Austin. "Urban Life and the Early Novel," in H. George Hahn, ed., *The Country Myth,* 61–62.

Garguilo, René. "*Pamela* et *Clarissa:* textes canoniques du roman sentimental," in Ellen Constans, ed., *Le roman sentimental,* 29–40.

Ghabris, Maryam. "La notion de destin dans les romans de Samuel Richardson." *Etudes Anglaises* 44 (1991), 169–75.

Grundy, Isobel. "'A novel in a series of letters by a lady': Richardson and Some Richardsonian Novels," in Margaret Anne Doody and Peter Sabor, eds., *Samuel Richardson,* 224–29, 231–35.

Gwilliam, Tassie. *Samuel Richardson's Fictions of Gender,* 50–110.

Hannaford, Richard. "Playing Her Dead Hand: Clarissa's Posthumous Letters." *Texas Stud in Lit and Lang* 35 (1993), 79–98.

Harries, Elizabeth W. "Fragments and Mastery: *Dora* and *Clarissa.*" *Eighteenth-Cent Fiction* 5 (1993), 217–38.

Harris, Jocelyn. "Protean Lovelace." *Eighteenth-Cent Fiction* 2 (1990), 327–46.

Harris, Jocelyn. "Richardson: Original or Learned Genius?," in Margaret Anne Doody and Peter Sabor, eds., *Samuel Richardson,* 190–201.

Hensley, David C. "Thomas Edwards and the Dialectics of Clarissa's Death Scene." *Eighteenth-Cent Life* 16:3 (1992), 130–48.

Hilliard, Raymond F. "*Clarissa* and Ritual Cannibalism." *PMLA* 105 (1990), 1083–94.

Hudson, Nicholas. "Arts of Seduction and the Rhetoric of *Clarissa.*" *Mod Lang Q* 51 (1990), 25–43.

Kahn, Madeleine. *Narrative Transvestism,* 103–50.

Keymer, Tom. "Richardson's *Meditations:* Clarissa's *Clarissa,*" in Margaret Anne Doody and Peter Sabor, eds., *Samuel Richardson,* 89–109.

Kraft, Elizabeth. *Character & Consciousness,* 8–11, 59–62.

Kraft, Elizabeth. "Public Nurturance and Private Civility: The Transposition of Values in Eighteenth-Century Fiction." *Stud in Eighteenth-Cent Culture* 22 (1992), 184–86.

Lehmann, Christine. *Das Modell Clarissa.*

Maaouni, Jamila. "Belford narrateur, double de Lovelace dans *Clarissa.*" *Etudes Anglaises* 44 (1991), 129–41.

McMaster, Juliet. "The Body inside the Skin: The Medical Model of Character in the Eighteenth-Century Novel." *Eighteenth-Cent Fiction* 4 (1992), 294–98.

McMaster, Juliet. *The Index of the Mind,* 23–24.

Moravetz, Monika. *Formen der Rezeptionslenkung,* 53–81, 137–79.

Mullan, John. *Sentiment and Sociability,* 63–79, 92–97.

Murray, Douglas. "Classical Myth in Richardson's *Clarissa:* Ovid Revised." *Eighteenth-Cent Fiction* 3 (1991), 113–24.

New, Melvyn. *Telling New Lies,* 39–40.

Ostovich, Helen M. " 'Our *Views* Must Now Be Different': Imprisonment and Friendship in *Clarissa.*" *Mod Lang Q* 52 (1991), 153–69.

Page, Norman. *Speech in the English Novel,* 50–52.

Perry, Ruth. "Colonizing the Breast: Sexuality and Maternity in Eighteenth-Century England." *Eighteenth-Cent Life* 16:1 (1992), 199–203.

Price, John Valdimir. "Patterns of Sexual Behavior in Some Eighteenth-Century Novels," in H. George Hahn, ed., *The Country Myth,* 125–37.

Probyn, Clive T. *English Fiction,* 61–69.

Robinson, David. "Unravelling the 'cord which ties good men to good men': Male Friendship in Richardson's Novels," in Margaret Anne Doody and Peter Sabor, eds., *Samuel Richardson,* 167–77.

Scheuermann, Mona. *Her Bread to Earn,* 60–95.

Spacks, Patricia. "The Novel as Ethical Paradigm," in Mark Spilka and Caroline McCracken-Flesher, eds., *Why the Novel Matters,* 200–202.

Spinner, Kaspar. "Samuel Richardson: *Clarissa, oder die Geschichte einer jungen Dame,*" in H. Kaspar Spinner and Frank-Rutger Hausmann, eds., *Eros—Liebe—Leidenschaft,* 52–69.

Stevenson, John Allen. *The British Novel,* 21–45.

Turner, James Grantham. "Lovelace and the Paradoxes of Libertinism," in Margaret Anne Doody and Peter Sabor, eds., *Samuel Richardson,* 70–88.

Uphaus, Robert W. *The Idea of the Novel,* 31–33.

Varey, Simon. *Space and the Eighteenth-Century English Novel,* 184–96.

Yoder, R. Paul. "Clarissa Regained: Richardson's Redemption of Eve." *Eighteenth-Cent Life* 13:2 (1989), 87–97.

Zimmerman, Everett. "*A Tale of a Tub* and *Clarissa:* A Battling of Books," in Frank Palmeri, ed., *Critical Essays,* 143–59.

Pamela, 1740

Aikins, Janet E. "Richardson's 'Speaking Pictures,'" in Margaret Anne Doody and Peter Sabor, eds., *Samuel Richardson,* 147–56.

Beer, Gillian. "*Pamela:* Rethinking *Arcadia,*" in Margaret Anne Doody and Peter Sabor, eds., *Samuel Richardson,* 23–39.

Brown, Murray L. "Learning to Read Richardson: *Pamela,* 'speaking pictures,' and the Visual Hermeneutic." *Stud in the Novel* 25 (1993), 129–45.

Butler, Gerald J. *Henry Fielding,* 43–46.

Butler, Gerald J. *Love and Reading,* 31–35, 50–53.

Chaber, Lois A. "From Moral Man to Godly Man: 'Mr. Locke' and Mr. B in Part 2 of *Pamela.*" *Stud in Eighteenth-Cent Culture* 18 (1988), 213–47.

Duggan, Margaret. "Gesture and Physical Attitude in Two Novels by Samuel Richardson." *Stud on Voltaire and the Eighteenth Cent* 265 (1989), 1608–10.

Dussinger, John A. "'The Glory of Motion': Carriages and Consciousness in the Early Novel," in H. George Hahn, ed., *The Country Myth,* 214–18.

Fasick, Laura. "The Edible Woman: Eating and Breast-Feeding in the Novels of Samuel Richardson." *South Atlantic R* 58:1 (1993), 19–23.

Fasick, Laura. "Sentiment, Authority, and the Female Body in the Novels of Samuel Richardson." *Essays in Lit* (Macomb) 19 (1992), 194–96.

Folkenflik, Robert. "*Pamela:* Domestic Servitude, Marriage, and the Novel." *Eighteenth-Cent Fiction* 5 (1993), 253–68.

Garguilo, René. "*Pamela* et *Clarissa:* textes canoniques du roman sentimental," in Ellen Constans, ed., *Le roman sentimental,* 29–40.

Georgia, Jennifer. "The Joys of Social Intercourse: Men, Women, and Conversation in the Eighteenth Century," in Kevin L. Cope, ed., *Compendious Conversations,* 252–53.

Ghabris, Maryam. "La notion de destin dans les romans de Samuel Richardson." *Etudes Anglaises* 44 (1991), 169–75.

Grundy, Isobel. "'A novel in a series of letters by a lady': Richardson and Some Richardsonian Novels," in Margaret Anne Doody and Peter Sabor, eds., *Samuel Richardson,* 225–27.

Gwilliam, Tassie. "*Pamela* and the Duplicitous Body of Femininity." *Representations* 34 (1991), 104–28.

Gwilliam, Tassie. *Samuel Richardson's Fictions of Gender,* 15–49.

Hall, K. G. *The Exalted Heroine,* 39–53.

Harris, Jocelyn. "Richardson: Original or Learned Genius?," in Margaret

Anne Doody and Peter Sabor, eds., *Samuel Richardson*, 191–93, 196–98.

Heilman, Robert Bechtold. *The Workings of Fiction*, 37–39.

Kibbie, Ann Louise. "Sentimental Properties: *Pamela* and *Memoirs of a Woman of Pleasure*." *ELH* 58 (1991), 561–68.

McAllister, Marie E. "Popean Echoes in *Pamela:* The Lady Davers Scene." *Papers on Lang & Lit* 28 (1992), 374–77.

McMaster, Juliet. *The Index of the Mind*, 22–29.

Martin, Catherine Gimelli. "On the Persistence of Quest-Romance in the Romantic Genre: The Strange Case of *Pamela*." *Poetics Today* 12 (1991), 87–108.

Mei, Huang. *Transforming the Cinderella Dream*, 7–19.

Mullan, John. *Sentiment and Sociability*, 72–75.

Nickel, Terri. "*Pamela* as Fetish: Masculine Anxiety in Henry Fielding's *Shamela* and James Parry's *The True Anti-Pamela*." *Stud in Eighteenth-Cent Culture* 22 (1992), 37–48.

Oakleaf, David. "Marks, Stamps, and Representations: Character in Eighteenth-Century Fiction." *Stud in the Novel* 23 (1991), 298–300.

Probyn, Clive T. *English Fiction*, 57–61, 78–83.

Schellenberg, Betty A. "Enclosing the Immovable: Structuring Social Authority in *Pamela*—Part II." *Eighteenth-Cent Fiction* 4 (1991), 27–42.

Scheuermann, Mona. *Her Bread to Earn*, 245–47.

Straub, Kristina. "Reconstructing the Gaze: Voyeurism in Richardson's *Pamela*." *Stud in Eighteenth-Cent Culture* 18 (1988), 419–30.

Stuber, Florian. "Teaching *Pamela*," in Margaret Anne Doody and Peter Sabor, eds., *Samuel Richardson*, 8–22.

Tatu, Chantal. "Morphologie des Ereignisses auf den ersten Seiten von 'Pamela oder die belohnte Tugend.'" *Wissenschaftliche Zeitschrift der Ernst Moritz Arndt-Universität Greifswald (Gesellschaftswissenschaftliche Reihe)* 38:2–3 (1989), 73–78.

Varey, Simon. *Space and the Eighteenth-Century English Novel*, 181–92.

Walker, William. "*Pamela* and Skepticism." *Eighteenth-Cent Life* 16:3 (1992), 68–84.

Yeazell, Ruth Bernard. *Fictions of Modesty*, 83–101.

Zhang, John Zaixin. "Free Play in Samuel Richardson's *Pamela*." *Papers on Lang & Lit* 27 (1991), 307–19.

Sir Charles Grandison, 1754

Aikins, Janet E. "Richardson's 'Speaking Pictures,'" in Margaret Anne Doody and Peter Sabor, eds., *Samuel Richardson*, 163–66.

Doody, Margaret Anne. "Identity and Character in *Sir Charles Grandison*," in Margaret Anne Doody and Peter Sabor, eds., *Samuel Richardson*, 110–32.

Duckworth, Alistair M. "Fiction and Some Uses of the Country House Setting from Richardson to Scott," in H. George Hahn, ed., *The Country Myth*, 225–33.

Fasick, Laura. "The Edible Woman: Eating and Breast-Feeding in the Novels of Samuel Richardson." *South Atlantic R* 58:1 (1993), 27–29.

Flynn, Carol Houlihan. "The Pains of Compliance in *Sir Charles Grandison*," in Margaret Anne Doody and Peter Sabor, eds., *Samuel Richardson*, 133–45.

Gard, Roger. *Jane Austen's Novels*, 29–32.

Ghabris, Maryam. "La notion de destin dans les romans de Samuel Richardson." *Etudes Anglaises* 44 (1991), 169–75.

Gordon, Robert C. "Heroism Demilitarized: The Grandison Example." *San José Stud* 15:3 (1989), 28–47.

Grundy, Isobel. "'A novel in a series of letters by a lady': Richardson and Some Richardsonian Novels," in Margaret Anne Doody and Peter Sabor, eds., *Samuel Richardson*, 224–33.

Gwilliam, Tassie. *Samuel Richardson's Fictions of Gender*, 111–60.

Haggerty, George E. "*Sir Charles Grandison* and the 'Language of Nature.'" *Eighteenth-Cent Fiction* 2 (1990), 127–40.

Harris, Jocelyn. "Richardson: Original or Learned Genius?," in Margaret Anne Doody and Peter Sabor, eds., *Samuel Richardson*, 190–94, 196–98.

Mullan, John. *Sentiment and Sociability*, 81–91.

Perry, Ruth. "Colonizing the Breast: Sexuality and Maternity in Eighteenth-Century England." *Eighteenth-Cent Life* 16:1 (1992), 203–5.

Probyn, Clive T. *English Fiction*, 69–74.

Robinson, David. "Unravelling the 'cord which ties good men to good men': Male Friendship in Richardson's Novels," in Margaret Anne Doody and Peter Sabor, eds., *Samuel Richardson*, 176–87.

Zykova, E. "*The History of Sir Charles Grandison* as a Moralistic Utopia of the Age of Enlightenment." *Stud on Voltaire and the Eighteenth Cent* 264 (1989), 1071–74.

ELIZABETH ROBINS

The Convert, 1907

Neetens, Wim. *Writing and Democracy*, 117–25.

Trodd, Anthea. *A Reader's Guide*, 69–71.

REGINA MARIA ROCHE

Clermont, 1798

Miles, Robert. *Gothic Writing*, 98–100.

JANE ROGERS

The Ice Is Singing, 1987

Hassam, Andrew. *Writing and Reality*, 122–24, 127–29.

GEORGINA ROSSETTI

Maude, 1897

Leighton, Angela. " 'When I Am Dead, My Dearest': The Secret of Christina Rossetti." *Mod Philology* 87 (1990), 373–88.

SALMAN RUSHDIE

Grimus, 1975

Cundy, Catherine. " 'Rehearsing Voices': Salman Rushdie's *Grimus." J of Commonwealth Lit* 27:1 (1992), 128–37.

Pathak, R. S. "Salman Rushdie's Treatment of Alienation," in R. S. Pathak, ed., *Indian Fiction in English,* 157–58.

Midnight's Children, 1981

Alexander, Marguerite. *Flights from Realism,* 137–44.

Booker, M. Keith. "Beauty and the Beast: Dualism as Despotism in the Fiction of Salman Rushdie." *ELH* 57 (1990), 977–88.

Cornwell, Neil. *The Literary Fantastic,* 185–87.

Harrison, James. "Reconstructing *Midnight's Children* and *Shame." Univ of Toronto Q* 59 (1990), 399–411.

Ireland, Kenneth R. "Doing Very Dangerous Things: *Die Blechtrommel* and *Midnight's Children." Compar Lit* 42 (1990), 335–59.

Lee, Alison. *Realism and Power,* 46–52, 115–19.

Merivale, Patricia. "Saleem Fathered by Oskar: Intertextual Strategies in *Midnight's Children* and *The Tin Drum." Ariel* 21:3 (1990), 5–19.

Pai, Sudha. "Expatriate Concerns in Salman Rushdie's *Midnight's Children." Liter Criterion* 23:4 (1988), 36–40.

Pathak, R. S. "Salman Rushdie's Treatment of Alienation," in R. S. Pathak, ed., *Indian Fiction in English,* 159–63.

Piwinki, David J. "Losing Eden in Modern Bombay: Rushdie's *Midnight's Children." Notes on Contemp Lit* 23:3 (1993), 10–12.

Rao, M. Madhusudhana. "Quest for Identity: A Study of the Narrative in Rushdie's *Midnight's Children." Liter Criterion* 25:4 (1990), 31–42.

Srivastava, Aruna. " 'The Empire Writes Back': Language and History in *Shame* and *Midnight's Children." Ariel* 20:4 (1989), 63–77.

Verma, Charu. "Padma's Tragedy: A Feminist Deconstruction of Rushdie's *Midnight's Children,"* in Sushila Singh, ed., *Feminism and Recent Fiction,* 154–61.

The Satanic Verses, 1988

Alexander, Marguerite. *Flights from Realism,* 200–206.

Al-Raheb, Hani. "Salman Rushdie's *The Satanic Verses:* Fantasy or Religious Satire." *Liter Criterion* 27:4 (1992), 31–41.

Bader, Rudolf. *"The Satanic Verses:* An Intercultural Experiment by Salman Rushdie." *Intl Fiction R* 19 (1992), 65–75.

Booker, M. Keith. "Beauty and the Beast: Dualism as Despotism in the Fiction of Salman Rushdie." *ELH* 57 (1990), 981–96.

Booker, M. Keith. *"Finnegans Wake* and *The Satanic Verses:* Two Modern Myths of the Fall." *Critique* (Washington, DC) 32 (1991), 190–205.

Close, Anthony. "The Empirical Author: Salman Rushdie's *The Satanic Verses." Philos and Lit* 14 (1990), 248–65.

Cornwell, Neil. *The Literary Fantastic,* 187–97, 219–29.

Donnerstag, Jürgen. " 'Of what type—satanic, angelic—was Farishta's song?' Dekonstruktion als Darstellungsprinzip in Salman Rushdies *The Satanic Verses." Zeitschrift für Anglistik und Amerikanistik* 40 (1992), 227–37.

Knönagel, Alex. *"The Satanic Verses:* Narrative Structure and Islamic Doctrine." *Intl Fiction R* 18 (1991), 69–75.

Malak, Amin. "Reading the Crisis: The Polemics of Salman Rushdie's *The Satanic Verses." Ariel* 20:4 (1989), 176–85.

Malik, Akbar Ali. *"The Satanic Verses,"* 19–71.

Newell, Stephanie. "The Other God: Salman Rushdie's 'New' Aesthetic." *Lit & Hist* 1:2 (1992), 67–85.

Pipes, Daniel. *The Rushdie Affair,* 53–61.

Prickett, Stephen. "Centring the Margins: Postmodernism and Fantasy," in Kath Filmer, ed., *Twentieth-Century Fantasists,* 183–91.

Shahid Ali, Agha. *"The Satanic Verses:* A Secular Muslim's Response." *Yale J of Criticism* 4:1 (1990), 295–300.

Suleri, Sara. "Contraband Histories: Salman Rushdie and the Embodiment of Blasphemy." *Yale R* 78 (1989), 604–24.

Verstraete, Beert C. "Classical References and Themes in Salman Rushdie's *The Satanic Verses." Classical and Mod Lit* 10 (1990), 327–34.

Whitlark, James. *Behind the Great Wall,* 178–79.

Shame, 1983

Booker, M. Keith. "Beauty and the Beast: Dualism as Despotism in the Fiction of Salman Rushdie." *ELH* 57 (1990), 985–96.

Harrison, James. "Reconstructing *Midnight's Children* and *Shame." Univ of Toronto Q* 59 (1990), 405–11.

Moss, Stephanie. "The Cream of the Crop: Female Characters in Salman Rushdie's *Shame." Intl Fiction R* 19 (1992), 28–30.

Pathak, R. S. "Salman Rushdie's Treatment of Alienation," in R. S. Pathak, ed., *Indian Fiction in English,* 163–68.

Srivastava, Aruna. " 'The Empire Writes Back': Language and History in *Shame* and *Midnight's Children." Ariel* 20:4 (1989), 63–77.

VITA SACKVILLE-WEST

All Passion Spent, 1931

Raitt, Suzanne. *Vita and Virginia,* 107–13.

Challenge, 1924

Raitt, Suzanne. *Vita and Virginia,* 92–97.

The Dragon in Shallow Waters, 1921
>   Raitt, Suzanne. *Vita and Virginia,* 58–61.

The Edwardians, 1930
>   Raitt, Suzanne. *Vita and Virginia,* 102–7.

Heritage, 1919
>   Raitt, Suzanne. *Vita and Virginia,* 49–53.

WILLIAM SANSOM

The Body, 1949
>   Bergonzi, Bernard. *Wartime and Aftermath,* 90–92.

SIEGFRIED SASSOON

The Complete Memoirs of George Sherston, 1928–1936
>   Onions, John. *English Fiction and Drama,* 135–49.

MARMION WILME SAVAGE

My Uncle the Curate, 1849
>   Norman, Paralee. "The Island of Higgledy-Piggledy: Marmion Savage's *My Uncle the Curate.*" *Eire-Ireland* 25:4 (1990), 93–110.

DOROTHY L. SAYERS

Busman's Honeymoon, 1937
>   Dale, Alzina Stone. *Maker & Craftsman,* 91–92, 139–40.
>   Reynolds, Barbara. *Dorothy L. Sayers,* 263–66, 270–71.
>   Reynolds, William. "Dorothy L. Sayers' *Busman's Honeymoon* and the Mind of its Maker." *Clues* 10:2 (1989), 65–79.

Clouds of Witness, 1926
>   McCrumb, Sharyn. "Where the Bodies Are Buried: The Real Murder Cases in the Crime Novels of Dorothy L. Sayers," in Alzina Stone Dale, ed., *Dorothy L. Sayers,* 93–95.

The Documents in the Case, 1930
>   Dale, Alzina Stone. *Maker & Craftsman,* 78–79.
>   Keating, H. R. F. "Dorothy L.'s Mickey Finn," in Alzina Stone Dale, ed., *Dorothy L. Sayers,* 134–38.
>   Reynolds, Barbara. *Dorothy L. Sayers,* 213–24.

Gaudy Night, 1936
>   Dale, Alzina Stone. *Maker & Craftsman,* 39–41.
>   Hart, Carolyn G. "*Gaudy Night:* Quintessential Sayers," in Alzina Stone Dale, ed., *Dorothy L. Sayers,* 45–50.

Rahn, B. J. "The Marriage of True Minds," in Alzina Stone Dale, ed., *Dorothy L. Sayers,* 57–63.

Reynolds, Barbara. *Dorothy L. Sayers,* 252–60.

Rossen, Janice. "Oxford *in loco parentis:* The College as Mother in Dorothy Sayers' *Gaudy Night,*" in David Bevan, ed., *University Fiction,* 139–55.

Rossen, Janice. *The University in Modern Fiction,* 36–38.

Say, Elizabeth A. *Evidence on Her Own Behalf,* 90–98.

Murder Must Advertise, 1933

Dale, Alzina Stone. *Maker & Craftsman,* 58–59, 80–81.

Patterson, Nancy-Lou. "A Comedy of Masks: Lord Peter as Harlequin in *Murder Must Advertise.*" *Mythlore* 15:3 (1989), 22–28.

Pitt, Valerie. "Dorothy Sayers: The Masks of Lord Peter," in Clive Bloom, ed., *Twentieth-Century Suspense,* 110–13.

The Nine Tailors, 1934

Kenney, Catherine. "The Comedy of Dorothy L. Sayers," in Alzina Stone Dale, ed., *Dorothy L. Sayers,* 141–43.

Patterson, Nancy-Lou. "A Ring of Good Bells: Providence and Judgement in Dorothy L. Sayers' *The Nine Tailors.*" *Mythlore* 16:1 (1989), 50–52.

Reynolds, Barbara. *Dorothy L. Sayers,* 239–42.

Strong Poison, 1930

Dale, Alzina Stone. *Maker & Craftsman,* 78–79.

McCrumb, Sharyn. "Where the Bodies Are Buried: The Real Murder Cases in the Crime Novels of Dorothy L. Sayers," in Alzina Stone Dale, ed., *Dorothy L. Sayers,* 89–91.

Rahn, B. J. "The Marriage of True Minds," in Alzina Stone Dale, ed., *Dorothy L. Sayers,* 51–55.

Unnatural Death, 1927

Kenney, Catherine. "Detecting a Novel Use for Spinsters in Sayers's Fiction," in Laura L. Doan, ed., *Old Maids,* 123–32.

The Unpleasantness at the Bellona Club, 1928

Pitt, Valerie. "Dorothy Sayers: The Masks of Lord Peter," in Clive Bloom, ed., *Twentieth-Century Suspense,* 106–10.

Whose Body?, 1923

Pitt, Valerie. "Dorothy Sayers: The Masks of Lord Peter," in Clive Bloom, ed., *Twentieth-Century Suspense,* 99–105.

Reynolds, Barbara. *Dorothy L. Sayers,* 101–3, 176–83.

OLIVE SCHREINER

From Man to Man, 1926

Barash, Carol L. "Virile Womanhood: Olive Schreiner's Narratives of a Master Race," in Elaine Showalter, ed., *Speaking of Gender,* 274–77.

Beeton, Ridley. *Facets of Olive Schreiner,* 281–93.

Berkman, Joyce Avrech. *The Healing Imagination,* 11–12, 58–60, 132–36, 147–49, 204–8, 219–21, 227–29.

Monsman, Gerald. *Olive Schreiner's Fiction,* 136–65.

Parkin-Gounelas, Ruth. *Fictions of the Female Self,* 105–18.

The Story of an African Farm, 1883

Ardis, Ann L. *New Women, New Novels,* 61–68.

Banerjee, Jacqueline. "Schreiner's *The Story of an African Farm.*" *Explicator* 48 (1989), 43–45.

Barash, Carol L. "Virile Womanhood: Olive Schreiner's Narratives of a Master Race," in Elaine Showalter, ed., *Speaking of Gender,* 272–74.

Berkman, Joyce Avrech. *The Healing Imagination,* 15–16, 46–51, 69–71, 145–49, 162–64, 202–9, 222–25.

Gorak, Irene E. "Olive Schreiner's Colonial Allegory: *The Story of an African Farm.*" *Ariel* 23:4 (1992), 53–71.

Haynes, Roslynn D. "Dream Allegory in Charles Kingsley and Olive Schreiner," in Kath Filmer, ed., *The Victorian Fantasists,* 161–69.

Holloway, Myles. "Thematic and Structural Organization in Olive Schreiner's *The Story of an African Farm.*" *Engl in Africa* 16:2 (1989), 77–88.

Humm, Maggie. *Border Traffic,* 42–44.

Monsman, Gerald. *Olive Schreiner's Fiction,* 48–107.

Parkin-Gounelas, Ruth. *Fictions of the Female Self,* 101–5.

Scherzinger, Karen. "The Problem of the Pure Woman: South African Pastoralism and Female Rites of Passage." *J of the Dept of Engl* (Calcutta) 29:2 (1991), 29–35.

Trooper Peter Halket, 1897

Berkman, Joyce Avrech. *The Healing Imagination,* 38–39, 109–13, 192, 198–99, 217–18, 223–24.

Jacob, Susan. "Sharers in a Common Hell: The Colonial Text in Schreiner, Conrad and Lessing." *Liter Criterion* 23:4 (1988), 84–86.

Monsman, Gerald. *Olive Schreiner's Fiction,* 110–23.

Undine, 1929

Berkman, Joyce Avrech. *The Healing Imagination,* 9–10, 54, 129–32, 162, 209, 226–27.

Monsman, Gerald. *Olive Schreiner's Fiction,* 36–47.

Parkin-Gounelas, Ruth. *Fictions of the Female Self,* 25–26, 85–86.

PAUL SCOTT

The Alien Sky, 1953

Spurling, Hilary. *Paul Scott,* 188–91.

Weinbaum, Francine S. *Paul Scott,* 16–23.

The Bender, 1963

Weinbaum, Francine S. *Paul Scott,* 62–68.

The Birds of Paradise, 1962

> Moore, Robin. *Paul Scott's Raj*, 34–44.
> Weinbaum, Francine S. *Paul Scott*, 47–61.

The Chinese Love Pavilion, 1960

> Weinbaum, Francine S. *Paul Scott*, 37–47.

The Corrida at San Feliu, 1964

> Spurling, Hilary. *Paul Scott*, 265–68.
> Weinbaum, Francine S. *Paul Scott*, 68–78.

The Day of the Scorpion, 1968

> Moore, Robin. *Paul Scott's Raj*, 77–89.
> Mukherjee, Sujit. *Forster and Further*, 99–102, 242–43.
> Spurling, Hilary. *Paul Scott*, 326–29.

A Division of the Spoils, 1975

> Moore, Robin. *Paul Scott's Raj*, 103–15.
> Mukherjee, Sujit. *Forster and Further*, 102–6.
> Spurling, Hilary. *Paul Scott*, 95–99, 359–70.

The Jewel in the Crown, 1966

> Moore, Robin. *Paul Scott's Raj*, 61–75, 126–28, 134–36.
> Sharpe, Jenny. *Allegories of Empire*, 137–61.
> Spurling, Hilary. *Paul Scott*, 299–311.

Johnnie Sahib, 1952

> Sharma, Lakshmi Raj. "Entering the Text of Paul Scott's *Johnnie Sahib.*"
>   *Liter Criterion* 27:1–2 (1992), 138–47.
> Spurling, Hilary. *Paul Scott*, 178–90.
> Weinbaum, Francine S. *Paul Scott*, 12–16.

A Male Child, 1956

> Spurling, Hilary. *Paul Scott*, 169–71, 205–8.
> Weinbaum, Francine S. *Paul Scott*, 23–30.

The Mark of the Warrior, 1958

> Spurling, Hilary. *Paul Scott*, 207–11.
> Weinbaum, Francine S. *Paul Scott*, 30–36.

The Raj Quartet, 1976

> Gooneratne, Yasmine. "The Expatriate Experience: The Novels of Ruth
>   Prawer Jhabvala and Paul Scott," in James Acheson, ed., *The British
>   and Irish Novel*, 54–57.
> Hannah, Donald. " 'Dirty Typescripts and Very Dirty Typescripts': Paul
>   Scott's Working Methods in *The Raj Quartet.*" *J of Commonwealth Lit*
>   27:1 (1992), 149–68.
> Moore, Robin. *Paul Scott's Raj*, 117–31.
> Petersone, Karina. "The Concept of History in Paul Scott's Tetralogy *The*

Raj Quartet." *Zeitschrift für Anglistik und Amerikanistik* 37 (1989), 228–33.

Spurling, Hilary. *Paul Scott,* 364–74.

Weinbaum, Francine S. *Paul Scott,* 79–191.

Staying On, 1977

Gooneratne, Yasmine. "The Expatriate Experience: The Novels of Ruth Prawer Jhabvala and Paul Scott," in James Acheson, ed., *The British and Irish Novel,* 57–60.

Moore, Robin. *Paul Scott's Raj,* 196–200.

Spurling, Hilary. *Paul Scott,* 378–94.

Weinbaum, Francine S. *Paul Scott,* 192–97.

The Towers of Silence, 1971

Moore, Robin. *Paul Scott's Raj,* 89–102, 171–73.

Spurling, Hilary. *Paul Scott,* 345–47.

SARAH SCOTT AND LADY BARBARA MONTAGU

A Description of Millenium Hall, 1762

Carretta, Vincent. "Utopia Limited: Sarah Scott's *Millenium Hall* and *The History of Sir George Ellison.*" *The Age of Johnson* 5 (1992), 303–23.

Lanser, Susan Sniader. *Fictions of Authority,* 225–31.

The History of Sir George Ellison, 1766

Carretta, Vincent. "Utopia Limited: Sarah Scott's *Millenium Hall* and *The History of Sir George Ellison.*" *The Age of Johnson* 5 (1992), 303–23.

WALTER SCOTT

The Antiquary, 1816

Goetsch, Paul. "Scott's *The Antiquary:* Tradition-Making as Process," in Joachim Schwend et al., eds., *Literatur im Kontext,* 91–106.

Letley, Emma. *From Galt to Douglas Brown,* 285–91.

The Bride of Lammermoor, 1819

Butterworth, Daniel S. "Tinto, Pattieson, and the Theories of Pictorial and Dramatic Representation in Scott's *The Bride of Lammermoor.*" *South Atlantic R* 56:1 (1991), 1–13.

Cairns, John W. "A Note on *The Bride of Lammermoor:* Why Scott did not Mention the Dalrymple Legend until 1830." *Scottish Liter J* 20:1 (1992), 19–33.

Polhemus, Robert M. *Erotic Faith,* 55–78.

Walsh, Catherine Henry. "The Sublime in the Historical Novel: Scott and Gil y Carrasco." *Compar Lit* 42 (1990), 29–37.

Count Robert of Paris, 1832

Simmons, Clare A. "A Man of Few Words: The Romantic Orang-Outang and Scott's *Count Robert of Paris.*" *Scottish Liter J* 17:1 (1990), 21–32.

The Fortunes of Nigel, 1822

Beiderwell, Bruce. *Power and Punishment,* 119–21.

Guy Mannering, 1815

Jordan, Frank. "The Vision of Pandemonium in Scott's Novels." *Scottish Liter J* 19:2 (1992), 24–29.

Orr, Marilyn. " 'The Return of the Different': Rereading in Scott and Calvino." *Dalhousie R* 71 (1991/92), 453–69.

Taylor, Michael. "Reluctant Romancers: Self-Consciousness and Derogation in Prose Romances." *Engl Stud in Canada* 17 (1991), 97–100.

The Heart of Midlothian, 1818

Beiderwell, Bruce. *Power and Punishment,* 62–80.

Duckworth, Alistair M. "Fiction and Some Uses of the Country House Setting from Richardson to Scott," in H. George Hahn, ed., *The Country Myth,* 239–46.

Goodrich, Norma Lorre. *Heroines,* 224–28.

Letley, Emma. *From Galt to Douglas Brown,* 16–22.

Manning, Susan. *The Puritan-Provincial Vision,* 171–81.

Millgate, Jane. "Scott and the Law: *The Heart of Midlothian,*" in M. L. Friedland, ed., *Rough Justice,* 95–108.

Page, Norman. *Speech in the English Novel,* 60–63.

Roy, Ross. "The Bible in Burns and Scott," in David F. Wright et al., eds., *The Bible in Scottish Life and Literature,* 88–89.

Schofield, Mary Anne. "The 'Heart' of Midlothian: Jeanie Deans as Narrator." *Stud in Eighteenth-Cent Culture* 19 (1989), 153–63.

Shaw, Harry E. "Scott's 'Daemon' and the Voices of Historical Narration." *JEGP* 88 (1989), 21–33.

Wagenknecht, Edward. *Sir Walter Scott,* 77–79.

Ivanhoe, 1819

Beiderwell, Bruce. *Power and Punishment,* 81–99.

Erlebach, Peter. *Theorie und Praxis des Romaneingangs,* 192–98.

Jordan, Frank. "The Vision of Pandemonium in Scott's Novels." *Scottish Liter J* 19:2 (1992), 32–34.

Ragussis, Michael. "Writing Nationalist History: England, the Conversion of the Jews, and *Ivanhoe.*" *ELH* 60 (1993), 181–213.

Wagenknecht, Edward. *Sir Walter Scott,* 81–83.

Walsh, Catherine Henry. "The Sublime in the Historical Novel: Scott and Gil y Carrasco." *Compar Lit* 42 (1990), 29–37.

Kenilworth, 1821

Alexander, J. H. "The Major Images in *Kenilworth.*" *Scottish Liter J* 17:2 (1990), 27–35.

The Legend of Montrose, 1819

Beiderwell, Bruce. *Power and Punishment,* 49–50.

Old Mortality, 1816

Beiderwell, Bruce. *Power and Punishment,* 28–44.

Dickson, Beth. "Sir Walter Scott and the Limits of Toleration." *Scottish Liter J* 18:2 (1991), 46–61.

Jordan, Frank. "The Vision of Pandemonium in Scott's Novels." *Scottish Liter J* 19:2 (1992), 31–32.

Letley, Emma. *From Galt to Douglas Brown,* 34–40.

McCracken-Flesher, Caroline. "Thinking Nationally/Writing Colonially? Scott, Stevenson, and England." *Novel* 24 (1991), 301–9.

Roy, Ross. "The Bible in Burns and Scott," in David F. Wright et al., eds., *The Bible in Scottish Life and Literature,* 86–87.

Wagenknecht, Edward. *Sir Walter Scott,* 72–75.

The Pirate, 1821

Orr, Marilyn. "Repetition, Reversal, and the Gothic: *The Pirate* and *St. Ronan's Well.*" *Engl Stud in Canada* 16 (1990), 187–92.

Quentin Durward, 1823

Lackey, Lionel. "Plausibility and the Romantic Plot Construction of *Quentin Durward.*" *Stud in Philology* 90 (1993), 101–14.

Wagenknecht, Edward. *Sir Walter Scott,* 87–89.

Redgauntlet, 1824

Beiderwell, Bruce. *Power and Punishment,* 100–117.

Beiderwell, Bruce. "Scott's *Redgauntlet* as a Romance of Power." *Stud in Romanticism* 28 (1989), 273–89.

Maitzen, Rohan. "'By No Means an Improbable Fiction': *Redgauntlet's* Novel Historicism." *Stud in the Novel* 25 (1993), 170–80.

Manning, Susan. *The Puritan-Provincial Vision,* 88–96.

Morère, Pierre. "Histoire et récit dans *Redgauntlet* de Walter Scott." *Caliban* 28 (1991), 25–35.

Wilkes, Joanne. "Scott's Use of Scottish Family History in *Redgauntlet.*" *R of Engl Stud* 41 (1990), 200–211.

Rob Roy, 1817

Agovi, K. E. *Novels of Social Change,* 111–30.

Beiderwell, Bruce. *Power and Punishment,* 45–61.

Roy, Ross. "The Bible in Burns and Scott," in David F. Wright et al., eds., *The Bible in Scottish Life and Literature,* 87–88.

Wagenknecht, Edward. *Sir Walter Scott,* 75–77, 105–7.

St. Ronan's Well, 1824

Buck, H. Michael. "A Message in her Madness: Socio-Political Bias in Scott's Portrayal of Mad Clara Mowbray of *St. Ronan's Well.*" *Stud in Scottish Lit* 24 (1989), 181–93.

Orr, Marilyn. "Repetition, Reversal, and the Gothic: *The Pirate* and *St. Ronan's Well.*" *Engl Stud in Canada* 16 (1990), 193–98.

The Talisman, 1825

Beiderwell, Bruce. *Power and Punishment,* 81–99.
Goodrich, Norma Lorre. *Heroines,* 224–25, 231–33.
Wagenknecht, Edward. *Sir Walter Scott,* 91–93.

Waverley, 1814

Agovi, K. E. *Novels of Social Change,* 79–111.
Beiderwell, Bruce. *Power and Punishment,* 11–27.
Bull, J. A. *The Framework of Fiction,* 90–103.
Crawford, Robert. *Devolving English Literature,* 121–33.
Elam, Diane. *Romancing the Postmodern,* 54–57, 60–62, 64–68, 76–78, 104–6.
Ferris, Ina. "Re-Positioning the Novel: *Waverley* and the Gender of Fiction." *Stud in Romanticism* 28 (1989), 291–301.
Garside, Peter. "Popular Fiction and the National Tale: Hidden Origins of Scott's *Waverley.*" *Nineteenth-Cent Lit* 46 (1991), 30–53.
Jordan, Frank. "The Vision of Pandemonium in Scott's Novels." *Scottish Liter J* 19:2 (1992), 29–31.
Lamont, Claire. "*Waverley* and the Battle of Culloden," in Angus Easson, ed., *History and the Novel,* 14–26.
Letley, Emma. *From Galt to Douglas Brown,* 11–16.
Oberhelman, David. "*Waverley,* Genealogy, History: Scott's Romance of Fathers and Sons." *Nineteenth-Cent Contexts* 15 (1991), 29–44.
Orr, Marilyn. "Real and Narrative Time: *Waverley* and the Education of Memory." *Stud in Engl Lit, 1500–1900* 31 (1991), 715–31.
Watts, Cedric. *Literature and Money,* 6–9.

Waverley Novels

Cochran, Peter. "*The Vision of Judgement* and the Waverley Novels." *Notes and Queries* 237 (1992), 168–72.

Woodstock, 1826

Wren, Keith. "*Cromwell* and *Woodstock,*" in A. R. W. James, ed., *Victor Hugo,* 27–38.

GEORGE BERNARD SHAW

An Unsocial Socialist, 1887

Morrison, Harry. *The Socialism of Bernard Shaw,* 6–12.
Neetens, Wim. *Writing and Democracy,* 131–38.

MARY SHELLEY

Falkner, 1837

Ellis, Kate Ferguson. "Subversive Surfaces: The Limits of Domestic Affection in Mary Shelley's Later Fiction," in Audrey A. Fisch et al., eds., *The Other Mary Shelley,* 231–33.
Mellor, Anne K. *Mary Shelley,* 187–91, 201–4.

Frankenstein, 1818

Aguirre, Manuel. *The Closed Space,* 131–34.

Albertazzi, Silvia. *Il sogno gotico,* 71–87.

Aldrich, Marcia, and Richard Isomaki. "The Woman Writer as Frankenstein," in Stephen C. Behrendt, ed., *Approaches,* 121–26.

Alexander, Meena. *Women in Romanticism,* 127–46, 181–83.

Basham, Diana. *The Trial of Woman,* 5–7.

Behrendt, Stephen C. "Language and Style in *Frankenstein,*" in Stephen C. Behrendt, ed., *Approaches,* 78–84.

Bennett, Betty T. "*Frankenstein* and the Uses of Biography," in Stephen C. Behrendt, ed., *Approaches,* 85–92.

Berman, Jeffrey. *Narcissism and the Novel,* 56–77.

Bewell, Alan. "An Issue of Monstrous Desire: *Frankenstein* and Obstetrics." *Yale J of Criticism* 2:1 (1988), 105–25.

Bök, Christian. "The Monstrosity of Representation: *Frankenstein* and Rousseau." *Engl Stud in Canada* 18 (1992), 415–31.

Botting, Fred. "*Frankenstein* and the Language of Monstrosity," in Philip W. Martin and Robin Jarvis, eds., *Reviewing Romanticism,* 51–58.

Botting, Fred. "*Frankenstein*'s French Revolution: The Dangerous Necessity of Monsters." *Lit & Hist* 2nd ser. 1:2 (1990), 29–39.

Botting, Fred. *Making Monstrous,* 36–204.

Bowerbank, Sylvia. "Bridging the Gulf: Teaching *Frankenstein* across the Curriculum," in Stephen C. Behrendt, ed., *Approaches,* 144–51.

Borgmaier, Raimund. "Das Monster und *Women's Lib:* Mary Shelleys *Frankenstein* aus feministischer Sicht," in Therese Fischer-Seidel, ed., *Frauen und Frauendarstellung,* 45–64.

Cantor, Paul A., and Michael Valdez Moses. "Teaching *Frankenstein* from the Creature's Perspective," in Stephen C. Behrendt, ed., *Approaches,* 127–32.

Clemit, Pamela. *The Godwinian Novel,* 139–74.

Clubbe, John. "The Tempest-toss'd Summer of 1816: Mary Shelley's *Frankenstein.*" *Byron J* 19 (1991), 26–40. (Also in Joachim Schwend et al., eds., *Literatur im Kontext,* 219–34.)

Conger, Syndy M. "Aporia and Radical Empathy: *Frankenstein* (Re)Trains the Reader," in Stephen C. Behrendt, ed., *Approaches,* 60–66.

Cornwall, Neil. *The Literary Fantastic,* 67–69, 70–74.

Covi, Giovanna. "The Matrushka Monster of Feminist Criticism." *Textus* 2:1–2 (1989), 217–36.

Davis, James P. "*Frankenstein* and the Subversion of the Masculine Voice." *Women's Stud* 21 (1992), 307–21.

Dixon, Wheeler Winston. "The Films of *Frankenstein,*" in Stephen C. Behrendt, ed., *Approaches,* 166–79.

Ellis, Reuben J. "Mary Shelley Reading Ludvig Holberg: A Subterranean Fantasy at the Outer Edge of *Frankenstein.*" *Extrapolation* 31 (1990), 317–24.

Favret, Mary A. *Romantic Correspondence,* 176–96.

Feldman, Paula R. "Probing the Psychological Mystery of *Frankenstein,*" in Stephen C. Behrendt, ed., *Approaches,* 67–77.

Ferguson, Frances. *Solitude and the Sublime,* 105–12.

Filmer, Kath. "The Spectre of the Self in *Frankenstein* and *Great Expectations,*" in Kath Filmer, ed., *The Victorian Fantasists,* 172–82.

Frantz, Andrea Breemer. *Redemption and Madness,* 25–33.

Goodwin, Sarah Webster. "Domesticity and Uncanny Kitsch in 'The Rime of the Ancient Mariner' and *Frankenstein.*" *Tulsa Stud in Women's Lit* 10 (1991), 93–104.

Graham, Kenneth W. *The Politics of Narrative,* 183–85.

Haggerty, George E. *Gothic Fiction,* 37–63.

Hall, Jean. "*Frankenstein:* The Horrifying Otherness of Family." *Essays in Lit* (Macomb) 17 (1990), 179–88.

Heller, Tamar. *Dead Secrets,* 29–37.

Hennlein, Elmar. *Religion und Phantastik,* 91–94.

Hindle, Maurice. "Vital Matters: Mary Shelley's *Frankenstein* and Romantic Science." *Crit Survey* 2:1 (1990), 29–35.

Hobbs, Colleen. "Reading the Symptoms: An Exploration of Repression and Hysteria in Mary Shelley's *Frankenstein.*" *Stud in the Novel* 25 (1993), 152–65.

Holt, Terrence. "Teaching *Frankenstein* as Science Fiction," in Stephen C. Behrendt, ed., *Approaches,* 112–20.

Hyles, Vernon. "Stoker, *Frankenstein, Dracula,* Sex, Violence, and Incompetence." *Round Table of the South Central Coll Engl Assoc* 27:1 (1986), 7–8.

Johnson, Donovan, and Linda Georgiana. "*Frankenstein* in a Humanities Course," in Stephen C. Behrendt, ed., *Approaches,* 138–43.

Joseph, Gerhard. "Virginal Sex, Vaginal Text: The 'Folds' of *Frankenstein,*" in Lloyd Davis, ed., *Virginal Sexuality,* 25–32.

Kayman, Martin A. *From Bow Street to Baker Street,* 144–50.

Kelly, David. "The Gothic Game." *Sydney Stud in Engl* 15 (1989–90), 110–22.

Keyishian, Harry. "Vindictiveness and the Search for Glory in Mary Shelley's *Frankenstein.*" *Am J of Psychoanalysis* 49 (1989), 201–10.

Kincaid, James R. "'Words Cannot Express': *Frankenstein's* Tripping on the Tongue." *Novel* 24 (1990), 26–47.

Lamb, John B. "Mary Shelley's *Frankenstein* and Milton's Monstrous Myth." *Nineteenth-Cent Lit* 47 (1992), 303–19.

Lanser, Susan Sniader. *Fictions of Authority,* 164–72.

Lehman, Steven. "The Motherless Child in Science Fiction: *Frankenstein* and *Moreau.*" *Science-Fiction Stud* 19 (1992), 49–55.

Lew, Joseph W. "The Deceptive Other: Mary Shelley's Critique of Orientalism in *Frankenstein.*" *Stud in Romanticism* 30 (1991), 255–83.

London, Bette. "Mary Shelley, *Frankenstein,* and the Spectacle of Masculinity." *PMLA* 108 (1993), 253–65.

Lowe-Evans, Mary. "*Frankenstein,*" 21–82.

Marder, Elissa. "The Mother Tongue in *Phèdre* and *Frankenstein.*" *Yale French Stud* 76 (1989), 59–77.

Margolis, Harriet E. "Lost Baggage: Or, The Hollywood Sidetrack," in Stephen C. Behrendt, ed., *Approaches,* 160–65.

Mellor, Anne K. "*Frankenstein* and the Sublime," in Stephen C. Behrendt, ed., *Approaches,* 99–104.

Mellor, Anne K. *Mary Shelley,* 38–51, 52–69, 70–88, 89–114, 115–40.

Mellor, Anne K. "Why Women Didn't Like Romanticism: The Views of Jane Austen and Mary Shelley," in Gene W. Ruoff, ed., *The Romantics and Us,* 281–86.

Michie, Elsie B. "*Frankenstein* and Marx's Theories of Alienated Labor," in Stephen C. Behrendt, ed., *Approaches,* 93–98.

Natarajan, Nalini. "*Frankenstein* de Mary Shelley como un contratexto de la Ilustración." *La Torre* 5:Suppl (1991), 265–73.

Newman, Jenny. "Mary and the Monster: Mary Shelley's *Frankenstein* and Maureen Duffy's *Gor Saga,*" in Lucie Armitt, ed., *Where No Man Has Gone Before,* 85–96.

O'Sullivan, Barbara Jane. "Beatrice in *Valperga:* A New Cassandra," in Audrey A. Fisch et al., eds., *The Other Mary Shelley,* 146–49.

Perkins, Margo V. "The Nature of Otherness: Class and Difference in Mary Shelley's *Frankenstein.*" *Stud in the Hum* 19 (1992), 27–41.

Punter, David. *The Romantic Unconscious,* 130–34.

Reed, John R. *Victorian Will,* 210–25.

Richardson, Alan. "From *Emile* to *Frankenstein:* The Education of Monsters." *European Romantic R* 1 (1991), 147–62.

Roberts, Marie. "Mary Shelley: Immortality, Gender and the Rosy Cross," in Philip W. Martin and Robin Jarvis, eds., *Reviewing Romanticism,* 60–67.

Rowen, Norma. "The Making of Frankenstein's Monster: Post-Golem, Pre-Robot," in Nicholas Ruddick, ed., *State of the Fantastic,* 169–77.

Rutelli, Romana. *Il desiderio del diverso,* 18–43.

Sadrin, Anny. "De la métaphore à la métamorphose: l'homme-machine de Descartes à la science-fiction, avec arrêt sur H. G. Wells." *Cahiers Victoriens et Edouardiens* 31 (1990), 123–24.

Soyka, David. "Frankenstein and the Miltonic Creation of Evil." *Extrapolation* 33 (1992), 166–76.

Thomas, Ronald R. *Dreams of Authority,* 72–74, 80–99.

Thompson, Terry. "Shelley's *Frankenstein.*" *Explicator* 50 (1992), 209–11.

Thornburg, Mary K. "Teaching *Frankenstein* in a General-Studies Literature Class: A Structural Approach," in Stephen C. Behrendt, ed., *Approaches,* 133–37.

Tropp, Martin. *Images of Fear,* 28–42.

Veeder, William. "Gender and Pedagogy: The Questions of *Frankenstein,*" in Stephen C. Behrendt, ed., *Approaches,* 38–49.

Vesterman, William. "Mastering the Free Spirit: Status and Contract in Some Fictional Polities." *Eighteenth-Cent Life* 16:3 (1992), 190–91.

Walling, William. "*Frankenstein* in the Context of English Romanticism," in Stephen C. Behrendt, ed., *Approaches,* 105–11.

Wolfson, Susan J. "Feminist Inquiry and *Frankenstein*," in Stephen C. Behrendt, ed., *Approaches*, 50–59.

Wolstenholme, Susan. *Gothic (Re)Visions*, 37–56.

Woodring, Carl. *Nature into Art*, 103–7.

Young, Arlene. "The Monster Within: The Alien Self in *Jane Eyre* and *Frankenstein*." *Stud in the Novel* 23 (1991), 325–37.

Young, Art. "Reading *Frankenstein:* Writing and the Classroom Community," in Stephen C. Behrendt, ed., *Approaches*, 152–59.

Youngquist, Paul. "*Frankenstein:* The Mother, the Daughter, and the Monster." *Philol Q* 70 (1991), 339–56.

Zonana, Joyce. " 'They Will Prove the Truth of My Tale': Safie's Letters as the Feminist Core of Mary Shelley's *Frankenstein*." *J of Narrative Technique* 21 (1991), 170–81.

The Last Man, 1826

Aaron, Jane. "The Return of the Repressed: Reading Mary Shelley's *The Last Man*," in Susan Sellers, ed., *Feminist Criticism*, 9–20.

Alexander, Meena. *Women in Romanticism*, 155–60, 185–91.

Clemit, Pamela. *The Godwinian Novel*, 183–210.

Ellis, Kate Ferguson. "Subversive Surfaces: The Limits of Domestic Affection in Mary Shelley's Later Fiction," in Audrey A. Fisch et al., eds., *The Other Mary Shelley*, 225–27.

Fisch, Audrey A. "Plaguing Politics: AIDS, Deconstruction, and *The Last Man*," in Audrey A. Fisch et al., eds., *The Other Mary Shelley*, 267–81.

Goldsmith, Steven. "Of Gender, Plague and Apocalypse: Mary Shelley's *Last Man*." *Yale J of Criticism* 4:1 (1990), 129–69.

Goldsmith, Steven. *Unbuilding Jerusalem*, 261–313.

Johnson, Barbara. " 'The Last Man,' " in Audrey A. Fisch et al., eds., *The Other Mary Shelley*, 258–66.

Mellor, Anne K. *Mary Shelley*, 144–69.

O'Dea, Gregory. "Prophetic History and Textuality in Mary Shelley's *The Last Man*." *Papers on Lang & Lit* 28 (1992), 283–303.

Paley, Morton D. "Mary Shelley's *The Last Man:* Apocalypse Without Millennium." *Keats-Shelley R* 4 (1989), 1–25. (Also in Audrey A. Fisch et al., eds., *The Other Mary Shelley*, 107–21.)

Zimmerman, Phyllis. "Some Lines of Italian Poetry in the Introduction to *The Last Man*." *Notes and Queries* 235 (1990), 31–32.

Lodore, 1835

Ellis, Kate Ferguson. "Subversive Surfaces: The Limits of Domestic Affection in Mary Shelley's Later Fiction," in Audrey A. Fisch et al., eds., *The Other Mary Shelley*, 230–32.

Mathilda, 1959

Alexander, Meena. *Women in Romanticism*, 160–66.

Ellis, Kate Ferguson. "Subversive Surfaces: The Limits of Domestic Affection in Mary Shelley's Later Fiction," in Audrey A. Fisch et al., eds., *The Other Mary Shelley*, 227–30.

Lanser, Susan Sniader. *Fictions of Authority*, 168–72.
Mellor, Anne K. *Mary Shelley*, 191–200.

Perkin Warbeck, 1830

O'Sullivan, Barbara Jane. "Beatrice in *Valperga:* A New Cassandra," in
Audrey A. Fisch et al., eds., *The Other Mary Shelley*, 152–54.

Valperga, 1823

Clemit, Pamela. *The Godwinian Novel*, 175–83.
Lew, Joseph W. "God's Sister: History and Ideology in *Valperga*," in
Audrey A. Fisch et al., eds., *The Other Mary Shelley*, 258–66.
O'Sullivan, Barbara Jane. "Beatrice in *Valperga:* A New Cassandra," in
Audrey A. Fisch et al., eds., *The Other Mary Shelley*, 140–56.

NAN SHEPHERD

A Pass in the Grampians, 1933

Watson, Roderick. " ' . . . to get leave to live': Patterns of Identity, Freedom and Defeat in the Fiction of Nan Shepherd," in Joachim Schwend
and Horst W. Drescher, eds., *Studies in Scottish Fiction*, 212–15.

The Quarry Wood, 1928

Watson, Roderick. " ' . . . to get leave to live': Patterns of Identity, Freedom and Defeat in the Fiction of Nan Shepherd," in Joachim Schwend
and Horst W. Drescher, eds., *Studies in Scottish Fiction*, 208–11.

The Weatherhouse, 1930

Watson, Roderick. " ' . . . to get leave to live': Patterns of Identity, Freedom and Defeat in the Fiction of Nan Shepherd," in Joachim Schwend
and Horst W. Drescher, eds., *Studies in Scottish Fiction*, 215–18.

ELIZABETH SHEPPARD

Charles Auchester, 1853

Auerbach, Emily. *Maestros, Dilettantes, and Philistines*, 56–59.

FRANCES SHERIDAN

The Memoirs of Miss Sidney Bidulph, 1761–1767

Hatch, Ronald B. " 'Lordship and Bondage': Women Novelists of the
Eighteenth Century." *REAL: Yrbk of Res in Engl and Am Lit* 8 (1991/
92), 233–34.

MARY MARTHA SHERWOOD

Caroline Mordaunt, 1835

Lanser, Susan Sniader. *Fictions of Authority*, 177–81.

M. P. SHIEL

The Purple Cloud, 1901

Ruddick, Nicholas. *Ultimate Island,* 110–12.

PHILIP SIDNEY

Arcadia, 1598

Beer, Gillian. *"Pamela:* Rethinking *Arcadia,"* in Margaret Anne Doody and Peter Sabor, eds., *Samuel Richardson,* 23–39.

Berrong, Richard M. "Changing Attitudes toward Material Wealth in Sidney's *Arcadias." Sixteenth Cent* J 22 (1991), 331–49.

Boss, J. A. "Sidney's *Arcadia* and Spenser's 'Sad Poutraict' (*The Faerie Queene* II.i.39–40)." *Notes and Queries* 236 (1991), 26–27.

Charles, Casey. "Heroes as Lovers: Attraction Between Men in Sidney's *New Arcadia." Criticism* 34 (1992), 467–90.

Erlebach, Peter. *Theorie und Praxis des Romaneingangs,* 119–27.

Hunt, Marvin. "Charactonymic Structures in Sidney's *Arcadias." Stud in Engl Lit, 1500–1900* 33 (1993), 1–15.

Kinney, Clare. "The Masks of Love: Desire and Metamorphosis in Sidney's *New Arcadia." Criticism* 33 (1991), 461–86.

Kinney, Clare. "On the Margins of Romance, at the Heart of the Matter: Revisionary Fabulation in Sidney's *New Arcadia." J of Narrative Technique* 21 (1991), 143–51.

Lindenbaum, Peter. "Sidney and the Active Life," in M. J. B. Allen et al., eds., *Sir Philip Sidney's Achievements,* 176–93.

Lucas, Caroline. *Writing for Women,* 118–34.

McCanles, Michael. *The Text of Sidney's Arcadian World,* 1–176.

McNeil, David. *The Grotesque Depiction of War,* 42–46.

Manganaro, Elise S. "Platonic Idealism in Sidney's Fallen *Arcadia." Engl Stud* 71 (1990), 105–12.

Partee, Morriss Henry. "The Genre of the *Arcadia." Univ of Mississippi Stud in Engl* 8 (1990), 212–23.

Pigeon, Renee. "'An Odious Marriage with a Stranger: Sidney's *Arcadias* and the French Match." *Engl Lang Notes* 31:1 (1993), 28–38.

Rees, Joan. "Justice, Mercy and a Shipwreck in *Arcadia." Stud in Philology* 87 (1990), 75–82.

Rees, Joan. *Sir Philip Sidney,* 27–141.

Roche, Thomas P., Jr. "Ending the *New Arcadia:* Virgil and Ariosto." *Sidney Newsl* 10:1 (1989), 3–12.

Shaver, Anne. "Woman's Place in the *New Arcadia." Sidney Newsl* 10:2 (1989–90), 3–15.

Skretkowicz, Victor. "'A More Lively Monument': Philisides in *Arcadia,"* in M. J. B. Allen et al., eds., *Sir Philip Sidney's Achievements,* 194–200.

Sullivan, Margaret M. "Amazons and Aristocrats: The Function of Pyrocles' Amazon Role in Sidney's Revised *Arcadia*," in Jean R. Brink et al., eds., *Playing with Gender*, 62–75.

Sullivan, Margaret Mary. "Getting Pamela out of the House: Gendering Genealogy in the *New Arcadia*." *Sidney Newsl* 9:2 (1988–89), 3–15.

Taylor, Michael. "Reluctant Romancers: Self-Consciousness and Derogation in Prose Romances." *Engl Stud in Canada* 17 (1991), 90–94.

Tennenhouse, Leonard. "Arcadian Rhetoric: Sidney and the Politics of Courtship," in M. J. B. Allen et al., eds., *Sir Philip Sidney's Achievements*, 201–13.

Woods, Susanne. "Freedom and Tyranny in Sidney's *Arcadia*," in M. J. B. Allen et al., eds., *Sir Philip Sidney's Achievements*, 166–75.

ALAN SILLITOE

The Death of William Posters, 1965

Hutchings, William. "Proletarian Byronism: Alan Sillitoe and the Romantic Tradition," in Allan Chavkin, ed., *English Romanticism and Modern Fiction*, 98–105.

Raw Material, 1972

Hutchings, William. "Proletarian Byronism: Alan Sillitoe and the Romantic Tradition," in Allan Chavkin, ed., *English Romanticism and Modern Fiction*, 85–87.

Saturday Night and Sunday Morning, 1958

Bergonzi, Bernard. *Wartime and Aftermath*, 149–51.

Hitchcock, Peter. *Working-Class Fiction*, 57–73.

Hutchings, William. "Proletarian Byronism: Alan Sillitoe and the Romantic Tradition," in Allan Chavkin, ed., *English Romanticism and Modern Fiction*, 91–93.

Singh, Avtar. "Nature of Rebellion in Alan Sillitoe's *Saturday Night and Sunday Morning* and *The Loneliness of the Long-Distance Runner*." *Panjab Univ Res Bull* 21:1 (1990), 43–53.

A Tree on Fire, 1967

Hutchings, William. "Proletarian Byronism: Alan Sillitoe and the Romantic Tradition," in Allan Chavkin, ed., *English Romanticism and Modern Fiction*, 105–10.

MAY SINCLAIR

Life and Death of Harriet Frean, 1922

Brown, Penny. *The Poison at the Source*, 36–49.

Mary Olivier, 1919

Brown, Penny. *The Poison at the Source*, 16–35.

The Three Sisters, 1914

Brown, Penny. *The Poison at the Source,* 14–16.

CHARLOTTE SMITH

The Banished Man, 1794

Schofield, Mary Anne. " 'The Witchery of Fiction': Charlotte Smith, Novelist," in Dale Spender, ed., *Living by the Pen,* 182–84.

Desmond, 1792

Elliott, Pat. "Charlotte Smith's Feminism: A Study of *Emmeline* and *Desmond,*" in Dale Spender, ed., *Living by the Pen,* 91–112.

Schofield, Mary Anne. " 'The Witchery of Fiction': Charlotte Smith, Novelist," in Dale Spender, ed., *Living by the Pen,* 180–82.

Emmeline, 1788

Elliott, Pat. "Charlotte Smith's Feminism: A Study of *Emmeline* and *Desmond,*" in Dale Spender, ed., *Living by the Pen,* 91–112.

Ethelinde, 1789

Schofield, Mary Anne. " 'The Witchery of Fiction': Charlotte Smith, Novelist," in Dale Spender, ed., *Living by the Pen,* 178–81.

Marchmont, 1796

Schofield, Mary Anne. " 'The Witchery of Fiction': Charlotte Smith, Novelist," in Dale Spender, ed., *Living by the Pen,* 184–87.

Montalbert, 1795

Schofield, Mary Anne. " 'The Witchery of Fiction': Charlotte Smith, Novelist," in Dale Spender, ed., *Living by the Pen,* 184–86.

The Old Manor House, 1793

Bartolomeo, Joseph F. "Subversion of Romance in *The Old Manor House.*" *Stud in Engl Lit, 1500–1900* 33 (1993), 645–56.

STEVIE SMITH

The Holiday, 1949

Sternlicht, Sanford. *Stevie Smith,* 23–25.

Novel on Yellow Paper, 1936

Gordon, Mary. "Preface to *Novel on Yellow Paper,*" in Sanford Sternlicht, ed., *In Search of Stevie Smith,* 57–61.

Oates, Joyce Carol. "A Child with a Cold, Cold Eye," in Sanford Sternlicht, ed., *In Search of Stevie Smith,* 65–70.

Sternlicht, Sanford. *Stevie Smith,* 18–20.

Over the Frontier, 1938

Sternlicht, Sanford. *Stevie Smith,* 20–23.

TOBIAS SMOLLETT

Ferdinand Count Fathom, 1753

Adamson, William Robert. *Cadences of Unreason,* 128–41, 201–5, 209–18.

Costopoulos-Almon, Olga. "Smollett's Central Characters: The Fictive Discoursing through the Fictile," in Kevin L. Cope, ed., *Compendious Conversations,* 198–200.

Probyn, Clive T. *English Fiction,* 115–22.

The History and Adventures of an Atom, 1769

Costopoulos-Almon, Olga. "A Note on Smollett's *Atom.*" *Notes and Queries* 236 (1991), 191–92.

McNeil, David. *The Grotesque Depiction of War,* 110–12.

Humphry Clinker, 1771

Adams, Percy G. "The Coach and the Inn," in H. George Hahn, ed., *The Country Myth,* 202–5.

Adamson, William Robert. *Cadences of Unreason,* 116–18, 141–50, 160–64, 200–205, 224–27, 232–36.

Carson, James P. "Commodification and the Figure of the Castrato in Smollett's *Humphry Clinker.*" *Eighteenth Cent* 33 (1992), 24–41.

Castronovo, David. *The English Gentleman,* 42–44.

Costopoulos-Almon, Olga. "Smollett's Central Characters: The Fictive Discoursing through the Fictile," in Kevin L. Cope, ed., *Compendious Conversations,* 202–4.

Crawford, Robert. *Devolving English Literature,* 64–75.

Duckworth, Alistair M. "Fiction and Some Uses of the Country House Setting from Richardson to Scott," in H. George Hahn, ed., *The Country Myth,* 233–36.

Duncan, Jeffrey L. "The Rural Ideal in Eighteenth-Century Fiction," in H. George Hahn, ed., *The Country Myth,* 258–61.

Kates, Carolyn J. "'Arcadia in Every Thing': Smollett's Use of the Pastoral in *Humphry Clinker.*" *Coll Lang Assoc* J 36 (1992), 73–84.

Krishman, R. S. "'The Vortex of Tumult': Order and Disorder in *Humphry Clinker.*" *Stud in Scottish Lit* 23 (1988), 239–51.

McMaster, Juliet. "The Body inside the Skin: The Medical Model of Character in the Eighteenth-Century Novel." *Eighteenth-Cent Fiction* 4 (1992), 290–94.

Mayer, Robert. "History, *Humphry Clinker,* and the Novel." *Eighteenth-Cent Fiction* 4 (1992), 239–55.

New, Melvyn. *Telling New Lies,* 42–44.

Probyn, Clive T. *English Fiction,* 123–29.

Richetti, John. "The Public Sphere and the Eighteenth-Century Novel: Social Criticism and Narrative Enactment." *Eighteenth-Cent Life* 16:3 (1992), 122–28.

Peregrine Pickle, 1751

Adamson, William Robert. *Cadences of Unreason,* 116–18, 119–28, 195–97, 201–8.

Costopoulos-Almon, Olga. "Smollett's Central Characters: The Fictive Discoursing through the Fictile," in Kevin L. Cope, ed., *Compendious Conversations,* 196–98.

Kraft, Elizabeth. *Character & Consciousness,* 123–36.

Paulson, Ronald. "The Pilgrimage and the Family: Structures in the Novels of Fielding and Smollett," in H. George Hahn, ed., *The Country Myth,* 181–98.

Price, John Valdimir. "Patterns of Sexual Behavior in Some Eighteenth-Century Novels," in H. George Hahn, ed., *The Country Myth,* 125–37.

Probyn, Clive T. *English Fiction,* 118–22.

Richetti, John. "The Old Order and the New Novel of the Mid-Eighteenth Century: Narrative Authority in Fielding and Smollett." *Eighteenth-Cent Fiction* 2 (1990), 193–96.

Roderick Random, 1748

Adamson, William Robert. *Cadences of Unreason,* 97–100, 119–28, 164–67, 181–95, 201–7, 218–20.

Boucé, Paul-Gabriel. " 'Scotorum praefervida ingenia': Violence in Smollett's *Roderick Random.*" *REAL: Yrbk of Res in Engl and Am Lit* 8 (1991/92), 243–51.

Costopoulos-Almon, Olga. "Smollett's Central Characters: The Fictive Discoursing through the Fictile," in Kevin L. Cope, ed., *Compendious Conversations,* 193–96.

Crawford, Robert. *Devolving English Literature,* 57–61.

Flanders, W. Austin. "Urban Life and the Early Novel," in H. George Hahn, ed., *The Country Myth,* 62–64.

Goode, Okey. "Finding a Character's Voice in Smollett's *Roderick Random.*" *Style* 24 (1990), 469–81. (Also in John V. Knapp, ed., *Literary Character,* 121–33.)

McMaster, Juliet. "The Body inside the Skin: The Medical Model of Character in the Eighteenth-Century Novel." *Eighteenth-Cent Fiction* 4 (1992), 289–90.

McNeil, David. *The Grotesque Depiction of War,* 86–110.

Probyn, Clive T. *English Fiction,* 111–13.

Zomchick, John P. " 'Inordinate Sallies of Desire' Restrained and 'Unutterable Rapture Possessed': The Emplotment of the Reader in *Roderick Random,*" in Carl R. Kropf, ed., *Reader Entrapment,* 201–25.

Sir Lancelot Greaves, 1762

Adamson, William Robert. *Cadences of Unreason,* 128–41, 168–70, 179–84, 201–4, 232–34.

Costopoulos-Almon, Olga. "Smollett's Central Characters: The Fictive Discoursing through the Fictile," in Kevin L. Cope, ed., *Compendious Conversations,* 200–202.

Kraft, Elizabeth. "Public Nurturance and Private Civility: The Transposition of Values in Eighteenth-Century Fiction." *Stud in Eighteenth-Cent Culture* 22 (1992), 187–91.

C. P. SNOW

The Affair, 1960

Rossen, Janice. *The University in Modern Fiction,* 119–38.
Shusterman, David. *C. P. Snow,* 90–94.

A Coat of Varnish, 1978

Shusterman, David. *C. P. Snow,* 127–31.

The Conscience of the Rich, 1958

Shusterman, David. *C. P. Snow,* 64–73.

Corridors of Power, 1964

Shusterman, David. *C. P. Snow,* 94–99.

Death under Sail, 1932

Shusterman, David. *C. P. Snow,* 25–28.

Homecomings, 1956

Shusterman, David. *C. P. Snow,* 47–55.

In Their Wisdom, 1974

Shusterman, David. *C. P. Snow,* 119–27.

Last Things, 1970

Shusterman, David. *C. P. Snow,* 110–14.

The Light and the Dark, 1947

Shusterman, David. *C. P. Snow,* 73–80.

The Malcontents, 1972

Shusterman, David. *C. P. Snow,* 115–19.

The Masters, 1951

Rossen, Janice. *The University in Modern Fiction,* 119–38.
Shusterman, David. *C. P. Snow,* 80–86.

New Lives for Old, 1933

Shusterman, David. *C. P. Snow,* 28–30.

The New Men, 1954

Munton, Alan. *English Fiction,* 96–99.
Shusterman, David. *C. P. Snow,* 86–90.

The Search, 1934

Shusterman, David. *C. P. Snow,* 30–38.

The Sleep of Reason, 1968

> Shusterman, David. *C. P. Snow,* 99–109.

Strangers and Brothers, 1940

> Bergonzi, Bernard. *Wartime and Aftermath,* 122–24.
> Shusterman, David. *C. P. Snow,* 56–64.

Time of Hope, 1949

> Shusterman, David. *C. P. Snow,* 39–47.

SOMERVILLE AND ROSS

The Big House of Inver, 1925

> Imhof, Rüdiger. "Somerville & Ross: *The Real Charlotte* and *The Big House of Inver,*" in Otto Rauchbauer, ed., *Ancestral Voices,* 101–4.

The Real Charlotte, 1894

> Imhof, Rüdiger. "Somerville & Ross: *The Real Charlotte* and *The Big House of Inver,*" in Otto Rauchbauer, ed., *Ancestral Voices,* 95–101.
> Weekes, Ann Owens. *Irish Women Writers,* 60–82.

MURIEL SPARK

The Abbess of Crewe, 1974

> Edgecombe, Rodney Stenning. *Vocation and Identity,* 89–110.
> Hynes, Joseph. *The Art of the Real,* 107–20.
> Little, Judy. "Muriel Spark's Grammars of Assent," in James Acheson, ed., *The British and Irish Novel,* 11–12.
> Page, Norman. *Muriel Spark,* 89–92.
> Randisi, Jennifer Lynn. *On Her Way Rejoicing,* 31–32, 86–88.
> Sproxton, Judy. *The Women of Muriel Spark,* 72–82.

The Bachelors, 1960

> Edgecombe, Rodney Stenning. *Vocation and Identity,* 7–33.
> Hynes, Joseph. *The Art of the Real,* 39–51.
> Page, Norman. *Muriel Spark,* 32–39.
> Randisi, Jennifer Lynn. *On Her Way Rejoicing,* 24–25, 90–91.
> Sproxton, Judy. *The Women of Muriel Spark,* 123–30.

The Ballad of Peckham Rye, 1960

> Hynes, Joseph. *The Art of the Real,* 51–53.
> Kane, Richard C. "Didactic Demons in Contemporary British Fiction." *Univ of Mississippi Stud in Engl* 8 (1990), 44–48.
> Page, Norman. *Muriel Spark,* 27–32.
> Randisi, Jennifer Lynn. *On Her Way Rejoicing,* 24–25, 89–90.

The Comforters, 1957

Hynes, Joseph. *The Art of the Real,* 136–48.
Page, Norman. *Muriel Spark,* 10–16.
Page, Norman. *Speech in the English Novel,* 13–15.
Randisi, Jennifer Lynn. *On Her Way Rejoicing,* 36–37, 38–50, 70–72.
Sproxton, Judy. *The Women of Muriel Spark,* 20–25.

The Driver's Seat, 1970

Hynes, Joseph. *The Art of the Real,* 80–87.
Little, Judy. " 'Endless Different Ways': Muriel Spark's Re-visions of the
    Spinster," in Laura L. Doan, ed., *Old Maids,* 28–31.
Page, Norman. *Muriel Spark,* 69–81.
Randisi, Jennifer Lynn. *On Her Way Rejoicing,* 24–28, 94–95.
Sproxton, Judy. *The Women of Muriel Spark,* 137–43.

A Far Cry from Kensington, 1988

Hynes, Joseph. "Muriel Spark and the Oxymoronic Vision," in Robert E.
    Hosmer, Jr., ed., *Contemporary British Women Writers,* 161–68.
Little, Judy. "Muriel Spark's Grammars of Assent," in James Acheson,
    ed., *The British and Irish Novel,* 12–14.
Page, Norman. *Muriel Spark,* 111–15.
Randisi, Jennifer Lynn. *On Her Way Rejoicing,* 79–80.
Sproxton, Judy. *The Women of Muriel Spark,* 48–59.

The Girls of Slender Means, 1963

Edgecombe, Rodney Stenning. *Vocation and Identity,* 35–60.
Hynes, Joseph. *The Art of the Real,* 58–69.
Little, Judy. "Muriel Spark's Grammars of Assent," in James Acheson,
    ed., *The British and Irish Novel,* 7–9.
Page, Norman. *Muriel Spark,* 44–50.
Sproxton, Judy. *The Women of Muriel Spark,* 82–90.

The Hothouse by the East River, 1973

Hynes, Joseph. *The Art of the Real,* 87–96.
Little, Judy. "Muriel Spark's Grammars of Assent," in James Acheson,
    ed., *The British and Irish Novel,* 10–11.
Page, Norman. *Muriel Spark,* 86–89.
Randisi, Jennifer Lynn. *On Her Way Rejoicing,* 28–31, 65–66, 95–96.

Loitering with Intent, 1981

Hynes, Joseph. *The Art of the Real,* 173–76.
Little, Judy. " 'Endless Different Ways': Muriel Spark's Re-visions of the
    Spinster," in Laura L. Doan, ed., *Old Maids,* 31–34.
Little, Judy. "Muriel Spark's Grammars of Assent," in James Acheson,
    ed., *The British and Irish Novel,* 12–14.
Page, Norman. *Muriel Spark,* 99–105.
Randisi, Jennifer Lynn. *On Her Way Rejoicing,* 16–18, 32–35, 75–77, 87–
    88.
Sproxton, Judy. *The Women of Muriel Spark,* 40–47.

The Mandelbaum Gate, 1965

Edgecombe, Rodney Stenning. *Vocation and Identity,* 61–88.
Harrison, Bernard. *Inconvenient Fictions,* 160–64.
Hynes, Joseph. *The Art of the Real,* 53–57.
Hynes, Joseph. "Muriel Spark and the Oxymoronic Vision," in Robert E.
  Hosmer, Jr., ed., *Contemporary British Women Writers,* 173–74.
Little, Judy. "Muriel Spark's Grammars of Assent," in James Acheson,
  ed., *The British and Irish Novel,* 4–6.
Page, Norman. *Muriel Spark,* 54–62.
Randisi, Jennifer Lynn. *On Her Way Rejoicing,* 68–71, 99–100.
Sproxton, Judy. *The Women of Muriel Spark,* 32–40.

Memento Mori, 1959

Bergonzi, Bernard. *Wartime and Aftermath,* 196–98.
Hynes, Joseph. *The Art of the Real,* 97–107.
Hynes, Joseph. "Muriel Spark and the Oxymoronic Vision," in Robert E.
  Hosmer, Jr., ed., *Contemporary British Women Writers,* 168–69.
Page, Norman. *Muriel Spark,* 20–27.
Randisi, Jennifer Lynn. *On Her Way Rejoicing,* 14–15, 66–67, 91–92.
Sproxton, Judy. *The Women of Muriel Spark,* 115–23.

Not to Disturb, 1971

Alexander, Marguerite. *Flights from Realism,* 182–85.
Hynes, Joseph. *The Art of the Real,* 155–73.
Hynes, Joseph. "Muriel Spark and the Oxymoronic Vision," in Robert E.
  Hosmer, Jr., ed., *Contemporary British Women Writers,* 177–78.
Page, Norman. *Muriel Spark,* 81–86.

The Only Problem, 1984

Harrison, Bernard. *Inconvenient Fictions,* 166–87.
Hynes, Joseph. *The Art of the Real,* 132–35.
Little, Judy. "Muriel Spark's Grammars of Assent," in James Acheson,
  ed., *The British and Irish Novel,* 12–13.
Page, Norman. *Muriel Spark,* 105–10.
Randisi, Jennifer Lynn. *On Her Way Rejoicing,* 37–50, 92–93.

The Prime of Miss Jean Brodie, 1961

Bower, Anne L. "The Narrative Structure of Muriel Spark's *The Prime of
  Miss Jean Brodie.*" *Midwest Q* 31 (1990), 488–98.
Harrison, Bernard. *Inconvenient Fictions,* 154–60.
Hynes, Joseph. *The Art of the Real,* 69–80.
Little, Judy. "'Endless Different Ways': Muriel Spark's Re-visions of the
  Spinster," in Laura L. Doan, ed., *Old Maids,* 23–28.
Little, Judy. "Muriel Spark's Grammars of Assent," in James Acheson,
  ed., *The British and Irish Novel,* 6–7.
Page, Norman. *Muriel Spark,* 39–44.
Sproxton, Judy. *The Women of Muriel Spark,* 63–71.

The Public Image, 1968

Hynes, Joseph. *The Art of the Real,* 148–55.
Little, Judy. "Muriel Spark's Grammars of Assent," in James Acheson, ed., *The British and Irish Novel,* 9.
Page, Norman. *Muriel Spark,* 64–69.
Randisi, Jennifer Lynn. *On Her Way Rejoicing,* 64–66, 96–97.
Sproxton, Judy. *The Women of Muriel Spark,* 130–37.

Robinson, 1958

Hynes, Joseph. *The Art of the Real,* 20–34.
Page, Norman. *Muriel Spark,* 17–20.
Randisi, Jennifer Lynn. *On Her Way Rejoicing,* 72–74, 88–89.
Sproxton, Judy. *The Women of Muriel Spark,* 25–32.

Symposium, 1990

Sproxton, Judy. *The Women of Muriel Spark,* 96–111.

The Takeover, 1976

Edgecombe, Rodney Stenning. *Vocation and Identity,* 89–110.
Hynes, Joseph. *The Art of the Real,* 120–27.
Page, Norman. *Muriel Spark,* 92–97.
Sproxton, Judy. *The Women of Muriel Spark,* 90–96.

Territorial Rights, 1979

Hynes, Joseph. *The Art of the Real,* 127–32.
Page, Norman. *Muriel Spark,* 97–99.

HENRIETTA STANNARD

A Blameless Woman, 1894

Ardis, Ann L. *New Women, New Novels,* 79–81.

OLAF STAPLEDON

Last and First Men, 1930

Bailey, K. V. "Time Scales and Culture Cycles in Olaf Stapledon." *Foundation* 46 (1989), 35–39.

Sirius, 1944

Crossley, Robert. "Censorship, Disguise, and Transfiguration: The Making and Revising of Stapledon's *Sirius.*" *Science-Fiction Stud* 20 (1993), 1–13.

The Star Maker, 1937

Bailey, K. V. "Time Scales and Culture Cycles in Olaf Stapledon." *Foundation* 46 (1989), 30–35.

FLORA ANNIE STEEL

On the Face of the Waters, 1896

Paxton, Nancy L. "Mobilizing Chivalry: Rape in British Novels about the Indian Uprising of 1857." *Victorian Stud* 36 (1992), 22–27.

JAMES STEPHENS

The Crock of Gold, 1912

Bramsbäck, Birgit. "James Stephens and *The Crock of Gold,*" in Birgit Bramsbäck, ed., *Homage to Ireland,* 31–44.

Deirdre, 1923

Tallone, Giovanna. "James Stephens' *Deirdre:* The Determining Word." *Canadian J of Irish Stud* 16:1 (1990), 75–79.

LAURENCE STERNE

A Sentimental Journey, 1768

Berthoud, Jacques. "The Beggar in *A Sentimental Journey.*" *Shandean* 3 (1991), 37–47.

Curley, Thomas M. "Sterne's *A Sentimental Journey* and the Tradition of Travel Literature," in John McVeagh, ed., *1660–1780,* 202–16.

Descargues, Madeleine. "Fonctions d'une lettre d'amour, de la correspondance de Sterne à *A Sentimental Journey.*" *Bull de la Société d'Etudes Anglo-Américaines des XVIIe et XVIIIe Siècles* 31 (1990), 143–57.

Duncan, Jeffrey L. "The Rural Ideal in Eighteenth-Century Fiction," in H. George Hahn, ed., *The Country Myth,* 264–67.

Kavanagh, Keryl. "Discounting Language: A Vehicle for Interpreting Laurence Sterne's *A Sentimental Journey.*" *J of Narrative Technique* 22 (1992), 136–43.

Lamb, Jonathan. *Sterne's Fiction,* 87–89.

Mullan, John. *Sentiment and Sociability,* 158–59, 189–97.

New, Melvyn. "Some Sterne Borrowings from Four Renaissance Authors." *Philol Q* 71 (1992), 302–5.

New, Melvyn. *Telling New Lies,* 138–51, 153–62.

O'Shea, Michael J. "Laurence Sterne's Display of Heraldry." *Shandean* 3 (1991), 61–68.

Peereboom, J. J. "Lachend naar het einde." *Maatstaf* 38:9–10 (1990), 128–33.

Probyn, Clive T. *English Fiction,* 142–45.

Soulier-Detis, Elisabeth. "Colliers, gants et manchon: Les Pulsions dévoilées." *Bull de la Société d'Etudes Anglo-Américaines des XVIIe et XVIIIe Siècles* 28 (1989), 145–62.

Zatta, Jane. "The Sentimental Journeys of Laurence Sterne and Italo Svevo." *Compar Lit* 44 (1992), 361–78.

Tristram Shandy, 1760–1767

Bandry, Anne. "Sterne, l'imitateur imité." *Bull de la Société d'Etudes Anglo-Américaines des XVIIe et XVIIIe Siècles* 32 (1991), 67–77.

Bandry, Anne. "*Tristram Shandy* et les fausses *Life and Opinions:* violences faites à un titre." *Cycnos* 6 (1990), 17–33.

Bandry, Anne. "*Tristram Shandy* ou le plaisir du tiret." *Etudes Anglaises* 41 (1988), 143–53.

Behrendt, Stephen C. "Multistability and Method in *Tristram Shandy,*" in Melvyn New, ed., *Approaches,* 146–51.

Benedict, Barbara M. " 'Dear Madam': Rhetoric, Cultural Politics and the Female Reader in Sterne's *Tristram Shandy.*" *Stud in Philology* 89 (1992), 485–98.

Blaydes, Sophia B. "Sterne and His Early Critics: The Outsider," in Melvyn New, ed., *Approaches,* 87–93.

Butler, Gerald J. *Henry Fielding,* 119–28.

Caldwell, Roy C. "*Tristram Shandy,* Bachelor Machine." *Eighteenth Cent* 34 (1993), 103–12.

Cash, Arthur H. "A South West Passage to the Intellectual World," in Melvyn New, ed., *Approaches,* 33–40.

Chibka, Robert L. "The Hobby-Horse's Epitaph: *Tristram Shandy, Hamlet,* and the Vehicles of Memory." *Eighteenth-Cent Fiction* 3 (1991), 125–51.

Cohan, Steven. "Figures beyond the Text: A Theory of Readable Character in the Novel," in Mark Spilka and Caroline McCracken-Flesher, eds., *Why the Novel Matters,* 119–20.

Davidson, Elizabeth Livingston. "Toward an Integrated Chronology for *Tristram Shandy.*" *Engl Lang Notes* 29:4 (1992), 48–56.

Erlebach, Peter. *Theorie und Praxis des Romaneingangs,* 168–73.

Fishelov, David. "Types of Character, Characteristics of Type," in John V. Knapp, ed., *Literary Character,* 81–83.

Frontain, Raymond-Jean. "Dinah and the Comedy of Castration in Sterne's *Tristram Shandy,*" in Raymond-Jean and Jan Wojcik, eds., *Old Testament Women,* 174–203.

Frontain, Raymond-Jean. " 'Madam, Spare That Mole!': Comic Responses to Psychosexual Threats in Sterne's *Tristram Shandy.*" *Publs of the Arkansas Philol Assoc* 16:1 (1990), 15–30.

Greene, Donald. "Pragmatism versus Dogmatism: The Ideology of *Tristram Shandy,*" in Melvyn New, ed., *Approaches,* 105–10.

Harries, Elizabeth W. "The Sorrows and Confessions of a Cross-Eyed 'Female-Reader' of Sterne," in Melvyn New, ed., *Approaches,* 111–17.

Harrison, Bernard. *Inconvenient Fictions,* 71–97.

Iser, Wolfgang. *Laurence Sterne,* 1–129.

Kantzenbach, Friedrich Wilhelm. *Traditionen Europas im Spiegel von Literatur,* 32–39.

Klein, Herbert G. "Wer ist Tristrams Vater? Paternität und Identität in

Laurence Sternes *Tristram Shandy.*" *Germanisch-Romanische Monats-schrift* 42 (1992), 415–24.

Klein, Jürgen. "Laurence Sterne's Novel of Consciousness: Identities of Selves and World Constructions in *Tristram Shandy.*" *Stud on Voltaire and the Eighteenth Cent* 265 (1989), 1544–47.

Konigsberg, Ira. "Tristram Shandy and the Spatial Imagination," in Melvyn New, ed., *Approaches,* 55–60.

Kraft, Elizabeth. *Character & Consciousness,* 100–102, 105–14, 116–18.

Kraft, Elizabeth. "*Tristram Shandy* and the Age That Begot Him," in Melvyn New, ed., *Approaches,* 123–30.

Lamb, Jonathan. *Sterne's Fiction,* 6–157.

Lee, Abigail E. "Sterne's Legacy to Juan Goytisolo: A Shandyian Reading of *Juan sin tierra.*" *Mod Lang R* 84 (1989), 351–57.

Loscocco, Paula. "Can't Live Without 'Em: Walter Shandy and the Woman Within." *Eighteenth Cent* 32 (1991), 166–78.

Loveridge, Mark. "Stories of COCKS and BULLS: The Ending of Tristram Shandy." *Eighteenth-Cent Fiction* 5 (1992), 35–54.

McCrea, Brian. "Stories That Should Be True? Locke, Sterne, and *Tristram Shandy,*" in Melvyn New, ed., *Approaches,* 94–99.

Macey, Samuel L. "The Linear and Circular Time Schemes in Sterne's *Tristram Shandy.*" *Notes and Queries* 234 (1989), 477–79.

McMaster, Juliet. "The Body inside the Skin: The Medical Model of Character in the Eighteenth-Century Novel." *Eighteenth-Cent Fiction* 4 (1992), 286–89.

McMaster, Juliet. *The Index of the Mind,* 1–2.

McMaster, Juliet. "'Uncrystalized Flesh and Blood': The Body in *Tristram Shandy.*" *Eighteenth-Cent Fiction* 2 (1990), 197–214.

McMaster, Juliet. "Walter Shandy, Sterne, and Gender: A Feminist Foray." *Engl Stud in Canada* 15 (1989), 441–57.

McNeil, David. *The Grotesque Depiction of War,* 144–67.

McNeil, David. "*Tristram Shandy:* The Grotesque View of War and the Military Character." *Stud on Voltaire and the Eighteenth Cent* 266 (1989), 411–32.

Matalene, H. W. "Sexual Scripting in Montaigne and Sterne." *Compar Lit* 41 (1989), 360–76.

Matteo, Sante. *Textual Exile,* 139–206.

Mullan, John. *Sentiment and Sociability,* 147–89.

New, Melvyn. "Job's Wife and Sterne's Other Women," in Laura Claridge and Elizabeth Langland, eds., *Out of Bounds,* 55–74.

New, Melvyn. "Some Sterne Borrowings from Four Renaissance Authors." *Philol Q* 71 (1992), 303–10.

New, Melvyn. "Sterne and the Narrative of Determinateness." *Eighteenth-Cent Fiction* 4 (1992), 315–29.

New, Melvyn. "Swift and Sterne: Two Tales, Several Sermons, and a Relationship Revisited," in Frank Palmeri, ed., *Critical Essays,* 171–73, 176–82.

New, Melvyn. *Telling New Lies,* 83–106.

Novak, Maximillian E. "Satirical Form and Realistic Fiction in *Tristram Shandy,*" in Melvyn New, ed., *Approaches,* 137–45.

Ogée, Frédéric. "Pli ou face? Autour d'un page de *Tristram Shandy.*" *Etudes Anglaises* 44 (1991), 257–71.

Page, Norman. *Speech in the English Novel,* 130–34.

Peereboom, J. J. "Lachend naar het einde." *Maatstaf* 38:9–10 (1990), 128–33.

Phelan, James. *Reading People,* 137–39.

Piper, William Bowman. "Understanding *Tristram Shandy,*" in Melvyn New, ed., *Approaches,* 41–48.

Porter, Roy. "'The whole secret of health': Mind, Body and Medicine in *Tristram Shandy,*" in John Christie and Sally Shuttleworth, eds., *Nature Transfigured,* 61–78.

Pott, Hans-Georg. *Neue Theorie des Romans,* 47–93.

Probyn, Clive T. *English Fiction,* 133–42.

Raymond, Michael. "Winding Up the Clock: Introducing *Tristram Shandy,*" in Melvyn New, ed., *Approaches,* 101–4.

Rizzo, Betty. "'How could you, Madam, be so inattentive?': Tristram's Relationship with the Reader," in Melvyn New, ed., *Approaches,* 67–71.

Rogers, Deborah D. "Tristram Shandy in a Restoration and Eighteenth-Century Course: Satire or Soap?," in Melvyn New, ed., *Approaches,* 131–35.

Rogers, Pat. "Ziggerzagger Shandy: Sterne and the Aesthetics of the Crooked Line." *English* 42 (1993), 97–106.

Seager, Dennis L. *Stories Within Stories,* 53–81.

Shipley, J. B. "Tristram's Dearly Beloved: Or, His Jenny's an ***." *Engl Lang Notes* 29:1 (1991), 45–49.

Siebenschuh, William R. "Sterne's Paradoxical Coherence: Some Principles of Unity in *Tristram Shandy,*" in Melvyn New, ed., *Approaches,* 72–79.

Spector, Robert D. "Structure as a Starting Point," in Melvyn New, ed., *Approaches,* 49–54.

Staves, Susan. "Toby Shandy: Sentiment and the Soldier," in Melvyn New, ed., *Approaches,* 80–86.

Stevenson, John Allen. *The British Novel,* 67–89.

Stockhammer, Robert. *Leseerzählungen,* 45–66.

Tave, Stuart M. *Lovers, Clowns, and Fairies,* 243–69.

Telotte, Leigh Ehlers. "'Fire, Water, Women, Wind': *Tristram Shandy* in the Classroom," in Melvyn New, ed., *Approaches,* 118–22.

Thomas, Calvin. "*Tristram Shandy*'s Consent to Incompleteness: Discourse, Disavowal, Disruption." *Lit and Psych* 36:3 (1990), 44–61.

Warren, Leland E. "Getting into the Talk: Tristram Shandy through Conversation," in Melvyn New, ed., *Approaches,* 61–66.

Wehrs, Donald R. "Sterne, Cervantes, Montaigne: Fideistic Skepticism and the Rhetoric of Desire." *Compar Lit Stud* 25:2 (1988), 127–51.

Weinsheimer, Joel. "History and Theory, Literature and Criticism: The

Two Knobs of Teaching *Tristram Shandy*," in Melvyn New, ed., *Approaches*, 152–56.

ROBERT LOUIS STEVENSON

The Black Arrow, 1888

McLynn, Frank. *Robert Louis Stevenson*, 225–27.

Catriona, 1891

Letley, Emma. *From Galt to Douglas Brown*, 170–87.
McLynn, Frank. *Robert Louis Stevenson*, 436–40.

Dr. Jekyll and Mr. Hyde, 1886

Aguirre, Manuel. *The Closed Space*, 147–49.
Cornwell, Neil. *The Literary Fantastic*, 94–97.
Doane, Janice, and Devon Hodges. "Demonic Disturbances of Sexual Identity: The Strange Case of Dr. Jekyll and Mr/s Hyde." *Novel* 23 (1989), 63–74.
Koestenbaum, Wayne. "The Shadow on the Bed: Dr. Jekyll, Mr. Hyde, and the Labouchère Amendment." *Crit Matrix* Special Issue 1 (1988), 31–55.
Leps, Marie-Christine. *Apprehending the Criminal*, 205–18.
McLynn, Frank. *Robert Louis Stevenson*, 254–66.
Manlove, Colin. "'Closer than an Eye': The Interconnection of Stevenson's *Dr. Jekyll and Mr. Hyde*." *Stud in Scottish Lit* 23 (1988), 87–101.
Pittock, Murray G. H. *Spectrum of Decadence*, 108–11.
Rutelli, Romana. *Il desiderio del diverso*, 44–64.
Shaw, Marion. "'To tell the truth of sex': Confession and Abjection in Late Victorian Writing," in Linda M. Shires, ed., *Rewriting the Victorians*, 92–97.
Thomas, Ronald R. *Dreams of Authority*, 237–53.
Tropp, Martin. *Images of Fear*, 99–109, 118–24, 126–29.

The Ebb-Tide, 1894

McLynn, Frank. *Robert Louis Stevenson*, 464–68.

Kidnapped, 1886

Letley, Emma. *From Galt to Douglas Brown*, 274–81.
McLynn, Frank. *Robert Louis Stevenson*, 266–69.

The Master of Ballantrae, 1889

Letley, Emma. *From Galt to Douglas Brown*, 192–206.
McLynn, Frank. *Robert Louis Stevenson*, 302–9.
Naugrette, Jean-Pierre. "*The Master of Ballantrae:* fragments d'un discours aventureux." *Etudes Anglaises* 43 (1990), 29–40.

Prince Otto, 1885

McLynn, Frank. *Robert Louis Stevenson*, 222–26.

Treasure Island, 1883

> Angus, David. "Youth on the Prow: The First Publication of *Treasure Island.*" *Stud in Scottish Lit* 25 (1990), 83–99.
> Bristow, Joseph. *Empire Boys,* 109–23.
> Cole, David. "Impressions: N. C. Wyeth and *Treasure Island.*" *Illinois Engl Bull* 79:2 (1992), 109–16.
> Loxley, Diana. *Problematic Shores,* 129–69.
> McLynn, Frank. *Robert Louis Stevenson,* 197–203.
> Mallardi, Rosella. " 'Tra il popolo del sogno': Riletture critica di *Treasure Island.*" *Confronto Letterario* 8:15 (1991), 35–63.
> Moore, John D. "Emphasis and Suppression in Stevenson's *Treasure Island:* Fabrication of the Self in Jim Hawkins' Narrative." *Coll Lang Assoc J* 34 (1991), 436–52.
> Wall, Barbara. *The Narrator's Voice,* 70–73.

Weir of Hermiston, 1896

> Letley, Emma. *From Galt to Douglas Brown,* 206–15.
> McLynn, Frank. *Robert Louis Stevenson,* 487–92.

J. I. M. STEWART

Death at the President's Lodging, 1936

> Carter, Ian. *Ancient Cultures of Conceit,* 26–30.

The Naylors, 1985

> Carter, Ian. *Ancient Cultures of Conceit,* 153–58.

MARY STEWART

Airs Above the Ground, 1965

> Friedman, Lenemaja. *Mary Stewart,* 42–46.

The Crystal Cave, 1970

> Friedman, Lenemaja. *Mary Stewart,* 60–71.
> Jurich, Marilyn. "Mithraic Aspects of Merlin in Mary Stewart's *The Crystal Cave,*" in Donald E. Morse et al., eds., *The Celebration of the Fantastic,* 91–99.

The Gabriel Hounds, 1967

> Friedman, Lenemaja. *Mary Stewart,* 46–52.

The Hollow Hills, 1973

> Friedman, Lenemaja. *Mary Stewart,* 72–84.

The Ivy Tree, 1961

> Friedman, Lenemaja. *Mary Stewart,* 29–34.

The Last Enchantment, 1979

> Friedman, Lenemaja. *Mary Stewart,* 85–96.

Madam, Will You Talk?, 1955

Friedman, Lenemaja. *Mary Stewart,* 10–14.

The Moon-Spinners, 1962

Friedman, Lenemaja. *Mary Stewart,* 34–38.

My Brother Michael, 1960

Friedman, Lenemaja. *Mary Stewart,* 26–29.

Nine Coaches Waiting, 1958

Friedman, Lenemaja. *Mary Stewart,* 19–24.

This Rough Magic, 1964

Friedman, Lenemaja. *Mary Stewart,* 39–42.

Thunder on the Right, 1957

Friedman, Lenemaja. *Mary Stewart,* 17–19.

Touch Not the Cat, 1976

Friedman, Lenemaja. *Mary Stewart,* 52–57.

The Wicked Day, 1983

Friedman, Lenemaja. *Mary Stewart,* 97–115.

Wildfire at Midnight, 1956

Friedman, Lenemaja. *Mary Stewart,* 14–17.

BRAM STOKER

Dracula, 1897

Aguirre, Manuel. *The Closed Space,* 139–41.

Appleby, Robin S. "*Dracula* and *Dora:* The Diagnosis and Treatment of Alternative Narratives." *Lit and Psych* 39:3 (1993), 16–35.

Arata, Stephen D. "The Occidental Tourist: Dracula and the Anxiety of Reverse Colonization." *Victorian Stud* 33 (1990), 621–45.

Bhalla, Alok. *Politics of Atrocity and Lust,* 35–56.

Bhalla, Alok. "Politics of Atrocity and Lust: Folklore of Vampirism and the Tales of Byron, Polidori, Prest and Le Fanu," in Jasodhara Bagchi, ed., *Literature, Society and Ideology,* 151–70.

Boone, Troy. " 'He is English and Therefore Adventurous': Politics, Decadence, and *Dracula.*" *Stud in the Novel* 25 (1993), 76–89.

Brennan, Matthew C. "Repression, Knowledge, and Saving Souls: The Role of the 'New Woman' in Stoker's *Dracula* and Murnau's *Nosferatu.*" *Stud in the Hum* 19 (1992), 1–8.

Cornwell, Neil. *The Literary Fantastic,* 107–12.

Craft, Christopher. " 'Kiss Me with Those Red Lips': Gender and Inversion in Bram Stoker's *Dracula,*" in Elaine Showalter, ed., *Speaking of Gender,* 216–38.

Dingley, R. J. "Count Dracula and the Martians," in Kath Filmer, ed., *The Victorian Fantasists,* 13–23.

Flood, David Hume. "Blood and Transfusion in Bram Stoker's *Dracula.*" *Univ of Mississippi Stud in Engl* 7 (1989), 180–89.

Gagnier, Regenia. "Evolution and Information, or Eroticism and Everyday Life, in *Dracula* and Late Victorian Aestheticism," in Regina Barreca, ed., *Sex and Death,* 140–54.

Geary, Robert F. "The Powers of Dracula." *J of the Fantastic in the Arts* 4:1 (1991), 81–91.

Hennlein, Elmar. *Religion und Phantastik,* 39–41, 104–5.

Hyles, Vernon. "Stoker, *Frankenstein, Dracula,* Sex, Violence, and Incompetence." *Round Table of the South Central Coll Engl Assoc* 27:1 (1986), 7–8.

Kayman, Martin A. *From Bow Street to Baker Street,* 229–34.

Keats, Patrick. "Stoker's *Dracula.*" *Explicator* 50 (1991), 26–27.

McDonald, Beth E. "The Vampire as Trickster Figure in Bram Stoker's *Dracula.*" *Extrapolation* 33 (1992), 128–41.

Nicholson, Mervyn. "Magic Food, Compulsive Eating, and Power Poetics," in Lilian R. Furst and Peter W. Graham, eds., *Disorderly Eaters,* 54–55.

Schliepsiek, Sue, and Karen Stone. "Why Teach *Dracula?*" *Illinois Engl Bull* 78:3 (1991), 67–76.

Smith, Malcolm. "*Dracula* and the Victorian Frame of Mind." *Trivium* 24 (1989), 76–97.

Spear, Jeffrey L. "Gender and Sexual Dis-Ease in *Dracula,*" in Lloyd Davis, ed., *Virginal Sexuality,* 179–92.

Spencer, Kathleen L. "Purity and Danger: *Dracula,* The Urban Gothic, and the Late Victorian Degeneracy Crisis." *ELH* 59 (1992), 197–210.

Tracy, Robert. "Loving You All Ways: Vamps, Vampires, Necrophiles and Necrofilles in Nineteenth-Century Fiction," in Regina Barreca, ed., *Sex and Death,* 39–47.

Tropp, Martin. *Images of Fear,* 133–69.

Whitehead, Gwendolyn. "The Vampire in Nineteenth-Century Literature." *Univ of Mississippi Stud in Engl* 8 (1990), 243–48.

Wicke, Jennifer. "Vampiric Typewriting: *Dracula* and its Media." *ELH* 59 (1992), 467–92.

Williams, Anne. "*Dracula:* Si(g)ns of the Fathers." *Texas Stud in Lit and Lang* 33 (1991), 445–59.

The Jewel of Seven Stars, 1903

Tracy, Robert. "Loving You All Ways: Vamps, Vampires, Necrophiles and Necrofilles in Nineteenth-Century Fiction," in Regina Barreca, ed., *Sex and Death,* 49–51.

Zeender, Marie-Noëlle. "L'érotisme et la mort: images de la mère dans trois des derniers romans de Bram Stoker," in Roger Bozzetto et al., eds., *Eros,* 62–65.

The Lady of the Shroud, 1909

Zeender, Marie-Noëlle. "L'érotisme et la mort: images de la mère dans trois des derniers romans de Bram Stoker," in Roger Bozzetto et al., eds., *Eros,* 59–62.

The Lair of the White Worm, 1911

Zeender, Marie-Noëlle. "L'érotisme et la mort: images de la mère dans trois des derniers romans de Bram Stoker," in Roger Bozzetto et al., eds., *Eros,* 65–68.

The Snake's Pass, 1890

Zeender, Marie Noëlle. "L'Irlande Romantique et Fantastique dans *The Snake's Pass.*" *Etudes Irlandaises* 18:1 (1993), 39–47.

ELIZABETH STONE

William Langshawe, 1842

Wheeler, Michael. "Two Tales of Manchester Life." *Gaskell Soc J* 3 (1989), 6–28.

MARIE STOPES

Love's Creation, 1928

Hall, Lesley A. "Uniting Science and Sensibility: Marie Stopes and the Narratives of Marriage in the 1920s," in Angela Ingram and Daphne Patai, eds., *Rediscovering Forgotten Radicals,* 125–28.

DAVID STOREY

Radcliffe, 1963

Lapaire, Jean-Rémi, and Wilfrid Rotge. "The Dynamics of Ambiguity in David Storey's *Radcliffe.*" *Caliban* 29 (1992), 85–100.

Pittock, Malcolm. "Storey's *Radcliffe.*" *Durham Univ J* 83 (1991), 235–48.

Saville, 1976

Brown, Dorothy H. "Breaking Away: A Yorkshire Working Class Family in David Storey's *Saville.*" *Round Table of the South Central Coll Engl Assoc* 27:1 (1986), 3–5.

This Sporting Life, 1960

Pittock, Malcolm. "Revealing the Sixties: *This Sporting Life* Revisited." *Forum for Mod Lang Stud* 26:2 (1990), 97–108.

FRANCIS STUART

Black List, Section H, 1971

Harmon, Maurice. "Francis Stuart," in Rüdiger Imhof, ed., *Contemporary Irish Novelists,* 16–19.

Molloy, Francis C. "A Life Reshaped: Francis Stuart's *Black List, Section H.*" *Canadian J of Irish Stud* 14:2 (1989), 37–47.

Schaffeld, Norbert. *Die Darstellung des nationalsozialistischen Deutsch-land,* 148–52.

A Hole in the Head, 1977

Harmon, Maurice. "Francis Stuart," in Rüdiger Imhof, ed., *Contemporary Irish Novelists,* 19–22.

The Pillar of Cloud, 1948

Harmon, Maurice. "Francis Stuart," in Rüdiger Imhof, ed., *Contemporary Irish Novelists,* 10–11.

Redemption, 1949

Harmon, Maurice. "Francis Stuart," in Rüdiger Imhof, ed., *Contemporary Irish Novelists,* 11–15.

GRAHAM SWIFT

Out of This World, 1988

Bernard, Catherine. "Les années quatre-vingt: vers une autre alchimie romanesque (A propos de deux romans de Graham Swift)." *Caliban* 27 (1990), 113–22.

Shuttlecock, 1981

Higdon, David Leon. " 'Unconfessed Confessions': The Narrators of Gra-ham Swift and Julian Barnes," in James Acheson, ed., *The British and Irish Novel,* 184–86.

The Sweet-Shop Owner, 1980

Higdon, David Leon. " 'Unconfessed Confessions': The Narrators of Gra-ham Swift and Julian Barnes," in James Acheson, ed., *The British and Irish Novel,* 181–84.

Waterland, 1983

Bernard, Catherine. "Les années quatre-vingt: vers une autre alchimie romanesque (A propos de deux romans de Graham Swift)." *Caliban* 27 (1990), 113–22.

Gallix, François. "Au nom de l'anguille: *Waterland,* de Graham Swift." *Etudes Anglaises* 45 (1992), 66–79.

Higdon, David Leon. " 'Unconfessed Confessions': The Narrators of Gra-ham Swift and Julian Barnes," in James Acheson, ed., *The British and Irish Novel,* 186–89.

Landow, George P. "History, His Story, and Stories in Graham Swift's *Waterland.*" *Stud in the Liter Imagination* 23:2 (1990), 197–211.

Lee, Alison. *Realism and Power,* 40–46.

Porée, Marc. "Différences et répétition dans *Waterland* de Graham Swift," in Jean-Jacques Lecercle, ed., *La Répétition,* 159–89.

Taylor, D. J. *A Vain Conceit,* 127–29.

JONATHAN SWIFT

Gulliver's Travels, 1726

Aikins, Janet E. "Reading 'with Conviction': Trial by Satire," in Frederik N. Smith, ed., *The Genres of "Gulliver's Travels,"* 203–25.

Alkon, Paul K. "*Gulliver* and the Origins of Science Fiction," in Frederik N. Smith, ed., *The Genres of "Gulliver's Travels,"* 163–76.

Barnett, Louise K. "Deconstructing *Gulliver's Travels:* Modern Readers and the Problematic of Genre," in Frederik N. Smith, ed., *The Genres of "Gulliver's Travels,"* 230–42.

Bellamy, Liz. *Jonathan Swift's "Gulliver's Travels,"* 29–118.

Bowden, Betsy. "Before the Houyhnhnms: Rational Horses in the Late Seventeenth Century." *Notes and Queries* 237 (1992), 38–40.

Brown, Laura. "Reading Race and Gender: Jonathan Swift," in Frank Palmeri, ed., *Critical Essays,* 128–38.

Burrow, Richard. "*Gulliver's Travels:* The Stunting of a Philosopher." *Interpretation* 21 (1993), 41–56.

Christie, John R. R. "Laputa Revisited," in John Christie and Sally Shuttleworth, eds., *Nature Transfigured,* 45–59.

Clark, John R. "Lures, Limetwigs, and the Swiftian Swindle," in Carl R. Kropf, ed., *Reader Entrapment,* 135–39.

Cunningham, John. "Perversions of the Eucharist in *Gulliver's Travels.*" *Christianity & Lit* 40 (1991), 345–60.

DePorte, Michael. "Avenging Naboth: Swift and Monarchy." *Philol Q* 69 (1990), 419–30.

Dixsaut, Jean. "Du modèle à la norme dans *Gulliver's Travels.*" *Bull de la Société d'Etudes Anglo-Américaines des XVIIe et XVIIIe Siècles* 28 (1989), 87–89.

Doll, Dan. "Swift and Brobdingnagian Law." *Univ of Hartford Stud in Lit* 22:1 (1990), 3–15.

Donnelly, Dorothy F. "*Utopia* and *Gulliver's Travels:* Another Perspective." *Moreana* 25 (1988), 115–24.

Downie, J. A. "The Political Significance of *Gulliver's Travels,*" in John Irwin Fischer et al., eds., *Swift and His Contexts,* 1–15.

Ehrenpreis, Irvin. "The Allegory of *Gulliver's Travels.*" *Swift Stud* 4 (1989), 13–28.

Emprin, Ginette. "Appearance and Reality in *Gulliver's Travels.*" *Etudes Irlandaises* 15:1 (1990), 37–44.

Fitzgerald, Robert P. "The Allegory of *Gulliver's Travels.*" *REAL: Yrbk of Res in Engl and Am Lit* 6 (1988/89), 187–214.

Flynn, Carol Houlihan. *The Body in Swift and Defoe,* 183–90.

Forster, Jean-Paul. *Jonathan Swift,* 47–54, 86–89, 92–96, 158–64, 176–79, 203–5.

Fox, Christopher. "The Myth of Narcissus in Swift's *Travels,*" in Carl R. Kropf, ed., *Reader Entrapment,* 89–102.

Géracht, Maurice A. "Pedro de Mendez: Marrano Jew and Good Samaritan in Swift's *Voyages.*" *Swift Stud* 5 (1990), 39–52.

Harpold, Terence. "The Anatomy of Satire: Aggressivity and Satirical Physick in *Gulliver's Travels.*" *Lit and Psych* 36:3 (1990), 32–39.

Hart, Vaughan. "Gulliver's Travels into the 'City of the Sun.'" *Swift Stud* 6 (1991), 111–14.

Heilman, Robert Bechtold. *The Workings of Fiction,* 143–48.

Hinnant, Charles H. "Swift and the 'Conjectural Histories' of the Eighteenth Century: The Case of the Fourth Voyage." *Stud in Eighteenth-Cent Culture* 21 (1991), 75–87.

Hunter, J. Paul. "*Gulliver's Travels* and the Novel," in Frederik N. Smith, ed., *The Genres of "Gulliver's Travels,"* 56–73.

Kantzenbach, Friedrich Wilhelm. *Traditionen Europas im Spiegel von Literatur,* 25–30.

Kennelly, Laura B. "Swift's Yahoo and King Jehu: Genesis of an Allusion." *Engl Lang Notes* 26:3 (1989), 37–43.

Knowles, Ronald. "Swift's Yahoos, Aphrodite and Hyginus Fabula CCXX." *Engl Lang Notes* 31:1 (1993), 44–45.

Lapraz-Severino, Françoise. *Relativité et communication dans les "Voyages de Gulliver" de Jonathan Swift.*

Leddy, Annette. "Borges and Swift: Dystopian Reflections." *Compar Lit Stud* 27 (1990), 113–22.

McNeil, David. *The Grotesque Depiction of War,* 65–83.

Manlove, C. N. "Swift and Fantasy," in Donald E. Morse and Csilla Bertha, eds., *More Real Than Reality,* 193–207.

Novak, Maximillian E. "*Gulliver's Travels* and the Picaresque Voyage: Some Reflections on the Hazards of Genre Criticism," in Frederik N. Smith, ed., *The Genres of "Gulliver's Travels,"* 23–35.

Patey, Douglas Lane. "Swift's Satire on 'Science' and the Structure of *Gulliver's Travels.*" *ELH* 58 (1991), 809–34.

Peterson, Leland D. "Gulliver's Travels: Antient and Modern History Corrected." *Swift Stud* 6 (1991), 83–110.

Philmus, Robert M. "Swift and the Question of Allegory: The Case of *Gulliver's Travels.*" *Engl Stud in Canada* 18 (1992), 157–72.

Piper, William Bowman. "Gulliver's Account of Houyhnhnmland as a Philosophical Treatise," in Frederik N. Smith, ed., *The Genres of "Gulliver's Travels,"* 179–200.

Pritchard, Allan. "The Houyhnhnms: Swift, Suetonius, and Marvell." *Notes and Queries* 235 (1990), 305–6.

Probyn, Clive T. *Jonathan Swift,* 31–109.

Probyn, Clive T. "Starting from the Margins: Teaching Swift in the Light of Poststructuralist Theories of Reading and Writing," in Peter J. Schakel, ed., *Critical Approaches,* 21–28.

Rodino, Richard H. "'Splendide Mendax': Authors, Characters, and Readers in *Gulliver's Travels.*" *PMLA* 106 (1991), 1054–68.

Rodino, Richard H. "The Study of *Gulliver's Travels,* Past and Future," in Peter J. Schakel, ed., *Critical Approaches,* 114–31.

Rothstein, Eric. "*Gulliver* 3; or The Progress of Clio," in Frank Palmeri, ed., *Critical Essays,* 104–19.

Salvaggio, Ruth. *Enlightened Absence,* 82–90, 99–101.

Sayers, William. "Gulliver's Wounded Knee." *Swift Stud* 7 (1992), 106–9.

Scott, John W. "The Uses of the Grotesque in *Gulliver's Travels* and *The Journey to the West.*" *Tamkang R* 19 (1988–89), 785–802.

Seidel, Michael. "Strange Dispositions: Swift's *Gulliver's Travels,*" in Frank Palmeri, ed., *Critical Essays,* 75–89.

Sena John F. "*Gulliver's Travels* and the Genre of the Illustrated Book," in Frederik N. Smith, ed., *The Genres of "Gulliver's Travels,"* 101–36.

Sitter, John. *Arguments of Augustan Wit,* 101–5, 112–14, 127–30, 145–53, 162–73.

Smedman, M. Sarah. "Like Me, Like Me Not: *Gulliver's Travels* as Children's Book," in Frederik N. Smith, ed., *The Genres of "Gulliver's Travels,"* 75–95.

Smith, Frederik N. "The Danger of Reading Swift: The Double Binds of *Gulliver's Travels,*" in Carl R. Kropf, ed., *Reader Entrapment,* 109–27.

Smith, Frederik N. "Science, Imagination, and Swift's Brobdingnagians." *Eighteenth-Cent Life* 14:1 (1990), 100–112.

Smith, Frederik N. "Scientific Discourse: *Gulliver's Travels* and *The Philosophical Transactions,*" in Frederik N. Smith, ed., *The Genres of "Gulliver's Travels,"* 139–59.

Smith, Frederik N. "Style, Swift's Reader, and the Genres of *Gulliver's Travels,*" in Frederik N. Smith, ed., *The Genres of "Gulliver's Travels,"* 246–58.

Smith, Frederik N. "Swift's View of Composition and the Meaning of *Gulliver's Travels,*" in Peter J. Schakel, ed., *Critical Approaches,* 91–113.

Stringfellow, Frank. "Irony and Ideals in *Gulliver's Travels,*" in Frank Palmeri, ed., *Critical Essays,* 104–19.

Takase, Fumiko. "Gulliver and Wasobee." *Swift Stud* 4 (1989), 91–94.

Todd, Dennis. "The Hairy Maid at the Harpsichord: Some Speculations on the Meaning of *Gulliver's Travels.*" *Texas Stud in Lit and Lang* 34 (1992), 239–72.

Varey, Simon. "Exemplary History and the Political Satire of *Gulliver's Travels,*" in Frederik N. Smith, ed., *The Genres of "Gulliver's Travels,"* 39–54.

Washington, Gene. "Fungible Gulliver: Fungible Flesh." *Engl Lang Notes* 30:1 (1992), 17–19.

Washington, Gene. "Swift's *Gulliver's Travels* Bk. 1, Ch. 5." *Explicator* 48 (1990), 251–52.

Watts, Cedric. *Literature and Money,* 112–14, 119–21.

Worth, Chris. "Swift's 'Flying Island': Buttons and Bomb-Vessels." *R of Engl Stud* 42 (1991), 343–60.

Wyrick, Deborah Baker. "*Gulliver's Travels* and the Early English Novel," in Peter J. Schakel, ed., *Critical Approaches,* 91–113.

ALGERNON CHARLES SWINBURNE

Lesbia Brandon, 1952

> Monneyron, Frédéric. "L'Androgyne dans *Lesbia Brandon* de Swin-
> burne." *Cahiers Victoriens et Edouardiens* 29 (1989), 55–63.

FRANK SWINNERTON

Nocturne, 1917

> Orel, Harold. *Popular Fiction in England,* 79–90.

NETTA SYRETT

Roseanne, 1902

> Ardis, Ann L. *New Women, New Novels,* 103–5.

ELIZABETH TAYLOR

At Mrs. Lippincote's, 1945

> Lassner, Phyllis. "The Quiet Revolution: World War II and the English
> Domestic Novel." *Mosaic* 23:3 (1990), 95–97. (Also in Evelyn J. Hinz,
> ed., *Troops versus Tropes,* 95–97.)

Palladian, 1946

> Baker, Niamh. *Happily Ever After?,* 89–91.

A View of the Harbour, 1947

> Baker, Niamh. *Happily Ever After?,* 99–102, 149–52.

MEADOWS TAYLOR

Seeta, 1872

> Paxton, Nancy L. "Mobilizing Chivalry: Rape in British Novels about the
> Indian Uprising of 1857." *Victorian Stud* 36 (1992), 16–19.

EMMA TENNANT

The Bad Sister, 1978

> Hassam, Andrew. *Writing and Reality,* 129–32, 149–51.

WILLIAM MAKEPEACE THACKERAY

Catherine, 1840

> Prawer, S. S. *Israel at Vanity Fair,* 49–55.

Denis Duval, 1864

Lund, Michael. *Reading Thackeray*, 127–29, 132–45.
Prawer, S. S. *Israel at Vanity Fair*, 400–405.

Henry Esmond, 1852

Clarke, Micael. "Thackeray's *Henry Esmond* and Eighteenth-Century Feminism: A Double Vision of Feminist Discourse and Literary Narrative." *Works and Days* 5:1 (1987), 85–107.
Crosby, Christina. *The Ends of History*, 44–68.
Lund, Michael. *Reading Thackeray*, 81–97, 100–102.
Peck, John. "Thackeray and Religion: The Evidence of *Henry Esmond*." *English* 40:168 (1991), 217–32.
Thomas, Deborah A. *Thackeray and Slavery*, 96–114.
Tierney, Terry. "Henry Esmond's Double Vision." *Stud in the Novel* 24 (192), 349–64.

The History of Samuel Titmarsh and the Great Hoggarty Diamond, 1841

Prawer, S. S. *Israel at Vanity Fair*, 82–90.

Lovel the Widower, 1860

Prawer, S. S. *Israel at Vanity Fair*, 367–69.
Sedgwick, Eve Kosofsky. "The Beast in the Closet: James and the Writing of Homosexual Panic," in Elaine Showalter, ed., *Speaking of Gender*, 249–52.

The Luck of Barry Lyndon, 1844

Castronovo, David. *The English Gentleman*, 22–24.
Decap, Roger. "*Barry Lyndon:* Thackeray et 'l'ailleurs.'" *Caliban* 28 (1991), 37–47.
Prawer, S. S. *Israel at Vanity Fair*, 131–40.
Thomas, Deborah A. *Thackeray and Slavery*, 32–40.
Tyson, Nancy Jane. "Thackeray and Bulwer: Between the Lines in *Barry Lyndon*." *Engl Lang Notes* 27:2 (1989), 53–55.

The Newcomes, 1854–1855

Auerbach, Emily. *Maestros, Dilettantes, and Philistines*, 104–9.
Datta, Kitty. "The Theme of Indian Fortunes in English Fiction from Mackenzie to Thackeray: Between Confrontain and Evasions," in Jasodhara Bagchi, ed., *Literature, Society and Ideology*, 263–66, 269–74.
Fasick, Laura. "Thackeray's Treatment of Writing and Painting." *Nineteenth-Cent Lit* 47 (1992), 72–90.
Lund, Michael. *Reading Thackeray*, 108–26.
McMaster, R. D. "London as a System of Signs in Thackeray's *The Newcomes*." *Victorian R* 16:1 (1990), 1–21.
McMaster, R. D. *Thackeray's Cultural Frame of Reference*, 8–171.
Perkin, J. Russell. "Thackeray and Orientalism: *Cornhill to Cairo* and *The Newcomes*." *Engl Stud in Canada* 16 (1990), 304–12.
Prawer, S. S. *Israel at Vanity Fair*, 290–335.

Reed, John R. *Victorian Will*, 300–302.

Thomas, Deborah A. *Thackeray and Slavery*, 121–25, 127–40.

Pendennis, 1849–1850

Baldridge, Cates. "The Problems of Worldliness in *Pendennis*." *Nineteenth-Cent Lit* 44 (1990), 492–513.

Datta, Kitty. "The Theme of Indian Fortunes in English Fiction from Mackenzie to Thackeray: Between Confrontatin and Evasions," in Jasodhara Bagchi, ed., *Literature, Society and Ideology*, 266–69.

Fasick, Laura. "Thackeray's Treatment of Writing and Painting." *Nineteenth-Cent Lit* 47 (1992), 72–90.

Knezevic, Borislav. "*Pendennis:* The Strategies of Discontent." *Studia Romanica et Anglica Zagrabiensia* 34 (1989), 129–48.

Lambert, Miles. "The Dandy in Thackeray's *Vanity Fair* and *Pendennis:* An Early Victorian View of the Regency Dandy." *Costume* 22 (1988), 60–69.

Lund, Michael. *Reading Thackeray*, 39–52, 68–72.

Prawer, S. S. *Israel at Vanity Fair*, 243–57.

Reed, John R. *Victorian Will*, 297–300.

Thomas, Deborah A. *Thackeray and Slavery*, 76–97.

Philip, 1862

Fasick, Laura. "Thackeray's Treatment of Writing and Painting." *Nineteenth-Cent Lit* 47 (1992), 72–90.

Prawer, S. S. *Israel at Vanity Fair*, 370–80.

Thomas, Deborah A. *Thackeray and Slavery*, 157–60, 164–87.

The Ravenswing, 1869

Auerbach, Emily. *Maestros, Dilettantes, and Philistines*, 94–101.

Rebecca and Rowena, 1850

Prawer, S. S. *Israel at Vanity Fair*, 263–70, 286–96.

The Rose and the Ring, 1854

Wall, Barbara. *The Narrator's Voice*, 50–52.

Vanity Fair, 1848

Auerbach, Emily. *Maestros, Dilettantes, and Philistines*, 101–4.

Chrétien, Maurice. "Miroirs de *Vanity Fair*." *Etudes Anglaises* 45 (1992), 424–31.

Fletcher, Robert P. "The Dandy and the Fogy: Thackeray and the Aesthetics/Ethics of the Literary Pragmatist." *ELH* 58 (1991), 383–403.

Jadwin, Lisa. "The Seductiveness of Female Duplicity in *Vanity Fair*." *Stud in Engl Lit, 1500–1900* 32 (1992), 663–84.

Lambert, Miles. "The Dandy in Thackeray's *Vanity Fair* and *Pendennis:* An Early Victorian View of the Regency Dandy." *Costume* 22 (1988), 60–69.

Lund, Michael. *Reading Thackeray*, 26–38.

MacKay, Carol Hanbery. "Controlling Death and Sex: Magnification v. the

Rhetoric of Rules in Dickens and Thackeray," in Regina Barreca, ed., *Sex and Death*, 129–35.

Miller, Andrew. "*Vanity Fair* through Plate Glass." *PMLA* 105 (1990), 1042–53.

Nicoletta, Daniela. *Vibrazione e risonanza*, 63–71.

Ortiz, Gloria. *The Dandy and the "Señorito,"* 33–37.

Phelan, James. *Reading People*, 138–39.

Phelan, James. "*Vanity Fair:* Listening as a Rhetorician—and a Feminist," in Laura Claridge and Elizabeth Langland, eds., *Out of Bounds*, 132–47.

Prawer, S. S. *Israel at Vanity Fair*, 213–42.

Ryals, Clyde de L. *A World of Possibilities*, 34–47.

Sherman, Joseph. "Race and Racism as Narrative Strategies in *Vanity Fair.*" *Engl Stud in Africa* 34 (1991), 76–101.

Steig, Michael. *Stories of Reading*, 14–16.

Thomas, Deborah A. *Thackeray and Slavery*, 49–76.

Thornton, Sarah. " 'Blind love and unbounded credit': l'argent et le texte dans *Vanity Fair.*" *Cahiers Victoriens et Edouardiens* 35 (1992), 169–76.

Woodring, Carl. *Nature into Art*, 130–33.

The Virginians, 1958–1959

Prawer, S. S. *Israel at Vanity Fair*, 351–66.

Thomas, Deborah A. *Thackeray and Slavery*, 140–58.

D. M. THOMAS

The White Hotel, 1981

Alexander, Marguerite. *Flights from Realism*, 97–103.

Bartkowski, Frances, and Catherine Stearns. "The Lost Icon in *The White Hotel.*" *J of the Hist of Sexuality* 1 (1990), 283–95.

Gabbard, Krin. "*The White Hotel* and the Traditions of Ring Composition." *Compar Lit Stud* 27 (1990), 230–46.

George, Diana. "Teaching the Nightmare World of *The White Hotel.*" *Proteus* 6:1 (1989), 57–60.

Lee, Alison. *Realism and Power*, 94–98.

Lougy, Robert E. "The Wolf-Man, Freud, and D. M. Thomas: Intertextuality, Interpretation, and Narration in *The White Hotel.*" *Mod Lang Stud* 21:3 (1991), 91–103.

Newman, Robert D. "D. M. Thomas' *The White Hotel:* Mirrors, Triangles, and Sublime Repression." *Mod Fiction Stud* 35 (1989), 193–207.

Phillips, K. J. "The Phalaris Syndrome: Alain Robbe-Grillet vs. D. M. Thomas," in Katherine Anne Ackley, ed., *Women and Violence in Literature*, 175–205.

Sauerberg, Lars Ole. "When the Soul Takes Wing: D. M. Thomas's *The White Hotel.*" *Critique* (Washington, DC) 31 (1989), 3–10.

Tanner, Laura E. "Sweet Pain and Charred Bodies: Figuring Violence in *The White Hotel.*" *Boundary 2* 18:2 (1991), 130–49.

Weber, Jim. "*The White Hotel:* Freud, Medusa, and the Missing Goddess." *Notes on Contemp Lit* 21:1 (1991), 10–11.

Weibel, Paul. *Reconstructing the Past,* 49–82, 97–122.

Zhang, Benzi. "The Chinese Box in D. M. Thomas's *The White Hotel.*" *Intl Fiction R* 20 (1993), 54–57.

J. R. R. TOLKIEN

The Hobbit, 1937

Bentinck, A. "Tolkien and De la Mare: The Fantastic Secondary Worlds of *The Hobbit* and *The Three Mulla-Mulgars.*" *Mythlore* 15:3 (1989), 39–43.

Christensen, Bonniejean. "Tolkien's Creative Technique: *Beowulf* and *The Hobbit.*" *Mythlore* 15:3 (1989), 4–10.

Couch, Christopher L. "From Under Mountains to Beyond Stars: The Process of Riddling in Leofric's *The Exeter Book* and *The Hobbit.*" *Mythlore* 14:1 (1987), 9–13, 55.

Ellison, John A. "The Structure of *The Hobbit.*" *Mallorn* 27 (1990), 29–32.

Hammond, Wayne G. "All the Comforts: The Image of Home in *The Hobbit* and *The Lord of the Rings.*" *Mythlore* 14:1 (1987), 29–33.

Miller, Miriam Youngerman. "J. R. R. Tolkien's Merlin: An Old Man with a Staff—Gandalf and the Magus Tradition," in Jeanie Watson and Maureen Fries, eds., *The Figure of Merlin,* 121–38.

O'Brien, Donald. "On the Origin of the Name 'Hobbit.'" *Mythlore* 16:2 (1989), 32–38.

Provost, William. "Language and Myth in the Fantasy Writings of J. R. R. Tolkien." *Mod Age* 33:1 (1990), 42–52.

Rosebury, Brian. *Tolkien,* 100–106.

Smith, Arden R. "I'm a Troll Man." *Vinyar Tengwar* 18 (1991), 33–34.

Smith, Arden R. "Who's Afraid of the Big, Bad Gollum?" *Vinyar Tengwar* 17 (1991), 23–24.

The Lord of the Rings, 1966

Abbott, Joe. "Tolkien's Monsters: Concept and Function in *The Lord of the Rings.*" *Mythlore* 16:1 (1989), 19–26, 33; 16:2 (1989), 40–47; 16:3 (1990), 51–59.

Aldrich, Kevin. "The Sense of Time in J. R. R. Tolkien's *The Lord of the Rings.*" *Mythlore* 15:1 (1988), 5–9.

Arthur, Elizabeth. "Above All Shadows Rides the Sun: Gollum as Hero." *Mythlore* 18:1 (1991), 19–27.

Attebery, Brian. "Fantasy and the Narrative Transaction," in Nicholas Ruddick, ed., *State of the Fantastic,* 19–21.

Attebery, Brian. "Tolkien, Crowley, and Postmodernism," in Olena H. Saciuk, ed., *The Shape of the Fantastic,* 23–25.

Bettridge, William Edwin. "Tolkien's 'New' Mythology." *Mythlore* 16:4 (1990), 27–31.

Boenig, Robert. "The Drums of Doom: H. G. Wells' *First Men in the Moon* and *The Lord of the Rings.*" *Mythlore* 14:3 (1988), 57–58.

Chance, Jane. *"The Lord of the Rings,"* 27–116.

Flieger, Verlyn B. "A Question of Time." *Mythlore* 16:3 (1990), 5–8.

Hammond, Wayne G. "All the Comforts: The Image of Home in *The Hobbit* and *The Lord of the Rings.*" *Mythlore* 14:1 (1987), 29–33.

Hargrove, Gene. "Who Is Tom Bombadil?" *Mythlore* 13:1 (1986), 20–24.

Harris, Mason. "The Psychology of Power in Tolkien's *The Lord of the Rings,* Orwell's *1984* and Le Guin's *A Wizard of Earthsea.*" *Mythlore* 15:1 (1988), 46–56.

Hennelly, Mark M., Jr. "The Road and the Ring: Solid Geometry in Tolkien's Middle-Earth." *Mythlore* 9:3 (1982), 3–13.

Higbie, Robert, and Joe E. Bryan, Jr. "Frodo and Childe Roland." *Mythlore* 14:1 (1987), 57.

Huttar, Charles A. "Tolkien, Epic Traditions, and Golden Age Myths," in Kath Filmer, ed., *Twentieth-Century Fantasists,* 92–104.

Irwin, Betty J. "Archaic Pronouns in *The Lord of the Rings.*" *Mythlore* 14:1 (1987), 46–47.

Keefer, Sarah Larratt. "'Work-Writing' to Create the Fictional Portrait: Tolkien's Inclusion of Lewis in *The Lord of the Rings.*" *Engl Stud in Canada* 18 (1992), 181–96.

Knowles, Sebastian D. G. *A Purgatorial Flame,* 135–37.

Kubinski, Wojciech. "Comprehending the Incomprehensible: On the Pragmatic Analysis of Elvish Texts in *The Lord of the Rings.*" *Inklings* 7 (1989), 63–81.

Langford, Jonathon D. "The Scouring of the Shire as a Hobbit Coming-of-Age." *Mythlore* 18:1 (1991), 4–9.

Lindsay, Sean. "The Dream System in *The Lord of the Rings.*" *Mythlore* 13:3 (1987), 7–14.

Madsen, Catherine. "Light from an Invisible Lamp: Natural Religion in *The Lord of the Rings.*" *Mythlore* 14:3 (1988), 43–47.

Mende, Lisa Anne. "Gondolin, Minas Tirith and the Eucatastrophe." *Mythlore* 13:2 (1986), 37–40.

Miller, Miriam Youngerman. "J. R. R. Tolkien's Merlin: An Old Man with a Staff—Gandalf and the Magus Tradition," in Jeanie Watson and Maureen Fries, eds., *The Figure of Merlin,* 121–38.

Obertino, James. "Moria and Hades: Underworld Journeys in Tolkien and Virgil." *Compar Lit Stud* 30 (1993), 153–67.

Potts, Stephen. "The Many Faces of the Hero in *The Lord of the Rings.*" *Mythlore* 17:4 (1991), 4–11.

Provost, William. "Language and Myth in the Fantasy Writings of J. R. R. Tolkien." *Mod Age* 33:1 (1990), 42–52.

Reckford, Kenneth. "'There and Back Again': Odysseus and Bilbo Baggins." *Mythlore* 14:3 (1988), 5–9.

Rosebury, Brian. *Tolkien,* 7–80.

Ryan, J. S. "The Mines of Mendip and of Moria." *Mythlore* 17:1 (1990), 25–27.

Scull, Christina. "On Reading and Re-Reading *The Lord of the Rings*." *Mallorn* 27 (1990), 11–14.

Smith, Arden R. "I'm a Troll Man." *Vinyar Tengwar* 18 (1991), 33–34.

Startzman, L. Eugene. "Goldberry and Galadriel: The Quality of Joy." *Mythlore* 16:2 (1989), 5–13.

Stratyner, Leslie. "Þe Us Þas Beagas Geaf (He Who Gave Us These Rings): Sauron and the Perversion of Anglo-Saxon Ethos." *Mythlore* 16:1 (1989), 5–8.

Treloar, John L. "The Middle-Earth Epic and the Seven Capital Vices." *Mythlore* 16:1 (1989), 37–42.

Wytenbroek, J. R. "Apocalyptic Vision in *The Lord of the Rings*." *Mythlore* 14:4 (1988), 7–12.

Silmarillion, 1977

Beach, Sarah. "Fire and Ice: The Traditional Heroine in *The Silmarillion*." *Mythlore* 18:1 (1991), 37–41.

Broadwell, Elizabeth. "Essë and Narn: Name, Identity and Narrative in the Tale of Túrin Turambar." *Mythlore* 17:2 (1990), 34–44.

Greenman, David. "*The Silmarillion* as Aristotelian Epic-Tragedy." *Mythlore* 14:3 (1988), 20–25.

Mende, Lisa Anne. "Gondolin, Minas Tirith and the Eucatastrophe." *Mythlore* 13:2 (1986), 37–40.

Rosebury, Brian. *Tolkien*, 92–99.

H. M. TOMLINSON

All Our Yesterdays, 1930

Onions, John. *English Fiction and Drama*, 109–15.

CHARLOTTE ELIZABETH TONNA

Helen Fleetwood, 1841

Krueger, Christine L. *The Reader's Repentance*, 138–45.

ROBERT TRESSELL

The Ragged Trousered Philanthropists, 1914

Neetens, Wim. *Writing and Democracy*, 145–56.

Trodd, Anthea. *A Reader's Guide*, 38–40.

Watts, Cedric. *Literature and Money*, 164–71.

WILLIAM TREVOR

The Boarding-House, 1965

Morrison, Kristin. *William Trevor*, 40–46.

The Children of Dynmouth, 1976

>   Morrison, Kristin. *William Trevor,* 148–63.

Elizabeth Alone, 1973

>   Morrison, Kristin. *William Trevor,* 26–29.

Fools of Fortune, 1983

>   Larsen, Max Deen. "Saints of the Ascendancy: William Trevor's Big-House Novels," in Otto Rauchbauer, ed., *Ancestral Voices,* 257–67.
>   Morrissey, Thomas. "Trevor's *Fools of Fortune:* The Rape of Ireland." *Notes on Mod Irish Lit* 2 (1990), 58–60.
>   Morrison, Kristin. *William Trevor,* 16–18, 117–19, 125–27, 129–32.

The Love Department, 1966

>   Morrison, Kristin. *William Trevor,* 46–53.

Miss Gomez and the Brethren, 1971

>   Morrison, Kristin. *William Trevor,* 55–64.

Mrs. Eckdorf in O'Neill's Hotel, 1969

>   Morrison, Kristin. *William Trevor,* 53–55, 97–106, 114–16.

Nights at the Alexandra, 1987

>   Morrison, Kristin. *William Trevor,* 133–37.

The Old Boys, 1964

>   Morrison, Kristin. *William Trevor,* 39–46.

Other People's Worlds, 1980

>   Morrison, Kristin. *William Trevor,* 29–36.

The Silence in the Garden, 1988

>   Larsen, Max Deen. "Saints of the Ascendancy: William Trevor's Big-House Novels," in Otto Rauchbauer, ed., *Ancestral Voices,* 267–76.
>   Morrison, Kristin. *William Trevor,* 65–74.

A Standard of Behaviour, 1958

>   Morrison, Kristin. *William Trevor,* 38–39.

ANTHONY TROLLOPE

The American Senator, 1877

>   Bell, Arnold Craig. *A Guide to Trollope,* 163–69.
>   Hall, N. John. *Trollope,* 421–25.
>   Heineman, Helen K. *Three Victorians in the New World,* 252–63.
>   Nardin, Jane. "The Social Critic in Anthony Trollope's Novels." *Stud in Engl Lit, 1500–1900* 30 (1990), 688–92.
>   Trotter, Jackson. "Foxhunting and the English Social Order in Trollope's *The American Senator." Stud in the Novel* 24 (192), 227–39.

Ayala's Angel, 1881

> Bell, Arnold Craig. *A Guide to Trollope,* 176–79.
> Hall, N. John. *Trollope,* 443–46.

Barchester Towers, 1857

> Auerbach, Emily. *Maestros, Dilettantes, and Philistines,* 118–19.
> Bell, Arnold Craig. *A Guide to Trollope,* 19–28.
> Blaisdell, Bob. "Can You Resist Her?" *Spectrum* 31 (1989), 68–70.
> Hall, N. John. *Trollope,* 143–53.
> Lyons, Paul. "The Morality of Irony and Unreliable Narrative in Trollope's *The Warden* and *Barchester Towers.*" *South Atlantic R* 54:1 (1989), 41–54.
> Wiesenfarth, Joseph. *Gothic Manners,* 41–59.

The Belton Estate, 1866

> Bell, Arnold Craig. *A Guide to Trollope,* 85–93.

The Bertrams, 1859

> Bell, Arnold Craig. *A Guide to Trollope,* 37–40.
> Dessner, Lawrence Jay. "The Autobiographical Matrix of Trollope's *The Bertrams.*" *Nineteenth-Cent Lit* 45 (1990), 26–58.
> Hall, N. John. *Trollope,* 161–64, 182–84.
> Swingle, L. J. *Romanticism and Anthony Trollope,* 84–87.

Can You Forgive Her?, 1864

> Bell, Arnold Craig. *A Guide to Trollope,* 65–77.
> Butler, Lance St. John. *Victorian Doubt,* 182–84.
> Chevalier, Jean-Louis. "La femme et la prudence dans les *Palliser Novels.*" *Cahiers Victoriens et Edouardiens* 31 (1990), 67–70.
> Hall, N. John. *Trollope,* 267–69.
> Halperin, John. *Jane Austen's Lovers,* 70–72, 93–94.
> Swingle, L. J. *Romanticism and Anthony Trollope,* 75–78, 145–47.

Castle Richmond, 1860

> Bell, Arnold Craig. *A Guide to Trollope,* 40–41.
> Johnston, Conor. "Parsons, Priests, and Politics: Anthony Trollope's Irish Clergy." *Eire-Ireland* 25:1 (1990), 82–97.

The Claverings, 1867

> Bell, Arnold Craig. *A Guide to Trollope,* 81–84.

Cousin Henry, 1879

> Bell, Arnold Craig. *A Guide to Trollope,* 179–82.
> Hall, N. John. *Trollope,* 458–60.
> Miller, J. Hillis. *Victorian Subjects,* 257–62.

Doctor Thorne, 1858

> Bell, Arnold Craig. *A Guide to Trollope,* 30–37.
> Hall, N. John. *Trollope,* 164–68.
> Johnston, Anne. "The Pleasant Surprise of Miss Dunstable." *Spectrum* 32 (1990), 149–53.

Dr. Wortle's School, 1881

Bell, Arnold Craig. *A Guide to Trollope,* 182–86.
Hall, N. John. *Trollope,* 462–64.
Swingle, L. J. *Romanticism and Anthony Trollope,* 23–25, 29–31, 240–42.

The Duke's Children, 1880

Bell, Arnold Craig. *A Guide to Trollope,* 170–71.
Chevalier, Jean-Louis. "La femme et la prudence dans les *Palliser Novels.*"
    Cahiers Victoriens et Edouardiens 31 (1990), 76–78.
Hall, N. John. *Trollope,* 465–69.
Halperin, John. *Jane Austen's Lovers,* 108–10, 112–15.
Kincaid, James R. "Anthony Trollope and the Unmannerly Novel," in
    Bege K. Bowers and Barbara Brothers, eds., *Reading and Writing,* 96–
    103.

The Eustace Diamonds, 1872

Bell, Arnold Craig. *A Guide to Trollope,* 135–42.
Chevalier, Jean-Louis. "La femme et la prudence dans les *Palliser Novels.*"
    Cahiers Victoriens et Edouardiens 31 (1990), 72–74.
Hall, N. John. *Trollope,* 377–79.

An Eye for an Eye, 1879

Bell, Arnold Craig. *A Guide to Trollope,* 142–44.
Johnston, Conor. "Parsons, Priests, and Politics: Anthony Trollope's Irish
    Clergy." *Eire-Ireland* 25:1 (1990), 90–97.

The Fixed Period, 1882

Bell, Arnold Craig. *A Guide to Trollope,* 188–90.
Hall, N. John. *Trollope,* 484–87.
Nardin, Jane. "The Social Critic in Anthony Trollope's Novels." *Stud in
    Engl Lit, 1500–1900* 30 (1990), 692–94.

Framley Parsonage, 1861

Bell, Arnold Craig. *A Guide to Trollope,* 41–46.
Hall, N. John. *Trollope,* 196–98.

The Golden Lion of Granpère, 1872

Bell, Arnold Craig. *A Guide to Trollope,* 96–97.
Swingle, L. J. *Romanticism and Anthony Trollope,* 153–57.

Harry Heathcote, 1874

Bell, Arnold Craig. *A Guide to Trollope,* 149.

He Knew He Was Right, 1869

Bell, Arnold Craig. *A Guide to Trollope,* 114–24.
Hall, N. John. *Trollope,* 337–44.
Halperin, John. *Jane Austen's Lovers,* 74–76, 108–11.
Swingle, L. J. *Romanticism and Anthony Trollope,* 157–59.

Is He Popenjoy?, 1878

> Bell, Arnold Craig. *A Guide to Trollope*, 161–62.
> Hall, N. John. *Trollope*, 437–40.

John Caldigate, 1879

> Bell, Arnold Craig. *A Guide to Trollope*, 171–75.
> Hall, N. John. *Trollope*, 456–58.

The Kellys and the O'Kellys, 1848

> Hall, N. John. *Trollope*, 102–5.
> Johnston, Conor. "Parsons, Priests, and Politics: Anthony Trollope's Irish
>   Clergy." *Eire-Ireland* 25:1 (1990), 81–87.

Kept in the Dark, 1882

> Bell, Arnold Craig. *A Guide to Trollope*, 186–87.

Lady Anna, 1874

> Bell, Arnold Craig. *A Guide to Trollope*, 148–49.
> Halperin, John. *Jane Austen's Lovers*, 64–66.
> Miller, J. Hillis. *Victorian Subjects*, 263–69.
> Swingle, L. J. *Romanticism and Anthony Trollope*, 8–11.

The Landleaguers, 1883

> Bell, Arnold Craig. *A Guide to Trollope*, 194–96.
> Johnston, Conor. "Parsons, Priests, and Politics: Anthony Trollope's Irish
>   Clergy." *Eire-Ireland* 25:1 (1990), 94–97.

The Last Chronicle of Barset, 1867

> Bell, Arnold Craig. *A Guide to Trollope*, 97–106.
> Blaisdell, Bob. "Can You Resist Her?" *Spectrum* 31 (1989), 67–68, 70–74.
> Hall, N. John. *Trollope*, 298–303.

Linda Tressel, 1868

> Bell, Arnold Craig. *A Guide to Trollope*, 95–96.

The Macdermotts of Ballycloran, 1847

> Hall, N. John. *Trollope*, 96–102.
> Johnston, Conor. "Parsons, Priests, and Politics: Anthony Trollope's Irish
>   Clergy." *Eire-Ireland* 25:1 (1990), 80–97.
> Swingle, L. J. *Romanticism and Anthony Trollope*, 40–42.

Marion Fay, 1882

> Swingle, L. J. *Romanticism and Anthony Trollope*, 241–43.

Miss Mackenzie, 1865

> Bell, Arnold Craig. *A Guide to Trollope*, 77–80.

Mr. Scarborough's Family, 1883

> Bell, Arnold Craig. *A Guide to Trollope*, 190–91.
> Delany, Paul. "Land, Money, and the Jews in the Later Trollope." *Stud in
>   Engl Lit, 1500–1900* 32 (1992), 772–84.
> Hall, N. John. *Trollope*, 490–93.

Nina Balatka, 1867

>   Bell, Arnold Craig. *A Guide to Trollope,* 94–95.
>   Hall, N. John. *Trollope,* 285–89.

An Old Man's Love, 1884

>   Bell, Arnold Craig. *A Guide to Trollope,* 192–93.

Orley Farm, 1862

>   Bell, Arnold Craig. *A Guide to Trollope,* 46–51.
>   Hall, N. John. *Trollope,* 213–15, 245–47.
>   Swingle, L. J. *Romanticism and Anthony Trollope,* 13–15, 122–24, 232–34.

Phineas Finn, 1869

>   Bell, Arnold Craig. *A Guide to Trollope,* 107–13.
>   Chevalier, Jean-Louis. "La femme et la prudence dans les *Palliser Novels.*"
>   *Cahiers Victoriens et Edouardiens* 31 (1990), 70–72.
>   Hall, N. John. *Trollope,* 334–37.
>   Halperin, John. *Jane Austen's Lovers,* 85–104.
>   Polhemus, Robert M. *Erotic Faith,* 196–222.
>   Swingle, L. J. *Romanticism and Anthony Trollope,* 160–63, 232–34, 242–
>   44.

Phineas Redux, 1874

>   Bell, Arnold Craig. *A Guide to Trollope,* 144–47.
>   Chevalier, Jean-Louis. "La femme et la prudence dans les *Palliser Novels.*"
>   *Cahiers Victoriens et Edouardiens* 31 (1990), 75–76.
>   Hall, N. John. *Trollope,* 393–98.
>   Polhemus, Robert M. *Erotic Faith,* 196–222.

The Prime Minister, 1876

>   Bell, Arnold Craig. *A Guide to Trollope,* 159–61.
>   Chevalier, Jean-Louis. "La femme et la prudence dans les *Palliser Novels.*"
>   *Cahiers Victoriens et Edouardiens* 31 (1990), 74–75.
>   Delany, Paul. "Land, Money, and the Jews in the Later Trollope." *Stud in
>   Engl Lit, 1500–1900* 32 (1992), 765–84.
>   Hall, N. John. *Trollope,* 398–401.
>   Harvie, Christopher. *The Centre of Things,* 94–97.
>   Roberts, Adam. "Trollope in *The Prime Minister.*" *Notes and Queries* 237
>   (1992), 183–84.
>   Swingle, L. J. *Romanticism and Anthony Trollope,* 88–91.

Rachel Ray, 1863

>   Bell, Arnold Craig. *A Guide to Trollope,* 59–65.
>   Hall, N. John. *Trollope,* 251–56.
>   Swingle, L. J. *Romanticism and Anthony Trollope,* 111–13.

Ralph the Heir, 1871

>   Bell, Arnold Craig. *A Guide to Trollope,* 132–35.
>   Hall, N. John. *Trollope,* 329–32.
>   Swingle, L. J. *Romanticism and Anthony Trollope,* 147–49.

Sir Harry Hotspur, 1870

Bell, Arnold Craig. *A Guide to Trollope,* 128–31.

The Small House at Allington, 1864

Bell, Arnold Craig. *A Guide to Trollope,* 52–59.
Hall, N. John. *Trollope,* 247–49.
Swingle, L. J. *Romanticism and Anthony Trollope,* 121–24.

The Three Clerks, 1858

Hall, N. John. *Trollope,* 153–58.

The Vicar of Bullhampton, 1870

Bell, Arnold Craig. *A Guide to Trollope,* 124–27.
Hall, N. John. *Trollope,* 357–59.

The Warden, 1855

Auerbach, Emily. *Maestros, Dilettantes, and Philistines,* 115–18.
Bell, Arnold Craig. *A Guide to Trollope,* 12–18.
Eade, J. C. " 'That's the Way the Money Goes': Accounting in *The Warden*." *Notes and Queries* 237 (1992), 182–83.
Hall, N. John. *Trollope,* 133–36.
Lyons, Paul. "The Morality of Irony and Unreliable Narrative in Trollope's *The Warden* and *Barchester Towers*." *South Atlantic R* 54:1 (1989), 41–54.
Miller, J. Hillis. *Victorian Subjects,* 221–23.
Nardin, Jane. "The Social Critic in Anthony Trollope's Novels." *Stud in Engl Lit, 1500–1900* 30 (1990), 686–87.

The Way We Live Now, 1875

Bell, Arnold Craig. *A Guide to Trollope,* 150–59.
Delany, Paul. "Land, Money, and the Jews in the Later Trollope." *Stud in Engl Lit, 1500–1900* 32 (1992), 769–84.
Hall, N. John. *Trollope,* 384–88.
Heineman, Helen K. *Three Victorians in the New World,* 240–45.
Swingle, L. J. *Romanticism and Anthony Trollope,* 61–63, 118–25.
Taylor, D. J. *A Vain Conceit,* 34–37.

FRANCES TROLLOPE

The Barnabys in America, 1843

Heineman, Helen K. *Three Victorians in the New World,* 67–74.

Jonathan Jefferson Whitlaw, 1836

Heineman, Helen K. *Three Victorians in the New World,* 61–66.

The Refugee in America, 1832

Heineman, Helen K. *Three Victorians in the New World,* 51–61.

JOHN WAIN

Hurry on Down, 1953

Bergonzi, Bernard. *Wartime and Aftermath,* 142–43.
Wilkinson, John. "Conventions of Comedies of Manners and British Novels about Academic Life," in Bege K. Bowers and Barbara Brothers, eds., *Reading and Writing,* 211–13.

Where the Rivers Meet, 1988

Rossen, Janice. *The University in Modern Fiction,* 69–74.

HORACE WALPOLE

The Castle of Otranto, 1765

Aguirre, Manuel. *The Closed Space,* 91–93.
Albertazzi, Silvia. *Il sogno gotico,* 13–32.
Cornwell, Neil. *The Literary Fantastic,* 47–49.
Dole, Carol M. "Three Tyrants in *The Castle of Otranto.*" *Engl Lang Notes* 26:1 (1988), 26–33.
Geary, Robert F. *The Supernatural in Gothic Fiction,* 24–31.
Haggerty, George E. *Gothic Fiction,* 15–17.
Miles, Robert. *Gothic Writing,* 105–12.
Napier, Elizabeth R. *The Failure of Gothic,* 73–99.
Probyn, Clive T. *English Fiction,* 170–72.
Punter, David. *The Romantic Unconscious,* 128–30.

MRS. HUMPHRY WARD

David Grieve, 1892

Collister, Peter. "A 'Legendary Hue': Henri Regnault and the Fiction of Henry James and Mrs Humphry Ward." *Mod Lang R* 87 (1992), 831–46.

Helbeck of Bannisdale, 1898

Butler, Lance St. John. *Victorian Doubt,* 124–25.
Fasick, Laura. "Culture, Nature, and Gender in Mary Ward's *Robert Elsmere* and *Helbeck of Bannisdale.*" *Victorian Newsl* 83 (1993), 25–31.
Rossen, Janice. *The University in Modern Fiction,* 24–26.
Schork, R. J. "Victorian Hagiography: A Pattern of Allusions in *Robert Elsmere* and *Helbeck of Bannisdale.*" *Stud in the Novel* 21 (1989), 296–302.

Marcella, 1894

Schmidt, Ricarda. "Radikalismus in konservativen Händen: Mrs. Humphry Wards *Marcella,*" in Gregory Claeys and Liselotte Glage, eds., *Radikalismus in Literatur und Gesellschaft,* 243–61.

Robert Elsmere, 1888

Bailey, Nancy I. "Ward's *Robert Elsmere.*" *Explicator* 49 (1991), 102.

Fasick, Laura. "Culture, Nature, and Gender in Mary Ward's *Robert Elsmere* and *Helbeck of Bannisdale.*" *Victorian Newsl* 83 (1993), 25–31.

Loesberg, Jonathan. "Deconstruction, Historicism, and Overdetermination: Dislocations of the Marriage Plots in *Robert Elsmere* and *Dombey and Son.*" *Victorian Stud* 33 (1990), 442–52, 460–64.

O'Connor, D. J. "Mrs. Humphry Ward's *Robert Elsmere* (1888) and Palacio Valdés's *La fe* (1892)." *Romance Q* 37 (1990), 331–36.

Reed, John R. *Victorian Will,* 365–67.

Schork, R. J. "Victorian Hagiography: A Pattern of Allusions in *Robert Elsmere* and *Helbeck of Bannisdale.*" *Stud in the Novel* 21 (1989), 292–96.

Udelson, Joseph H. *Dreamers of the Ghetto,* 37–39.

Sir George Tressady, 1896

Ardis, Ann L. *New Women, New Novels,* 157–59.

REX WARNER

The Professor, 1938

Croft, Andy. *Red Letter Days,* 301–4.

The Wild Goose Chase, 1937

Croft, Andy. *Red Letter Days,* 284–88.

SYLVIA TOWNSEND WARNER

Lolly Willowes, 1926

Brothers, Barbara. "Flying the Nets at Forty: *Lolly Willowes* as Female Bildungsroman," in Laura L. Doan, ed., *Old Maids,* 195–211.

Summer Will Show, 1936

Castle, Terry. "Sylvia Townsend Warner and the Counterplot of Lesbian Fiction." *Textual Practice* 4 (1990), 218–31.

Montefiore, Janet. "Listening to Minna: Realism, Feminism and the Politics of Reading." *Paragraph* 14 (1991), 197–216.

SAMUEL WARREN

Now and Then: Through a Glass, Darkly, 1848

Drexler, Peter. *Literatur, Recht, Kriminalität,* 168–70.

KEITH WATERHOUSE

Jubb, 1963

Prince, John. "Angus Wilson, Keith Waterhouse and the New Towns." *Caliban* 27 (1990), 19–21.

IAN WATSON

Chekhov's Journey, 1983

Lee, Alison. *Realism and Power,* 73–79.

THEODORE WATTS-DUNTON

Aylwin, 1898

Reed, John R. *Victorian Will,* 355–58.

ALEC WAUGH

The Loom of Youth, 1917

Orel, Harold. *Popular Fiction in England,* 91–103.

EVELYN WAUGH

Black Mischief, 1932

Beaty, Frederick L. *The Ironic World,* 67–83.
Crabbe, Katharyn W. *Evelyn Waugh,* 46–58.
Garnett, Robert R. *From Grimes to Brideshead,* 78–97.
Kolek, Leszek S. "*Black Mischief* as a Comic Structure," in Alain Blayac, ed., *Evelyn Waugh,* 1–20.
McDonnell, Jacqueline. *Evelyn Waugh,* 61–66.
Myers, William. *Evelyn Waugh and the Problem of Evil,* 30–39.

Brideshead Revisited, 1945

Beaty, Frederick L. *The Ironic World,* 145–65.
Bergonzi, Bernard. *Wartime and Aftermath,* 36–39.
Bittner, David. "The Long-Awaited Solution to the Nada Alapov Puzzle, or Saving the 'Jest' Till Last." *Evelyn Waugh Newsl and Stud* 25:2 (1991), 4–7.
Bittner, David. "Sebastian and Charles—More Than Friends?" *Evelyn Waugh Newsl and Stud* 24:2 (1990), 1–3.
Bittner, David. " 'Serious Measure': Assessing Sebastian Flyte's Intellect." *Evelyn Waugh Newsl and Stud* 26:2 (1992), 1–3.
Burch, Francis F. "Robert Hugh Benson, Roger Martin du Gard, and Evelyn Waugh's *Brideshead Revisited.*" *Notes and Queries* 235 (1990), 68.
Chevalier, Jean-Louis. "Arcadian Minutiae: Notes on *Brideshead Revisited,*" in Alain Blayac, ed., *Evelyn Waugh,* 35–58.
Crabbe, Katharyn W. *Evelyn Waugh,* 94–106.
Davis, Robert M. "Imagined Space in *Brideshead Revisited,*" in Alain Blayac, ed., *Evelyn Waugh,* 22–33.
Davis, Robert Murray. "*Brideshead Revisited,*" 23–135.
Garnett, Robert R. *From Grimes to Brideshead,* 145–60.

Gorra, Michael. *The English Novel*, 180–90.

Greene, Donald. "Charles Ryder's 'Conversion' Once More." *Evelyn Waugh Newsl and Stud* 25:1 (1991), 2–3.

Greene, Donald. "More on Charles Ryder's Conversion." *Evelyn Waugh Newsl* 23:3 (1989), 1–3.

Hitt, Ann. "The Fountain at Brideshead Castle." *Evelyn Waugh Newsl* 23:3 (1989), 6–7.

Kennedy, Valerie. "Evelyn Waugh's *Brideshead Revisited:* Paradise Lost or Paradise Regained?" *Ariel* 21:1 (1990), 23–37.

Knowles, Sebastian D. G. *A Purgatorial Flame*, 190–202.

Linholm, Rhonda, and Elaine E. Whitaker. "Jerusalem Revisited." *Evelyn Waugh Newsl and Stud* 24:3 (1990), 1–2.

McCartney, George. "The Being and Becoming of Evelyn Waugh," in Alain Blayac, ed., *Evelyn Waugh*, 144–45.

McDonnell, Jacqueline. *Evelyn Waugh*, 27–30, 90–105, 108–10.

Myers, William. *Evelyn Waugh and the Problem of Evil*, 67–77.

Osborne, John. "The Character of Bridey." *Evelyn Waugh Newsl and Stud* 27:2 (1993), 7–8.

Osborne, John. "The Character of Cara in *Brideshead Revisited*." *Evelyn Waugh Newsl and Stud* 26:2 (1992), 3–4.

Osborne, John W. "The Character of Mr. Samgrass." *Evelyn Waugh Newsl and Stud* 26:3 (1992), 5–6.

Osborne, John W. "Charles Ryder's Conversion Revisited." *Evelyn Waugh Newsl and Stud* 24:2 (1990), 3–4.

Osborne, John W. "The Relationship of Charles and Sebastian." *Evelyn Waugh Newsl and Stud* 25:1 (1991), 4–5.

Osborne, John W. "Sebastian Flyte as a Homosexual." *Evelyn Waugh Newsl* 23:3 (1989), 7–8.

Rossen, Janice. *The University in Modern Fiction*, 93–103.

Schönberg, Ulf. "Architecture and Environment in Evelyn Waugh's *Brideshead Revisited.*" *Orbis Litterarum* 45 (1990), 84–95.

Tindall, Gillian. *Countries of the Mind*, 72–78.

Whitaker, Elaine E. "The Awakening Conscience in *Brideshead Revisited.*" *Evelyn Waugh Newsl and Stud* 27:2 (1993), 1–2.

Wilson, John Howard. "Mary Waugh and Julia's Daughter in *Brideshead Revisited.*" *Evelyn Waugh Newsl and Stud* 26:1 (1992), 5–7.

Wirth, Annette. *The Loss of Traditional Values*, 53–98.

Decline and Fall, 1928

Beaty, Frederick L. *The Ironic World*, 32–50.

Crabbe, Katharyn W. *Evelyn Waugh*, 25–36.

Frick, Robert. "Style and Structure in the Early Novels of Evelyn Waugh." *Papers on Lang & Lit* 28 (1992), 421.

Garnett, Robert R. *From Grimes to Brideshead*, 37–57.

Gorra, Michael. *The English Novel*, 156–62.

Hager, Thomas. "*Decline and Fall:* The Modern Man." *Evelyn Waugh Newsl and Stud* 24:3 (1990), 4–5.

McCartney, George. "The Being and Becoming of Evelyn Waugh," in Alain Blayac, ed., *Evelyn Waugh,* 10–44.

McDonnell, Jacqueline. *Evelyn Waugh,* 46–52.

Myers, William. *Evelyn Waugh and the Problem of Evil,* 4–13.

Rossen, Janice. *The University in Modern Fiction,* 22–24.

Stovel, Bruce. "The Genesis of Evelyn Waugh's Comic Vision: Waugh, Captain Grimes, and *Decline and Fall.*" *Thalia* 11:1 (1989), 14–24.

Wilson, John Howard. "The Hero's Misadventure in *Decline and Fall.*" *Evelyn Waugh Newsl and Stud* 27:1 (1993), 4–7.

A Handful of Dust, 1934

Beaty, Frederick L. *The Ironic World,* 84–110.

Crabbe, Katharyn W. *Evelyn Waugh,* 59–69.

Drewry, Thomas. "Tony Last's Two Children in *A Handful of Dust.*" *Evelyn Waugh Newsl and Stud* 25:3 (1991), 5–8.

Frick, Robert. "Style and Structure in the Early Novels of Evelyn Waugh." *Papers on Lang & Lit* 28 (1992), 421–41.

Garnett, Robert R. *From Grimes to Brideshead,* 98–118.

Gorra, Michael. *The English Novel,* 172–78.

Greene, Donald. "A Note on Hetton and Some Other Abbeys." *Evelyn Waugh Newsl and Stud* 26:3 (1992), 1–3.

Jager, Eric. "A Handful of Dusty Books: Orality and Literacy in Waugh." *Evelyn Waugh Newsl and Stud* 24:2 (1990), 4–5.

Kloss, Robert J. "Waugh's *A Handful of Dust* as Autobiography." *J of Evolutionary Psych* 10 (1989), 372–82.

McDonnell, Jacqueline. *Evelyn Waugh,* 67–73.

Wilson, John Howard. "A Note on the Ending of *A Handful of Dust.*" *Evelyn Waugh Newsl and Stud* 24:3 (1990), 2.

Wirth, Annette. *The Loss of Traditional Values,* 25–51.

Helena, 1950

Crabbe, Katharyn W. *Evelyn Waugh,* 117–24.

McCartney, George. "The Being and Becoming of Evelyn Waugh," in Alain Blayac, ed., *Evelyn Waugh,* 151–54.

McDonnell, Jacqueline. *Evelyn Waugh,* 110–14.

Myers, William. *Evelyn Waugh and the Problem of Evil,* 89–95.

Love Among the Ruins, 1953

Beaty, Frederick L. *The Ironic World,* 20–22.

Myers, William. *Evelyn Waugh and the Problem of Evil,* 83–87.

The Loved One, 1948

Babiak, Peter R. "A Brief Philosophy of Stoneless Peaches." *Evelyn Waugh Newsl and Stud* 25:3 (1991), 5.

Beaty, Frederick L. *The Ironic World,* 166–82.

Crabbe, Katharyn W. *Evelyn Waugh,* 106–17.

Doyle, Paul A. "Liam O'Flaherty and Waugh's *Loved One.*" *Evelyn Waugh Newsl and Stud* 25:1 (1991), 3–4.

McDonnell, Jacqueline. *Evelyn Waugh*, 118–27.
Myers, William. *Evelyn Waugh and the Problem of Evil*, 84–89.

Men at Arms, 1952

Crabbe, Katharyn W. *Evelyn Waugh*, 125–28, 147–51.
Hitt, Ann. "Virginia Troy." *Evelyn Waugh Newsl and Stud* 27:2 (1993), 3.
McDonnell, Jacqueline. *Evelyn Waugh*, 131–34.
Munton, Alan. *English Fiction*, 83–85.

Officers and Gentlemen, 1955

Crabbe, Katharyn W. *Evelyn Waugh*, 128–32, 142–45.
Hitt, Ann. "Virginia Troy." *Evelyn Waugh Newsl and Stud* 27:2 (1993), 3–4.
McDonnell, Jacqueline. *Evelyn Waugh*, 42–44.
Munton, Alan. *English Fiction*, 83–86.
Myers, William. *Evelyn Waugh and the Problem of Evil*, 110–11, 116–18, 127–29.

The Ordeal of Gilbert Pinfold, 1957

Crabbe, Katharyn W. *Evelyn Waugh*, 157–67.
Gorra, Michael. *The English Novel*, 194–97.
McDonnell, Jacqueline. *Evelyn Waugh*, 114–17.
Myers, William. *Evelyn Waugh and the Problem of Evil*, 98–106.

Put Out More Flags, 1942

Crabbe, Katharyn W. *Evelyn Waugh*, 80–91.
Garnett, Robert R. *From Grimes to Brideshead*, 142–45.
Gorra, Michael. *The English Novel*, 178–80.
Knowles, Sebastian D. G. *A Purgatorial Flame*, 179–90.
McDonnell, Jacqueline. *Evelyn Waugh*, 82–86.
Myers, William. *Evelyn Waugh and the Problem of Evil*, 58–67.

Scoop, 1938

Beaty, Frederick L. *The Ironic World*, 111–30.
Crabbe, Katharyn W. *Evelyn Waugh*, 69–80.
Garnett, Robert R. *From Grimes to Brideshead*, 120–33.
Horsley, Lee. *Political Fiction*, 37–39, 80–89.
McDonnell, Jacqueline. *Evelyn Waugh*, 77–82.
Manheim, Leonard H. "Oh What a Lovely War: The Television Version of *Scoop*." *Evelyn Waugh Newsl and Stud* 25:1 (1991), 5–6.
Myers, William. *Evelyn Waugh and the Problem of Evil*, 47–51.

Sword of Honour, 1965

Garnett, Robert R. *From Grimes to Brideshead*, 161–64.
Gorra, Michael. *The English Novel*, 190–94.
Knowles, Sebastian D. G. *A Purgatorial Flame*, 202–13.
McDonnell, Jacqueline. *Evelyn Waugh*, 131–41.
Munton, Alan. *English Fiction*, 83–86.

Myers, William. *Evelyn Waugh and the Problem of Evil*, 107–31.
Wirth, Annette. *The Loss of Traditional Values*, 99–139.

Unconditional Surrender, 1961

Crabbe, Katharyn W. *Evelyn Waugh*, 132–40, 145–50.
Hitt, Ann. "Virginia Troy." *Evelyn Waugh Newsl and Stud* 27:2 (1993), 4–6.
McDonnell, Jacqueline. *Evelyn Waugh*, 137–40.
Munton, Alan. *English Fiction*, 83–93.
Myers, William. *Evelyn Waugh and the Problem of Evil*, 108–30.

Vile Bodies, 1930

Ames, Christopher. *The Life of the Party*, 176–202.
Beaty, Frederick L. *The Ironic World*, 51–66.
Blayac, Alain. "Evelyn Waugh and Humour," in Alain Blayac, ed., *Evelyn Waugh*, 124–27.
Crabbe, Katharyn W. *Evelyn Waugh*, 36–46.
Frick, Robert. "Style and Structure in the Early Novels of Evelyn Waugh." *Papers on Lang & Lit* 28 (1992), 421–22.
Garnett, Robert R. *From Grimes to Brideshead*, 58–75.
Gorra, Michael. *The English Novel*, 162–66.
McCartney, George. "The Being and Becoming of Evelyn Waugh," in Alain Blayac, ed., *Evelyn Waugh*, 148–51.
McDonnell, Jacqueline. *Evelyn Waugh*, 52–61.
Mahler, Andreas. "Zwischenkriegsbewusstsein und die Inszenierung satirischen Erzählens am Beispiel von Evelyn Waughs *Vile Bodies.*" *Deutsche Vierteljahrsschrift für Literaturwissenschaft und Geistesgeschichte* 64 (1990), 311–37.
Myers, William. *Evelyn Waugh and the Problem of Evil*, 13–20.

Work Suspended, 1943

Beaty, Frederick L. *The Ironic World*, 131–44.
Garnett, Robert R. *From Grimes to Brideshead*, 135–41.
McDonnell, Jacqueline. *Evelyn Waugh*, 87–90.
Myers, William. *Evelyn Waugh and the Problem of Evil*, 52–58.

MARY WEBB

Armour Wherein He Trusted, 1929

Coles, Gladys Mary. *Mary Webb*, 135–39.

The Golden Arrow, 1915

Coles, Gladys Mary. *Mary Webb*, 53–62.
Orel, Harold. *Popular Fiction in England*, 107–15.

Gone to Earth, 1917

Coles, Gladys Mary. *Mary Webb*, 71–79.

The House in Dormer Forest, 1920

Coles, Gladys Mary. *Mary Webb*, 84–90.

Precious Bane, 1924

Coles, Gladys Mary. *Mary Webb,* 115–24.

Seven for a Secret, 1922

Coles, Gladys Mary. *Mary Webb,* 104–9.
Cusick, Edmund. "Mary Webb's Borderland." *New Welsh R* 3:4 (1991), 26–33.

FAY WELDON

Down Among the Women, 1971

Salzmann-Brunner, Brigitte. *Amanuenses to the Present,* 183–87.

The Fat Woman's Joke, 1967

Greene, Gayle. *Changing the Story,* 75–76.
Newman, Jenny. "'See Me As Sisyphus, But Having A Good Time': The Fiction of Fay Weldon," in Robert E. Hosmer, Jr., ed., *Contemporary British Women Writers,* 189–90.

Female Friends, 1975

Salzmann-Brunner, Brigitte. *Amanuenses to the Present,* 188–95.

The Heart of the Country, 1987

Newman, Jenny. "'See Me As Sisyphus, But Having A Good Time': The Fiction of Fay Weldon," in Robert E. Hosmer, Jr., ed., *Contemporary British Women Writers,* 202–4.

The Life and Loves of a She-Devil, 1983

Newman, Jenny. "'See Me As Sisyphus, But Having A Good Time': The Fiction of Fay Weldon," in Robert E. Hosmer, Jr., ed., *Contemporary British Women Writers,* 198–200.
Salzmann-Brunner, Brigitte. *Amanuenses to the Present,* 203–10.

Praxis, 1978

Newman, Jenny. "'See Me As Sisyphus, But Having A Good Time': The Fiction of Fay Weldon," in Robert E. Hosmer, Jr., ed., *Contemporary British Women Writers,* 191–94.
Salzmann-Brunner, Brigitte. *Amanuenses to the Present,* 196–202.

The President's Child, 1982

Newman, Jenny. "'See Me As Sisyphus, But Having A Good Time': The Fiction of Fay Weldon," in Robert E. Hosmer, Jr., ed., *Contemporary British Women Writers,* 196–97.

Puffball, 1980

Newman, Jenny. "'See Me As Sisyphus, But Having A Good Time': The Fiction of Fay Weldon," in Robert E. Hosmer, Jr., ed., *Contemporary British Women Writers,* 194–95.

The Shrapnel Academy, 1986

> Newman, Jenny. " 'See Me As Sisyphus, But Having A Good Time': The Fiction of Fay Weldon," in Robert E. Hosmer, Jr., ed., *Contemporary British Women Writers,* 200–202.
>
> Salzmann-Brunner, Brigitte. *Amanuenses to the Present,* 211–21.

H. G. WELLS

Ann Veronica, 1909

> Coren, Michael. *The Invisible Man,* 84–86.
>
> Ducamp, Josette. "La signification historique de *Ann Veronica.*" *Cahiers Victoriens et Edouardiens* 30 (1989), 79–91.
>
> Harris, Janice H. "Lawrence and the Edwardian Feminists," in Michael Squires and Keith Cushman, eds., *The Challenge of D. H. Lawrence,* 64–66.
>
> Murray, Brian. *H. G. Wells,* 128–31.
>
> Simpson, Anne B. "Struggling with the Family in the Novels of H. G. Wells." *Cahiers Victoriens et Edouardiens* 30 (1989), 72–76.
>
> Trodd, Anthea. *A Reader's Guide,* 62–66.

The Autocracy of Mr. Parham, 1930

> Coren, Michael. *The Invisible Man,* 185–87.

Boon, 1915

> Hammond, J. R. *H. G. Wells and Rebecca West,* 87–89.
>
> Murray, Brian. *H. G. Wells,* 56–58.

The Bulpington of Blup, 1932

> Hammond, J. R. *H. G. Wells and Rebecca West,* 180–82.

Christina Alberta's Father, 1925

> Murray, Brian. *H. G. Wells,* 135–37.

The Croquet Player, 1936

> Coren, Michael. *The Invisible Man,* 199–200.
>
> Hammond, J. R. *H. G. Wells and Rebecca West,* 197–99.
>
> Murray, Brian. *H. G. Wells,* 142–44.

The Dream, 1924

> Hammond, J. R. *H. G. Wells and Rebecca West,* 146–49.

The First Men in the Moon, 1901

> Boenig, Robert. "The Drums of Doom: H. G. Wells' *First Men in the Moon* and *The Lord of the Rings.*" *Mythlore* 14:3 (1988), 57–58.
>
> Hillegas, Mark R. "A Road Not Taken." *Extrapolation* 30 (1989), 364–70.
>
> Lake, David. "Mr Bedford's Brush with God: Fantastic Tradition and Mysticism in *The First Men in the Moon.*" *Wellsian* 13 (1990), 2–16.
>
> Lake, David. "Wells, *The First Men in the Moon,* and Lewis's Ransom Trilogy," in Kath Filmer, ed., *Twentieth-Century Fantasists,* 24–28.

Murray, Brian. *H. G. Wells,* 97–100.

Parrinder, Patrick. "H. G. Wells and the Fall of Empires." *Foundation* 57 (1993), 54–56.

Renzi, Thomas C. *H. G. Wells,* 148–67.

Sadrin, Anny. "De la métaphore à la métamorphose: l'homme-machine de Descartes à la science-fiction, avec arrêt sur H. G. Wells." *Cahiers Victoriens et Edouardiens* 31 (1990), 130–34.

The Food of the Gods, 1904

Bailey, Kenneth V. "The Road to Cheasing Eyebright." *Cahiers Victoriens et Edouardiens* 30 (1989), 45–53.

Renzi, Thomas C. *H. G. Wells,* 173–87.

Russell, W. M. S. "H. G. Wells and Ecology," in Patrick Parrinder and Christopher Rolfe, eds., *H. G. Wells Under Revision,* 145–52.

The History of Mr. Polly, 1910

Brown, Richard. "Little England: On Triviality in the Naive Comic Fictions of H. G. Wells." *Cahiers Victoriens et Edouardiens* 30 (1989), 61–65.

Davies, Christie. "Making Fun of Work: Humor as Sociology in the Work of H. G. Wells," in Patrick Parrinder and Christopher Rolfe, eds., *H. G. Wells Under Revision,* 82–96.

Murray, Brian. *H. G. Wells,* 120–24.

In the Days of the Comet, 1906

Murray, Brian. *H. G. Wells,* 50–52, 102–6.

The Invisible Man, 1897

Holt, Philip. "H. G. Wells and the Ring of Gyges." *Science-Fiction Stud* 19 (1992), 236–45.

Renzi, Thomas C. *H. G. Wells,* 90–116.

Simpson, Anne B. "The 'Tangible Antagonist': H. G. Wells and the Discourse of Otherness." *Extrapolation* 31 (1990), 134–41.

Stetz, Margaret Diane. "Visible & Invisible Ills: H. G. Wells's 'Scientific Romances' as Social Criticism." *Victorians Inst J* 19 (1991), 14–24.

The Island of Dr. Moreau, 1896

Bozzetto, Roger. "Moreau's Tragi-Farcical Island." *Science-Fiction Stud* 20 (1993), 34–41.

Chialant, Maria Teresa. "A proposito dell'isola del Dottor Moreau," in Carlo Pagetti, ed., *Nel tempo del sogno,* 77–93.

Coren, Michael. *The Invisible Man,* 53–54.

Haynes, R. D. "The Unholy Alliance of Science in *The Island of Dr. Moreau.*" *Wellsian* 11 (1988), 13–24.

Lehman, Steven. "The Motherless Child in Science Fiction: *Frankenstein* and *Moreau.*" *Science-Fiction Stud* 19 (1992), 49–55.

Milling, Jill. "The Ambiguous Animal: Evolution of the Beast-Man in Scientific Creation Myths," in Olena H. Saciuk, ed., *The Shape of the Fantastic,* 106–7.

Murray, Brian. *H. G. Wells,* 90–93.

Philmus, Robert M. "Revisions of *Moreau.*" *Cahiers Victoriens et Edouardiens* 30 (1989), 117–36.

Philmus, Robert M. "The Strange Case of *Moreau* Gets Stranger." *Science-Fiction Stud* 19 (1992), 248–50.

Philmus, Robert M. "Textual Authority: The Strange Case of *The Island of Doctor Moreau.*" *Science-Fiction Stud* 17 (1990), 64–68.

Pittock, Murray G. H. *Spectrum of Decadence,* 111–12.

Reed, John R. "The Vanity of Law in *The Island of Doctor Moreau,*" in Patrick Parrinder and Christopher Rolfe, eds., *H. G. Wells Under Revision,* 134–44.

Renzi, Thomas C. *H. G. Wells,* 60–87.

Ruddick, Nicholas. *Ultimate Island,* 64–67.

Sadrin, Anny. "De la métaphore à la métamorphose: l'homme-machine de Descartes à la science-fiction, avec arrêt sur H. G. Wells." *Cahiers Victoriens et Edouardiens* 31 (1990), 132–34.

Shaw, Marion. " 'To tell the truth of sex': Confession and Abjection in Late Victorian Writing," in Linda M. Shires, ed., *Rewriting the Victorians,* 97–100.

Joan and Peter, 1918

Coren, Michael. *The Invisible Man,* 148–49.

Hammond, J. R. *H. G. Wells and Rebecca West,* 113–17.

Kipps, 1905

Davies, Christie. "Making Fun of Work: Humor as Sociology in the Work of H. G. Wells," in Patrick Parrinder and Christopher Rolfe, eds., *H. G. Wells Under Revision,* 82–96.

Hammond, J. R. *H. G. Wells and Rebecca West,* 39–41.

Murray, Brian. *H. G. Wells,* 111–14.

Love and Mr. Lewisham, 1900

Brown, Richard. "Little England: On Triviality in the Naive Comic Fictions of H. G. Wells." *Cahiers Victoriens et Edouardiens* 30 (1989), 60–61.

Marriage, 1912

Cheyette, Bryan. "Beyond Rationality: H. G. Wells and the Jewish Question." *Wellsian* 14 (1991), 50–54.

Simpson, Anne B. "Struggling with the Family in the Novels of H. G. Wells." *Cahiers Victoriens et Edouardiens* 30 (1989), 71–72.

Men Like Gods, 1923

Coren, Michael. *The Invisible Man,* 173–75.

Hammond, J. R. *H. G. Wells and Rebecca West,* 134–37.

Murray, Brian. *H. G. Wells,* 65–67.

Russell, W. M. S. "H. G. Wells and Ecology," in Patrick Parrinder and Christopher Rolfe, eds., *H. G. Wells Under Revision,* 145–52.

Manlove, Colin. "Charles Kingsley, H. G. Wells, and the Machine in Victorian Fiction." *Nineteenth-Cent Lit* 48 (1993), 227–33.

Manlove, Colin. "Dualism in Wells's *The Time Machine* and *The War of the Worlds.*" *Riverside Q* 8 (1990), 173–81.

Moddelmog, Debra A. *Readers and Mythic Signs,* 43–51.

Murray, Brian. *H. G. Wells,* 87–90.

Parrinder, Patrick. "H. G. Wells and the Fall of Empires." *Foundation* 57 (1993), 52–54.

Peters, Mary, and Ruth Fennick. "Reconstructing the Writer's Process Narrative Revisions in H. G. Wells' *Fin de Siècle* Vision: *The Time Machine.*" *Illinois Engl Bull* 79:3 (1992), 11–25.

Pittock, Murray G. H. *Spectrum of Decadence,* 112–13.

Renzi, Thomas C. *H. G. Wells,* 18–55.

Sadrin, Anny. "De la métaphore à la métamorphose: l'homme-machine de Descartes à la science-fiction, avec arrêt sur H. G. Wells." *Cahiers Victoriens et Edouardiens* 31 (1990), 127–34.

Stetz, Margaret Diane. "Visible & Invisible Ills: H. G. Wells's 'Scientific Romances' as Social Criticism." *Victorians Inst J* 19 (1991), 8–14.

Watts, Cedric. *Literature and Money,* 188–92.

Tono-Bungay, 1909

Allett, John. "The Durkheimian Theme of Suicide in *Tono-Bungay.*" *Wellsian* 13 (1990), 35–41.

Allett, John. "*Tono-Bungay:* A Study of Suicide." *Univ of Toronto Q* 60 (1991), 469–74.

Allett, John. "*Tono-Bungay:* The Metaphor of Disease." *Wellsian* 10 (1987), 2–9.

Cheyette, Bryan. "Beyond Rationality: H. G. Wells and the Jewish Question." *Wellsian* 14 (1991), 45–50.

Chialant, Maria Teresa. "Dickensian Motifs in Wells's Novels: The Disease Metaphor in *Tono-Bungay,*" in Patrick Parrinder and Christopher Rolfe, eds., *H. G. Wells Under Revision,* 97–107.

Hammond, J. R. "The Narrative Voice in *Tono-Bungay.*" *Wellsian* 12 (1989), 16–21.

Hammond, J. R. "The Timescale of *Tono-Bungay.*" *Wellsian* 14 (1991), 34–36.

Murray, Brian. *H. G. Wells,* 114–20.

Trodd, Anthea. *A Reader's Guide,* 44–46, 103–4.

The War in the Air, 1908

Parrinder, Patrick. "H. G. Wells and the Fall of Empires." *Foundation* 57 (1993), 56–57.

The War of the Worlds, 1898

Carey, John. *The Intellectuals and the Masses,* 130–32.

Dingley, R. J. "Count Dracula and the Martians," in Kath Filmer, ed., *The Victorian Fantasists,* 13–23.

Hughes, David Y. "The Revisions of *The War of the Worlds.*" *Cahiers Victoriens et Edouardiens* 30 (1989), 141–48.

Lowentrout, Peter. "*The War of the Worlds* Revisited: Science Fiction and the Angst of Secularization." *Extrapolation* 33 (1992), 351–58.

Manlove, Colin. "Charles Kingsley, H. G. Wells, and the Machine in Victorian Fiction." *Nineteenth-Cent Lit* 48 (1993), 233–39.

Manlove, Colin. "Dualism in Wells's *The Time Machine* and *The War of the Worlds.*" *Riverside Q* 8 (1990), 173–81.

Murray, Brian. *H. G. Wells,* 94–97.

Renzi, Thomas C. *H. G. Wells,* 119–42.

Simpson, Anne B. "The 'Tangible Antagonist': H. G. Wells and the Discourse of Otherness." *Extrapolation* 31 (1990), 141–46.

Stetz, Margaret Diane. "Visible & Invisible Ills: H. G. Wells's 'Scientific Romances' as Social Criticism." *Victorians Inst J* 19 (1991), 4–5.

Wakeford, Iain. "Wells, Working and *The War of the Worlds.*" *Wellsian* 14 (1991), 18–29.

The Wheels of Chance, 1896

Brown, Richard. "Little England: On Triviality in the Naive Comic Fictions of H. G. Wells." *Cahiers Victoriens et Edouardiens* 30 (1989), 57–60.

The Wonderful Visit, 1895

Scheick, William J. *Fictional Structure & Ethics,* 75–91.

The World of William Clissold, 1926

Coren, Michael. *The Invisible Man,* 183–85.

Hammond, J. R. *H. G. Wells and Rebecca West,* 152–57.

Murray, Brian. *H. G. Wells,* 68–70, 137–41.

The World Set Free, 1914

Coren, Michael. *The Invisible Man,* 129–30.

Murray, Brian. *H. G. Wells,* 107–9.

You Can't Be Too Careful, 1941

Bailey, K. V. "Homo Tewler and the Undine: Evolutionary and Mythic Images in Wells's Late Fiction." *Foundation* 56 (1992), 63–66, 70–75.

Hammond, J. R. *H. G. Wells and Rebecca West,* 207–9.

REBECCA WEST

The Fountain Overflows, 1956

Hammond, J. R. *H. G. Wells and Rebecca West,* 55–57, 228–33.

Harriet Hume, 1929

Hammond, J. R. *H. G. Wells and Rebecca West,* 167–70.

Scott, Bonnie Kime. "Refiguring the Binary, Breaking the Cycle: Rebecca West as Feminist Modernist." *Twentieth Cent Lit* 37 (1991), 180–86.

The Judge, 1922

>   Hammond, J. R. *H. G. Wells and Rebecca West,* 124–28.
>   Norton, Ann. "Rebecca West's Ironic Heroine: Beauty as Tragedy in *The Judge.*" *Engl Lit in Transition* 34 (1991), 295–307.
>   Scott, Bonnie Kime. "Refiguring the Binary, Breaking the Cycle: Rebecca West as Feminist Modernist." *Twentieth Cent Lit* 37 (1991), 173–80.

The Return of the Soldier, 1918

>   Breen, Jennifer. *In Her Own Write,* 99–102.
>   Tylee, Claire M. *The Great War,* 144–50.

The Thinking Reed, 1936

>   Hammond, J. R. *H. G. Wells and Rebecca West,* 219–21.

MICHAEL WESTLAKE

The Utopian, 1989

>   Collier, Andrew. "The Interpretation of Political Dreams: Michael Westlake's *The Utopian.*" *News From Nowhere* 9 (1991), 82–91.

ANTONIA WHITE

Beyond the Glass, 1954

>   Brown, Penny. *The Poison at the Source,* 142–49.

Frost in May, 1933

>   Benson, Julietta. "'Varieties of Dis-belief': Antonia White and the Discourses of Faith and Scepticism." *Lit & Theology* 7 (1993), 284–301.
>   Brown, Penny. *The Poison at the Source,* 124–31.
>   Palmer, Pauline. "Antonia White's *Frost in May:* A Lesbian Feminist Reading," in Susan Sellers, ed., *Feminist Criticism,* 89–106.
>   Rose, Ellen Cronan. "Antonia White: Portrait of the Artist as a Dutiful Daughter." *LIT* 2 (1991), 239–48.

The Lost Traveller, 1950

>   Brown, Penny. *The Poison at the Source,* 131–37.

The Sugar House, 1952

>   Brown, Penny. *The Poison at the Source,* 137–42.

T. H. WHITE

The Once and Future King, 1958

>   Hanks, D. Thomas, Jr. "T. H. White's Merlyn: More Than Malory Made Him," in Jeanie Watson and Maureen Fries, eds., *The Figure of Merlin,* 101–18.

WILLIAM HALE WHITE

The Autobiography of Mark Rutherford, 1881

> Goode, John. "Mark Rutherford and Spinoza." *Engl Lit in Transition* 34 (1991), 435–45.

Clara Hopgood, 1896

> Ardis, Ann L. *New Women, New Novels,* 145–48.
> Goode, John. "Mark Rutherford and Spinoza." *Engl Lit in Transition* 34 (1991), 445–52.

Miriam's Schooling, 1890

> Goode, John. "Mark Rutherford and Spinoza." *Engl Lit in Transition* 34 (1991), 430–34.

The Revolution in Tanner's Lane, 1887

> Swann, Charles. "Re-Forming the Novel: Politics, History and Narrative Structure in *The Revolution in Tanner's Lane.*" *Engl Lit in Transition* 34 (1991), 45–67.

OSCAR WILDE

The Picture of Dorian Gray, 1891

> Behrendt, Patricia Flanagan. *Oscar Wilde,* 103–5.
> Berman, Jeffrey. *Narcissism and the Novel,* 155–69, 173–75.
> Bernstein, Carol L. *The Celebration of Scandal,* 121–24.
> Buckler, William E. "*The Picture of Dorian Gray:* An Essay in Aesthetic Exploration." *Victorians Inst J* 18 (1990), 135–71.
> Cornwell, Neil. *The Literary Fantastic,* 102–6.
> Edelman, Lee. "Homographesis." *Yale J of Criticism* 3 (1989), 189–207.
> Felski, Rita. "The Counterdiscourse of the Feminine in Three Texts by Wilde, Huysmans, and Sacher-Masoch." *PMLA* 106 (1991), 1094–1104.
> Gall, John. "The Pregnant Death of Dorian Gray." *Victorian Newsl* 82 (1992), 55–57.
> Gillespie, Michael Patrick. "Picturing Dorian Gray: Resistant Readings in Wilde's Novel." *Engl Lit in Transition* 35 (1992), 7–23.
> Hannon, Patrice. "Theatre and Theory in the Language of *Dorian Gray.*" *Victorian Lit and Culture* 19 (1991), 143–63.
> Humphreys, Kathryn. "The Artistic Exchange: *Dorian Gray* at the *Sacred Fount.*" *Texas Stud in Lit and Lang* 32 (1990), 524–28.
> Kohl, Norbert. *Oscar Wilde,* 138–75.
> Litvak, Joseph. *Caught in the Act,* 271–75.
> McGowan, John. "From Pater to Wilde to Joyce: Modernist Epiphany and the Soulful Self." *Texas Stud in Lit and Lang* 32 (1990), 428–30.
> Manganiello, Dominic. "Through a Cracked Looking Glass: *The Picture of Dorian Gray* and *A Portrait of the Artist as a Young Man,*" in Diana A. Ben-Merre and Maureen Murphy, eds., *James Joyce,* 89–94.
> Molino, Michael R. "Narrator/Voice in *The Picture of Dorian Gray:* A

Question of Consistency, Control, and Perspective." *J of Irish Lit* 20:3 (1991), 6–18.

Nunokawa, Jeff. "Homosexual Desire and the Effacement of the Self in *The Picture of Dorian Gray.*" *Am Imago* 49 (1992), 311–20.

Pfister, Manfred. "Kult und Krise des Ich: Zur Subjektkonstitution in Wildes *Dorian Gray,*" in Manfred Pfister, ed., *Die Modernisierung des Ich,* 254–68.

Pittock, Murray G. H. *Spectrum of Decadence,* 37–39.

Rindisbacher, Hans J. *The Smell of Books,* 189–93.

Schenk, Christiane. *Venedig im Spiegel,* 478–79.

Schroeder, Horst. "A Quotation in *Dorian Gray.*" *Notes and Queries* 236 (1991), 327–28.

Snider, Clifton. *The Stuff That Dreams Are Made On,* 72–84.

Summers, Claude J. *Gay Fictions,* 42–51.

Swann, Charles. "*The Picture of Dorian Gray,* the Bible, and the Unpardonable Sin." *Notes and Queries* 236 (1991), 326–27.

Tuss, Alex J., SM. *The Inward Revolution,* 159–88.

Weintraub, Stanley. "Disraeli and Wilde's Dorian Gray." *Cahiers Victoriens et Edouardiens* 36 (1992), 19–26.

Whissen, Thomas Reed. *The Devil's Advocates,* 7–8, 46–47, 59–60, 88–89, 91–92, 95–96, 109–10.

Woodring, Carl. *Nature into Art,* 222–24.

CHARLES WILLIAMS

All Hallows' Eve, 1945

Anderson, Angelee Sailer. "The Nature of the City: Visions of the Kingdom and Its Saints in Charles Williams' *All Hallows' Eve.*" *Mythlore* 15:3 (1989), 16–21.

Bosky, Bernadette. "Grace and Goetia: Magic as Forced Compensation in *All Hallows' Eve.*" *Mythlore* 12:3 (1986), 19–23.

Knowles, Sebastian D. G. *A Purgatorial Flame,* 151–54, 169–72.

McKinley, Marlene Marie. "'To Life from a New Root': The Uneasy Consolation of *All Hallows' Eve.*" *Mythlore* 16:1 (1989), 13–17.

Reynolds, George. "Dante and Williams: Pilgrims in Purgatory." *Mythlore* 13:1 (1986), 3–7.

Tilley, Elizabeth S. "Language in Charles Williams's *All Hallows' Eve.*" *Renascence* 44 (1992), 303–18.

Weeks, Dennis L. *Steps Toward Salvation,* 70–74, 86–89.

Descent into Hell, 1937

Knowles, Sebastian D. G. *A Purgatorial Flame,* 153–72.

McKinley, Marlene. "Viewing 'the Immense Panorama or Futility and Anarchy that is Contemporary History' in the First Six Novels of Charles Williams," in Kath Filmer, ed., *Twentieth-Century Fantasists,* 78–88.

Warren, Colleen. "Wentworth in the Garden of Gomorrah: A Study of the Anima in *Descent into Hell*." *Mythlore* 13:2 (1986), 41–44, 54.

Weeks, Dennis L. *Steps Toward Salvation*, 64–69, 86–89, 101–2.

The Greater Trumps, 1932

Knowles, Sebastian D. G. *A Purgatorial Flame*, 154–56.

McKinley, Marlene. "Viewing 'the Immense Panorama or Futility and Anarchy that is Contemporary History' in the First Six Novels of Charles Williams," in Kath Filmer, ed., *Twentieth-Century Fantasists*, 81–88.

Weeks, Dennis L. *Steps Toward Salvation*, 58–63, 101–2.

White, Donna R. "Priestess and Goddess: Evolution of Human Consciousness in *The Greater Trumps*." *Mythlore* 14:3 (1988), 15–19.

Many Dimensions, 1931

McKinley, Marlene. "Viewing 'the Immense Panorama or Futility and Anarchy that is Contemporary History' in the First Six Novels of Charles Williams," in Kath Filmer, ed., *Twentieth-Century Fantasists*, 78–88.

Weeks, Dennis L. *Steps Toward Salvation*, 39–48, 92–93.

The Place of the Lion, 1931

Doyle, Barry B. "The Ways of the Images in Charles Williams' *The Place of the Lion*." *Mythlore* 16:3 (1990), 15–19.

McKinley, Marlene. "Viewing 'the Immense Panorama or Futility and Anarchy that is Contemporary History' in the First Six Novels of Charles Williams," in Kath Filmer, ed., *Twentieth-Century Fantasists*, 80–88.

Weeks, Dennis L. *Steps Toward Salvation*, 51–53, 55–57.

Shadows of Ecstasy, 1933

McKinley, Marlene. "Viewing 'the Immense Panorama or Futility and Anarchy that is Contemporary History' in the First Six Novels of Charles Williams," in Kath Filmer, ed., *Twentieth-Century Fantasists*, 72–88.

Weeks, Dennis L. *Steps Toward Salvation*, 22–31.

War in Heaven, 1930

McKinley, Marlene. "Viewing 'the Immense Panorama or Futility and Anarchy that is Contemporary History' in the First Six Novels of Charles Williams," in Kath Filmer, ed., *Twentieth-Century Fantasists*, 77–88.

Weeks, Dennis L. *Steps Toward Salvation*, 29–40.

NIGEL WILLIAMS

Star Turn, 1985

Lee, Alison. *Realism and Power*, 60–66.

HENRY WILLIAMSON

The Patriot's Progress, 1930

Onions, John. *English Fiction and Drama*, 76–83.

ANGUS WILSON

Late Call, 1964

> Prince, John. "Angus Wilson, Keith Waterhouse and the New Towns." *Caliban* 27 (1990), 21–24.

No Laughing Matter, 1967

> Gasiorek, Andrzej. "Resisting Postmodernism: The Parodic Mode of Angus Wilson's *No Laughing Matter.*" *Engl Stud in Canada* 19 (1993), 45–61.

Setting the World on Fire, 1980

> Wicht, Wolfgang. "Intertextualität als Modus vorsätzlicher Vieldeutigkeit in Angus Wilsons *Setting the World on Fire.*" *Zeitschrift für Anglistik und Amerikanistik* 39 (1991), 102–12.

COLIN WILSON

Adrift in Soho, 1961

> Stanley, Colin. "The Nature of Freedom: Colin Wilson's *Adrift in Soho.*" *Colin Wilson Stud* 2 (1990), 1–6.

The Glass Cage, 1966

> Dossor, Howard F. *Colin Wilson,* 266–69.

The Mind Parasites, 1968

> Dossor, Howard F. *Colin Wilson,* 274–79.
> Stanley, Colin. "The Ultimate Allegory: Colin Wilson's *The Mind Parasites.*" *Colin Wilson Stud* 2 (1990), 19–25.

Ritual in the Dark, 1960

> Dossor, Howard F. *Colin Wilson,* 256–58.

The Space Vampires, 1976

> Dossor, Howard F. *Colin Wilson,* 278–80.
> Marigny, Jean. "Science-fiction et fantastique: *The Space Vampires* de Colin Wilson." *Etudes Anglaises* 41 (1988), 319–26.

The World of Violence, 1963

> Dossor, Howard F. *Colin Wilson,* 263–65.

P. G. WODEHOUSE

Jeeves and the Feudal Spirit, 1954

> Kiernan, Robert F. *Frivolity Unbound,* 117–24.

Joy in the Morning, 1946

> Kiernan, Robert F. *Frivolity Unbound,* 104–11.

The Mating Season, 1949

>   Kiernan, Robert F. *Frivolity Unbound,* 111–17.

Mike, 1909

>   Richards, Jeffrey. *Happiest Days,* 125–40

Right Ho, Jeeves, 1934

>   Kiernan, Robert F. *Frivolity Unbound,* 97–104.

MARY WOLLSTONECRAFT

Maria, or The Wrongs of Woman, 1798

>   Alexander, Meena. *Women in Romanticism,* 50–57.
>   Cole, Lucinda. "(Anti)Feminist Sympathies: The Politics of Relationship in Smith, Wollstonecraft, and More." *ELH* 58 (1991), 129–31.
>   Frost, Cy. "Autocracy and the Matrix of Power: Issues of Propriety and Economics in the Work of Mary Wollstonecraft, Jane Austen, and Harriet Martineau." *Tulsa Stud in Women's Lit* 10 (1991), 258–60.
>   Heller, Tamar. *Dead Secrets,* 25–29.
>   Lanser, Susan Sniader. *Fictions of Authority,* 230–37.
>   Lorch, Jennifer. *Mary Wollstonecraft,* 90–99.
>   Maurer, Shawn Lisa. "The Female (As) Reader: Sex, Sensibility, and the Maternal in Wollstonecraft's Fictions." *Essays in Lit* (Macomb) 19 (1992), 36–41, 45–51.
>   Michaelson, Patricia Howell. "*The Wrongs of Woman* as a Feminist *Amelia.*" *J of Narrative Technique* 21 (1991), 250–59.
>   Scheuermann, Mona. *Her Bread to Earn,* 175–98.
>   Spencer, Jane. " 'Of Use to Her Daughter': Maternal Authority and Early Women Novelists," in Dale Spender, ed., *Living by the Pen,* 206–7.
>   Tomalin, Claire. *The Life and Death of Mary Wollstonecraft,* 253–54.

Mary, A Fiction, 1787

>   Alexander, Meena. *Women in Romanticism,* 40–43.
>   Frost, Cy. "Autocracy and the Matrix of Power: Issues of Propriety and Economics in the Work of Mary Wollstonecraft, Jane Austen, and Harriet Martineau." *Tulsa Stud in Women's Lit* 10 (1991), 258–60.
>   Hatch, Ronald B. " 'Lordship and Bondage': Women Novelists of the Eighteenth Century." *REAL: Yrbk of Res in Engl and Am Lit* 8 (1991/92), 236–37.
>   Lorch, Jennifer. *Mary Wollstonecraft,* 28–29, 72–73.
>   Maurer, Shawn Lisa. "The Female (As) Reader: Sex, Sensibility, and the Maternal in Wollstonecraft's Fictions." *Essays in Lit* (Macomb) 19 (1992), 36–41, 41–45.
>   Parke, Catherine N. "What Kind of Heroine Is Mary Wollstonecraft?," in Syndy McMillen Conger, ed., *Sensibility in Transformation,* 107–12.
>   Tomalin, Claire. *The Life and Death of Mary Wollstonecraft,* 84–86.

MRS. HENRY WOOD

East Lynne, 1861

Cvetkovich, Ann. *Mixed Feelings,* 97–127.

Shuttleworth, Sally. "Demonic Mothers: Ideologies of Bourgeois Motherhood in the Mid-Victorian Era," in Linda M. Shires, ed., *Rewriting the Victorians,* 47–50.

St. Martin's Eve, 1866

Shuttleworth, Sally. "Demonic Mothers: Ideologies of Bourgeois Motherhood in the Mid-Victorian Era," in Linda M. Shires, ed., *Rewriting the Victorians,* 45–47, 49–50.

LEONARD SIDNEY WOOLF

The Village in the Jungle, 1913

Alexander, Peter F. *Leonard and Virginia Woolf,* 72–74.

Poole, Roger. *The Unknown Virginia Woolf,* 74–78.

The Wise Virgins, 1914

Alexander, Peter F. *Leonard and Virginia Woolf,* 80–84.

Hussey, Mark. "Refractions of Desire: The Early Fiction of Virginia and Leonard Woolf." *Mod Fiction Stud* 38:1 (1992), 129–44.

Poole, Roger. *The Unknown Virginia Woolf,* 78–102.

VIRGINIA WOOLF

Between the Acts, 1941

Abbott, Reginald. "What Miss Kilman's Petticoat Means: Virginia Woolf, Shopping, and Spectacle." *Mod Fiction Stud* 38:1 (1992), 211–14.

Abel, Elizabeth. *Virginia Woolf,* 108–30.

Ames, Christopher. *The Life of the Party,* 107–24.

Ames, Christopher. "The Modernist Canon Narrative: Woolf's *Between the Acts* and Joyce's 'Oxen of the Sun.'" *'Twentieth Cent Lit* 37 (1991), 390–403.

Babcock, Barbara A. "Mud, Mirrors, and Making Up: Liminality and Reflexivity in *Between the Acts,*" in Kathleen M. Ashley, ed., *Victor Turner,* 86–116.

Barzilai, Shuli. "The Principle of the Chinese Dagger: Synecdoche in *Between the Acts.*" *Bull of Res in the Hum* 87:1 (1986–87), 128–46.

Batchelor, John. *Virginia Woolf,* 132–46.

Bazin, Nancy Topping, and Jane Hamovit Lauter. "Virginia Woolf's Keen Sensitivity to War: Its Roots and Its Impact on Her Novels," in Mark Hussey, ed., *Virginia Woolf and War,* 33–39.

Bergonzi, Bernard. *Wartime and Aftermath,* 27–29.

Booth, Alison. *Greatness Engendered,* 143–50, 236–55, 264–84.

Bowlby, Rachel. *Virginia Woolf,* 45–59.

Buckman, Jacqueline. "Virginia Woolf's *Between the Acts* and Some Problems of Periodisation." *Durham Univ J* 84 (1992), 279–88.

Cuddy-Keane, Melba. "The Politics of Comic Modes in Virginia Woolf's *Between the Acts*." *PMLA* 105 (1990), 273–84.

Daugherty, Beth Rigel. "Face to Face with 'Ourselves' in Virginia Woolf's *Between the Acts*," in Vara Neverow-Turk and Mark Hussey, eds., *Virginia Woolf*, 76–81.

Dick, Susan. *Virginia Woolf*, 74–81.

Evans, William A. *Virginia Woolf*, 209–26.

Ferrer, Daniel. *Virginia Woolf and the Madness of Language*, 97–140.

Fox, Alice. *Virginia Woolf*, 153–58.

Gindin, James. *British Fiction*, 215–17.

Haller, Evelyn. "Her Quill Drawn from the Firebird: Virginia Woolf and the Russian Dancers," in Diane F. Gillespie, ed., *The Multiple Muses*, 207–8, 221–25.

Haller, Evelyn. "Virginia Woolf and Katherine Mansfield, or The Case of the Déclassé Wild Child," in Mark Hussey and Vara Neverow-Turk, eds., *Virginia Woolf Miscellanies*, 96–104.

Hussey, Mark. " ' "I" Rejected; "We" Substituted': Self and Society in *Between the Acts*," in Bege K. Bowers and Barbara Brothers, eds., *Reading and Writing*, 141–52.

Hyman, Virginia R. *"To the Lighthouse" and Beyond*, 273–75.

Joplin, Patricia Klindienst. "The Authority of Illusion: Feminism and Fascism in Virginia Woolf's *Between the Acts*." *South Central R* 6:2 (1989), 88–104.

Kaivola, Karen. *All Contraries Confounded*, 4–6, 44–58.

Knowles, Sebastian D. G. *A Purgatorial Flame*, 36–61, 179–90.

Kurtz, Marilyn. *Virginia Woolf*, 103–13, 129–35.

Lambert, Elizabeth. "Evolution and Imagination in *Pointz Hall* and *Between the Acts*," in Vara Neverow-Turk and Mark Hussey, eds., *Virginia Woolf*, 83–88.

Lanser, Susan Sniader. *Fictions of Authority*, 117–19.

Laurence, Patricia. "The Facts and Fugue of War: From *Three Guineas* to *Between the Acts*," in Mark Hussey, ed., *Virginia Woolf and War*, 238–45.

Laurence, Patricia Ondek. *The Reading of Silence*, 42–49, 170–213.

McNichol, Stella. *Virginia Woolf*, 141–47.

McWhirter, David. "The Novel, the Play, and the Book: *Between the Acts* and the Tragicomedy of History." *ELH* 60 (1993), 787–808.

Mepham, John. *Virginia Woolf*, 198–204.

Miller, C. Ruth. *Virginia Woolf*, 5–8, 31–34, 60–64, 72–74, 92–100.

Mills, Pamela. "Narrative Techniques in *Between the Acts*." *Ilha do Desterro* 24:2 (1990), 27–37.

Oldfield, Sybil. "From Rachel's Aunt to Miss La Trobe: Spinsters in the Fiction of Virginia Woolf," in Laura L. Doan, ed., *Old Maids*, 99–101.

Pawlowski, Merry. "Virginia Woolf's *Between the Acts:* Fascism in the

Heart of England," in Mark Hussey and Vara Neverow-Turk, eds., *Virginia Woolf Miscellanies*, 188–91.

Poole, Roger. *The Unknown Virginia Woolf*, 219–27, 232–45.

Poole, Roger. "'We all put up with you Virginia': Irreceivable Wisdom about War," in Mark Hussey, ed., *Virginia Woolf and War*, 90–96.

Ray, Sangeeta. "The Discourse of Silence: Narrative Interruption and Female Speech in Woolf's *Between the Acts*." *Works and Days* 15 (1990), 37–48.

Reed, Christopher. "Through Formalism: Feminism and Virginia Woolf's Relation to Bloomsbury Aesthetics," in Diane F. Gillespie, ed., *The Multiple Muses*, 31–34.

Roe, Sue. *Writing and Gender*, 143–69.

Schneider, Karen. "Of Two Minds: Woolf, the War and *Between the Acts*." *J of Mod Lit* 16:1 (1989), 93–112.

Scott, Bonnie Kime. "Woolf, Barnes and the Ends of Modernism: An *Antiphon* to *Between the Acts*," in Vara Neverow-Turk and Mark Hussey, eds., *Virginia Woolf*, 25–32.

Tindall, Gillian. *Countries of the Mind*, 91–93.

Wright, G. Patton. "Virginia Woolf's Uncommon Reader: Allusions in *Between the Acts*," in Mark Hussey and Vara Neverow-Turk, eds., *Virginia Woolf Miscellanies*, 230–33.

Jacob's Room, 1922

Asbee, Sue. *Virginia Woolf*, 43–46.

Batchelor, John. *Virginia Woolf*, 56–72.

Bazin, Nancy Topping, and Jane Hamovit Lauter. "Virginia Woolf's Keen Sensitivity to War: Its Roots and Its Impact on Her Novels," in Mark Hussey, ed., *Virginia Woolf and War*, 15–17.

Bishop, Edward L. "The Subject in *Jacob's Room*." *Mod Fiction Stud* 38:1 (1992), 147–73.

Booth, Alison. *Greatness Engendered*, 161–63.

Bowlby, Rachel. *Virginia Woolf*, 98–116.

Caramagno, Thomas C. *The Flight of the Mind*, 185–210.

Chamberlain, Daniel Frank. *Narrative Perspective in Fiction*, 198–225.

Dick, Susan. *Virginia Woolf*, 13–29.

Evans, William A. *Virginia Woolf*, 45–69.

Flint, Kate. "Revising Jacob's Room: Virginia Woolf, Women, and Language." *R of Engl Stud* 42 (1991), 361–79.

Fox, Alice. *Virginia Woolf*, 39–41.

Galef, David. "Disfigured Figures: Virginia Woolf's Disabled List." *Univ of Mississippi Stud in Engl* 9 (1991), 135–36.

Garvey, Johanna X. K. "Woolf and Joyce: Reading and Re/Vision," in Vincent J. Cheng and Timothy Martin, eds., *Joyce in Context*, 40–51.

Handley, William R. *Virginia Woolf*, 10–36.

Handley, William R. "War and the Politics of Narration in *Jacob's Room*," in Mark Hussey, ed., *Virginia Woolf and War*, 110–32.

Kurtz, Marilyn. *Virginia Woolf*, 64–65.

Lanser, Susan Sniader. *Fictions of Authority,* 113–17.

McCluskey, Kathleen, CSJ. *Reverberations,* 31–53.

McNichol, Stella. *Virginia Woolf,* 39–61.

Mepham, John. *Virginia Woolf,* 76–84.

Miller, C. Ruth. *Virginia Woolf,* 5–8, 77–80, 84–87.

Schaefer, Josephine O'Brien. "The Great War and 'This late age of world's experience' in Cather and Woolf," in Mark Hussey, ed., *Virginia Woolf and War,* 134–35, 138–40.

Mrs. Dalloway, 1925

Abbott, Reginald. "What Miss Kilman's Petticoat Means: Virginia Woolf, Shopping, and Spectacle." *Mod Fiction Stud* 38:1 (1992), 198–210.

Abel, Elizabeth. *Virginia Woolf,* 30–44.

Ames, Christopher. "Death and Woolf's Festive Vision," in Mark Hussey and Vara Neverow-Turk, eds., *Virginia Woolf Miscellanies,* 62–63.

Ames, Christopher. *The Life of the Party,* 81–109.

Asbee, Sue. *Virginia Woolf,* 46–56.

Baldwin, Dean R. *Virginia Woolf,* 130–32, 134–38.

Batchelor, John. *Virginia Woolf,* 73–90.

Berman, Jeffrey. *Narcissism and the Novel,* 226–52.

Booth, Alison. *Greatness Engendered,* 139–41, 163–65.

Bouson, J. Brooks. *The Empathic Reader,* 138–53.

Bowlby, Rachel. *Still Crazy After All These Years,* 13–16.

Bowlby, Rachel. *Virginia Woolf,* 80–98.

Brimstone, Lyndie. "Towards a New Cartography: Radclyffe Hall, Virginia Woolf and the Working of Common Land," in Elaine Hobby and Chris White, eds., *What Lesbians Do in Books,* 99–104.

Burroughs, Megan C. "Septimus Smith: A Man of Many Words." *Univ of Windsor R* 22:1 (1989), 70–78.

Caramagno, Thomas C. *The Flight of the Mind,* 210–43.

Clayton, John J. *Gestures of Healing,* 177–81.

Cohan, Steven. "Figures beyond the Text: A Theory of Readable Character in the Novel," in Mark Spilka and Caroline McCracken-Flesher, eds., *Why the Novel Matters,* 125–29.

Cramer, Patricia. "Notes from Underground: Lesbian Ritual in the Writings of Virginia Woolf," in Mark Hussey and Vara Neverow-Turk, eds., *Virginia Woolf Miscellanies,* 178–81.

Dick, Susan. *Virginia Woolf,* 30–43.

Dodd, Elizabeth. " 'No, she said, she did not want a pear': Women's Relation to Food in *To the Lighthouse* and *Mrs. Dalloway,*" in Vara Neverow-Turk and Mark Hussey, eds., *Virginia Woolf,* 150–57.

Donaldson, Sandra M. "Where Does Q Leave Mr. Ramsay?" *Tulsa Stud in Women's Lit* 11 (1992), 329–34.

Dowling, David. *"Mrs. Dalloway,"* 39–127.

Evans, William A. *Virginia Woolf,* 71–100.

Ferrer, Daniel. *Virginia Woolf and the Madness of Language,* 8–39.

Fiérobe, Claude. "Eros médusé," in Roger Bozzetto et al., eds., *Eros*, 16–17.

Fox, Alice. *Virginia Woolf*, 116–19, 129–32.

Garvey, Johanna X. K. "'A Voice Bubbling Up': *Mrs Dalloway* in Dialogue with *Ulysses*," in Vara Neverow-Turk and Mark Hussey, eds., *Virginia Woolf*, 299–306.

Guth, Deborah. "Rituals of Self-Deception: Clarissa Dalloway's Final Moment of Vision." *Twentieth Cent Lit* 36 (1990), 35–41.

Handley, William R. *Virginia Woolf*, 36–52.

Hankins, Leslie K. "The Doctor and the Woolf: Reel Challenges—*The Cabinet of Dr. Caligari* and *Mrs. Dalloway*," in Vara Neverow-Turk and Mark Hussey, eds., *Virginia Woolf*, 40–49.

Hoff, Molly. "The Midday Topos in *Mrs. Dalloway*." *Twentieth Cent Lit* 36 (1990), 449–62.

Hoff, Molly. "Woolf's *Mrs Dalloway*." *Explicator* 50 (1992), 161–63.

Horner, Avril, and Sue Zlosnik. *Landscapes of Desire*, 91–114.

Kanwar, Asha. *Virginia Woolf and Anita Desai*, 20–32.

Kurtz, Marilyn. *Virginia Woolf*, 43–47, 65–73.

Laurence, Patricia Ondek. *The Reading of Silence*, 45–53, 174–79.

Lee, So-Hee. "Madness, Marginalization and Power in *Mrs. Dalloway*." *J of Engl Lang and Lit* 36 (1990), 691–712.

Lynch, Eve M. "The Cook, the Nurse, the Maid, and the Mother: Woolf's Working Women," in Vara Neverow-Turk and Mark Hussey, eds., *Virginia Woolf*, 68–75.

McNaron, Toni A. H. "'The Albanians, or was it the Armenians?': Virginia Woolf's Lesbianism as Gloss on Her Modernism," in Vara Neverow-Turk and Mark Hussey, eds., *Virginia Woolf*, 136–41.

McNichol, Stella. *Virginia Woolf*, 62–90.

Marek, Heidi. "Die Rezeption von Virginia Woolfs *Mrs Dalloway* in Elio Vittorinis *Piccola Borghesia*." *Arcadia* 25 (1990), 287–303.

Mepham, John. *Virginia Woolf*, 92–100.

Miller, C. Ruth. *Virginia Woolf*, 15–18, 37–39, 54–57, 90–94, 107–9.

Munday, Kathryn. "Marcel Proust and Virginia Woolf: An Excuse for a Party." *Engl Stud in Africa* 35 (1992), 39–43, 48–50.

Muzina, Matej. "Virginia Woolf's *Mrs Dalloway:* A Study in the Integration of the Personality." *Studia Romanica et Anglica Zagrabiensia* 35 (1990), 23–28.

Oldfield, Sybil. "From Rachel's Aunt to Miss La Trobe: Spinsters in the Fiction of Virginia Woolf," in Laura L. Doan, ed., *Old Maids*, 92–94.

Page, Norman. *Speech in the English Novel*, 43–45.

Pearce, Richard. *The Politics of Narration*, 146–55.

Pearce, Richard. "Who Comes First, Joyce or Woolf?," in Vara Neverow-Turk and Mark Hussey, eds., *Virginia Woolf*, 59–67.

Phelan, James. *Reading People*, 202–205.

Poole, Roger. *The Unknown Virginia Woolf*, 138–47, 161–72, 176–83, 185–99.

Poole, Roger. "'We all put up with you Virginia': Irreceivable Wisdom about War," in Mark Hussey, ed., *Virginia Woolf and War,* 81–83, 90–92.

Reichman, Brunilda Tempel. "The Concurrence of the Spatio-Temporal and Psychological Planes in *Tess of the D'Urbervilles* and *Mrs. Dalloway.*" *Ilha do Desterro* 24:2 (1990), 21–26.

Richter, Harvena. "The *Ulysses* Connection: Clarissa Dalloway's Bloomsday." *Stud in the Novel* 21 (1989), 305–17.

Schulze, Robin Gail. "Design in Motion: Words, Music, and the Search for Coherence in the Works of Virginia Woolf and Arnold Schoenberg." *Stud in the Liter Imagination* 25:2 (1992), 6–8.

Schwartz, Beth C. "Thinking Back through Our Mothers: Virginia Woolf Reads Shakespeare." *ELH* 58 (1991), 731–32.

Schwarz, Daniel R. *The Transformation of the English Novel,* 264–84.

Searles, Susan. " 'Accesses of emotion—bursting into tears': Why All the Crying in Virginia Woolf's *Mrs. Dalloway,*" in Vara Neverow-Turk and Mark Hussey, eds., *Virginia Woolf,* 112–18.

Seidl, Michael. "The Pathology of the Everyday: Uses of Madness in *Mrs. Dalloway* and *Ulysses,*" in Vara Neverow-Turk and Mark Hussey, eds., *Virginia Woolf,* 52–58.

Shaffer, Brian W. *The Blinding Torch,* 80–81, 84–89, 93–98.

Smith, Lenora. "Rooms and the Construction of the Feminine Self," in Vara Neverow-Turk and Mark Hussey, eds., *Virginia Woolf,* 219–22.

Tambling, Jeremy. "Repression in Mrs Dalloway's London." *Essays in Criticism* 39 (1989), 137–55.

Taylor, Nancy. "Erasure of Definition: Androgyny in *Mrs. Dalloway.*" *Women's Stud* 18 (1991), 367–77.

Tylee, Claire M. *The Great War,* 150–67.

Usui, Masami. "The Female Victims of the War in *Mrs. Dalloway,*" in Mark Hussey, ed., *Virginia Woolf and War,* 151–63.

Wang, Ban. " 'I' on the Run: Crisis of Identity in *Mrs. Dalloway.*" *Mod Fiction Stud* 38:1 (1992), 177–90.

Night and Day, 1919

Asbee, Sue. *Virginia Woolf,* 40–43.

Booth, Alison. *Greatness Engendered,* 153–57.

Cooley, Elizabeth. "Discovering the 'Enchanted Region': A Revisionary Reading of *Night and Day.*" *CEA Critic* 54:3 (1992), 4–16.

Da Silva, N Takei. *Modernism and Virginia Woolf,* 196–200.

Evans, William A. *Virginia Woolf,* 25–43.

Fisher, Jane. " 'Silent as the Grave': Painting, Narrative, and the Reader in *Night and Day* and *To the Lighthouse,*" in Diane F. Gillespie, ed., *The Multiple Muses,* 95–99.

Fox, Alice. *Virginia Woolf,* 120–26.

Hussey, Mark. "Refractions of Desire: The Early Fiction of Virginia and Leonard Woolf." *Mod Fiction Stud* 38:1 (1992), 129–44.

Hyman, Virginia R. *"To the Lighthouse" and Beyond,* 88–93.

Kurtz, Marilyn. *Virginia Woolf,* 32–37, 61–64.

Lynch, Eve M. "The Cook, the Nurse, the Maid, and the Mother: Woolf's Working Women," in Vara Neverow-Turk and Mark Hussey, eds., *Virginia Woolf*, 68–75.

McNichol, Stella. *Virginia Woolf*, 16–38.

Malamud, Randy. "Splitting the Husks: Woolf's Modernist Language in *Night and Day*." *South Central R* 6:1 (1989), 32–45.

Mepham, John. *Virginia Woolf*, 48–54.

Miller, C. Ruth. *Virginia Woolf*, 80–82.

Oldfield, Sybil. "From Rachel's Aunt to Miss La Trobe: Spinsters in the Fiction of Virginia Woolf," in Laura L. Doan, ed., *Old Maids*, 90–92.

Poole, Roger. *The Unknown Virginia Woolf*, 46–49, 67–70.

Smith, Lenora. "Rooms and the Construction of the Feminine Self," in Vara Neverow-Turk and Mark Hussey, eds., *Virginia Woolf*, 223–24.

Wussow, Helen. "Conflict of Language in Virginia Woolf's *Night and Day*." *J of Mod Lit* 16:1 (1989), 61–73.

Orlando, 1928

Alexander, Peter F. *Leonard and Virginia Woolf*, 154–56.

Batchelor, John. *Virginia Woolf*, 15–21.

Boehm, Beth A. "Fact, Fiction, and Metafiction: Blurred Gen(d)res in *Orlando* and *A Room of One's Own*." *J of Narrative Technique* 22 (1992), 191–202.

Booth, Alison. *Greatness Engendered*, 168–203.

Bowlby, Rachel. *Virginia Woolf*, 48–61, 128–45.

Cavalieri, Ruth Villela. "O Fascínio de *Orlando*." *Minas Gerais, Suplemento Literário* 23:1145 (1990), 12–13.

Cooley, Elizabeth. "Revolutionizing Biography: *Orlando, Roger Fry,* and the Tradition." *South Atlantic R* 55:2 (1990), 71–81.

Evans, William A. *Virginia Woolf*, 133–47.

Fox, Alice. *Virginia Woolf*, 46–50.

Horner, Avril. "Virginia Woolf, History, and the Metaphors of *Orlando*," in Angus Easson, ed., *History and the Novel*, 70–87.

Jones, Danell. "The Chase of the Wild Goose: The Ladies of Llangollen and *Orlando*," in Vara Neverow-Turk and Mark Hussey, eds., *Virginia Woolf*, 181–88.

Lawrence, Karen R. "Orlando's Voyage Out." *Mod Fiction Stud* 38:1 (1992), 253–75.

Lokke, Kari Elise. "*Orlando* and Incandescence: Virginia Woolf's Comic Sublime." *Mod Fiction Stud* 38:1 (1992), 235–50.

Meese, Elizabeth A. *(SeM)erotics*, 25–42.

Mepham, John. *Virginia Woolf*, 125–28.

Moses, John W. "Orlando's 'Caricature Value': Virginia Woolf's Portrait of the Artist as a Romantic Poet," in Allan Chavkin, ed., *English Romanticism and Modern Fiction*, 39–73.

Nelson-McDermott, Catherine. "Virginia Woolf and Murasaki Shikibu: A Question of Perception," in Mark Hussey and Vara Neverow-Turk, eds., *Virginia Woolf Miscellanies*, 134–43.

Raitt, Suzanne. *Vita and Virginia,* 17–40.

Roe, Sue. *Writing and Gender,* 91–102.

Roessel, David. "The Significance of Constantinople in *Orlando.*" *Papers on Lang & Lit* 28 (1992), 398–415.

Snider, Clifton. *The Stuff That Dreams Are Made On,* 87–94.

To the Lighthouse, 1927

Abbott, Reginald. "What Miss Kilman's Petticoat Means: Virginia Woolf, Shopping, and Spectacle." *Mod Fiction Stud* 38:1 (1992), 210–11.

Abel, Elizabeth. *Virginia Woolf,* 45–83.

Alexander, Peter F. *Leonard and Virginia Woolf,* 149–53.

Asbee, Sue. *Virginia Woolf,* 57–72.

Barr, Tina. "Divine Politics: Virginia Woolf's Journey toward Eleusis in *To the Lighthouse.*" *Boundary 2* 20:1 (1993), 125–45.

Batchelor, John. *Virginia Woolf,* 39–41, 49–51, 53–55, 91–113.

Bazin, Nancy Topping, and Jane Hamovit Lauter. "Virginia Woolf's Keen Sensitivity to War: Its Roots and Its Impact on Her Novels," in Mark Hussey, ed., *Virginia Woolf and War,* 19–22, 29–31.

Booth, Alison. *Greatness Engendered,* 8–10, 41–43, 113–16, 163–67.

Bowlby, Rachel. *Virginia Woolf,* 60–79.

Breen, Jennifer. *In Her Own Write,* 11–15, 68–70.

Caramagno, Thomas C. *The Flight of the Mind,* 244–69.

Caughie, Pamela L. "Virginia Woolf and Postmodernism: Returning to the Lighthouse," in Kevin J. H. Dettmar, ed., *Rereading the New,* 310–15.

Clark, Miriam Marty. "Consciousness, Stream and Quanta, in *To the Lighthouse.*" *Stud in the Novel* 21 (1989), 413–22.

Clayton, John J. *Gestures of Healing,* 172–74.

Daugherty, Beth Rigel. "'There she sat': The Power of the Feminist Imagination in *To the Lighthouse.*" *Twentieth Cent Lit* 37 (1991), 289–304.

Davies, Stevie. *Virginia Woolf: "To the Lighthouse,"* 1–141.

Dick, Susan. *Virginia Woolf,* 44–57.

Dodd, Elizabeth. "'No, she said, she did not want a pear': Women's Relation to Food in *To the Lighthouse* and *Mrs. Dalloway,*" in Vara Neverow-Turk and Mark Hussey, eds., *Virginia Woolf,* 150–57.

Emery, Mary Lou. "'Robbed of Meaning': The Work at the Center of *To the Lighthouse.*" *Mod Fiction Stud* 38:1 (1992), 217–33.

Erlebach, Peter. *Theorie und Praxis des Romaneingangs,* 261–70.

Evans, William A. *Virginia Woolf,* 101–32.

Faria, Thereza Maria Lustosa de Castro. "*To the Lighthouse:* A Unidade da Obra-Prima na Cumplicidade da Prosa Poética com a Pintura e o Cinema." *Ilha do Desterro* 24:2 (1990), 65–91.

Ferrer, Daniel. *Virginia Woolf and the Madness of Language,* 40–64.

Fisher, Jane. "'Silent as the Grave': Painting, Narrative, and the Reader in *Night and Day* and *To the Lighthouse,*" in Diane F. Gillespie, ed., *The Multiple Muses,* 100–109.

Fox, Alice. *Virginia Woolf,* 41–46.

Fraiman, Susan. *Unbecoming Women,* 137–39.

Galef, David. "Disfigured Figures: Virginia Woolf's Disabled List." *Univ of Mississippi Stud in Engl* 9 (1991), 137–39.

Halperin, John. *Jane Austen's Lovers*, 186–89.

Handley, William R. "The Housemaid and the Kitchen Table: Judgment, Economy, and Representation in *To the Lighthouse*," in Vara Neverow-Turk and Mark Hussey, eds., *Virginia Woolf*, 309–19.

Haule, James M. "*To the Lighthouse* and the Great War: The Evidence of Virginia Woolf's Revisions of 'Time Passes,'" in Mark Hussey, ed., *Virginia Woolf and War*, 164–78.

Hirsch, Marianne. *The Mother/Daughter Plot*, 108–18.

Horner, Avril, and Sue Zlosnik. *Landscapes of Desire*, 114–32.

Hyman, Virginia R. *"To the Lighthouse" and Beyond*, 103–55, 199–206, 212–20.

Ingersoll, Earl G. "Woolf's *To the Lighthouse*." *Explicator* 50 (1992), 93–96.

Kaivola, Karen. *All Contraries Confounded*, 26–37.

Kanwar, Asha. *Virginia Woolf and Anita Desai*, 34–47.

Kunat, John. "The Function of Augustus Carmichael in Virginia Woolf's *To the Lighthouse*." *Xanadu* 13 (1990), 48–59.

Kurtz, Marilyn. *Virginia Woolf*, 47–51, 73–78.

Lanser, Susan Sniader. *Fictions of Authority*, 115–17.

Laurence, Patricia Ondek. *The Reading of Silence*, 1–9, 43–50, 115–19, 172–79, 184–90.

Lilienfeld, Jane. "'Like a Lion Seeking Whom He Could Devour': Domestic Violence in *To the Lighthouse*," in Mark Hussey and Vara Neverow-Turk, eds., *Virginia Woolf Miscellanies*, 154–62.

Lund, Roger D. "We Perished Each Alone: 'The Castaway' and *To the Lighthouse*." *J of Mod Lit* 16:1 (1989), 75–92.

Lynch, Eve M. "The Cook, the Nurse, the Maid, and the Mother: Woolf's Working Women," in Vara Neverow-Turk and Mark Hussey, eds., *Virginia Woolf*, 68–75.

McCluskey, Kathleen, CSJ. *Reverberations*, 79–118.

McCombie, Frank. "Flounders in *To the Lighthouse*." *Notes and Queries* 236 (1991), 343–45.

McCracken, LuAnn. "'The synthesis of my being': Autobiography and the Reproduction of Identity in Virginia Woolf." *Tulsa Stud in Women's Lit* 9 (1990), 59–67.

McNichol, Stella. *Virginia Woolf*, 91–116.

McVicker, Jeanette. "Vast Nests of Chinese Boxes, or Getting from Q to R: Critiquing Empire in 'Kew Gardens' and *To the Lighthouse*," in Mark Hussey and Vara Neverow-Turk, eds., *Virginia Woolf Miscellanies*, 40–42.

Mares, C. J. "Reading Proust: Woolf and the Painter's Perspective." *Compar Lit* 41 (1989), 344–45.

Martin, Bill. "*To the Lighthouse* and the Feminist Path to Postmodernity." *Philos and Lit* 13 (1989), 307–13.

Melia, Margaret E. "Portrait of an Artist as a Mature Woman: A Study of Virginia Woolf's Androgynous Aesthetics in *To the Lighthouse.*" *Emporia State Res Stud* 37:1 (1988), 5–15.

Mepham, John. *Virginia Woolf*, 100–116.

Miller, C. Ruth. *Virginia Woolf*, 13–14, 17–18, 22–26, 36–40, 48–50, 68–70, 89–94.

Miller, J. Hillis. *Tropes, Parables, Performatives*, 151–70.

Moser, Christian. "Der Blick der Künstlerin: Zur Revision ästhetischer Wahrnehmungsformen in Virginia Woolfs *To the Lighthouse.*" *Poetica* 22 (1990), 384–412.

Munday, Kathryn. "Marcel Proust and Virginia Woolf: An Excuse for a Party." *Engl Stud in Africa* 35 (1992), 43–46.

Oldfield, Sybil. "From Rachel's Aunt to Miss La Trobe: Spinsters in the Fiction of Virginia Woolf," in Laura L. Doan, ed., *Old Maids*, 94–96.

Oliveira, Solange Ribeiro de. "A Arte como Conhecimento: *To the Lighthouse* de Virginia Woolf." *Ilha do Desterro* 24:2 (1990), 39–63.

Pearce, Richard. *The Politics of Narration*, 130–43.

Phillips, K. J. *Dying Gods in Twentieth-Century Fiction*, 179–92.

Polhemus, Robert M. *Erotic Faith*, 307–10.

Poole, Roger. *The Unknown Virginia Woolf*, 7–20, 271–73.

Poole, Roger. "'We all put up with you Virginia': Irreceivable Wisdom about War," in Mark Hussey, ed., *Virginia Woolf and War*, 83–90.

Raitt, Suzanne. *Virginia Woolf's "To the Lighthouse,"* 29–114.

Reynier, Christine. "'A Haunted House': Or, The Genesis of *To the Lighthouse.*" *J of the Short Story in Engl* 14 (1990), 63–78.

Risolo, Donna. "Outing Mrs. Ramsay: Reading the Lesbian Subtext in Virginia Woolf's *To the Lighthouse*," in Vara Neverow-Turk and Mark Hussey, eds., *Virginia Woolf*, 238–46.

Roe, Sue. *Writing and Gender*, 63–80.

Saunders, Rebecca. "Language, Subject, Self: Reading the Style of *To the Lighthouse.*" *Novel* 26 (1993), 192–211.

Schulze, Robin Gail. "Design in Motion: Words, Music, and the Search for Coherence in the Works of Virginia Woolf and Arnold Schoenberg." *Stud in the Liter Imagination* 25:2 (1992), 8–10.

Schwarz, Daniel R. *The Transformation of the English Novel*, 284–310.

Shaffer, Brian W. *The Blinding Torch*, 80–81, 89–94.

Steinberg, Erwin R. "G. E. Moore's Table and Chair in *To the Lighthouse.*" *J of Mod Lit* 15:1 (1988), 161–68.

Stevenson, Randall. *Modernist Fiction*, 55–58, 79–81, 159–63.

Tremper, Ellen. "In Her Father's House: *To the Lighthouse* as a Record of Virginia Woolf's Literary Patrimony." *Texas Stud in Lit and Lang* 34 (1992), 1–33.

The Voyage Out, 1915

Asbee, Sue. *Virginia Woolf*, 33–40.

Batchelor, John. *Virginia Woolf*, 13–15, 19–20.

Da Silva, N Takei. *Modernism and Virginia Woolf*, 196–200.

Davis-Clapper, Laura. "Why Did Rachel Vinrace Die? Tracing the Clues from *Melymbrosia* to *The Voyage Out,*" in Mark Hussey and Vara Neverow-Turk, eds., *Virginia Woolf Miscellanies*, 225–27.

Evans, William A. *Virginia Woolf*, 7–23.

Fox, Alice. *Virginia Woolf*, 22–31.

Friedman, Susan Stanford. "Virginia Woolf's Pedagogical Scenes of Reading: *The Voyage Out, The Common Reader,* and Her 'Common Readers.'" *Mod Fiction Stud* 38:1 (1992), 101–22.

Gillespie, Diane F. "'Her Kodak Pointed at His Head': Virginia Woolf and Photography," in Diane F. Gillespie, ed., *The Multiple Muses*, 121–23.

Handley, William R. *Virginia Woolf*, 6–10.

Horner, Avril, and Sue Zlosnik. *Landscapes of Desire*, 73–91.

Kurtz, Marilyn. *Virginia Woolf*, 47–51, 73–78.

Lambert, Elizabeth G. "'and Darwin says they are nearer the cow': Evolutionary Discourse in *Melymbrosia* and *The Voyage Out.*" *Twentieth Cent Lit* 37 (1991), 1–19.

Laurence, Patricia Ondek. *The Reading of Silence*, 7–12, 123–69.

McCracken, LuAnn. "'The synthesis of my being': Autobiography and the Reproduction of Identity in Virginia Woolf." *Tulsa Stud in Women's Lit* 9 (1990), 67–72.

McNichol, Stella. *Virginia Woolf*, 1–15.

Mepham, John. *Virginia Woolf*, 41–46.

Oldfield, Sybil. "From Rachel's Aunt to Miss La Trobe: Spinsters in the Fiction of Virginia Woolf," in Laura L. Doan, ed., *Old Maids*, 87–90.

Poole, Roger. *The Unknown Virginia Woolf*, 33–38, 42–46, 293–95.

Trodd, Anthea. *A Reader's Guide*, 76–78.

Tvordi, Jessica. "*The Voyage Out:* Virginia Woolf's First Lesbian Novel," in Vara Neverow-Turk and Mark Hussey, eds., *Virginia Woolf*, 226–37.

Wussow, Helen. "War and Conflict in *The Voyage Out,*" in Mark Hussey, ed., *Virginia Woolf and War*, 101–9.

The Waves, 1931

Alexander, Peter F. *Leonard and Virginia Woolf*, 159–68.

Ascher, Carol. "Reading to Write: *The Waves* as Muse," in Mark Hussey and Vara Neverow-Turk, eds., *Virginia Woolf Miscellanies*, 47–56.

Batchelor, John. *Virginia Woolf*, 114–31.

Booker, M. Keith. "Tradition, Authority, and Subjectivity: Narrative Constitution of the Self in *The Waves.*" *LIT* 3 (1991), 33–55.

Caramagno, Thomas C. *The Flight of the Mind*, 270–95.

Dick, Susan. *Virginia Woolf*, 58–69.

Evans, William A. *Virginia Woolf*, 149–89.

Ferrer, Daniel. *Virginia Woolf and the Madness of Language*, 65–96.

Fox, Alice. *Virginia Woolf*, 133–38.

Gibbons, Thomas, and David Ormerod. "'The Whitsun Weddings' and *The Waves.*" *Notes and Queries* 238 (1993), 69–70.

Haller, Evelyn. "Her Quill Drawn from the Firebird: Virginia Woolf and the Russian Dancers," in Diane F. Gillespie, ed., *The Multiple Muses*, 199–205, 212–14.

Hodge, Robert. *Literature as Discourse,* 32–35.

Hyman, Virginia R. *"To the Lighthouse" and Beyond,* 193–208.

Johnston, Judith L. " 'A Necessary Bore' or Brilliant Novelist?: What Yourcenar Understood About Woolf's *The Waves,"* in Mark Hussey and Vara Neverow-Turk, eds., *Virginia Woolf Miscellanies,* 125–32.

Kaivola, Karen. *All Contraries Confounded,* 37–44.

Kanwar, Asha. *Virginia Woolf and Anita Desai,* 49–61.

Kurtz, Marilyn. *Virginia Woolf,* 81–92, 125–27.

Lanser, Susan Sniader. *Fictions of Authority,* 111–16.

Laurence, Patricia Ondek. *The Reading of Silence,* 21–28, 49–54, 123–69, 170–213.

Lee, Judith. " 'This Hideous Shaping and Moulding': War and *The Waves,"* in Mark Hussey, ed., *Virginia Woolf and War,* 180–200.

McCluskey, Kathleen, CSJ. *Reverberations,* 55–78.

McGee, Patrick. "The Politics of Modernist Form; or, Who Rules *The Waves?" Mod Fiction Stud* 38 (1992), 631–49.

McGee, Patrick. "Woolf's Other: The University in Her Eye." *Novel* 23 (1990), 241–46.

McNichol, Stella. *Virginia Woolf,* 117–40.

Mares, C. J. "Reading Proust: Woolf and the Painter's Perspective." *Compar Lit* 41 (1989), 345–48. (Also in Diane F. Gillespie, ed., *The Multiple Muses,* 77–81.)

Mepham, John. *Virginia Woolf,* 139–45.

Miller, C. Ruth. *Virginia Woolf,* 38–40, 45–49, 51–56, 78–81, 90–96, 102–4.

Munday, Kathryn. "Marcel Proust and Virginia Woolf: An Excuse for a Party." *Engl Stud in Africa* 35 (1992), 46–50.

Oxindine, Annette. "Sapphist Semiotics in Woolf's *The Waves:* Untelling and Retelling What Cannot Be Told," in Vara Neverow-Turk and Mark Hussey, eds., *Virginia Woolf,* 171–80.

Pearce, Richard. *The Politics of Narration,* 156–59, 161–67.

Phelan, James. "Character and Judgment in Narrative and in Lyric: Toward an Understanding of the Audience's Engagement in *The Waves." Style* 24 (1990), 408–19. (Also in John V. Knapp, ed., *Literary Character,* 60–71.)

Phillips, K. J. *Dying Gods in Twentieth-Century Fiction,* 29–37.

Pillai, A. S. D. "Spatial Form in Modern Fiction: A Reading of *Ulysses* and *The Waves." Aligarh J of Engl Stud* 14:1 (1989), 108–22.

Poole, Roger. *The Unknown Virginia Woolf,* 195–97, 199–216, 268–70.

Poresky, Louise. "Eternal Renewal: Life and Death in Virginia Woolf's *The Waves,"* in Mark Hussey and Vara Neverow-Turk, eds., *Virginia Woolf Miscellanies,* 64–69.

Porritt, Ruth. "Surpassing Derrida's Deconstructed Self: Virginia Woolf's Poetic Disarticulation of the Self." *Women's Stud* 21 (1992), 326–31.

Raitt, Suzanne. *Vita and Virginia,* 146–65.

Roe, Sue. *Writing and Gender,* 103–19.

Schulze, Robin Gail. "Design in Motion: Words, Music, and the Search

for Coherence in the Works of Virginia Woolf and Arnold Schoenberg.''
Stud in the Liter Imagination 25:2 (1992), 10–14.

Schwartz, Beth C. "Thinking Back through Our Mothers: Virginia Woolf
Reads Shakespeare." *ELH* 58 (1991), 732–36.

Snider, Clifton. *The Stuff That Dreams Are Made On*, 94–104.

Topia, André. "La Double Ecriture dans *Les Vagues*." *Roman 20–50* 9
(1990), 139–48.

Usui, Masami. "A Portrait of Alexander, Princess of Wales and Queen of
England, in Virginia Woolf's *The Waves*," in Vara Neverow-Turk and
Mark Hussey, eds., *Virginia Woolf*, 121–25.

Wilt, Judith. "God's Spies: The Knower in *The Waves*." *JEGP* 92 (1993),
179–99.

The Years, 1937

Alexander, Peter F. *Leonard and Virginia Woolf*, 171–77.

Bazin, Nancy Topping, and Jane Hamovit Lauter. "Virginia Woolf's Keen
Sensitivity to War: Its Roots and Its Impact on Her Novels," in Mark
Hussey, ed., *Virginia Woolf and War*, 22–23.

Booth, Alison. *Greatness Engendered*, 204–37.

Bowlby, Rachel. *Virginia Woolf*, 123–27.

Cramer, Patricia. "'Loving in the War Years': The War of Images in *The
Years*," in Mark Hussey, ed., *Virginia Woolf and War*, 203–23.

Dick, Susan. *Virginia Woolf*, 70–74.

DuPlessis, Rachel Blau. "Feminist Narrative in Virginia Woolf," in Mark
Spilka and Caroline McCracken-Flesher, eds., *Why the Novel Matters*,
345–48.

Evans, William A. *Virginia Woolf*, 191–208.

Fox, Alice. *Virginia Woolf*, 143–53.

Galef, David. "Disfigured Figures: Virginia Woolf's Disabled List." *Univ
of Mississippi Stud in Engl* 9 (1991), 135–37.

Gindin, James. *British Fiction*, 213–15.

Hyman, Virginia R. *"To the Lighthouse" and Beyond*, 225–35, 237–62.

Kurtz, Marilyn. *Virginia Woolf*, 92–103, 128–29.

Laurence, Patricia Ondek. *The Reading of Silence*, 102–8.

Lucy, Michael. "Voice to Voice: Self-Affirmation in *The Years*." *Novel* 24
(1991), 257–81.

McNichol, Stella. *Virginia Woolf*, 146–48.

Mepham, John. *Virginia Woolf*, 153–59.

Miller, C. Ruth. *Virginia Woolf*, 27–30, 51–54, 75–78, 89–92, 100–102.

Phillips, Kathy J. "Woolf's Criticism of the British Empire in *The Years*,"
in Mark Hussey and Vara Neverow-Turk, eds., *Virginia Woolf Miscellanies*, 30–31.

Poole, Roger. *The Unknown Virginia Woolf*, 36–38.

Roe, Sue. *Writing and Gender*, 121–42.

Squier, Susan. "Woolf Studies Through *The Years:* Nationalism, Methodological Politics, and Critical Reproduction," in Vara Neverow-Turk
and Mark Hussey, eds., *Virginia Woolf*, 16–23.

S. FOWLER WRIGHT

Deluge: A Romance, 1927

  Ruddick, Nicholas. *Ultimate Island,* 120–23.

The Island of Captain Sparrow, 1928

  Ruddick, Nicholas. *Ultimate Island,* 72–74.

LADY MARY WROTH

Urania, 1621

  Krontiris, Tina. Oppositional Voices, 121–40.
  Roberts, Josephine A. "Labyrinths of Desire: Lady Mary Wroth's Recon-
  struction of Romance." *Women's Stud* 19 (1991), 183–91.
  Roberts, Josephine A. "Radigund Revisited: Perspectives on Women Rul-
  ers in Lady Mary Wroth's *Urania,*" in Anne M. Haselkorn and Betty S.
  Travitsky, eds., *The Renaissance Englishwoman,* 187–207.

JOHN WYNDHAM

The Chrysalids, 1955

  Wymer, Rowland. "How 'Safe' is John Wyndham? A Closer Look at his
  Work, with Particular Reference to *The Chrysalids.*" *Foundation* 55
  (1992), 25–34.

The Day of the Triffids, 1951

  Ruddick, Nicholas. *Ultimate Island,* 137–42.

The Kraken Wakes, 1953

  Ruddick, Nicholas. *Ultimate Island,* 137–42.

CHARLOTTE YONGE

Countess Kate, 1862

  Wall, Barbara. *The Narrator's Voice,* 79–81.

The Little Duke, 1854

  Wall, Barbara. *The Narrator's Voice,* 60–62, 64–65, 79–80.

ISRAEL ZANGWILL

Children of the Ghetto, 1892

  Udelson, Joseph H. *Dreamers of the Ghetto,* 81–109.

ANONYMOUS NOVEL

The Love of an Unknown Soldier: Found in a Dug-Out, 1918?
Orel, Harold. *Popular Fiction in England,* 215–22.

Abel, Elizabeth. *Virginia Woolf and the Fictions of Psychoanalysis.* Chicago and London: University of Chicago Press, 1989.

Acheson, James, ed. *The British and Irish Novel Since 1960.* New York: St. Martin's, 1991.

Ackley, Katherine Anne, ed. *Women and Violence in Literature: An Essay Collection.* New York: Garland, 1990.

Ackroyd, Peter. *Dickens.* London: Sinclair-Stevenson, 1990.

Ackroyd, Peter. *Introduction to Dickens.* London: Sinclair-Stevenson, 1991.

Adamson, Judith. *Graham Greene: The Dangerous Edge—Where Art and Politics Meet.* London: Macmillan, 1990.

Adamson, William Robert. *Cadences of Unreason: A Study of Pride and Madness in the Novels of Tobias Smollett.* Frankfurt: Peter Lang, 1990.

Adelman, Gary. *"Jude the Obscure": A Paradise of Despair.* New York: Twayne, 1992.

Adelman, Gary. *Snow of Fire: Symbolic Meaning in "The Rainbow" and "Women in Love."* New York and London: Garland, 1991.

Agovi, K. E. *Novels of Social Change.* Tema: Ghana Publishing Corporation, 1988.

Aguirre, Manuel. *The Closed Space: Horror Literature and Western Symbolism.* Manchester and New York: Manchester University Press, 1990.

Ahrends, Günter, and Hans-Jürgen Diller, eds. *English Romantic Prose: Papers delivered at the Bochum Symposium, September 30 to October 1, 1988.* Essen: Die Blaue Eule, 1990.

Albertazzi, Silvia. *Il sogno gotico: Fantasia onirica e coscienza femminile da Horace Walpole a Charlotte Brontë.* Imola: Galeati, 1980.

Alexander, Doris. *Creating Characters with Charles Dickens.* University Park: Pennsylvania State University Press, 1991.

Alexander, Marguerite. *Flights from Realism: Themes and Strategies in Postmodernist British and American Fiction.* London: Edward Arnold, 1990.

Alexander, Meena. *Women in Romanticism: Mary Wollstonecraft, Dorothy Wordsworth and Mary Shelley.* Savage, MD: Barnes & Noble, 1989.

Alexander, Peter F. *Leonard and Virginia Woolf: A Literary Partnership.* New York: Harvester Wheatsheaf, 1992.

Allen, M. J. B., Dominic Baker-Smith, Arthur F. Kinney, and Margaret Sullivan, eds. *Sir Philip Sidney's Achievements.* New York: AMS Press, 1990.

Alvarez, A. *Beckett.* 2nd ed. London: Fontana Press, 1992.

Ames, Christopher. *The Life of the Party: Festive Vision in Modern Fiction.* Athens (GA) and London: University of Georgia Press, 1991.

Amiran, Eyal. *Wandering and Home: Beckett's Metaphysical Narrative.* University Park: Pennsylvania State University Press, 1993.

Ardis, Ann L. *New Women, New Novels: Feminism and Early Modernism.* New Brunswick (NJ) and London: Rutgers University Press, 1990.

Armitt, Lucie, ed. *Where No Man Has Gone Before: Women and Science Fiction.* London and New York: Routledge, 1991.

Armstrong, Frances. *Dickens and the Concept of Home*. Ann Arbor (MI) and London: UMI Research Press, 1990.

Armstrong, Isobel. *Jane Austen: "Mansfield Park."* London: Penguin, 1988.

Arnold, Bruce. *The Scandal of "Ulysses": The Sensational Life of a Twentieth-Century Masterpiece*. New York: St. Martin's, 1992.

Arnold, David Scott. *Liminal Readings: Forms of Otherness in Melville, Joyce and Murdoch*. New York: St. Martin's, 1993.

Arru, A., and M. T. Chialant, eds. *Il racconto delle donne: voci autobiografie figurazioni*. Naples: Liguori, 1990.

Asbee, Sue. *Flann O'Brien*. Boston: Twayne, 1991.

Asbee, Sue. *Virginia Woolf*. Vero Beach, FL: Rourke Corporation, 1990.

Ashley, Kathleen M., ed. *Victor Turner and the Construction of Cultural Criticism*. Bloomington: Indiana University Press, 1990.

Astro, Alan. *Understanding Samuel Beckett*. Columbia: University of South Carolina Press, 1990.

Attridge, Derek, ed. *The Cambridge Companion to James Joyce*. Cambridge: Cambridge University Press, 1990.

Attridge, Derek, and Daniel Ferrer, eds. *Post-structuralist Joyce: Essays from the French*. Cambridge: Cambridge University Press, 1984.

Aubrey, James R. *John Fowles: A Reference Companion*. New York: Greenwood, 1991.

Auerbach, Emily. *Maestros, Dilettantes, and Philistines: The Musician in the Victorian Novel*. New York: Peter Lang, 1989.

Avery, Gillian, and Julia Briggs, eds. *Children and Their Books: A Celebration of the Work of Iona and Peter Opie*. Oxford: Clarendon, 1989.

Axelrod, M. R. *The Politics of Style in the Fiction of Balzac, Beckett and Cortázar*. New York: St. Martin's, 1992.

Ayers, David. *Wyndham Lewis and Western Man*. New York: St. Martin's, 1992.

Backscheider, Paula R. *"Moll Flanders": The Making of a Criminal Mind*. Boston: Twayne, 1990.

Backus, Guy. *Iris Murdoch: The Novelist as Philosopher, the Philosopher as Novelist—"The Unicorn" as a Philosophical Novel*. Bern: Peter Lang, 1986.

Bagchi, Jasodhara, ed. *Literature, Society and Ideology in the Victorian Era*. New Delhi: Sterling Publishers, 1991.

Baker, Niamh. *Happily Ever After? Women's Fiction in Postwar Britain, 1945–60*. New York: St. Martin's, 1989.

Baldwin, Dean R. *Virginia Woolf: A Study of the Short Fiction*. Boston: Twayne, 1989.

Baldwin, Louis. *One Woman's Liberation: The Story of Fanny Burney*. Wakefield, NH: Longwood Academic, 1990.

Barnes, Jim. *Fiction of Malcolm Lowry and Thomas Mann: Structural Tradition*. Kirksville, MO: Thomas Jefferson University Press, 1990.

Barreca, Regina, ed. *Sex and Death in Victorian Literature*. Bloomington and Indianapolis: Indiana University Press, 1990.

Basham, Diana. *The Trial of Woman: Feminism and the Occult Sciences in Victorian Literature and Society*. London: Macmillan, 1992.

sion, Technological Innovation and Poetic Imagination. Heidelberg: Carl Winter, 1990.

Bergonzi, Bernard. *Wartime and Aftermath: English Literature and its Background, 1939–60.* Oxford and New York: Oxford University Press, 1993.

Berkman, Joyce Avrech. *The Healing Imagination of Olive Schreiner: Beyond South African Colonialism.* Amherst: University of Massachusetts Press, 1989.

Berman, Jeffrey. *Narcissism and the Novel.* New York and London: New York University Press, 1990.

Bernstein, Carol L. *The Celebration of Scandal: Toward the Sublime in Victorian Urban Fiction.* University Park: Pennsylvania State University Press, 1991.

Bersani, Leo. *The Culture of Redemption.* Cambridge (MA) and London: Harvard University Press, 1990.

Bevan, David, ed. *Literature and War.* Amsterdam: Rodopi, 1990.

Bevan, David, ed. *University Fiction.* Amsterdam and Atlanta: Rodopi, 1990.

Bhalla, Alok. *Politics of Atrocity and Lust: The Vampire Tale as a Nightmare History of England in the Nineteenth Century.* New Delhi: Sterling Publishers, 1990.

Black, Michael. *D. H. Lawrence: The Early Philosophical Works—A Commentary.* London: Macmillan, 1991.

Black, Michael. *D. H. Lawrence: "Sons and Lovers."* Cambridge: Cambridge University Press, 1992.

Blake, Kathleen, ed. *Approaches to Teaching Eliot's "Middlemarch."* New York: Modern Language Association of America, 1990.

Blayac, Alain, ed. *Evelyn Waugh: New Directions.* London: Macmillan, 1992.

Bloch, R. Howard, and Frances Ferguson, eds. *Misogyny, Misandry, and Misanthropy.* Berkeley: University of California Press, 1989.

Bloom, Clive, ed. *Spy Thrillers: From Buchan to le Carré.* London: Macmillan, 1990.

Bloom, Clive, ed. *Twentieth-Century Suspense: The Thriller Comes of Age.* New York: St. Martin's, 1990.

Boardman, Michael M. *Narrative Innovation and Incoherence: Ideology in Defoe, Goldsmith, Austen, Eliot, and Hemingway.* Durham (NC) and London: Duke University Press, 1992.

Bock, Carol. *Charlotte Brontë and the Storyteller's Audience.* Iowa City: University of Iowa Press, 1992.

Boheemen, Christine van. *The Novel as Family Romance: Language, Gender, and Authority from Fielding to Joyce.* Ithaca (NY) and London: Cornell University Press, 1987.

Boheemen, Christine van, ed. *Joyce, Modernity, and its Mediation.* Amsterdam and Atlanta: Rodopi, 1989.

Bohlmann, Otto. *Conrad's Existentialism.* New York: St. Martin's, 1991.

Bolletieri Bosinelli, Rosa Maria, Carla Marengo Vaglio, and Christine van Boheemen, eds. *The Languages of Joyce: Selected Papers from the 11th International James Joyce Symposium, Venice, 12–18 June 1988.* Philadelphia and Amsterdam: John Benjamins, 1992.

Flynn, Carol Houlihan. *The Body in Swift and Defoe.* Cambridge: Cambridge University Press, 1990.

Folsom, Marcia McClintock, ed. *Approaches to Teaching Austen's "Pride and Prejudice."* New York: Modern Language Association of America, 1993.

Forster, Jean-Paul. *Jonathan Swift: The Fictions of the Satirist.* Bern: Peter Lang, 1991.

Foster, Paul. *Beckett and Zen: A Study of Dilemma in the Novels of Samuel Beckett.* London: Wisdom Publishers, 1989.

Fox, Alice. *Virginia Woolf and the Literature of the English Renaissance.* Oxford: Clarendon, 1990.

Fraiman, Susan. *Unbecoming Women: British Women Writers and the Novel of Development.* New York: Columbia University Press, 1993.

Frantz, Andrea Breemer. *Redemption and Madness: Three Nineteenth-Century Feminist Views on Motherhood and Childbearing.* Las Colinas, TX: Ide House, 1993.

Fraser, Hilary. *The Victorians and Renaissance Italy.* Oxford and Cambridge (MA): Blackwell, 1992.

Frickey, Pierrette M., ed. *Critical Perspectives on Jean Rhys.* Washington, DC: Three Continents Press, 1990.

Friedland, M. L., ed. *Rough Justice: Essays on Crime in Literature.* Toronto: University of Toronto Press, 1991.

Friedman, Lawrence S. *William Golding.* New York: Continuum, 1993.

Friedman, Lenemaja. *Mary Stewart.* Boston: Twayne, 1990.

Friedman, Susan Stanford, ed. *Joyce: The Return of the Repressed.* Ithaca (NY) and London: Cornell University Press, 1993.

Frontain, Raymond-Jean, and Jan Wojcik, eds. *Old Testament Women in Western Literature.* Conway, AR: UCA Press, 1991.

Fuller, David. *James Joyce's "Ulysses."* New York: Harvester Wheatsheaf, 1992.

Furst, Lilian R. *Through the Lens of the Reader: Explorations of European Narrative.* Albany: State University of New York Press, 1992.

Furst, Lilian R., and Peter W. Graham, eds. *Disorderly Eaters: Texts in Self-Empowerment.* University Park: Pennsylvania State University Press, 1992.

Gallagher, Monique. *Flann O'Brien: Myles from Dublin—A Lecture Given at the Princess Grace Irish Library on Monday 18 September 1989.* Gerrards Cross, Bucks: Colin Smythe, 1991.

Ganguly, Adwaita P. *India: Mystic, Complex and Real—A Detailed Study of E. M. Forster's "A Passage to India": His Treatment of India's Landscape, History, Social Anthropology, Religion, Philosophy, Music and Art.* Delhi: Motilal Banarsidass, 1990.

Ganz, Margaret. *Humor, Irony, and the Realm of Madness: Psychological Studies in Dickens, Butler, and Others.* New York: AMS Press, 1990.

Garard, Charles. *Point of View in Fiction and Film: Focus on John Fowles.* New York: Peter Lang, 1991.

Gard, Roger. *Jane Austen's Novels: The Art of Clarity.* New Haven and London: Yale University Press, 1992.

Grace, Sherrill, ed. *Swinging the Maelstrom: New Perspectives on Malcolm Lowry*. Montreal and Kingston: McGill-Queen's University Press, 1992.

Graham, Kenneth W. *The Politics of Narrative: Ideology and Social Change in William Godwin's "Caleb Williams."* New York: AMS Press, 1990.

Graham, Kenneth W., ed. *Gothic Fictions: Prohibition/Transgression*. New York: AMS Press, 1989.

Graham, Kenneth W., ed. *"Vathek" and the Escape from Time: Bicentenary Revaluations*. New York: AMS Press, 1990.

Gray, Beryl. *George Eliot and Music*. New York: St. Martin's, 1989.

Greene, Donald. *Samuel Johnson*. Updated ed. Boston: Twayne, 1989.

Greene, Gayle. *Changing the Story: Feminist Fiction and the Tradition*. Bloomington and Indianapolis: Indiana University Press, 1991.

Guy, Josephine M. *The British Avant-Garde: The Theory and Politics of Tradition*. New York: Harvester Wheatsheaf, 1991.

Gwilliam, Tassie. *Samuel Richardson's Fictions of Gender*. Stanford, CA: Stanford University Press, 1993.

Haggerty, George E. *Gothic Fiction/Gothic Form*. University Park and London: Pennsylvania State University Press, 1989.

Hagstrum, Jean H. *Eros and Vision: The Restoration to Romanticism*. Evanston, IL: Northwestern University Press, 1989.

Hahn, H. George, ed. *The Country Myth: Motifs in the British Novel from Defoe to Smollett*. Frankfurt: Peter Lang, 1991.

Haight, Gordon S. *George Eliot's Originals and Contemporaries: Essays in Victorian Literary History and Biography*. Edited by Hugh Witemeyer. Ann Arbor: University of Michigan Press, 1992.

Hall, K. G. *The Exalted Heroine and the Triumph of Order: Class, Women and Religion in the English Novel, 1740–1800*. Lanham, MD: Barnes & Noble, 1993.

Hall, N. John. *Trollope: A Biography*. Oxford: Clarendon, 1991.

Halperin, John. *Jane Austen's Lovers: and Other Studies in Fiction and History from Austen to le Carré*. London: Macmillan, 1988.

Halperin, John. *Novelists in their Youth*. New York: St. Martin's, 1990.

Hammond, J. R. *A Defoe Companion*. London: Macmillan; Lanham, MD: Barnes & Noble, 1993.

Hammond, J. R. *H. G. Wells and Rebecca West*. New York: St. Martin's, 1991.

Hampson, Robert. *Joseph Conrad: Betrayal and Identity*. London: Macmillan; New York: St. Martin's, 1992.

Handley, Graham. *George Eliot's Midlands: Passion in Exile*. London: Allison & Busby, 1991.

Handley, Graham. *State of the Art George Eliot: A Guide through the Critical Maze*. Bristol: Bristol Press, 1990.

Handley, Graham. *Thomas Hardy: "Tess of the d'Urbervilles."* London: Penguin, 1991.

Handley, William R. *Virginia Woolf: The Politics of Narration*. Stanford, CA: Stanford University Humanities Honors Program, 1988.

Hands, Timothy. *Thomas Hardy: Distracted Preacher?—Hardy's Religious Biography and Its Influence on His Novels*. New York: St. Martin's, 1989.

Hanks, D. Thomas, Jr., ed. *Sir Thomas Malory: Views and Re-views*. New York: AMS Press, 1992.

Hanley, Lynne. *Writing War: Fiction, Gender, and Memory*. Amherst: University of Massachusetts Press, 1991.

Harkness, Marguerite. *"A Portrait of the Artist as a Young Man": Voices of the Text*. Boston: Twayne, 1990.

Harper, Margaret Mills. *The Aristocracy of Art in Joyce and Wolfe*. Baton Rouge and London: Louisiana State University Press, 1990.

Harrington, John P. *The Irish Beckett*. Syracuse, NY: Syracuse University Press, 1991.

Harris, G. T., and P. M. Wetherill, eds. *Littérature et révolutions en France*. Amsterdam: Rodopi, 1990.

Harrison, Antony H., and Beverly Taylor, eds. *Gender and Discourse in Victorian Literature and Art*. DeKalb: Northern Illinois University Press, 1992.

Harrison, Bernard. *Inconvenient Fictions: Literature and the Limits of Theory*. New Haven (CT) and London: Yale University Press, 1991.

Harvie, Christopher. *The Centre of Things: Political Fiction in Britain from Disraeli to the Present*. London: Unwin Hyman, 1991.

Haselkorn, Anne M., and Betty S. Travitsky, eds. *The Renaissance Englishwoman in Print: Counterbalancing the Canon*. Amherst: University of Massachusetts Press, 1990.

Hassam, Andrew. *Writing and Reality: A Study of Modern British Diary Fiction*. Westport (CT) and London: Greenwood, 1993.

Hassan, Dolly Zulakha. *V. S. Naipaul and the West Indies*. New York: Peter Lang, 1989.

Hawthorn, Jeremy. *Joseph Conrad: Narrative Technique and Ideological Commitment*. London: Edward Arnold, 1990.

Hayman, David. *The "Wake" in Transit*. Ithaca (NY) and London: Cornell University Press, 1990.

Heilman, Robert Bechtold. *The Workings of Fiction: Essays by Robert Bechtold Heilman*. Columbia and London: University of Missouri Press, 1991.

Heineman, Helen K. *Three Victorians in the New World: Interpretations of the New World in the Works of Frances Trollope, Charles Dickens, and Anthony Trollope*. New York: Peter Lang, 1992.

Heller, Tamar. *Dead Secrets: Wilkie Collins and the Female Gothic*. New Haven (CT) and London: Yale University Press, 1992.

Hendrix, Howard V. *The Ecstasy of Catastrophe: A Study of Apocalyptic Narrative from Langland to Milton*. New York: Peter Lang, 1990.

Hennlein, Elmar. *Religion und Phantastik: Zur Rolle des Christentums in der phantastischen Literatur*. Essen: Die Blaue Eule, 1989.

Henricksen, Bruce. *Nomadic Voices: Conrad and the Subject of Narrative*. Urbana and Chicago: University of Illinois Press, 1992.

Henson, Eithne. *"The Fictions of Romantick Chivalry": Samuel Johnson and Romance*. Rutherford, NJ: Fairleigh Dickinson University Press, 1992.

Herget, Winfried, ed. *Sentimentality in Modern Literature and Popular Culture*. Tübingen: Gunter Narr, 1991.

tion. Carbondale and Edwardsville: Southern Illinois University Press, 1990.

Jaffe, Audrey. *Vanishing Points: Dickens, Narrative, and the Subject of Omniscience.* Berkeley: University of California Press, 1991.

Jain, Nalini. *The Mind's Extensive View: Samuel Johnson on Poetic Language.* Strathtay, Perths: Roland Harris Education Trust, 1991.

James, A. R. W., ed. *Victor Hugo et la Grande-Bretagne.* Liverpool: Cairns, 1986.

Jordan, Richard Douglas. *The Quiet Hero: Figures of Temperance in Spenser, Donne, Milton, and Joyce.* Washington, DC: Catholic University of America Press, 1989.

Joshi, S. T. *The Weird Tale: Arthur Machen, Lord Dunsany, Algernon Blackwood, M. R. James, Ambrose Bierce, H. P. Lovecraft.* Austin: University of Texas Press, 1990.

Kahn, Madeleine. *Narrative Transvestism: Rhetoric and Gender in the Eighteenth-Century English Novel.* Ithaca (NY) and London: Cornell University Press, 1991.

Kaivola, Karen. *All Contraries Confounded: The Lyrical Fiction of Virginia Woolf, Djuna Barnes, and Marguerite Duras.* Iowa City: University of Iowa Press, 1991.

Kamra, Shashi. *The Novels of V. S. Naipaul: A Study in Theme and Form.* New Delhi: Prestige Books, 1990.

Kantzenbach, Friedrich Wilhelm. *Traditionen Europas im Spiegel von Literatur: Privatheit und Öffentlichkeit der christlichen Religion zwischen Thomas Morus und Denis Diderot.* Saarbrücken: Rita Dadder, 1988.

Kanwar, Asha. *Virginia Woolf and Anita Desai: A Comparative Study.* New Delhi: Prestige Books, 1989.

Kaplan, Carey, and Ellen Cronan Rose, eds. *Approaches to Teaching Lessing's "The Golden Notebook."* New York: Modern Language Association of America, 1989.

Kaplan, Deborah. *Jane Austen among Women.* Baltimore and London: Johns Hopkins University Press, 1992.

Kayman, Martin A. *From Bow Street to Baker Street: Mystery, Detection and Narrative.* London: Macmillan, 1992.

Kelly, Richard. *Lewis Carroll.* Rev. ed. Boston: Twayne, 1990.

Kelsey, Nigel. *D. H. Lawrence: Sexual Crisis.* London: Macmillan, 1991.

Kemeny, Tomaso, ed. *Differences Similar: More Jottings on Joyce.* Udine: Campanotto, 1990.

Kennedy, Beverly. *Knighthood in the "Morte Darthur."* 2nd ed. Cambridge: D. S. Brewer, 1992.

Kenyon, Olga. *Writing Women: Contemporary Women Novelists.* London: Pluto Press, 1991.

Kersnowski, Frank L., ed. *Into the Labyrinth: Essays on the Art of Lawrence Durrell.* Ann Arbor (MI) and London: UMI Research Press, 1989.

Kiernan, Robert F. *Frivolity Unbound: Six Masters of the Camp Novel—Thomas Love Peacock, Max Beerbohm, Ronald Firbank, E. F. Benson, P. G. Wodehouse, Ivy Compton-Burnett.* New York: Continuum, 1990.

Kushigian, Nancy. *Pictures and Fictions: Visual Modernism and the Pre-War Novels of D. H. Lawrence*. New York: Peter Lang, 1990.

La Cassagnère, Christian, ed. *Visages de l'angoisse*. Clermont-Ferrand: Publications de la Faculté des Lettres de Clermont, 1989.

Lamb, Jonathan. *Sterne's Fiction and the Double Principle*. Cambridge: Cambridge University Press, 1989.

Land, Stephen K. *Challenge and Conventionality in the Fiction of E. M. Forster*. New York: AMS Press, 1990.

Lane, Denis, ed. *In the Spirit of Powys: New Essays*. Lewisburg, PA: Bucknell University Press; London and Toronto: Associated University Presses, 1990.

Lang, Frederick K. *"Ulysses" and the Irish God*. Lewisburg, PA: Bucknell University Press; London and Toronto: Associated University Presses, 1993.

Langland, Elizabeth. *Anne Brontë: The Other One*. Totowa, NJ: Barnes & Noble, 1989.

Lanser, Susan Sniader. *Fictions of Authority: Women Writers and Narrative Voice*. Ithaca (NY) and London: Cornell University Press, 1992.

Lapraz-Severino, Françoise. *Relativité et communication dans les "Voyages de Gulliver" de Jonathan Swift*. Lille: Université de Lille III; Paris: Didier, 1989.

Lassner, Phyllis. *Elizabeth Bowen*. Savage, MD: Barnes & Noble, 1989.

Lauber, John. *Jane Austen*. New York: Twayne, 1993.

Laurence, Anne, W. R. Owens, and Stuart Sim, eds. *John Bunyan and His England, 1628–88*. London and Ronceverte: Hambledon Press, 1990.

Laurence, Patricia Ondek. *The Reading of Silence: Virginia Woolf in the English Tradition*. Stanford, CA: Stanford University Press, 1991.

Leavy, Barbara Fass. *To Blight with Plague: Studies in a Literary Theme*. New York and London: New York University Press, 1992.

Lecercle, Jean-Jacques, ed. *La Répétition*. Paris: Centre de Recherches Anglo-Américaines, Université de Paris, 1989.

Le Gallez, Paula. *The Rhys Woman*. London: Macmillan, 1990.

Lee, Alison. *Realism and Power: Postmodern British Fiction*. London and New York: Routledge, 1990.

Lehmann, Christine. *Das Modell Clarissa: Liebe, Verführung, Sexualität und Tod der Romanheldinnen des 18. und 19. Jahrhunderts*. Stuttgart: Metzler, 1991.

Leps, Marie-Christine. *Apprehending the Criminal: The Production of Deviance in Nineteenth-Century Discourse*. Durham (NC) and London: Duke University Press, 1992.

Lernout, Geert, ed. *"Finnegans Wake": Fifty Years*. Amsterdam and Atlanta: Rodopi, 1990.

Letley, Emma. *From Galt to Douglas Brown: Nineteenth-Century Fiction and Scots Language*. Edinburgh: Scottish Academic Press, 1988.

Levin, Amy K. *The Suppressed Sister: A Relationship in Novels by Nineteenth- and Twentieth-Century British Women*. Lewisburg, PA: Bucknell University Press; London and Toronto: Associated University Presses, 1992.

Sheridan Le Fanu, Yeats and Bowen. Manchester and New York: Manchester University Press, 1993.

MacDonagh, Oliver. *Jane Austen: Real and Imagined Worlds.* New Haven (CT) and London: Yale University Press, 1991.

MacDonald, Ruth K. *Christian's Children: The Influence of John Bunyan's "The Pilgrim's Progress" on American Children's Literature.* New York: Peter Lang, 1989.

McDonnell, Jacqueline. *Evelyn Waugh.* New York: St. Martin's, 1988.

McEwan, Neil. *Anthony Powell.* New York: St. Martin's, 1991.

McGann, Jerome J., ed. *Victorian Connections.* Charlottesville: University Press of Virginia, 1989.

McGavran, James Holt, Jr., ed. *Romanticism and Children's Literature in Nineteenth-Century England.* Athens (GA) and London: University of Georgia Press, 1991.

McGillis, Roderick, ed. *For the Childlike: George MacDonald's Fantasies For Children.* Metuchen (NJ) and London: Children's Literature Association and Scarecrow Press, 1992.

McKay, Margaret. *Peacock's Progress: Aspects of Artistic Development in the Novels of Thomas Love Peacock.* Uppsala and Stockholm: Almqvist & Wiksell, 1992.

McKnight, Natalie. *Idiots, Madmen, and Other Prisoners in Dickens.* New York: St. Martin's, 1993.

McLynn, Frank. *Robert Louis Stevenson: A Biography.* London: Hutchinson, 1993.

McMaster, Juliet. *The Index of the Mind: Physiognomy in the Novel.* Lethbridge, Alberta: University of Lethbridge Press, 1990.

McMaster, R. D. *Thackeray's Cultural Frame of Reference: Allusion in "The Newcomes."* Montreal and Kingston: McGill-Queen's University Press, 1991.

McMichael, James. *"Ulysses" and Justice.* Princeton, NJ: Princeton University Press, 1991.

McMinn, Joseph. *John Banville: A Critical Study.* Dublin: Gill and Macmillan, 1991.

McNeil, David. *The Grotesque Depiction of War and the Military in Eighteenth-Century English Fiction.* Newark: University of Delaware Press; London and Toronto: Associated University Presses, 1990.

McNichol, Stella. *Virginia Woolf and the Poetry of Fiction.* London and New York: Routledge, 1990.

Macpherson, Pat. *Reflecting on Jane Eyre.* London and New York: Routledge, 1989.

McSweeney, Kerry. *George Eliot (Marian Evans): A Literary Life.* London: Macmillan, 1991.

McVeagh, John, ed. *1660–1780: All the World Before Them.* London: Ashfield, 1990.

Malik, Akbar Ali. *"The Satanic Verses": Was It Worth All the Fuss?—A Muslim Lawyer's Viewpoint.* London: Unique Books, 1993.

Miles, Peter. *"Wuthering Heights."* London: Macmillan, 1990.

Miles, Robert. *Gothic Writing, 1750–1820: A Genealogy.* London and New York: Routledge, 1993.

Miles, Robert. *"Jane Eyre" by Charlotte Brontë.* London: Macmillan, 1988.

Miller, C. Ruth. *Virginia Woolf: The Frames of Art and Life.* New York: St. Martin's, 1988.

Miller, David. *W. H. Hudson and the Elusive Paradise.* New York: St. Martin's, 1990.

Miller, J. Hillis. *Tropes, Parables, Performatives: Essays on Twentieth-Century Literature.* Durham, NC: Duke University Press, 1991.

Miller, J. Hillis. *Victorian Subjects.* Durham, NC: Duke University Press, 1991.

Miller, R. H. *Understanding Graham Greene.* Columbia: University of South Carolina Press, 1990.

Milligan, Ian. *Studying Jane Austen.* Beirut: York Press; Harlow, England: Longman, 1988.

Mills, Sara, Lynne Pearce, Sue Spaull, and Elaine Millard. *Feminist Readings/ Feminists Reading.* Charlottesville: University Press of Virginia, 1989.

Mink, JoAnna Stephens, and Janet Doubler Ward, eds. *Joinings and Disjoinings: The Significance of Marital Status in Literature.* Bowling Green, OH: Bowling Green State University Popular Press, 1991.

Minogue, Sally, ed. *Problems for Feminist Criticism.* London and New York: Routledge, 1990.

Mizejewski, Linda. *Divine Decadence: Fascism, Female Spectacle, and the Makings of Sally Bowles.* Princeton, NJ: Princeton University Press, 1992.

Moddelmog, Debra A. *Readers and Mythic Signs: The Oedipus Myth in Twentieth-Century Fiction.* Carbondale and Edwardsville: Southern Illinois University Press, 1993.

Moler, Kenneth L. *"Pride and Prejudice": A Study in Artistic Economy.* Boston: Twayne, 1988.

Monsman, Gerald. *Olive Schreiner's Fiction: Landscape and Power.* New Brunswick, NJ: Rutgers University Press, 1991.

Montgomery, Martin, Alan Durant, Nigel Fabb, Tom Furniss, and Sara Mills. *Ways of Reading: Advanced Reading Skills for Students of English Literature.* London and New York: Routledge, 1992.

Moore, Gene M., ed. *Conrad's Cities: Essays for Hans van Marle.* Amsterdam and Atlanta: Rodopi, 1992.

Moore, Robin. *Paul Scott's Raj.* London: Heinemann, 1990.

Moravetz, Monika. *Formen der Rezeptionslenkung im Briefroman des 18. Jahrhunderts: Richardsons "Clarissa," Rousseaus "Nouvelle Héloïse" und Laclos' "Liaisons Dangereuses."* Tübingen: Gunter Narr, 1990.

Morgan, Janice, Colette T. Hall, and Carol L. Snyder, eds. *Redefining Autobiography in Twentieth-Century Women's Fiction: An Essay Collection.* New York: Garland, 1991.

Morgan, Nicholas H. *Secret Journeys: Theory and Practice in Reading Dickens.* Rutherford, NJ: Fairleigh Dickinson University Press; London and Toronto: Associated University Presses, 1992.

Pleithner, Regina, ed. *Reisen des Barock: Selbst- und Fremderfahrung und ihre Darstellung*. Bonn: Romanistischer Verlag, 1991.

Polhemus, Robert M. *Erotic Faith: Being in Love from Jane Austen to D. H. Lawrence*. Chicago and London: University of Chicago Press, 1990.

Poole, Roger. *The Unknown Virginia Woolf*. 3rd ed. Atlantic Highlands (NJ) and London: Humanities Press International, 1990.

Pott, Hans-Georg. *Neue Theorie des Romans: Sterne, Jean Paul, Joyce, Schmidt*. Munich: Wilhelm Fink, 1990.

Potter, Rosanne G., ed. *Literary Computing and Literary Criticism: Theoretical and Practical Essays on Theme and Rhetoric*. Philadelphia: University of Pennsylvania Press, 1989.

Prasad, Nityanand. *Fission and Fusion: A Thematic Study of Mrs. Gaskell's Novels*. New Delhi: Wisdom Publications, 1989.

Prawer, S. S. *Israel at Vanity Fair: Jews and Judaism in the Writings of W. M. Thackeray*. Leiden: E. J. Brill, 1992.

Probyn, Clive T. *English Fiction of the Eighteenth Century, 1700–1789*. London and New York: Longman, 1987.

Probyn, Clive T. *Jonathan Swift: "Gulliver's Travels."* London: Penguin, 1987.

Punter, David. *The Romantic Unconscious: A Study in Narcissism and Patriarchy*. New York: New York University Press, 1990.

Putnam, Walter C., III. *L'Aventure littéraire de Joseph Conrad et d'André Gide*. Saratoga, CA: ANMA Libri, 1990.

Rabaté, Jean-Michel. *James Joyce, Authorized Reader*. Baltimore and London: Johns Hopkins University Press, 1991.

Rabaté, Jean-Michel. *Joyce upon the Void: The Genesis of Doubt*. London: Macmillan, 1991.

Rabinovitz, Rubin. *Innovation in Samuel Beckett's Fiction*. Urbana and Chicago: University of Illinois Press, 1992.

Raby, Peter. *Samuel Butler: A Biography*. London: Hogarth Press, 1991.

Raeper, William, ed. *The Gold Thread: Essays on George MacDonald*. Edinburgh: Edinburgh University Press, 1990.

Rai, Alok. *Orwell and the Politics of Despair: A Critical Study of the Writings of George Orwell*. Cambridge: Cambridge University Press, 1988.

Raitt, Suzanne. *Virginia Woolf's "To the Lighthouse."* New York: Harvester Wheatsheaf, 1990.

Raitt, Suzanne. *Vita and Virginia: The Work and Friendship of V. Sackville-West and Virginia Woolf*. Oxford: Clarendon, 1993.

Ralph, Phyllis C. *Victorian Transformations: Fairy Tales, Adolescence, and the Novel of Female Development*. New York: Peter Lang, 1989.

Ramanathan, Suguna. *Iris Murdoch: Figures of Good*. New York: St. Martin's, 1990.

Randisi, Jennifer Lynn. *On Her Way Rejoicing: The Fiction of Muriel Spark*. Washington, DC: Catholic University of America Press, 1991.

Randriambeloma-Rakotoanosy, Ginette. *Rencontres avec les soeurs Brontë en terre malagache*. Paris: L'Harmattan, 1989.

Raphael, Frederic. *Somerset Maugham*. London: Cardinal, 1989.

Rauchbauer, Otto, ed. *Ancestral Voices: The Big House in Anglo-Irish Literature—A Collection of Interpretations*. Hildesheim: Georg Olms, 1992.

Reece, Benny R. *The Mystery of Edwin Drood Solved*. New York: Vantage Press, 1989.

Reed, John R. *Victorian Will*. Athens: Ohio University Press, 1989.

Rees, Joan. *Sir Philip Sidney and "Arcadia."* Rutherford, NJ: Fairleigh Dickinson University Press, 1991.

Reilly, Jim. *Joseph Conrad*. Vero Beach, FL: Rourke Corporation, 1990.

Reilly, Jim. *Shadowtime: History and Representation in Hardy, Conrad and George Eliot*. London and New York: Routledge, 1993.

Reilly, Patrick. *"Lord of the Flies": Fathers and Sons*. New York: Twayne, 1992.

Reilly, Patrick. *"Tom Jones": Adventure and Providence*. Boston: Twayne, 1991.

Reinstein, P. Gila. *Alice in Context*. New York and London: Garland, 1988.

Renzi, Thomas C. *H. G. Wells: Six Scientific Romances Adapted for Film*. Metuchen (NJ) and London: Scarecrow Press, 1992.

Restuccia, Frances L. *Joyce and the Law of the Father*. New Haven (CT) and London: Yale University Press, 1989.

Reynolds, Barbara. *Dorothy L. Sayers: Her Life and Soul*. London: Hodder & Stoughton, 1993.

Richards, Jeffrey. *Happiest Days: The Public Schools in English Fiction*. Manchester: Manchester University Press, 1988.

Ricks, Christopher. *Beckett's Dying Words: The Clarendon Lectures, 1990*. Oxford: Clarendon, 1993.

Riesen, Beat. *Thomas Hardy's Minor Novels*. Bern: Peter Lang, 1990.

Riewald, J. G. *Remembering Max Beerbohm: Correspondence, Conversations, Criticisms*. Assen and Maastricht: Van Gorcum, 1991.

Rifelj, Carol de Dobay. *Reading the Other: Novels and the Problem of Other Minds*. Ann Arbor: University of Michigan Press, 1992.

Rindisbacher, Hans J. *The Smell of Books: A Cultural-Historical Study of Olfactory Perception in Literature*. Ann Arbor: University of Michigan Press, 1992.

Rising, Catharine. *Darkness at Heart: Fathers and Sons in Conrad*. New York: Greenwood, 1990.

Robb, David S. *George MacDonald*. Edinburgh: Scottish Academic Press, 1987.

Robinson, Sally. *Engendering the Subject: Gender and Self-Representation in Contemporary Women's Fiction*. Albany: State University of New York Press, 1991.

Rodden, John. *The Politics of Literary Reputation: The Making and Claiming of 'St. George' Orwell*. New York and Oxford: Oxford University Press, 1989.

Roe, Sue. *Writing and Gender: Virginia Woolf's Writing Practice*. New York: St. Martin's, 1990.

Rogers, Katharine M. *Frances Burney: The World of "Female Difficulties."* New York: Harvester Wheatsheaf, 1990.

Rose, Jonathan, ed. *The Revised Orwell*. East Lansing: Michigan State University Press, 1992.

Rosebury, Brian. *Tolkien: A Critical Assessment*. London: Macmillan; New York: St. Martin's, 1992.

Ross, Charles L. *"Women in Love": A Novel of Mythic Realism*. Boston: Twayne, 1991.

Ross, Deborah. *The Excellence of Falsehood: Romance, Realism, and Women's Contribution to the Novel*. Lexington: University Press of Kentucky, 1991.

Rossen, Janice. *The University in Modern Fiction: When Power Is Academic*. London: Macmillan; New York: St. Martin's, 1993.

Rotkin, Charlotte. *Deception in Dickens' "Little Dorrit."* New York: Peter Lang, 1989.

Roughley, Alan. *James Joyce and Critical Theory: An Introduction*. New York: Harvester Wheatsheaf, 1991.

Rousseau, G. S., and Roy Porter, eds. *Sexual Underworlds of the Enlightenment*. Chapel Hill: University of North Carolina Press, 1988.

Ru, Yi-ling. *The Family Novel: Toward a Generic Definition*. New York: Peter Lang, 1992.

Ruddick, Nicholas. *Ultimate Island: On the Nature of British Science Fiction*. Westport, CT: Greenwood Press, 1993.

Ruddick, Nicholas, ed. *State of the Fantastic: Studies in the Theory and Practice of Fantastic Literature and Film—Selected Essays from the Eleventh International Conference on the Fantastic in the Arts, 1990*. Westport (CT) and London: Greenwood, 1992.

Ruoff, Gene W. *Jane Austen's "Sense and Sensibility."* New York: St. Martin's, 1992.

Ruoff, Gene W., ed. *The Romantics and Us: Essays on Literature and Culture*. New Brunswick (NJ) and London: Rutgers University Press, 1990.

Rutelli, Romana. *Il desiderio del diverso: Saggio sul doppio*. Naples: Liguori, 1984.

Ryals, Clyde de L. *A World of Possibilities: Romantic Irony in Victorian Literature*. Columbus: Ohio State University Press, 1990.

Saciuk, Olena H., ed. *The Shape of the Fantastic: Selected Essays from the Seventh International Conference on the Fantastic in the Arts*. New York: Greenwood, 1990.

Sadler, Lynn Veach. *Anita Brookner*. Boston: Twayne, 1990.

Sadrin, Anny. *Dickens ou le roman-théâtre*. Paris: Presses Universitaires de France, 1992.

Salami, Mahmoud. *John Fowles's Fiction and the Poetics of Postmodernism*. Rutherford, NJ: Fairleigh Dickinson University Press; London and Toronto: Associated University Presses, 1992.

Salvaggio, Ruth. *Enlightened Absence: Neoclassical Configurations of the Feminine*. Urbana and Chicago: University of Illinois Press, 1988.

Salwak, Dale, ed. *Kingsley Amis: In Life and Letters*. London: Macmillan, 1990.

Salzmann-Brunner, Brigitte. *Amanuenses to the Present: Protagonists in the Fic-*

Storey, Graham. *"David Copperfield": Interweaving Truth and Fiction.* Boston: Twayne, 1991.

Stratton, Jon. *Writing Sites: A Genealogy of the Postmodern World.* Ann Arbor: University of Michigan Press, 1990.

Sullivan, Zohreh T. *Narratives of Empire: The Fictions of Rudyard Kipling.* Cambridge: Cambridge University Press, 1993.

Summers, Claude J. *Gay Fictions: Wilde to Stonewall—Studies in a Male Homosexual Literary Tradition.* New York: Continuum, 1990.

Suzuki, Takashi, and Tsuyoshi Mukai, eds. *Arthurian and Other Studies: Presented to Shunichi Noguchi.* Cambridge: D. S. Brewer, 1993.

Swingle, L. J. *Romanticism and Anthony Trollope: A Study in the Continuities of Nineteenth-Century Literary Thought.* Ann Arbor: University of Michigan Press, 1990.

Tave, Stuart M. *Lovers, Clowns, and Fairies: An Essay on Comedies.* Chicago and London: University of Chicago Press, 1993.

Tayler, Irene. *Holy Ghosts: The Male Muses of Emily and Charlotte Brontë.* New York: Columbia University Press, 1990.

Taylor, D. J. *A Vain Conceit: British Fiction in the 1980s.* London: Bloomsbury, 1989.

Templeton, Wayne. *States of Estrangement: The Novels of D. H. Lawrence, 1912–1917.* Troy, NY: Whitston, 1989.

Thacker, John. *"Edwin Drood": Antichrist in the Cathedral.* London: Vision Press; New York: St. Martin's, 1990.

Theoharis, Theoharis Constantine. *Joyce's "Ulysses": An Anatomy of the Soul.* Chapel Hill and London: University of North Carolina Press, 1988.

Thomas, Deborah A. *Thackeray and Slavery.* Athens: Ohio University Press, 1993.

Thomas, Ronald R. *Dreams of Authority: Freud and the Fictions of the Unconscious.* Ithaca (NY) and London: Cornell University Press, 1990.

Thoms, Peter. *The Windings of the Labyrinth: Quest and Structure in the Major Novels of Wilkie Collins.* Athens: Ohio University Press, 1992.

Tiessen, Paul, ed. *Apparently Incongruous Parts: The Worlds of Malcolm Lowry.* Metuchen (NJ) and London: Scarecrow Press, 1990.

Tigges, Wim. *An Anatomy of Literary Nonsense.* Amsterdam: Rodopi, 1988.

Tindall, Gillian. *Countries of the Mind: The Meaning of Place to Writers.* London: Hogarth Press, 1991.

Toker, Leona. *Eloquent Reticence: Withholding Information in Fictional Narrative.* Lexington: University Press of Kentucky, 1993.

Tomalin, Claire. *The Life and Death of Mary Wollstonecraft.* Rev. ed. London: Penguin, 1992.

Tomarken, Edward. *Johnson, "Rasselas," and the Choice of Criticism.* Lexington: University Press of Kentucky, 1989.

Topsfield, Valerie. *The Humour of Samuel Beckett.* New York: St. Martin's, 1988.

Toyama, Jean Yamasaki. *Beckett's Game: Self and Language in the Trilogy.* New York: Peter Lang, 1991.

Watt, Stephen. *Joyce, O'Casey, and the Irish Popular Theater.* Syracuse, NY: Syracuse University Press, 1991.

Watts, Cedric. *Joseph Conrad: A Literary Life.* New York: St. Martin's, 1989.

Watts, Cedric. *Literature and Money: Financial Myth and Literary Truth.* New York: Harvester Wheatsheaf, 1990.

Watts, Cedric. *A Preface to Conrad.* 2nd ed. London and New York: Longman, 1993.

Watts, Cedric. *Thomas Hardy: "Jude the Obscure."* London: Penguin, 1992.

Weber, Jean Jacques. *Critical Analysis of Fiction: Essays in Discourse Stylistics.* Amsterdam and Atlanta: Rodopi, 1992.

Weekes, Ann Owens. *Irish Women Writers: An Uncharted Tradition.* Lexington: University Press of Kentucky, 1990.

Weeks, Dennis L. *Steps Toward Salvation: An Examination of Coinherence and Substitution in the Seven Novels of Charles Williams.* New York: Peter Lang, 1991.

Weibel, Paul. *Reconstructing the Past: "G." and "The White Hotel," Two Contemporary 'Historical' Novels.* Bern: Peter Lang, 1989.

Weinbaum, Francine S. *Paul Scott: A Critical Study.* Austin: University of Texas Press, 1992.

Weir, Lorraine. *Writing Joyce: A Semiotics of the Joyce System.* Bloomington and Indianapolis: Indiana University Press, 1989.

Weiss, Timothy F. *On the Margins: The Art of Exile in V. S. Naipaul.* Amherst: University of Massachusetts Press, 1992.

Weld, Annette. *Barbara Pym and the Novel of Manners.* London: Macmillan, 1992.

Whissen, Thomas Reed. *The Devil's Advocates: Decadence in Modern Literature.* New York: Greenwood Press, 1989.

White, Allon. *Carnival, Hysteria, and Writing: Collected Essays and Autobiography.* Oxford: Clarendon, 1993.

Whitlark, James. *Behind the Great Wall: A Post-Jungian Approach to Kafkaesque Literature.* Rutherford, NJ: Fairleigh Dickinson University Press; London and Toronto: Associated University Presses, 1991.

Widmer, Kingsley. *Defiant Desire: Some Dialectical Legacies of D. H. Lawrence.* Carbondale and Edwardsville: Southern Illinois University Press, 1992.

Wiesenfarth, Joseph. *Gothic Manners and the Classic English Novel.* Madison: University of Wisconsin Press, 1988.

Williams, Judith. *Perception and Expression in the Novels of Charlotte Brontë.* Ann Arbor (MI) and London: UMI Research Press, 1988.

Williams, Meg Harris, and Margot Waddell. *The Chamber of Maiden Thought: Literary Origins of the Psychoanalytic Model of the Mind.* London and New York: Routledge, 1991.

Williams, Merryn. *A Preface to Hardy.* 2nd ed. London and New York: Longman, 1993.

Williamson, Marilyn L. *Raising Their Voices: British Women Writers, 1650–1750.* Detroit, MI: Wayne State University Press, 1990.

Wilmer, S. E., ed. *Beckett in Dublin.* Dublin: Lilliput Press, 1992.